Israeli Foreign Policy since the End of the Cold War

This is the first study of Israeli foreign policy towards the Middle East and selected world powers including China, India, the European Union and the United States since the end of the Cold War. It provides an integrated account of these foreign policy spheres and serves as an essential historical context for the domestic political scene during these pivotal decades. The book demonstrates how foreign policy is shaped by domestic factors, which are represented as three concentric circles of decision-makers, the security network and Israeli national identity. Told from this perspective, Amnon Aran highlights the contributions of the central individuals, societal actors, domestic institutions and political parties that have informed and shaped Israeli foreign policy decisions, implementation and outcomes. Aran demonstrates that Israel has pursued three foreign policy stances since the end of the Cold War – entrenchment, engagement and unilateralism – and explains why.

AMNON ARAN is Senior Lecturer in International Politics of the Middle East at City, University of London where his main research focuses on the Arab-Israeli conflict and the foreign policy of Middle Eastern states. He has contributed to the EU's Middle East Peace Task Force and he comments on Middle Eastern affairs for the BBC, Bloomberg, *Financial Times* and the *Guardian*.

Cambridge Middle East Studies

Editorial Board

Charles Tripp (general editor)
Julia Clancy-Smith
F. Gregory Gause
Yezid Sayigh
Avi Shlaim
Judith E. Tucker

Cambridge Middle East Studies has been established to publish books on the nineteenth- to twenty-first-century Middle East and North Africa. The series offers new and original interpretations of aspects of Middle Eastern societies and their histories. To achieve disciplinary diversity, books are solicited from authors writing in a wide range of fields including history, sociology, anthropology, political science, and political economy. The emphasis is on producing books affording an original approach along theoretical and empirical lines. The series is intended for students and academics, but the more accessible and wide-ranging studies will also appeal to the interested general reader.

A list of books in the series can be found after the index.

Israeli Foreign Policy since the End of the Cold War

Amnon Aran
City, University of London

CAMBRIDGE
UNIVERSITY PRESS

University Printing House, Cambridge CB2 8BS, United Kingdom

One Liberty Plaza, 20th Floor, New York, NY 10006, USA

477 Williamstown Road, Port Melbourne, VIC 3207, Australia

314–321, 3rd Floor, Plot 3, Splendor Forum, Jasola District Centre, New Delhi – 110025, India

79 Anson Road, #06–04/06, Singapore 079906

Cambridge University Press is part of the University of Cambridge.

It furthers the University's mission by disseminating knowledge in the pursuit of education, learning, and research at the highest international levels of excellence.

www.cambridge.org
Information on this title: www.cambridge.org/9781107052499
DOI: 10.1017/9781107280618

© Amnon Aran 2021

This publication is in copyright. Subject to statutory exception and to the provisions of relevant collective licensing agreements, no reproduction of any part may take place without the written permission of Cambridge University Press.

First published 2021

A catalogue record for this publication is available from the British Library.

ISBN 978-1-107-05249-9 Hardback

Cambridge University Press has no responsibility for the persistence or accuracy of URLs for external or third-party internet websites referred to in this publication and does not guarantee that any content on such websites is, or will remain, accurate or appropriate.

To my family

Contents

	List of Maps	*page* ix
	List of Figures	x
	Acknowledgements	xi
	Chronology	xiii
	List of Abbreviations	xx
	Introduction	1
1	Entrenchment	12
2	Redirection	33
3	On the Brink of Peace?	59
4	Engagement Incomplete	87
5	Engagement under Assault	104
6	The Dividends of Engagement	124
7	Unpicking the Oslo Accords	148
8	Backtracking	169
9	Just Beyond Reach	195
10	Between Engagement and Unilateralism	215
11	In Search of a Foreign Policy Paradigm	239
12	A Perfect Storm	262
13	The Road Map for Regime Change	283
14	The Resurgence of Unilateralism	300
15	Events Dear Boy, Events	326

viii   Contents

16 The End of the Road   342

17 Vulnerable Ties   366

Epilogue   387

Appendix: List of Persons Interviewed   403
References   405
Index   419

Maps

0.1 Israel and its neighbours	*page* xxii
0.2 Israel political map	xxiii
2.1 The Golan Heights	43

Figures

5.1	Rubble of building and car	*page* 120
5.2	Prime Minister Shamir delivering a speech	121
5.3	Shimon Peres (L) Yitzhak Rabin, Hosni Mubarak, Yasser Arafat and Warren Christopher (R)	121
5.4	Yasser Arafat and Yitzhak Rabin	122
5.5	Blown-up Egged bus	122
5.6	Caricature of Yasser Arafat	123
5.7	Yitzhak Rabin, King Hussein and President Clinton	123
14.1	Soldiers and family in Hebron	322
14.2	Separation barrier	322
14.3	Handshake between Foreign Minister Levy and his Chinese counterpart	323
14.4	Prime Ministers Sharon and Vajpayee	323
14.5	PM Ehud Barak, Chief of Staff Shaul Mofaz and Major General Gabi Ashkenazi	324
14.6	Acting PM Ehud Olmert and Cabinet Secretary Israel Maimon	324
14.7	Mass demonstration	325
14.8	Prime Minister Netanyahu and President Barak Obama	325

Acknowledgements

I have been extremely fortunate along the journey that led to the publication of this book. My colleagues at the Department of International Politics at City, University of London, provided me with invaluable support. Anastasia Nesvetailova, Ronen Palan and Inderjeet Parmer, who served as heads of department, deserve special mention, as well as Dina Fainberg, Leonie Fleischmann, Iosif Kovras, Sandy Hager, Stefano Pagliari and Gadi Yishayahu. I am also grateful to a number of colleagues in other institutions including Chris Alden, Ronit Ben Dor, Klaus Brummer, Katerina Dalacoura, Rami Ginat, Christopher Hill, Clive Jones, Juliet Kaarbo, George Lawson, Cynthia Little, Oren Barak, Colin Shindler, Asaf Siniver, Karen Smith and Charles Tripp. All of them have been helpful in so many ways. My deep appreciation is extended to my friend, Dr Moshe Fox, for his continuous support of my research, and my interviewees, who spared the time to see me and answer my questions. My thanks go also to the team at Cambridge University Press, Maria Marsh, Daniel Brown and Atifa Jiwa, who were patient, responsive, professional and attentive to detail.

I owe an immensely profound debt of gratitude and friendship to Avi Shlaim, who has redefined and transformed our understanding of Israel's foreign relations with the Arab world. For the past twenty years, Avi has been a constant source of stalwart support, inspiration and guidance. Avi read every chapter of this book since I began writing, and met with me over lunches at St Antony's College, University of Oxford, to provide me with the most extensive and insightful feedback I could have asked for. I also would like to extend my deepest thanks to Rory Miller, a brilliant scholar of the international relations of the Middle East. Throughout my career, I have benefited from Rory's resolute support, stimulating intellectual engagements, friendship and guidance.

Over the years of writing this book, I have been extremely fortunate to receive love and support from my dear family and friends: Natalie Aran, Tom and Mog Aslan, Tony Ducket, Shai Eisen, Ezra Gabbai, Amina Harris, Keren, Guy, Lea and Thea Gelkoff, clan Gera, Itamar, Ifat and

xii   Acknowledgements

Amit Orgad, Nechemya Orgad, Gil Rabinovich, Guy Shinar, Yoav Shaked, Ophir, Jonathan and Abigail Salomon, Atalya (Kipi) and Kobi Wolf. Having reached the end of writing this book, I cannot but express my heartfelt feelings and love to my parents, Shai and Michael Aran, who, through thick and thin, were always there for me. To my wife, Shani Orgad, thank you for all your care, love and support. You are everything I have ever wished for from a partner to life, the ultimate companion with whom I have been blessed to be singing our own 'songs in the key of life'. Last, but by no means least, my sons, the Aran brothers, Yoav and Assaf. Every day you fill my life with love, light, meaning and joy. All the above deserve my deepest thanks and gratitude.

For any shortcomings the book might have, I alone am responsible.

Chronology

1990
11 – June Yitzhak Shamir forms a government.
2 – August Iraqi Invasion of Kuwait.

1991
17 – January to 28 February The Gulf War.
25 – December Dissolution of the USSR.

1992
24 – January Israel and China establish diplomatic relations.
29 – January Israel and India establish diplomatic relations.
23 – June Labour defeats Likud in national election.
13 – July Yitzhak Rabin becomes prime minister.
16 – December Israeli deportation of 415 Hamas activists.

1993
19 – January Knesset repeals ban on contact with the PLO.
25 – July Israel launches Operation Accountability.
4 – August Assad rejects the Rabin 'deposit'.
29 – August Israeli cabinet approves the DoP.
10 – September Israel and the PLO exchange formal letters of recognition.
13 – September Israel-PLO DoP signed in Washington, DC.
10–17 – October first state visit to China by an Israeli prime minister, by Yitzhak Rabin.

1994
25 – February Massacre of Palestinians at Tomb of the Patriarchs in Hebron.
6 – April Hamas's first suicide attack kills eight people in Afula.
4 – May Israel and the PLO reach agreement in Cairo on limited Palestinian autonomy and establishment of the Palestinian Authority (Oslo I).
1 – July Yasser Arafat enters the Gaza Strip.

xiv Chronology

25 – July Washington Declaration ends state of war between Israel and Jordan.

26 – October Israel and Jordan sign a peace treaty in the Arava desert.

27 – October Failed Clinton-Assad summit in Damascus.

30 – October–1 – November First MENA Economic Summit in Casablanca.

1995

27 – June Commencement of second round of negotiations between Israel's and Syria's military chiefs of staff.

28 – September Signing of the Israel-PLO Interim Agreement on the West Bank and the Gaza Strip (Oslo II).

29–31 – October Second MENA Economic Summit in Amman.

4 – November Prime Minister Yitzhak Rabin is assassinated by a Jewish fanatic.

20 – November Israel and the EU sign an Association Agreement.

27–28 – November Launch of the European Mediterranean Partnership or Barcelona Process.

1996

5 – January Hamas chief bomb maker and terrorist, Yahya Ayash, assassinated by Israel.

20 – January Yasser Arafat elected president in first Palestinian elections.

25 – February A Hamas suicide bomber blows up a bus in Jerusalem.

2–4 – March Four Hamas suicide bombs kill fifty-nine Israelis.

13 March Peacemakers summit held in Sharm el-Sheik.

11 – April Israel launches Operation Grapes of Wrath in Lebanon.

29 – May Binyamin Netanyahu defeats Shimon Peres by less than 1 percent in Israeli elections.

25 – September Deadly clashes following opening of tunnel in the Old City of Jerusalem.

13 – November Third MENA Economic Summit in Cairo.

1997

15 – January Israel and the PLO sign the Hebron Protocol.

26 – February 1997 Israel authorizes construction of 6,300 units for Jewish housing at Har Homa in East Jerusalem.

Chronology xv

14 – March Ahmed Dakamesh, a Jordanian soldier, kills seven Israeli schoolgirls.

1998
23 – October Netanyahu and Arafat sign the Wye River Memorandum.
2 – December 1998 Israeli government decides to suspend implementation of the Wye River Memorandum.

1999
17 – May Ehud Barak defeats Binyamin Netanyahu in Israeli elections.
26 – May–26 – July Israel supplies weapons to India during its Kargil conflict with Pakistan.
26 – July Israeli-Syrian negotiations resume.
4 – September Israel and the PLO sign the Sharm el-Sheik Memorandum.
15 – December Israel-Syria Blair House Summit.

2000
3–10 – January Israel-Syria Shepherdstown Summit.
26 – March Failure of Assad-Clinton Geneva Summit, effectively ending Israeli-Syrian negotiations under Barak.
24 – May Israel withdraws unilaterally from southern Lebanon, ending a twenty-two-year military presence in the country.
1 – June EU-Israel Association Agreement comes into force.
10 – June Hafez al-Assad dies; Bashar al-Assad assumes Syrian presidency.
13 – July Israel cancels plan to sell Phalcon air radar to China after US pressure.
11–25 – July Failed Camp David Summit.
28 – September Outbreak of the al-Aqsa Intifada.
7 – October Hezbollah attempts to kidnap IDF soldiers in the Mount Dov area.
23 – December President Clinton presents his peace plan to end to the Israeli-Palestinian conflict.

2001
7 – March Ariel Sharon inaugurated as prime minister.
11 – September al-Qaeda terrorist attacks on the World Trade Centre and the Pentagon.
17 – October PFLP assassinates Israeli minister, Rehavam Ze'evi.

2002

3 – January Israeli naval commandos seize the *Karin A*, carrying weapons to the Palestinian Authority, in international waters in the Red Sea.

27 – March Hamas suicide bomber kills twenty-nine and wounds close to 150 in Park Hotel, Netanya.

28 – March Arab League summit in Beirut approves Saudi peace initiative.

29 – March Israel launches Operation Defensive Shield.

24 – June President Bush delivers speech, calling for a 'provisional' Palestinian state under new leadership.

5 – November Sharon dissolves national unity government following the departure of One Israel from the coalition.

2003

28 – January Likud wins thirty-eight seats in the Israeli elections, securing a second Sharon government.

19 – March Abu Mazen appointed as Palestinian prime minister

20 – March USA and Britain invade Iraq.

30 – April 'The Quartet' issues the road map.

25 – May Israeli government announces fourteen reservations on the road map.

3 – June Arab leaders' summit with President Bush in Sharm el-Sheik.

4 – June Summit in Aqaba to launch the road map.

8–10 – October First state visit of an Israeli prime minister to India, by Ariel Sharon. The Delhi Statement of Friendship and Cooperation between Israel and India is signed.

2004

22 – March Israel assassinates Hamas's founder and leader, Sheik Ahmed Yassin.

14 – April Letter from Bush to Sharon backing disengagement from Gaza, supports the incorporation of the major 'settlement blocks' in Israel in any future agreement with the Palestinians.

6 – June Israeli cabinet approved the disengagement plan from the Gaza Strip.

26 – October Knesset approves the disengagement plan from the Gaza Strip.

11 – November Yasser Arafat dies, prompting elections for the Palestinian presidency.

Chronology

2005

9 – January Mahmoud Abbas elected Palestinian president.

10 – January Third Sharon government sworn in.

15–22 – August Israel carries out the unilateral withdrawal from the Gaza Strip.

29 – April Syria withdraws its forces from Lebanon after a twenty-nine-year military presence.

2006

4 – January Ariel Sharon falls into a coma; Ehud Olmert becomes acting prime minister.

26 – January Hamas has a landslide victory in the Palestinian elections.

28 – March Kadima wins Israeli elections.

4 – May Ehud Olmert becomes prime minister.

25 – June Corporal Gilad Shalit is abducted by members of three Palestinian cells – Hamas, the Popular Resistance Committees and the Army of Islam.

12 – July Hezbollah launches raid across the Israeli border, killing eight soldiers and kidnapping two others.

12 – July-14 – August Israel-Hezbollah 2006 War.

2007

February Israel and Syria restart indirect peace negotiations via Turkish mediation.

8 – February Saudi Arabia brokers the Mecca Agreement between Fatah and Hamas, leading to a Palestinian national unity government.

14 – June Hamas's military takeover of the Gaza Strip; Mahmoud Abbas dissolves the national unity government.

6 – September Israel destroys the Syrian nuclear reactor in Dir el-Zur.

27 – November The Annapolis Conference.

2008

3 – May Ehud Olmert presents US Secretary of State with his idea for a final peace agreement with the Palestinians.

18 – June Egypt brokers a cease fire between Israel and Hamas.

16 – September Ehud Olmert presents his peace offer to Mahmoud Abbas.

15 – October US Congress passes the Naval Vessel Transfer Act, which legally grounds US commitment to Israel to maintain its Qualitative Military Edge in the Middle East.

27 – December Israel launches Operation Cast Lead.

xviii Chronology

2009

31 – March Binyamin Netanyahu sworn in as prime minister for second time.

14 – June Netanyahu concedes the need for a Palestinian state in his Bar-Ilan speech.

25 – November Israeli security cabinet approves partial ten-month settlement freeze.

2010

17 – December Arab uprisings erupt.

2011

11 – February Egyptian president, Hosni Mubarak, ousted.

2012

14 – November Israel launches Operation Pillar of Defence.

2013

22 – January Likud wins Israeli elections.

18 – March Netanyahu becomes prime minister for the third time.

2014

7 – July–26 – August Israel-Hamas war or Operation Protective Edge.

2015

14 – May Netanyahu becomes prime minister for the fourth time.

14 – July Iran nuclear deal signed between the Islamic Republic of Iran, five members of the UN Security Council plus Germany and the EU.

2016

13 – September The USA finalizes a $38 billion package over ten years, of military aid to Israel.

21 – February US Secretary of State, John Kerry, presents his peace plan to Binyamin Netanya in Aqaba, Jordan; Netanyahu rejects the proposal.

2017

6 – December President Trump recognizes Jerusalem as Israel's capital and orders the US Embassy to move there.

2018

8 – May USA withdraws from the Iran nuclear deal.

Chronology   xix

2019

19 – July Israel passes nationhood basic law.

2020

28 – January US President Donald Trump launches 'Deal of the
Century Peace Plan'.

Abbreviations

AIPAC	American Israeli Public Affairs Committee
API	Arab Peace Initiative
BJP	Bharatiya Janata Party
CIA	Central Intelligence Agency
CNPC	China National Petroleum Corporation
DIC	Disseminated Intravascular Coagulation
DoP	Declaration of Principles
EEC	European Economic Community
EESP	Economic Emergency Stability Plan
EMP	European Mediterranean Partnership
ENP	European Neighbourhood Policy
EU	European Union
FAPS	Framework Agreement on Permanent Status
FTA	Free Trade Agreement
GCC	Gulf Cooperation Council
GSS	General Security Service
GWoT	Global War on Terror
IAEA	International Atomic Energy Association
IAF	Israeli Air Force
MENA	Middle East and North Africa
MFA	Ministry of Foreign Affairs
MIT	Massachusetts Institute of Technology
MK	Member of Knesset
MSM	Million Cubic Metres
NATO	North Atlantic Treaty Organization
NPT	Non-Proliferation (of Nuclear Weapons) Treaty
NSC	National Security Council
OECD	Organization for Economic Cooperation and Development
PA	Palestinian Authority
PFLP	Popular Front for the Liberation of Palestine
PIJ	Palestinian Islamic Jihad

PKK	Kurdistan Workers' Party
PLO	Palestinian Liberation Organization
PRC	People's Republic of China
QME	Qualitative Military Edge
SLA	South Lebanese Army
UK	United Kingdom
UN	United Nations
UNIFIL	United Nations Interim Force in Lebanon
UNSC	United Nations Security Council
UNSCOM	United Nations Special Commission
UNSCR	United Nations Security Council Resolution
USA	United States of America
WWI	World War I
WWII	World War II

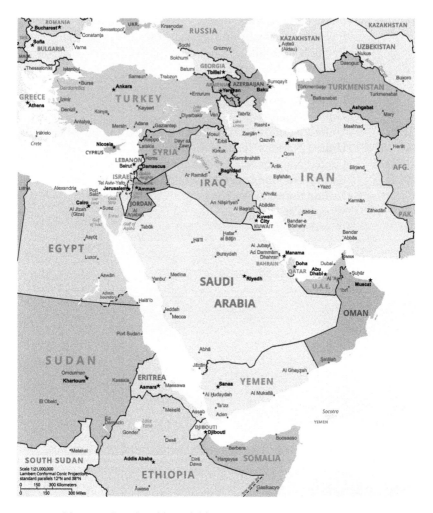

Map 0.1 Israel and its neighbours

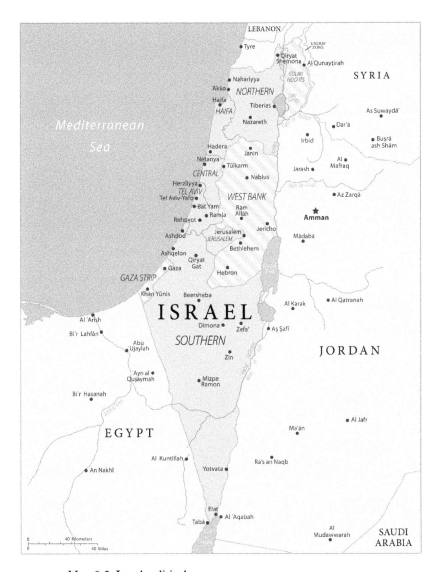

Map 0.2 Israel political map

Introduction

The end of the Cold War ushered in a new period in Israeli foreign policy, situating it in an unprecedentedly strong strategic position. The collapse of the Soviet Union, which had supported Israel's Arab foes, ended the bipolar world order and established the United States, Israel's closest ally, as the world's sole superpower. Shortly, thereafter, in the 1990–1 Gulf War, a US-led coalition expelled Iraqi forces from Kuwait, exposed deep divisions within the Arab world and weakened the Palestinian Liberation Organization (PLO), which supported Iraqi president Saddam Hussein during the conflict. These dramatic international shifts were coupled with changes within Israel. The successful restructuring of the Israeli economy via the 1985 Economic Emergency Stability Plan (EESP) and arrival of close to a million immigrants from the former USSR greatly increased Israel's state capacity to seize the opportunities and tackle the challenges generated by the end of the Cold War.

This book accounts for Israeli foreign policy since the end of the Cold War by proposing a new argument, namely, that it revolved around three foreign policy stances: entrenchment, engagement and unilateralism. As the Cold War drew to a close, Israeli foreign policymakers were deeply divided about which of these foreign policies to pursue. Prime Ministers Binyamin Netanyahu and Yitzhak Shamir, leaders of Likud, Israel's largest centre-right party, opted for retaining what I describe as Israel's foreign policy of entrenchment. This foreign policy position hinged on basing Israel's regional foreign policy on its iron wall of military might rather than on diplomacy and making peace with the Arab world in exchange for peace not territory. The Palestinians residing in the West Bank and Gaza Strip, which Israel had captured during the 1967 Arab-Israeli war, would be granted limited autonomy, but remain under Israeli military occupation.

Prime Ministers Yitzhak Rabin and Shimon Peres, the leaders of the Labour party, Israel's largest centre-left party at the time, favoured a different foreign policy stance. Both were more optimistic than Shamir about the opportunities presented by the end of the Cold War,

2   Introduction

but were more pessimistic about the prospects of prolonged occupation of the West Bank and the Gaza Strip. Rabin and Peres pursued what I term Israel's foreign policy of engagement. This involved making peace with the Arab world in exchange for returning territories that Israel had occupied in the 1967 Arab-Israeli war, putting a premium on diplomacy rather than on military force when engaging with the Middle East and downscaling the Israeli occupation.

The limits to entrenchment and engagement became clear within the decade after the end of the Cold War, giving rise to what I call Israel's foreign policy of unilateralism. It will be seen that unilateralism was associated mostly with prime Ministers Ehud Barak, Ariel Sharon and, to a lesser extent, Ehud Olmert. It was based on the recognition that downscaling the occupation was in Israel's national interest, but not via an agreement with an Arab counterpart, once Israeli foreign policymakers deemed it unachievable. Instead, Israel would negotiate its unilateral territorial withdrawal to recognized borders with the international community. Since the withdrawals were carried out without mutually binding agreements, Israel would manage the consequences of unilateralism by deploying military, diplomatic and economic foreign policy tools.

Thus, unilateralism, like engagement, embodied an understanding that was shared by five of the seven Israeli prime ministers since the end of the Cold War. Although Yitzhak Rabin, Shimon Peres, Ehud Barak, Ariel Sharon and Ehud Olmert were of different political persuasions, they all concluded that occupation of the Gaza Strip and the whole of the West Bank was not in Israel's interest. During their periods of office, to lesser or greater degrees, all sought to change the territorial status quo that had emerged following the 1967 Arab-Israeli war and Israel's 1982 invasion of Lebanon. In contrast, Yitzhak Shamir and Binyamin Netanyahu, during their premierships, opposed engagement, citing ideological and security reasons and had no faith in unilateral foreign policy moves. Why did Israel's prime ministers choose to pursue these particular foreign policy stances? What explained their respective foreign policy records? These vital questions are explored by this book.

Israel's foreign policy towards its most immediate and acute foreign policy arena, the Middle East, was linked inextricably to its wider foreign policy. The end of the Cold War presented Israel with some fundamental questions concerning its relations with the USA. The strategic alliance between the two states was forged during the Cold War as the USA identified Israel as a bulwark against Communism. Could the alliance survive the collapse of the USSR? Israel also faced serious dilemmas over its relations with the European Economic Community (EEC), harbinger of the European Union (EU), which, towards the end of the Cold War,

Introduction

backed the Palestinian struggle for an independent state more vocally and explicitly than in the past. Could Israel's ties with the EEC, its largest trading partner, endure amid the deepening rift?

Shifting the spotlight to the east, Israeli foreign policymakers had other matters to consider. Russia, which emerged as a weak state following the collapse of the USSR, was constrained in its ability to exert influence externally; it took the best part of ten years for it to rebuild itself amid US international domination. Meanwhile, China and India became rising powers. These countries, which are the world's most populous, have space programmes and nuclear weapons and rapidly developing economies, had refused to normalize relations with Israel during the Cold War. In fact, China and India were strongly supportive of the Arab states and especially the Palestinians. China was the first non-Arab country to recognize the PLO in 1965, while India likened the Palestinian struggle against Israel to its own anti-colonial path to independence from Britain. Did the end of the Cold War create an opportunity for Israel to normalize relations with these erstwhile hostile states? These intriguing questions are explored in Chapters 6 and 17, which draw links between Israel's foreign policy towards the Middle East, established powers, such as the EU and the USA, and rising powers, namely, China and India. These chapters are designed to place Israel's policy in the Middle East in a global context rather than to provide a comprehensive account of Israel's relations with these established and emerging powers.

Israeli foreign policy since the end of the Cold War is hardly a neglected topic. As the Cold War drew to a close a group called the Israeli revisionist, or 'new' historians, Avi Shlaim, Benny Morris, Ilan Pappe and Simha Flapan, closely scrutinized the standard Zionist version of the Arab-Israeli conflict. Avi Shlaim's monumental study, *The Iron Wall: Israel and the Arab World* and Benny Morris's own history of the conflict from 1881 to 2001, entitled *Righteous Victims*, remain the most enduring contributions of the new historians.[1] These ground-breaking studies challenged the claim that the fundamental cause of the Arab-Israeli conflict since 1948, including during the post-Cold War period, was the Arabs' rejection of Israel's legitimacy to exist and Arab diplomatic intransigence. Although Benny Morris changed his political views in the wake of the Palestinian al-Aqsa intifada, laying the blame at the door of the Palestinians, the impact of the new historians is irreversible. The Zionist and pro-Zionist historiography's portrayal of Israel as a country

[1] Avi Shlaim, *The Iron Wall: Israel and the Arab World* (London: Penguin, 2000); Avi Shlaim, *The Iron Wall: Israel and the Arab World* (London: Penguin, 2014, 2nd ed.); Benny Morris, *Righteous Victims: A History of the Zionist-Arab Conflict 1881–2001* (New York: Vintage Books, 2001).

4   Introduction

that goes to war only when there is no other choice has been shattered beyond repair.

In addition to the literature generated by Israeli foreign policy towards the Arab world, students have benefitted from excellent studies on Israel's bilateral relations with, inter alia, Iran, the USA, the EU, India and China, in addition to the several excellent scholarly accounts of particular episodes in Israeli foreign policy.[2] However, the extremely rich studies of Israeli foreign policy towards various arenas – the Middle East, the EU, the USA and Asia – are usually kept in separate compartments.

I have tried in this book to provide a more integrated narrative by placing Israel's foreign policy towards the Middle East in the context of its relations with the EU, USA, China and India. The structure of the book reflects the relative weight of each foreign policy arena. For example, US-Israeli relations attract more attention because they are more significant to Israeli foreign policy than any of the other bilateral relations. Similarly, Israel's most fateful foreign policy decisions – concerning war and peace – are taken in relation not to the EU, China or India, but to the Middle East, which dominates this book. However, in a departure from current debate, I place Israel's Middle Eastern foreign policy within the wider context of its relations beyond the region. The story I present examines how, when and why Israel's distinct approaches – entrenchment engagement, and unilateralism – to the Middle East, intersect with its foreign policy further afield, but also how each foreign policy trajectory evolved separately.

The Domestic Sources of Israeli Foreign Policy

The story of Israeli foreign policy since the end of the Cold War is told here from the perspective of how domestic factors shape foreign policy.[3] The emphasis on the domestic arena does not imply that the external environment is less important – Israel's regional environment is compelling and its ties with external powers, above all the USA, are crucial. Rather, the focus on the internal environment is informed by the assumption that the effects produced by the regional and broader international external environments depend on how they are filtered, understood and interpreted by the domestic actors, which then shaped Israeli foreign policy towards a range of issues, in significant ways. However, my

---

[2] The literature on these bilateral relations is reviewed extensively throughout the book.

[3] Explaining foreign policy in terms of its domestic sources is a well-established approach in foreign policy analysis, which I and others have developed elsewhere. See Chris Alden and Amnon Aran, *Foreign Policy Analysis: New Approaches* (London: Routledge, 2016); Christopher Hill, *Foreign Policy in the 21st Century* (London: Palgrave, 2016).

The Domestic Sources of Israeli Foreign Policy 5

approach does not follow Henry Kissinger's dictum that Israel has no foreign policy, only domestic politics. Instead, the book is based on a novel analytical framework that locates the domestic sources of Israeli foreign policy within three concentric circles, each of which represents the proximity of certain factors to, and their influence on, Israeli foreign policy.

The Decision-Makers

The decision-makers, above all the prime minister, comprise the most inner and influential circle. They operate in a particular decision-making structure, which is conditioned strongly by Israel's proportional representation electoral system. Parties need to pass an electoral threshold defined by the minimum number of votes needed to win a seat in the Knesset, Israel's parliament, which comprises 120 members. This electoral threshold of 3.25 per cent of the votes is low and has resulted in Israeli governments consisting of coalitions of several parties that govern according to a coalition-cabinet system.[4]

Political scientist, Charles Freilich, has observed that Israeli prime ministers have no institutionalized or formal sources of control over their ministers – especially those from rival parties. This severely constrains the prime minister's political authority over his cabinet members, who are political figures in their own right, with their own political agendas. Consequently, the task of maintaining the coalition becomes all-consuming and affects the decision-making process; even the most junior coalition partners can topple the government based on a narrow parliamentary majority. As a result, Israeli cabinets are prone to leaks and political discord.[5]

Nevertheless, and in contrast to the conventional wisdom in relation to studies of Israeli foreign policy decision-making, Israeli prime ministers tend not to be buffeted by the political forces of the government.[6] They rely on a small, private and loyal circle of trust rather than using their cabinets and the government to formulate and deliberate on sensitive foreign policy matters. It is within the narrow confines of this intimate circle of individually appointed confidants that, often fateful

---

[4] 'Elections for the Knesset, *Knesset Official Website*, https://main.knesset.gov.il/en/mk/pag es/elections.aspx, accessed 15 February 2019.
[5] Charles D. Freileich, 'National Security Decision Making in Israel', *Middle East Journal*, 60, 4, 2006: 645, 649.
[6] Studies following this conventional wisdom include Yehuda Ben Meir, *Civil-Military Relations in Israel* (New York: Columbia University Press, 1995); Yehezkel Dror, *Israeli Statecraft* (London: Routledge, 2011); Charles D. Freileich, *Zion's Dilemmas: How Israel Makes National Security Policy* (Cornell: Cornell University Press, 2013).

6   Introduction

decisions are deliberated and agreed. This represents the relative autonomy of the prime minister to set the direction of Israeli foreign policy, an autonomy that is enhanced by the political, symbolic and institutional resources accompanying the office. The chapters in this book trace how Israeli prime ministers bypassed and marginalized formal state institutions, especially the Ministry of Foreign Affairs (MFA), which often is led by a political rival of the prime minister. We will see how prime ministers sidestepped the MFA by deploying personal envoys, Mossad and General Security Services (GSS) personnel reporting directly to the prime minister, and even family members. Some have also assumed the position of defence minister alongside their position as prime minister, marginalizing the MFA still further. Since the government enjoys an almost automatic parliamentary majority, the Knesset cannot exercise significant oversight over the course of Israeli foreign policy once it has been established. Moreover, the Foreign Affairs and Defence Committee, responsible mainly for statutory oversight to manage government foreign policy, has historically been under-resourced and, thus, weak.

However, it would be a mistake to assume that Israeli prime ministers enjoy complete independence in decision-making, which is why I prefer the term 'relative autonomy' to describe their ability to shape Israel's foreign policy. The government, cabinet and parliament can – and often do – resist the prime minister's chosen foreign policy course. Yet this is far from a straightforward political task. To begin with, the prime minister has the prerogative to decide the agenda of government meetings. More significantly, however, confronting the prime minister over his chosen foreign policy path often involves also challenging the US president. Every one of Israel's prime ministers has sought to secure their most fateful foreign policy decisions by obtaining US backing before the issue was presented to the Israeli government. This direct and exclusive access to the US administration constitutes one of the most significant sources of the relative autonomy of Israeli prime ministers. Any attempt to oppose the prime minister's chosen foreign policy path, once it received US blessing, could be construed as opposing the US president. The political costs of such a confrontation, in terms of political standing within the Israeli public, would be significant, which has helped to suppress cabinet revolts.

The Security Network and its Limits

If the prime minister and the decision-makers comprise the inner circle of Israeli foreign policymaking, then the second concentric circle is

The Domestic Sources of Israeli Foreign Policy 7

constituted by the 'security network'.[7] Israel's highly informal, but very potent security network includes serving and retired Israeli Defence Force (IDF) generals, members of Israel's broader defence establishment, politicians, bureaucrats and private entrepreneurs. Their tight-knit structure around the defence establishment socializes them and instils shared values, perceptions and material interests, pursued via their influential civil roles, to determine key foreign policy issues.

The influence of the security network on Israeli foreign policy is compounded by institutionalized and formalized inroads into foreign policy-making made by the IDF over time. Of crucial importance is the Military Intelligence Directorate – Israel's main military intelligence-collecting agency and analyst of regional and international strategic developments. It produces the annual National Intelligence Estimate, which is the main strategic assessment made available to Israeli foreign policymakers on issues such as war and peace and regional and global processes. The IDF's Planning and Policy Directorate, which, since the early 1970s, has been the main unit in the military providing strategic and political assessments, represents the military's second institutional inroad into foreign policymaking.[8]

At the same time, the IDF's influence is tempered by a number of factors. The legal framework, in the form of the Military Basic Law (enacted in 1976) and later amendments to it, defines the relationship between the military and the government. The influence of the defence establishment is tempered also by its reliance, for its daily functioning, on resources generated by the civil sphere. For instance, the IDF is dependent on a constant civilian presence in its large reserve core, which, for many years, epitomized the notion of the IDF as a 'people's army'. Thus, the IDF is not a closed corporate entity insulated, as professional militaries are, from the civil sphere.[9] Consequently, extra-parliamentary movements and the media have developed mechanisms for calling the IDF to account.[10] On balance, therefore, the security network is significant in shaping foreign policy, although not outright determining it.

---

[7] Gabriel Sheffer and Oren Barak, *Israel's Security Networks* (Cambridge: Cambridge University Press, 2013).

[8] Yoram Peri, *Generals in the Cabinet Room: How the Israeli Military Shapes Israeli Policy* (Washington: United State Institute for Peace, 2006), pp. 50–76.

[9] Dan Horwitz, 'The Israeli Defense Forces' in Roman Kolowicz and Andrzej Korbonski (eds.), *Soldiers, Peasants and Bureaucrats* (London: George Allen & Unwin, 1982), pp. 77–106; Peri, *Generals in the Cabinet Room*, pp. 19, 23; Sheffer and Barak, *Israel's Security Network*, p. 2.

[10] Ben Meir, *Civil-Military Relations in Israel*, pp. 43–50; Stuart Cohen, 'Changing Civil-Military Relations in Israel', *Israel Affairs*, 12, 4, 2006: 775; Yagil Levy, *Israel's Materialist Militarism* (Lanham: Lexington Books, 2007), p. 52.

8   Introduction

Beyond Decision-Makers and the Security Network

A third concentric circle that shapes Israeli foreign policy is comprised of national narratives, which constitute Israeli identity. In thinking about the link between national narratives and foreign policy, five national discourses stand out. The first is Israel as a Jewish state. Although the specific meanings and practices of what being a Jewish state entails are disputed, there is a virtual consensus among the Jewish majority in Israel that religion must play some part in defining the state and everyday life.[11] The second is Israel as a Zionist state, which has different expressions. However, all strands of Zionism converge around the core idea that rather than being only a religious community the Jews are a nation, with the right to self-determination in the Land of Israel or parts of it. This view of Zionism is adopted by the majority of Israelis (bar some ultra-orthodox Jews and Palestinian citizens of Israel) as an integral part of their national identity.[12]

A third aspect of Israel's national narratives is the notion of Israel as a 'start-up nation', which developed since the mid-1980s in tandem with the advances of the Israeli economy, technological pioneering and innovation. The restructuring of the economy by the aforementioned EESP created access, for the first time in Israel's history, to capital that was not allocated by the government. This fundamental shift enabled the rise of an Israeli business community, which forged ties with global elites, global institutions and private sectors abroad. This vibrant, assertive, and independent-of-government, globally oriented business community, plays a pivotal role in shaping Israel's economic and diplomatic ties beyond the Middle East.[13]

The fourth national discourse concerns the Holocaust, which is deeply embedded in Israeli identity via a national Commemoration Day, legislation and museums, such as Yad Vashem. It emerges strongly in moments of crisis and conflict and has led political leaders to brand Israel's foes – from the PLO to Iran – as Nazi incarnations, amplifying the already high perception of Israeli foreign policymakers of the threats under which they operate.[14] The Holocaust is a long and threatening shadow that looms large over Israel and its foreign policy.

---

[11] See the excellent survey of the state of religion in Israel by Guy Ben Porat, *Between State and Synagogue* (Cambridge: Cambridge University Press, 2013).

[12] Shlomo Avineri, *The Making of Modern Zionism* (London: Basic Books, 1983); Gershon Shafir and Yoav Peled, *Being Israeli: The Dynamics of Multiple Citizenship* (Cambridge: Cambridge University Press, 2002).

[13] See Gershon Shafir and Yoav Peled, *The New Israel* (Boulder: Westview Press, 2000); Dan Senor and Saul Singer, *Start Up Nation: The Story of Israel's Economic Miracle* (New York: Twelve, 2011).

[14] Idit Zertal, *Israel's Holocaust and the Politics of Nationhood* (Cambridge: Cambridge University Press, 2011).

The fifth narrative is Israel as a democracy – within its 1967 borders it has a free press, free and fair elections, a competitive party system, universal suffrage and respect for freedom of speech. However, Israeli democracy has been seriously impaired by the prolonged and deepening occupation of the Gaza Strip (until 2005) and the West Bank where Palestinians are not granted Israeli citizenship, cannot vote for the Israeli Parliament and are subject to severe limitations on their personal movement and their movement of goods.[15]

These national narratives impose certain contours that determine what is possible and impossible and legitimate and illegitimate in the context of Israeli foreign policy. Israeli foreign policymakers use these categories to justify and legitimize certain foreign policy positions and to suppress others. Political parties – by dint of their central role in mobilizing group action, defining policy options and articulating alternative future paths – also play a critical role in shaping the contours of Israel's foreign policy. As the end of the Cold War approached, two political parties, Labour and Likud, dominated the Israeli domestic political landscape. The narrative supported by Likud was based on the saga of unceasing persecution of the Jews, the redemption and protection provided by Jewish military power and the right to settle the whole of Israel and the occupied territories. The Labour party was less clear on these issues. It articulated a narrative of Israel as sustainable without the territories, which offers a more hopeful appraisal of progress and peaceful coexistence.[16]

The debate over foreign policy issues between the two parties was part of a broader conflict over defining the domestic contours of Israeli foreign policy. The Jewish Settler Movement, the most powerful grassroots movement to have been established in Israel, supported Likud and its narrative. Its ideo-theology, which hinged on the idea that the people of Israel and the Land of Israel must remain inseparable if national salvation were to be achieved, was consistent with the political programme proposed by Likud. In contrast, Labour drew its popular support from individuals and organizations affiliated to Kibbutzim and the

---

[15] There are several studies on the Israeli occupation, for example Yael Berda, *Living Emergency: Israel's Permit Regime in the Occupied West Bank* (Stanford: Stanford University Press, 2017); Neve Gordon, *Israel's Occupation* (Berkeley: University of California Press, 2008). There is a debate about the degree to which Israeli democracy is applied to its 20 per cent strong Palestinian minority. For two opposing views see Dan Shiftan, *Palestinians in Israel: The Arab Minority and the Jewish States* (Or Yehuda: Kineret, Zmora Bitan, 2011) (in Hebrew); Ilan Peleg and Dov Waxman, *Israel's Palestinians: The Conflict Within* (Cambridge: Cambridge University Press, 2011).

[16] Yaron Ezrahi, *Rubber Bullets* (New York: Farrar Straus, & Giroux, 1997); Colin Shindler, 'Likud and the Search for Eretz Israel, *Israel Affairs*, 8, 1–2, 2001: 91–117.

10   Introduction

Histadroot, or the Labour Federation. By the end of the Cold War, Kibbutzim and the Histadroot had significantly declined as Israel was no longer a socialist country promoting collectivist economic and social policies to nation-build, which severely weakened the grassroots support for Labour. In the successive chapters of this book, I show how the unbalanced grassroots' support in favour of the centre-right impeded certain foreign policy options and facilitated others.

A Note on Sources

I should state at the outset that this is not an all-encompassing account of Israeli foreign policy since the end of the Cold War. The emphasis throughout is on Israel – on the perceptions, attitudes and thinking of its leaders, the influence of particular institutions and specific foreign policy determinants that lie beyond government and the Israeli state. The structure of the book is chronological, although I have made every effort to critically evaluate Israeli foreign policy rather than simply to provide a sequential narrative of events. In my reconstruction of Israel's foreign policy, I have relied, wherever possible, on primary sources. It is to Israel's credit that much of its foreign policy documents are freely available to researchers. Students of Israel's foreign policy are well served by the Israeli Ministry of Foreign Affairs series *Documents on the Foreign Policy of Israel*, which is now digitized and is available in different formats on the MFA website. I used this excellent resource extensively.

However, under the thirty-year rule, official documents from the Israeli archives pertaining to the period covered by this book are not yet available. I have tried to bridge this gap by using other types of primary sources and triangulating them. I have consulted memoirs in English, Hebrew and Arabic, authored by the leading decision-makers and practitioners, diplomatic diaries, media interviews and transcripts of Knesset debates and public lectures, government-appointed commissions of enquiry, US Congressional reports and documents released via the WikiLeaks website.

I have also made extensive use of information gained from almost thirty interviews I conducted with the chief policymakers and participants in the events described here: pollsters, leading political activists, heads of Israel's security services and foreign ministry, parliamentarians, ministers and one prime minister. As Avi Shlaim observed long ago, using interviews as evidence involves several problems, including faulty memory, self-serving accounts, distortions and deliberate falsifications.[17]

---

[17] Shlaim, *The Iron Wall*, p. xvii.

Nevertheless, the interviews I conducted were indispensable for filling some of the blanks. Interviews cannot replace documented history, but they are an essential complementary tool. I list my interviewees in the bibliography and I am grateful to all of them for their time and generosity in responding to my questions.

A final word refers to the debate over Israeli foreign policy, which evokes strong sentiment. For some, the very word 'Israel' is as toxic as the term apartheid was before its final demise. For others, 'Israel' is synonymous with a country that struggles to defend itself in the face of an implacably hostile region. These perceptions are unhelpful; they mask the intricacies of Israel and its foreign policy. The final call, therefore, is for scepticism towards categorical readings of Israel's foreign policy and the embracing of complex interpretations in their stead.

1 Entrenchment

Introduction

In August 1989, Solidarity, the first non-Communist party-controlled trade union in a Warsaw pact country, formed a government in Poland. The leader of Solidarity, Lech Wałesa, became president of Poland in December 1989, replacing General Wojciech Jaruzelski, Poland's last Communist leader. These dramatic events marked the end of Communist rule in Poland, precipitating and also giving momentum to the collapse of the entire Communist bloc in Eastern Europe and the end of the Cold War. These momentous events were observed closely by Israel. By 1990, its key foreign policymakers were left in no doubt that the 'vast political, social, and economic construct of the USSR and its satellites [had] lurched and crashed.'[1] Israel's foreign policymakers, like Robert Frost's traveller, stood long, and looked down as far as they could. The time had come to choose between the foreign policy course less travelled or keeping to familiar ways.

Foreign Policy Orientation and the Decision-Making Circle

The government tasked with responding to the end of the Cold War was established by Likud leader and prime minister, Yitzhak Shamir, on 11 June 1990. Apart from Likud, the coalition government included three ultra-orthodox parties, Agudat Israel, Shas and Degel HaTora, and three ultra-nationalist parties, Tehiya, Tzomet and the National-Religious Party, Mafdal. This ultra-religious ultra-nationalist coalition government, which, on its inception, commanded a slim majority of two members of the Knesset (MKs), had a clear foreign policy orientation.[2]

---

[1] Moshe Arens, *Broken Covenant: American Foreign Policy and the Crisis between the US and Israel* (New York: Simon & Schuster, 1995), pp. 104–5.
[2] Party and government composition, Knesset Official Website, https://main.knesset.gov.il /About/History/Pages/FactionHistory12.aspx, accessed 31 October 2018.

Its basic lines reflected its resolute opposition to relinquishing any territories Israel had occupied during the 1967 Arab-Israeli war in exchange for peace. In addition, the government was committed to expanding Jewish settlements established by Israel in the Golan Heights, the West Bank, Gaza Strip and East Jerusalem.[3]

The core foreign policy decision-making circle consisted of Prime Minister Yitzhak Shamir, Defence Minister Moshe Arens and their confidants. These included the newly appointed minister of justice, Dan Meridor, his brother, Sallai Meridor, Arens's chief aide, and two civil servants, Elyakim Rubinstein, and the prime minister's military secretary, Brigadier Azriel Nevo. David Levy, the foreign minister, who Shamir deemed as 'unfit to serve in the highest policy-making posts', was bypassed in sensitive foreign policy matters.[4] Another vocal rival the prime minister sidestepped was former general and defence minister, Ariel Sharon, who was appointed minister for construction and housing and was a cabinet member.[5]

Yitzhak Shamir and Moshe Arens brought considerable experience to the decision-making table. Shamir formed his 1990 government following three previous terms as Israel's prime minister while Arens, prior to his re-appointment as defence minister, had served terms as Israel's ambassador to the USA (1982–3), defence minister (1983–4), and foreign minister (1988–90). Both men were Likud veterans and political allies, and had long service in Israel's security network. Shamir was a member of Mossad between 1956 and 1965, while Arens was appointed chief engineer in the Israeli aircraft industry in 1962.[6]

Prime Minister Shamir, the chief decision-maker, was born Yitzhak Yzernitsky in 1915, in the small Polish town of Rzhnoi, in a household that blended ardent Zionism with Jewish tradition or *Yidishkeit*. However, Shamir was a deeply secular man and held in contempt the rabbinical institution that opposed Zionism.[7] In 1935, Shamir emigrated – or in Zionist parlance, 'made Aliya' – from Poland to British Mandated Palestine, which saved him from the fate met by the rest of his family.

---

[3] Government Policy Guidelines, 8 June, 1990, in Meron Medzini, *Israel's Foreign Relations: Selected Documents, 1988–1992* (vol. 12) (Jerusalem: Ministry of Foreign Affairs, 1993), pp. 345–9.

[4] Yitzhak Shamir, *Summing Up* (Tel Aviv: Yedioth Ahronoth, 1994), p. 176 (in Hebrew); Interview Sallai Meridor, 9 July, 2014, Jerusalem; Interview 1 Dan Meridor, 7 July, 2014, Jerusalem.

[5] Ariel Sharon, Knesset Official Website, https://main.knesset.gov.il/mk/Pages/MKGovRoles.aspx?MKID=125, accessed 31 October, 2018.

[6] Shamir, *Summing Up*, pp. 100–8, 119–29, 139–75; Arens, *Broken Covenant*, pp. 10–12, 140.

[7] Interview 1 Dan Meridor.

14   Entrenchment

Shamir's father, mother and two sisters were murdered in the Holocaust. Shamir summed up his feelings thus: 'I can't forget and I will never forgive.'[8]

This searing experience coloured Shamir's view of the world and of the Arab-Israeli conflict in particular. He was convinced that the Arab stance towards Zionism had 'nothing to do with the quest for self-determination', but rather was an extension of anti-Semitism and, hence, was perpetual.[9] Shamir's bleak conviction was that there was nothing Israel could offer the Arab side in exchange for recognizing its existence, and that Israel should not make peace with the Arab states until they realized that fighting against Israel was futile. Only then could peace be exchanged for peace, rather than territory.[10] This Hobbesian zero-sum -game approach was emblematic of the views espoused traditionally by the Israeli right, which formed the political and ideological core of the Shamir government.

Prime Minister Shamir and his defence minister personified another core ideological and political tenet of the Israeli right. Throughout his career in Likud, Shamir was renowned for his staunch support for retaining the territories Israel occupied during the 1967 Arab-Israeli war. Shamir's position was grounded in the belief that Jews had a more just claim to the Land of Israel than the Arabs' claim to that land.[11] Somewhat differently, Arens supported Israel's retention of the territories it occupied in the 1967 war, on the grounds of the strategic depth they provided to Israel rather than on purely nationalistic grounds. Through this prism, Arens saw the Gaza Strip, which Israel captured from Egypt in the 1967 war, as a demographic liability. It was heavily populated by 642,000 Palestinians while the Jewish presence amounted to only a few thousand settlers, who physically controlled just 25 per cent of the Strip, but 40 per cent of its arable land.[12]

The zero-sum-game view of the Arab-Israeli conflict and the opposition to a land-for-peace exchange, hinged on the assumption that time was on Israel's side. Shamir personified the view that prevailed among the Israeli right that, as the years went by, Israel could compel its Arab foes to accept its existence by building an impregnable iron wall of military strength.[13] However, until then, Israel must survive by the sword.

---

[8] Shamir, *Summing Up*, pp. 9–16.   [9] Shamir, *Summing Up*, p. 30.
[10] Haim Misgav, *Conversations with Yitzhak Shamir* (Tel Aviv: Sifriyat Poalim, 1997) (in Hebrew).
[11] Shamir, *Summing Up*, p. 177; Arens, *Broken Covenant*, p. 18.
[12] Arens, *Broken Covenant*, p. 208; population data from Israeli Central Bureau of Statistics, *Statistical Abstract of Israel* (Jerusalem: Government of Israel, 1993), p. 758.
[13] Shamir, *Summing Up*, p. 22.

Prime Minister Shamir and Defence Minister Arens concurred that premature deviation from this course could lead only to the Arab side making further demands on Israel, which then would be dealing with them from a significantly weaker position.[14]

Shamir's belief in the iron wall was ingrained in his political outlook by the fate met by his family, his leadership roles in the pre-state Jewish resistance group – the Fighters for the Freedom of Israel (Lehi) or the Stern Gang – and his service in Mossad.[15] His long experience of service in clandestine militarized organizations left him sceptical and suspicious of diplomacy, which was anathema to his secretive, distrustful and reserved personality.[16] Instead, Shamir subscribed heavily to the view that military force was the most effective means to a political end and he had no inherent commitment to democracy.[17]

Integral to the foreign policy orientation of Shamir, Arens and their confidants, was the view that strategic alliance with the USA was indispensable to Israel's security and prosperity.[18] Arens was convinced that the US-Israeli alliance was forged on the basis of these two countries' common ideals and democratic values.[19] Shamir, adopting a realpolitik approach, opined that the alliance would endure as long as Israel did not burden the USA and was confident that differences – short of a direct clash of interests – could be resolved within the ongoing US-Israeli dialogue. Accordingly, Shamir's foreign policy approach to the USA hinged on manoeuvring between safeguarding what the Israeli leadership defined as its 'red lines' and the demands imposed on Israel by the USA.[20]

A Threat from Iraq

Israel's initial reaction to the end of the Cold War was made crystal clear in a meeting of top US and Israeli officials, held on 20 July 1990. In attendance on the American side were Defence Secretary Dick Cheney, Undersecretary for Defence Paul Wolfowitz and Defence Intelligence Agency Head Lieutenant General Harry Soster. Israel was represented by the IDF head of intelligence, Major General Amnon Shahak, the head of Mossad, Shabtai Shavit and Defence Minister Arens, who laid out Israel's position: 'Whereas in Eastern Europe there is glasnost and the

---

[14] Misgav, *Conversations*, p. 66; Arens *Broken Covenant*, pp. 35–6.
[15] Shamir, *Summing Up*, p. 193.   [16] Shamir, *Summing Up*, pp. 22–38.
[17] Shamir, *Summing Up*, pp. 111–12; Avishai Margalit, 'The Violent Life of Yitzhak Shamir, *New York Review of Books*, 14 May 1992.
[18] Arens, *Broken Covenant*, p. 191.
[19] Interview with Moshe Arens, 8 July, 2014, Savion.
[20] Interview Sallai Meridor; Interview 1 Dan Meridor; Misgav, *Conversations*, pp. 108–9.

16   Entrenchment

beginnings of democracy', Arens explained, 'the Middle East, except for Israel, continued to be ruled by dictators, and Muslim fundamentalism was running rampant. The Soviet Union and the Eastern European countries were disarming while the arms race in the Middle East was intensifying.'[21]

The message coming out of Israel via its defence minister, regarding the significance of the end of Cold War for the Middle East, was that nothing much had changed. From the Israeli vantage point, the significance of the end of the Cold War lay elsewhere, most crucially, in the 'opening up of the gates' to a massive Jewish Aliya from the Soviet Union to Israel. In addition, the ending of the conflict between the two super powers was seen in Jerusalem as creating the conditions that might prompt Eastern European countries and the USSR to renew the diplomatic relations with Israel that had been severed in 1967.[22] By February 1990, former Czechoslovakia, Hungary and Poland had restored diplomatic relations with Israel.[23] Through this lens, the end of the Cold War was perceived not as requiring a foreign policy rethink but rather confirmed that the foreign policy course Israel had pursued during the Cold War was sound. Israel now should take advantage of the new opportunities to consolidate in order to confront the challenges that lay ahead.[24]

One of those challenges was the threat posed by Iraq, whose president, Saddam Hussein, issued a clear warning to Israel. In a speech he delivered on 2 April 1990, Hussein threatened that, were Israel to attempt to launch another strike similar to the one in 1981 that had destroyed the Iraqi Osirak nuclear reactor, Iraq would retaliate with binary chemical weapons: 'By God, we will make the fire eat up half of Israel if it tries to do anything against Iraq.'[25] It is unclear whether there was an Israeli plan afoot to attack Iraq. However, it is apparent that the Israelis viewed Iraq's concern over a potential Israeli strike as a threat in and of itself.[26] The Israeli view was shaped in part by the prime minister's and defence minister's perception of Saddam Hussein as a new Hitler after the Iraqi president authorized use of chemical weapons in 1984 against Iranian troops and in 1988 against Iraqi-Kurdish civilians in the village of Halabja.[27] Understandably, in early 1990, following completion of the construction of six Scud missile launchers in western Iraq, Israel saw itself

---

[21] Arens, *Broken Covenant*, p. 149.

[22] Shamir, *Summing Up*, pp. 251–4; Arens, *Broken Covenant*, pp. 104–6; Efraim Halevy, *Man in the Shadows: Inside the Middle East Crisis with a Man Who Led the Mossad* (Tel Aviv: Matar, 2006), p. 24 (in Hebrew).

[23] Medzini, *Israel's Foreign Relations*, p. 332.   [24] Interview 1 Dan Meridor.

[25] Quoted in Arens, *Broken Covenant*, p. 130.   [26] Arens, *Broken Covenant*, p. 147.

[27] Arens, *Broken Covenant*, pp. 150, 213; On Iraqi attacks, see Charles Tripp, *A History of Iraq* (Cambridge: Cambridge University Press, 2007), p. 236.

A Threat from Iraq

as vulnerable to a ballistic attack that might have a chemical component.[28] Another source of Israeli concern was the lack of direct communication lines with Iraq, which risked misperceptions, miscalculations and misunderstandings, on both sides, resulting in an unintended escalation. In these circumstances, Israeli intelligence rendered the threat posed by Saddam Hussein's 2 April speech, 'an immediate danger'.[29]

From this point, events moved quickly. On 2 August 1990, Iraqi forces invaded Kuwait, which was occupied and claimed by Saddam Hussein as the nineteenth province of Iraq. The invasion was followed by a long period of waiting, during which a US-led coalition of western states, the USSR and Arab states was built to evict the Iraqi forces from occupied Kuwait. The countdown to the military showdown began on 29 November 1990, after the passing of Resolution 678 by the United Nations Security Council (UNSC), authorizing the use of 'all necessary means' against Iraq unless it withdrew its forces from Kuwait by 15 January 1991.[30]

It was clear to Prime Minister Shamir that, if the US-led coalition attacked militarily, then Iraq would seek to drive a wedge between the Arab states and the rest of the US-led coalition by drawing Israel into the conflict.[31] Israel was particularly concerned about an Iraqi attack from Jordan, which shared the longest international border with Israel. These concerns were well founded. In early 1990, Iraq and Jordan had forged a military alliance and established a joint air squadron, enabling Iraq to reconnoitre the Israeli side of the Jordan valley from Jordanian airspace. King Hussein of Jordan, a close friend of the Iraqi president, believed wholeheartedly that Saddam Hussein could provide the leadership needed to restore pride and dignity to the Arab world. His assessment of the Iraqi president, which he repeated in private conversations, including with his Israeli Mossad contact, Efraim Halevy, was echoed by the wide pro-Iraqi sentiment within Jordan itself.[32]

Speaking in the Knesset on 7 August, 1990, Arens issued the stern warning that were Israel to see any 'entry of the Iraqi army into Jordan, we shall act'.[33] The warning was acknowledged by King Hussein, who, a few

---

[28] James A. Baker, *The Politics of Diplomacy: Revolution, War, and Peace* (New York: G.P. Putnam's Sons, 1995), p.267; Arens, *Broken Covenant*, p. 163.

[29] Arens, *Broken Covenant*, pp. 135, 148; Shlaim, *The Iron Wall*, p. 472; Dick Cheney, *In My Time: A Personal and Political Memoir* (New York: Threshold Editions, 2011), p. 182.

[30] UNSCR Resolution 678, http://unscr.com/en/resolutions/678, accessed 5 November 2018.

[31] Shamir, *Summing Up*, p. 264.

[32] Halevy, *Man in the Shadows*, pp. 31–3; Nigel Ashton, *King Hussein of Jordan: A Political Life* (New Haven: Yale University Press, 2008), pp. 258–60.

[33] Arens, *Broken Covenant*, p. 153.

18 Entrenchment

days later, announced publicly that Jordan would 'not open its borders to "tourist visits" by foreign armies from either East or West'.[34]

At the same time, Israel and Jordan had cooperated covertly for many years, on a wide range of strategic issues and, especially, following the 1970–71 'Black September' events. During that period, the PLO had tried to topple King Hussein, who had fended off the attempt with the aid of Israel and Jordan's Western backers, Britain and the USA.[35] Subsequently, Israel and Jordan had established an infrastructure for secret collaboration, which was also used following the Iraqi invasion of Kuwait. On 4–5 January, 1991, Israeli and Jordanian top brass met in King Hussein's home in Ascot, England. The Jordanian side was represented by King Hussein and his military advisor, General Zeid bin Shaker.[36] Representing Israel were Prime Minister Shamir, Mossad's Efraim Halevy, IDF Deputy Chief of Staff Ehud Barak, Cabinet Secretary Elyakim Rubinstein and Director General of the Prime Minister's Office, Yossi Ben Aharon. The main objective of the meeting was to avoid an unintended clash between the IDF and the Jordanian army. To this effect, King Hussein pledged to the Israelis that his armed forces would be mobilized solely for defensive purposes and that he would not allow Iraqi forces to use Jordanian sovereign space. However, he emphasized that he could not control 'the outer space', which would be penetrated if Iraq launched a missile attack against Israel.[37] Equally, King Hussein refused to grant the Israeli request to use Jordanian airspace in the event of an Iraqi attack on Israel.[38] The meeting assuaged the tensions in Jerusalem regarding the threat posed to Israel from its immediate eastern flank. However, not all were persuaded. Minister of housing and cabinet member, Ariel Sharon, for instance, opposed the diplomatic signals the government sent to Jordan. He advocated using military force in the event of an Iraqi attack, irrespective of the Jordanian position.[39]

The long waiting period also required liaison with the USA. On 8 August 1990, US ambassador to Israel, Bill Brown, met Defence Minister Arens. The ambassador relayed the US request that Israel exercise the utmost restraint during the crisis and take no pre-emptive action against Iraq. The Israeli leadership construed the request as a US decision to sideline Israel in order to secure Arab cooperation with the US-led international effort against Iraq and, possibly, beyond. It was in sharp

---

[34] Ibid.
[35] Moshe Zak, *King Hussein Makes Peace* (Ramat-Gan: Bar-Ilan University Press, 1996) (in Hebrew).
[36] Shlaim, *The Iron Wall*, p. 478.   [37] Interview 1 Dan Meridor.
[38] Ashton, *King Hussein of Jordan*, pp. 275–6; Halevy, *Man in the Shadows*, pp. 35–6.
[39] Shlaim, *The Iron* Wall, p. 479.

A Threat from Iraq   19

contrast to the strategic-ally role previous US administrations had ascribed to Israel during most of the Cold War. Now, as the first major post-Cold War international crisis was unfolding, Israel was, at best, immaterial to realization of US interests in the Middle East and, at worst, a liability.[40]

Tellingly, as Israel's ambassador to the US, Zalman Shuval, recalls, Israel was not among the countries the USA had briefed about how to prepare for a possible war against Iraq.[41] In fact, the waiting period was fraught with US-Israeli tensions. The USA stalled over Israeli requests for cooperation. Instead, it provided assurances that the US air force would neutralize any threat to Israel, especially in western Iraq. The USA also offered to deploy US-manned Patriot anti-ballistic weapons systems in Israel, an offer that Israel declined.[42] In summing up the view from Jerusalem regarding cooperation with the USA, Minister of Defence Arens noted that he was 'frustrated by the distrust that coloured' the US attitude towards Israel.[43]

Political strains compounded the tensions generated by the disagreements over the extent of US-Israeli military cooperation. In 1990, the popular uprising by the Palestinians against Israeli occupation of the West Bank, East Jerusalem and the Gaza Strip, dubbed the Intifada, entered its third year. Saddam Hussein sought to exploit the prolonged conflict by suggesting, early in the crisis, on 12 August, that Iraq might withdraw from Kuwait if Israel withdrew from all the occupied territories and Syria withdrew from Lebanon. Clearly, Saddam Hussein was trying to transform the conflict that had begun as a dispute between Iraq and a wide-based international coalition into an Arab-Israeli clash. This would put political pressure on the Arab states to leave the US-led coalition or be perceived as cooperating with Israel in a war against another Arab country.[44] Linking the Israeli-Palestinian conflict and the Kuwait crisis was a cunning move. It created a source of concern throughout the waiting period since there was virtually no prospect of a change of the Shamir government policy towards the Palestinian Intifada. In fact, senior cabinet colleagues, such as Ariel Sharon and former chief of staff, Raphael Eitan, chided Prime Minister Shamir and Defence Minister Arens for being 'too soft' on the Palestinian insurgency.[45]

---

[40] Shamir, *Summing Up*, pp. 265–8; Arens, *Broken Covenant*, p. 151.
[41] Zalman Shuval, *Diplomat* (Rishon Le Zion: Miskal, 2016), p. 174 (in Hebrew).
[42] Arens, *Broken Covenant*, pp. 158, 171; Halevy, *Man in the Shadows*, p. 34; Cheney, *In My Time*, p. 211.
[43] Arens, *Broken Covenant*, p. 175.
[44] Shlaim, *The Iron Wall*, pp. 475–6; Baker, *The Politics of Diplomacy*, p. 292.
[45] Arens, *Broken Covenant*, p. 163.

20   Entrenchment

By early January 1991, military confrontation between the US-led coalition and Iraq was inevitable. The Israeli government had significantly stepped up preparations on the home front and had begun distributing gasmasks to the entire population. Concurrently, cooperation with the USA was tightened. A secure telephone line, codenamed 'Hammer Rick', was installed to enable direct communication between Defence Minister Arens and his US counterpart, Dick Cheney. A system was put in place to allow US satellites to provide early warning of Iraqi missiles launched against Israel, directly to the Israeli ministry of defence, via Hammer Rick. Nevertheless, the cooperation fell short of what Israel wanted. The USA continued to reject Israeli requests for real-time intelligence and a framework for military cooperation. It was concerned that the information might be exploited by Israel for a pre-emptive attack against Iraq, which could break up the US-led international coalition.[46]

The 1991 Gulf War

On 17 January 1991, two days after expiry of the international ultimatum issued to Iraq to withdraw its forces from Kuwait, the US-led coalition launched an attack on the Iraqi forces. The 1991 Gulf War, which came to be known as Operation Desert Storm, lasted for six weeks, from 17 January to 28 February. It consisted of a long period of airstrikes by the US-led coalition, coupled with a ground invasion on 24–28 February.[47]

The war reflected the fast moving geopolitical changes following the end of the Cold War. The USA and USSR cooperating with Arab countries, including Syria, which until recently had been a Soviet client, to fight a fellow Arab country, Iraq. Israel, officially at least, was not part of the conflict. However, Iraqi President Saddam Hussein confirmed the earlier intelligence prediction that he would try and draw Israel into the war. Throughout Operation Desert Storm, Israel was subjected to salvos of ground-to-ground missiles from Iraq. Some thirty-eight Iraqi versions of Scud missiles fell in nineteen missile attacks, targeting Israel's most densely populated areas. Shortly after the attacks began, Defence Minister Arens reversed the earlier Israeli decision and requested US Secretary of Defence Dick Cheney, that US-manned Patriot missile batteries be deployed in Israel. However, as the USA eventually

---

[46] Arens, *Broken Covenant*, pp. 169–71; Cheney, *In My Time*, p. 211; Shamir, *Summing Up*, p. 266.

[47] For an extended account of the conflict, see Ephraim Karsh and Lawrence Freedman, *The Gulf Conflict, 1990–1991: Diplomacy and War in the New World Order* (London: Faber & Faber, 1993).

The 1991 Gulf War

conceded, the Patriot missiles proved ineffective for intercepting the Scud missiles launched by Iraq on Israel. A report by the Israeli Air Force (IAF), which was presented to the Americans by Defence Minister Arens, concluded that Patriots succeeded in eliminating Scud missiles in only 20 per cent of attempts.[48] Nonetheless, the total damage caused by the attacks was limited: one direct fatality, 208 injured and 7,667 properties hit.[49] Even so, the Scud attacks had a demoralizing effect; they caused significant disruption to everyday life as residents of Haifa and the greater Tel-Aviv area sought refuge in areas that were not targeted by the Iraqi missiles. Also, the fear that Iraq would launch a chemical attack against Israel remained acute throughout the war.[50]

Israeli foreign policymakers fiercely debated Israel's response in regular meetings between cabinet ministers and senior IDF members during the war. Israel needed to strike a balance between stopping (or at least limiting) the Scud attacks, the real risk of an Iraqi chemical strike against Israel, and the impact of Israeli foreign policy actions on the US-led international coalition. Two factions emerged. There was a group of hardliners within the cabinet – Likud's Ariel Sharon, Tzomet's leader and former general chief of staff, Rafael Eitan, and Professor Yuval Ne'eman from Tehiya – who demanded a military response with or without US approval: 'Send the aircraft to photograph!', demanded Sharon of Defence Minister Arens in the cabinet meeting following the first Scud attack. 'Even without coordinating with the US', queried Arens? 'Notify them and fly!', thundered Sharon.[51] As the Scud attacks continued, these hardliners, more explicitly and more publicly, demanded that Israel put a stop to them and punish Iraq.[52]

Prime Minister Shamir, Defence Minister Arens, their confidants and Foreign Minister Levy, took a different line centred on the notion that Israel must have US permission and a joint military framework for such an attack. Failing this, Israel must continue to comply with the US demand for forbearance in order to thwart the Iraqi attempt to drive a wedge

---

[48] Shuval, *Diplomat*, p. 207.

[49] Israeli Ministry of Foreign Affairs, *The Gulf War* (1991), http://mfa.gov.il/MFA/AboutI srael/History/Pages/The%20Gulf%20War%20-%201991.aspx, accessed 5 November, 2018.

[50] Confirmed by former Head of the Iraqi Intelligence, General Wafiq al-Sammarai in Cheney, *In My Time*, p. 220; for the Israeli awareness see Shamir, *Summing Up*, p. 270; Baker, *The Politics of Diplomacy*, p. 408.

[51] Arens, *Broken Covenant*, p. 180.

[52] Ibid, p. 197; David Landau, *Arik: The Life of Ariel Sharon* (New York: Alfred A. Knopf, 2013), p.263.

22   Entrenchment

between the USA and the Arab members of the coalition by drawing Israel into the conflict.[53]

Forbearance was untypical of Israel, whose deterrence policy hinged on not just response to military attacks, simple tit-for-tat, but on escalation.[54] However, the understandings reached with King Hussein on the eve of the war were a significant factor in restraining the Israeli response.[55] More significant, however, was the US stance. The US president's special envoy to Israel during the conflict, Lawrence Eagleburger, emphasized the resolute US objection to an Israeli military strike on Iraq. The USA, he stressed, 'would do nothing to enable an Israeli attack'.[56] Matching words to deeds, throughout the war, the intelligence provided by the USA to Israel was out of date, and the USA refused to create a joint military framework.[57]

Domestic factors also mattered. The IDF's top brass does not seem to have been eager for Israel to 'go it alone' against Iraq.[58] This was very evident in the diplomatic mission to the USA by Major General Ehud Barak, the deputy chief of staff, and the director general of the ministry of defence, David Ivri, on 27–29 January, 1991, in the midst of the conflict. Their brief from Defence Minister Arens was to relay Israel's determination to take military action, even if the Americans withheld the coordination needed for such an operation. After their debriefing on their return to Israel, Arens felt that the generals 'had not made that point with sufficient emphasis'.[59] The IDF's preparations for attacking the Scud launchers in western Iraq continued notwithstanding, but the view of the military was that 'the potential gains of such a mission were balanced by the attendant risk'.[60] Furthermore, the Israeli politico-military top brass itself was sceptical about whether an attack by the IDF would yield a better military result than the combined US and UK airstrikes that were pounding western Iraq daily.[61]

However, the most significant restraint on Israel's response to the Iraqi attacks was the posture of forbearance championed by Prime Minister Yitzhak Shamir. Although in the midst of the war, Arens veered increasingly towards the view that Israel should react militarily to the Iraqi attacks, Shamir remained resolute. Throughout the war, he put all his political weight in the cabinet on preserving Israel's restraint, a decision

---

[53] Arens, *Broken Covenant*, p. 191; Shamir, *Summing Up*, p. 270.
[54] Avner Yaniv, *Deterrence without the Bomb: The Politics of Israeli Strategy* (Lanham: Lexington Books, 1987), pp. 164–6.
[55] Conversation with Professor Avi Shlaim.
[56] Baker, *The Politics of Diplomacy*, p. 389; Cheney, *In My Time*, p. 214.
[57] Interview 1 Dan Meridor.   [58] Interviews 1 Dan Meridor; Interview Arens.
[59] Arens, *Broken Covenant*, p. 198.   [60] Ibid, pp. 200, 208, 211.
[61] Interview 1 Dan Meridor.

that the prime minister described as the most difficult in his political career.[62] Opting for forbearance was driven by a simple calculation, which was consistent with Shamir's realpolitik world view. Shamir was intensely aware of the risk of the US-led international coalition splintering were Israel to retaliate, and that this would significantly undermine the already strained US-Israeli relations and spare Iraq. Shamir reasoned that the price exacted from Israel would be higher than any gains that could be achieved by a targeted Israeli attack on Iraq's Scud launchers. A majority in the cabinet sided with the Prime Minister, as did the majority of the Israeli public according to opinion polls conducted during the war, and this kept the hardliners in the cabinet in the minority.[63]

A mixed picture emerged as the dust of Desert Storm began to settle. The 1991 Gulf War was the first time that the Israeli heartland had been hit. Israel's untypical forbearance response had created a sense of humiliation and concern that Israeli deterrence had been dented, and had highlighted Israel's vulnerability to a ballistic attack. The result was more investment in anti-missile technology, such as the Arrow missile, which was designed to intercept tactical-ballistic missiles.[64] At the same time, Iraq had been defeated, its army dealt a mighty blow and the country subjected to harsh sanctions and Saddam Hussein's international standing had been weakened significantly. Within six weeks, Iraq had been transformed from a formidable threat to Israel to that of a contained risk. The demise of the USSR, the patron of Israel's Arab foes during the Cold War, meant that no Arab state – including either Syria or Libya – was capable of taking on Iraq's aim to lead the Arab world in an assault against Israel.

Preparing Arab-Israeli Negotiations

Following the end of the Gulf War, policy makers in the USA estimated that its credibility was at its highest since the end of World War II, and at the zenith of its influence in the Middle East. A jubilant USA set out to establish a 'new world order' that would include Arab-Israeli peace.[65] Having emerged as the sole world super power and leader of the coalition that had defeated Iraq, the USA was well placed to act as the sole mediator in the Arab-Israeli conflict. Negotiations would be based on UN Security Council Resolutions (UNSCR) 242 and 338, which stipulated that Israel withdraw from

[62] Interview 1 Dan Meridor; Interview Sallai Meridor; Shamir, *Summing Up*, p. 263.
[63] Shamir, *Summing Up*, pp. 270–71; Arens, *Broken Covenant*, p. 203.
[64] Ze'ev Schif, 'Israel after the War', *Foreign Affairs*, 70, 2, 1991: 19–33.
[65] Baker, *The Politics of Diplomacy*, pp. 412–15.

24   Entrenchment

lands it occupied in 1967 in exchange for peace with the Arabs.[66] Crucially, its overwhelming power notwithstanding, the USA would not try to enforce peace. Rather, it saw its role as a catalyst for peace through the breaking of the taboo on direct talks between Israel and the Arab governments. Hitherto, bar Egypt, Arab governments had refused to engage directly with Israel.[67]

US Secretary of State James Baker, who led the US mediation team, used sticks and carrots to draw Israel and the Arabs into direct negotiations. He sought to get the parties to the negotiations invested in the process 'so it's not so easy to walk away from it'. 'We want them to build their stake in its success', Baker wrote, 'and increase the cost to them of failure'.[68] In this vein, Secretary of State Baker threatened to 'lay the dead cat at the doorstep' of any party he deemed responsible for failing his diplomatic mission.[69] Equipped with this mediation 'toolkit' Baker embarked on a shuttle-diplomacy mission where he would try and take ideas that Israel could 'live with' and 'sell' them, to the Arab negotiators.[70]

The launch of Baker's shuttle diplomacy mission, during a two-day visit to Israel, on 9–10 April 1991, was sensitive; previous US mediation efforts in 1988–9 had ended in failure, which Baker attributed to Prime Minister Shamir's intransigence and reluctance to respect his previous commitments.[71] 'Battered, beaten, and betrayed', was how Baker and President Bush felt during that acrimonious round of negotiations.[72] The Israelis felt equally let down, particularly by Baker's demand to 'lay aside once and for all the unrealistic vision of a Greater Israel'.[73] How, wondered Shamir, could the adjective 'Greater' be applied to a tiny country like Israel?[74] Further, on 1 March 1990, the USA conditioned $US400 million of loan guarantees for housing for Soviet Jewish immigrants, on Israel's agreement to halt the construction of new settlements in the occupied territories.[75] Aghast, Prime Minister Shamir charged the USA with pressurising Israel to make political concessions to the Arab side by curtailing its capacity to deal with the 'humanitarian issue' – housing for new immigrants.[76]

---

[66] Ibid, pp. 415-17.
[67] Dennis Ross, *The Missing Peace: The Inside Story of the Fight for Middle East Peace, 1988–2000* (New York: Farrar, Straus, & Giroux, 2004) pp. 65–6.
    Baker, *The Politics of Diplomacy*, p. 506.   [68] Ibid, p. 444.   [69] Ibid, pp. 443–70.
[70] Ibid, p. 416; Ross, *The Missing Peace*, p. 55.   [71] Ibid, p. 116.   [72] Ibid, pp. 123, 128.
[73] Ibid, p. 121.   [74] Shamir, *Summing Up*, p. 244.
[75] Baker, *The Politics of Diplomacy*, pp. 123–8, 542.
[76] Shamir, *Summing Up*, pp. 255–8.

Preparing Arab-Israeli Negotiations 25

The cloud of the previous encounter hung over the 9 April 1991 meeting between Baker and the Israeli leadership.[77] However, on hearing Israel's opening positions, Baker felt 'relieved' that they had 'moved a little' from some of their previous stances.[78] Israel agreed to participate in a one-off regional 'meeting', to be followed immediately by direct Arab-Israeli negotiations, whereas in the past the Israelis had rejected outright participation in an international conference. The Israelis consented to the USA and the USSR co-hosting the meeting, but objected to active roles of the EEC and the United Nations (UN), both of which Israel perceived as biased towards the Arab side.

During the following eight months, Secretary of State Baker made eight visits to the Middle East, which focused on negotiating the conditions for opening an Arab-Israeli dialogue. Israel's position was shaped by two sets of determinants that pushed and tugged in different directions. On the one hand, there was a set of domestic factors that included the decision-makers' ideological commitment to the integrity of the Land of Israel, the political requirement to keep intact the right-wing Shamir government, and lobbying from the settlers. Members of Likud, especially and, most vocally, Ariel Sharon, were subjecting the prime minister and his allies to intense political criticism and accusing the prime minister of making too many concessions to US demands. The ultra-right wing parties, Tzomet, Tehiya and Moledet – a party that Shamir had brought into the government during the Gulf War and which advocated physical transfer of Palestinians from Israel – added to the prime minister's coalition woes. This troika, which threatened to topple the government, accused the prime minister of selling out the Land of Israel. At the same time, the USA was insisting that Israel find some common ground with the Arab positions, which, by definition, were far removed from the Israeli right agenda.[79]

Balancing this two-level game, Israel conceded to US demands concerning procedural matters. It retracted its initial objections to calling the meeting a 'conference' and where such a 'conference' might be held. The Israelis settled ultimately for Madrid after initially insisting it should take place in the Middle East. They also agreed to EEC participation in the meeting, with UN presence as an observer.[80] These concessions on procedural matters were a shrewd tactic to increase Israel's ability to

---

[77] The content of this meeting is derived from: Baker, *The Politics of Diplomacy*, pp. 444–7; Interview 1 Dan Meridor; Arens, *Broken Covenant*, pp. 224–6; Ross, *The Missing Peace*, pp. 70–71.

[78] Baker, *The Politics of Diplomacy*, p. 444.

[79] Interviews Sallai and Dan Meridor; Arens, *Broken Covenant*, pp. 226, 238; Shamir, *Summing Up*, p. 278.

[80] Israeli Ministry of Foreign Affairs, 'Madrid Letter of Invitation', 30 October 1991, www .mfa.gov.il/mfa/foreignpolicy/peace/guide/pages/madrid%20letter%20of%20invitation

26   Entrenchment

hold firm on issues its decision-makers deemed substantive or irreconcilable with domestic politics. For example, it was clear to the Israelis that the USA, the USSR and the Europeans wanted to see a return to the 1967 borders and this was what the Arabs would demand.[81] Thus, the opening positions of most of the prospective participants in the conference were in stark contrast to the stance of the Israeli government, which was staunchly opposed to the land-for-peace formula. Israel was, a priori, in a vulnerable minority position, which was why it objected to negotiating within the format of an international conference.[82]

Israel also resisted any negotiating format that would afford the Palestinians statehood status, not least through independent Palestinian delegation participation in the conference.[83] In this context, Israel rejected the PLO as a negotiating partner, in spite of its recognition by the Arab League since 1974 as the 'sole, legitimate, representative of the Palestinian people'. Israel still regarded the PLO as a terrorist organization, which had publicly supported Saddam Hussein's invasion of Kuwait and the recent Iraqi attacks on Israel. On this point, there was cross-party consensus within both the government and the Israeli parliament. Also, Prime Minister Shamir was convinced that negotiating with the PLO would lead inevitably to negotiation over establishing a Palestinian state on part of the Land of Israel. Herein 'lay the seeds for the destruction of Israel', argued Shamir, personifying the revisionist Zionist claim that the indivisibility between the people of Israel and the Land of Israel was at the heart of Israeli spiritual and material fortitude.[84] Moreover, Shamir was convinced that the territorial strategic depth afforded by controlling the 'Land of Israel' was a *sine qua non* for Israeli security.[85] It was the only way that Israel could limit its enemies' ability to use the territory as a launch pad for attacks against Israelis.[86]

As Baker conceded, Israel ultimately got its way. The Palestinians participated in the Madrid peace conference as part of a joint Jordanian-Palestinian delegation, and their representatives were vetted by Israel. Palestinian representatives who were residents of Jerusalem were banned from participation lest it be construed as Israel acknowledging Palestinian claims to the city that Israel insisted was its eternal indivisible capital. The PLO also was banned from attendance and confined to its headquarters

---

.aspx, accessed 5 November 2018; Shamir, *Summing Up*, pp. 274–8; Arens, *Broken Covenant*, p. 227.

[81] Arens, *Broken Covenant*, p. 242.   [82] Interview Arens.

[83] Shamir, *Summing Up*, p. 242; Interview Sallai Meridor.

[84] Interview, Sallai Meridor; Misgav, *Conversations with Yitzhak Shamir*, p. 96.

[85] Interview Sallai Meridor; Misgav, *Conversations with Yitzhak Shamir*, pp. 100–1, 131.

[86] Misgav, *Conversations with Yitzhak Shamir*, pp. 111–12; Interview Sallai Meridor.

in the Tunisian capital, Tunis, from where it communicated with the Palestinian representatives at the conference via fax. The outcome strongly reflected the weak position of the PLO and Jordan, which, publicly supported Iraq in the 1991 Gulf War. This strategically flawed decision was at the cost of Jordan and the PLO losing both support of the Arab Gulf States and the USA.

Israel stood firm on another issue, namely, expanding its settlements. The uncompromising Israeli stance was determined by an absolute belief in the integrity of the Land of Israel and the political requirement to keep the ultra-right Shamir government intact. The implications of settlement expansion to deepen the occupation of a growing non-citizen Palestinian population played no role in informing the Israeli stance on this issue. Among the points on which Israel did not budge, settlement was the most charged. The occupied Palestinians considered that the land expropriated by Israel and used for settlement expansion, belonged to them. For the Arab governments, the issue of settlements was a yardstick to gauge US even-handedness with respect to the peace process. Amid these high stakes, the USA rendered the settlements and their chief patron, Ariel Sharon, 'an obstacle to peace' in the Middle East.[87]

The Loan Guarantees Feud

US-Israeli differences over the settlement issue came to a head in September 1991.[88] On 6 September, Israel submitted a request to the US Congress for $US10 billion in loan guarantees, for finance it intended to raise in loans from the international markets to fund the absorption of Soviet immigrants. In the period 1989 to 1991 alone, approximately 345,000 immigrants had arrived in Israel from the Soviet Union.[89]

The request for loan guarantees was tendered at a very sensitive moment; it coincided with the final stages in the resolution of issues related to convening the Madrid peace conference. Were the USA to accept the Israeli request without a clear commitment to a settlement freeze, the Arab side would perceive the USA as economically endorsing Likud's commitment to the integrity of the Land of Israel. At the same time, a public US-Israeli dispute over the settlement question risked Shamir refusing to participate in the Madrid conference and calls for new elections in Israel, which would derail the budding peace process.

---

[87] Baker, *The Politics of Diplomacy*, pp. 542, 545, 547.
[88] I draw on a number of sources to describe the unfolding events: Ross, *The Missing Peace*, p, 83; Arens, *Broken Covenant*, pp. 245–54; Shamir, *Summing Up*, pp. 281–2.
[89] Yinon Cohen et al., 'Who went where? Jewish Immigration from the Former Soviet Union to Israel, the USA, and Germany, 1990–2000, *Israel Affairs*, 17, 1, 2011: 9.

28   Entrenchment

Therefore, the Bush administration did not reject the Israeli request outright. Instead, it suggested, cunningly, that Congress 'defer' discussion of the request for loan guarantees for 120 days, that is, until after the direct Arab-Israeli negotiations had begun and the process was well underway. However, the Israelis refused to link the loan guarantees and the peace process and rejected this formula, setting the Shamir government and the Bush administration on a collision course. The Israeli government, via the American Israeli Public Affairs Committee (AIPAC), the most powerful pro-Israeli advocacy group, lobbied Congress to vote in favour of Israel's request for loan guarantees. The Bush Administration, whose influence was still high following the Gulf War, counter-campaigned. President Bush weighed in by publicly criticizing what he defined as 'powerful political forces amounting to thousands of lobbyists' fighting 'one lonely guy'.[90] In a televised address, he stated that US citizens and representatives must choose between supporting the administration's efforts towards peace or not.[91]

Ultimately, the administration triumphed after Congress and Senate approved deferral of discussion of the Israeli request for 120 days. Prime Minister Shamir was decisive in Israel's participation in the Madrid conference, the American decision notwithstanding. In contrast to the conventional wisdom that he was an uncompromising arch ideologist, Shamir's response, in this instance, reflected his foreign policy manoeuvring among Israeli 'red lines', and avoiding a direct clash with US interests. As he told Baker: '[T]his is an American decision, we'd like it to be otherwise, but we'll live with this decision.'[92]

The Madrid Peace Conference

Resolution of the loan guarantee feud paved the way for the Madrid peace conference. The delegations were positioned to form three sides of a rectangle table, facing the conference presidency, comprising the USA and the USSR, the co-hosts. The conference, which included representatives of Israel, Syria, Egypt, Jordan, Lebanon and the Palestinians, was scheduled for 30 October to 2 November 1991. Then US President George H. Bush and his Soviet counterpart, Mikhail Gorbachev, represented the co-host countries. The Arab states were represented by their

---

[90] Baker, *The Politics of Diplomacy*, p. 552.
[91] Associated Press, 'Excerpts from President Bush's News Session on Israeli Loan Guarantees, *New-York Times*, 13 September 1991, www.nytimes.com/1991/09/13/world/excerpts-from-president-bush-s-news-session-on-israeli-loan-guarantees.html, accessed 1 November 2018.
[92] Baker, *The Politics of Diplomacy*, p. 553.

The Madrid Peace Conference 29

foreign ministers, and Israel by Prime Minister Shamir; Foreign Minister David Levy was left out. The conference had no authority to impose solutions on the parties or to veto any agreements that might be reached; it had no authority to make decisions for the parties and no power to vote on results; the conference could be reconvened only with the consent of all the parties.[93]

In hindsight, the Madrid peace conference seems primarily a ceremonial event. Although, after forty-three years of bloody conflict, the taboo against Arabs talking directly to Israelis was broken in Madrid, the ensuing discussions were a 'dialogue of the deaf'. The Arab participants and Israel used the occasion polemically to reiterate their previous positions of entrenchment towards each other rather than to advance peace negotiations.[94] Syria's foreign minister, Farouk al-Shara focused on criticizing Israeli foreign policy, branding it as 'settler-colonialist' and 'inhumane'. Shamir, in his turn, delivered a hardline speech, which focused on Arab rejection of Israel and questioned the Arab's basic desire for peace. Only one speech, delivered by the head of the Palestinian contingent of the joint Palestinian-Jordanian delegation, Dr Haidar Abdel-Shafi, was forward looking and showed empathy for the other side.[95]

The Israeli delegation left the conference on Friday 1 November – one day before its official conclusion – on the pretext that it could not observe the Jewish Sabbath outside the borders of Israel. This was perplexing even to some Israeli diplomats since Israeli government representatives routinely observed the Sabbath outside Israel. One prominent Israeli diplomat questioned whether his country was signalling that the Madrid peace conference was a trivial affair and not an event that could constitute a cornerstone of a peace process.[96]

---

[93] Israel Ministry of Foreign Affairs, 'Madrid Letter of Invitation', http://mfa.gov.il/MFA/ForeignPolicy/Peace/Guide/Pages/Madrid%20Letter%20of%20Invitation.aspx, accessed 17 July 2014.

[94] Eytan Bentsur, *Making Peace: A First-Hand Account of the Arab-Israeli Peace Process* (Westport: Praeger Publishers, 2001), pp. 120–7; Shamir, *Summing Up*, pp. 285–91; Baker, *The Politics of Diplomacy*, p. 512.

[95] 'Statement of Mr Farouk al-Shara 31 October 91', *IMFA*, www.mfa.gov.il/MFA/ForeignPolicy/Peace/MFADocuments/Pages/STATEMENT%20OF%20MR%20FAROUK%20AL-SHARA%20-%2031-Oct-91.aspx; 'Address by Mr Yitzhak Shamir', 31 October 1991, *IMFA* www.mfa.gov.il/MFA/ForeignPolicy/Peace/MFADocuments/Pages/ADDRESS%20BY%20MR%20YITZHAK%20SHAMIR%20-%2031-Oct-91.aspx Statement by Dr Haider Abdul Shafi, 31 October 1991, IMFA, https://mfa.gov.il/mfa/foreignpolicy/peace/mfadocuments/pages/address%20by%20dr%20haider%20abdul%20shafi-%20-%2031-oct-91.aspx, links accessed 5 November 2018 and 1 March 2019.

[96] Bentsur, *Making Peace*, p. 124.

30   Entrenchment

Both the tone of the dialogue and the decision to leave the peace conference early reflected the Israeli foreign policy position towards a possible peace, which was outlined by prominent Likud MK, Benny Begin. Under Likud, Israel entered the process assuming that it had complied fully with the stipulation in UNSCR 242 – to exchange land for peace – well before the Madrid conference, in 1979 in fact, by returning to Egypt the Sinai Peninsula which comprised 90 per cent of the territories Israel occupied in 1967. Thus, in Madrid, Israel was prepared to accept peace in exchange for peace but not territory. In relation to the Palestinians in the occupied territories, Israel was willing to grant them religious and cultural autonomy and responsibility for administrating various spheres: justice, finance, budgeting, taxation and a local police. However, they would remain under Israeli 'sovereignty', a euphemism for deepening occupation.[97] This Israeli foreign policy posture represented a yawning divide with Arab demands, which centred on return of the land lost in 1967, an end to the Israeli occupation and establishment of a Palestinian state.

Israel's foreign policy position remained unchanged during the bilateral negotiations, which opened in December 1991 in Washington, following the Madrid peace conference. The talks continued in January in Moscow and later transferred to other European capitals. Israel's position consisted of hard negotiating over procedural matters and no substantial concessions. Likewise, the Arab countries and the Palestinians remained fixed in their position. Unsurprisingly, as two senior participants in the negotiations observed, the negotiations yielded no significant results.[98]

So why the Israeli government decided to participate in the Madrid peace conference and the ensuing negotiations is a question that has not received sufficient attention. Shamir saw participation as an opportunity to rehearse the Israeli 'narrative' of the Arab-Israeli conflict on a global stage, which was one of the main reasons why he decided to represent Israel at the peace conference and to deliver the speech that he did.[99] More importantly, however, was the willingness of the Arab governments to hold direct bilateral talks with Israel, which made no concessions over any matters of substance. Although the conference and ensuing talks might not have yielded a peace agreement, Arab readiness to directly engage with Israel without preconditions gave further support to grudging acceptance of Israel into the Middle East region. Shamir, as Dan Meridor

[97] Binyamin Ze'ev Begin, 'The Likud Vision for Israel at Peace', *Foreign Affairs*, 70, 4, 1991: 21–35.
[98] Bentsur, *Making Peace*; Hannan Ashrawi, *This Side of Peace* (New York: Touchstone Books, 1996), p.200.
[99] Shamir, *Summing Up*, pp. 284–90.

presciently observed, saw this as an achievement in itself.[100] Meanwhile, the Palestinians attended the conference as part of a joint delegation with Jordan, which symbolically underlined the tie between Jordan and the Palestinians rather than Palestinian claims to being an independent entity.

Finally, the decision to participate in Madrid reflected Israeli foreign policy manoeuvring within a two-level game. On one level, conceding to some of the requests made by the USA; on another, using these compromises as leverage in the negotiations to increase Israeli influence over what were deemed core issues such as maintaining the integrity of the Land of Israel and not negotiating with the PLO. In these circumstances, the Israelis were willing to go along with the process on the assumption that they could prolong negotiations for years without making further concessions, which, ultimately, might cause the Arab but not the Israeli side to derail the process. It was a question of who blinked first.[101]

Keeping to Familiar Ways

The end of the Cold War was viewed by Israel through the prism of how it could exploit the changing international landscape to consolidate, amid what was perceived as an essentially unchanged and implacable Arab world. In contrast, US decision-makers were intent on creating a new world order within which the role of Israel was uncertain. Accordingly, Israel manoeuvred between responding to the demands made by the USA and the limits imposed by domestic determinants. These included the deeply entrenched world view, images and perceptions of the key decision-makers regarding the Arab-Israeli conflict; the political composition of the government; and a defence establishment that was reluctant to take risks in war or peacemaking.

The logic of a two-level game defined Israel's foreign policy during this period. As long as its foe, Iraq, was being dealt a severe blow, Israel would hold its fire despite being attacked. The defeat of Iraq removed the main Arab country with the capability to pose an existential threat to Israel. However, even as the dispersing fog of war highlighted the enfeebling of Iraq and demise of the USSR, Israel offered a vision of peace that was a far cry from what the Arab side was willing to entertain. Essentially, Israel continued to subscribe to a foreign policy of entrenchment towards the Middle East that was based on the notion of peace for peace not territory; remaining committed to relying on its iron wall of military force rather

[100] Interview 1 Dan Meridor.
[101] Shamir Interview with Yosef Harif, *Ma'ariv*, 26 June, 1992; Interview Sallai Meridor.

than engaging more in diplomacy, and granting limited autonomy to the Palestinians as long as they remained under Israeli military occupation. Shackled by politics, the past and the deeply entrenched views of its leadership, the government of Yitzhak Shamir showed itself disinclined to travel the road not yet taken.

2 Redirection

Introduction

The 1991 Madrid peace conference left Yitzhak Shamir's Likud-led government between a rock and a hard place. The USA had exerted pressure on Israel to advance the budding peace process and stop settlement expansion. Elements within Likud and its right-wing coalition partners – Tzomet, Tehiya and Moledet – strongly resisted these demands. In February 1992, the Shamir government collapsed after these three parties announced their departure from the coalition, prompting a national election on 23 June 1992.[1]

The election campaign pitted two post-Cold War visions against one another. Likud, claiming that the end of the Cold War had little significance for Israel's position in the Middle East, advocated its entrenchment foreign policy stance. Labour, opposing this view, stressed that the end of the Cold War, the Iraqi debacle and the influx of Soviet immigrants placed Israel in an unprecedentedly strong strategic position. Labour's election campaign accused Likud of stalling the peace process, weakening the strategic relationship with the USA, further slowing the Israeli economy and undermining immigrant absorption.[2] Between 1990 and 1992 alone, 400,000 immigrants, mostly from the crumbling

---

[1] My account of the 1992 election draws on Arens, *Broken Covenant*, pp. 270–2; Barry Rubin, 'US–Israeli Relations and Israel's 1992 Elections', in Asher Arian and Michal Shamir, *The 1992 Elections in Israel* (New York: State University of New York Press, 1992); Leon T. Hadar, 'The 1992 Electoral Earthquake and the Fall of the "Second Israeli Republic"', *Middle East Journal*, 46, 4, 1992: 594–616; Sammy Smooha and Don Peretz, 'Israel's 1992 Knesset Elections: Are they Critical?' *Middle East Journal*, 47, 3, 1993: 444–63; Asher Arian and Michal Shamir, 'Two Reversals in Israeli Politics: Why 1992 Was not 1977?' *Electoral Studies*, 12, 4, 1993: 315–41.

[2] For unemployment rates, see 'Israel Unemployment Rate', *Trading Economics*, www.tradingeconomics.com/israel/unemployment-rate; for inflation rates, see 'Key Indicators for the Israeli Market', *Bank of Israel*, www.boi.org.il/he/DataAndStatistics/Pages/IndicatorsDynamic.aspx?Level=1&IndicatorId=7&sId=2, both links accessed 20 March 2015.

34   Redirection

USSR, arrived in Israel, increasing its 4.8 million population by 8 per cent.[3]

Foreign Policy Orientation and the Decision-Making Circle

On election night, Labour won a clear parliamentary majority over Likud, of forty-four to thirty-two seats. Although the Likud-led right-wing bloc received a larger number of votes, many were effectively lost because they were cast for right-wing splinter parties that did not achieve the electoral threshold. Thus, there was a significant gap between the resounding parliamentary victory of Labour over Likud and actual public support, which, in terms of the number of votes cast, favoured the political centre-right. Indeed, Labour's ability to form a government hinged on support from the centre-left bloc comprising Labour, Meretz – a threesome of secular-liberal pro-peace factions – and two Palestinian-Israeli parties: the Arab Democratic Party and the Palestinian-Israeli-led New Communist List. This centre-left bloc of parties accounted for sixty-one of the 120 Knesset seats, the slimmest possible majority.

Against this complex domestic background, in 13 July 1992, Yitzhak Rabin became prime minister for the second time. Rabin was born on 1 March 1922 in the Yishuv, the pre-state of Israel Jewish community in mandated Palestine. At the age of nineteen, he was drafted to the Haganah, the underground military arm of the Jewish agency in man-dated Palestine and joined its leading fighting unit, the Palmach. He spent the next twenty-five years in the Israeli military before being appointed IDF chief of staff in 1963. The climax of his military career was the resounding Israeli military victory in the 1967 Arab-Israeli war. During his time in the IDF, Rabin grappled with the issue that was to most shape his foreign policy views – security. Rabin viewed the world through a state-centric lens and placed great emphasis on his country's security needs and the military means to promote them. He saw the Arab states – rather than the Palestinians – as the main threat, encountered in war and at the negotiating table.[4] A strong IDF was indispensable to Israel's

---

[3] Lili Galili and Roman Bronfman, *The Million that Changed the Middle East: The Soviet Aliya to Israel* (Tel Aviv: Matar, 2013), p. 47 (in Hebrew); Nurit Yafe, 'The Population of Israel 1990–2009: Demographic Statistics', *The Israeli Central Bureau of Statistics* (Jerusalem: Central Bureau of Statistics, 2010), p.1; Yinon Cohen, Yitchak Haberfeld and Irene Kogan, 'Who Went Where? *Israel* Affairs, 17, 1, 2011: pp. 8–9.

[4] Yitzhak Rabin, *The Rabin Memoirs* (Berkeley: University of California Press, 1996), pp. 331–4.

Foreign Policy Orientation and Decision-Making 35

survival and convincing 'the Arab leaders that the only course open to them was political negotiations'.[5]

Yitzhak Rabin's foreign policy outlook was also influenced strongly by his experience as Israeli ambassador to the USA, following his retirement from the IDF in 1968. He was captivated by the USA and this experience instilled in Rabin a deep conviction that US support of Israel was absolutely essential.[6] As his Chief of Staff, Eytan Haber, put it: 'Yitzhak Rabin believed that, for Israel, there was no life without the US, we would simply not be here, and we would simply not exist.'[7] His term as ambassador also spared him from implication in Israel's debacle during the 1973 Arab-Israeli War, which stood him in good stead for his election in 1974 to Israeli prime minister on his return from the USA.

During his first term as premier, Rabin's main foreign policy objective was to gain time. Rabin explained to the then Director General of the Foreign Ministry, Shlomo Avineri, that Israel had been weakened by its performance in the 1973 Arab-Israeli War, the hike in oil prices, Europe's dependence on oil and continuing superpower rivalry in the Middle East.[8] Therefore, it was imperative that Israel rebuild itself strategically, psychologically and diplomatically before attempting to negotiate a peace accord with neighbouring Arab states, in exchange for Israel withdrawing from most of the territories it occupied in the 1967 Arab-Israeli war. Rabin explained to Avineri that areas with dense Arab populations in the West Bank and the Gaza Strip could not remain under Israeli rule indefinitely. However, Jerusalem, the Jordan Valley and specific locations of strategic value were envisaged by Rabin as continuing under Israeli control in any future peace deal. Meanwhile, all Israel could do was buy time without alienating the USA or conceding to Arab demands that Israel withdraw to the 4 June 1967 borders and establish a Palestinian state.[9] Thus, throughout his first term, Rabin espoused a relatively hawkish line, which consisted of refusing to recognize or talk to the PLO or to relinquish the Golan Heights. At the same time, Rabin advocated that Israel should give up a 'piece of land' in return for a 'piece of peace', a principle that informed his successful negotiation of the Sinai I and II agreements with Egypt – harbingers of the permanent 1979 Israeli-Egyptian peace treaty.[10]

---

[5] Ibid, p. 242.   [6] Ibid, p. 172.

[7] Interview 2 Eitan Haber, 2 November 2015, Ramat Gan.

[8] Shlaim, *The Iron Wall*, p. 328.

[9] Shlomo Avineri, 'Leader in the Grip of Political Constraints', *Ha'aretz*, 1 December, 1995.

[10] Rabin, *The Rabin* Memoirs, p. 245.

36   Redirection

Unlike his predecessor, Yitzhak Shamir, Rabin was not haunted by European anti-Semitism, neither was he driven by 'big ideas' or fixed ideologies. In fact, he was somewhat disdainful of intellectual deliberations and thought that committing his thoughts to paper was a waste of time.[11] Eitan Haber, his loyal and diligent chief of staff, did that for him. A quintessential 'doer', Rabin derived his foreign policy outlook from the lessons drawn from his first-hand experience as statesman, chief of staff, diplomat and politician. Rabin applied this experience to his foreign policy, which he was known to pursue cautiously, through trial and error, paying great attention to detail.[12]

During his first term in office, Rabin was scarred by domestic politics. A political novice, he lacked the political acumen to control his government. The burden of the rivalry with his minister of defence and arch political rival, Shimon Peres, hampered the whole of this first term.[13] During their numerous political confrontations, Rabin branded Peres a 'relentless subverter', a label that tainted Peres's entire political career.[14] Having been the first Labour prime minister to lead his party to an election defeat against Likud, in 1977, Rabin was extremely sensitive to the potential for Israeli parliamentary politics to upset the government's foreign policy.[15] Thus, he approached his second premiership with determination and a sense of urgency.[16]

Boasting one of the most distinguished military track records in Israel, Rabin's ability to exercise authority over the security network was undisputed. He was well aware of his reputation and his image as Israel's 'Mr. Security'. This led to his assuming the position of defence minister (a post he had held twice before during the 1984–90 Likud-Labour national unity governments) alongside his position as prime minister. Taking on the defence portfolio had a clear political dimension: it marginalized the influence of Shimon Peres on foreign policy decision-making. However, Rabin could not completely overlook Peres, who had received the votes of more than one-third of the party members. So he grudgingly appointed him foreign minister, but with significantly reduced functions. A written agreement signed by both Peres and Rabin, barred the former from engaging in US-Israeli relations and participation in the

[11] Interview 1 Dr Yossi Beilin, 5 November 2014, Tel Aviv.
[12] Interview 1 Haber; Interview 1 Beilin.
[13] Rabin, *The Rabin Memoirs.*, pp. 239–40, 289, 307–8; Michael Bar-Zohar, *Shimon Peres: The Biography* (New York: Random House, 2007), pp. 295, 299, 301, 305–6, 321–4, 328, 338–44, 348.
[14] Bar Zohar, *Shimon Peres*, pp. 347–8; Interview 1 Beilin .
[15] Shimon Peres led the Labour party during the elections following Rabin's resignation, but it was Rabin who led the party during the period that led to Labour's defeat.
[16] Interview Professor Itamar Rabinovich, 2 November, 2015, Tel Aviv.

Foreign Policy Orientation and Decision-Making · 37

bilateral Arab-Israeli negotiations prompted by the Madrid peace conference. Being limited only to participation in Arab-Israeli multilateral talks, which were not expected to form a political basis for resolving the Arab-Israeli conflict, left Peres 'humiliated, constrained, and gloomy'.[17]

In addition to the personal divide between Rabin and Peres, the government's foreign policy decision-making process was heavily politicized. The coalition government, comprising sixty-two MKs, included the Labour party, Meretz and Shas. Meretz, the senior coalition partner, championed the land-for-peace foreign policy approach, was staunchly secular and advocated the separation between church and state. Shas or the Association of Sephardic Torah Keepers, the junior coalition partner, was of a different ilk. It advocated a strong anti-liberal agenda, seeking to subordinate the state to religious authority and instil Judaism in Israeli public and private life.[18] On foreign policy and, especially, the prospect of exchanging land-for-peace, its position was opaque. It derived from a religious opinion, published by its spiritual and political leader, Rabbi Ovadia Yosef, in 1979, in the context of the Israeli-Egyptian peace negotiations. In it, Yosef stated that it was permissible – rather than necessary or preferable – in the name of Pikuch Nefesh or the primacy of preserving Jewish lives, to relinquish parts of the Land of Israel in exchange for peace.[19]

In formulating his foreign policy, Rabin was wary about using his politicized cabinet, which was prone to leaks. He preferred to conduct foreign policy by exploiting his exclusive access to US officials, his control over the defence establishment, the prime minister's office and the support he derived from his circle of confidants. These included IDF Chief of Staff, Ehud Barak, and Rabin's military secretary, Danny Yatom. The General Manager of the Prime Minister's Office, Shimon Sheves, and Rabin's Chief of Staff, Eitan Haber, were also significant. Rabin kept his confidants in distinct clusters in preference to having a single cohesive forum, which enabled decision-making in small, intimate groups. This gave Rabin exclusive control of all information, which was divulged selectively to his clusters of confidants.[20] To secure internal government support for his policies, Rabin appointed his

---

[17] Interview 1 Beilin.
[18] Ami Pedahtzur, *The Triumph of Israel's Radical Right* (Oxford: Oxford University Press, 2012), p. 7; Peled, 'Towards a Redefinition of Jewish nationalism in Israel', pp. 717–21.
[19] Ricky Tesler, *In the Name of God: Shas and the Religious Revolution* (Jerusalem: Keter Books, 2003), pp. 59–60 (in Hebrew).
[20] Interview 1 Haber; Interview Mr Kalman Gayer, 22 December 2014, Tel Aviv; Itamar Rabinovich, *The Brink of Peace: The Israeli-Syrian Negotiations* (Princeton: Princeton University Press, 1998), p. 57.

38   Redirection

political allies in the Labour party, such as Efraim Sneh and David Libai, to ministerial posts.[21]

Rabin set out his foreign policy agenda on 13 July 1992, in a speech delivered to the Knesset when presenting his government. He emphasized that Israel must find a fit with the changing world around it. 'No longer are we necessarily "a people that dwells alone"', he proclaimed, 'and no longer is it true that "the whole world is against us".'[22] Rabin urged Israelis to overcome the sense of isolation to which Israel had been in thrall since its establishment. As he put it: 'We must join the international movement toward peace, reconciliation and cooperation that is spreading over the entire globe these days – lest we be the last to remain, all alone, in the station.'[23] He emphasized that ending the Arab-Israeli conflict by taking vigorous steps towards peace, was a central goal of his government.[24] The prime minister's remarks conveyed the sense that time was of the essence if Israel were to seize the opportunities presented by the collapse of the USSR, growing Jewish immigration and the Iraq debacle, which Rabin and his government described as creating 'new and great possibilities' for the state of Israel.[25]

However, since Rabin was a realist, his view of the post-Cold War world was not wholly sanguine. He stressed that the Middle East was still 'fraught with danger', meaning that Israel would 'concede nothing' when it came to security, which 'took preference over peace'.[26] The possibility that one of Israel's enemies – especially Iraq or Iran – would develop nuclear weapons, concerned Rabin deeply. Therefore, achieving Arab-Israeli peace was urgent in that it could facilitate a US-led effort 'against nuclear arms proliferation, including Iran'.[27] Contemplating failure to achieve this was particularly worrying for Rabin; he believed firmly that, increasingly, secular pro-Western Arab regimes were being threatened by the rise of Islamist forces.[28]

---

[21] For the composition of Rabin's government see Knesset official website, www .knesset.gov.il/govt/heb/GovtByNumber.asp?govt=25, accessed 14 November 2018.

[22] Yitzhak Rabin, 'Address to the Knesset by Prime Minister Rabin Presenting his Government – 13 July 1992', www.mfa.gov.il/mfa/foreignpolicy/mfadocuments/year book9/pages/1%20%20address%20to%20the%20knesset%20by%20prime%20minis ter%20rabin.aspx, accessed 20 March 2015.

[23] Ibid.   [24] Ibid   [25] Ibid.

[26] Rabin, 'Address to the Knesset by Prime Minister Rabin Presenting his Government'13 July 1992', www.mfa.gov.il/mfa/foreignpolicy/mfadocuments/year book9/pages/1%20%20address%20to%20the%20knesset%20by%20prime%20minis ter%20rabin.aspx, accessed 20 March 2015.

[27] Interview Prime Minister Rabin on Israel Television – 15 July, 1992, *Israeli Ministry of Foreign Affairs*, http://mfa.gov.il/MFA/ForeignPolicy/MFADocuments/Yearbook9/Page s/3%20Interview%20with%20Prime%20Minister%20Rabin%20on%20Israel%20Te .aspx, accessed 17 March 2015.

[28] Interview 1 Dr Efraim Sneh, 25 December 2014, Herzliya.

As those around him observed, Prime Minister Rabin was worried also that Israelis had 'grown soft' and was doubtful about how long they could withstand the taxing price of the Arab-Israeli conflict. In this respect, the exodus of Israelis from Tel Aviv during the 1991 Gulf War and the increasingly materialist lifestyles – especially of the social circles surrounding Rabin himself – made him extremely apprehensive.[29] Finally, Rabin had harboured a concern about the ability of Israel, amid its deepening occupation of the Palestinians, to remain a Jewish and a democratic state. Therefore, during his election campaign, Rabin vowed to reach agreement on Palestinian autonomy in six to nine months.[30] Moreover, his government promised to redirect the vast resources invested by Likud in the occupied territories, to Israel proper, and to impose a freeze on what Rabin described as 'political settlements' – settlements established solely to serve the ideology of the Jewish settlers and Likud.[31]

Stalemate in the Madrid Peace Process

This speech from Rabin revealed his approach to peacemaking, which he saw not as an end in itself, but rather as a tool to advance Israel's interests. This line of thinking informed Israel's approach to the negotiations that emerged from the Madrid peace conference, which Rabin's Labour-led government inherited from Likud. They involved three tracks: between Israel and Syria, between Israel and Lebanon and between Israel and a joint Palestinian-Jordanian delegation. According to Professor Itamar Rabinovich, a seasoned academic and Syria expert, appointed by Rabin as the leading Israeli negotiator with the Syrians, Rabin had some reservations about the Madrid framework. For instance, he felt it was wrong to 'predicate an Arab-Israeli peace process on a negotiation between Israel and the Arab collective' because this meant negotiations would 'be radicalized by the most extreme Arab participant'.[32] However, since Israel had committed to the Madrid framework under the Shamir government,

---

[29] Interview 1 Beilin; Itamar Rabinovich, *Yitzhak Rabin: Soldier, Leader, Statesman* (New Haven: Yale University Press, 2017), p. 193.

[30] Yair P. Hirschfeld, *Oslo: A Formula for Peace from Negotiations to Implementation* (Tel Aviv: Am Oved, 2000), p. 111 (in Hebrew); Rabinovich, *The Brink of Peace*, p. 47; Uri Savir, *The Process* (Tel Aviv: Yedioth Ahronoth, 1998), p. 19 (in Hebrew).

[31] The Israeli Labour Party, *The Israeli Labour Party Manifesto to the 13th Knesset* (Tel Aviv: The Israeli Labour Party, 1992) (in Hebrew); Basic Policy Guidelines of the 25th Government, *Israeli Ministry of Foreign Affairs*, http://mfa.gov.il/MFA/AboutIsrael/Stat e/Government/Pages/2%20Basic%20Policy%20Guidelines%20of%20the%2025th%2 0Government-.aspx, accessed 1 December 2018.

[32] Rabinovich, *Yitzhak Rabin*, p. 175.

40   Redirection

Rabin 'saw no point in trying to rattle or alter the Madrid framework right at the outset' and resigned himself to it.[33]

According to Jacques Neriah, one of Rabin's chief policy advisors between 1992 and 1994, Rabin fully understood the importance of negotiating with the Palestinians. From Rabin's perspective, Neriah explains: '[T]he Palestinians were the nub of the conflict. An agreement with them would remove the main motivation of the Arab states to fight against Israel.'[34] In addition, according to Itamar Rabinovich, Rabin estimated that 'King Hussein [of Jordan] would not move before any actions he might take were legitimized by an earlier agreement by either Syria or the Palestinians.'[35]

This was the background to the sixth and seventh rounds of negotiations between Israel and the Palestinian contingent of the joint Palestinian-Jordanian delegation. Elyakim Rubenstein, who had been appointed by Likud and was retained by Rabin, led the Israeli delegation. The Palestinian contingent of the joint delegation, which was headed by Dr Haider Abdel-Shafi, comprised residents of the West Bank and Gaza Strip, but no PLO activists. The profound gaps between Israel and the Palestinians quickly emerged during these negotiations, which convened during August and November 1992 in Washington, DC. According to a chief Palestinian negotiator, Hannan Ashrawi, the Palestinians came to the negotiations with a clear aim in mind: concluding an interim self-government arrangement, which would pave the way to ending Israeli occupation on the basis of UNSC 242, and establishing a Palestinian state.[36] Israel, however, was hell-bent on Palestinian self-rule as the end point of the process.[37]

The format of the negotiations was unsuitable for bridging this fundamental gap. Although the Palestinian delegation was described as officially representing the Palestinian population in the occupied territories, they were no more than messengers. Abdel-Shafi and his colleagues were bound by the decisions made by the PLO leadership in Tunis, which, as long as it remained officially excluded from the negotiations, was determined to obstruct them. Writing rather somberly in her memoirs, Hannan Ashrawi described the Palestinian delegation as being 'haunted by the question' of its 'mandate and mission'.[38] The profound differences

---

[33] Ibid.

[34] Jaques Neriah, *Between Rabin and Arafat: A Political Diary* (Jerusalem: Jerusalem Centre for Public Affairs, 2016), p. 26 (in Hebrew).

[35] Rabinovich, *Yitzhak Rabin*, p. 177.

[36] Hanan Ashrawi, *This Side of Peace* (New York: Touchstone, 1996), pp. 212–18.

[37] Interview Prime Minister Rabin, Israel Television, 15 July, 1992; Basic Policy Guidelines of the 25th Government – July 1992.

[38] Ashrawi, *This Side of Peace*, p. 245.

Stalemate in the Madrid Peace Process

over substance, which were compounded by the flawed negotiating format, resulted in the sixth and seventh rounds of Israeli-Palestinian negotiations ending in stalemate.

The sixth and seventh rounds, which were held in Washington, also involved discussion of the Israeli-Syrian track. Following the Israeli elections, US Secretary of State, James Baker, travelled to Israel to relay the message from the then Syrian President, Hafez al-Assad, that he was interested in making peace with Israel. This appealed to Rabin on several grounds. Syria had all but turned Lebanon into a client state following its 1976 invasion of that country. For this reason, Rabin was confident that an Israeli-Syrian peace accord would lead to an Israeli-Lebanese treaty. Also, Rabin hoped that an Israeli-Syrian peace accord would undermine Syria's alliance with Iran, forged following the 1979 Iranian revolution. Finally, Rabin estimated that an Israeli-Syrian deal would pressurize the Palestinians into concluding a deal with Israel, freeing the Arab states in North Africa and the Gulf to normalize relations with Israel.[39]

To realize this ambitious foreign policy agenda, Rabin departed from the 'peace-for-peace stance' propagated by Shamir's government during the Madrid peace conference. However, he imposed some conditions of his own. He stated publicly that Israel expected that any withdrawal from the Golan Heights would be part of a comprehensive Israeli-Syrian peace accord, which would be concluded irrespective of progress in the parallel peace tracks. Until Syria would agree to these conditions, Israel was unwilling to discuss the possible scope of its withdrawal from the Golan Heights.[40] Syria responded by underlining its demand for Israel to withdraw from the Golan regardless of whether a full Syrian-Israeli peace agreement was concluded. Itamar Rabinovich, Rabin's chief negotiator with Syria, described the Syrian proposal as an offer of 'glorified non-belligerenly in return for full withdrawal'.[41]

The format of the negotiations did not help to bridge the gaps. The discussions, which were public, received intensive coverage in the Arab and Israeli media. This intense scrutiny forced the Israeli and Syrian diplomats to maintain their traditional and irreconcilable positions. In this context, the Israeli delegation faced serious domestic political constrains. Most of the Golan settlers and, certainly, their leadership, formed

---

[39] Rabinovich, *The Brink of Peace*, p. 47; Martin Indyk, *Innocent Abroad: An Intimate Account of the American Peace Diplomacy in the Middle East* (New York: Simon & Schuster, 2009), pp.18, 21; Aaron David Miller, *The Much Too Promised Land* (New-York: Bantam Books, 2009), p. 247.

[40] Rabinovich, *The Brink of Peace*, pp. 57–8, 72, 75–7; Rabin, 'Opening speech of the Knesset Winter Session', 26 October 1992, *Pursing Peace: The Peace Speeches of Prime Minister Yitzhak Rabin* (Tel Aviv: Zmora Bitan, 1995), pp. 74–5 (in Hebrew).

[41] Miller, *The Much Too Promised Land*, p. 253; Rabinovich, *The Brink of Peace*, p. 62.

42   Redirection

a single-issue constituency, focused on thwarting an Israeli-Syrian agreement. The Golan lobby, as it came to be known, had several allies, including the inhabitants of northern Galilee, the settlers in the West Bank and the Gaza Strip and Israeli right-wing political parties. The Golan lobby's anti-withdrawal campaign was extremely effective and stressed the critical importance of the Golan Heights (see Map 2.1) for dominating northern Galilee and controlling the main water sources feeding Israel's sweet water reservoir, the Sea of Galilee. US and Israeli negotiators observed that President Assad's cold and enigmatic public statements and speeches during the September–December 1992 negotiation phase helped the settlers to make a case against any withdrawal from the Golan.[42]

Rabin and his negotiating team had to take serious account of the Golan lobby. A majority of the Golan settlers, who had moved to the area when the prospect of peace with Syria was very remote, supported Labour but, more specifically, Rabin. Moreover, the prime minister had vowed, during the election campaign, not to withdraw from the Golan Heights. Rabin and the Israeli negotiators with Syria were walking a tightrope between soothing the Golan settlers without, ipso facto, sending a message to the Syrians that domestic politics rendered an Israeli-Syrian peace impossible.[43] This delicate balancing act resulted in Israel's flexible foreign policy position towards the negotiations with Syria that 'the depth of the withdrawal will reflect the depth of peace'.[44] However, fettered by domestic constraints and faced with an obstinate Syrian counterpart, the sixth and seventh rounds of Israeli-Syrian negotiations in Washington yielded no significant progress.

The Arab-Israeli talks following the Madrid peace conference, which entered their eighth round in December 1992, were rudely interrupted by a spate of attacks launched by the military wing of Hamas, between 7 and 13 December. The perpetrators killed three Israeli soldiers in the Gaza Strip and kidnapped an Israeli border policeman, who was found dead two days later. The Arabic word *hamas* means zeal and is also an acronym of Harakat al-Muqawamah al-Islamiyya, the Islamic Resistance Movement. The movement was formed in 1987 as the military wing of the long-established Muslim Brotherhood Movement in Palestine, which Israel initially supported in the hope of dividing the Palestinian camp and weakening the PLO. As the Palestinian Intifada progressed, Hamas retained some features of the Muslim Brotherhood. It developed an elaborate welfare system and established deep roots in Palestinian

---

[42] Rabinovich, *The Brink of Peace*, p. 73; Miller, *The Much Too Promised Land*, p. 256.
[43] Rabinovich, *The Brink of Peace*, pp. 67, 72–3, 81–3.   [44] Ibid, p. 83.

Map 2.1 The Golan Heights

politics, society and culture. At the same time, Hamas adopted an uncompromising stance towards Israel, which it refused to recognize and vowed to destroy. Hamas rendered negotiations with Israel invalid,

44   Redirection

insisting that the end of Israeli occupation could be achieved only through the use of military force. Accordingly, Hamas objected to Palestinian participation in the Madrid peace process, which it sought to derail by attacking Israeli military and civilian targets. Presenting a clear political alternative, Hamas would emerge as the most significant challenge to the leadership and authority of the secular PLO.[45]

In response to Hamas's December attacks, which were an early indication of the disruptive impact terrorism was to have on the peace negotiations, Rabin decided on 16 December on the unorthodox and dramatic step of deporting 415 Hamas members to Lebanon for a maximum two-year exile. This decision, taken in consultation with his closest confidants, but, significantly, not the government, was presented to the cabinet as a fait accompli, which the supine cabinet approved. From Rabin's perspective, the logic behind the deportation decision was straightforward. As a prime minister who had once lost an election to Likud, Rabin was particularly aware that the negotiation timeframe could exceed his four-year term of office.[46] Rabin was convinced that the key to securing domestic support from the public – critical for his re-election – was drastic security measures, such as the deportation, amid any attempts to derail the peace process. As he stated in his opening speech, it would signal to Israelis that security took precedence over peace and would deter Hamas.[47]

However, the domestic gains Rabin sought were outweighed by the international repercussions of his decision. In the wake of the deportations, the Arab delegations withdrew their participation in the eighth round of the Washington talks and refused to set a date for their resumption. Active US mediation might have prevented this outcome, but the American team, established following the election victory of the Democratic presidential candidate, Bill Clinton, was ineffective. Presided over by the newly appointed Secretary of State, Warren Christopher, the US mediators exhibited 'hesitancy and vagueness, in which loose ends would be left to threaten the whole process'.[48] Rabin

---

[45] Hamas has attracted wide academic interests see, inter alia, Tareq Baconi, *Hamas Contained: The Rise and Pacification of Palestinian Resistance* (Stanford: Stanford University Press, 2018); Khaled Hroub, *Hamas: Political Thought and Practice* (Washington: Institute for Palestine Studies, 2000); Beverly Milton Edwards and Stephen Farrel, *Hamas* (Cambridge: Polity, 2010); Shaul Mishal and Avraham Sela, *The Palestinian Hamas: Vision, Violence and Co-Existence* (New York: Columbia University Press, 2006).
[46] Interview Rabinovich.
[47] Interview Rabinovich; Interview 1 Haber; Rabinovich, *The Brink of Peace*, p. 84; Hirschfeld, *Oslo*, p. 105.
[48] Ashrawi, *This Side of Peace*, p. 236; Interview 1 Beilin.

also had to reckon with international condemnation of the deportation and critique of Israel's flagrant violation of international law.[49] Ultimately, in February 1993, Israel had to readmit the deportees as a condition for renewal of the peace talks in Washington – the sojourn in south Lebanon proving a blessing in disguise for Hamas. The deportees had worked to consolidate relations with Hezbollah and Iran's revolutionary guard. The leadership cadre of Hamas was boosted as was Hamas's popularity and recognition among the Palestinians and across the Middle East.[50]

Establishing the Oslo Process

In December 1992, amid the stalemate in the peace negotiations, the Knesset began to debate cancellation of a six-year old law prohibiting meetings between Israelis and PLO members. The debate, which was driven by Deputy Foreign Minister, Yossi Beilin, led to the law being repealed on 19 January 1993. This legislative change ushered in a period in which, initially in a private capacity, Israelis could meet with members of the PLO to explore how to break the evident deadlock in the Washington talks. In this context, two Israeli academics and peace activists, Dr Yair Hirschfeld and Dr Ron Pundak, met privately with a team led by Ahmed Qurie, known also as Abu Ala, who was Yasser Arafat's most important economic advisor and director of the Sumud fund.[51] Dan Kurtzer of the US State Department was kept informed. Terje Rod Larsen, from the Oslo-based Fafo research foundation, secured financial and logistical support from the Norwegian government for this secret channel, which became known as the Oslo process. During the first phase of the discussions, December 1992–February 1993, Abu Ala and his team reported directly to Yasser Arafat and Mahmoud Abbas, who oversaw all aspects of Israeli-PLO negotiations; however, initially only one Israeli government official – Deputy Foreign Minister Dr Yossi Beilin – was informed of the talks.[52]

Hirschfeld's and Pundak's decision to seek support from Beilin was not coincidental. Beilin was a confidant of foreign minister Peres. As cabinet secretary, political general manager of the Israeli MFA, a MK and deputy

---

[49] Ashrawai, *This Side of Peace*, pp. 221–5; Rabinovich, *The Brink of Peace*, p. 84; Shlaim, *The Iron Wall*, pp. 509–10.

[50] Milton-Edwards and Farrell, *Hamas*, p. 65; Rabinovich, *Yitzhak Rabin*, p. 179.

[51] Ron Pundak, *Secret Channel* (Tel Aviv: Aliyat Gag, 2013), pp. 104–5 (in Hebrew); Yossi Beilin, *Touching Peace: From the Oslo Accord to a Final Agreement* (London: Weidenfeld & Nicolson, 1999), p. 51.

[52] Pundak, *Secret Channel*, pp. 40–68, 104; Hirschfeld, *Oslo*, pp. 90–7; Beilin, *Touching Peace*, pp. 51, 56.

46   Redirection

minister of finance, Beilin was a strong advocate of a liberal-progressive domestic agenda, negotiations with the PLO and the establishment of a Palestinian state.[53] His political views, policy experience and proximity to Foreign Minister Peres combined to render Beilin ideal for potentially translating the Oslo process into official Israeli foreign policy.[54]

The political rivalry between Rabin and Peres significantly influenced how Beilin approached these early and informal liaisons with the PLO. Initially, he decided not to inform Rabin, Peres or the government about the secret Oslo channel. He believed that were he to report the negotiations to Peres, the foreign minister would be obliged to inform Rabin, who, given his mistrust of Peres, would 'demand an end to the process before it had begun'.[55] Beilin, exploiting Israel's informal decision-making structure to the full, authorized Hirschfeld and Pundak to proceed with the talks and to report exclusively to him. As the talks unfolded, the PLO representatives expressed views that departed from the organization's hitherto complete rejection of dialogue with Israel. They agreed to unprecedented economic cooperation with Israel and to Israeli withdrawal from Gaza as the preliminaries to a gradual, phased, peace process.[56]

The revised PLO position reflects its weakness following the end of the Cold War. It had lost an important supporter – the USSR – and remained on the US State Department's terrorism list.[57] The PLO's coffers were empty as the rich Gulf States had withdrawn their financial support following the PLO's gravely mistaken support for the 1990 Iraqi invasion of Kuwait. In the meantime, the PLO was losing ground domestically to Hamas.[58]

Phase two of the Oslo process began on 9 February 1993, when Beilin presented Peres with a position paper summarizing the understandings reached by Hirschfeld and Pundak, operating in a private capacity, with the team led by Abu Ala. Peres, terrified of again being branded by Rabin a relentless subverter and suffering retaliation, duly informed the prime minister of the secret channel.[59] Rabin authorized its continuation, but insisted it remain a private initiative, which allowed the Israelis to deny any involvement if these negotiations were revealed. In fact, at this stage, Rabin decided to treat the Oslo process as auxiliary to the stalled Washington talks.[60]

---

[53] Shayke Ben-Porat, *Talks with Yossi Beilin* (Tel Aviv: Ha Kibbutz Hameuchad, 1996), pp. 49–50, 79–80, 83–4, 102, 112 (in Hebrew).
[54] Hirschfeld, *Oslo*, pp. 92–102, 106.   [55] Beilin, *Touching Peace*, p. 62.
[56] Ibid, pp. 65–7.   [57] Indyk, *Innocent Abroad*, pp. 19–20.
[58] Milton-Edwards and Farrel, *Hamas*, p. 65.   [59] Interview 1 Beilin.
[60] Hirscheld, *Oslo*, pp. 110–17; Pundak, *Secret Channel*, pp. 90–146; Beilin, *Touching Peace*, pp. 65–6, 73; Bar-Zohar, *Shimon Peres*, pp. 427–9.

The balance between the two negotiation tracks changed gradually, with the Oslo process taking precedence over the official Washington talks. The main driver of this shift was Foreign Minister Peres, who brought his full political and personal clout to bear to control the Oslo process and persuade Rabin to prioritize it. Peres was convinced that the Washington negotiations were futile because the Palestinian delegation could not effect a breakthrough without the PLO's agreement. In this sense, Peres was more realistic than Rabin about Palestinian politics. With an eye to Israeli domestic politics, Peres realized that a breakthrough in Oslo would pave the way to his return to the centre of foreign policymaking, from which he had been excluded by Rabin since Labour's election victory.[61] In other words, there was a strong personal domestic political incentive driving Peres's support for a secret Israel-PLO channel.

Ultimately, Rabin's decision to prioritize the Oslo secret channel over the Washington talks was also driven by domestic considerations. The Washington talks, which Rabin was sceptical about, continued to dither, while the tide of violence increased. In March 1993 alone, thirteen Israelis were murdered in attacks carried out primarily by members of Hamas's military wing. Israeli reaction continued to reflect Rabin's proclivity to shore up his domestic support by combining drastic security measures with his peace efforts. In response to the attacks, Israel imposed a closure on the West Bank and Gaza Strip, which barred Palestinian workers from entering Israel and restricted movement of people and goods within the occupied territories. The closure policy had the immediate effect of reducing Israeli casualties and the longer term effect of initiating social and economic separation between Israelis and Palestinians in the occupied territories. Also, it set the pattern for Israel's response to attacks on its soldiers and civilians – by Hamas or other Palestinian factions – of punishing the Palestinian population in the West Bank and the Gaza Strip collectively.

It was increasingly clear to Rabin that he was in danger of not fulfilling his election campaign promise to complete negotiations within nine months on an interim settlement on a Palestinian autonomy. The prospect of failing to meet his pledge precipitated his May 1993 decision to upgrade the Oslo secret channel. Rabin authorized Uri Savir, general director of the foreign ministry, to meet secretly with Abu Ala and his team on the condition that the Washington talks resumed. Hence, almost a year after his re-election, Rabin finally aligned his peace strategy to the

---

[61] Ben Porat, *Conversations with Yossi Beilin*, p. 115; Interview 1 Beilin; Pundak, *Secret Channel*, pp. 134–5, 169–70.

48   Redirection

balance of power in Palestinian politics, which clearly favoured PLO leadership over the participation of Palestinian delegates in the Washington talks. Savir was given the task of exploring the progress made by the academics involved in the Oslo process and reporting back to Rabin and Peres.[62]

In addition, at the prime minister's request, Yoel Singer became an official member of the Israeli negotiating team and Rabin's de facto representative at the Oslo talks. At the time, Singer was employed by the Washington-based law firm, Sidely & Austin; previously, he had headed the IDF's international law section when Rabin was minister of defence. Trusted by both the prime minister and the group of men surrounding Peres, Singer became legal advisor to the Israeli delegation at the Oslo talks.[63]

To all intents and purposes, Israel was embarking on direct and official negotiations with the PLO, breaking one of the strongest taboos that had shaped Israeli foreign policy since 1967. The option of denying that Israeli-PLO talks were taking place, possible only as long as only Hirschfeld and Pundak were meeting with the PLO officials in a private capacity, was no longer available. It is telling that this momentous decision was taken by the Israeli prime minister without consultation with his close confidants or the relevant state agencies – Mossad, GSS and the IDF. The Israeli government was kept in ignorance in spite of varying levels of involvement in the Oslo process from the Egyptian, US and Norwegian governments.[64]

Rabin's ability to exploit his position as prime minister to advance the secret negotiations with the PLO was indispensable for maintaining the Oslo negotiations. However, at the same time, several Israeli ministers, who were unaware of the Oslo channel, had been authorized by Rabin to effect a breakthrough in the stalled Washington talks. These efforts included private talks between Dr Nabil Shaath and the Israeli health minister, Dr Efraim Sneh, contact between the Head of Meretz, Shulamit Aloni and PLO officials and a secret channel that had been established between Haim Ramon, an influential Labour leader and the minister of health, and Mahmoud Abbas.[65]

The flurry of secret talks reflected Rabin's proclivity to explore several options in parallel, while keeping them separate, before making a final

[62] Savir, *The Process*, pp. 18, 20; Pundak, *Secret Chanel*, pp. 195, 205–7, 216–20; Beilin, *Touching Peace*, pp. 84–5; Bar Zohar, *Shimon Peres*, pp. 433–4.
[63] Pundak, *Secret Channel*, p. 233; Beilin, *Touching Peace*, p. 89.
[64] Ben Porat, *Conversations with Yossi Beilin*, pp. 113–14; Savir, *The Process*, pp. 59–63; Hirschfeld, *Oslo*, p. 122.
[65] Beilin, *Touching Peace*, p. 75; Rabinovich, *Yitzhak Rabin*, p. 189.

decision.[66] This foreign policy tactic risked misperceptions and miscalculations and, therefore, was risky. For instance, the PLO leadership suspected the Israelis of speaking with a forked tongue 'with the intention of dragging the negotiations across the two tracks – Oslo and Washington – indefinitely'.[67] The PLO feared that Israel would try to use the Oslo process to achieve superficial agreement in Washington and accelerate progress to making deals with Jordan and Syria, leaving the Palestinians out in the cold.[68] In June 1993, Rabin, who understood that Israel's foreign policy cacophony was jeopardizing the budding peace process, decreed that the Oslo process should be the sole secret channel between Israel and the PLO representatives.[69] Henceforth, having received intelligence reports that Arafat was 'determined to avoid any alternative to Oslo', Rabin would personally oversee the process.[70]

Forcing the Prime Minister's Hand

During July and August 1993, several processes came together. The Israeli-Syrian track had made almost no progress in the ninth round of the Washington talks held in April 1993.[71] This virtual stalemate was exacerbated by the ongoing conflict between Israel and Hezbollah. Hezbollah, which in Arabic means the 'Party of God', was established in 1982 against the backdrop of the Israeli invasion of Lebanon and by Iran, which was keen to export its 1979 revolution model to other parts of the Middle East. During the 1980s and 1990s, Hezbollah developed into a proxy of Iran, which provided it with political, military and financial support. Syria, Iran's ally, supported and facilitated Iran's backing of Hezbollah and its attacks on the IDF in south Lebanon.[72]

Lebanon defined the IDF presence in the south of the country as outright occupation. Meanwhile, Israel insisted that the area was a 'security zone' that was indispensable to its defence of its northern border. This security zone was established by Israel in 1985 as part of a broader redeployment of its army following its 1982 invasion of Lebanon. It comprised two elements. One was a Mossad and IDF presence, which, in clear violation of Lebanese sovereignty, erected a chain of

---

[66] This tendency of Rabin is reported in Rabinovich, *Yitzhak Rabin*, p. 183.
[67] Pundak, *Secret Channel*, pp. 246, 269, 271.   [68] Beilin, *Touching Peace*, pp. 75, 102.
[69] Pundak, *Secret Channel*, p. 271; Ahmed Qurie, *From Oslo to Jerusalem: The Palestinian Story of the Secret Negotiations* (London: I.B. Tauris, 2006), pp. 167, 179.
[70] Pundak, *Secret Channel*, pp. 298–301; Qurie, *From Oslo to Jerusalem*, pp. 157, 161; Beilin, *Touching Peace*, pp. 94–6; Rabinovich, *Yitzhak Rabin*, p. 190.
[71] Rabinovich, *The Brink of Peace*, pp. 85, 93–9; Ross, *The Missing Peace*, p. 100.
[72] Yaakov Amidror, 'The Hezbollah-Syria-Iran Triangle', *Middle East Review of International Affairs*, 11, 1, 2007: 1–5.

50   Redirection

military posts stretching ten kilometres north of the Israeli border. The second was a local militia, the South Lebanese Army (SLA), composed primarily of Lebanese Christians, commanded by General Antoine Lahad and backed financially and militarily by Israel.[73]

Iran and Syria supported Hezbollah's attacks on the IDF, which were primarily aimed at achieving an Israeli withdrawal from south Lebanon. However, since the beginning of the Israeli-Syrian peace negotiations, Syria's support for Hezbollah had acquired another dimension. Assad refused to extend any confidence-building measures or public diplomacy towards Israel until a breakthrough in negotiations and an agreement in principle had been achieved. Instead, he supported Hezbollah's guerrilla campaign against the IDF as a means to put pressure on Israel in the negotiations.[74]

Hezbollah increased its rocket attacks on Israel proper during July 1993, arguing that its attacks were retaliation for Israel's use of military force beyond the borders of the security zone. Israel rejected the claims. Instead, it contended that Hezbollah's attacks were part of Assad's foreign policy tactics of influencing the Syrian-Israeli negotiations through the use of force. Against this combustible backdrop, in 25 July 1993, the IDF launched Operation Accountability, which escalated the violence several notches. In addition to targeting Syrian positions, the logic underlying Operation Accountability was to set in motion an exodus of Shi'ite Lebanese civilians towards Beirut. The Israelis assumed mistakenly that this would put pressure on the Lebanese government to plead with Assad to rein in Hezbollah's attacks on Israel proper. However, the Lebanese government lacked the capacity to exert this pressure on the Syrian president, who remained unperturbed by the plight of the southern Lebanese.[75]

Ultimately, the feud between Israel and Hezbollah was settled by a US-brokered ceasefire. Boosted by this success, US Secretary of State Christopher began a pre-planned visit to the Middle East from 1 to 5 August 1993.[76] On 3 August, Christopher held a critical meeting with Rabin. Dennis Ross and Itamar Rabinovich sat in as notes takers. In the meeting, Rabin requested Christopher to pose three questions to President Assad. These came to be known as Rabin's 'deposit' because

---

[73] Gal Luft, 'The Israeli Security Zone – A Tragedy? *Middle East Report*, 3, 2000: 13–20, www
.meforum.org/70/israels-security-zone-in-lebanon-a-tragedy, accessed 20 March 2015.
[74] Rabinovich, *The Brink of Peace*, pp. 101–2.
[75] Rabinovich, *The Brink of Peace*, pp. 102–3; Ross, *The Missing Peace*, p. 110.
[76] My account of the meeting between 3 and 5 August 1993 is based on Rabinovich, *The
Brink of Peace*, pp. 104–6; Ross, *The Missing Peace*, pp. 111–12; Miller, *The Much Too
Promised Land*, p. 254; Warren Christopher, *Chances of a Lifetime: A Memoir* (New York:
Scribner, 2001), pp. 220–2.

Rabin intended for the Americans to raise these questions to Assad hypothetically rather than as an official Israeli position. Only if the Syrians agreed to the conditions outlined by Rabin would the Israeli offer change from hypothetical and indirect to direct and affirmative.

The questions were as follows. Would Syria agree to sign a peace treaty with Israel in return for an Israeli commitment to the USA to withdraw fully from the Golan, irrespective of progress in other peace tracks? Was Syria ready for a peace that encompassed trade, tourism, diplomatic relations and other attributes of 'normalization'? Was Syria ready to offer elements of peace before Israel withdrew fully from the Golan, which Rabin proposed would be achieved within five years? Rabin sought satisfactory security arrangements based on the USA manning the early-warning sites in the Golan and guarantees to safeguard Israel's water supply. Finally, Rabin stated explicitly that Israel could not move forward along two peace tracks simultaneously because the Israeli public would not stomach the concessions demanded by the conclusion of multiple agreements. Therefore, Rabin preferred, first, to make progress with Syria and Lebanon and then to settle for limited simultaneous progress with the Palestinians on the basis of a 'Gaza First' plan.

On 4 August 1993, Christopher and Ross presented Rabin's questions to the Syrian President and, on 5 August, they flew back to meet with Rabin. They reported that Assad had refused to accept the principle underlying the proposal made by Rabin – that Israeli-Syrian normalization and the first phase of Israeli withdrawal from the Golan would occur simultaneously. Neither was Assad willing to accept the five-year time-frame envisaged by Rabin for an Israeli withdrawal – his counter-suggestion being six months. Finally, Assad's response as to whether Syria would be willing to move forward irrespective of the progress made in other tracks was extremely vague although his discomfort with the term 'normalization' was explicit. Rabin was deeply disappointed by Assad's reaction. Given the similarity of his requests to the principles underlying the peace accords signed by Israel and Egypt in 1979, Rabin had hoped Assad would respond positively. Rabin told Dennis Ross and Warren Christopher that the Syrian response was minimal and indicative that Assad was not minded to move quickly to a peace agreement. At this point, the US mediators perhaps expected Rabin to haggle with Assad, but their mediation tactic had made a critical mistake. Immediately after reporting back to Rabin, Christopher and his team announced their return to the USA for their summer vacation, which left Rabin completely unclear about whether he had a Syrian option.[77]

---

[77] Rabinovich, *The Brink of Peace*, p. 139; Rabinovich, *Yitzhak Rabin*, p. 197.

52   Redirection

Assad's tepid response tilted the main thrust of Israeli peace negotiations towards the Palestinians. This foreign policy redirection was far from self-evident in that the Israeli-Palestinian track was patently more complicated than negotiation with Syria. In August 1993, Israel and the PLO officially still refused to recognize one another, which made it unclear who would be negotiating with Israel on behalf of the Palestinians. In contrast, the identity of Syria's negotiating partner was unambiguous. In addition, the argument with Syria hinged on the single issue: the relationship between the extent of Israeli withdrawal from the Golan and the degree of normalization of relations between the two states. By contrast, the range of issues Israel was required to resolve with the Palestinians, was wide and diverse. It included, inter alia, Palestinian statehood, the fate of Jerusalem, security arrangements, Palestinian refugees and Jewish settlements.

So, did the decision to prioritize the Palestinian track, following the response from Assad, reflect Rabin's reconciliation towards endorsement of the stance towards the PLO purported by Peres's confidants, whom, according to Peres's closest confidant, Rabin 'loathed'?[78] The evidence suggests that this was far from true. In fact, as late as June 1993, Rabin ordered Peres, in writing, to stop the negotiations on the grounds that the Israeli negotiators were conceding too much to PLO demands. It was only after assurances to the contrary from his confidant Yoel Singer, that Rabin authorized renewal of the negotiations on 10 June, 1993.[79] However, as a participant, intimately involved in the peace negotiations, recalls, Rabin remained 'ambivalent about making a deal with the PLO and suspicious of Peres'.[80] Indeed, according to Avi Gil, Peres' closest confidant, Rabin informed his foreign minister in a private conversation, held 2 August 1993, that he is 'inclined to go with the Syrian option'.[81]

So why did a cautious statesman such as Rabin decide, on his own, against further bargaining with Assad in favour of a more complex and multifarious peace track with the Palestinians? The fundamental explanation is that Rabin's hand was forced. By July–August, 1993, after five rounds of tough negotiating in the Oslo process, the Israeli-Palestinian negotiators felt that the moment was nigh for their respective political leaders to clinch a deal.[82] At this stage, as Rabin's closest advisor on

---

[78] Avi Gil, *The Peres Formula: Diary of a Confidant* (Hevel Mod'iin: Kineret, Zmora Bitan, 2018), p. 115 (in Hebrew).
[79] The full version of the letter is provided in Gil, *The Peres Formula*, pp. 129–30.
[80] Rabinovich, *Yitzhak Rabin*, p. 189.   [81] Gil, *The Peres Formula*, p. 134.
[82] Qurie, *From Oslo to Jerusalem*, pp. 165–236; Savir, *The Process*, 53–9, 63; Pundak, *Secret Channel*, pp. 275–356; Beilin, *Touching Peace*, pp. 102–16.

The Israeli-PLO Declaration of Principles 53

negotiations with Syria, Itamar Rabinovich, explains, it was virtually impossible for Rabin to continue to prioritize the Syrian track:

Opting for the Syrian track over the Palestinian track in August 1993 would have entailed a direct political confrontation with Peres. If Rabin had a concrete Syrian offer he could have perhaps done so, but the elusive response from Assad made that impossible. Rabin was convinced that if he continued to prioritize the Syrian track over the Oslo Process, Peres would have portrayed him as the enemy of peace, perhaps even split the Labour party, which would lead Rabin to losing his majority in the Knesset.[83] This nightmare scenario, which haunted Rabin during his constant conflicts with Peres in his first premiership, proved decisive in the decision by Rabin in August 1993 to prioritize the Israeli-PLO track over the negotiations with Syria.[84]

Rabin's concerns were real. As Peres's closest confidant, Avi Gil, recalls, Peres clearly outlined the stakes to Rabin. 'I can', Peres told the prime minister, 'have with you a gentlemen's agreement. If you proceed in the path of peace, you will find in me your most loyal friend. However, if you deviate from it, you will not recognize me. I will be a predator.'[85]

The Israeli-PLO Declaration of Principles

Unless he was willing to risk an open clash with his arch rival, Shimon Peres, Rabin had no choice, but to endorse the Oslo peace process. Taking advantage of a prescheduled diplomatic visit to Scandinavia, Rabin authorized Peres to conduct a telephone conversation with PLO leader, Yasser Arafat, on the night of 17 to 18 August, with Norwegian Foreign Minister, Joergen Holst, acting as go-between. During this seven-hour phone call, which was interrupted nine times for Peres to confer with Rabin, Peres and Arafat finalized agreement on what became known as the Declaration of Principles (DoP) on Interim Self-Government Arrangements. On 19 August, in Oslo, the agreement was initialled in secret by Uri Savir and Abu Ala and, on 27 August, it was presented by Foreign Minister Peres and his Norwegian counterpart, Joergen Holst, to an utterly surprised Secretary of State Warren Christopher and Dennis Ross.[86] The Clinton administration quickly recognized Oslo as an opportunity that had dropped into its lap, and the 'president was smart and ambitious enough to know that it could not let it go.'[87] The USA affirmed its enthusiastic support for

---

[83] Interview Rabinovich.   [84] Interview Rabinovich.
[85] Gil, *The Peres Formula*, p. 124.
[86] Qurie, *From Oslo to Jerusalem*, pp. 237–60; Savir, *The Process*, pp. 76–84; Pundak, *Secret Channel*, pp. 356–65.
[87] Miller, *The Much Too Promised Land*, p. 251.

54   Redirection

the accord, despite having had no involvement in the process that had led to its conclusion.[88]

US backing, a sine qua non for Rabin, paved the way to the presentation of the DoP before the Israeli government in a special meeting held on 29 August 1993. Ministers were asked to vote on the agreement and all bar two – Labour's Shimon Shitrit and Shas's Arye Deri – supported it. How was this transformation of the PLO from being utterly reprehensible and unmentioned in any official communication into a potential peace partner achieved so swiftly as to result in a near consensus government vote? It was based simply on Rabin's and Peres's complete identification with support for the DoP, which meant a vote against the initial agreement would be tantamount to a vote of no confidence in the prime minister and his foreign minister.[89] This simple domestic political fact trumped any misgivings government ministers might have had.

The issue of who would sign the DoP was settled duly, thereafter, with the exchange of two letters via Foreign Minister Holst on 10 September. In a letter from Chairman Arafat to Prime Minister Yitzhak Rabin, the PLO described the DoP as representing a 'new era in the history of the Middle East'. Accordingly, the PLO committed to Israel's right to exist in peace and security and accepted UNSCR 242 and 338. The PLO confirmed that those articles and provisions of the Palestinian Covenant that denied Israel's right to exist, were invalid and, in due course, would be submitted to the Palestinian National Council for formal amendment. Pledging itself to peaceful resolution of the conflict, the PLO rejected all forms of terrorism and other acts of violence, although other Palestinian organizations – most importantly Hamas – were not bound by this commitment. Tersely, Rabin responded that in light of the commitments set out in the PLO letter, the government of Israel would recognize the PLO as the representative of the Palestinian people and commence negotiations with the PLO within the Middle East peace process.[90]

The exchange of these letters of mutual recognition removed a serious obstacle to the signing of the Israeli-PLO DoP by Foreign Minister Peres and the PLO's Mahmoud Abbas. It took place on the south lawn of the White

---

[88] Beilin, *Touching Peace*, pp. 120–3; Ross, *The Missing Peace*, pp. 117–18.

[89] Beilin, *Touching Peace*, pp. 123–6.

[90] 'Israel-PLO Mutual Recognition, Letters and Speeches, 10 September 1993', *Israeli Ministry of Foreign* Affairs, www.mfa.gov.il/mfa/foreignpolicy/mfadocuments/year book9/pages/107%20israel-plo%20mutual%20recognition-%20letters%20and%20spe .aspx, accessed 17 March 2015; Beilin, *Touching Peace*, pp. 127–31; Qurie, *From Oslo to Jerusalem*, pp. 263–4, 266–71, 278–83; Pundak, *Secret Channel*, pp. 372–6.

House on 13 September 1993. President Bill Clinton, acting as master of ceremonies, had to nudge Prime Minister Rabin and Chairman Arafat to seal the document's signing with a historic handshake.

At the time, the DoP was perceived by many as symbolizing a new era of Israeli-Palestinian peace, but it was not a peace agreement. Rather, it was a statement of intent related to a number of issues over which Israel and the PLO agreed to negotiate within a finite time-frame. The two sides agreed to establish a 'Palestinian Interim Self-Government Authority' in the West Bank and the Gaza Strip, for a transitional period 'not exceeding five years'. Its composition would be determined by Palestinian elections to be held no later than nine months after the DoP came into force. In addition, the DoP laid down that Israel and the PLO should reach agreement – within two months – about Israel's withdrawal from populated areas in the Gaza Strip and the Jericho region. Then, within a further two months, Israel would physically redeploy its forces. Concurrently, the Israeli military government and its Civil Administration would begin trans-ferring authority to 'authorized Palestinians', who would assume responsibility for five key issues: education and culture, health, social welfare, direct taxation and tourism. While it was agreed that the Palestinians would also establish 'a strong police force', comprised primarily of Arafat supporters, Israel would retain overall responsibil-ity for external security, foreign affairs, Jerusalem, settlers and mili-tary locations.

The gradual, phased peacemaking approach stipulated by the DoP meant that the negotiators had to address multiple issues during the five-year 'interim period'. To this end, a joint Israeli-Palestinian Liaison Committee and an Israeli Palestinian Economic Cooperation Committee were set up to develop and promote joint ventures related to water, electricity and energy production, transport and communica-tions, trade, industry and the environment. In addition, Israel and the PLO agreed to cooperate to establish an emergency fund to encourage financial and economic support of the multilateral peace efforts in the Middle East, with a focus on the West Bank and the Gaza Strip. The Development Programme for the Middle East, as described in the DoP, would be initiated by the G7, Organisation for Economic Cooperation and Development members, regional Arab states and institutions and the private sector. The DoP did not include issues such as the future of Jerusalem, Jewish settlements, Palestinian refugees, Palestinian state-hood, the status of the Israeli occupation or the Israeli record of human rights violations in the West Bank and the Gaza Strip. These aspects

56   Redirection

were left to negotiations between the two parties during the interim period.[91]

Thus, the DoP presented Israel with two major advantages, which, as Rabin was later to explain, constituted key considerations in his decision to sign the DoP.[92] First, the PLO signed the agreement – albeit interim – while Israel retained sovereignty over Jerusalem. Second, the DoP reversed the precedent set by the Israeli-Egyptian Camp David accords, which included evacuating Jewish settlements in the Sinai; the interim agreement signed between Israel and the PLO stipulated clearly that all settlements would remain intact. Nonetheless, the DoP merited the appellation 'historic' in that it was the first mutual recognition by Israel and the Palestinians after years of mutual negation. Had either side tried to address some of the more fundamental disagreements between them, there would likely have been no accord.[93]

Between Engagement and Entrenchment

Labour's victory over Likud in the 1992 national elections prompted a redirection of Israeli foreign policy, which was shaped significantly by domestic factors. Prime Minister Rabin's ability to exploit the foreign policy decision-making structure was the most significant. He adopted a highly personalized, secretive, foreign policy decision-making style, which compartmentalized his closest aides, marginalized his foreign minister and state agencies and virtually excluded the government. Consequently, the key decisions during this period – to deport 415 members of Hamas, reprioritize the PLO track over the negotiations with Syria and recognize the PLO – were made by Rabin alone or in consultation with only a handful of individuals.

Consequently, Israeli foreign policy post-1992 bore the strong imprint of Rabin's personal foreign policy outlook. The prime minister was utterly convinced that Israel's fortunes were tied to US support and power. Thus, the emergence of the USA as the sole superpower after the Soviet collapse was perceived by Rabin as presenting Israel with unprecedented opportunities. Rabin's own Labour party and the coalition's senior

---

[91] Declaration of Principles on Interim Self-Government Arrangements 13 September 1993, *Israeli Ministry of Foreign Affairs*, www.mfa.gov.il/mfa/foreignpolicy/peace/guide/pages/declaration%20of%20principles.aspx, accessed 17 March 2015.

[92] 'Remarks by Prime Minister Rabin to the Committee of Editors of the Israeli Newspapers' 8 December 1993, IMFA, http://mfa.gov.il/MFA/ForeignPolicy/MFADocuments/Yearbook9/Pages/140%20Remarks%20by%20Prime%20Minister%20Rabin%20to%20the%20Committ.aspx, accessed 26 January 2016.

[93] Shlaim, *The Iron Wall*, p. 517.

member, Meretz, shared the prime minister's foreign policy outlook. This contrasted starkly with the view of Yitzhak Shamir and his government that the ending of the Cold War was of small significance to Israel. These distinct interpretations of what this period promised explain why, within a period of three years, in the wake of that international event, Israeli foreign policy took two distinct directions – entrenchment or engagement.

However, even as dominant a prime minister as Rabin did not operate in a domestic political vacuum. His main foreign policy decisions during this period were shaped partly by the domestic constraints he faced and his reading of how to deal with them. Accordingly, to shore up his domestic support, he implemented drastic security measures, such as deportation and closures, which amounted to collective punishment. Rabin realized that, unless he switched between the Syrian and Palestinian tracks, he would be unable to fulfil his election promise to reach an agreement with the Palestinians within six to nine months. Unfettered by ideology, the question of whether to engage with the PLO, for Rabin, ultimately was tactical.

In contrast to his first premiership, in his second term, Rabin was intent on making foreign policy gains rather than gaining time. It was Rabin's disappointment at Assad's tepid response to the three questions posed to him by the US secretary of state that led him to prioritize the Palestinian track over negotiations with Syria. At that point, domestic dictates meant that further bargaining with Assad was not an option. The elusive Syrian response made it politically impossible for Rabin to present it as a viable peace alternative to the Peres-led Oslo framework without risking his arch political rival launching a direct challenge to his leadership. The relentless political rivalry between the two Labour leaders, which so significantly influenced the course of the negotiations with Syria, also had serious bearing on the breakthrough with the PLO. Peres's support of the Israel-PLO negotiations was shaped significantly by his analysis that a breakthrough would pave the way to his return to the centre of Israeli foreign policymaking.

Nevertheless, Rabin remained master of his own house. In just over a year after the elections, his government had broken a historic taboo by recognizing the PLO and signing the DoP. The significance of the Israeli-PLO accord lay beyond the breakthrough it represented in the relationship with Israel's erstwhile nemesis. Signing the DoP marked a historical juncture in that it pitted two clear foreign policy alternatives against one another. The accord with the PLO launched Labour's foreign policy of engagement, which hinged on scaling down the Israeli occupation, relinquishing territory in exchange for peace agreements with the Arabs and putting a premium on diplomacy while keeping military force as a viable foreign policy tool. The alternative, entrenchment, championed by Likud, was based on the notion of peace for peace not territory, retaining the Palestinians under Israeli occupation and basing Israel's regional foreign policy on its military might. The contours of the debate over Israeli foreign policy following the end of the Cold War were finally set.

3   On the Brink of Peace?

Rabin's Security-Driven Approach to Implementing the DoP

Yitzhak Rabin, who spent his life leading Israel's fight against the PLO, remained profoundly suspicious of the organization and of Arafat's intentions towards Israel. Initially, recalled Eitan Haber, 'Rabin did not believe one word of Arafat and would not rely on him for one second.'[1] Thus, Rabin approached the first stage of implementing the DoP, which involved redeployment of the IDF in the Gaza Strip and the Jericho area, with great caution. He told the Knesset that its implementation would be 'a quasi-test of the ability of the Palestinians to implement the DoP' and to 'pacify' those areas subject to the transfer of control.[2] Rabin commented, rather condescendingly, that, unlike the IDF, the PLO could 'deal with the problems in the Gaza Strip without being accountable to B'Tselem' [the leading Israeli Human Rights organization] and the Israeli Supreme Court'.[3]

Suspicious and cautious, Rabin adopted a security-driven approach towards the negotiations for the implementation of the DoP, which caused him to restructure the Israeli negotiating team to the peace process. Ahead of the official talks, which were due to start on 13 October 1993 in the Egyptian resort of Taba, Rabin sidelined Deputy Foreign Minister Yossi Beilin and Uri Savir. Both men, who had been instrumental in the success of the Oslo secret channel, were replaced, respectively by the then IDF Deputy Chief of Staff, Amnon Likpkin-Shahak, and Generals Dani Rothschild and Uzi Dayan, who took charge of negotiations with the PLO.[4]

---

[1] Interview 1 Haber; Savir, *The Process*, p. 128.
[2] Yitzhak Rabin, 'Statement in the Knesset by Prime Minister Rabin on the Israel-PLO Declaration of Principles—21 September 1993, https://mfa.gov.il/MFA/ForeignPolicy/MFADocuments/Yearbook9/Pages/110%20Statement%20in%20the%20Knesset%20by%20Prime%20Minister%20Rab.aspx, accessed 30 November, 2018.
[3] *Yedioth Ahoronoth*, 3 September, 1993 (in Hebrew).
[4] Savir, *The Process*, p. 118; Interview 1 Beilin.

60   On the Brink of Peace?

The changes Rabin put in place were significant. Yossi Beilin, Uri Savir and the Israeli academics who had established the Oslo secret channel with the PLO were rooted in the Israeli peace movement while Generals Shahak, Rothschild and Dayan came from the IDF. Close observers of the negotiations noticed that the generals were unable to make the transition from considering the Palestinians as 'prisoners' and 'subjects' to seeing them as equals.[5] Serving in leading positions within the very organization that enforced the West Bank and Gaza Strip occupations instilled in the generals a sense of entitlement to impose the Israeli agenda on their Palestinian interlocutors. Arafat was to complain repeatedly, but unsuccessfully, to Rabin that the Israelis were imposing decisions because 'prime minister, your Excellency, you have the upper hand'.[6]

Instead of the win–win approach underpinning the negotiations during the secret phase of the Oslo peace process, the generals were guided by a zero-sum-game attitude. This negotiation method, as Uri Savir noted while observing the negotiations, was problematic. It hinged on plans for a worst case scenario and was predicated on deterrence rather than confidence-building measures.[7] Gradually, the generals subordinated the DoP implementation process to Israel's short-term security concerns, which, by definition, were unaccommodating to Palestinian political aspirations.[8]

Why did Rabin decide to restructure the Israeli negotiating team, given the success of the Oslo secret channel? His decision seems to have been shaped by two domestic factors, which, from the outset, had haunted Rabin's premiership: maintaining Israel's day-to-day security and preserving domestic support for and the legitimacy of the peace process with the PLO. Retaining legitimacy became a particularly acute concern as Rabin's coalition government began to fray. By September 1993, as the breakthrough with the PLO was announced, the Israeli police brought charges of bribery against Raphael Pinchasi and Arie Deri from Shas. Shas responded by resigning from the government, rendering it a minority government of fifty-six MKs rather than the former majority of sixty-two.[9] Rabin was convinced that Shas's departure undermined the legitimacy of the peace process with the PLO because the government had lost its 'Jewish majority' in parliament. This apprehension was one of

---

[5] Halevy, *Man in the Shadows*, p. 68; Savir, *The Process*, pp. 195, 228, 237, 245; Interview 2 Haber.

[6] Interview 2 Beilin; Interview 2 Haber.

[7] Uri Savir, *Peace First* (Tel Aviv: Yedioth Ahronoth Books, 2007), p. 60 (in Hebrew).

[8] Savir, *The Process*, p. 121.

[9] Reuven Y. Hazan, 'Intraparty Politics and Peace-Making in Democratic Societies: Israel's Labour Party and the Middle East Process, 1992–1996', *Journal of Peace Research*, 37, 3, 2000: 367.

the main reasons why Rabin incorporated the IDF into the negotiations. As the then head of the GSS recalled, Rabin was sending a clear signal to Israeli Jews that the IDF approved the nascent peace process and that Israeli security remained Rabin's utmost consideration.[10]

Rabin's security-driven approach to implementing the DoP contrasted starkly with the goals the PLO set out to achieve. According to leading Palestinian negotiator, Dr Nabil Sha'ath, these goals included separating from Israel, ending the occupation and creating the conditions for an independent Palestinian state.[11] In contrast, Israel's opening position reflected its historical negation of Palestinian statehood and the unchanged positions of Rabin and Peres in this regard. Tellingly, the Israelis refused adamantly, in the official documentation, to refer to Arafat as 'President' lest this should imply that he was the head of a state in the making, or to describe the Palestinian Interim Self-Government Authority as a 'national' authority.[12]

The security-driven approach of Rabin and the generals seriously impinged on the negotiations. This was evident in Israeli demands regarding Jewish settlements, especially in the Gaza Strip. Israel insisted on retaining control over the settlements, the land usurped by the settlers for agriculture, plus the three main lateral routes joining the settlements to the Green Line.[13] Consequently, the lives of the approximately 750,000 Palestinian residents of the Gaza Strip at the time were severely impinged by the short-term security concerns of some 6,234 Jewish settlers.[14]

In refusing to recognize any aspect of Palestinian statehood and by privileging security over Palestinian political aspirations, the Israeli approach to the negotiations perpetuated the existing power asymmetry favouring Israel – an occupying state – and the non-state actor status of the PLO. This diminished the principle of Israeli-PLO parity underpinning the DoP and the Israeli-PLO letters of mutual recognition. These documents explicitly acknowledged the mutual 'legitimate and political rights' of Israel and the Palestinian people, and was understood by the PLO as ushering in a period of Palestinian statehood.

---

[10] Carmi Gillon, *Shin-Beth Between the Schisms* (Tel-Aviv: Yedioth Ahronoth, 2000), pp. 149, 284 (in Hebrew).

[11] Nabil Shaath, 'The Oslo Agreement. An Interview with Nabil Shaath', *Journal of Palestine Studies*, 23, 1, 1993: 12.

[12] Hirschfeld, *Oslo*, pp. 152–4; Ross, *The Missing Peace*, p. 123.

[13] Savir, *The Process*, p. 120.

[14] Data on settlers drawn from 'Twenty Years after Oslo the Two State Solution Is Still Alive', *Peace Now Official Website*, http://peacenow.org.il/20-years-to-oslo, accessed 5 March 2019.

62   On the Brink of Peace?

Domestic Response to the DoP

Once the DoP became public knowledge it sparked a visceral anti-peace campaign led by Likud, the Yesha Council and settler splinter groups such as Zoo Artzeinu or This is Our Land. They accused the prime minister of losing his moorings, of betraying the Land of Israel, Judaism and Zionism, of not disclosing to Israelis that the DoP was the midwife of Palestinian statehood and of transferring responsibility for Israeli security from the IDF to the PLO.[15] In a scathing critique of the DoP when it was presented to the Knesset, the then leader of the opposition, Binyamin Netanyahu, asked rhetorically: when the DoP talks about 'the mutual political rights between us and the Palestinians what does that mean? A state for them too.'[16]

This anti-peace campaign, which involved fierce attacks on the government in parliament, mounting mass demonstrations and increasingly rabid public rallies, was determined to expose what it described as the 'dangers and delusions' of negotiating with the PLO.[17] Significantly, there was no counter-campaign mounted during this turbulent period. The main Israeli pro-peace umbrella organization, Peace Now, was well aware of the unpatriotic stigma, which, for many years, had marked the peace movement. Therefore, it feared that campaigning openly in support of the government's policy towards the PLO could delegitimize the entire peace process and the government itself.[18]

Did the fierce anti-peace campaign affect Israeli foreign policy towards the peace negotiations? By all accounts, Rabin was neither by nature nor ideology an ardent solicitor of public affection.[19] Therefore, the public campaign did not cause him to divert from seeking a political settlement with the PLO. However, it did have a bearing on the negotiations. One of Rabin's first actions as newly elected prime minister in 1992 was to nominate Kalman Guyer as special advisor for surveys. Guyer implemented surveys on a variety of political issues and presented the results to Rabin. Rabin's need to retain the public's support for his ambition and

---

[15] Interview Mr Israel Harel, 4 November 2014, Tel-Aviv; Interview Mr Elyakim Haetzni, 6 November 2014, Kiryat Arba; Feiglein Moshe, *In the Place Where There Are No People Strive to Be a Person* (Jerusalem: Metzuda, 1997), pp. 34, 36 (in Hebrew); Uri Elitzur and Hagai Uberman, *The Oslo Agreement: A Report on Its Achievements, September 93– September 94* (Beit-El: Ha Likud, Mafdal, Tzomet, and Yesha Council, 1994) (in Hebrew).
[16] Divrei Yemei Ha-Knesset, Knesset Archives, 21 September 1993 (in Hebrew).
[17] Interviews Harel and Haetzni.
[18] Tamar Hermann, *The Israeli Peace Movement: A Shattered Dream* (Cambridge: Cambridge University Press, 2009), pp. 123, 135.
[19] Interview 2 Haber; Interview former Head of Mossad, Efraim Halevy, 5 November, 2015, Tel-Aviv.

Domestic Response to the DoP

ability to pursue his foreign policy pushed him to recheck on and consider public opinion in his decision-making process.[20]

In this context, Guyer was keeping close tabs on the level of support for the Oslo process among the Israeli public – especially Jews – amid attempts by Likud and the settlers to discredit the peace process. The data, which were presented to the prime minister at frequent intervals, showed consistent support from more than half of the Israelis surveyed for the government-led peace process. However, the polls also revealed that this support hinged on Rabin's showing complete resolve to continue the process and make the Palestinians 'work hard' to get something out of the negotiations.[21] This is one explanation for the slow and painstaking process pursued by the Israeli negotiators, which tallied with preserving public support for and enhancing the credibility of Rabin in the wake of the anti-peace campaign.

Another explanation was the personalized, secretive and exclusionary foreign policy style, adopted by Rabin during the secret phase of the negotiations, which did not allow government and relevant state agencies to plan ahead. As a result, the Israeli and Palestinian negotiators faced many unexpected problems in the course of implementation of the DoP and, especially, the security arrangements related to the areas to be transferred to Palestinian control and Israel proper.[22]

The deceleration of the peace process undermined another key principle of the DoP: its self-imposed timeframe. It was not until April 1994 that Israel and the PLO finalized agreement to Palestinian rule in the Gaza Strip and Jericho area, which the DoP decreed should be concluded in two months. For Arafat, as Dennis Ross recalls, to miss this date was 'to violate the agreement'.[23] In contrast, Rabin declared that 'there were no sacred dates'.[24] 'That was a terrible mistake', lamented former Deputy Foreign Minister Beilin and rightly so.[25] Declaring that there were 'no sacred dates' legitimized breaching of the commitments stipulated by the DoP and slowing the pace of negotiations. Inadvertently perhaps, Rabin had undermined this important mechanism of a self-imposed timeframe, which would have held Israel and the PLO accountable simultaneously. Without it, Israel, the occupying power, retained firm control over the scope and pace of DoP implementation.

---

[20] Interview Mr Kalman Gayer, 22 December 2014, Ramat Gan; References to poll data in interview given by Rabin in Haaretz, 6 July 1994 in http://mfa.gov.il/MFA/ForeignPolicy/MFADocuments/Yearbook9/Pages/197%20Interview%20with%20Prime%20Minister%20Rabin%20in%20Haaretz.aspx, accessed 26 November 2018.

[21] Interview Gayer.   [22] Interview 2 Haber; Savir, The Process, pp. 126–31, 136–44.

[23] Ross, The Missing Peace, p. 124.

[24] Interview 2 Beilin; Ross, The Missing Peace, p. 124.   [25] Interview 2 Beilin.

64   On the Brink of Peace?

Assaulting the DoP: the Settlers and Hamas

Besides opposition using democratic means, the settlers resorted to direct and often illegal actions, aimed at reversing the peace process. The most important of these was expanding the settlements in spite of the restrictions imposed by the Rabin government. As senior figures in the settler movement confirm, its leadership was well aware of the contrasting reading of the DoP by Israel and the PLO and the lack of trust between Rabin and Arafat. Therefore, they reasoned correctly, that 'settlement activity at this stage had the potential of neutralizing the whole [peace] process.'[26] To this end, the Yesha Council spearheaded the expansion of settlements, whose population increased between 1992 and 1996 from 105,400 to 146,900.[27] The expansion of settlements may not have violated the letter of Oslo per se, but it seriously undermined the logic of gradually scaling down the Israeli occupation.

However, the most direct attempt to derail the peace process within the first few months was the growing violence of the settlers, which culminated in a terrorist act committed by a US-born practising physician and settler from Kiryat Arba, Dr Baruch Goldstein. On 25 February 1994, Goldstein entered the Tomb of the Patriarchs wearing an IDF uniform. Then, in a shooting spree, he singlehandedly murdered twenty-nine Palestinians and wounded another 125 as they knelt in prayer during the holy month of Ramadan. The massacre was followed by clashes between the Israeli security forces and Palestinians protestors, in which five more Palestinians were killed; following this, Hebron was placed under curfew.[28] The victims, it seems, had to pay the price for the actions of their perpetrator and the monumental incompetence and systematic failure of Israeli security forces to enforce the law against armed Jewish settlers.[29]

The massacre, which was perpetrated as Israeli and PLO negotiators were finalizing the agreement on Palestinian self-rule in the Gaza Strip and the Jericho area, was clearly timed to derail the peace process.[30] In the wake of the carnage, the PLO suspended talks, agreeing to their

---

[26] Interview Haetzni; Feiglin, *In the Place*, pp. 52, 73.

[27] Feiglein, *In the Place*, pp. 62–89; for the data on the number of settlers, see 'The Number of Settlers Per Year, *Peace Now Official* Website, http://peacenow.org.il/settlements-watch/matzav/population, accessed 5 March 2019.

[28] Danny Yatom, *The Confidant: From Sayeret Matkal to the Mossad* (Tel Aviv: Yedioth Ahronoth, 2009), p. 96 (Hebrew); Ross, *The Missing Piece*, p. 126.

[29] For key security flaws, see Yatom, *The Confidant*, p. 105.

[30] Israel-PLO statement on the Cairo Talks, 23 February 1994, *Israel Ministry of Foreign Affairs*, https://mfa.gov.il/MFA/ForeignPolicy/MFADocuments/Yearbook9/Pages/159%20Israel-PLO%20Statement%20on%20the%20Cairo%20Talks-%2023%20Fe.aspx, accessed 29 November 2018.

Assaulting the DoP: the Settlers and Hamas

resumption on condition that Israel removed Jewish settlers from the Tel-Rumeida area in Hebron to the settlement of Kiryat Arba, established a Palestinian police force in Hebron and deployed an international force to protect the city's Palestinian population. In addition, the PLO sought a UNSCR condemning the massacre, holding Israel accountable and allowing the despatch of an international force to Hebron.

The Israeli response to the crisis and the demands made by the PLO are telling in terms of the influence the settlers were able to exert on decision-making. On 15 March 1993, a delegation headed by Shahak, clarified to the PLO that these conditions were unacceptable to Israel, which halted the negotiations. On 19 March, Peres and Rabin considered options for how to respond to the crisis. Initially, they were inclined to remove some of the settlers from Hebron, both to defuse the tensions in the city and as a gesture of goodwill to Arafat.[31] However, when the Yesha Council became aware of the government's idea for a partial settler evacuation, it sent a discreet, but clear message via the security services and members of the opposition. It threatened that any attempt to evacuate the settlers from Hebron would be met with stiff resistance and that each evacuated settler would be replaced by a new cohort. This increased the IDF's and the GSS's opposition to the idea of a partial evacuation of the settlers from Hebron.[32]

Rabin was clearly taken aback by this clear threat, which was why, ultimately, he decided against the partial evacuation. On 20 March, Shahak informed Arafat of the prime minister's decision, adding that Israel would consider establishing an international observer presence in Hebron in the form of the Red Cross. Following two days of extremely tense deliberations in Tunis, Arafat accepted the Israeli offer, despite its being designed to avoid conflict with the settlers rather than to deal with the crisis prompted by the Hebron massacre.[33]

Two factors influenced Arafat's decision. First, Israel and the USA had recently announced Syria's return to the negotiations, which the Palestinians were concerned would weaken their bargaining position with Israel.[34] Second, at this crucial juncture in the peace process, Arafat remained politically committed to the DoP. It is revealing that he rejected outright the suggestions from some of his aides to revert to armed struggle rather than accepting the Israeli proposal to progress

[31] Savir, *The Process*, pp. 147, 149–54; Hirschfeld, *Oslo*, p. 156.
[32] Interview Harel; Ross, *The Missing Peace*, p. 126.   [33] Savir, *The Process*, pp. 149–56.
[34] Joint Press Conference Clinton-Rabin, the White House, 16 March 1994, *Israeli Ministry of Foreign Affairs*, www.mfa.gov.il/mfa/foreignpolicy/mfadocuments/yearbook9/pages/1 70%20joint%20press%20conference%20clinton-rabin-%20the%20whit.aspx, accessed 22 June 2015.

66   On the Brink of Peace?

negotiations. Dennis Ross and Uri Savir, who had held meetings directly with Arafat during this tense period, both noted his unambiguity on this point.[35]

Furthermore, Arafat told Shahak and Savir that 'he trusted that Prime Minister Rabin would deal with the settlers appropriately in due course.'[36] However, Rabin never did, which was a grave mistake on his part. It sent a clear message to the settlers that the government was susceptible to their threats and that they could break democratic rules and norms with impunity. For Arafat, in turn, it eventually became clear that his calculated personal and political risk had not paid off. Ultimately, Israel conceded little in the wake of the massacre. It authorized a toothless commission of inquiry, outlawed the Jewish settler movement fringes and accepted the rather innocuous UNSCR 904.[37]

The tame response of Rabin's government to the Hebron massacre assisted Hamas. It provided a pretext to scale up its terror campaign against the Israelis, aimed at promoting the 'relentless war' Hamas had declared on the peace process from the outset. Hamas argued, deceivingly, that the massacre demonstrated Israel's indiscriminate distinction between fighters and unarmed civilians, which 'forced [Hamas] to treat the Zionists in a similar manner'.[38] The unambiguous threat in Hamas's statements was realized once the official forty-day period of mourning for the victims of the massacre ended. In the following two weeks, Hamas introduced a new weapon in its conflict with Israel: suicide bombers, who, in the space of a week, blew up two packed commuter buses in the Israeli towns of Afula and Hadera, killing thirteen Israelis and wounding several others.[39]

This was a deliberate political attack by Hamas on the peace process and compounded the impact of the Hebron massacre. These terrorist attacks undermined one of the cornerstones of the DoP, namely, use of the interim period to create a network of cooperation that would facilitate resolution of the more difficult issues in a more benign climate. Instead, amid the Goldstein massacre and the suicide bombing campaign by Hamas, negotiations over the interim settlements were marred by

---

[35] Ross, *The Missing Peace*, pp. 132–3; Savir, *The Process*, pp. 149–56, 158.

[36] Savir, *The Process*, p. 158.

[37] United Nations Website, http://daccess-dds-ny.un.org/doc/UNDOC/GEN/N94/139/8 5/PDF/N9413985.pdf?OpenElement, accessed 13 January 2016.

[38] Milton-Edwards and Farrel, *Hamas*, pp. 70–1, 78.

[39] Suicide and Other Bombing Attacks in Israel Since the Declaration of Principles (Sept 1993), *IMFA*, http://www.mfa.gov.il/mfa/foreignpolicy/terrorism/palestinian/pages/suicide%20and%20other%20bombing%20attacks%20in%20israel%20since.aspx, accessed 22 November 2018.

distrust, violence and dissolution, which spread among Israelis, Palestinians and their respective leaderships.

The Oslo I Agreement

By May 1994 – eight months after the signing of the DoP – the peace process was marked by contradictions. Despite several setbacks, Israel and the PLO had made some progress. On 4 May, in Cairo, the DoP was finally translated into specifics when Israel and the PLO signed the Agreement on the Gaza Strip and the Jericho Area, which became known as the Oslo I Agreement. An economic appendix to the agreement was signed in Paris on 29 April.[40] Oslo I paved the way to Yasser Arafat's return to the Gaza Strip on 1 July 1994, amid fierce demonstrations in Israel, which revealed the visceral hatred still felt by many towards the Palestinian leader. Arafat would preside over a twenty-four-member Palestinian Authority (PA), which was set up by the agreement, for a period of five years. The PA would be in charge for all the legislative and executive powers and responsibilities, transferred to it by Israel, within parts of the Gaza Strip and the Jericho area.

Oslo I also established a joint Coordination and Cooperation Committee and three District Coordination and Cooperation Offices – for the Gaza, Khan Yunis and the Jericho districts – to institutionalize cooperation between the Israeli security forces and their nascent Palestinian counterparts. Further, Oslo I stipulated that responsibility for tourism, education and culture, health, social welfare and direct taxation would be transferred from Israel's civil administration to the PA. Importantly, the accord set a final deadline, 4 May 1999, for concluding final agreement on all outstanding issues. In all these respects, the Oslo I agreement constituted a scaling down of the Israeli occupation and a partial transfer of authority from Israel to the PA.

However, Oslo I also reflected the extent to which Rabin's security-driven approach dismantled the original framework created by DoP. Tellingly, rather than ending the occupation of Gaza – as the term Gaza initially implies – Israel merely redeployed the IDF. The areas that fell under PA jurisdiction remained firmly within reach of the IDF, which still occupied 35 per cent of the Gaza Strip through deployment in the Gush Katif settlement block, the Erez settlements, the Gaza Strip-Egyptian border and the lateral roads in the Gaza Strip.

---

[40] Gaza-Jericho Agreement Annex IV – Economic Protocol, IMFA, http://mfa.gov.il/MFA/ForeignPolicy/Peace/Guide/Pages/Gaza-Jericho%20Agreement%20Annex%20IV%20-%20Economic%20Protoco.aspx, accessed 13 January 2016.

68 On the Brink of Peace?

Reflecting the continuing objections of Rabin and Peres to establishing a Palestinian state and in order to preserve public support, the government ensured that Oslo I denied almost all expression of Palestinian statehood. Israel retained control over foreign affairs, external security, the airspace and the vetting of people and goods moving in and out of the areas under Palestinian self-rule. Furthermore, the PA was, in several respects, a seriously constrained institution, which reflected Israel's ability to impose its demands on the PLO. For instance, Oslo I included a stipulation that Israel be kept informed of the names of the twenty-four members comprising the PA. Any change in the PA's membership would require an exchange of letters between the PLO and the Israeli government. It also decreed that Israel had the right to veto members of the Palestinian police force. Similarly, Oslo I allowed Israel to challenge proposed PA legislation if it was deemed not to accord with Israel's security, to 'threaten other significant Israeli interests' or if Israel judged it likely to cause 'irreparable damage or harm'. Reflecting the asymmetry of power between the occupier, Israel, and the PLO, the agreement meant that the Palestinians were not afforded similar rights over Israeli legislation. In fact, in certain respects Oslo I prolonged Israel's occupier status: it allowed its occupation laws and military orders to remain in force unless amended or abrogated by mutual agreement. Consequently, any issue that could not be resolved by negotiation was subject to the provisions of Israeli rather than international law and, particularly, the Fourth Geneva Convention. Although it seemingly went unnoticed at the time, Oslo I embodied a trend that ultimately would seriously undermine the peace process. The facade of short-term success suggesting progress obscured the dismantling of the foundations underpinning the DoP, through Rabin's security-driven approach to the negotiations. The infrastructure supporting the peace process in the longer term was weakened significantly in this process.

Prioritizing the Jordanian Track

As Rabin had anticipated, the signing of the DoP in September 1993 created new opportunities for Israeli foreign policy towards the Arab states. A charged debate developed within the Israeli foreign policy community and between the Israeli and the US leaderships on how to proceed. The IDF, via the military intelligence directorate, recommended that Israel pursue a 'Syria first' approach. The US administration, including President Clinton, supported this approach on the grounds that were negotiations with Syria to be postponed, President Assad would seek to derail the whole peace process. In contrast, a peace deal with Syria would

Prioritizing the Jordanian Track   69

surely pave the way to a deal with both Jordan and the Palestinians. However, Rabin and Peres took a very different view. They were convinced that the Jordanian peace track should be prioritized because, compared to the Syrian and Palestinian tracks, the areas of dispute between Israel and Jordan – over territory, water and Jerusalem – were minor.[41]

In addition, both Israel and Jordan had a clear interest in concluding a peace accord. For Israel, a peace agreement would dramatically diminish the prospect of an Arab invasion from the east. It was also in line with Israel's tactic of playing off the Palestinian, Syrian and Jordanian tracks against one another: headway in one direction meant Rabin would slow progress in the other two. For Jordan, a peace agreement represented the only way it could ensure that implementation of the DoP would not threaten its interests. Specifically, Jordan sought to guarantee that further Israeli-PLO agreement would not undermine the Hashemite Monarchy's status as Guardian of the Holy Muslim Shrines in Jerusalem and would address the issue of Palestinian refugees in Jordan. The Jordanians also perceived that an accord with Israel would be the key to restoring its erstwhile strategic relationship with the USA, which had collapsed following King Hussein's decision to support Iraq during the 1990–1 Gulf War. Realizing the economic potential of an Arab-Israeli peace, which was crucial for the feeble Jordanian economy, was another important consideration.[42] The convergence of interests between the two countries was reflected in the Israel-Jordan Common Agenda, signed on 14 September 1993, which held that a peace treaty was a mutual objective.[43]

Nonetheless, initial relations with King Hussein following the signing of the DoP were complicated. Hussein felt betrayed and threatened by his exclusion from the secret negotiations that led to the Israeli-PLO DoP, which referred to Jordan only once, in the 12th clause.[44] At the same time,

---

[41] Indyk, *Innocent Abroad*, pp. 95–96; Rabinovich, *The Brink of Peace*, p. 124.
    Savir, *The Process*, p. 107.
[42] On Jordanian and Israeli interests, see Ashton, *King Hussein of Jordan*, pp. 292–4, 302–3; Shimon Shamir, *The Rise and Decline of the Warm Peace with Jordan: Israeli Diplomacy in the Hussein Years* (Tel Aviv: Hakibbutrz Hameuchad Publishing House, 2012), pp. 52–9 (in Hebrew); Halevy, *Man in the Shadows*, p. 75.
[43] Israel-Jordan Common Agenda, *Israeli Ministry of Foreign Affairs*, http://mfa.gov.il/MFA/ForeignPolicy/Peace/Guide/Pages/Israel-Jordan%20Common%20Agenda.aspx, accessed 30 November 2018.
[44] Mahmoud Abbas, *Through Secret Channels* (Reading: Garnett, 1995), p. 187; Avi Shlaim, *Lion of Jordan: The Life of King Hussein in War and Peace* (London: Penguin, 2007), pp. 522–4; Declaration of Principles on Interim Self-Government Arrangements, 13 September 1993, *Israeli Ministry of Foreign Affairs*, www.mfa.gov.il/mfa/foreignpolicy/peace/guide/pages/declaration%20of%20principles.aspx, accessed 30 November 2018.

70 On the Brink of Peace?

Hussein recognized the advantages of the DoP. While the Madrid conference removed the Arab taboo on negotiating with Israel, the Oslo process removed the Palestinian taboo, which conferred on King Hussein the legitimacy previously lacking, to pursue an independent peace accord with Israel.[45]

Against this background, on 6 October 1993 King Hussein met secretly with the Israeli prime minister. Rabin was keen to restore King Hussein's trust, following his exclusion from the Oslo process, and to explore how Israeli-Jordanian relations might develop in light of the Israeli-PLO breakthrough.[46] Thus, Rabin assured Hussein that Israel remained firmly committed to upholding his regime, to protecting Jordanian interests while dealing with the Palestinians and to coordinating closely on a future peace strategy. This meeting was significant: King Hussein emphasized to Rabin that Jordan would be willing to conclude a peace deal with Israel irrespective of progress on the other peace tracks. However, the two leaders could not agree on the sequence of the negotiations. The Israelis were keen to sign a peace treaty and then attend to the detail later. The Jordanians, in contrast, would not agree to sign until outstanding issues related to borders, border crossings, security, refugees, trade, water and the environment had been resolved. This resulted in a 'real stalemate'.[47]

Nevertheless, the convergence of interests between the two countries kept the peace process on track. On 1 October 1993, Foreign Minister Peres met publicly with Crown Prince Hassan in Washington, during the international donor conference for the Middle East. This encounter, which was presided over by President Clinton, produced the Israeli-US-Jordanian Trilateral Economic Community, whose remit was to promote a common economic and environmental agenda.[48] Therefore, despite the Rabin-Hussein stalemate, Peres believed that Jordan was ready to sign an independent peace accord with Israel.[49]

The opportunity to test his thesis came on 2 November 1993. Accompanied by Mossad's Efraim Halevy, who was sent by Rabin to

---

[45] Ashton, *King Hussein of Jordan*, p. 300.
[46] My account of this meeting draws on Rabin's Military Secretary Danny Yatom's, recollections of the meeting, in Yatom, *The Confidant*, pp. 277–9; Efraim Halevy's interview with Ari Shavit in Ari Shavit, 'Smiley Stopped Smiling', *Ha'aretz*, 2 September, 2003 (in Hebrew); Shlaim, *Lion of Jordan*, p. 525; Ashton, *King Hussein of Jordan*, p. 301; Indyk, *Innocent Abroad*, pp. 93, 95.
[47] Halevy, *Man in the Shadows*, p. 90.
[48] Statements by President Clinton, Crown Prince Hassan and Foreign Minister Peres, the White House, 1 October 1993, http://mfa.gov.il/MFA/ForeignPolicy/MFADocuments/Yearbook9/Pages/113%20Statements%20by%20President%20Clinton-%20Crown%20Prince.aspx, accessed 30 November 2018.
[49] Savir, *The Process*, p. 107.

monitor his foreign minister, Peres met King Hussein in Amman. The conditions of the meeting were that it be kept secret because King Hussein was fearful of Assad's reaction; should the Syrian president discover that the Jordanian monarch was meeting with the Israelis, he would likely try to derail the process. At this meeting, Peres presented a far-reaching economic vision for an Israeli-Jordanian peace and ways to secure Jordan's custodianship of the Holy Muslim Shrines in Jerusalem.

However, on his return to Israel, Peres acted recklessly. 'Put 3 November in your calendars as a historic date', he told journalists, insinuating that Israel and Jordan were on the verge of a peace agreement. According to Efraim Halevy's account of the meeting and the memoirs of US diplomats, Peres conveyed a similar message to the Americans and Rabin, without consulting King Hussein.[50] In addition to breaking the promise of a secret meeting, Peres seriously misrepresented the content of his encounter with Hussein. It is true that, in their meeting, Peres and King Hussein had agreed on the general parameters to an Israeli-Jordanian peace, summarized in a 'non-paper' initialled by Peres and Hussein.[51] However, fundamental disagreements remained. The thorniest problem was border demarcation. During the late 1960s, Israel absorbed 380 square kilometres, which, according to the borders outlined in the 1949 armistice agreement, was Jordanian land.[52] Peres claimed that, in the meeting, Hussein had agreed to Israel's leasing the area. In turn, Halevy contended that the King had rejected this proposal outright, which seems more plausible since the issue of this contested piece of land resurfaced in later Israeli-Jordanian negotiations.[53]

What explains Peres's reckless behaviour? Some attribute it to his 'overexcited' and 'euphoric' mood following the meeting.[54] However, this explanation fails to convince since, according to those who worked closely with Peres, he had a very measured temperament, seldom displayed his feelings and thoroughly thought through his public statements.[55] What is more conceivable is that Peres's personal rivalry with Rabin led to concern over whether the prime minister would allow him to be part of the negotiations with Jordan. His press leaks were cunning and designed to secure for himself a central role in Israeli peace-making with Jordan, based on public perception that he and not Rabin had been the main driving force. However, since it was not the first time

---

[50] My account of the content of the meeting is based on Halevy, *Man in the Shadows*, p. 91; Ross, *The Missing Peace*, p. 167; Indyk, *Innocent Abroad*, pp. 102–3.
[51] Shamir, *The Rise and Decline of the Warm Peace*, p. 63.
[52] Shlaim, *The Iron Wall*, p. 543. [53] Halevy, *Man in the Shadows*, p. 89.
[54] Bar-Zohar, *Shimon Peres*, p. 455; Shlaim, *The Iron Wall*, p. 529.
[55] Interview 1 Beilin; Savir, *The Process*, p. 175; Yatom, *The Confidant*, p. 284.

72   On the Brink of Peace?

that Peres had reneged on commitments made to King Hussein, his plan backfired.[56] Hussein lost all faith in Peres and insisted that he be excluded from the peace process.[57]

Cooperation across the Jordan

Rabin used Peres's calamitous handling of the meeting to exclude his foreign minister from covert negotiations with Jordan. Thereafter, they were conducted by the tight-knit political-military elite surrounding King Hussein and Rabin's confidants from the prime minister's office and Mossad. The Israeli group included Eitan Haber, Danny Yatom and Efraim Halevy, the last of whom was the most instrumental of the three subordinates. Halevy had been Mossad's representative in Washington when Rabin was ambassador; he had established a working relationship with Rabin, which extended over more than twenty-five years and had gained his full trust. Likewise, as the key Israeli interlocutor with Jordan, Halevy had King Hussein's complete trust. Reflecting the enduring impact of the Peres-Rabin rivalry on foreign policymaking, Halevy was under strict orders from Rabin not to brief Peres or his ministerial staff on developments.[58]

The concentration of secret talks in a handful of individuals inside the Jordanian and Israeli military-political elites is key to understanding the success of the negotiations between the two countries. In April 1994, King Hussein felt increasingly threatened by the imminent signing of the Oslo I agreement, which established PLO rule over parts of the Gaza strip and the Jericho area. The agreement constituted a steppingstone to an extended PLO presence in other parts of the West Bank. It made more real the prospect of Israel and the PLO signing further agreements that might jeopardize Jordan's core interests. Against this background, Hussein sent a message to Rabin, via Halevy, that Jordan was keen to move towards a permanent agreement.[59] According to Hussein, Syria, which in the past had been fiercely opposed to any Arab country negotiating independently with Israel, would not object. However, Halevy stressed that progress with Israel was contingent on the USA restoring its strategic relationship with Jordan to its pre-1990–1 Gulf War status.

---

[56] Previously, Peres had reneged on the commitment he made to Hussein during negotiations over the botched 1987 London agreement. See Shlaim, *The Iron Wall*, pp. 442–7.
[57] Interview 2 Haber; Yatom, *The Confidant*, p. 282.
[58] Halevy, *Man in the Shadows*, p. 77.
[59] My account of the May–April breakthrough is based on Halevy, *Man in the Shadows*, pp. 71–5; Indyk, *Innocent Abroad*, pp. 126–7, 129; Ross, *The Missing Peace*, pp. 168–9.

His position in Mossad and Rabin's and Hussein's trust in him stood Halevy in excellent stead to break the Israeli-Jordanian stalemate. Halevy used the message from the King to pave the way to a secret meeting between Hussein and Rabin, in London, on 19 May 1994. In this meeting, Rabin was more forthcoming than he had been in the talks held in the previous September. He assured Hussein that Israel would exert its influence in Washington in relation to accession to the Jordanian requests and would consider positively Jordan's demands relating to borders, water and preservation of Hashemite guardianship of the Muslim Holy Shrines in Jerusalem. Martyn Indyk's memoirs cast light on the domestic considerations driving Rabin to be more amenable to King Hussein's demands in May than in their October meeting:

A warm peace was worth a great deal to Rabin at that point when the latter was trying to convince his people of the wisdom of his deal with Arafat while preparing them for full withdrawal from the Golan. For that, Rabin would be willing to pay.[60]

Halevy used his unique position as deputy director of Mossad and confidant of Rabin and Hussein to translate the understandings from the London meeting into specifics. The first task was to harness the support of the US negotiating team, which was sceptical about the prospects of an Israeli-Jordanian peace. The opportunity arose during a visit by the US mediators in late May 1994. Secretary of State Christopher, in a move that once more reflects his poor instinct in the context of peacemaking, preferred to retire to his hotel room rather than to be briefed by Halevy on progress in the Israeli-Jordanian talks. Halevy was left to communicate King Hussein's keenness for a breakthrough with Israel to Dennis Ross, who, through his own contacts in Jordan, verified Halevy's version.

During a formal visit to Washington by King Hussein on 18 June 1994, the advantages of pursuing negotiations with Jordan via Mossad were made further apparent. King Hussein sought to achieve a number of goals in exchange for Jordan publicly breaking the mould with the Israelis. These goals included lifting of the maritime quarantine imposed by the USA on Jordan during the 1990–1 Gulf War, resumption of US military support to Jordan and the passing of a bill by Congress to wipe out the $700 million Jordanian debt. It is significant that, throughout the US-Jordanian high-level talks, Halevy acted as liaison between the Israelis, the Jordanians and the Americans. His lobbying of the Americans to support the *Jordanian* case was so fervent as to prompt Dennis Ross to

---

[60] Indyk, *Innocent Abroad*, p. 135.

74   On the Brink of Peace?

ask whether he were representing Israel or Jordan. 'Both', replied Halevy, without batting an eyelid.[61]

In a key meeting between President Clinton and King Hussein, the USA outlined its proposal. It conditioned acceding to Jordan's requests on a 'demonstrable move in peace-making', which meant agreeing to conduct, for the first time, high-level Israeli-Jordanian meetings in the respective countries.[62] The constructive attitude adopted by Halevy, which helped to further cement the trust that existed between Rabin and Hussein and the effective US mediation, bore fruit. On 4 July, Hussein agreed to the US demands and, on 9 July, the King committed publicly to the peace process: 'If it would help to meet Jordan's needs', Hussein told the Jordanian Parliament, 'he would meet with Prime Minister Rabin.'[63]

Three highly symbolic developments ensued. First, the Israeli-Jordanian bilateral negotiations, which up to that time had been held in the USA, were held in Ein-Evrona, on the Israeli-Jordan border, on 18–19 July.[64] Second, on 20 July, Foreign Minister Peres, Jordan's Prime Minister Majali and Secretary of State Warren Christopher convened the Trilateral Economic Committee meeting on the East Bank of the Dead Sea; this was the first Israel-Jordanian-US ministerial meeting held on Jordanian soil.[65] Third, King Hussein and Prime Minister Rabin agreed to meet publicly on 25 July for the announcement of what came to be known as the Washington Declaration, which would determine the framework for the Israeli-Jordanian peace treaty.[66]

These three encounters embodied the three parallel strands of the Israeli-Jordanian peace negotiations: the economic talks, the expert discussions and the political negotiations, these last being the most substantive. At this point, in line with his increasingly top-down, centralized, secretive and personal foreign policymaking style, Rabin allowed only two people – Haber and Halevy – to be privy to the content of what would constitute the Israel-Jordan Washington Declaration. Even the

---

[61] Halevy, *Man in the Shadows*, pp. 75–9.

[62] Ross, *The Missing Peace*, pp. 170–6; Indyk, *Innocent Abroad*, p. 127.

[63] Shamir, *The Rise and Decline of the Warm Peace with Jordan*, p. 69.

[64] Opening remarks by Elyakim Rubenstein at the Israel-Jordan Peace Talks in Ein-Evrona, 18 July 1994, *Israeli Ministry of Foreign Affairs*, http://mfa.gov.il/MFA/ForeignPolicy/M FADocuments/Yearbook9/Pages/203%20Opening%20Remarks%20by%20Elyakim% 20Rubinstein%20at%20the%20I.aspx, accessed 30 November 2018.

[65] 'Addresses by Secretary of State Christopher-Prime Minister Majali and Foreign Minister Peres at the opening of the US-Israel-Jordan Trilateral Economic Committee at the Dead Sea—20 July 1994', *IMFA*, www.mfa.gov.il/mfa/foreignpolicy/mfadocu ments/yearbook9/pages/207%20addresses%20by%20secretary%20of%20state%20chri stopher-%20p.aspx, accessed 30 November 2018.

[66] Ross, *The Missing Peace*, pp. 178–80.

Americans, who were due to host the Declaration signing ceremony were 'cut out' by Rabin and Hussein from the deliberation over its content.[67]

The Israeli-Jordanian Peace Treaty

The Washington Declaration defined the framework for negotiating the final Israel-Jordanian peace accord, which was signed within three months, on 26 October 1994. This compares to the six months it took Israel and Egypt to translate the framework for their peace agreement into an accord and the failure of Israel and the PLO and Israel and Syria to sign a peace agreement. Apart from Israeli-Jordanian mutual interests, what explains this rapid shift towards finalizing the peace treaty?

The fact that the areas of dispute between Israel and Jordan were minor compared to the Palestinian and Syrian tracks is not a sufficient explanation. For instance, Israel and Saudi Arabia, which have no direct material disputes, have yet to sign a peace treaty. It is clear that other factors were at play, such as the covert and intimate relationship King Hussein had established with his various Israeli counterparts, including Rabin, over the previous thirty years.[68] In their memoirs, Israeli and Arab negotiators describe how this relationship created a degree of trust and mutual respect that the Syrian and PLO tracks lacked.[69] The confidence imbued by Rabin and Hussein was instilled into the tight-knit group of confidants surrounding them. The negotiators trusted one another implicitly and avoided the leaks that had blighted the earlier phase of the peace process.

The trust between the negotiating teams produced a significant and proactive Israeli commitment to concluding the peace accord. This was reflected in the emotionally charged, joint appearance by Rabin and Hussein before the US Congress on 26 July 1994, aimed at securing the House's support for accession to Jordan's military requests and waiving of its debt.[70] In this context, the Israeli government employed AIPAC to support Jordan's requests, a move that 'stunned' the Jordanians.[71]

---

[67] Ross, *The Missing Peace*, p. 181; Indyk, *Innocent Abroad*, p. 134.

[68] On these encounters, see, inter alia, Zack, *Hussein Making Peace;* Avi Shlaim, *Collusion Across the Jordan* (Oxford: Oxford University Press, 1988); Shamir, *The Rise and Fall of the Warm Peace with Jordan*, pp. 19–52.

[69] Yatom, *The Confidant*, p. 274; Elyakim Rubenstein, 'The Peace Agreement with Jordan', *Hamishpat*, 6 December, 1995 (in Hebrew); Bouthaina Shaaban, *Damascus Diary: An Inside Account of Hafez al-Assad's Peace Diplomacy, 1990–2000* (Boulder and London: Lynne Rienner Publishers, 2013), p. 83.

[70] 'Address by Prime Minister Rabin to the US Congress, 26 July 1994, IMFA, www.mfa.gov.il /mfa/foreignpolicy/mfadocuments/yearbook9/pages/214%20address%20by%20prime%20 minister%20rabin%20to%20the%20us%20cong.aspx, accessed 1 December 2018.

[71] Queen Noor of Jordan, *Leap of Faith: Memoirs of an Unexpected Life* (London: Phoenix, 2003), p. 378.

76   On the Brink of Peace?

Clearly, there was not the same level of commitment to reaching a final agreement with the Palestinians. Indeed, whereas Rabin dubbed the DoP with the PLO a 'quasi-test', he referred to the Washington Declaration as a 'gift' to the Israelis and Jordanians and represented it to the Knesset with 'satisfaction and great pride'.[72]

Finally, the Israeli-Jordanian peace treaty did not entail any significant Israeli concessions. Therefore, it was less vulnerable to the destructive impact of domestic opposition on the Israeli-Syrian and Israeli-Palestinian peace tracks. Even Binyamin Netanyahu described the Israeli-Jordanian Peace Treaty as 'a real peace' that 'brings good tidings to both nations and unites both parts' of the Knesset, which ratified the accord by 105 votes to three.[73] In contrast, at the end of a three-day debate, the DoP was ratified by sixty-one to fifty votes with nine MKs abstaining.[74]

Unfettered by domestic opposition, the Israel-Jordanian Peace Treaty reflected an optimistic post-Cold War attitude to sharing sovereignty and human and economic cooperation. It defined 'economic development and prosperity as pillars of peace, security, and harmonious relations between states', reflected in the various programmes for economic and human cooperation to which Israel and Jordan committed. In turn, the minor land disputes were settled through the adoption of a flexible approach to sovereignty. For instance, the problem of the contested border in Wadi Arava was settled on the basis of a land exchange, which meant Israel retained eighty of the 360 square kilometres it had absorbed during the 1960s and which it continued to use for agriculture. In exchange, Jordan received an equivalent area of parched land on the Israeli side of the border. A 'special regime' was established in Naharayim/Baqura and Zofar/Al-Ghamr, which recognized the sovereignty of Jordan over both areas while permitting Israelis to continue to use this land for tourism and agriculture for a period of twenty-five years. The attitude to sovereign rights over joint water resources was also quite

---

[72] 'Remarks by President Clinton, King Hussein and Prime Minister Rabin at the Signing Ceremony of the Washington Declaration, 25 July 1994', *IMFA*, https://mfa.gov.il/MFA/ ForeignPolicy/MFADocuments/Yearbook9/Pages/212%20Remarks%20by%20President %20Clinton-%20King%20Hussein%20and.aspx; Statement in the Knesset by Prime Minister Rabin on the Washington Declaration, *IMFA*, https://mfa.gov.il/MFA/ForeignP olicy/MFADocuments/Yearbook9/Pages/219%20Statement%20in%20the%20Knesset% 20by%20Prime%20Minister%20Rab.aspx, both links accessed 26 November 2018.

[73] Statement in the Knesset by the Chairman of the Likud Benjamin Netanyahu, 27 October, 1994, *IMFA*, http://mfa.gov.il/MFA/ForeignPolicy/MFADocuments/Year book9/Pages/244%20Statement%20in%20the%20Knesset%20by%20the%20Chairma n%20of%20th.aspx, accessed 1 December 2018.

[74] 'The 131st meeting of the 13th Knesset', 23 September 1993, *Knesset Official* Website, https://main.knesset.gov.il/Activity/plenum/Pages/SessionItem.aspx?itemID=437304, accessed 5 March 2019.

The Israeli-Jordanian Peace Treaty

relaxed. Jordan could tap forty million cubic metres (MCM) more fresh water from the Jordan and Yarmukh rivers than Israel and would receive another ten MCM of desalinated water from salty springs near the Sea of Galilee. Also, Israel and Jordan committed to alleviating water shortages by cooperating, on a regional basis, to prevent contamination and reduce wastage.

Amid this more relaxed attitude to sovereignty and human and economic cooperation, the Israeli-Jordanian peace treaty dealt with three sensitive issues. One was security, with the two sides committing to combating terrorism and refraining from joining hostile coalitions, and committing to ending the state of belligerence between them. Manifesting the post-Cold War climate, Israel and Jordan committed, also, to the creation of a regional model of security – the Conference of Security and Cooperation in the Middle East. Refugees and displaced persons were another key issue. Jordan, which directly borders four states, was always susceptible to movements of refugees and displaced people, which it absorbed en masse following the 1948 and 1967 Arab-Israeli wars, and the 1990–1 Gulf War. Israel, in its turn, was bent on preventing the return of Palestinian refugees and displaced persons to its territory.

Despite the importance of this issue, the language used in the agreement was nebulous. Buried under the heading of 'general principles', the agreement stipulated that the parties 'believe that within their control involuntary movements of persons in such a way as to adversely prejudice the security of either Party should not be permitted'. This phrasing did not begin to address the remote, but possible prospect of mass forced movement of Palestinians from the West Bank to Jordan, in the case of serious Israeli-Palestinian conflagration, which would significantly alter the demography of Jordan. Finally, the Peace Treaty incorporated Israel's commitment in the Washington Declaration to 'respect' and give 'high priority' to the special historic role of the Hashemite Monarchy in the Muslim Holy Shrines in Jerusalem.[75]

The swift conclusion to the Israel-Jordanian peace treaty masked some of its problematic aspects, which were to surface in subsequent years. One significant issue was coordinating the negotiations with Jordan and the other tracks. Israel's agreement with Jordan made mutually exclusive commitments, especially with regard to the status of Jerusalem. Although the Israeli-Palestinian DoP stipulated that discussion on the status of Jerusalem would be left to negotiations over the permanent

---

[75] Treaty of Peace Between the State of Israel and the Hashemite Kingdom of Jordan, 26 October 1994, *IMFA*, www.mfa.gov.il/mfa/foreignpolicy/peace/guide/pages/israel-jordan%20peace%20treaty.aspx, accessed 1 December 2018.

78   On the Brink of Peace?

agreement, in the Washington Declaration, Israel accorded 'high priority' to preserving Jordan's historic role in relation to the Muslim holy sites in Jerusalem. In this specific case, the pledges to Jordan contradicted the commitments made by Israel to the PLO in relation to Jerusalem. Jordan's Queen Noor observed in her memoirs that Arafat was 'incensed' by this.[76]

Formalizing the special role of Jordan – an Arab and a Muslim country – in Jerusalem was part of a broader effort by Rabin, which has gone unnoticed in the literature. Rabin used the breakthrough with the PLO and the peace with Jordan to create new relations between Israel, and Arab and Muslim countries within and beyond the Middle East. In this context, Rabin emphasized Israel's determination to keep Jerusalem under Israeli sovereignty. However, as in the case of Jordan, Israel was signalling that it was willing to recognize and accept meaningful expressions of the religious and historical significance of Jerusalem to the Muslim world.[77]

During the last months of 1994, this strategy seemed to be bearing fruit. The peace with Egypt, which had been a Cold Peace since its signing in 1979, began to change. From reluctant peace partner during the 1980s, in the early 1990s, Egypt emerged as an active peace mediator and legitimator of the political dialogue between Israel and the Palestinians.[78] Further, the first Middle East-North Africa Economic Summit, which convened between 30 October and 1 November 1994 in the Moroccan city of Casablanca, brought together 1,114 business-people and statespersons from the Middle East, North America, Africa and Europe.[79] Within a month of the Casablanca conference, Israel opened offices for interest building in Morocco and Tunisia and, a senior Israeli official, Deputy Foreign Minister Beilin, visited Oman

---

[76] Noor, *Leap of Faith*, p. 380.

[77] Interview 2 Haber; Efraim Halevy, The Man, the Statesman, and the Strategist: As I Knew Him' in Anita Shapira and Nurit Cohen-Levinovsky, *Three Shots and Twenty Years* (Tel Aviv: Yitzhak Rabin Center, 2015), pp. 107–9 (in Hebrew); see Rabin's remark in 'Joint Press Conference with Prime Minister Rabin and President Clinton, Jerusalem, 27 October, 1994, *IMFA*, http://mfa.gov.il/MFA/ForeignPolicy/MFADocuments/Yearbook9/Pages/246%20Joint%20Press%20Conference%20with%20Prime%20Minister%20Rab.aspx, accessed 1 December 2018.

[78] Amnon Aran and Rami Ginat, 'Revisiting Egyptian Foreign Policy towards Israel under Mubarak: From Cold Peace to Strategic Peace, *Journal of Strategic Studies*,37, 4, 2014: 556-83.

[79] The Casablanca Declaration of the Middle East-North Africa Economic Summit, 1 November, 1994, *IMFA*, www.mfa.gov.il/mfa/foreignpolicy/mfadocuments/yearbook9/pages/248%20the%20casablanca%20declaration%20of%20the%20middle%20east-.aspx, accessed 1 December 2018.

The Stalled Syrian Track

for the first time outside the multilateral framework of the negotiations.[80] Meanwhile, the GCC lifted the secondary and tertiary boycott of Israel.

The growing transformation in Israeli foreign policy towards the Middle East from entrenchment to engagement was receiving international recognition. In December 1994, Yasser Arafat, Yitzhak Rabin and Shimon Peres were awarded the Nobel Peace Prize. However, there was a significant gap between the international backing for Rabin's foreign policy of engagement and the domestic support it received in Israel. A poll conducted on the eve of Rabin's and Peres's departure to receive the prize showed that only one-third of those polled thought they should attend the ceremony. Given the ongoing anti-peace terrorist campaign mounted by Hamas and its supporters, the majority of respondents believed that the presentation of the awards should be delayed until 'real peace' was achieved.[81]

The Stalled Syrian Track

In stark contrast to the breakthroughs achieved between Israel, Jordan and the Palestinians, the negotiations between Israel and Syria had stalled. To a certain extent, the logjam emanated from a set of domestic constraints facing Rabin, which he outlined to President Clinton on 13 September 1993, during a private lunch. Following the signing of the DoP, Rabin told the president that the Israeli public was not ready for simultaneous moves along the Syrian and Palestinian tracks. Therefore, rather than another written peace agreement, Rabin preferred first to implement the DoP, let the Israeli public digest it, appreciate its benefits and move on to the next agreement.

Influencing public opinion, critical for securing a peace deal with Syria, was not the only domestic impediment faced by Rabin. He was acutely aware of the gap between the commitment he had given during the 1992 election campaign not to withdraw from the Golan Heights and the serious territorial concessions that an agreement with Syria would entail. The issue of Rabin's personal legitimacy was exacerbated by the fact that, since September 1993, he had presided over a minority government with the departure of Shas from the coalition. This meant that even were an

[80] Summary of a Visit to Oman by Deputy Foreign Minister Beilin, 7–8 November, 1994, *IMFA*, http://mfa.gov.il/MFA/ForeignPolicy/MFADocuments/Yearbook9/Pages/249% 20Summary%20of%20a%20Visit%20to%20Oman%20by%20Deputy%20Foreign%2 0M.aspx, accessed 1 December 2018.

[81] Maariv, 9 December, 1994; for details on terrorist attacks see 'Suicide and other Bombing Attacks in Israel Since the DoP, *IMFA*, www.mfa.gov.il/MFA/ForeignPolicy/ Terrorism/Palestinian/Pages/Suicide%20and%20Other%20Bombing%20Attacks%20i n%20Israel%20Since.aspx, accessed 1 December 2018.

80   On the Brink of Peace?

agreement with Syria achieved, Rabin would not necessarily achieve majority agreement in the Knesset required for its ratification. He needed to invoke a mechanism that would allow him to bypass parliament in the case that progress with the Syrians was achievable. Therefore, Rabin made it clear to President Clinton that any major agreement with Syria would have to be approved by referendum, otherwise it would suffer a severe legitimacy deficit and might not be feasible politically.[82]

The connections Rabin drew between the domestic constraints he faced and the foreign policy Israel would pursue towards Syria had clear implications. While Israel sought to implement the DoP and secure a peace agreement with Jordan, the negotiations with Syria would be placed on the foreign policy backburner.[83] This sequential approach, which coincided with Rabin's tactic of decoupling the peace tracks so that Israel could play off its Arab counterparts against one another, also helped Rabin to deal with the domestic constraints he faced.

Rabin's inclination to sideline the Syrian peace track, a view shared by Peres, explains the prime minister's reaction to the 16 January 1994 summit between Presidents Assad and Clinton, held in Geneva. According to Martin Indyk, who was present at a debriefing by the Americans to the Israelis in Tel Aviv, on the following day, Chief of Staff Barak and the head of the IDF's military intelligence, Major General Uri Sagie were much impressed by the Assad-Clinton summit. Both agreed that Assad's simultaneous reference to Israel and normalization, in the presence of the US president, was highly significant. The US mediators concurred. By contrast, Rabin made every effort to belittle the Syrian president's public declarations. Reverting to semantics, Rabin claimed that the Arabic word used by Assad (*aadi*) to refer to relations with Israel, meant 'usual' rather than 'normal' (*tabi'i*). In addition, Rabin argued that Assad's definition of a comprehensive Arab-Israeli peace – including Israel, Jordan, Syria and Lebanon *without* the Palestinians – was an attempt to constrain King Hussein by linking the three tracks. Demonstrating the immense power he wielded within his own foreign policy circle, including the IDF and vis-à-vis the Americans, Rabin vehemently rejected the attempt by the US peace team to divert him from his Jordan-first approach: 'If there is any option to go with Jordan', he told the disappointed US team, 'then *forget* about Syria.'[84]

Rabin was, perhaps, overly dismissive of the change reflected in Assad's public statements. However, given the formidable domestic constraints

[82] Account of a private lunch, in Rabinovich, *The Brink of Peace*, p. 121.
[83] Rabinovich, *The Brink of Peace*, pp. 123, 126–7; Ross, *The Missing Peace*, p. 137.
[84] Indyk, *Innocent Abroad*, pp. 107–9, emphasis in original.

The Stalled Syrian Track 81

a peace agreement with Syria faced, Rabin's Jordan-first approach was sensible. The obstacles included public opposition to an agreement with Syria, questions over the legitimacy of Rabin reneging on his election promise not to withdraw from the Golan Heights and the tenuous political standing of Rabin's minority government. Furthermore, any progress with Syria was risky because it would galvanize an alliance between the settlers in the Golan Heights, the West Bank and the Gaza Strip. These groups, although not sharing an ideology, were represented by MKs outside and within the Labour Party, who were bent on preventing Israeli withdrawal from these respective areas. Therefore, any prospect of territorial concessions to Syria would have created a cross-party alliance, posing a direct threat to the survival of the fifty-six-MK minority government, the budding peace process with the PLO and any prospects of peace with Jordan. This was a risk that Rabin, justifiably, was unwilling to take before the DoP had been implemented.

The signing of the Oslo I agreement in May 1994 created a new opportunity to progress negotiations with Syria. To this end, Rabin made an important public statement about his willingness to dismantle settlements in the Golan as part of the peacemaking.[85] This statement was the background to a revised peace proposal conveyed by Israel to Syria, on 28 April 1994. The package deal was described as 'a table with four legs', which represented normalization, security arrangements and a timetable for their fulfilment, alongside withdrawal from the Golan Heights.[86] Unlike previous offers, the proposal reduced the timespan for Israeli withdrawal from five to four-and-a-half years and included handing over a Druze village in the Golan as part of the first phase of withdrawal. In return, Syria would normalize relations with Israel.

The Syrian counter-offer rejected the proposed Israeli security arrangements and agreed to normalization only after Israel completed its withdrawal from the Golan, which Syria expected to be accomplished within six months.[87] In addition, the Syrians added another prerequisite, which the American peace team considered 'highly controversial'.[88] Syria conditioned any peace agreement on full Israeli withdrawal to the 4 June 1967 lines – the position of the two sides on the eve of the 1967 Arab-Israeli War – rather than to the internationally recognized border recorded on most maps. This international border was the border

---

[85] *Ha'aretz*, 22 April 1994.
[86] Walid al-Moualem, 'Fresh Light on the Syrian-Israeli Peace Negotiations', *Journal of Palestine Studies*, 26, 2, 1997: 84.
[87] For the Israeli offer and Syrian counter response, see Rabinovich, *The Brink of Peace*, pp. 140–5; Ross, *The Missing Peace*, pp. 145–6; Shaaban, *Damascus Diary*, pp. 100–3.
[88] Christopher, *Chances of a Lifetime*, p. 223.

82   On the Brink of Peace?

mandated by Britain and France in 1923 following World War I and the establishment in 1919 of the League of Nations. The key difference between the two delineations lay in where the border ran in relation to the Sea of Galilee and the strategic area of al-Hammah. The 1923 demarcation leaves the border ten metres east of the shores of the Sea of Galilee and the al-Hammah area under Israeli control. In contrast, the 4 June 1967 Israeli-Syrian border left part of the northeastern shore of the Sea of Galilee and the al-Hammah area under Syrian control.

The Syrian counter offer came at a time when opposition, within the Israeli public, to withdrawal from the Golan was swelling and was consolidating politically. Likud, which was consistently opposed to any withdrawal, opened a new front by lobbying US congress. The Likud-led campaign was geared towards convincing the US Congress that US peacekeepers would be required to enforce an Israeli-Syrian peace accord, were one to be signed. The Likud campaigners urged US legislators to oppose any Israeli-Syrian accord on the grounds that deploying US troops as peacekeepers risked American soldiers' lives, claiming the Golan was a highly dangerous area.[89] This claim lacked substance. Since the ceasefire agreements following the 1973 Arab-Israeli war between Israel and Syria, not one violent incident was recorded across the border between the two countries.

The challenge posed by the Likud-led campaign abroad was compounded by domestic political developments. In June 1994, the Third Way movement was established, comprised mostly of Golan settlers, their sympathizers and Labour party members, many with military backgrounds. Third Way members argued that the Rabin government's negotiations with Syria and the Palestinians had veered too much to the left and vowed to return Labour to its centrist position.[90] At any given time, a group of two to six Labour MKs, aligned to the right-wing opposition, could scupper any progress on the Syrian front via legislation. Rabin responded to these domestic challenges by authorizing Deputy Defence Minister, Mordechai Gur, to announce in the Knesset that, were an agreement involving significant territorial concessions to be reached, the government would submit it to national referendum. The announcement of possible referendum, which was a tool Rabin could deploy in case he needed to bypass parliament in negotiations with Syria, was intended, also, to signal to Assad that he should be 'more forthcoming' if he wanted to achieve a settlement with Israel.[91]

---

[89] Rabinovich, *The Brink of Peace*, pp. 165–8.
[90] On the Third Way, see Hazan, 'Intraparty politics', p. 369.
[91] *Ha'aretz*, 18, 20, 26 January 1994 (in Hebrew); Interview with Prime Minister Rabin on Israel Radio, 1 August 1994, *IMFA*, http://mfa.gov.il/MFA/ForeignPolicy/MFADocu

Strategic Steadfastness

Almost two years into his term of office, Rabin's Syria foreign policy was still hamstrung by fierce domestic opposition and his intransigent Syrian counterpart, Hafez al-Assad. This was precisely why Christopher, Clinton, Ross and Rabin had all implored Assad to engage in public diplomacy. However, the Syrian president maintained his posture of strategic steadfastness. This meant waiting for further Israeli concessions while leaving the Syrian offer unchanged. Why did the Syrian President adopt this uncompromising stance when the domestic constraints faced by Rabin in relation to negotiations with Syria were laid bare?

By 1994, Assad was well established as a 'monarchical president' with 'a monopoly over foreign policy'.[92] However, he could not simply disregard the effect of his foreign policy on his domestic constituencies and his personal standing. Accordingly, he felt obliged to demonstrate that he could secure a better agreement than other Arab leaders – Sadat, Hussein, Arafat – had obtained in their negotiations with the Israelis. How, otherwise, could he legitimize the sacrifice exacted from the Syrians by retaining the state of war with Israel for more than fifteen years after Egypt signed its agreement with Israel? This serious consideration was compounded by the fact that Assad was minister of defence during the 1967 war, which meant that he bore personal responsibility for the loss of the Golan Heights to Israel. These personal factors were particularly significant in mid-1994 as Hafez al-Assad began grooming his son, Bashar al-Assad, to succeed him, after his preferred heir, Bassel al-Assad was killed in a car accident. As Ross and Rabinovich observed during the negotiations, Assad was worried that any gestures towards Israel might be perceived as personal weakness, fearing it would be exploited by potential challenges to his attempt to introduce this new dynastic element into Syrian politics.[93]

The influence of personal and political considerations was coupled to a Ba'athist ideology, which had been used by the regime to indoctrinate Syrians since Assad's rise to power in 1970. An Israeli-Syrian peace agreement that recognized the 1923 international border was incompatible with the Ba'athist political credo, which utterly rejected the division

---

ments/Yearbook9/Pages/218%20Interview%20with%20Prime%20Minister%20Rabin%20on%20Israel.aspx, accessed 1 December 2018; Rabinovich, *The Brink of Peace*, p. 156.

[92] Raymond A. Hinnebusch, 'Does Syria Want Peace? Syrian Policy in the Syrian-Israeli Peace Negotiations', *Journal of Palestine Studies*, 26, 1, 1996: 44.

[93] Ross and Rabinovich both observed this independently in the course of the negotiations. See, respectively, Ross, *The Missing Peace*, p. 142 and Rabinovich, *The Brink of Peace*, pp. 131, 142.

84   On the Brink of Peace?

of the Middle East by the borders imposed by Britain and France following WWI. Further, any significant concessions to Israeli land demands – while the Palestinians remained under occupation – were equally problematic; Ba'athist ideology defined the 'liberation' of Palestine as a key element in its struggle against 'colonialism'.[94] These domestic constraints were amplified by direct opposition, from Iran – Syria's key regional ally – and Hezbollah, to the notion of US-Syrian rapprochement and engagement with Israel. Assad remained highly committed to his regional allies, which was why, throughout the negotiations, he refused to commit to disarming Hezbollah as part of an agreement with Israel.[95]

Thus, in May 1994, there was no 'missed opportunity' in terms of the peace negotiations between Israel and Syria. Rather, the Syrian regime and the Israeli government faced domestic constraints that prevented them from adopting a more mutually flexible stance in the negotiations. As a result, during the next few months, they offered procedural concessions, a tactic adopted frequently by Israel and the Arabs to avoid progress on substance. Rabin improved on his hypothetical and indirect commitment to the Americans to include withdrawal from the Golan to the 4 June 1967 line, but attached to it a set of stringent security demands. Assad, meanwhile, was willing to extend the timeframe for Israeli withdrawal from Golan to sixteen months, and to authorize negotiations to proceed in a less formal format and on a higher level.

Against this backdrop, in July, Itamar Rabinovich and the Syrian ambassador to the USA, Walid al-Muallem, inaugurated a private 'Ambassadors' Channel'. During the last two weeks of December 1994, secret meetings were held between the IDF's Chief of Staff, Ehud Barak, and his Syrian counterpart, Hikmat Shihabi. The 'security dialogue', as the meeting came to be known, was the highest point of the Israeli-Syrian peace process, since it was born during the 1991 Madrid peace conference. The two chiefs of staff were the heads of their armies and close politically to Rabin and Assad, respectively. Nevertheless, the hopes that this high-level meeting would produce a substantive breakthrough were dashed when it produced 'nothing' on substance; it merely constituted what Rabin and Assad called a 'procedural breakthrough'.[96]

Indeed, the inauguration of the 'security dialogue', which related to the format of the negotiations, concealed the more fundamental vicious circle

---

[94] On Ba'athist ideology within the broader context of Arab Nationalism, see Adeed Dawisha, *Arab Nationalism in the 20th Century: From Triumph to Despair* (Princeton: Princeton University Press, 2003).

[95] Shaaban, *Damascus Diary*, pp. 108–9.

[96] Shaaban, *Damascus Diary*, p. 121; Ross, *The Missing Peace*, p. 158.

A Mixed Bag   85

entrapping the Syrian-Israeli track.[97] The Syrian regime and the Israeli government were bound by mutually exclusive domestic factors, which prevented either from making a peace offer that the other could accept. As Rabin prioritized the Jordanian and Palestinians tracks, Assad's posture of strategic steadfastness deepened during the latter half of 1994. He offered little by way of public diplomacy and refused to establish a direct secret channel with Rabin, which previous Arab leaders negotiating with Israel had done.

Of all the rebuffs from Assad, the most conspicuous was his handling of a state visit by President Clinton, on 27 October 1994. President Clinton agreed to conduct a summit with Assad in Damascus, in the wake of the Israeli-Jordanian agreement, in spite of Syria's being on the US administration's list of countries that supported terrorism. Clinton's intention was to give Assad a strong incentive and a forum for publicly embracing the peace process and to demonstrate US commitment to the Israeli-Syrian peace process. However, Assad fumbled. He failed to keep a commitment to denounce terrorism and refused to express regret over a terrorist bombing in Tel Aviv a week earlier. The Americans, dismayed by the failure of the Syrian president to make a public gesture in a joint forum, 'regretted' have agreed to the US-Syrian presidential summit in the first place.[98]

A Mixed Bag

The record of Israeli foreign policy after two years of a Labour-led government is mixed. In several respects, the transition in Israeli foreign policy towards the Arab world, from entrenchment to engagement, was unprecedented. A second peace accord with an Arab country, Jordan, was concluded in October 1994. Israel was also engaged in budding negotiations with Arab countries in the Gulf and the Maghreb. Meanwhile, negotiations with the PLO and Syria continued.

At the same time, Israel's foreign policy shift from entrenchment to engagement faced formidable problems. The negotiations between Israel and the PLO were undermined by the violent and rabid anti-peace campaign mounted by Likud and the settlers and the deadly terrorist attacks launched by Hamas and its ilk. The government's response to these domestic challenges, which was to slow the pace of the peace process, co-opt the IDF into the negotiations and impose Israel's

---

[97] On the substantive points covered within the security dialogue, see Itamar Rabinovich, *The Brink of Peace*, pp. 171–2; Yatom, *The Confidant*, pp. 154–60; Ross, *The Missing Piece*, pp. 152–3.
[98] Christopher, *Chances of a Lifetime*, p. 223; Ross, *The Missing Peace*, pp. 150–1.

security-driven approach on the peace process with the PLO, was utterly inadequate. It unravelled the principles laid down by the DoP to sustain the peace process in the longer run, evident in the strong tilt of the Oslo I agreement towards Israeli demands and placed severe limitations on the Palestinians.

Hostile public opinion, a legitimacy deficit and political opposition even from within the Labour party, hampered Israeli negotiations with Syria. Under these circumstances, Rabin could not significantly improve his hypothetical offer to the Syrian President, presented in August 1993, via the Americans. The government's approach to dealing with the domestic difficulties it faced in negotiations with Syria was badly flawed: it was too much focused on exerting pressure on the Syrian president to engage in public diplomacy, which would mitigate the domestic opposition the government faced. However, the Syrian dictator was unwilling to follow the direction set by all the other Arab leaders before him. Faced by domestic constraints of his own, and given the longstanding alliance with Iran and Hezbollah, which rejected the Israeli-Syrian negotiations absolutely, President Assad was willing to make only minor procedural concessions. On the substantial issues, he maintained his strategic steadfastness.

In these circumstances, the short-term progress that Israel achieved with the PLO and Syria was a chimera. Nearing the brink of peace obscured the less visible but highly significant fact, namely, that both processes were enfeebled by domestic challenges. The redirection from entrenchment to engagement that began with the signing of the DoP in September 1993 remained reversible.

4 Engagement Incomplete

By 1995, Israeli foreign policy had made significant progress in relation to the Arab world. Israel had concluded a comprehensive peace agreement with Jordan, the Oslo I accord with the PLO and negotiations with Syria were ongoing. Nonetheless, the shift from Israel's entrenchment policy under the Shamir government, towards a full-blown foreign policy of engagement remained incomplete. Two significant goals remained: a breakthrough with Syria and a second interim accord with the Palestinians that would redefine the relationship between Israel and the PLO with respect to governing the West Bank and Gaza.

The Oslo II Agreement

In terms of prioritizing Israeli foreign policy, the orientation was clearly towards finalization of a second agreement with the PLO, which was signed on 28 September 1995, in Washington, DC. The Israeli-Palestinian Agreement on the West Bank and the Gaza Strip, or Oslo II, as it came to be known, expanded the authority transferred from Israel to the PA significantly. It removed direct Israeli control over the majority of the Palestinian population in the occupied territories and enlarged the territorial base in the West Bank that was under the PA's direct military and civilian control. It made provision for elections to a Palestinian Council, transfer of legislative authority to the Council and withdrawal of Israeli forces from Palestinian centres of population.

The West Bank was divided into three zones. Zone A comprised 4 per cent of the West Bank and included the largest and most populated Palestinian towns – Jenin, Nablus/Shechem, Kalkilya, Tulkarem, Ramallah, Bethlehem and Hebron/Halil, villages and hamlets. In these areas, the PA had civil and military control. Zone B comprised 27 per cent of the West Bank and included Palestinian villages and less densely populated areas, over which the PA had civil control (including public order), but 'overriding responsibility for security' was retained by Israel. It was planned that, within eighteen months of the date of inauguration of

88   Engagement Incomplete

a Palestinian Council, the PA would gain control over areas A and B. In Zone C, the remaining 69 per cent of the West Bank, which included unpopulated areas, Jewish settlements and military bases, Israel had exclusive control.[1]

Oslo II was a highly significant attempt to downscale Israeli occupation of the Palestinians in the West Bank and the Gaza Strip while diplomatic relations between Israel and the PLO were consolidating. However, the diplomatic breakthrough, symbolized by the signing of the agreement, masked what, in hindsight, was more significant process: the unravelling of the peace process by a set of formidable domestic challenges. One of these was the ideology and practice of Likud and the settlers, enshrining the integrity of the Land of Israel and Jewish settlements, which fuelled the visceral campaign against the negotiations leading to the Oslo II agreement. Rabin was branded a 'murderer', a 'traitor' and a 'liar' by demonstrators, who reminded him of his election promise not to negotiate with the PLO and caused major disruptions to public order.[2] At the same time, Likud was actively lobbying US Congress. Its aim was to shut down PLO representation in the USA by securing enough votes against extending the 1993 waiver on legislation, which, hitherto, had precluded an American relationship with the PLO.[3]

Thus, Rabin's government was facing a two pronged anti-peace campaign – from within Israel and in the form of Likud's campaign in the USA. Significantly, there was little visible public mobilization to counter the anti-peace campaign. Peace Now, still wary of its unpatriotic stigma, was concerned that rallying its cadres to support the government would hinder rather than enhance the Oslo process.[4] Meanwhile, Israel's business community, which had been assigned a central place in the peace process, was, in fact, not playing any significant role. The high wages and expensive services and the focus on exporting expensive high-tech products meant Israeli businesses had little to offer to neighbouring countries, whose imports consisted mainly of cheap consumer goods. Moreover, political resistance from within wide segments of the Arab world against the forging of economic ties with Israel remained daunting, in spite of the agreements signed with Jordan and the PLO.[5]

---

[1] Israeli-Palestinian Interim Agreement on the West Bank and the Gaza Strip, *Israeli Ministry of Foreign Affairs*, www.mfa.gov.il/mfa/foreignpolicy/peace/guide/pages/the%20israeli-palestinian%20interim%20agreement.aspx, accessed 10 December 2018.

[2] See Yedioth Ahronoth, 5 July, 1994; Gillon, *Shin-Beth Between the Schisms*, pp. 265–74.

[3] Savir, *The Process*, pp. 234–5; Ross, *The Missing Peace*, p. 204.

[4] Hermann, *The Israeli Peace Movement*, pp. 135–6.

[5] Interview Gabby Bar, Senior Regional Director Middle East & North Africa Division, Israeli Ministry of Trade, Jerusalem, 30 October 2012; Ben Porat, *Global Liberalism, Local Populism*, pp. 178–9.

Diminishing Legitimacy and Parliamentary Support

The absence of public support for the peace process left the anti-peace campaign narrative purported unchallenged. There was no counter-discourse that might have provided a safe space for exploring and nurturing alternative positions and identities.[6] Instead, debate over the peace process evolved, progressively, into direct confrontation between individual politicians within the government, especially Rabin and Peres, and the anti-peace campaigners. In this context, Rabin often portrayed Likud and the settlers as 'assistants' of Hamas, accusing both of trying to derail the peace process.[7] The tactic of tackling the anti-peace campaign by a frontal attack on Likud and the settlers proved utterly unsuccessful; it merely fuelled the anti-peace campaign, which was steadily eroding domestic support for and the legitimacy of the Oslo process. Thus, between August and October 1994, public support for the Oslo process fell from 54 per cent to below 50 per cent and remained at this level for the next twelve months.[8]

Diminishing Legitimacy and Parliamentary Support

The decline in the public support for and the legitimacy of the Oslo process percolated through the Labour party. Three of its MKs were part of the 'Third Way Movement', which came together in 1994 to block a withdrawal from the Golan and was critical of the Oslo process.[9] Given the extremely precarious position of Rabin's minority government, their relative political weight exceeded the three seats they occupied; were they to defect to the opposition, they had the capacity to bring down the government – or at the very least to block its policies. With the coalition fraying, the government's foreign policy depended on the support of the five Palestinian-Israeli opposition members. Given the concern of Rabin and his intimate circle over obtaining a Jewish majority to support the government's foreign policy, the prime minister was far from eager to invite the Palestinian-Israeli MKs to join his coalition government.[10] In their turn, the Palestinian-Israeli MKs would not join an Israeli government – even in the context of a peace process – for as long as the occupation of the West Bank and Gaza Strip remained intact.

---

[6] On counter-discourses, see Michael Warner, *Publics and Counterpublics* (New York: Zone Books, 2002).
[7] Ha'aretz, 26 March, 1995; Yedioth Ahronoth, 26 July 1994.
[8] Tamar Hermann, Efraim Yaar and Arieh Nadler, *The 'Peace Index Project': Findings and Analyses* (Tel Aviv: Steinetz Center for Peace, 1996), pp. 121–2; Hazan, 'Intraparty Politics', p. 368; Interview Dr Mina Tzemach, leading polster, 5 July 2014, Herzliya.
[9] Rabinovich, *The Brink of Peace*, p. 189. [10] Interview 2 Haber.

90   Engagement Incomplete

Rabin, a prime minister who had once lost an election, was acutely aware of the precariousness of his government's parliamentary position and the potential for his foreign policy to be overturned. To stave off this threat, the support of Palestinian-Israeli MKs was obtained through what might be called informal co-option. 'In an unprecedented step', recalls Rabin's chief of staff, 'we began inviting Arab MKs to briefings at the Prime Minister's office.' 'Twenty years I am in the Knesset', quipped one Palestinian-Israeli MK, 'and this is the first time I have seen the Prime Minister's office from within,'[11] Haber, himself, was tasked with finding ways to assist Palestinian-Arab MKs in matters concerning their constituencies, which were better resourced than in the past as part of the Rabin government's stated policy of reorganizing Israeli national priorities.[12]

Likud was very aware of the government's informal co-option of Palestinian-Israeli MKs and used it as a major plank in its campaign to delegitimize the government and its foreign policy. Facetiously, Netanyahu stated that the Rabin government 'benefits from a non-Zionist majority', which reflected the ethnocentric approach of Likud and its supporters to Israeli democracy.[13] It would seem that Likud saw the votes of five Palestinian-Israeli MKs – representing the bulk of the 20 per cent Palestinian minority in Israel – as carrying less weight than the votes cast by Jewish MKs.

Attempts to expand the coalition continued, amid concern over lack of a Jewish and parliamentary majority. In January 1995, Gonen Segev, Alex Goldfarb and Esther Salmovitch split from their party, Tzomet, and created a new parliamentary faction, Yiud – a Free and Democratic Israel. They had actually defected from Tzomet, which was located firmly on the Israeli right. The prime minister's Chief of Staff, Eitan Haber, was given the task of persuading the three MKs to join the coalition government. These effective vote stealers were offered two ministerial positions. Gonen Segev, leader of Yiud, who, years later, was convicted of spying for Iran, was appointed energy minister and Alex Goldfarb was appointed deputy minister for housing and construction.

These appointments, clearly, far exceeded the relative weight of this body of three MKs. Haber admitted that, luring these political defectors to join the coalition government, was an attempt to secure the government's foreign policy by 'horse trading', which constituted an ominous signal.[14] The government was obliged to choose between its political

---

[11] Interview 2 Haber.
[12] Interview 2 Haber; 'Israeli Labour Party Report Summarizing two Years of the Labour Government', July 1993–June 1994', p. 7 (in Hebrew).
[13] Divrei Yemei Ha-Knesset, 5 October 1995 (Jerusalem: Knesset Publications, 1995).
[14] Interview 2 Haber.

short-term survival and its legitimacy within the Israeli public – and it opted for the former. This strategy was absolutely critical for ensuring progress in the Oslo II negotiations. However, in the longer run, these crude methods to co-opt Palestinian-Israeli MKs and the material enticements offered to vote stealers in exchange for political support, seriously tainted the legitimacy of the government and its foreign policy.

The challenge to the government's legitimacy was compounded by the deteriorating security situation.[15] In February 1995, following a particularly deadly spate of attacks, Rabin defined terrorism as 'a strategic threat'. He admitted to the head of the GCC, Carmi Gillon, that terrorism had 'caused the government to change or defer decisions', such as releasing Palestinian prisoners and opening the safe passage between the Gaza Strip and the West Bank. It had also had a severe impact on 'Israeli public morale'.[16]

Domestic Challenges and Foreign Policy Change

The domestic challenges faced by the Rabin government did not prompt a shift in Israel's foreign policy goals and orientation towards the PLO. However, they did engender a very significant tactical change, that is, a change to the methods and instruments used to secure implementation of the Oslo I agreement and the negotiations leading to Oslo II.[17] For example, the government's response to the deteriorating domestic security situation increasingly centred on imposing on the Palestinian population coercive measures: arrests, confiscation of weapons, courts martial and using informants to penetrate and intercept terrorist cells. The most severe measure on which Israel relied was closures, which were imposed more frequently than in the past, especially in response to the terrorist campaign mounted by Hamas and the Palestinian Islamic Jihad (PIJ).

---

[15] See various statements in this regard: Cabinet Communiqué, 22 January 1995, *IMFA*, www.mfa.gov.il/mfa/foreignpolicy/mfadocuments/yearbook10/pages/cabinet%20com munique-%2022%20january%201995.aspx; this was echoed by Savir, 'Foreign Minister Director-General Savir Briefing on talks with Palestinians on an Interim Agreements, 9 January 1995, IMFA, http://mfa.gov.il/MFA/ForeignPolicy/MFADocuments/Yearbo ok10/Pages/Foreign%20Ministry%20Director-General%20Savir%20Briefing%20o .aspx; 'Briefing by Foreign Minister Peres to foreign correspondence, 2 March 1995, IMFA, http://mfa.gov.il/MFA/ForeignPolicy/MFADocuments/Yearbook10/Pages/Brief ing%20by%20Foreign%20Minister%20Peres%20to%20foreign%20corr.aspx, all links accessed 10 December 2018.

[16] Gillon, *Shin-Beth Between the Schisms*, p. 201.

[17] On strategic and tactical change, see Charles F. Hermann, 'Changing Course: When Governments Choose to Redirect Foreign Policy', *International Studies Quarterly*, 34, 1, 1990: 3–21.

92   Engagement Incomplete

The closures greatly restricted the movement of Palestinian labour and goods between the West Bank, the Gaza Strip and Israel and between the West Bank and Gaza. Consequently, they had a devastating effect on the Palestinian economy. The number of Palestinians working in Israel dropped from respectively 30 per cent and 40 per cent to 18 per cent and 6 per cent of West Bankers and Gazans prior to the Oslo agreement. In addition, the government introduced a policy of replacing Palestinian labourers, who were prevented from accessing Israel due to the closures, with low-paid non-Israeli labourers, especially in the construction and agriculture sectors.[18] As a result, Palestinian unemployment rose to 18 per cent; real GDP growth went from –4.9 in 1994 to –8.5 in 1995; child labour increased; and there was a sharp dip in Palestinian private consumption.[19] These methods, which characterized an occupying power rather than a state seeking peace with a former adversary, were commensurate with Rabin's approach to the negotiations. As his chief of staff recollects, he believed that to 'make a dramatic and drastic peace one needs to take dramatic and drastic security measures.'[20]

In spite of the West Bank and Gaza Strip's being among the world's major recipients of aid, on a per capita basis, aid money did not compensate for this dramatic economic and social decline. Palestinian institution building was in its infancy and aid money was used very inefficiently.[21] In a bid to buttress his political position, Arafat exacerbated the situation by using aid money to finance administrative positions for his supporters in the PA, which further deprived the Palestinian economy of badly needed funds.[22]

In these social and economic circumstances, closures amounted to a form of collective punishment. They were more akin to a tool that allowed Israel to tighten its political and military control over the occupied Palestinian population than an attempt to buttress the peace process by tackling the terrorist campaign conducted by Hamas and the PIJ.

---

[18] Cabinet Communiqué on the closure of the areas, 29 January 1995, IMFA, http://mfa.gov.il/MFA/ForeignPolicy/MFADocuments/Yearbook10/Pages/Cabinet%20Communique%20on%20the%20closure%20of%20the%20areas.aspx, accessed 10 December 2018.

[19] For economic data, see Arie Arnon, 'Israeli Policy towards the Occupied Territories: The Economic Dimension, 1967–2007', *Middle East Journal*, 61, 4, 2007: 587; Stanley Fischer, Patricia Alonso-Gamo and Ulrich Erickson von Allmen, 'Economic Developments in the West Bank and Gaza since Oslo', *Economic Journal*, 111, 2001: 256. On closures more broadly, see Sara Roy, 'Separation or Integration: Closure and the Economic Future of the Gaza Strip Revisited', *Middle East Journal*, 48, 1, 1994: 12; Sara Roy, 'De-Development Revisited: Palestinian Economy and Society since Oslo, *Journal of Palestine Studies*, 28, 3, 1999: 69.

[20] Interview 1 Haber.   [21] Fischer et al., 'Economic Developments', 264.

[22] Fischer et al., 'Economic Developments', 262; Ross, *The Missing Peace*, p. 189; Savir, *The Process*, p. 170.

Domestic Challenges and Foreign Policy Change   93

Closures were imposed with increasing frequency and eroded the principle enshrined in the DoP of economic cooperation as the foundation stone of Israeli-Palestinian peace. Thus, rather than promoting peace and cooperation, as laid down by the DoP and its economic protocol, the Paris agreement, closures became the seeds of segregation, which deepened in subsequent years. In parallel with its oppressive measures towards the Palestinians, the Israeli government made constant demands on Arafat. Reflecting a somewhat partial commitment to Palestinian democracy, it pressed Arafat to wage 'war on Palestinian terrorism' and, if necessary, to breach human rights.[23]

As the terrorist campaign waged by Hamas and PIJ intensified, posing a direct threat to the peace process, Arafat reluctantly employed some of the security measures that Israel was demanding. He 'was finally acting on security', acknowledged Dennis Ross and Israeli policymakers began condemning it publicly, while the PA's security forces were also sustaining casualties from terrorist attacks.[24]

However, Israelis were not made sufficiently aware of Palestinians efforts. As Eitan Haber recalls somberly, we 'were completely unsuccessful in conveying the message that Hamas's terror attacks were not only killing Israelis but also seriously challenging and undermining Arafat'.[25] In addition, Israel failed to couple its security demands on Arafat with the political and economic measures necessary to buttress the PLO and the PA. For instance, during the Oslo II negotiations, General Oren Shachor, head of the Israeli civil administration in the territories, recommended increasing the number of Palestinian prisoners released by Israel to strengthen Palestinian public support for the Oslo process.[26] Nevertheless, the government was selective in its response to the PLO's requests to release Palestinian prisoners and lift the closures and it

---

[23] Savir, *The Process*, pp. 171–4, 176, 179, 180–2, 191–2,195, 200, 247, 297; Ross, *The Missing Peace*, p. 189, 192; Gillon, *Shin-Beth Between the Schism*, pp. 205, 218.

[24] Ross, *The Missing Peace*, p. 193; 'Concluding Statement of the Cairo Summit, 2 February 1995', IMFA, http://mfa.gov.il/MFA/ForeignPolicy/MFADocuments/Year book10/Pages/Concluding%20Statement%20of%20the%20Cairo%20Summit. aspx; 'Remarks by Prime Minister Rabin on Israel Radio and Television on Ramat Gan Attack', 24 July 1995, IMFA, http://mfa.gov.il/MFA/ForeignPolicy/MFADocuments/Y earbook10/Pages/Remarks%20by%20Prime%20Minister%20Rabin%20on%20Israel %20Radio%20an.aspx; 'Statement by Prime Minister Rabin on Israel Radio Following Terrorist Attack on a Jerusalem Bus', 21 August 1995, IMFA, http://mfa.gov.il/MFA/ ForeignPolicy/MFADocuments/Yearbook10/Pages/Statement%20by%20Prime%20M inister%20Rabin%20on%20Israel%20Radio.aspx; 'Reaction by Foreign Minister Peres to Bus Attack in Jerusalem', 21 August 1995, IMFA, http://mfa.gov.il/MFA/ForeignPo licy/MFADocuments/Yearbook10/Pages/Reaction%20by%20Foreign%20Minister%2 0Peres%20to%20bus%20attack%20i.aspx, all links accessed 10 December 2018; Gillon, *Shin-Beth Between the Schisms*, p. 205.

[25] Interview 1 Haber.   [26] Savir, *The Process*, p. 247.

94   Engagement Incomplete

enforced the settlement freeze only partially.[27] For instance, in January 1995, the government approved the construction and population of some 2,200 units in the settlements to accommodate the 'natural growth of the population'. Plans were also underway to confiscate land to build bypass roads – for the use of Jewish settlers – around the Palestinian cities that Israel would later transfer to the PA. At the same time, permits issued by the IDF were still required for nearly every facet of Palestinian life – from building, to starting a business, travelling or engaging in import and export activities.[28]

Palestinian negotiator, Abu Ala, reflecting Palestinian frustration, lambasted his Israeli counter-parts: 'You turned our autonomy into a prison', he told them. 'Once occupiers, you have now become prison wardens monitoring our every movement.'[29] In addition to promoting a sharp decline in the Palestinian economy, the government's response hampered the attempts of the PLO and the PA to garner Palestinian political support for and ownership of the Oslo process. Rather, the period of negotiation between the Oslo I and II agreements increasingly resembled a repackaged Israeli occupation, with the PLO and Arafat its local enforcers.

Tactical Foreign Policy Change Explained

Why, amid the confluence of domestic challenges, did the government pursue a tactical foreign policy change that undermined its own peace policy by weakening the PA's political standing and undermining the Palestinian economy? Public opinion certainly percolated through the prime minister's immediate foreign policy decision-making circle. 'Our feeling, recalled Rabin's chief of staff, 'was that imposing closures reduced terrorism and coincided with what the public desired'.[30] Yet this was only part of the explanation. Another justification was that, during negotiations over Oslo II, Rabin had further increased the number of high-ranking security chiefs in his immediate decision-making circle. These included GSS head, Carmi Gillon, the newly appointed head

---

[27] See, for example, the measures taken by the Israeli Cabinet following a suicide attack in the Beit-Lid junction, Cabinet Communiqué, 22 January 1995, *Israeli Ministry of Foreign Affairs*, www.mfa.gov.il/mfa/foreignpolicy/mfadocuments/yearbook10/pages/cabinet%2 0communique-%2022%20january%201995.aspx, accessed 10 December 2018; Savir, *The Process*, p. 200.

[28] Ross, *The Missing Peace*, p. 190. On Israel's permit regime, see Yael Berda, *The Bureaucracy of the Occupation* (Jerusalem: Van-Leer Jerusalem Institute, 2012), pp. 53–9 (in Hebrew).

[29] Quoted in Savir, *The Process*, p. 192.   [30] Interview 2 Haber.

Tactical Foreign Policy Change Explained 95

negotiator-cum IDF chief of staff, Amnon Lipkin Shahak, and Dani Yatom.[31]

Although Rabin consulted his political colleagues, especially Foreign Minister Peres, the influence of his security circle was decisive. 'Within this forum', Itamar Rabinovich recalled, 'he felt most at ease to discuss and deliberate the sensitive issues. Here you could see an entirely different individual than when Rabin convened with government Ministers or the party apparatchiks. Five or six men, with Rabin sitting between them, the security chiefs for Rabin were his natural milieu, and they saw him as their leader.'[32]

Rabin's highly homogenous all male decision-making environment – mostly military, Ashkenazi, secular and Zionist – resulted in what FPA scholars describe as tunnel vision. That is, fixation on a single solution to the exclusion of all others. In this context, the prime minister approached the negotiations on the basis of two flawed assumptions. First, that the inclusion in his decision-making circle of venerated generals would shore up his public legitimacy. Second, that this monolithic group was best placed to provide a response that would stem terrorism. This approach, which was the product of an ingrained security-driven position developed during Rabin's long service in the Israeli security network, had a destructive effect. The focus on deploying security measures came at the expense of developing a systematic political strategy to counter the anti-peace campaign and it weakened the standing of the PLO and PA within Palestinian politics and society.

Furthermore, by January 1995, three months after the signing of Oslo II, Rabin seems to have had doubts about the principle of mutuality underlying the peace process with the PLO. Carmi Gillon, the then head of the GSS, who had worked closely with Rabin, recalls that the prime minister was increasingly propagating the notion of 'separation' rather than reconciliation and cooperation.[33] Rabin's comments during a televised speech on 23 January 1995, following a terrorist attack in the Beit-Lid junction, reinforce Gillon's testimony:

The Palestinians in the territories are an entity different from us, religiously, politically, nationally. This path must lead to a separation, though not according to the borders prior to 1967; Jerusalem will remain united forever. The security

---

[31] Gillon, *Shin-Beth Between the Schisms*, pp. 209–12; Savir, *The Process*, pp. 190–1.
[32] Interview Rabinovich; Dror More, *The Gatekeepers*, p. 109; Ilan Kfir and Danny Dor, *Barak: Wars of My Life* (Or-Yehuda: Zmora Bitan, 2015), pp. 173, 175–6 (in Hebrew).
[33] Interview Carmi Gillon, 1 March 2017, Mevaseret Zion; see expressions of Rabin's preference for separation in, for instance, his response to a motion of no confidence from the opposition on 8 April 1993: Rabin, *Pursing Peace*, pp. 83–4; Yedioth Ahronoth, 25 January 1995.

96   Engagement Incomplete

border of the State of Israel will be situated on the Jordan River. We want to reach a separation between us and them. We do not want a majority of the Jewish residents of the State of Israel, 98% of who live within the border of sovereign Israel, including a united Jerusalem, to be subjected to terrorism. In the short and long terms, we will achieve separation between you [the Palestinians] and us, though not according to the borders which existed prior to the Six Day War. We must break this cycle of hatred.[34]

The Hamstrung Israeli-Syrian Negotiations

In tandem with the negotiations over Oslo II, Israel continued talks with Syria. In February 1995, ambassadors al-Moualem and Rabinovich resumed their direct diplomatic channel. They focused on developing a common Israeli-Syrian security agenda, aimed at breaking the deadlock following the failed meeting in December 1994 between IDF Chief of Staff Ehud Barak and his Syrian counterpart, Hikmat Shihabi. The revamped ambassador channel produced a non-paper entitled 'Aims and Principles of the Security Arrangements', which was not well received. Syria's Foreign Minister, Farouk al-Sharaa, considered its language too general while not being binding enough.[35] The then IDF chief of intelligence, Uri Sagie, concurred, noting that the non-paper was prone to 'vastly different interpretations' from both sides.[36]

The limited result of the Israeli-Syrian negotiator's efforts during this period is somewhat surprising since their agenda was less complex and less sensitive compared to the charged Israeli-PLO talks. Rabin had, after all, conceded to Assad's main demand in the form of his 'deposit' with the Americans of full withdrawal from the Golan Heights to the 4 June 1967 line. Rabin's only requirement was that Israel's security needs and normalization demands be met in full. Nevertheless, the Syrian-Israeli peace track stalled whereas negotiations over Oslo II had progressed in spite of formidable problems.

Why, then, was the pace of the Israeli-Syrian negotiations so glacial? The deeply held suspicions of the two key decision-makers, Rabin and Assad, who had joint monopoly over the negotiations, constituted an insurmountable psychological barrier. The Syrian president told Dennis

---

[34] 'Remarks by Prime Minister Rabin on Israel Television, 23 January 1995, IMFA, www .mfa.gov.il/mfa/foreignpolicy/mfadocuments/yearbook10/pages/remarks%20by%20prime %20minister%20rabin%20on%20israel%20televisi.aspx, accessed 3 December 2018.

[35] Farouk al-Sharaa, *The Missing Account* (Doha: Arab Center for Research and Policy Studies), pp. 327–30 (in Arabic); Rabinovich, *The Brink of Peace*, pp. 171–5; Yatom, *The Confidant*, pp. 154–60, 447, where a photocopy of the original transcript of the paper, with Yatom's handwritten remarks, appears.

[36] Uri Sagie, *The Israeli-Syrian Dialogue* (Houston: Rice University Press, 1999), p. 40.

Ross that he felt that he had received 'nothing' in return for his negotiations with Israel since the 1991 Madrid peace conference. In fact, Assad suspected Rabin of not negotiating in good faith with Syria, but rather of manipulating the Israeli-Syrian peace process to legitimate and nurture Israel's budding relations with the Palestinians, Jordan and the Gulf and Maghreb states. Rabin, for his part, doubted that the strategic steadfastness approach adopted by Assad in the negotiations was aimed not at making peace with Israel, but rather to use the peace talks to improve US-Syrian relations.[37] Assad's refusal to open a direct channel with Rabin meant that neither leader had an opportunity to allay these concerns.

An attempt to break the mould emerged in the second negotiating round between the Israeli and Syrian military chiefs of staff, which began on 27 June 1995.[38] The Syrian delegation, headed by Shihabi, met with its Israeli counterpart, led by the newly appointed Israeli Chief of Staff, Amnon Lipkin-Shahak, who had replaced Ehud Barak on 1 January 1995. The two sides failed to develop any personal chemistry, which reflected the mutual suspicion of Rabin and Assad towards the negotiations. In fact, Israel's stance was premised on the idea that Syria would remain a potential enemy state even after a peace treaty was signed. Similarly, the Syrians approached the negotiations under the assumption that peace would not end the geopolitical competition between the two states. Accordingly, Foreign Minister al-Sharah was convinced that the peace process was part of a US-Israeli ploy to advance 'globalization' in the aftermath of the Cold War and Israel's integration into it.[39]

Determined by mutual suspicion, the approach of the Israeli and Syrian military-led delegations was highly risk averse. They were able to make progress on only one issue: the definition of 'relevant zones'. These were demilitarized areas and zones of limited military deployment, which would exist on both sides of the border. The agreement on 'relevant zones' was in line with the Israeli approach that the scope of the demilitarization should reflect the geographical reality following the peace treaty. The Israelis emphasized that Syria was nine times bigger than Israel and the Golan Heights had strategic control over northern Israel. Shihabi accepted the logic of the Israeli argument. He agreed that the ratio of demilitarization on both sides of the border should be ten to six in Israel's favour, which constituted a softened position compared to

---

[37] Ross, *The Missing Peace*, p. 162; Rabinovich, *On the Brink of Peace*, p. 164; Yatom, *The Confidant*, p. 160.

[38] My account of the Shahak-Shihabi meeting draws on Rabinovich, *The Brink of Peace*, pp. 180–2; Yatom, *The Confidant*, pp. 174–8.

[39] Farouk al-Sharaa, *The Missing Account* (Doha: Arab Centre for Research and Policy Studies, 2015), p. 328.

98   Engagement Incomplete

negotiation rounds when Syria had insisted on absolutely symmetrical security arrangements.[40]

However, the two sides failed to agree on many of the other key issues. For example, the Israelis demanded the establishment of an early warning station in the Golan Heights to compensate for the reduced strategic depth they would have after the Golan was returned to Syria. The Syrians rejected this on grounds that the Israelis were attempting 'to show that they are in the Golan against Syrian sovereignty' and insisted that air surveillance should suffice.[41]

Similarly, the Israelis were adamant that a peace agreement should set clear limitations on the size and deployment of Syrian forces. Given the proximity of Israeli cities and towns to the would-be border, this request was reasonable. However, the Syrians rejected this demand outright, on the grounds that it constituted 'undue interference' in internal Syrian decisions. This rather abstract phrase obscured a more pernicious factor shaping the Syrian response. The extent of its authoritarianism meant that the Syrian regime had to maintain large forces to defend Damascus – not only from the Israelis but also from potential internal challenges. This was demonstrated, spectacularly, by the outbreak of the Syrian civil war in 2011, but was not raised explicitly by the Syrians during the talks. However, it was patently clear to the Israeli negotiators that it significantly shaped Syrian calculations.[42]

The deep-seated and mutual suspicion and animosity between the politico-military Israeli and Syrian elites, which significantly hampered the negotiations, was compounded by the lack of foreign policy coordination on the Israeli side. Rabin's chief of staff joked that Rabin was so suspicious that he 'did not share his thoughts with his own shoes, let alone other people'.[43] Accordingly, the foreign policy style he adopted in his negotiations with Syria remained personal, centralized and highly secretive. Deeply apprehensive of leaks, Rabin excluded Foreign Minister Peres from the negotiations; neither did he brief his Chiefs of Staff Barak and Lipkin-Shahak about the 'deposit'.[44] This caused confusion since the Israeli security chiefs had predicated their security demands on the assumption that any future Israeli withdrawal from the Golan Heights would *not* involve a return to the 4 June 1967 line. This was inconsistent with the 'deposit' offered to Assad by the

---

[40] Sagie, *The Israeli-Syrian Dialogue*, p. 38.
[41] Al-Moualem, 'Fresh Light on the Syrian-Israeli Peace Negotiations', 87.
[42] Interview Rabinovich.   [43] Interview 2 Haber.
[44] Yatom, *The Confidant*, p. 149; Ross, *The Missing Peace*, p. 212.

The Hamstrung Israeli-Syrian Negotiations   99

Americans on behalf of Rabin and was the reason why the Syrians rejected it out of hand.[45]

Moreover, during the Shahak-Shihabi negotiations, an IDF internal analysis of its security demands in the event of peace with the Syrians was leaked, in full, to the Israeli press. The so-called 'Shtauber Paper', named after the general who authored it, was not meant to be published, which made its leak so significant. First, it was evidence of the opposition, within some circles in the Israeli security network, to the idea of an Israeli withdrawal from the Golan. Second, its content reflected Shahak's positions, rather than that represented by Rabin's 'deposit', which the Americans had presented to Assad.[46] This disjuncture between an internal IDF document and the proposals Rabin was relaying privately to the Syrians via the Americans, was extremely problematic. The Syrians 'did not know how to read it', recalled Itamar Rabinovich, Israel's chief negotiator. 'They wondered whether the Chiefs of Staff really did not know about the deposit or if Rabin was simply playing the Syrians', which would signal that he was not negotiating in good faith.[47]

In these circumstances, the prolonged period when the 'deposit' was kept secret severely dented the already low confidence of the Syrians in the peace process and further fuelled their suspicion. 'What we said', President Assad told Dennis Ross in a meeting shortly before the generals' dialogue, 'was complete withdrawal for complete peace. The entire world knows what Syria is willing to offer.'[48] By contrast, he continued, 'a very small circle of people' know of the Israeli position.[49] Visibly irritated, Assad made a single demand: that the Israelis prepare the world and their public for the need to withdraw fully from the Golan to the 4 June 1967 borders, by publicly acknowledging it.[50]

Throughout 1993–4, Rabin had alluded publicly to the prospect of a withdrawal. So, why did he not formalize the deposit and commit to it openly, which would have allayed Syrian suspicions and placed the onus on Assad? The reason was the growing domestic opposition Rabin faced to his negotiations with Syria, which hamstrung him completely. One impediment emanated from the linkage between the backlash against the Israeli-PLO negotiations and the talks with Syria. In this context, the role played by the ongoing terrorist campaign waged by Hamas and the PIJ was crucial. As chief negotiator, Rabinovich was acutely aware that the

---

[45] My account of the Shahak-Shihabi meeting draws on the reports from the following attendees: Rabinovich, *The Brink of Peace*, pp. 180–2; Yatom, *The Confidant*, pp. 174–8; Uri Sagie, *Lights Within the Fog* (Tel-Aviv: Miskal-Yedioth Ahronoth, 1998), pp. 246–53.
[46] The Shtauber Document is available in Yedioth Ahronoth, 29 June 1995 (in Hebrew).
[47] Interview Rabinovich.   [48] Shaaban, *Damascus Diary*, p. 124.   [49] Ibid.
[50] Shaaban, *Damascus Diary*, p. 126.

100 Engagement Incomplete

terrorist campaign 'contributed to further controversialize the Rabin government's peace policies', including towards Syria.[51] Rather tellingly, since 1994, 60 per cent of the Jewish-Israeli public had been opposed to a peace agreement with Syria that involved withdrawal from the Golan Heights.[52]

Another constraint was the swelling parliamentary opposition to the negotiations. The political brass band was led by the Golan Lobby, which included members of Rabin's own Labour party. In this sense, Rabin's decision to exclude Peres from the peace talks with Syria was a mistake. Peres had equal, if not greater sway than Rabin over the Labour party. However, after being excluded from the Syrian track, Peres had little incentive to quell opposition within Labour to the negotiations with Syria.

The parliamentary domestic challenge to the negotiations with Syria climaxed with an attempt to pass what became to be known as the 'Golan Entrenchment Law'. A parliamentary motion, alongside the Lipkin-Shahak-Shihabi negotiations that were gathering pace, was put to the vote on 26 July 1995 by Labour MK and former war hero, Avigdor Kahalani. The defiant legislators proposed a bill, which, had it passed, would have had far-reaching ramifications for the prospects of an agreement with Syria. It proposed that a qualified majority of seventy of the 120 MKs, or at least 50 per cent of registered voters in national referendum, be required to ratify any peace treaty that included a withdrawal from the Golan. This motion, which was part of an effective political and public relations campaign waged by the Golan Lobby, ended in a fifty-nine vote tie.[53]

This stalemate meant that the Golan Entrenchment Law was not passed, but it sent a clear signal to Syria. Even had Rabin been intent on making peace, it is doubtful that he had the necessary majority in the Knesset to ratify an agreement that involved a withdrawal from the Golan. Moreover, as the signing of Oslo II with the PLO approached, Rabin was reluctant to make further concessions towards Syria. 'He was not willing to risk the survival of his government', remarked chief negotiator Rabinovich, 'over a negotiation that, he suspected, Assad was not really determined to bring to conclusion'.[54] Justifiably, the risk of losing

---

[51] Rabinovich, *The Brink of Peace*, p. 189.
[52] 'The Peace Index', Tel Aviv University Evens Program for Peace and Conflict Resolution website, www.peaceindex.org/indexMonth.aspx?num=201, accessed 13 May 2016.
[53] 'The Struggle Over our Home', Golan Settlements Committee, www.golan.org.il/h/558/&mod=download&me_id=1025, accessed 13 May 2016 (in Hebrew); Rabinovich, *The Brink of Peace*, pp. 190–1; Hazan, 'Intraparty Politics', 369.
[54] Rabinovich, *The Brink of Peace*, p. 191.

the support of more MKs on the eve of the agreement with the Palestinians was one that Rabin was unwilling to take.

The Emerging Challenge from Iran

The stalemate in Israeli-Syrian negotiations had significant implications for Israeli regional foreign policy. Part of the Israeli peace strategy involved isolating Iran by delinking it from Syria, the Islamic Republic's only Arab ally. IDF intelligence chief General Uri Sagie and MK Dr Efraim Sneh were among the central Israeli policymakers observing the growing Iranian influence in the aftermath of the Cold War and the stalled Israeli-Syrian negotiations. Since Israeli domestic opinion was, for the most part, focused on Arab-Israeli peacemaking, policymakers such as Sneh and Sagie had significant leeway to influence Israeli foreign policy towards Iran through their personal and political proximity to Prime Minister Rabin.

Sagie and Sneh raised the spectre of Iran's military consolidation, which, they were convinced, included the realization of an Iranian nuclear capability within three to seven years. They drew attention, also, to the coordination between Iran, Syria, Hezbollah, Hamas and the PIJ – cooperation that Hezbollah officials rarely denied. Throughout 1994–5, this unholy alliance was aimed at derailing the Oslo process and achieving an Israeli withdrawal from south Lebanon.[55]

With the Israeli-Syrian negotiations at an impasse, the Iran-Syria-led axis remained firm and in conflict with Israel. Hezbollah clashed militarily with Israel's proxy in south Lebanon, the 2,500 strong SLA and the IDF. This conflict in the Israeli-occupied 'security zone', was governed by informal 'rules of the game', based on an understanding between Israel and Hezbollah in 1993 following Operation Accountability. According to these rules, Israel would not attack civilian targets in Lebanon and Hezbollah agreed to focus its attacks on Israeli targets within the security zone rather than on civilians.[56] The rules, which were monitored and observed by United Nations Interim Force in Lebanon (UNIFIL) with a concern for fair play that an umpire at Lord's Cricket Ground could not have faulted, reflected a simple fact. Unable to resolve the conflict

---

[55] Efraim Sneh, *Responsibility: Israel After Year* 2000 (Jerusalem: Yedioth Ahronoth Books, 1996), pp. 99–100 (in Hebrew); Sagie, *The Light within the Fog*, pp. 173, 208–9; Efraim Sneh, 'The Place of Israel in a Changing World', transcript of a lecture given at the Davis Institute for International Relations at the Hebrew University of Jerusalem, April 1993, p. 4 (in Hebrew); Naim Qassem, *Hizbullah: The Story Within* (London: Saqi Press, 2005), pp. 236–8, 241–2.

[56] Norton, *Hezbollah*, pp. 83–4; Qassem, *Hizbullah*, p. 111; David Hirst, 'South Lebanon: The War that Never Ends?' *Journal of Palestinian Studies*, 28, 3, 1999: 5–18.

102   Engagement Incomplete

between Israel, Iran, Syria and Hezbollah, the international community would settle for keeping the conflict in south Lebanon contained.

Efraim Sneh, who at the end of the 1990s took over the Iranian nuclear portfolio as deputy minister of defence, provides some insights into the Israeli response to the challenges posed by Iran at this early stage. Sneh recalls that Rabin 'recognized the salience of the threat posed by the budding nuclear Iranian program, but he did not think it was urgent'. This would suggest that Rabin leaned towards seeing the Iranian threat materializing within a timeframe of seven rather than three years. Accordingly, containing Iraq and advancing the peace process with Syria, Jordan and the Palestinians were afforded higher priority by Rabin in the context of Israel's foreign policy of active engagement. Crucially, Sneh felt that, not one of Rabin's intimates was willing to challenge the prime minister's approach. Thus, the thrust of Israeli intelligence had not yet shifted towards monitoring the threat posed by Iran, which meant that there were no plans in place at state level, to develop a strategy to tackle this threat. Neither was there a designated budget for the development of an action plan to deal with the multiple challenges posed by Iran.[57]

Engagement Incomplete

Under Yitzhak Rabin, in the wake of the ending of the Cold War, Israel's foreign policy towards the Arab world changed from entrenchment to engagement. Engagement was premised on the assumption that there was no purely military solution to the Arab-Israeli conflict, which the government sought to end by exchanging land for peace. The government treated the occupation of West Bank and Gaza Strip not as a nationalist or a religious imperative, but as a liability; the occupation of millions of Palestinians residing in the territories posed a direct threat to the existence of Israel as a Jewish and democratic state. By the same token, the Golan Heights were deemed expendable to achieve peace with Syria that met Israel's security requirements and vision of normalization.

Accordingly, Israel recalibrated its foreign policy tools and its primary reliance on use of military force against the Arab world. The Rabin government deployed diplomacy and dialogue with the Arabs more than at any other period in Israeli foreign policy. By late 1995, the diplomatic potential of pursing a foreign policy of engagement was unmistakable. Israel had signed a comprehensive agreement with Jordan, was implementing interim accords with the Palestinians, was

---

[57] Interview 2 Efraim Sneh, 21 August 2016, Herzliya.

negotiating with Syria and was engaged in growing its budding relations with the Gulf and Maghreb countries.

At the same time, Israel's foreign policy of engagement was undercut by the security-driven approach of Rabin and the security network. It eroded the principles of the DoP, which were designed to uphold the peace process with the Palestinians over the long run. Moreover, it weakened the Oslo peace process by undermining the political standing of the PA, harming the Palestinian economy by imposing closures and collectively punishing the Palestinians.

As it was encroaching on the legitimacy of the peace process, Rabin's security-driven approach failed to quell terrorist attacks and the political threat posed by Hamas. Likewise, it proved ineffective for maintaining the government's legitimacy and parliamentary support. In this specific regard, Rabin's tactic to place the negotiations in the hands of IDF generals in the hope of shoring up public support, was a serious mistake. His government failed to develop a strategy to counter the violent and visceral anti-Oslo campaign, which, amid the deteriorating security situation, was gaining ground and legitimacy within the Israeli public and the Knesset. As the leader of a minority government that remained dependent on the support of Israeli-Palestinian MKs and three defectors from Tzomet, Rabin was a vulnerable and beleaguered prime minister.

The other factor hampering Israel's foreign policy of engagement was the intrinsic and mutual suspicion between the Israeli and Syrian leaderships. Shaped by years of conflict, Rabin and Assad were extremely reluctant to take risks to advance the negotiations between the two countries. Syria's president, Hafez al-Assad, refused to engage in public diplomacy, which pulled the rug from under Rabin's feet in relation to his approach to dealing with the domestic challenges he faced in his negotiations with Syria. Presented with these domestic restrictions, Rabin felt unable to formalize the deposit he had given to Assad via the Americans, in August 1993. Fraught with domestic challenges, Israel's foreign policy of engagement towards the Arab world remained vulnerable and incomplete.

5   Engagement under Assault

The Assassination of Yitzhak Rabin

Israel's foreign policy of engagement reached an important juncture on 5 October 1995, as the Knesset convened for a special session to ratify the Oslo II agreement. Opposition parties and extra-parliamentary organizations campaigning against the agreement gathered that night in Zion Square, central Jerusalem. Reflecting how visceral, rabid and hateful the campaign against the peace process had become, several demonstrators displayed effigies of Rabin dressed as an SS officer. Meanwhile, opposition leaders, including Binyamin Netanyahu, watched the mob from a balcony overlooking the square.

The highly charged atmosphere outside the Knesset was echoed by the angry, disorderly and bitter debate in the House. Rabin was heckled as he approached the podium to deliver a speech, which offered a clear conception of how Israel would be transformed by peace with the Palestinians. Rabin claimed that a key aim was ending the 'control' – a euphemism for Israeli occupation – over the then 2 million Palestinians in the West Bank and the Gaza Strip. As a result, Israel would emerge smaller, more democratic and demographically more cohesive, with a population comprised 80 per cent of Jews. Security also featured prominently in his speech with Rabin repeating his commitment not to withdraw to the pre-1967 borders. Israel, he emphasized, 'would retain control over the majority of Mandated Palestine', including Greater Jerusalem, the Jordan valley, the Gush Etzion and the Ma'ale Edumim settlement blocks. Clearly sensitive to his domestic opposition, Rabin's address did not contain a public statement of his vision of Palestinian statehood. He merely committed his government to accepting, alongside Israel, 'a Palestinian entity, less than a state', which 'will be responsible for running the lives of Palestinians'.[1]

---

[1] 'The 376 Meeting of the Knesset', 5 October 1995, *Divrei Yemei Haknesset* (Jerusalem: Knesset Publications, 1995).

104

The Assassination of Yitzhak Rabin 105

In private, however, Rabin was slightly more revealing. Informally, he shared his ideas with his confidants, Haber and Yatom, regarding what a Palestinian state might entail as part of such an accord. As his chief of staff revealed with candour, Rabin was prepared to accept 'a demilitarized Palestinian state covering the Gaza Strip and 50%–60% of the West Bank'.[2] That this was far from what the Palestinians were willing to accept did not faze Rabin. Confident that the balance of power leaned firmly towards Israel, Rabin was convinced that Israel could impose on the Palestinians this weak and geographically divided state, which would be utterly dependent on Israel – both militarily and economically.[3]

It is telling that the Oslo II agreement, which made no explicit commitment to a Palestinian state, was ratified in the Knesset by the slimmest of majorities, sixty-one to fifty-nine votes. To the opposition's chagrin, the votes cast by the two defectors from Yiud tilted the balance in favour of the coalition government. The unavoidable feeling that the government was buying support for the Oslo II accord was underscored by the scathing remarks from the opposition during the charged debate.

Also, the government had to rely on the support of five MKs from the Arab and the ex-Communist parties, neither of which was a part of the coalition and that primarily represented Palestinian-Israeli constituents. Consistent with its ethnocentric, religious and nationalist approach to Israeli democracy, the opposition made a unique demand. It insisted that Oslo II be ratified by a specific majority to neutralize the 'Arab votes' in the Knesset, which were held to be Arafat's stooges and, therefore, were considered disqualified from deciding on matters so vital to Jewish people in Israel and abroad.[4] That the Oslo II agreement might have significance for the Palestinian-Israelis, who constituted 20 per cent of the population, was a fact that the opposition members chose to gloss over.

The serious allegations made by the opposition certainly struck a chord within the Jewish-Israeli public, the majority of whom opposed the Oslo II agreement.[5] It was against this clear challenge to the legitimacy of the foreign policy course of Rabin's government that Peace Now, the largest umbrella group of Israeli peace organizations, launched a peace rally in support of the Oslo Process and the Rabin government. The gathering of some 150,000 demonstrators in Tel Aviv's central square was the largest show of public support for the peace process since the DoP was signed in 1993. In a short, but powerful speech at the rally, Rabin voiced his most

---

[2] Interview 2 Haber.   [3] Interview 2 Haber; Yatom, *The Confidant*, pp. 302–3.
[4] The 376th meeting of the Knesset, pp. 51, 54, 55, 56, 83, 91.
[5] Ephraim Yuchtman-Yaar, Tamar Herman and Arieh Nadler, *Peace Index Project: Findings and Analysis, June 1994–May 1996* (Tel Aviv: Steinmetz Centre for Peace Research, 1996).

public endorsement of the PLO to date by referring to it as a 'partner for peace'. 'This rally', he continued, brimming with vitality as he was reaching his closing remarks, 'must send a message to the Israeli people, to the Jewish people around the world, to the many people in the Arab world, and indeed to the entire world, that the people of Israel want peace, support peace.'[6]

Yet, ever the realist, Rabin also referred in his speech to the deep divide in Israeli society and its ominous presence since the beginning of the Oslo process. 'Violence', Rabin cautioned, 'erodes the essence of Israeli democracy. It must be condemned and isolated.'[7] These comments, which were made in reference to the ad hominem anti-peace campaign that had haunted Rabin since the signing of the DoP, proved harrowingly to be apt. As he descended the steps of the podium, walking towards his car at the Kings of Israel Square in Tel Aviv, three bullets fired from a pistol at close range on that Saturday evening, 4 November 1995, by a Jewish fanatic, Yigal Amir, fatally wounded Yitzhak Rabin, who died in hospital an hour later. By assassinating Rabin, Amir told his interrogators, he wanted to 'change the course of history'.[8]

Yigal Amir had received his formative education in mainstream religious institutions. In Yishuv Hadah, an elitist Haredi institution where Amir spent his high school years, teachers emphasized the precepts of Jewish law and preached contempt for secular state law. Accordingly, for Amir and his ilk, if civil law and democracy clashed with religious dictate and law, civil law and democracy must yield. During his subsequent studies at Kerem D'Yavneh Yeshiva, where most students were the sons of religious-nationalist families, Amir developed his belief in the supremacy of the people of Israel, the Torah of Israel and the Land of Israel. Through this prism, Amir told the Shamgar State Commission of Inquiry, which investigated the assassination of Yitzhak Rabin, 'The Arabs' are 'our antithesis in every way. We can't live peacefully with them.'[9] In line with his extreme views, in the 1992 elections, Amir cast his ballot for Moledet, the Homeland Party, which was led by the retired racist general, Rehavam Ze'evi, and which preached the doctrine of 'transfer': expulsion of the Palestinians and annexation of the occupied territories. Evidently, to Yigal Amir the Oslo agreement was abhorrent and must be opposed.

---

[6] Rabin, *Pursing Peace*, p. 253. [7] Ibid.
[8] Quoted in Eldar and Zartal, *The Settlers and the State of Israel 1967–2004* (Or-Yehuda: Kinneret-Zmora Bitan, 2005), p. 111 (in Hebrew).
[9] Quoted in Michael Karpin and Ina Friedman, *Murder in the Name of God: The Plot to Kill Yitzhak Rabin* (London: Granta Publications), p. 9.

The Assassination of Yitzhak Rabin 107

Yigal Amir was influenced heavily by a broader group of vigilantes within the settler movement, who promoted violence – first against the Palestinians, later against IDF officers, policemen, soldiers and politicians. Not all had the capacity to murder, but those who inspired Amir did. They included the perpetrator of the Hebron Massacre, Baruch Goldstein, and Yehuda Etzion, who in 1984 was sentenced to seven years' imprisonment. Etzion was a member of a Jewish underground, which, during the 1980s, seriously injured a number of prominent Palestinian mayors, planned to blow up buses packed with Palestinian commuters and conspired to blow up a mosque on the Temple Mount in Jerusalem.[10]

Vigilantes such as Amir and Goldstein did not operate in a vacuum. They were part of a highly significant minority within the settler movement that was politically organized within the ranks of the Kach and Kahane Chai movements. Affiliates of these organizations, which were outlawed after the Hebron massacre, idealized Baruch Goldstein in a book written in his honour, *Baruch HaGever, Blessed Be the Man*.[11] The vigilantes were inspired also by a group of militant orthodox rabbis living in Israel and abroad. By January 1995, a prominent group of rabbis – Eliezer Melamed, Dov Lior Daniel Shilo and Nachum Rabinovitvh – had embarked on an exchange with their counterparts in Israel and abroad. They debated whether two ancient religious edicts, *din mosser* and *din rodef*, which laid down the duty to kill a Jew who imperils the life or property of another Jew, could be applied to Prime Minister Rabin.[12]

The significance of this debate, which was summarized in a document circulated by the GSS to the higher echelons of the Israeli government, was that it gave religious sanction to an assassination attempt on Rabin.[13] The debate over reviving *din mosser* and *din rodef* echoed the accusations levelled at Rabin of 'murderer' and 'traitor' in the public rallies organized by Likud, the settlers and their followers. In operating in the political and intellectual context that emerged from within the settler movement, Yigal Amir was not alone. Rather, he personified the maturing of a messianic and militant domestic constituency that posed a direct threat to the

---

[10] My account of Amir's background draws on Karpin's and Friedman's excellent investigative book: Karpin and Friedman, *Murder in the Name of God*, pp. 7–28; Hagai Segal, *Dear Brothers: The West Bank Jewish Underground* (Jerusalem: Keter, 1987) (in Hebrew).
[11] Michael Ben-Horin et al., *Blessed Be the Man* (Jerusalem: Shalom Al-Yisrael, 1995) (in Hebrew).
[12] Karpin and Friedman, *Murder in the Name of God*, pp. 114–20.
[13] Gillon, *Shabak Between the Schisms*, pp. 243, 319.

108 Engagement under Assault

democratic ability of any Israeli government to implement a foreign policy of peace towards the Arab world.

Flying High and Fast

Shimon Peres succeeded Yitzhak Rabin as both prime minister and defence minister. One of his first tasks on assuming the premiership for the second time in his career was to attend to Rabin's funeral. The leaders of more than eighty countries gathered in Jerusalem, at twenty-four hours' notice, to pay tribute to Rabin. The impressive international cohort included President Clinton and several Western and Arab leaders, including President Mubarak of Egypt, King Hussein of Jordan and the foreign ministers of Oman, Qatar, Tunisia and Morocco. This impressive show of international solidarity shattered the notion of Israel as a people who dwell alone.

However, Peres and his close foreign policy circle realized that the unprecedented international embrace by Israel and its foreign policy of engagement towards the Arab world could not compensate for the waning domestic support and legitimacy prior to the assassination. Therefore, domestic factors figured prominently in determining how to proceed with the peace process, and at what pace. 'For now', as Uri Savir put it to Dennis Ross, 'the right in Israel was on the defensive' and, as a result of the assassination, public opinion shifted sharply towards supporting the peace process.[14] Presciently, added the seasoned negotiator, 'no one could tell how long it would last.'[15]

This domestic and international context following the assassination of Rabin was the backdrop to Shimon Peres's emergence as chief foreign policy decision-maker. Ehud Barak, former IDF chief of staff, was appointed foreign minister and included in the close decision-making circle surrounding Peres. This coterie of intimates included, also, Peres's aide, Avi Gil, Uri Savir, director general of the foreign ministry and confidant of Peres, and Yossi Beilin, who was appointed minister without portfolio.[16]

Peres faced a dilemma on assuming the premiership. During the previous two years, former deputy foreign minister Yossi Beilin had been negotiating secretly with the PLO's number two, Mahmoud Abbas, popularly known as Abu Mazen, over the parameters to a final Israeli-Palestinian peace accord. The informal talks, which were held without the

[14] Herman, *The Israeli Peace Movement*, p. 276.
[15] Ross, *The Missing Peace*, p. 213; Savir, *The Process*, p. 296.
[16] Savir, *The Process*, p. 296; Kfir and Dor, *Barak: Wars of My Life*, pp. 187–8.

knowledge of both Rabin and Peres, were not binding. Nonetheless, crafted as it was by two political figures with direct access to Peres and Arafat, the document was significant.

On 11 November 1995, Beilin presented the document to Peres. What became known as the Abu Mazen-Beilin agreement, advocated establishing Israeli and Palestinian states – the two-state solution. The territory that was home to the majority of the settlers – around 100,000 – would be annexed to Israel. In addition, Israel would retain a military presence in the Jordan valley, which would remain its eastern border. In return, the Palestinians would receive an equivalent area of territory, adjacent to the Gaza Strip, in Holot Halutza. The settlers remaining in the area designated a Palestinian state could choose between remaining under Palestinian rule or relocating to Israel and receiving compensation.

The document also laid down that there should be no en masse return of Palestinian refugees to Israel. Areas populated by Palestinians in the Greater Jerusalem area would be transferred to the Palestinians, including an ex-territorial area that included the Dome of the Rock, which Jews were prohibited to enter and would be administered by the Jerusalem Waqf. Israel would retain control over the remainder of Jerusalem, although the final status of the city would be decided by further negotiations after the peace was signed.

Beilin recalls that, during the meeting, 'Peres seemed like someone who did not exactly realize what was happening to him', so shortly after the assassination of Rabin.[17] Avi Gil, another of Peres's close confidants, concurred, noting that 'the horrors of the murder and the burden of his new post made Peres lose sleep ... Since the murder, it seemed to me that Peres had aged rapidly.'[18] Still visibly shocked, Peres did not seem able to muster the energy to adopt the ambitious plan. He was concerned that there was a serious risk that finalizing the negotiations over the Abu Mazen-Beilin document would extend beyond the date set for the forthcoming Israeli elections. Focusing on implementing the Oslo II agreement rather than seeking a comprehensive Israeli-Palestinian peace appeared to be a more realistic goal to Peres. Without further consultation, he flatly rejected Beilin's document.[19]

Peres prioritized, instead, the concluding of a comprehensive Israeli-Syrian peace agreement within a year.[20] This chimed with his penchant for bold and ambitious moves, which, in the past, he had found difficult to realize because he lacked sufficient credibility and legitimacy within

---

[17] Interview 2 Beilin.   [18] Gil, *The Peres Formula*, pp. 208–9.
[19] Beilin, *Touching Peace*, pp. 181–4.
[20] Ross, *The Missing Peace*, p. 212; Savir, *The Process*, p. 299.

110   Engagement under Assault

Israel. Peres presented his vision of peace to Dennis Ross, during their first working meeting on 20 November 1995. His plan was shaped significantly by public opinion. A deal with Syria that required giving up the Golan, explained Peres, could 'only be sold if it really ended the Arab-Israeli conflict'. It had to be part of a 'deal with the region' on which Peres hoped to base his re-election platform. Therefore, and unlike the slow negotiation pace adopted by Rabin, Peres was inclined towards swift implementation of an Israeli-Syrian peace accord, which would be part of a comprehensive regional peace agreement signed between Israel and at least fifteen other Arab states.[21]

Swift implementation was not the only aspect that distinguished Shimon Peres's and his predecessor's approaches to the negotiations with Syria. As Peres told Ross bluntly, the IDF 'tended to be stubborn when it came to its security needs' and it was advocating to slow down the negotiations with Syria following Rabin's assassination. By contrast, Peres and his close circle wanted to 'fly high and fast' in order to capitalize on the shift in public opinion in support of the peace process and the Israeli right being on the defence.[22] In this regard, the IDF was perceived by Peres as a potential liability in the negotiations.

Uri Savir was appointed to lead negotiations with the Palestinians and Syria, which was a clear signal that Israel's approach to the negotiations would differ from the military-led security-driven agenda promoted by Rabin. It would be premised, instead, on the New Middle East Vision, which Peres had been advocating since the 1993 Arab-Israeli breakthrough.[23] This vision was inspired by a liberal reading of how European economic cooperation had transformed historical enmity into peaceful political cooperation.[24] This chequered reading of European history overlooked the fact that European economic cooperation emerged only after the great European empires could no longer fight following two devastating world wars and were facing a common enemy, the USSR. By contrast, the Middle East states had no common enemy and their military capabilities were intact. The new Middle East vision was also based on

---

[21] Ross, *The Missing Peace*, p. 226; Rabinovich, *The Brink of Peace*, pp. 200, 215, 216; Yatom, *The Confidant*, p. 183.

[22] Ross, *The Missing Peace*, pp. 219, 223–4, 234.

[23] Savir, *The Process*, p. 302; Rabinovich, *The Process*, p. 201; Yatom, *The Confidant*, pp. 182–3.

[24] Shimon Peres, *The New Middle East: A Framework and Processes Towards an Era of Peace* (Tel Aviv: Steimatzky, 1993) pp. 19, 93 (in Hebrew); Shimon Peres, 'Address by Foreign Minister Peres to the Jerusalem International Business Forum, 31 October 1993', in *Israeli Ministry of Foreign Affairs*, http://mfa.gov.il/MFA/ForeignPolicy/MFADocuments/Yearbook9/Pages/127%20Address%20by%20Foreign%20Minister%20Peres%20to%20the%20Jerus.aspx, accessed 14 December 2018.

a flawed reading of what the end of the Cold War signified. The end of the conflict between the two powers, Peres was convinced, marked a new epoch in human history, distinguished by the triumph of capitalism, democracy and the retreat of the nation state. In this brave new world, state power no longer derived primarily from military force, but from technological capacity, ability to compete in the global economy and the extent to which states were democratic. Therefore, at the heart of Peres's notion of a New Middle East were peace economies – economies that would be sustained by investments from developed states, multinational corporations (MNCs) and foundations and would be geared towards enhancing human development.

The New Middle East of Shimon Peres was, effectively, a post-sovereign vision for the region that left no room for an independent Palestinian state. Instead, Peres advocated that the Palestinians form a political confederation with Jordan, which would be economically con-nected to Israel via 'soft' borders – that is, borders that would allow complete freedom of passage of people and goods. In this sense, the New Middle East vision was far less radical than how it was actually presented by Prime Minister Peres. Essentially, it repackaged his erst-while preferred solution to the Israeli-Palestinian conflict – the 'Jordanian option' – in a post-Cold War framework.[25] For Peres, the New Middle East vision would provide the foundations of an Israeli-Syrian peace accord, which would be guaranteed by shared economic interests and stakes rather than by security arrangements.

The direct Israeli-Syrian negotiations, held at the Aspen Institute's Wye River Plantation, which extended from end of December 1995 to end of February 1996, were shaped by Peres' New Middle East approach. Whereas previous negotiations had been conducted by military delega-tions and focused on security, the Wye negotiations brought together several Israeli and Syrian experts with a mandate to discuss the multiple issues underlying Israeli-Syrian relations: a comprehensive regional agreement, its timeline, normalization, security arrangements and eco-nomic cooperation. In a move that was without precedent, the members of the Syrian delegation were permitted by Assad to spend a lengthy period with their Israeli counterparts and to socialize with them. Another promising sign was that Israel and Syria committed to restraining their respective forces in south Lebanon during the negotiations, to avoid clashes between the IDF and Hezbollah.[26]

[25] Peres, *The New Middle East*, pp. 68–71, 88, 149–150.
[26] Ross, *The Missing Peace*, pp. 228–34, 237–8; Savir, *The Process*, pp. 304–5, 308–15; Rabinovich, *The Brink of Peace*, pp. 212, 218–22; Yatom, *The Confidant*, pp. 184–7; Shaaban, *Damascus Diary*, p. 133.

112   Engagement under Assault

The high hopes generated by this auspicious setting were dashed by the limited progress made in the Wye negotiations. The main obstacle was Syria's intransigence. Although the Israeli's leaned towards rapid implementation of an agreement, the Syrians remained entrenched in their erstwhile position. They insisted on a sequence of Israeli withdrawal to 4 June 1967 lines followed by partial normalization only and rejected establishment of mutually binding bilateral economic relations. By implication, Israeli-Syrian economic cooperation in the Golan Heights was a non-starter.[27]

The rejection of Peres's terms and failure to provide any real prospect of a timely agreement was due to Assad's and his foreign policy circle's deep-seated suspicion towards Israel and its intentions. For example, Syria's then foreign minister commented that Israel 'negotiated only to procrastinate and evade the requirements of peace', whereas Peres was explicit that he wanted to move quickly.[28] Likewise, rather than treating the New Middle East vision as an economically driven peace plan, the Syrians construed it as a ploy to enhance Israeli hegemony in the Middle East. What Peres viewed as an economically driven peace vision for a borderless Middle East, Assad interpreted as Israeli economic colonialism by stealth.[29]

These innate apprehensions were exacerbated by the impact of internal Israeli politics and foreign policy discord in the Wye negotiations. By the time negotiations began, members of the Third Way movement had split from Labour to form their own independent faction, which left Shimon Peres presiding over a minority government. He was faced with the choice of calling a snap election or sticking to the original 29 October 1996 election date. With an eye to the prospect of party primaries in the event of an early election, several members of his Labour party became critical of the negotiations with Syria. Particularly significant in this regard were the statements made by Foreign Minister Barak. Appealing to a sceptical Israeli public regarding the talks with Syria, Barak said that 'we will do everything to prevent the Syrians from [dipping] their toes in the Kinneret' (the Sea of Galilee).[30]

Such statements, which contradicted what Savir was conveying privately to the Syrians, created discord at the heart of Israeli foreign policymaking. Assad, whose grip on Syrian foreign policymaking was absolute, saw the dispute between the Israeli prime minister and his foreign

---

[27] Rabinovich, *The Brink of Peace*, pp. 213, 219.
[28] Al-Sharaa, *The Missing Account*, p. 334.   [29] Rabinovich, *The Brink of Peace*, p. 213.
[30] Kfir and Dor, *Barak: Wars of My Life*, p. 190.

Flying High and Fast

minister as ominous. In his view, Peres was either acting duplicitously towards him or was unable to deliver on his peace plan.[31]

The doubts harboured by the Syrian leadership were compounded by how it viewed the cementing of relations between Israel and other regional powers, especially Turkey. In February 1996, Israel and Turkey signed a defence cooperation pact and, in March, they set up a free trade zone agreement. On the Turkish side, the agreement with Israel was central to the internal political contest between the Islamist government, led by Necmettin Erbakan, and the Turkish military establishment, which had long been the protector of the secular Kemalist legacy. The agreement with Israel was supported – at least in part – by the Turkish military establishment, because Erbakan and the Islamists were campaigning against it. Interstate interests, such as the potential for economic and security cooperation and the common threat posed to the two states by a rising Iran, also played a role.[32]

Syrian assessments of the evolving Israel-Turkish relations were skewed by their inherent suspicion and distrust of the Israelis. The entente between the two countries, which clearly served multifaceted goals, was seen by Walid al-Moualem as serving *one* purpose only and that was 'isolating Syria'.[33] It was this deep-seated suspicion, risk aversion and hostility towards Israel's intentions that prompted Assad to decline the several public and private requests from Peres for a summit.[34] Assad was evasive, telling the Americans that 'he could not commit to a date'.[35] Peres interpreted this correctly as a stalling tactic that removed any support for the re-election strategy Peres had devised.

[31] Ross, *The Missing Peace*, p. 242; Savir, *The Process*, pp. 315–6.
[32] On the Israeli-Turkish Alliance, see Ofra Bengio, *The Turkish-Israeli Relationship* (Basingstoke: Palgrave, 2004); Neil Lochery, 'Israel and Turkey: Deepening Ties and Strategic Implications, 1995–1998', *Israel Affairs*, 5, 1, 1998: 48.
[33] Al-Moualem, 'Fresh Light on the Syrian-Israeli Peace Negotiations', 88.
[34] Gil, *The Peres Formula*, p. 211; Shaaban, *Damascus Diary*, p. 134; 'Statement to the Knesset by Acting Prime Minister Peres', *IMFA*, http://mfa.gov.il/MFA/ForeignPolic y/MFADocuments/Yearbook10/Pages/Statement%20to%20the%20Knesset%20by% 20Acting%20Prime%20Minister.aspx, assessed 14 December 2018; 'Interview with Prime Minister Peres in US News and World Report', *IMFA*, www.mfa.gov.il/mfa/fo reignpolicy/mfadocuments/yearbook10/pages/interview%20with%20prime%20minis ter%20peres%20in%20us%20news%20and.aspx, accessed 14 December 2018; 'Address by Prime Minister Peres to a Joint Session of the US Congress', 12 December 1995, http://mfa.gov.il/MFA/ForeignPolicy/MFADocuments/Yearboo k10/Pages/Address%20by%20Prime%20Minister%20Peres%20to%20a%20Joint%2 0Session.aspx, accessed 14 December 2018.
[35] Savir, *The Process*, p. 316.

114   Engagement under Assault

Fateful Decisions

From the start of the negotiations with Syria, Peres had been guided by a simple principle: he was willing to 'lose the Golan or the elections, but not both'.[36] Assad's tepid response to Israeli overtures, in mid-February 1996, prompted Peres to announce that the elections would be brought forward to 29 May 1996. An electoral law, which became effective with the elections to the 14th Knesset, stipulated two separate ballots: one for prime minister and one for the list of party members of the Knesset.[37] Peres, Israel's veteran politician, entered the 1996 national election campaign from a seemingly advantageous position. Initially, the assassination of Yitzhak Rabin had produced a rallying effect around the Labour camp. Also, the Israeli economy had improved significantly since 1992 and US President Bill Clinton, considered a hero by many Israelis since Rabin's funeral, supported Shimon Peres throughout the campaign.[38]

However, Peres's campaign was to encounter serious challenges. A month before the announcement to bring forward the elections, the GSS had devised a plan to assassinate Hamas's most notorious bomb-maker, known as Yahya 'the Engineer' Ayash. As the then head of the Israeli GSS, Carmi Gillon, recollected years later, Ayash 'not only had a highly advanced technological sense of how to build bombs. He was also an excellent military tactician and, above all, he had endless charisma ... after all he needed to recruit individuals to give their lives away. That is no simple matter.'[39] Israel had been in pursuit of Yahya Ayash since 1991. In 1994, Rabin authorized the GSS to arrest or kill Ayash should the opportunity arise. 'Rabin would drive me crazy on this matter', recalled Carmi Gillon. 'Every meeting he would ask me if there is "anything new on this issue".'[40] On assuming office, Peres retained the authorization given by Rabin to assassinate or imprison Ayash.[41] On 5 January 1996, the GSS acted on the prime minister's authorization, carrying out the successful assassination of Ayash in Beit Lahiya, northern Gaza. 'The Engineer' was killed by an explosive device hidden inside a mobile telephone supplied by Israeli intelligence agents to a Palestinian collaborator.

Ayash's assassination occurred at a particularly sensitive moment. During this period, Palestinian factions were in the midst of inter-factional dialogue, to try to resolve the ongoing frictions between the PA and Hamas. Towards the end of 1995, they had reached agreement

---

[36] Ross, *The Missing Peace*, p. 225.
[37] Gregory S. Mahler, 'The Forming of the Netanyahu Government: Coalition-Forming in a Quasi-Parliamentary Setting', *Israel Affairs*, 3, 3–4, 1997: 3.
[38] Giora Goldberg, 'The Electoral Fall of the Israeli Left' in Daniel J. Elazar and Shmuel Sandler, *Israel at the Polls 1996* (London: Frank Cass, 1998).
[39] Interview Gillon.   [40] Interview Gillon.   [41] Interview Gillon.

Fateful Decisions 115

on a period of calm (Tahdiyah) that included suspending attacks on Israeli targets.[42] Indeed, since August 1995 suicide and other bombing attacks on Israelis had ceased.[43]

According to an Israeli investigative journalist, Shlomi Eldar, who has researched Hamas thoroughly, Arafat sought to build on this promising political climate. He began negotiations with Hamas, via his emissary, Samir Masharawi, to incorporate Hamas's military wing in the PA's security forces. Had this succeeded, it would have been the first significant step towards disarming Hamas and creating a single, unified Palestinian security force. The emerging agreement laid down that, in return for ceasing its military activities and accepting the Oslo agreements, Israel would desist from pursuit of Hamas leaders, whom would be allowed to resume routine life in the PA's territories. Throughout, the Israeli secret services were kept abreast of these negotiations.[44]

Eldar's narrative, which strongly suggests that the assassination of Ayash was a critical factor in scuppering the imitative, is inadequate. It ignores a significant factor, namely, the influence of Hamas's external leadership under Khaled Mashal, based in Damascus. According to then GSS head, Carmi Gillon, Hamas's external leadership was more antagonistic towards the PA than the Gaza-based leadership of the movement, which is why it vetoed Masharawi's budding initiative.[45] From this perspective, it would appear that Ayash's assassination was important not for torpedoing the Palestinians intra-factional reconciliation, but rather for facilitating the resumption of Hamas's terrorist campaign. Soon after the traditional forty-day mourning period ended, Hamas launched its deadliest terrorist campaign since the onset of the peace process. In the space of nine days, between 25 February and 5 March 1996, fifty-nine Israelis were killed in just four terrorist attacks.[46]

Was Hamas, through its slew of terrorist attacks, attempting to interfere in the Israeli elections by politically weakening Peres – the champion of the Oslo process? According to chief of the Israeli GSS, Carmi Gillon, and his successor, Ami Ayalon, there is no evidence that this was the case.[47] Also, a leading Hamas figure, Musa Abu Marzuk, denied that Hamas was trying to influence the Israeli elections, explaining that: 'We can't tie our future with the Labour party or Likud party or who wins the elections.'[48] So was

[42] Milton-Edwards and Farell, *Hamas*, p. 218.
[43] 'Suicide and Other Bombing Attacks in Israel since the Declaration of Principles', *IMFA*.
[44] Shlomi Eldar, *Eyeless in Gaza: Recollection of an Israeli Reporter* (Tel Aviv: Miskal, 2005), pp. 203–7.
[45] Interview Gillon.   [46] Savir, *The Process*, p. 318.
[47] Interview 2 Ami Ayalon, 12 July 2017, Tel Aviv. Interview Gillon.
[48] Quoted in Milton-Edwards and Farrell, *Hamas*, p. 82.

116 Engagement under Assault

the spate of suicide bombings prepared and executed in revenge for the assassination of Ayash? Former heads of the Israeli GSS thought this unlikely. The timeframe necessary for recruiting the suicide bombers, preparing the devices and executing four devastating attacks would require longer than the fifty days that had elapsed since the assassination.[49]

This assessment suggests strongly that the attacks launched by Hamas had been planned and prepared during the period of calm, possibly under Ayash's instructions. Their execution after Ayash's assassination had an element of revenge, but, more fundamentally, were part of a Hamas tactic. The Islamic Resistance Movement sought to establish a balance of deterrence with Israel by retaliating to the killing of one of its leaders with suicide attacks. Beyond this, the February–March spate of terrorist attacks was commensurate with Hamas's political stance towards Israel. Just nine years after its establishment, Hamas was still a highly zealous movement. The preamble to its 1988 covenant stated that 'Israel will exist and will continue to exist until Islam will obliterate it, just as it obliterated others before it.' Article 11 of the covenant discounted any prospect of a two-state solution in stating that 'Palestine is an Islamic Waqf land consecrated for Moslem generations until Judgement Day.'[50]

Did Peres take an undue risk in maintaining the authorization to assassinate Ayash when Palestinian inter-factional dialogue was underway and he was contemplating bringing forward the Israeli elections? After all, since August 1995, as part of the Palestinian inter-factional dialogue, Hamas had ceased its suicide and other bombing attacks against Israelis. In theory, Peres could have overturned Rabin's decision, but, in practice, this would have been an extremely tall task from the prime minister. Reversing his decision would have shattered his security credentials vis-à-vis the security network and, if it had become known more widely, with the broader public. Indeed, for Peres, his standing with the security network was a sensitive issue. Unlike Yitzhak Rabin, Ariel Sharon, Ezer Weitzman and every other political leader of his generation, Peres had never served in the IDF. He had climbed the ranks via his successes in civil service and government roles. Peres's official biography shows that his not serving in the IDF haunted him throughout his entire political career. Despite his heavy involvement in establishing and developing Israel's security network, Peres never succeeded in fully establishing his credentials as someone who could be trusted on security matters[51]

---

[49] Interview Gillon; Interview 2 Ami Ayalon.

[50] Hams Covenant, 1988, The Avalone Project: Documents in Law, History, and Diplomacy, http://avalon.law.yale.edu/20th_century/hamas.asp, accessed 6 December 2018.

[51] Bar Zohar, *Shimon Peres*, pp. 68–74.

Fateful Decisions

Therefore, claims Peres's close confidant, Avi Gil, Peres chose to retain the defence portfolio following Rabin's assassination, rather than to appoint Ehud Barak defence minister. He was determined to shore up his security record by proving that, like Rabin, he could manage both roles simultaneously and successfully.[52] Revoking the authorization to assassinate Ayash that Rabin had maintained for years would have dealt a devastating blow to Peres's already weak security credentials. Psychologically and politically, this was something he absolutely could not contemplate.

Conscious of Peres's precarious position, President Clinton convened the Summit of Peacemakers on 13 March 1996, in Sharm El-Sheik. The meeting brought together representatives from Israel, the PLO and twenty-nine states including fourteen Arab countries. Two months earlier, on 20 January 1996, Yasser Arafat was elected Palestinian president with a landslide majority, in the first free and fair elections conducted under PA rule. His victory reinforced the mandate he had from the Palestinians for his policy towards Israel. The summit represented an unprecedented demonstration of international support for the beleaguered Israeli premier in the wake of the terrorist campaign waged by Hamas during February–March 1996.[53]

The Summit of Peacemakers had a limited influence; Peres's security credentials were tested again, although this time not by Hamas. By March 1996, both Israel and Hezbollah were more frequently breaching the verbal understandings reached after Operation Accountability in 1993. On 9 April 1996, the 'rules of the game' collapsed entirely. Peres, who was engaged in a hard-fought election campaign, with the polls showing a tie between him and his rival, Binyamin Netanyahu, needed to demonstrate his security standing to a disillusioned Israeli public. As Ehud Barak, who was intimately involved in the campaign, wrote in his memoirs: '[T]he last thing Shimon wanted was for tens of thousands of people in the north of Israel to be cowering in shelters during the final stretch of the campaign.'[54]

This domestic consideration was the background to authorizing the launching of Operation Grapes of Wrath.[55] The operation was designed to trigger a chain effect by displacing half a million south Lebanese. The underlying logic was that a civilian stampede would compel the Lebanese government to pressure Syria to curb activities of Hezbollah, its ally.

---

[52] Gil, *The Peres Formula*, p. 221.   [53] Ross, *The Missing Peace*, pp. 248–9, 257.
[54] Ehud Barak, *My Country My Life: Fighting for Israel, Searching for Peace* (New York: Macmillan, 2018), p. 296.
[55] On the operation from an Israeli perspective, see Savir, *The Process*, pp. 323–5; Ross, *The Missing Peace*, pp. 249–55; Barak, *My Country My Life*, p. 296.

118   Engagement under Assault

However, this Machiavellian logic backfired. On 18 April 1996, a stray artillery missile, launched by the IDF in the midst of the operation hit the UN base in Qana killing 102 refugees and prompting a frantic diplomatic effort by the USA to bring an end to hostilities on 27 April. Thus, Peres's attempt to assert himself as 'Mr Security' failed utterly as the limits to what could be achieved by use of military force were glaringly exposed. All Operation Grapes of Wrath had achieved was a return to the status quo ante, whereby the rules of the game governing the conflict between Israel and its ally, the SLA, Iran, Syria and Hezbollah were restored.

Rejecting Engagement

Rabin, one of Israel's least eloquent prime ministers, had left no written text explaining his foreign policy creed. Instead, the legacy of Yitzhak Rabin's foreign policy of engagement was marked by his bold measures during his dynamic premiership. There was a common denominator to his peace accord with Jordan, budding relations with the Gulf and Maghreb countries and his negotiations with Syria and the PLO. Israel's foreign policy of engagement under Rabin hinged on relinquishing territory in exchange for peace agreements with the Arabs. It relied on prioritizing diplomacy and keeping military force as a viable alternative. It was based on scaling down the Israeli occupation, resulting in a smaller, more democratic and demographically more cohesive Israel, with 80 per cent of the population Jews.

Rabin's foreign policy engagement was under constant attack. It was challenged by the Israeli right and was contested continuously by parliament, the public and the vigilante segments of the Jewish settler movement. It was assaulted, too, by the relentless anti-peace terror campaigns launched by Hamas and the PIJ. Rabin's efforts to shore up his domestic support through his negotiations with his Arab counterparts were only partially successful. Crucially, his counterpart in his negotiations with Syria was Hafez al-Assad, whom Rabin found to be extremely reluctant and elusive and not willing to extend any positive gestures towards Rabin or engage in public diplomacy. The lethal damage inflicted by Yigal Amir, Rabin's assassin, to Rabin's foreign policy of engagement was clear. What is less obvious is what might have resulted had Rabin not been killed. Given the challenges he faced, could he have brought his foreign policy of engagement to fruition. We will never know. History does not disclose alternatives.

On becoming (acting) prime minister, Shimon Peres sought to advance Israel's foreign policy of engagement in line with his New Middle East vision, but this was ill conceived. It took no account of the discrepancies

Rejecting Engagement

between post-World War II Europe and the Middle East and was insensitive to the deep-seated hostility within large segments of the Arab world towards potential Israeli economic dominance. This was reflected most strongly in talks with Syrian negotiators, who proved inflexible and inherently suspicious of Israeli intentions. Despite Peres's overtures, Assad persistently opposed the idea of peace with Israel being based on mutually beneficial economic ties. In fact, the New Middle East utopia continued to be bedevilled by old and familiar challenges: terrorism, mutual suspicion between Israeli and Arab elites and domestic opposition to peace.

Still reeling from the assassination of Yitzhak Rabin and rocked by the confrontations with Hamas and Hezbollah, Shimon Peres proved unable to champion Israel's foreign policy of engagement in an election campaign. Rabin's murder seemed to have sapped the energy for which Peres was renowned, while the party he led entered the 1996 election campaign with an institutional deficit. Its core political institutions, such as the once mighty Workers' Federation, Histadroot, as well as the Labour movement, were in decline.[56]

In contrast, Peres's opponents, the ultra-orthodox community, the settlers and the well-prepared Likud, were the most politically mobilized in Israeli society. Their ranks were expanded by the vast former Soviet Union immigrant community, which, in 1992, had supported Labour en masse. However, by 1996, it was no longer committed to Labour. As a result of its grievances towards the absorption policies of Likud and Labour, several of its more prominent figures, led by former Refusnik, Natan Sheranski, joined forces to establish a new political party, Israel Ascending (Israel Ba'aliya). The party centred on representing the new Russian immigrants and was highly sceptical of Israel's engagement foreign policy.[57]

This nationalist, religious and ethnocentric coalition accused Labour of abandoning immigrants and ties to the Land of Israel, and forsaking the Jewish nature of the Israeli state and Zionism. Its campaign culminated in the divisive rallying cry, 'Netanyahu – Good for the Jews', around the leader of the opposition.[58] Meanwhile, Peres was accused of planning to 'divide Jerusalem' and Likud was running an effective campaign to position itself at the centre of Israeli politics.[59] Without referring explicitly to the Oslo Accords, the Likud platform stated that 'the party will continue

---

[56] Lev. L Greenberg, *The Histadroot Above All* (Jerusalem: Nevo, 1993) (in Hebrew).
[57] Galili and Bronfman, *The Million that Changed the Middle East*, pp. 89–102.
[58] Sam Lehman-Wilzig, 'The Media Campaign: The Negative Effects of Positive Campaigning' in Daniel J. Elazar and Shmuel Sandler, *Israel at the Polls 1996* (London: Frank Cass, 1998), p. 183.
[59] Obituary Shimon Peres, *Guardian*, 28 September 2016, www.theguardian.com/world/2016/sep/28/shimon-peres-obituary, accessed 8 March 2017.

to respect international agreements' and 'abide by the facts created by them'.[60] Promising 'peace and security', it committed to 'firmly resist a Palestinian state'.[61]

The fierce terrorist campaign waged by Hamas and the institutional advantage of Likud, combined with its shrewd election campaign, resulted in the victory of Binyamin Netanyahu. Peres, who lost the election by just 1 per cent, had reinforced his reputation as the candidate who won every poll and lost every election. No wonder Orly Azoulay titled her 1996 biography of him *The Man Who Didn't Know How to Win*.[62] A significant yet often overlooked result of the campaign was the 7 per cent reduction in the number of votes cast for centre-left political parties.[63] Israelis had delivered a clear verdict rejecting the Rabin-Peres government policy of engagement.

Figure 5.1 Rubble of building and car
Security forces among the ruins in south Tel Aviv following an Iraqi Scud missile attack. Taken 18 January 1991. Courtesy Nathan Alpert, Israel Government Press Office

[60] Likud-Gesher-Tzomet, *A Platform: A Plan for Action, Elections 1996* (Jerusalem: Knesset Publications, 1996), p. 3 (in Hebrew).
[61] Ibid.
[62] Orly Azoulay, *The Man Who Didn't Know How to Win* (Tel Aviv: Yedioth Ahronoth, 1996) (in Hebrew).
[63] Appendix to the Results of the Elections to the 14th Knesset (Jerusalem: Central Elections Committee), p. 3 quoted in Elazar and Sandler, *Israel at the Polls 1996*, p. 28.

Figure 5.2 Prime Minister Shamir delivering a speech
Prime Minister Yitzhak Shamir addressing the Madrid peace conference. Taken 30 October 1991. Courtesy Ya'acov Sa'ar, Israel Government Press Office

Figure 5.3 Shimon Peres (L) Yitzhak Rabin, Hosni Mubarak, Yasser Arafat and Warren Christopher (R)
Foreign Minister Shimon Peres, Prime Minister Yitzhak Rabin, Egyptian President Mubarak and US Secretary of State Warren Christopher, trying to convince PLO Chairman Yasser Arafat to sign maps of Oslo I agreement. Taken 4 May 1994. Courtesy Tzvika Israeli, Israel Government Press Office

Figure 5.4 Yasser Arafat and Yitzhak Rabin
Prime Minister Yitzhak Rabin meeting in Casablanca with PLO Chairman Yasser Arafat. Taken 30 October 1994. Courtesy Ya'acov Sa'ar, Israel Government Press Office

Figure 5.5 Blown–up Egged bus
The shell of a number 18 Jerusalem bus blown up by a Hamas suicide bomber at the intersection of Jaffa and Shlomzion Hamalka Streets. Taken 3 March 1996. Courtesy Avi Ohayon, Israel Government Press Office

Figure 5.6 Caricature of Yasser Arafat
Hamas propaganda against PLO Chairman Yasser Arafat portrayed as a dove and his dreams of peace. Taken 3 February 1993. Courtesy Tzvika Israeli, Israel Government Press Office

Figure 5.7 Yitzhak Rabin, King Hussein and President Clinton
Prime Minister Yitzhak Rabin (R) and Jordan's King Hussein shake hands after signing the Israel-Jordan Peace Accord as US President Bill Clinton applauds on the White House lawn. Taken 25 July 1994. Courtesy Ya'acov Sa'ar, Israel Government Press Office

6   The Dividends of Engagement

Post-Cold War Dilemmas beyond the Middle East

The end of the Cold War presented Israeli foreign policymakers with challenges and opportunities beyond the Middle East. The disintegration of the USSR gave birth to a weak, fractured and unstable Russian Federation, shifting attention towards rising powers, such as China and India. Both countries had recognized Israel, but throughout the Cold War had refused to establish diplomatic relations. Could Israel exploit the end of the Cold War to forge new relations with these two Asian powers?

The stakes were even higher in the case of the established powers. Israeli relations with the European Economic Community (EEC), harbinger of the EU and Israel's largest trading partner, were increasingly strained because of diverging views towards the Arab-Israeli conflict. Could the end of the Cold War be harnessed to narrow the deepening disagreements? Paramount, however, were relationships with the USA. With the US-USSR conflict drawing to a close, would the Israeli-US strategic relationship endure or was it set to decline?

The Evolution of the US-Israeli 'Special Relationship'

Contrary to claims made by US presidents and Israeli prime ministers, the alliance between the two states was not 'eternal' or 'forever'.[1] The special relationship dated back to the 1970s and the specific circumstances produced by the Cold War during that period. Following the embroilment of the USA in Vietnam, its approach to the Cold War shifted. US policymakers abandoned the 1957 Eisenhower Doctrine, which stipulated direct intervention by the USA in countries seeking its

---

[1] 'Barak Obama Hails Eternal US-Israeli Alliance at Start of Middle East Visit', *Guardian*, 20 March 2013, available at www.theguardian.com/world/2013/mar/20/obama-eternal-us-israel-alliance, accessed 20 December 2018.

'protection from "international communism"'.[2] Instead, in 1969, the USA adopted the Nixon Doctrine, which advocated US containment of the USSR via regional proxies. The recalibration of US foreign policy came shortly after the 1967 Arab-Israeli war. Having displayed its military prowess, Israel was designated a US proxy in the Middle East, alongside Turkey and Iran.[3]

The useful role played by Israel as a bulwark against Soviet expansionism quickly became apparent. In 1970, King Hussein of Jordan – an important Western ally in the region – faced a PLO attempt to topple his regime that became known as 'Black September'. Israel played an important part in foiling the challenge. It positioned IDF forces near the Jordanian-Syrian border, which deterred Syria, a key Soviet ally, from deploying military to support PLO forces. The events in Jordan were a catalyst for the development of the Israeli-US alliance.[4] During the 1970s and 1980s, it consolidated rapidly and was grounded in Memoranda of Agreements and Memoranda of Understandings on Strategic Cooperation. The memoranda, which were signed by consecutive US administrations, codified and formalized the military, economic and political aspects of Israel-US relations.[5] They were defined as 'executive agreements' and differ, legally, from 'international agreements'. Whereas executive agreements have a constitutional basis, international agreements enter into force, with respect to the USA, only after two-thirds of the US Senate has given its advice and consent.[6]

The benefits accruing to Israel from the evolving special relationship were immense. In 1986, the USA designated Israel a 'major non-NATO ally', which increased the range of Pentagon contracts for which Israeli companies could bid and gave Israel's defence industries access to previously restricted US technologies. Also, US economic assistance to Israel grew substantially. In the early years of the Cold War, it comprised

---

[2] Michael C. Hudson, 'The United States in the Middle East' in Louise Fawcett, *International Relations of the Middle East* (Oxford: Oxford University Press, 2013), p. 323.
[3] Shlaim, *The Iron Wall*, p. 313.
[4] Bernard Reich, *Securing the Covenant: United States-Israel Relations after the Cold War* (Westport, Praeger, 1995), pp. 37–9.
[5] See Israeli-United States Memorandum of Understanding, 1 September 1975, *IMFA*, www.mfa.gov.il/mfa/foreignpolicy/mfadocuments/yearbook2/pages/112%20israel-united %20states%20memorandum%20of%20understandi.aspx; US-Israel Memorandum of Understanding on Strategic Cooperation, *IMFA*, 30 November 1981, www.mfa.gov.il/ mfa/foreignpolicy/peace/guide/pages/us-israel%20memorandum%20of%20understand ing.aspx; Memorandum of Agreement between Israel and the United States *IMFA*, 21 April 1988, www.mfa.gov.il/mfa/foreignpolicy/mfadocuments/yearbook7/pages/355 %20memorandum%20of%20agreement%20between%20israel%20and%20the.aspx, all links accessed 20 December 2018.
[6] 'Treaty vs. Executive Agreement', US Department of State website, www.state.gov/s/l/tr eaty/faqs/70133.htm, accessed 20 December 2018.

126   The Dividends of Engagement

economic and humanitarian aid; by the 1980s, it included a significant military component. Out of a $3 billion package of grant aid provided by the USA to Israel annually, which marked Israel as the top recipient of US aid, $1.8 billion was earmarked for military assistance. In trade terms, in 1970 the US market accounted for 10 per cent of Israeli exports, but, by the end of the Cold War, this had grown to 30 per cent. In 1985, the two countries signed a free trade agreement, the first FTA ever signed by the USA.[7]

The special relationship was also marked by cooperation in spheres such as counterterrorism, intelligence, military and civilian research and by joint manoeuvres between the IDF and the US army.[8] The deepening security cooperation gave rise to US-Israeli joint security forums, including the Joint Military Political Group (JMPG), established in 1984 to coordinate common security issues, and the 1988 Joint Security Assistance Planning (JSAP) Group, which reviews Israel's requests for security assistance.[9] Thus, as the Cold War came to an end, the foundations of the special relationship seemed firm.

However, the 1990–1 Gulf War underscored the potential challenges to the special relationship in a post-Cold War era. Israel's foreign policy-makers could not fail to notice Israel's exclusion from the US-led anti-Iraq coalition during the Gulf War, which raised concerns that its strategic importance for the USA was diminishing.[10] In this context, ensuing feuds between Shamir's government and the Bush administration were deeply problematic. The disputes over settlement expansion, the deepening Israeli occupation and the Palestinian Intifada – ongoing since 1987 – cast doubts over whether the notion of US-Israeli 'common values' could be sustained. Personal tensions, for example, between Prime Minister Shamir and Secretary of State Baker, exacerbated the deepening rift. Shamir was 'appalled' by the strong hints given by Baker to the Palestinians, in a meeting two weeks after the end of the Gulf War, that the USA would not tolerate the continued Israeli occupation.[11] Similarly,

---

[7] 'Israel-US Free Trade Area Agreement', *IMFA*, www.mfa.gov.il/mfa/mfa-archive/1980–1989/pages/israel-us%20free%20trade%20area%20agreement.aspx, accessed 21 July, 2018.

[8] Reich, *Securing the Covenant*, pp. 45, 92–3, 95–6; see BIRD website, www.birdf.com/?CategoryID=317&ArticleID=374, accessed 16 September, 2016; Elyakim Rubenstein, *Ways of Peace* (Tel Aviv: Maarachot, 1992), p. 179 (in Hebrew).

[9] Reich, *Securing the Covenant*, p. 43; Memorandum of Agreement between Israel and the United States, 21 April 1988.

[10] Shamir, *Summing Up*, p. 265; report produced by the Jaffe Centre for Strategic Studies, a leading Israeli think tank: Dore Gold, 'Following the American Elections: Preparing for Trends in Israel-US Relations', Memorandum No. 37, December, 1992, p. 1 (in Hebrew); Interview Moshe Arens.

[11] Shamir, *Summing Up*, pp. 274–5.

Evolution of the US-Israeli 'Special Relationship' 127

according to Zalman Shuval, then Israeli ambassador to the USA, the meetings between Prime Minister Shamir and President Bush were 'usually tense'.[12] Shuval wrote that the two men 'fundamentally disagreed over how to handle the Arab-Israeli conflict and Israel's settlement policy'.[13]

The growing tensions were reflected during several incidents following the 1990–1 Gulf War. For instance, in March 1992, the US administration withdrew military aid over and above the annual $1.8 billion that had been approved by Congress. More significant was the leaking of documents to the American press by US officials, accusing Israel of passing US technology to South Africa and Ethiopia and selling Patriot parts and technology to China.[14] Indeed, Secretary of state Cheney raised this issue in a meeting with his Israeli counterpart, Moshe Arens, on 16 March 1992.[15]

Dismayed, Arens was convinced of a decision to 'put the screws on Israel'. 'Poison arrows', he concluded, were 'fired at Israel and directed first and foremost, against the Likud government to show the Israeli public that no improvement should be expected in US-Israeli relations as long as the Likud was in power'.[16] Arens's melodramatic language reflected deep concern within Israel's inner foreign policy decision-making circle that a continuing Israeli entrenchment foreign policy post the Cold War would stall relations with the USA in the short run and might threaten the alliance in the long run.

This was precisely why the Israeli foreign policy shift under Yitzhak Rabin, from entrenchment to engagement, significantly influenced US-Israeli relations. The memoirs of Ambassador Shuval, who had been appointed by a Likud government and, hence, could not be suspected of being overly biased towards Prime Minister Rabin, are pertinent in this context. Shuval recalls that Rabin was received by the president's administration, Congress, the organized Jewish community and the press as a 'hero' and a 'saviour'.[17]

Rabin's foreign policy style towards the USA differed from that of his predecessor. The fraught relationship with George H. Bush compelled Yitzhak Shamir to adopt a highly confrontational style towards Bush's administration via Congress and the Israel lobby – defined as 'a loose coalition of individuals and groups that seeks to influence American foreign policy in ways that will benefit Israel'.[18] This aggressive approach,

---

[12] Shuval, *Diplomat*, p. 191.   [13] Ibid.
[14] Arens, *Broken Covenant*, pp. 281–4; Shuval, *Diplomat*, pp. 286–7.
[15] Arens, *Broken Covenant*, p. 280.   [16] Arens, *Broken Covenant*, p. 281.
[17] Shuval, *Diplomat*, pp. 300, 311.
[18] John Mearsheimer and Stephen Walt, *The Israel Lobby and US Foreign Policy* (New York: Farrar, Straus, & Giroux, 2007), p. viii.

128   The Dividends of Engagement

which produced the loan guarantee crisis, contrasted starkly with the personal, centralized and direct foreign policy style of Rabin. 'Visits to the US', recalls his chief of staff, 'were integral to his routine. Every three or four months we aimed to travel to the US for what Rabin referred to as "maintenance visits", which were geared towards reinforcing the bilateral relationship and the personal networks Rabin had in the US since his ambassadorial days.'[19]

Indeed, Rabin sought to limit the Israel lobby's intermediation in Israel's relations with the USA. Instead, he used intergovernmental ties and his personal relationship with the president to bolster the special relationship with the USA. To assert his primacy over the Israel lobby, during his first visit to the USA as prime minister in August 1992, Rabin lambasted AIPAC for confronting the administration in the feud over the loan guarantees. Typically gruff, he informed his audience that it was his and his government's responsibility not AIPAC's, to negotiate with the administration.[20] This approach, which was consistent with his foreign policy style, had a clear political rationale. As we have seen, the Israel lobby had strongly supported the previous Likud government by being against negotiating with the PLO and territorial concessions, which was counter to the posture of engagement pursued by Rabin.

The personalized foreign policy style of Rabin and the shift from entrenchment to engagement had immediate effects on US-Israeli relations. Secretary of State Baker recalls how 'the unremitting friction' over the settlement issue was immediately removed.[21] Subsequently, President Clinton's memoirs reveal the extent of his special relationship with Rabin:

> In the two and half years we had worked together, Rabin and I had developed an unusually close relationship, marked by candour, trust, and an extraordinary understanding of each other's political positions and thought processes ... with every encounter, I came to respect and care for him more. By the time he was killed, I had come to love him as I had rarely loved another man.[22]

Moreover, in positioning itself at the forefront of the peace process, Israel became an indispensable partner in US efforts during the post-Cold War era, to reshape the Middle East in line with three principles: containing Iran and Iraq, achieving Arab-Israeli peace and securing a reasonably priced free flow of oil from the Gulf. The contrast with Israel's peripheral strategic position during the 1990–1 Gulf War could not have been greater. Israel's foreign policy shift under Rabin had normative

[19] Interview 1 Haber.   [20] *New York Times*, 22 August 1992.
[21] Baker, *The Politics of Diplomacy*, p. 557.
[22] Bill Clinton, *My Life* (New York: Knopf Publishing Group, 2004) p. 679.

implications for US-Israeli relations, too. Its limitations notwithstanding, engagement entailed a commitment to scaling down the Israeli occupation, which was critical for sustaining the notion that Israel and the USA had shared values of democracy and individual freedom.

The convergence of personalities, strategies and normative directions between the USA and Israel under Rabin and Peres, marked a high in the US-Israeli special relationship. On 5 October 1992, Congress authorized payment of $10 billion of the previously deferred loan guarantees, for a period of five years.[23] In addition, a US inspection team concluded that the accusations of sales of Patriot parts to China were unfounded. Concurrently, according to Samuel W. Lewis, who directed the State Department's Policy Planning in 1993 and 1994, during the Clinton administration, security cooperation between the USA and Israel strengthened. The USA agreed to sell F-15i fighter jets to Israel and authorized exports of Israeli space equipment and technology to the USA.[24]

The Changing Ties between Israel and the EEC/EU

Israeli foreign policy towards the EEC, established by the 1957 Treaty of Rome, stands in stark contrast to US-Israeli ties. The centuries of Jewish persecution in Europe, culminating in the Holocaust, left significant residues of mistrust and alienation. Relations with West Germany remained extremely sensitive in the aftermath of the Holocaust, while liaison with France experienced extremes. The close military and political alliance forged between Israel and France during the first twenty years of Israel's existence, collapsed in the wake of the 1967 Arab-Israeli War. The then French President, Charles de Gaulle, imposed a weapons embargo on Israel, holding it responsible for the outbreak of hostilities. Israel's foreign policy elite perceived the French volte face as 'betrayal'.[25]

This uneasy relationship between Israel and the EEC, evidenced in its ties with two of the founding member states, Germany and France, was

[23] Shimon Peres, 'Ministry of Foreign Affairs Brief', IMFA, May 1993, p. 2 (in Hebrew); Baker, *The Politics of Diplomacy*, p. 557.

[24] 'Two Years of a Labour Government Brief', p. 4; Shuval, *Diplomat*, p. 316; 'Letter from President Clinton to Prime Minister Rabin Authorizing the Export of Israeli Space Equipment and Technology to the US, 19 January 1994' *IMFA*, http://mfa.gov.il/MF A/ForeignPolicy/MFADocuments/Yearbook9/Pages/155%20Letter%20from%20Presi dent%20Clinton%20to%20Prime%20Ministe.aspx, accessed 21 September 2016.

Samuel W. Lewis, 'The United States and Israel: Evolution of an Unwritten Alliance', *Middle East Journal*, 53, 3, 1999: 371.

[25] Yochanan Meroz, 'The Role of Europe in the State's Foreign Policy System' in Moshe Yegar et al., *The Ministry of Foreign Affairs: The First 50 Years* (Jerusalem: Keter, 2002), p. 336 (in Hebrew).

130   The Dividends of Engagement

compounded by growing divergence towards the Arab-Israeli conflict. The EEC Summit of the Nine, held in Copenhagen on 6 November 1973, reflects this. Its closing statement laid down that UNSCR 242 required Israel to withdraw from all the territories it occupied in 1967, although the original phrasing of the resolution does not state this explicitly; it called for Israel to withdraw from 'territories' – rather than *the* territories – it occupied in 1967.

Thus, the November 1973 Copenhagen summit reflected a shift in EEC foreign policy towards supporting the Palestinian struggle for independence and ending the Israeli occupation. This shift was completed seven years later when the 1980 Venice Declaration included EEC endorsement of the PLO, support for full Palestinian self-determination and direct criticism of Israeli territorial occupation.[26] This contrasted with Israel's stance, which, during the 1980s, constituted a deepening of the occupation, refusal to recognize the PLO, and denial of Palestinian right to self-determination. This increased divergence was a source of serious friction in EEC-Israel relations.

The political friction between Israel and the EU was contrasted by their bilateral economic relations. Historically, Israeli foreign policymakers had always recognized the significance of Europe for Israel's economic prosperity. When the EEC was established, Israel's first Prime Minister, David Ben-Gurion predicted that it would become a central force in world affairs and strove to forge close ties with it. Consequently, Israel became the third country to establish a diplomatic mission with full ambassadorial status in Brussels, which was critical to its budding trade relations with the EEC. On 4 June 1964, Israel signed its first trade agreement with the EEC, which, on 29 June 1970, was upgraded to a Preferential Agreement, leading to a phased reduction of Israeli tariffs. In 1975, despite considerable diplomatic pressure from the Arab world, Israel was the first Mediterranean country to sign a major FTA with the EEC, opening Western European markets to Israeli industrial goods and agricultural produce.[27]

The waning of the Cold War and the demise of the USSR raised the stakes for Israeli foreign policy and its relations with the EEC. The

---

[26] Rory Miller, *Inglorious Disarray: Europe, Israel and the Palestinians since 1967* (London: Hurst, 2010), pp. 7–14, 34, 36, 52, 78–80, 83. 'Agreement between the European Economic Community and Israel—11 May 1975, IMFA; Venice Declaration, 13 June 1980', European Union official website, https://eeas.europa.eu/mepp/docs/veni ce_declaration_1980_en.pdf, accessed 20 December 2018.

[27] 'Agreement between the European Economic Community and Israel—11 May 1975', *IMFA*, http://mfa.gov.il/MFA/ForeignPolicy/MFADocuments/Yearbook2/Pages/82%2 0Agreement%20between%20the%20European%20Economic%20Communi.aspx, accessed 20 December 2018.

Maastricht Treaty, negotiated in 1991 and made effective in 1993, would transform the EEC into a twelve-member state EU comprising three pillars. The first was the single market, which included free movement of goods, services, people and money. The second, admittedly less developed, consisted of a common foreign policy and security framework. The third entailed deepening cooperation on justice and home affairs issues and was geared towards combating international crime.[28] Thus, as leading academic, Karen Smith, argues convincingly, the end of the Cold War raised 'internal and external expectations that the Community would take a greater international role'.[29]

However, this seems not to have been imprinted on Israeli foreign policymakers at that time. Yossef Ben-Aharon, director general of the Israeli prime minister's office, was quite clear about Israel's predicament at this crucial juncture. In a publicized press conference, he stated that 'we are very closely tied, economically, to the European Community and the European Market.' Yet, he added, Israel had 'a problem with the Community' because it adopted a 'very clear-cut position in support of total withdrawal [and] the PLO'.[30]

Prime Minister Shamir's attitude to the EEC was also affected by a black-and-white perception of EEC hostility to Israel's position.[31] He claimed, before EEC officials, that, in Europe, 'there is insufficient understanding of all the problems which Israel confronts – with respect to both its foreign relations and its treatment of internal problems.'[32] That the EEC's stance was not due to a misunderstanding of Israel's problems, but rather reflected increased endorsement of the PLO from segments of the international community and criticism of the Israeli occupation, was conveniently overlooked. Indeed, in his meetings with EEC officials, Shamir urged the EEC to revise the 1975 FTA while refusing to modify Likud's foreign policy position in the Arab-Israeli peace process. Shamir remained committed to granting the Palestinians

---

[28] Karen E. Smith, *European Union Foreign Policy in a Changing World*, 3rd ed. (Cambridge: Polity, 2014), pp. 28–43.

[29] Smith, *European Union Foreign Policy in a Changing World*, p. 27.

[30] 'Press Conference with Director General of the Prime Minister's Office Ben-Aharon', 23 May 1991, *Israel's Foreign Relations*, p. 523.

[31] 'Interview with Prime Minister Shamir in the Jerusalem Post', 15 June 1990', *IMFA* ht tps://mfa.gov.il/MFA/ForeignPolicy/MFADocuments/Yearbook8/Pages/145%20Intervi ew%20with%20Prime%20Minister%20Shamir%20in%20the%20Je.aspx, accessed 18 December 2018.

[32] Summary of meeting between Prime Minister Shamir and EEC Commissioner Matutes, 11 July 1991, *IMFA*, https://mfa.gov.il/MFA/ForeignPolicy/MFADocuments/Yearboo k8/Pages/221%20Summary%20of%20a%20meeting%20between%20Prime%20Minis ter%20Sh.aspx, accessed 18 December 2018.

132   The Dividends of Engagement

autonomy – rather than an independent state and securing peace between Israel and the Arab states, in exchange for peace not territory.[33]

Seeking revisions to the EEC-Israel 1975 FTA while rejecting the EEC's stance towards the budding Arab-Israeli peace process was a deeply flawed foreign policy approach. Israeli Ambassador to the EEC Avi Primor's recollection of this period help explain the fundamental problem in Israel's EEC foreign policy stance under Shamir:

> The deterioration of our image in European public opinion meant that the achievement of securing the 1975 free trade agreement was gradually lost. Although the Europeans never annulled the agreement, due to political reasons they refused to update it or adjust it to the changing nature of the EEC and the world economy. Consequently, by 1991, the value of the 1975 free trade agreement for Israel had substantially decreased.[34]

It was precisely for this reason that the shift from entrenchment to engagement under Rabin was so significant for Israeli-EEC/EU relations. It collapsed the political differences marking EEC-Israeli relations since the publication of the 1980 Venice Declaration. What seemed impossible under Likud – that Israeli and EU foreign policies towards the Arab-Israeli conflict would converge significantly – came to pass under Labour. The effect was transformative. As Ambassador Primor recalls: '[T]he atmosphere after the signing of the Oslo Agreements changed. We could now enter into negotiations over adjusting, updating, and even expanding the 1975 agreement.'[35]

Primor's comments capture the thrust of Israeli foreign policy tactics towards the EEC during the period of engagement. They hinged on convincing the EEC to reward Israel for the risks it took to achieve peace, by renegotiating the obsolete 1975 FTA.[36] Cunningly, as a quintessential US-centrist, Prime Minister Rabin would consign Europe to a secondary role in the peace process. In an address to the European Parliament in Strasburg, Prime Minister Rabin showed some degree of *hutzpa* in all but demanding that his European audience play a limited role in the peace process by assisting it economically, mitigating

---

[33] 'Summary of a Meeting between Prime Minister Shamir and EEC Ministerial Delegation', 7 March, 1991, *IMFA*, https://mfa.gov.il/MFA/ForeignPolicy/MFADocuments/Yearbook8/Pages/193%20Summary%20of%20a%20meeting%20between%20Prime%20Minister%20Sh.aspx, accessed 18 December 2018.

[34] Avi Primor, *Israel and the EU* in Yager et al., *The Ministry of Foreign Affairs: The First 50 Years*, p. 342 (in Hebrew).

[35] Primor, *Israel and the EU*, p. 342.

[36] 'Address by Prime Minister Rabin to the Hebrew University Conference on Europe-Middle East Relations', 8 November 1993, *IMFA*, http://mfa.gov.il/MFA/ForeignPolicy/MFADocuments/Yearbook9/Pages/128%20Address%20by%20Prime%20Minister%20Rabin%20at%20the%20Hebrew.aspx, accessed 20 December 2018.

opposition to it from the Arab world and working to end the Arab boycott on Israel.[37]

Israel's foreign policy towards the EEC bore fruit rapidly. In December 1994, just over a year after the signing of the DoP, the EU Foreign Ministers Council, held in Essen, declared that: 'Israel should enjoy a special status in its relations with the EU on the basis of reciprocity and common interests.'[38] On 31 October 1995, Israel and the EU concluded a Research and Development Agreement, which meant Israel became the first non-European country to be fully associated with the EU framework programmes.[39]

On 20 November 1995, Israel and the EU signed an Association Agreement (AA), which dramatically expanded the erstwhile 1975 FTA. Previously, political dialogue between Israel and the EEC had been occasional and, usually, within broad ministerial forums; the AA provided for annual meetings, at all working levels, to be devoted to discussing myriad issues defining EU-Israeli relations. Also, the AA reshaped EU-Israeli economic relations by expanding the free trade parameters. Among the key advantages for Israel were improved access to public and government procurement markets, removal of customs duties on imports and exports between the parties, updated rules of origin, regulation of flows of agricultural goods, phased freedom of movement in financial services and a call to abolish the restrictions on capital movements. Israeli companies, which were operating in a far more economically liberalized domestic environment than when the 1975 FTA was signed, were permitted to establish branches in European countries and vice versa.[40]

In spite of the EU's becoming the largest contributor of international efforts to support the Palestinian economy and Israel's foremost trading

---

[37] 'Address by Prime Minister Rabin to the Parliamentary Assembly of the Council of Europe', Strasbourg, 26 January 1994, *IMFA*, http://mfa.gov.il/MFA/ForeignPolicy/M FADocuments/Yearbook9/Pages/156%20Address%20by%20Prime%20Minister%20R abin%20to%20the%20Parliam.aspx, accessed 20 December 2018.

[38] 'European Council Meeting on 9 and 10 December in Essen Presidency Conclusions', *European Parliament*, www.europarl.europa.eu/summits/ess1_en.htm, accessed 6 October 2016.

[39] Sharon Pardo and Joel Peters, *Uneasy Neighbours: Israel and the European Union* (Lanham: Lexington Books, 2010), p.50.

[40] For the full text of the Association Agreement, see European Mediterranean Agreement Establishing an Association between the European Communities and their Member States, of the one Part, and the State of Israel, of the other part, Delegation of the European Union to Israel official website, http://eeas.europa.eu/delegations/israel/docu ments/eu_israel/asso_agree_en.pdf; 'Israel-EU Trade Agreement' to be signed, 20 November 1995, IMFA, www.mfa.gov.il/mfa/pressroom/1995/pages/israel-european%20union%20trade%20agreement%20to%20be%20signed.aspx, both links accessed 20 December 2018.

134   The Dividends of Engagement

partner, it failed to become a political player in the peace process. There were a number of factors that determined this outcome. These included the proclivity of Israeli foreign policy towards the USA, which wanted to retain its monopoly over the peace process, the belief on the Arab side that only the Americans could deliver Israel and the EU's internal competition and lack of cohesion. Thus, Israeli foreign policy towards the EU during its engagement phase endowed it with what its foreign policymakers perceived as the best of both worlds. European political influence in the Arab-Israeli conflict was kept at bay, while EU-Israeli economic cooperation and financial support for the peace process was maximized.

This was demonstrated by Israel's reluctant participation in the European Mediterranean Partnership or the Barcelona Process, launched by the EU in 1995. The Barcelona Process was an ambitious attempt by the EU to reposition itself centre stage in the Arab-Israeli peace process. The initiative was driven by the EU's prevailing perception that economic underdevelopment and social inequality were the main causes of instability in the Mediterranean basin. It believed that these issues should be tackled in a multilateral framework, based on economic incentives, promotion of democracy and cultural dialogue across the Mediterranean region.[41]

However, Israel was reluctant to shift the balance in its bilateral liaison with the Arab states via US mediation. Furthermore, the Mediterranean basin was still perceived by Israel as tainted by Arab-Israeli relations, while the EU continued to be seen as far less attractive than the USA as leader of the peace process. Consequently, the focus of Israeli activity on economic cooperation with its neighbours was maintained in the MENA Economic Summits held in Rabat (1994) and Amman (1995). These summits, which were linked more closely to a US-led bilateral Arab-Israeli peace process, cast a shadow over Europe's attempt to integrate the Mediterranean basin in its leadership.[42] As eminent historian, Rory Miller, put it, the EU remained a payer but not a player.

Walking through the Cracks of the Great Wall of China

Israeli foreign policy towards the People's Republic of China (PRC) evolved differently from that of its ties with Western powers.[43] In 1949,

---

[41] Constanza Musu, *European Union Policy towards the Arab-Israeli Peace Process* (Basingstoke: Palgrave-Macmillan, 2010), p. 57.

[42] Pardo and Peters, *Uneasy Neighbours*, pp. 33–7.

[43] My background account draws closely on the following works: P.R. Kumaraswamy, *Israel's China Odyssey* (New Delhi: Institute for Defence Studies and Analysis, 1994); E. Zev Sufott, *A China Diary: Towards the Establishment of China-Israel Diplomatic*

Israel adopted a foreign policy of non-identification and, on 9 January 1950, was the seventh non-Western state and the first Middle Eastern country to recognize the PRC. However, amid the eruption of conflict between the PRC and the USA in the Korean War (1950–3), Israel abandoned its non-identification policy. Cautious of antagonizing the USA, Israel hesitated to establish full diplomatic relations with the PRC. Consequently, Israel-China liaisons during the first years of statehood were sporadic.

The prospects of establishing full diplomatic relations were diminished greatly by the April 1955 conference of non-aligned states, which was convened in Bandung, Indonesia. Following strong pressure from the Arab states, Israel was excluded from the conference, during which the PRC was recognized by the Arab League. A year later, during the 1956 Suez Crisis, which involved a coordinated Israeli-British-French attack on Egypt, the Chinese leadership and media described Israel as an instrument of Western imperialism. From that moment, until the late 1970s, the PRC supported the Arab states in their conflict with Israel, becoming, in 1965, the first non-Arab country to recognize the PLO officially and to provide the organization with political and military support. Relations with Israel were all but severed. The PRC's stance towards the Arab-Israeli conflict should be viewed in light of the deterioration of Soviet-Chinese relations during the early 1960s. During this period, the PRC challenged the notion of 'peaceful coexistence' with the capitalist world, advocated by the USSR. Instead, it promoted an antagonistic stance towards the capitalist West. Its position towards Israel was integral to its efforts to raise its international standing in the anti-West camp.

However, China's foreign policy stance mollified following its admission to the UN on 25 October 1971, the ensuing thaw in US-Chinese relations, the death of Mao Ze Dong and the end of the Cultural Revolution. Under Mao's successor, Deng Xiaoping, the PRC moderated its foreign policy, aimed at economic development and modernization reforms in agriculture, science and technology, national defence and industry. The change in China's foreign policy coincided with the Israeli-Egyptian peace agreement, prompting a limited shift in Chinese-Israeli relations. From 1979, the two countries engaged in covert military trade, consisting of Israeli upgrading of Soviet supplied and designed, near

---

Relations (London: Frank Cass, 1997); Moshe Yegar, *The Long Journey to Asia: A Chapter in the Diplomatic History of Israel* (Haifa: Haifa University Press, 2004), pp. 237–72 (in Hebrew); Aron Shai, *China and Israel: Equivocal Ties: Jews, Chinese, Jerusalem, Beijing* (Tel Aviv: Miskal, 2016), pp. 39–65, 88–91, 106–10 (in Hebrew); Jonathan Goldstein and Yitzhak Shichor, *China and Israel: From Discord to Concord* (Jerusalem: Magnes, 2016).

136 The Dividends of Engagement

obsolete weapons and systems, seized during the 1973 Arab-Israeli war. This military assistance to China, which in 1979 was engaged in a bloody and unsuccessful conflict with Vietnam, was significant. An Israeli tycoon, Shaul Eisenberg, presided over this covert trade via his global company, United Development Incorporated, which had a network of businesses in China. Exploiting his ties to Israeli security policymakers, Eisenberg charged a commission for his services as the middleman between Israeli defence companies and the Chinese. In the absence of reliable data, it is difficult to estimate the volume of trade during this period; valuations vary from values of around $27 million to $3.5 billion per annum.[44]

Against this backdrop, the waning of the Cold War proved particularly significant for Israeli foreign policy towards the PRC. A few years earlier, in 19 December 1984, the UK and PRC governments concluded an agreement on the restoration of Hong Kong to China by 1 July 1997.[45] The agreement was significant in that it laid the legal foundations for establishing official Israeli representation in China after the recovery of Hong Kong. Clause XI of the agreement states:

Foreign consular and other official or semi-official missions may be established in the Hong Kong Special Administrative Region with the approval of the Central People's Government. Consular and other official missions established in Hong Kong by states which have established formal diplomatic relations with the People's Republic of China, may be maintained. According to the circumstances of each case, consular and other official missions of states having no formal diplomatic relations with the People's Republic of China may either be maintained or changed to semi-official missions.[46]

This resulted in Mossad veteran, Reuven Merhav, being installed by Prime Minister Yitzhak Shamir in Israel's foreign affairs ministry. The epitome of an entrepreneurial civil servant, in 1985, Merhav was appointed Israeli general consul in Hong-Kong. His previous experience was in unconventional diplomacy in Iran, Kenya, Ethiopia and Arab countries. For ten months during 1983, he had manned an Israeli liaison office in Beirut, during which time he reported directly to Prime Minister Shamir and Defence Minister Arens. This hugely competent and discreet

---

[44] See, respectively, Yitzhak Shichor, 'Israel Military Transfers to China and Taiwan, *Survival*, 40, 1, 1998: 68–91; Yegar, *The Long Journey to Asia*, p. 266.

[45] 'Joint Declaration of the Government of the United Kingdom of Great Britain and Northern Ireland and the Government of the People's Republic of China on the Question of Hong Kong', UK Legislation official website, www.legislation.gov.hk/blis_pdf.nsf/6799165D2FEE3FA94825755E0033E532/84A057ECA380F51D482575E F00291C2F/$FILE/CAP_2301_e_b5.pdf, accessed 14 October 2016.

[46] Joint Declaration, p. 7.

individual, who had the trust of both Arens and Shamir, was given the task of setting up a base in Hong Kong from which Israel could seek to establish formal diplomatic relations with the PRC. Accountable directly to Shamir and Arens – rather than the MFA bureaucracy that opposed his appointment – Merhav led a small and intimate group, which had a virtual 'free hand' to formulate Israeli foreign policy towards the PRC.[47]

The approach adopted by Israel, which was chronicled carefully by Merhav, was linked inextricably to the waning of the Cold War.[48] In December 1985, reflecting the mellowing international context, the then Chinese Foreign Minister, Wu Xueqian, made an important declaration during an official visit to Cairo. He stated that: 'There needs to be a distinction between the Israeli authorities and the Israeli people … Israeli experts and academics are allowed to visit China as individuals to attend conferences organized by international organizations and scholarly associations.'[49] This stark departure from previous Chinese policy, which excluded any contact with Israelis, created an opportunity to forge scientific ties. During an academic visit to China in April 1986, Yehoshua Yortner, Vice President of the National Israel Academy of Sciences, obtained authorization for Israeli scientists to participate in conferences held in China.

These promising academic links proved invaluable. Merhav debriefed the tens of Israeli scientists who visited China, which provided him with intelligence about the PRC's scientific needs. The information was used to further bilateral relations with Israel. This was a core component of the tactic of bypassing the Chinese foreign ministry, which, Merhav concluded, remained biased after years of advocating support for Arab states in their conflict with Israel. Therefore, in his efforts to forge initial ties, Merhav focused on the ministerial committee for technology, which, he determined, had more political clout than the MFA with the PRC's bureaucratic hierarchy.[50]

Concurrently, informal diplomatic exchanges continued. In September 1987, Israeli Foreign Minister Shimon Peres met his Chinese counterpart on the neutral territory of a UN General Assembly session. This encounter, the first of its kind at this high level, set a precedent for subsequent annual meetings. Moreover, in April 1987, Merhav achieved

---

[47] Interview Reuven Merhav, 22 August 2016, Jerusalem.
[48] My account of evolving Israel-China relations during the late 1980s draws heavily on Reuven Merhav, 'The Dream of the Red Chambers – from the Scented Port to the Forbidden City/from Hong-Kong to Beijing' in *The Ministry of Foreign Affairs: The First 50 Years*.
[49] Quoted in Merhav, 'The Dream of the Red Chambers', p. 570.
[50] Interview Merhav.

138   The Dividends of Engagement

a first covert meeting with a Chinese official, in the Lee Gardens Hotel in Hong Kong. Merhav used the opportunity to make a strong case for Israel-PRC cooperation. He emphasized the historical lack of animosity between Jews and Chinese; the potential contribution to international stability of relations between Israel and the PRC, a permanent member of the UNSC; and the common interest of the PRC and Israel in agricultural, scientific and technological cooperation.

The Israeli consulate followed up by the provision of a list of some 200 relevant Chinese officials seeking to expand unofficial economic ties, who were sent print and audio-visual material on Israel. On the Consulate's recommendation, in 1988, the Israeli MFA purchased Copeco – a dormant company registered in Hong Kong – which, henceforth, was coordinated by the MFA and the Ministries of Agriculture, Finance, Trade and Industry. Its aim was to represent civilian Israeli companies seeking to do business in China, informally and indirectly.[51]

The three foreign policy tools Israel employed towards the PRC – covert diplomacy, exchange of scientific knowledge and indirect economic relations – resulted in the first secret, but official visit by Merhav to mainland China in 1988. Merhav achieved a formal agreement between the PRC and Israel to establish non-governmental offices. Israel would set up the Beijing Liaison Office of the Israel Academy of Sciences and Humanities while China would open the China International Tourist Service in Tel Aviv.

The idea behind the establishment of the Beijing Liaison Office was relayed by the MFA to its designated head, water-use efficiency expert, Professor Yoseph Shalhevet. He was told that: 'The academic centre, which constituted the first institutionalized Israeli presence in China, was in fact an embassy in the making.'[52] A full-time diplomat, Yoel Gilat, worked alongside Shalhevet and Copeco was integrated with the Liaison Office to form an economic branch. Meanwhile, Merhav, who had been recalled to Israel to follow up on the progress of bilateral relations with China from Jerusalem, was promoted to director of the MFA.[53]

The Israeli Liaison Office, which was officially opened on 15 June 1990, encountered formidable political obstacles from the outset. Its expanding activities to disseminate Israeli agricultural technology in China, coordinate scientific exchanges and cooperate on renewable energy generated limited coverage in the official Chinese press. The

---

[51] Merhav, 'The Dream of the Red Chambers', p. 571; Interview Merhav.
[52] Joseph Shalhevet, *China and Israel: Science in the Service of Diplomacy* (Kiryat Ono: Smirim, 2009), p. 14 (in Hebrew).
[53] Merhav, 'The Dream of the Red Chambers', pp. 571–6; Shalhevet, *China and Israel*, pp. 12–13.

Chinese authorities urged foreign embassies not to engage with Israeli representatives. The amount of business created by Copeco under its new director, Amos Yoden, was modest. Meetings proved difficult to arrange since, in several quarters, Israel was still perceived as a hostile state. Indeed, PRC officials made it clear to the Israeli delegation that China's relationship with Israel would remain at the people-to-people not the state level. With some frustration, Shalhevet noted that the Chinese 'were keen to receive Israeli expertise and technologies at the lowest political costs', which meant the Chinese MFA remained out of bounds.[54] In a sobering note to the Israeli MFA, Shalhevet pinpointed the cause of the political confines in which he was operating: 'A significant change in the diplomatic relationship between the PRC and Israel', he concluded, 'could only arrive were there a salient shift in Israeli-Palestinian relations.'[55]

Shalhevet was not alone in this assessment. In early March 1991, he was joined in Beijing by Zev Sufott, who was appointed special advisor to the academic liaison office. This somewhat innocuous title concealed Suffot's actual role; as a seasoned diplomat, he was sent to Beijing as an ambassador in the making.

Suffot, who was ideally positioned to assess the evolving ties between Israel and the PRC, chronicled events in his *China Diary*.[56] Shortly after his arrival, an important precedent was set by the first official – albeit covert – meeting between the PRC and Israeli officials in Beijing. The Israeli side was led by Special Advisor Sufott and Merhav. The Chinese delegation was headed by Vice Foreign Minister, Yang Fuchang. The following month, between 22 and 26 April, a reciprocal meeting was held in Israel. These meetings provided a good opportunity for the Israelis to assess the prospects of advancing existing contacts, which the Chinese viewed 'favourably.' However, PRC officials emphasized that 'their further development would be a process, extending over a period of time, the hope being that favourable developments in the Middle East and in Arab-Israeli relations would make possible the establishment of diplomatic relations'.[57] The PRC delegates stressed, also, that 'the Palestine question and the Israeli-Arab dispute are at the heart of the Middle East problem and the main cause for regional instability'. Its solution, they emphasized, should be addressed through 'direct Israeli-PLO negotiations'.[58]

At the same time, Chinese perceptions were by no means fixed. The Chinese were critical of the PLO for supporting Iraq during the 1990–1

---

[54] Shalhevet, *China and Israel*, pp. 31, 36, 128, 138, 172, 187–8, 197–8.   [55] Ibid, p. 193.
[56] Zev E. Sufott, *A China Diary: Towards the Establishment of China-Israel Diplomatic Relations* (London: Frank Cass, 1997).
[57] Sufott, *A China Diary*, p. 19.   [58] Ibid, pp. 39, 42.

140   The Dividends of Engagement

Gulf War, but commended Israel for its forbearance in the wake of the Iraqi Scud attacks. This restraint was considered by the Chinese as having prevented the war from descending into a 'chaos' that would have harmed China's material interests in the Middle East. Also, the intra-Arab conflict entailed by the Gulf War challenged the erstwhile Chinese view that the Arab-Israeli conflict was the main source of instability in the Middle East.[59]

Thus, Israel's forbearance stance was an important element in creating the opportunity for normalization between Israel and China following the 1990–1 Gulf War. Equally significant was the international context produced by the shuttle diplomacy being conducted by US Secretary of State Baker, which led to the Madrid peace conference. The small Israeli decision-making circle engaging with China sought to link Israel's participation in the US-led peace initiative with the normalizing of relations with the PRC. China's goal, Suffot observed presciently, 'was to participate and play a role in the peace conference process and framework – not to be excluded by the lack of relations with a major party to the dispute'.[60] He believed that China's 'delayed participation could only prove negative for her international standing, including her position in the Middle East and the Arab World'.[61]

Israel's approach towards the PRC built on Suffot's insights. It was shrewd and can be summarized as no (Chinese) participation in the peace process without normalization of relations with Israel. The yields were swift and significant. In early October 1991, Chinese officials were discussing normalization with Israel being achieved within one to three years. However, following assurances in mid-October that the Madrid peace conference would go ahead, the Chinese began work on imminent normalization of relations. As a result, meetings between Chinese and Israeli officials were upgraded to government-to-government level, culminating in Vice Foreign Minister Yang's official visit to Israel, where he extended an official invitation to establish formal relations.[62] The decision to expedite normalization, according to Sufott, was taken to facilitate participation of China in the multilateral working group sessions resulting from the Madrid conference, which were due to start on 28 January 1992, in Moscow.[63]

The Israeli strategy of linking the Arab-Israeli peace process to relations with the PRC was reinforced by the launch of the Oslo process. Merhav, who had maintained close ties with his Chinese colleagues, believed that it

---

[59] Interview Merhav.   [60] Sufott, *A China Diary*, p. 93.
[61] Sufott, *A China Diary*, p. 117.   [62] Sufott, *A China Diary*, pp. 102–5, 109–12, 114–25.
[63] Ibid, p. 125.

Forging the Israel-India Partnership

was a key 'enabling factor'; it allowed Israel to fend off 'any criticism in the Chinese MFA by pointing to the process with the Palestinians, the peace accord with Jordan, and Egypt'.[64] Moshe Yegar, head of the Asia, Africa, Oceania section of the Israeli MFA, concurred. He recounts how relations expanded rapidly in tandem with the Oslo process. Public diplomatic exchanges at the highest levels became routine and a series of bilateral agreements, including a most favoured nation trade agreement, were signed. Trade between the two states increased between 1991 and 1997, from $22.8 million to $71.3 million annually. Scientific cooperation in agriculture and technological ventures thrived and involved thousands of participants.[65]

At the same time, some constraints to trade continued. They included growing US concern that Israeli military exports to China would result in the transfer of American technology to the PRC. Consequently, as leading Sinologist Ytizhak Shichor explains, the USA had imposed restrictions on Israeli military exports to the PRC, although these were loosened during the early 1990s.[66] Another limitation was the unsuccessful Israeli attempts to reduce Chinese arms sales to Arab countries, an issue that was raised directly by Prime Minister Rabin during Foreign Minister Qian Qichen's visit to Israel on 17 September 1992. A third constraint was China's demand that Israel should not sell weapons to Taiwan, to which the Israelis acquiesced.[67]

These conditions notwithstanding, Israel's strategy of linking the Arab-Israeli peace process to PRC-Israel bilateral relations was resoundingly successful in that it redefined the remit of Israeli diplomacy. As the Cold War drew to a close, Israel had, for the first time, full diplomatic ties with all five permanent members of the UNSC. Moreover, the limited concessions made by Israel during the Madrid peace conference and the Oslo peace process created further opportunities in Asia.

Forging the Israel-India Partnership

One of these opportunities was to forge official diplomatic ties with India, which had rejected several attempts to establish full diplomatic relations since it recognized Israel on 16 September 1950.[68] Having freed India

---

[64] Interview Merhav.   [65] Yegar, *The Long Journey to Asia*, pp. 280–1.
[66] Shichor, 'Israel Military Transfers to China and Taiwan', p. 74.
[67] 'Summary of a Meeting between Prime Minister Rabin and Foreign Minister Qian Qichen of China', 17 September 1992, *IMFA*, http://mfa.gov.il/MFA/ForeignPolicy/M FADocuments/Yearbook9/Pages/15%20Summary%20of%20a%20meeting%20betwee n%20Prime%20Minister%20Rab.aspx, accessed 18 December 2018.
[68] My background account of Israeli-India relations during the Cold War is based on Yegar, *The Long Journey to Asia*, pp. 140–63; P.R. Kumaraswamy, *India's Israel Policy* (New York: Columbia University Press, 2010).

142   The Dividends of Engagement

from the yoke of British imperialism, India's founding fathers, Mahatma Gandhi and Jawaharlal Nehru and their Indian Congress Party, opposed political relations with Israel. From their standpoint, especially following the 1956 Suez Crisis, Israel was identified with European imperialism and perceived as a foreign implant in the Middle East.

Domestic political considerations also impeded diplomatic ties. Successive Indian governments were concerned that formal relations with Israel would prompt a harsh reaction from the sizeable Muslim minority in India. These worries were exacerbated by India's relations with Pakistan, which defined itself as an Islamic republic that had been in conflict with India since partition. The prospect of Pakistan manipulating diplomatic ties between India and Israel, to agitate Indian Muslims and forge an anti-Indian international Islamic block, were a formidable obstacle to Israeli-Indian rapprochement.

These political considerations were accompanied by economic concerns. A growing number of the Indian nationals working in the Arab world since the 1973 oil boom, were sending home valuable foreign exchange remittances, which had become an important source of capital for the Indian economy. Senior Indian officials were concerned that relations with Israel might prompt repatriation.[69] In addition, India's modernization and trade depended on imported Arab oil and free navigation through the Suez Canal. Upgrading relations with Israel posed a risk to these material interests in the Arab world. Finally, establishing diplomatic ties with Israel could jeopardize India's leading role in the non-aligned movement, which hinged on anti-colonialist African-Asian solidarity and was personified by bonhomie between Nasser and Nehru.

India's foreign policy behaviour towards Israel throughout the Cold War reflected these considerations. It wholly supported the Arab states during the main Arab-Israeli wars; it backed the oil embargo imposed by OPEC in the wake of the 1973 Arab-Israeli war; and it voted in favour of UN General Assembly Resolution 3379, which 'determined that Zionism is a form of racism and racial discrimination'.[70] Consistently, India conditioned normalization on Israeli withdrawal to the pre-1967 borders and endorsed the right to Palestinian self-determination.[71]

Significantly, throughout the Cold War, Israeli representation in India was confined to a small, remote and heavily restricted consulate in

---

[69] J.N. Dixit, *My South Block Years: Memoirs of a Foreign Secretary* (New Delhi: UBS Publishers, 1996), p. 310.
[70] 'Elimination of All Forms of Racial Discrimination', UN official website, https://documents-dds-ny.un.org/doc/RESOLUTION/GEN/NR0/000/92/IMG/NR000092.pdf?OpenElement, accessed 2 November 2016.
[71] Kumaraswamy, *India's Israel Policy*, p. 125.

Bombay, 1,200 km from New Delhi, the capital city and centre of political activity. Israeli efforts to reverse India's foreign policy stance via personal diplomacy, and supplying India with weapons during its major conflicts with China (1962) and Pakistan (1965, 1971), proved futile. For almost four decades, non-relations remained the hallmark of India's foreign policy towards Israel.

The shift to formal diplomatic ties between Israel and India, in some respects, resembled the pattern of Israel-China relations.[72] The rise of India's Prime Minister Rajiv Gandhi, following the assassination of his mother, Indira Gandhi, in 1984, was a watershed moment. Rajiv Gandhi, like Deng Xiaoping, led a dramatic shift by moving away from the socialist tradition instilled by his Congress Party, towards modernization, liberalization and closer ties with the West. Consequently, his government's foreign policy position was less informed by anti-Western stances and the legacy of colonialism. This significant change in India's domestic politics, combined with the waning of the Cold War, prompted Israeli foreign policymakers to renew their efforts to establish formal ties with India.

Giora Bechar, Israel's first consul general in Bombay since 1982, who had arrived in August 1989, was entrusted with this job. The brief he received from General Director Merhav was laconic. He was to present 'the Israeli positions to Indian policy-makers' and establish 'a framework for routine diplomatic contacts'.[73] However, as Bechar's memoirs reveal, the close circle surrounding Israeli Prime Minister Shamir was focused on the more strategic aim of establishing formal diplomatic ties.[74]

The young diplomat was dealt a weak hand. Entrenchment, the foreign policy stance pursued by the Shamir-led government in the Middle East, exacerbated the deeply seated historical and political impediments to Indian-Israeli rapprochement. Entrenchment was certain to deepen the Israeli occupation, expand Israeli settlements and prolong the Palestinian Intifada, which resonated with the non-violent anti-colonialist struggle, championed by Gandhi, against the British. Thus, despite feverish efforts by Bechar to instigate normalization, relations remained 'completely frozen' well into 1991.[75]

Nonetheless, the foreign policy environment of the consul and his small team was changing. In the run-up to the 1990–1 Gulf War, the Israeli

---

[72] This background information is drawn from Kumaraswamy, *India's Israel Policy*, pp. 224–9.

[73] Giora Bachar, *India – A Diplomatic Diary: The Story of Forging Diplomatic Relations between India and Israel 1989–1992 From a Personal Perspective* (Azur: Reuveni Books, 2013), p. 15 (in Hebrew).

[74] Bachar, *India – A Diplomatic Diary*, p. 15.

[75] Bachar, *India – A Diplomatic Diary*, pp. 16–36, 41; Kumaraswamy, *India's Israel Policy*, p. 233.

144   The Dividends of Engagement

Consulate issued entry visas for leading Indian journalists keen to cover the Gulf War from Israel. This was a strategic move: reports of Israeli forbearance and images of gasmasked Israelis prompted an attitudinal change. As Bechar notes in his diary: '[G]eneral public opinion, parts of the intelligentsia, the media, and even state bureaucrats, were more sympathetic towards us.'[76]

The mindset changes observed by Bechar were significant in the wake of the international changes provoked by the Gulf War and the onset of peace diplomacy by the USA. Hitherto, as a possessor of a common socialist economic outlook with the USSR, India had pursued an anti-American foreign policy during long periods of the Cold War. However, the demise of the USSR, which was a key ally of India and its chief weapons supplier, coupled with reforms to liberalize the economy, prompted the Indian government to seek closer ties with the USA. American support was critical for successful implementation of the economic liberalization reforms promoted by the Indian government in the immediate aftermath of the Cold War.

A report from Bechar to the MFA in Jerusalem reveals that the intimate circle of Israeli foreign policymakers working on normalizing relations with India, were well aware of the opportunity created by these dramatic changes.[77] Indeed, Israel sought to exploit the imminent Madrid peace conference to challenge previous Indian positions. 'Why', the Israelis asked their counterparts in Delhi, 'was India still boycotting Israel when the Arab states are willing to meet?'[78] Furthermore, in the absence of direct diplomatic ties, the Israelis piggybacked on the US Embassy in Delhi to relay diplomatic proposals. Bill Clark, US Ambassador to India, clarified to his Indian counterparts that any Indian participation in the Arab-Israeli peace process would be conditioned on normalization with Israel.[79]

Moshe Yegar, head of the Asia-African-Oceania section of the Israeli MFA, had an excellent vantage point from which to observe the subsequent unfolding of events. On 2 July 1991, he was dispatched from Jerusalem on what was portrayed as a purely humanitarian diplomatic mission: releasing an Israeli backpacker kidnapped by Jammu and the Kashmir Liberation Front. However, on Merhav's instruction, he also used the visit to hold informal talks in Delhi on Israeli-Indian relations.[80]

---

[76] Bachar, *India – A Diplomatic Diary*, pp. 47, 49–50, 54, 81, 83.
[77] Bachar, *India – A Diplomatic Diary*, p. 110; Yegar, *The Long Journey to Asia*, p. 163.
[78] Bachar, *India – A Diplomatic Diary*, pp. 84, 92.
[79] Bachar, *India – A Diplomatic Diary*, pp. 88–9, 94; Yegar, *The Long Journey to Asia*, p. 163.
[80] Interview Merhav.

Forging the Israel-India Partnership 145

His recollections from this period reveal that Israeli-India normalization was not just connected to the budding peace process. It was also tightly linked to Indian interest in strengthening ties with the USA to improve India's feeble economy and, specifically, to secure a $2–$5 billion loan from the International Monetary Fund (IMF) and the World Bank. In this context, the Israelis mounted a significant campaign in the USA, via the Israel lobby. The goal was to relay to the Indian government, via US officials, that the Americans would not support India's request for economic assistance unless it changed its policy towards Israel. Bill Clark, US Ambassador to India, who coordinated with Bechar, conveyed the same stern message to his Indian counterparts.[81]

The significance of this concerted foreign policy activity became evident in India's timing of its official announcement of official diplomatic ties with Israel, on 29 January 1992. The proclamation came a day after the opening in Moscow of multilateral talks following the Madrid conference from which India was excluded because it lacked diplomatic relations with Israel. In addition, 29 January 1992, was the day before a state visit to the USA by the Indian prime minister. Meanwhile, China announced its intention to normalize relations with Israel on 24 January 1992.

In his declaration of diplomatic relations, Prime Minister Rao of India sought to resolve these outstanding issues. Indeed, India's softened stance towards Israel resulted from a 'fundamental re-examination' of its non-relations position. Indian Foreign Secretary Dixit, who was close to Rao, presided over the process. Dixit's memoirs confirm that, after lengthy deliberations, Prime Minister Rao and the majority of his cabinet accepted that relations with Israel should be resumed. It was considered that, in the aftermath of the Cold War, a position of non-relations was more costly than beneficial.[82]

Nevertheless, the general normalization trajectory following the establishment of diplomatic relations was linked closely to the shift in Israeli foreign policy from entrenchment to engagement. While Israel maintained its entrenchment approach to the Arab world, India was willing to make only small steps towards normalization. For instance, Prime Minister Rao did not respond to an invitation from Yitzhak Shamir to visit Israel. Diplomatic contacts were restricted to the bureaucratic level. Moreover, according to Foreign Secretary Dixit, rapprochement with Israel was linked to Israel-PLO ties. India, Dixit claims in his memoirs,

---

[81] Yegar, *The Long Journey to Asia*, pp. 165–7; Bachar, *India-A Diplomatic Diary*, pp. 88–9.
[82] 'Historical Overview', Embassy of Israel in India, http://embassies.gov.il/delhi/AboutT heEmbassy/India-Israel-Relations/Pages/default.aspx, accessed 7 November, 2016; Bachar, *India – A Diplomatic Diary*, p. 112; Dixit, *My South Block Years*, pp. 310–15.

146   The Dividends of Engagement

was made aware of informal Israeli-PLO talks as early as 1991. This timing is highly unlikely given that the Shamir government was in power in that period. However, the broader point conveyed by Dixit, namely, that India's decision to normalize and improve relations was linked closely to and facilitated by the PLO's own 'normalization' with Israel, is significant.[83]

It might explain why, as unconfirmed reports of Israeli-PLO relations were emerging, in May 1993 Shimon Peres was the first Israeli foreign minister to be granted an official visit to India. Accompanying Peres was a delegation including chief executives from Israel's defence industry, such as Israeli Aerospace Industries Ltd, Elbit Systems Ltd and Elul Technologies Ltd. During this visit, Peres signed an economic memorandum of understanding and a delegation of Israeli businessmen participated in a symposium with their Indian counterparts.[84]

Also in May 1993, Indian Defence Minister Sharad Pawar visited Israel. These high-profile diplomatic exchanges effectively laid the foundations for Israeli-India security and military trade cooperation. India's Foreign Secretary Dixit recollects being attracted by Israeli experience in counterterrorism and proven ability in improving Soviet origin weapons systems that could be utilized by India.[85] In this context, the Israeli security network was extremely well placed to play a paramount role in enabling Israeli foreign policymakers to forge rapid and closer ties with India. To this end, a visit to India by Deputy Foreign Minister Yossi Beilin, focused on the potential sale of Israeli unmanned aerial vehicles to India. In the same year, a large delegation comprising the chiefs of Israel's defence industries and ministry of defence, general director of the Defence Ministry, David Ivri, also visited India to increase military ties.[86]

The foundations for security cooperation were coupled with intensive activity to develop non-military economic ties. Mutual visits by Israeli and Indian officials kickstarted agricultural, medical and scientific cooperation, tourism and the start of direct flights between India and Israel. By 1993, these meetings were upgraded to ministerial level and resulted in the signing of several agreements on cooperation in agriculture (1993) and telecommunications (1994), economic and commercial cooperation (1996) and promotion and protection of investments

---

[83] Dixit, *My South Block Years*, p. 309.
[84] 'Summary of a Visit to India by Foreign Minister Peres', 18 May 1993, *IMFA*, http://mfa.gov
.il/MFA/ForeignPolicy/MFADocuments/Yearbook9/Pages/79%20Summary%20of%20a%
20Visit%20to%20India%20by%20Foreign%20Minister.aspx, accessed 20 December 2018.
[85] Dixit, *My South Block Years*, p. 310.   [86] Yegar, *The Long Journey to Asia*, pp. 172–3.

(1996).[87] The economic yields were significant, with bilateral trade – excluding defence – rising steadily from \$200 million in 1992 to \$500 million in 1995.[88]

The Dividends from Engagement

It is impossible to say whether, in the absence of the Madrid conference and ensuing Oslo process, Israel would have established diplomatic ties with India and China and significantly upgraded its relations with the EU and USA. However, it is obvious that the gradual, but clear transition from entrenchment to engagement had a transforming effect on Israeli foreign policy. By the end of the Rabin–Peres government, Israeli foreign policy had a truly global remit. Also, Israel had established full diplomatic relations with all five members of the Security Council, the foundations for trade relations with emerging powers had been laid and the economic and diplomatic ties with the USA and EU had greatly expanded. This impressive diplomatic record refutes the claims made by the Israeli right that the shift to engagement – with the Oslo process at its centre – was a disaster for Israel. Far from it: the dividends from engagement secured Israel's relations with established powers and created the global remit Israeli foreign policymakers had craved since the establishment of the State of Israel. These substantial rewards reflected the prevailing view within the international community that engagement was pursued in good faith and was on course for success. This optimistic assumption was to be put to the test with the rise to power of a young and as yet inexperienced Israeli prime minister: Binyamin Netanyahu.

---

[87] Nicolas Blarel, *The Evolution of India's Israel Policy: Continuity, Change, and Compromise since 1922* (Oxford: Oxford University Press, 2015), pp. 262, 267, 331; 'Overview of India-Israel Bilateral Trade and Economic Relations', Israeli Ministry of Economy and Industry, http://itrade.gov.il/india/israel-india/, accessed 8 November 2016.

[88] Yegar, *The Long Journey to Asia*, p. 177.

7 Unpicking the Oslo Accords

Binyamin Netanyahu and his Coalition Government

On assuming power at the age of forty-seven, Binyamin Netanyahu was the first prime minister of Israel born after the state had been established. When Netanyahu was fourteen, his family emigrated to the USA, where his father, Ben-Zion Netanyahu, a hardline revisionist Zionist, historian and onetime political secretary to Ze'ev Jabotinski, secured an academic post. On achieving the age of eighteen, Netanyahu returned to Israel and spent five years serving in the IDF as a captain in the elite commando unit, Sayeret Matkal.

Prior to his election to the highest position in the land, he had graduated from the Massachusetts Institute of Technology (MIT) and embarked on a short-lived and not particularly successful business marketing career. He subsequently established and directed an antiterrorism institute in the USA, which attracted the attention of the then Israeli ambassador to Washington and future foreign minister, Moshe Arens. In 1982, Arens appointed Netanyahu Deputy Head of the Mission in Washington, which launched Netanyahu's public life. Fluent in English and a powerful speaker, Netanyahu soon became a familiar face on US television and was an effective advocate of the case for Israel. In 1984, he was appointed Israel's permanent representative at the UN in New York, which instilled in his political thinking the conviction that conveying powerful messages in public was 'an indispensable element in the waging of political and military struggles'.[1] On his return to Israel in 1988, Netanyahu was elected to the Knesset and soon was appointed deputy foreign minister.[2]

---

[1] Binyamin Netanyahu, *A Place among the Nations* (London: Bantam, 1993), p. 379.
[2] For biographical notes on Netanyahu, see official Knesset website, www.knesset.gov.il/mk/heb/mk.asp?mk_individual_id_t=90, accessed 2 January 2019; Michael Keren, 'Elections 1996: The Candidates and the "New Politics"' in Elazar and Sandler, *Israel at the Polls 1996*, pp. 263, 265.

Following the 1992 defeat of Likud by Labour, in March 1993 Netanyahu was elected chairman of Likud. The contest with his rival, David Levy, had been bitter and acrimonious and resulted, in autumn 1995, in Levy leaving Likud to form his own party, Gesher. However, in an effort to buttress the Israeli political right prior to the 1996 elections, Netanyahu lured Levy back with the promise of a cabinet position. In addition, seven 'safe' seats in the ranking of Likud to the Knesset were allocated to members of Gesher, which, together with another centre-right faction, Tzomet, was incorporated into the Likud-Gesher-Tzomet union.[3]

The Likud-Gesher-Tzomet triumvirate was a highly fractured political construct. Indeed, the relationship between Binyamin Netanyahu and his inner cabinet may be described as a war without peace. Netanyahu's personal and political rival, David Levy, who was appointed foreign minister based on his strong position in the Likud, challenged him from the outset.[4] In response, as a key insider's account reveals, 'foreign minister Levy was excluded from the majority of decisions that concerned his office', which eventually caused him to resign.[5] Equally problematic were the liaisons between Netanyahu and his Defence Minister, Yitzhak Mordechai, which were described by Cabinet Minister Danny Nave, as 'replete with tensions and distrust'.[6] Netanyahu suspected his defence minister, a member of his own party, was continuously 'trying to consolidate himself politically and publicly to compete with Netanyahu for the premiership'.[7] Another Likud heavyweight, Ariel Sharon, was appointed to the inner cabinet, albeit 'grudgingly' and only after Levy made it a precondition of his joining the government.[8]

These fraught relations were compounded by the complex composition of the coalition government. Under the new electoral system, it was possible to vote directly for the prime minister and to vote separately for the Knesset. In other words, the choice of political party did not have to coincide with the prime ministerial candidate vote. This resulted in a clear increase in the number of smaller parties in the Knesset and a corresponding contraction in the number of Labour and Likud seats, respectively ten and five fewer compared to the previous elections.[9]

---

[3] Mahler, 'The Forming of the Netanyahu Government', 12; Efraim Inbar, 'Netanyahu Takes Over' in Elazar and Sandler, *Israel at the Polls 1996*, p. 34.
[4] Mahler, 'The Forming of the Netanyahu Government', 20–2.
[5] Avigdor Liberman, *My Truth* (Tel Aviv: Ma'ariv, 2004), p. 74 (in Hebrew); Interview with high-level MFA official on condition of anonymity.
[6] Danny Nave, *Executive Secrets* (Tel Aviv: Yedioth Ahronoth, 1999), p. 17. Hebrew
[7] Ibid, p. 18.   [8] Mahler, 'The Forming of the Netanyahu Government', 20–2.
[9] See the Israeli Knesset official website for the 1996 and 1992 party composition, http:// main.knesset.gov.il/About/History/Pages/FactionHistory14.aspx, http://main .knesset.gov.il/About/History/Pages/FactionHistory13.aspx, accessed 4 January 2017.

150   Unpicking the Oslo Accords

This change marked a significant shift. Since 1977, the year that Likud first rose to power after defeating Labour, Israeli politics had been based on Labour and Likud. While the smaller parties could tip the balance in either's favour, the coalition government was dominated by one or the other main party. However, in 1996, Labour and Likud won only 27.5 per cent and 25.8 per cent respectively of the votes.[10] These decreased shares significantly expanded the number of parties required by Netanyahu to form his coalition government, which commanded a majority of sixty-six seats in the Knesset. These included the National Religious Party, the United Torah Party, Shas, Yisrael BaAliya and the Third Way – a Labour party breakaway group opposing withdrawal from the Golan.[11]

The Prime Minister's Inner Decision-Making Circle and its Foreign Policy Outlook

When Binyamin Netanyahu assumed power as the ninth prime minister of Israel, he had no seasoned political allies, his relations with his inner cabinet were tense and he was presiding over a multiparty, fragmented coalition. Conscious of the threat posed by his coalition government, Netanyahu exploited the new direct system for electing the prime minister to develop a presidential-style foreign policy decision-making structure. It hinged on marginalizing his inner cabinet as much as possible and distancing his political rivals in the coalition from the locus of decision-making. As a result, the inner foreign policy decision-making circle surrounding Binyamin Netanyahu comprised the prime minister, a small group of non-elected trusted aides and some of Netanyahu's personal acquaintances.

The political thinking of Binyamin Netanyahu, the key decision-maker, had developed under the towering influence of his father, his long stay in the USA and the traumatic death of his brother, Yonatan Netanyahu, who had commanded the daring Israeli Entebbe raid in 1976 and was accorded mythic status of national hero in Israel.[12] Prior to his election, Netanyahu published *A Place among the Nations*, commonly perceived to be the blueprint for his political thinking. The book proposes a purist

---

[10] The Israeli Knesset official website, http://main.knesset.gov.il/About/History/Pages/Fac tionHistory14.aspx, accessed 4 January 2017.

[11] Shlaim, *The Iron Wall*, p. 590.

[12] Ari Shavit, 'In the Shadow of History', *Ha'aretz*, 1 May 2012. Binyamin Netanyahu and Ido Netanyahu, *The Letters of Jonathan Netanyahu* (Jerusalem: Gefen, 1980), Kindle edition, www.amazon.com/Letters-Jonathan-Netanyahu/dp/9652296295, accessed 17 November 2016.

Foreign Policy Outlook and Decision-Making 151

conception of Zionism and of the Israeli cause. It provides a blinkered portrayal of the absolute, inalienable and exclusive right of the Jews to the Land of Israel. Accordingly, the establishment of the state of Israel was reduced to the Zionist idea of the Jewish Return to the ancient homeland and the myth that it was empty of any other people.[13] The Palestinians are depicted as a 'phantom nation' with no 'expressed ties' to Palestine;[14] 'there is a Palestinian state', wrote Netanyahu, 'in Jordan'.[15]

At the same time, and somewhat conflictingly, Netanyahu was a territorial maximalist. Throughout the book, he repeated the claim that the rightful borders of Israel – promised to the Zionist movement at the 1919 Versailles conference – include the east bank of the River Jordan. In his words, 'the creation of Transjordan by the British lopped off nearly 80 percent of the land promised [to] the Jewish people.'[16] Revealingly, he depicts Israel within its internationally recognized pre-1967 borders as a 'truncated ghetto-state squeezed onto a narrow shoreline'.[17]

Like Aristotle's world of the excluded middle, Arab-Israeli relations are depicted in binary terms. The core cause of conflict in the Middle East is attributed to Arab aggression, which is portrayed as deriving from a number of sources. These include 'the Pan-Arab nationalist rejection of any non-Arab sovereignty in the Middle East, the Islamic fundamentalist drive to cleanse the region of non-Islamic influences, and the particularly bitter historic resentment of the West'.[18]

Arab politics are described as predisposed to 'violence and strife', which is a rather limited depiction.[19] It ignores, for instance, Egypt's decision in 1979 to sign a peace agreement with Israel, which clearly limited Egypt's ability to use violence. Also, in 1994, Jordan signed a similar agreement. Moreover, it implies that Israel lacked agency to shape the conflict. Indeed, throughout the book, Israel is portrayed as the perpetual 'victim'. Criticisms levelled against it are reduced to Arab 'propaganda', the pernicious influence of the UN, pro-Arab Western diplomats and anti-Semitism.[20]

Accordingly, 'the real root of the [Arab-Israeli] conflict' is 'the persistent Arab refusal to recognize Israel within any boundaries'.[21] Furthermore, Netanyahu argues, the 'theology of Arab resentment treats Israel as a weapon by which the Western governments can inflict further

---

[13] Netanyahu, *A Place Among the* Nations, pp. 36–41, 180–4.   [14] Ibid, pp. 24–7, 42.

[15] Ibid, pp. 148, 343–5, 357. In later versions, these references to a Palestinian state in Jordan were caveated to allay Jordanian concerns about Netanyahu. On this point, see Shamir, *The Rise and Decline of the Warm Peace with Jordan*, pp. 322–3.

[16] Netanyahu, *A Place among the Nations*, pp. 50, 348.   [17] Ibid, p. 6.   [18] Ibid, p. 124.

[19] Ibid, p. 238.   [20] Ibid, pp. 79–83, 88.   [21] Ibid, pp. 149, 187.

152   Unpicking the Oslo Accords

defeats and humiliations upon the Arab nation.'[22] Therefore, Netanyahu contends, *'the Arabs do not hate the West because of Israel; they hate Israel because of the West'*.[23]

This stark, monochromatic vision informed the type of peace that Netanyahu envisaged between Israel and its neighbours: a peace of deterrence. Any other type of peace is depicted as a prelude to the next war. Therefore, Netanyahu insisted that peace is 'proportional to Israel's ability to project a strong deterrent posture'.[24] It consists of military strength, warning time and the minimum space required by Israel's army to deploy.[25] In this context, the protective wall of the West Bank is rendered invaluable. Contrastingly, a state under the control of the PLO – with whom Israel was negotiating – is presented as 'a hand poised to strangle Israel's vital artery along the sea'.[26] Indeed, Netanyahu advocated that the Palestinians should be granted autonomy, not a state, *'primarily applicable to urban centres'*, consigning them to perpetual subservience under Israeli occupation.[27]

Netanyahu's notion of a peace of deterrence is devoid of Israeli-Palestinian reconciliation and dialogue. It is based on a skewed analysis of demographics, discussed exclusively in terms of whether Jews can outnumber Palestinians.[28] Even if Netanyahu's somewhat contestable demographic projection of an assured Jewish majority within mandated Palestine is accepted, there remains the fundamental problem of reconciling Israel's self-definition of being a democracy, with the deprivation of the millions of Palestinians under its occupation, of their basic rights, including citizenship. This fundamental issue is not tackled in the book's 467 pages, which refuse to recognize any Arab contribution to either history or civilization.

What guided the foreign policy outlook of Israel's primary decision-maker was a cosmos of his own construction, which created a gap between his psychological environment and the actual foreign policy environment in which he operated. This gap was compounded by the long shadow of the Holocaust, which looms over the entire political thinking presented in the book. For instance, Netanyahu takes great pains to demonstrate the links that existed between Haj-Amin al Husseini and the Nazis, implying – and not so subtly – a direct linkage between the Nazis and the Palestinian leadership. Perceiving Israeli-Palestinian relations in Holocaustian terms at a time when the Jewish nation was indisputably more powerful than it was during WWII, reflects the prime minister's perception of an amplified

---

[22] Ibid, direct quotes pp. 78, 116; see also pp. 91–103, 106–16.
[23] Ibid, p. 123, emphasis in original.   [24] Ibid, p. 253, 342.   [25] Ibid, p. 260.
[26] Ibid, pp. 271, 282.   [27] Ibid, p. 351, emphasis in original, 352–4.
[28] Ibid, pp. 294–328.

threat and a pessimistic world view. A minister who had worked for many years with Netanyahu, elaborates: 'Prime Minister Netanyahu sees the world as a place ridden by conflict. The Jews, Netanyahu is convinced, have been hated and rejected by the world throughout history. This is an axiom in the eyes of the Prime Minister; a fact that does not need proving.'[29]

The Inner Decision-Making Circle

Binyamin Netanyahu's inner circle, which shared the prime minister's inexperience and lack of a decision-making track record, was cast in Netanyahu's monolithic and bleak foreign policy outlook. Cabinet Secretary Danny Nave, who was a key confidant, is a good example. Nave was thirty-six when he was appointed cabinet secretary. His only experience was in a bureaucratic role in the Israeli national health service and as media advisor to former Defence and Foreign Minister, Moshe Arens. Nave had a nationalist religious background and described himself as an ardent follower of the Land of Israel dream and the political tradition of Herut – the political offspring of Zeev Jabotinsky. He referred to the pre-1967 borders of Israel as the 'Auschwitz Borders' and was adamantly opposed to the Oslo agreements.[30]

Nave's involvement in student politics led him to an encounter with another key member of the inner decision-making circle, Avigdor (Ivet) Liberman. Like Binyamin Netanyahu, Liberman was a Likud outsider and a political novice. He was born in Kishinev (Moldova) and emigrated to Israel in 1978, aged twenty. He lived in the Jewish settlement of Nokdim and quickly became involved in Likud after his military service and was close to Netanyahu from 1988. After Netanyahu was elected party chairman, he appointed Liberman General Manager of Likud.[31] At the age of thirty-eight, following Likud's 1996 election victory, Liberman was appointed Director General of the Prime Minister's Office, which provoked significant tensions among Likud's old guard.[32] In a book he wrote, *My Truth*, Liberman describes his political outlook. The book derives from the thinking of revisionist Russian Zionist intellectuals but above all, from Jabotinski, whose ideas Liberman sought to adjust and to apply to modern Israel and its foreign policy.[33]

The composition of the group of aides and confidants surrounding Binyamin Netanyahu had a significant influence on the foreign policy

---

[29] Interview 2 Meridor.   [30] Nave, *Executive Secrets*, pp. 10–11, 65–66.
[31] Liberman, *My Truth*, p. 119.   [32] Ibid, pp. 145, 149–50.
[33] Liberman, *My Truth*, pp. 24, 28, 29, 31–3.

154   Unpicking the Oslo Accords

decision-making structure. 'Netanyahu', observed Efraim Halevy, who worked under Netanyahu as head of Mossad, 'lacked someone that would dare to tell him to stop, wait, and think through the issues carefully before he makes a final decision'.[34] Also, unlike the prime ministerial regimes of Rabin and Shamir, Netanyahu and his close group had no experience of negotiating with Arab leaders within or outside of Israel. Consequently, as a senior GSS official, who was involved intimately in the decision-making process, observed: 'Netanyahu and his group around him could not put themselves in the shoes of the Arab side. They could not understand how the situation looks from the perspective of the Arabs.'[35]

The ideologically monolithic and inexperienced foreign policy structure created a serious blind spot in Israeli decision-making, especially in relation to the Arab world. The only person close to Binyamin Netanyahu who could challenge the group's thinking was Yitzhak Molcho, who was Netanyahu's personal attorney and confidant. Acting as his personal emissary, he was given a leading role in negotiations with the Palestinians and the Americans. Molcho's political centre-left leanings meant he was the only member of the prime minister's immediate inner circle who did not perceive Arafat as the 'ultimate demon'.[36]

However, the relative influence of this pragmatic envoy on the decision-making process was limited because he lacked a political power base. The views of similarly pragmatic cabinet members with experience of dealing with the Arabs, such as David Levy and Yitzhak Mordechai, did not have sufficient weight. The more rational foreign policy direction espoused by them was perceived by Netanyahu and his immediate circle as motivated by rivalry with the prime minister rather than an impartial assessment of Israel's foreign policy interests.[37]

An Unmistakable Threat to Peace

Given the hardline foreign policy outlook of Netanyahu and his closest confidants, it was not surprising that US President Bill Clinton deemed Netanyahu's potential election 'an unmistakable threat to peace'.[38] The foreign policy pursued by the Netanyahu-led government confirmed the deep concerns harboured by the US president. During the first three months after his election, Netanyahu refused to meet Arafat. The sombre

---

[34] Halevy, *Man in the Shadows*, p. 121.
[35] Interview 1 Ami Ayalon, 27 February 2017, Tel Aviv.
[36] Ross, *The Missing Peace*, p. 352; Iinterview 1 Ayalon.
[37] Interview 1 Ayalon; Interview with former media advisor to Binyamin Netanyahu, Mr Aviv Bushinsky, Tel Aviv, 27 February 2017.
[38] Ross, *The Missing Peace*, p. 257.

An Unmistakable Threat to Peace 155

handshake between the two men when they finally met, on 4 September 1996, as the result of mounting US pressure, reflected the deep chasm between Israel and the PLO. The widening of the gulf between the two sides was caused primarily by Israel's unilateral measures since Netanyahu's rise to power. Most significantly, the Netanyahu government reversed the settlement-freeze policy imposed by the Rabin-Peres government and authorized the construction of 1,500 new settlement units in the West bank.[39]

Settlement expansion was a particularly sensitive matter. The former GSS head, Ami Ayalon, explained that: '[T]hrough my meetings with the Palestinians I witnessed how they felt increasingly deceived by the Oslo Process. They were concerned that in continuing to build settlements and roads [Israel] was trying to buy time and reach a situation where eventually it will be "too bloody late" for the Palestinians to have a state.'[40]

The deterioration in Israeli-PLO relations was precipitated by a self-inflicted crisis. On 24 September 1996, the government decided to open a second gate to the second-century BC, eighty-metre long Hasmonean Tunnel in East Jerusalem. The Waqf or Muslim Religious Authority had previously opposed the opening of a second gate because it was located just outside the perimeter of Haram al-Sharif. Waqf believed that opening this second gate to the tunnel would alter the character of the Muslim quarter in East Jerusalem and claimed it could affect the mosques located in Haram al-Sharif – known to the Islamic world as the Noble Sanctuary – the third holiest Muslim shrine. The Waqf's allegations were exaggerated. Since 1967, Israel had taken significant measures to safeguard the mosques, including foiling a plot hatched by the Jewish Resistance to blow them up.[41] Nonetheless, the Waqf's declarations rendered the question of whether or not to open a second gate to the tunnel an extremely sensitive political issue. According to Dennis Ross, every Israeli government since the tunnel had been excavated in 1987 had refrained from opening it.[42] The signing of the Oslo agreements raised another objection to opening the second gate: creating a second exit went directly against the spirit of Israel's commitment in the Oslo agreements,

---

[39] Ross, *The Missing Peace*, p. 263; 'Guidelines of the Government of Israel, 17 June 1996, *IMFA*, http://mfa.gov.il/mfa/foreignpolicy/mfadocuments/year book11/pages/2%20address%20in%20the%20knesset%20by%20president%20weiz man%20on%20t.aspx, accessed 15 December 2016; 'Government Communiqué on Settlement Activities in Judea and Samaria, 2 August 1996, *IMFA*, http://mfa.gov.il/ MFA/ForeignPolicy/MFADocuments/Yearbook11/Pages/18%20Government%20co mmunique%20on%20settlement%20activities.aspx, accessed 15 December 2016.
[40] Interview 1 Ayalon.   [41] Hagai Segal, *Dear Brothers.*
[42] Ross, *The Missing Peace*, p. 254.

156   Unpicking the Oslo Accords

to do nothing to change the status quo in Jerusalem before it was negotiated.

What was the reason for this provocative decision? It reflected the substance and style of the prime minister and his immediate foreign policy decision-making circle. The intimate group around Prime Minister Netanyahu ignored the Palestinian connection to Jerusalem and was unwilling to assess the situation from a Palestinian perspective. Moreover, the prime minister and his immediate circle were inexperienced and complacent, which is why the decision was taken with no consultation. According to the former head of the GSS, Ami Ayalon, the Israeli internal security service was excluded from the process and there was no serious liaison with the Palestinians.[43] Astonishingly, the prime minister also paid no heed to a written warning from the MFA. In a report compiled by the head of the MFA's research division, David Afek, the MFA issued a stark warning against the opening of the second exit to the tunnel, predicting that it would plunge the peace process into violent crisis.[44] However, the prime minister authorized its opening, this unambiguous warning notwithstanding, and left immediately for Europe. Foreign Minister David Levy was also abroad.[45]

As the MFA had predicted, the opening of the second gate to the tunnel sparked a violent crisis, which posed a direct threat to the Oslo peace process. It became clear that, throughout the crisis, Netanyahu's pre-existing views of the PLO were guiding his decision-making. In his conversations with the Americans and the Europeans, Netanyahu refused to concede that his unilateral actions had caused the violence to erupt. Instead, the Israeli prime minister accused Arafat of using the incident 'to unleash violence and exert pressure on Israel'.[46]

In pinning the blame on the Palestinians, the Israeli prime minister ignored the role of his own policies since his election in generating the crisis. Netanyahu refused to acknowledge that, to some degree, the tunnel crisis emanated from the stalemate in the Oslo peace process following the February–March 1996 terror attacks waged by Hamas and the 1996 May elections. Since that time, the new Israeli premier had shunned the Palestinians and negotiations all but stopped. In addition, Israel had reversed the settlement-freeze policy imposed by the Rabin-Peres government and the prime minister had broken the commitment to maintain the status quo in Jerusalem, by his unilateral decision to open the Hasmonean Tunnel. In these circumstances, Arafat had no incentive to cooperate

[43] More, *Gate Keepers*, pp. 212–13.
[44] Interview 1 Eitan Bentsur, 28 February 2017, Tel Aviv.
[45] Shamir, *The Rise and Fall of the Warm Peace with Jordan*, p. 223.
[46] Nave, *Executive Secrets*, p. 37.

The October 1996 Washington Summit   157

with a government he did not trust. Instead, he opted to consolidate his ranks by supporting Palestinian rioters, backing the Palestinian police who were firing on Israeli soldiers and being vociferous about the threat posed by the tunnel to the Haram. As the crisis spread quickly, from Jerusalem to Joseph's Tomb in Nablus/Shchem, where rioting Palestinians engulfed an Israeli platoon, Netanyahu was focused on exerting pressure on Arafat. He told the Palestinian leader that 'he [would] not allow him to yield any political fruits from the crisis' and threatened 'massive military reprisal' if the violence continued.[47]

The October 1996 Washington Summit

After three days of violence, the stakes were extremely high, with fourteen Israelis and fifty-four Palestinians killed.[48] It was clear that the ability to resolve problems directly with the PLO, which had characterized the Rabin-Peres era, had been shattered by Netanyahu's advent to power. Indeed, resolution of the tunnel crisis depended on direct intervention from President Clinton, who invited Netanyahu and Arafat to attend a summit in Washington. During this summit, held between 30 September and 2 October 1996, Netanyahu was 'riveted on his political base rather than on the needs of the [peace] process', in other words, the Israelis were making no concessions.[49]

The obstinacy displayed by the prime minister at the summit was integral to his domestic political strategy since his election campaign. A former minister in his government observed that, gradually, Netanyahu transformed Likud from a nationalist-liberal movement to a more pure nationalist political party. Netanyahu formulated a political strategy that was predicated on his being the political leader of the Israeli national-religious right, which became his power base.[50] A high-level MFA official echoed Meridor's views. He recalled that: 'The settlers were represented disproportionally in the Prime Minister's office. Netanyahu was very attentive to the relatively high political weight of this group.'[51]

The prime minister's domestic political moorings shaped his position in the summit. According to Cabinet Secretary Danny Nave, who was present throughout the negotiations, Netanyahu was hoping to use the summit to 'lay the seeds for renegotiating the redeployment in Hebron',

---

[47] See quotations in, respectively, Nave, *Executive Secrets*, p. 37; Ross, *The Missing Peace*, p. 265.
[48] Shlaim, *Lion of Jordan*, p. 562.   [49] Ross, *The Missing Peace*, p. 267.
[50] Interview 2 Dan Meridor, Jerusalem, 26 February 2017.
[51] Interview with high-level MFA official on condition of anonymity.

158   Unpicking the Oslo Accords

which had been postponed by the Peres government following the terrorist attacks waged by Hamas in February and March 1996.[52] Netanyahu argued that 'the security arrangements agreed by the Rabin-Peres government needed to be modified.'[53]

The discussions during the October 1996 summit made it clear that the resolution to the tunnel crisis hinged on Netanyahu's abiding by the Oslo II agreement and redeploying the IDF in Hebron. This represented a highly symbolic decision for the prime minister. Jews and Muslims venerate the city of Hebron because of its association with Abraham. In addition, it is the only major Palestinian city that is also home to a small but particularly zealous community of 400 Jewish settlers. Redeploying the IDF was a litmus test that would determine whether the Netanyahu government would honour the Oslo agreements and breach an important taboo of both Likud and the prime minister: exchanging land for peace. Sitting side by side with Arafat during the Washington Summit, Netanyahu assured him that: 'We can surprise the world, we can reach an agreement quickly.'[54]

However, the prime minister faced stiff opposition. The GSS was strongly opposed to signing an agreement without exacting a price from the Palestinians for the deaths of seventeen IDF soldiers killed during the tunnel crisis. The GSS believed that signing a deal under these circumstances would be seen by the Palestinians as 'surrender by Israel'.[55] The GSS's opposition was compounded by the profound symbolism of an agreement over Hebron and the political opposition Netanyahu faced from within his political power base, which resulted in extremely tedious negotiations.

The Palestinians also contributed to slowing the negotiations. By October 1996, Arafat had lost all trust in Binyamin Netanyahu. Reluctant to renegotiate the Hebron Agreement he had signed with the Rabin-Peres government, throughout the negotiations Arafat's behaviour was erratic; he constantly backtracked from agreements he had reached with Dennis Ross. In turn, the chief American negotiator could not fail to note the transformed role of the USA in the negotiations. From being a presence in the background during the Rabin-Peres negotiations, the USA had become a full-time mediator and was indispensable for brokering compromises. This was the reason why the Hebron Protocol was sealed only after Secretary of State Christopher had set a precedent in the Oslo peace process by providing his own letter of assurances.[56]

---

[52] Nave, *Executive Secrets*, p. 41.   [53] Ibid.   [54] Ross, *The Missing Peace*, p. 267.
[55] Interview 1 Ayalon.
[56] Ross, *The Missing Peace*, pp. 268, 286, 291, 316, 320; Nave, *Executive Secrets*, pp. 32, 48, 52; Miller, *The Much Too Promised Land*, p. 269; 'Comments by Prime Minister Netanyahu on the Security Situation and Political Negotiations', 3 November 1996,

The Hebron Protocol and its Significance

The revised Hebron Protocol was significant in that it marked the first agreement between Likud and the PLO that involved ceding land to the Palestinians in the context of a peace process. Hebron was divided into two areas, H-1 and H-2, governed by different security arrangements. The Palestinian police assumed control over H-1, the Palestinian zone, which covered about 80 per cent of the city. H-2, which was located in Hebron's commercial centre, remained under Israeli control and was home to 400 Jewish settlers and 20,000 of Hebron's then 160,000 strong Palestinian population.[57]

The redrafted Hebron protocol was important in another sense. It established the Israeli foreign policy tactic under Likud, of unpicking the Oslo accords, but not breeching the framework completely. The method adopted by Prime Minister Netanyahu in this context, outlined in his statement to the Knesset over the Hebron protocol, was extremely shrewd. He explained that it was based on a meticulous and intricate legalistic distinction between the 'written and oral laws' of the Oslo agreements.[58] By exploiting this distinction, Netanyahu was able to impose his own reading of the agreements and alter them accordingly.

The Hebron Protocol strongly reflects this. While the original Interim agreement laid down that Israel should redeploy from 60 per cent of the West Bank by September 1997, the Hebron Protocol extended the time-frame to 'no later than mid-1998'.[59] Furthermore, based on a letter of assurances provided by the US Secretary of State Warren Christopher, the Israelis obtained the support of the USA for Israel to determine the nature and scope of further redeployments. Christopher's letter confirmed, also, that 'The key element in the US approach to the deal' was 'recognition of Israel's security requirements'.[60] Thus, the division of Hebron into H-1 and H-2, which disproportionately favoured the 400

IMFA, vol. 16, 1996–1997; 'Letter from Secretary of State Christopher', January 1997, *IMFA*, www.mfa.gov.il/MFA/ForeignPolicy/Peace/Guide/Pages/Letter%20from%20Se cretary%20of%20State%20Christopher.aspx, accessed 2 January 2019.

[57] Shlaim, *The Iron Wall*, p. 682; 'Protocol Concerning Redeployment in Hebron, *IMFA*, www.mfa.gov.il/mfa/foreignpolicy/peace/guide/pages/protocol%20concerning%20the% 20redeployment%20in%20hebron.aspx, accessed 20 December 2016.

[58] Statement to the Knesset by Prime Minister Benjamin Netanyahu 'On the Protocol Concerning Hebron', *IMFA*, http://mfa.gov.il/MFA/MFA-Archive/1997/Pages/PM% 20Netanyahu%20Statement%20to%20Knesset%20on%20Hebron%20Protoc.aspx, accessed 20 December 2016.

[59] Letter to be provided by US Secretary of State Christopher to Benjamin Netanyahu at the time of the signing of the Heron Protocol, *IMFA*, www.mfa.gov.il/MFA/ForeignP olicy/Peace/Guide/Pages/Letter%20from%20Secretary%20of%20State%20Christop her.aspx, accessed 20 December 2016.

[60] Ibid.

160   Unpicking the Oslo Accords

Jewish settlers in the Israeli-controlled 20 per cent of the city, laid the groundwork for a permanent division of the city along those lines.

The added Note for the Record of the Hebron Protocol incorporated the new principle of reciprocity into the Israel-PLO framework of the negotiations.[61] Accordingly, Israel assumed certain obligations, which included reaffirming commitment to Israeli redeployments in the West Bank, release of female Palestinian prisoners and resumption of negotiations over the issues underpinning the interim and permanent agreements. However, in line with the principle of reciprocity, Israel was expected to fulfil its side of the bargain only after the Palestinians had met a number of conditions. These included combating terrorism and incitement, collecting illegal weapons, amending the Palestinian National Covenant, extraditing Palestinians to Israel on the latter's request and reducing the size of the Palestinian police force.[62]

The 'reciprocity' requirement, constituted a complete reversal of the principle laid down by Yitzhak Rabin, who pledged to fight terrorism as if there were no peace process and to pursue the peace process as if there were no terrorism.[63] Viewed through a strict security prism, it made sense to more strongly condition progress in the Oslo peace process on a Palestinian commitment to confront the terrorist campaign being waged by Hamas. However, within the fraught and untrusting relationship that had developed between Israel and the PLO under Likud, demand for reciprocity meant something other. It linked Israel's commitment to continue with the peace process to Palestinian ability to ensure Israel's security, as defined by a nationalist, pro-settler government, which was explicit about its dissatisfaction with the Oslo peace process.

Therefore, the Palestinians found this demand for reciprocity hard to digest, particularly in view of the intentions proclaimed by the Israeli government following the agreement over Hebron. In his statement to the Knesset concerning the Hebron protocol, the prime minister stated simply that his government was committed to 'preserving and consolidating' the Jewish community in Hebron, which he vowed not to leave and that further redeployments were postponed.[64] Thus, ten months after his

---

[61] Note for the Record, *IMFA*, www.mfa.gov.il/MFA/ForeignPolicy/Peace/Guide/Pages/Note%20for%20the%20Record.aspx, accessed 20 December 2016.

[62] Nave, *Executive Secrets*, 'Protocol Concerning Redeployment in Hebron', pp. 56–7.

[63] The policy dictum paraphrased Ben-Gurion's presentation of his strategy related to the need to fight the British White Paper while supporting Britain in its war against Hitler. See Shlomo Ben-Ami, *Scars of War Wounds of Peace: The Israeli-Arab Tragedy* (London: Weidenfeld & Nicolson, 2005), p. 215.

[64] 'Statement to the Knesset by Prime Minister Benjamin Netanyahu on the Protocol Concerning Hebron', *IMFA*, http://mfa.gov.il/MFA/MFA-Archive/1997/Pages/PM%

assuming power, the Palestinians had only civil and security responsibilities in area 'A', which comprised 2.9 per cent of the West Bank.

Although for Likud to sign an agreement with the PLO and cede territory in Hebron was unprecedented, Israel's foreign policy towards the Palestinians under Netanyahu was diverging from its previous engagement posture. Nevertheless, the Hebron protocol met with stiff resistance from the government, especially Ministers Ariel Sharon and Benny Begin. It was passed on 14 January 1997, by eleven votes to seven, not before Benny Begin resigned, protesting that it set a dangerous precedent and declaring he could not support the further Israeli redeployments suggested.[65] The backlash was exacerbated by the settler lobby's criticism of the new government's policies. In a publication, '100 Days of Disappointment', the settlers branded the government's settlements expansion record as too modest.[66] Meanwhile, former Prime Minister Yitzhak Shamir, accused Netanyahu of 'betraying the idea of Greater Israel' and called on Likud to find 'an alternative candidate to lead the national camp'.[67]

The campaign waged by the settler lobby and government members opposing the Hebron deal was effective. In line with his domestic political strategy, it prompted the prime minister to try to regain his standing within his power base – the ethnocentric, nationalist and religious coalition that had got him elected. Accordingly, the government took a decision that significantly reversed the progress represented by the signing of the Hebron protocol. Despite US requests to reconsider, Israel authorized the building of '2,000 housing units for Jews in the Har Homa neighbourhood' – known in Arabic as Jabal Abu-Ghneim – on the outskirts of Jerusalem and 3,500 homes for Palestinians throughout the city.[68] 'I have no choice', claimed Netanyahu in making his case to Dennis Ross.[69]

The seeming equilibrium in the construction of houses for Jews and Palestinians was as false as the prime minister's claim that he had no alternative. As Cabinet Secretary Nave recalls, the Har Homa construction was aimed clearly at 'creating a continuity of Jewish neighbourhoods

---

20Netanyahu%20Statement%20to%20Knesset%20on%20Hebron%20Protoc.aspx, accessed 20 December 2016.

[65] Nave, *Executive Secrets*, p. 52.

[66] The publication is quoted in Eldar and Zartal, *Lords of the Land*, p. 218.

[67] Yedioth Ahoronoth, 16 January 1997.

[68] 'Conversation between Prime Minister Netanyahu and President Mubarak', 26 February 1997, *IMFA*, http://mfa.gov.il/MFA/ForeignPolicy/MFADocuments/Yearbook11/Pages/88%20Conversation%20between%20Prime%20Minister%20Netanyahu%20a.aspx, accessed 22 December 2016.

[69] Ross, *The Missing Peace*, p. 330.

162   Unpicking the Oslo Accords

in southern Jerusalem to prevent any future territorial contiguity between Bethlehem and Eastern Jerusalem's Arab neighbourhoods'.[70] In contrast, the Palestinian homes would blend into existing neighbourhoods.

Consistent with the opening of the Hasmonean Tunnel, the decision to build in Har Homa went directly against the understanding in the Oslo accords about not changing the status quo in Jerusalem, in a way that was likely to prejudge the final settlement. A UNSC debate, which called for Israel to halt construction in the neighbourhood, underlines this point. Only a US veto on a resolution condemning Israel protected the Netanyahu government from mounting international pressure.[71]

However, by imposing this veto, the USA was all but condoning the decision to build in Har Homa, which compromised its honest broker role. The Israeli MFA, which was seeking a more proactive Israeli peace policy, was becoming increasingly frustrated. As a well-placed official observed: '[T]he US peace team always reacted to events, rather than tried to shape them' and 'focused on adapting themselves to every new US administration, every new Secretary of State, and to the stronger political current in Israel at any given moment. They were as conjectural as they come.'[72]

Backsliding

The tensions created by the decision to build in Har Homa were increased by the Israeli interpretation of the Hebron Protocol in relation to Israel's Further Redeployments in the West Bank. According to Binyamin Netanyahu, Arafat told the Israelis that the Palestinians always expected to receive 90 per cent of the West Bank before the start of negotiations over the permanent status agreement.[73] Uri Savir, chief Israeli negotiator in the Rabin-Peres government, recalls that the expectation was a minimum of 51 per cent, which still would give the Palestinians control over a majority of the West Bank before negotiations over the permanent agreement.[74] However, under Netanyahu, the Israelis' proposed that the second phase of the Further Redeployments would include the transfer of just 9 per cent of the West Bank to full PA control: 7 per cent of this

---

[70] Nave, *Executive Secrets*, p. 60.
[71] Paul Lewis, 'US again Vetoes a Move by UN Condemning Israel', *New York Times*, 22 March 1997.
[72] Interview with high-level MFA official on condition of anonymity.
[73] 'Statement by Prime Minister Netanyahu upon his Return from Washington', 25 October, 1998, *IMFA*, https://mfa.gov.il/MFA/ForeignPolicy/MFADocuments/Yea rbook12/Pages/78%20Statement%20by%20Prime%20Minister%20Netanyahu%20up on%20his.aspx, accessed 29 March 1998.
[74] Ross, *The Missing Peace*, p. 363.

Backsliding

would be included in the transfer of security authority from Israel to the PA in area B, where the Palestinians already had civil responsibility, the other 2 per cent to include areas in which the Palestinian had not had control prior to the signing of the Hebron Protocol.[75]

The PA rejected Israel's proposal outright; it was far from the area of land they had expected to receive as part of Israel's Further Redeployments. At the same time, the PA reduced the pressure it imposed on Hamas and Islamic Jihad following the February–March 1996 terror attacks. Arafat began to reach out to these organizations via what he described as 'national reconciliation dialogue'.[76] The Israeli-PLO negotiations had reached an impasse that was deepened in March 1997 by two anti-Israel terrorist attacks. On 14 March, Ahmed Dakamesh, a Jordanian soldier, killed seven Israeli schoolgirls who were visiting a shared patch of land in the Jordan Valley known as the Island of Peace. A week later, a Palestinian suicide bomber killed four Israelis in Apropos, a Tel Aviv café.[77]

Israel's response was to adopt a foreign policy of backsliding the peace process, which, combined with terrorist attacks, caused a deadlock of several months in the negotiations. During this period, there was fierce debate within the Israeli security network. The IDF military intelligence claimed that the Palestinian 'national reconciliation dialogue' was an Arafat ploy and that Arafat had authorized Hamas and Islamic Jihad with the 'green light' to carry out terrorist attacks in Israel. Netanyahu's immediate decision-making circle accepted the IDF's analysis, although it contradicted the views of the GSS – the specialist agency dealing with the Palestinians.[78]

With characteristic candour, the then head of the GSS, Ami Ayalon, challenged the claim that Arafat had authorized the Hamas and Islamic Jihad terrorist attacks. He believed that: '[U]nder the Netanyahu government cooperation with the Palestinian security services was as important as the work of the GSS itself in the increased security of Israelis.'[79] 'It was not because they believed Bibi', he continued, 'but because they had faith in Clinton. The Palestinians believed that Clinton would act on their behalf, provided that they tackled Hamas.'[80] This required Arafat's agreement, which seriously questioned the IDF intelligence assessment.

---

[75] Nave, *Executive Secrets*, p. 63; Ross, *The Missing Peace*, p. 374.

[76] Ross, *The Missing Peace*, p. 318.

[77] Serge Schmemann, 'Jordanian Soldier Kills 7 Israeli School Girls', *New York Times*, 14 March 1997; Serge Schmemann, '4 Arabs Killed in a Suicide Bombing in Tel Aviv', *New York Times*, 22 March 1997; Ashton, *King Hussein of Jordan*, p. 330.

[78] Nave, *Executive Secrets*, pp. 72–3.

[79] Moreh, *Gate Keepers*, pp. 223–4. Ayalon's deputy, Yuval Diskin, dismissed this view absolutely.

[80] Interview 1 Ayalon.

164   Unpicking the Oslo Accords

American sources echoed the views expressed by Ami Ayalon, as negotiator Aaron David Miller explained:

Our focus on security performance would also witness the CIA's open involvement in the peace process. And we milked this aspect of the relationship with Arafat for all we could get ... [CIA Director] Tenet and Arafat developed an unusually close relationship that ... contributed significantly to giving Arafat a stake – at least during the [Netanyahu] years in delivering more than he'd ever done and would do again on security.[81]

Nevertheless, the ingrained hostility of the prime minister's decision-making circle to the Oslo process, the PLO and Arafat, skewed its judgement in relation to uncritical acceptance of the IDF intelligence view. Subscribing to the IDF's assessment of the Palestinians was in line with Likud's foreign policy tactic, which consisted of backsliding in relation to the negotiations and holding the PA and Arafat responsible for the terrorism. Accordingly, following two suicide bombings, on 30 July and 4 September, 1997, which killed twenty-one Israelis, the cabinet's response was decisive. It announced that 'the political process will not move forward' – especially the second and third Further Redeployments mandated by the Oslo II agreement – for 'as long as the PA does not fight terrorism'.[82]

The result, which only consolidated the stalemate, was fuelled by domestic politics, which Efraim Halevy, head of Mossad under Netanyahu, felt were always paramount in the prime minister's decision-making calculus.[83] Dennis Ross concurs, observing presciently that Netanyahu was content 'to go slow, satisfy his cabinet, and show that he did not have to make concession after concession – indeed, any concessions at all'.[84] Ross elaborated that this brought the Palestinians to believe that the Israeli game plan was 'creating the illusion of progress while

---

[81] Miller, *The Much Too Promised Land*, pp. 272.
[82] 'Conversation between Prime Minister Netanyahu and PA Chairman Arafat Following Bombing in Jerusalem', 30 July 1997, *IMFA*, http://mfa.gov.il/MFA/Fore ignPolicy/MFADocuments/Yearbook11/Pages/127%20Conversation%20between% 20Prime%20Minister%20Netanyahu.aspx, 'Cabinet Communiqué on Bombing in Jerusalem, 30 July 1997, IMFA, http://mfa.gov.il/MFA/ForeignPolicy/MFADocum ents/Yearbook11/Pages/129%20Cabinet%20communique%20on%20bombing%20i n%20Jerusalem-%2030.aspx, 'Government Communiqué on the Struggle against Terror', 3 August 1997, *IMFA*, www.mfa.gov.il/MFA/ForeignPolicy/MFADocume nts/Yearbook11/Pages/131%20Government%20communique%20on%20the%20str uggle%20against.aspx, 'Cabinet Communiqué on the Peace Process, 23 November', 1997, *IMFA*, www.mfa.gov.il/MFA/ForeignPolicy/MFADocuments/Yeabook11/Pa ges/161%20Cabinet%20communique%20on%20the%20peace%20process-%2023 %20No.aspx, all accessed 4 January 2017.
[83] Interview Ephraim Ha-Levy, Tel Aviv, 5 November 2015.
[84] Ross, *The Missing Peace*, p. 350.

Backsliding 165

actually trying to reverse the Oslo process'.[85] Palestinian suspicions were understandable given Israel's provocation in Har Homa, its meagre offer regarding the second Further Redeployment and the accelerated settlement expansion in the West Bank, which, as Cabinet Secretary Nave revealed, was designed to 'enhance the Jewish grip over the land.'[86]

By late 1997, the divergence of Israeli foreign policy from its previous engagement position was well underway. The Oslo peace process, which under Rabin and Peres, had been driven by Israel and the PLO, was kept intact by international stakeholders. The EU remained the largest funder of the peace process, while the Clinton administration focused its efforts on effecting the second Israeli Further Redeployment in the West Bank. To this end, newly appointed Secretary of State Madeleine Albright made her first visit to the region in early September to try to restart the negotiations. Albright's first stab at the Israeli-Palestinian peace process reflected the USA's 'light touch' mediation. She demanded of the Palestinians a '100 percent effort to fight terror' and that the Israelis should refrain from 'taking unilateral steps such as the Har Homa construction'.[87] However, she did not attach a price to a renege by either side. The effectiveness of US mediation was weakened further by the Monica Lewinski scandal. On 21 January 1998, the *Washington Post* led with a story that President Clinton had had inappropriate relations with a White House intern, one Monica Lewinski. This, as both the president and his chief negotiator, Dennis Ross, observed, reduced President Clinton's clout over Israel and the Palestinians.[88]

Meanwhile, the coalition government in Israel was coming under strain. The moderate Foreign Minister, David Levy, resigned in December 1997, accusing the prime minister of constructing 'obstacles for peace'.[89] The Third Way, government's moderate centre-left partner, threatened to leave if Israel continued to reject the US Further Redeployment proposal for the West Bank of 10 per cent to 15 per cent. At the same time, a group of seventeen politicians loyal to the settlers, the Eretz Yisrael Front, threatened to topple the government if Netanyahu conceded to America's demand.[90]

Netanyahu exploited his political predicament astutely. He played down the objections from the moderates while highlighting the

---

[85] Ibid, p. 349.   [86] Nave, *Executive Secrets*, p. 84.
[87] Madeleine Albright, *Madam Secretary* (New York: Hyperion, 2003), p. 374.
[88] Ross, *The Missing* Peace, pp. 398, 401; Clinton, *My Life*, p. 774.
[89] Levy's Choice, *Haaretz Editorial*, 4 January 1998.
[90] Nave, *Executive Secrets*, p. 91; 'Cabinet Communiqué', 4 January 1998, *IMFA*, www .mfa.gov.il/MFA/ForeignPolicy/MFADocuments/Yearbook12/Pages/1%20Cabinet%2 0communique-%204%20January%201998.aspx, accessed 5 January 2017.

166   Unpicking the Oslo Accords

opposition from the hardliners as an insurmountable domestic political obstacle to acceptance of the package proposed by the Americans. At the core of the American plan was the idea that Israel would complete the overdue second Further Redeployment by transferring 13 per cent of the West Bank to PA control. In exchange, the Palestinians would devise and implement a plan, vetted by the Israelis, to clamp down on terrorism.

The negotiations over a deal combining these elements, which began in March 1998 and was to last a year, was dogged by the Monica Lewinski scandal that dominated the Clinton administration. The US president and Foreign Secretary Madeleine Albright were keen to get Israel and the Palestinians to attend a summit in the USA, to demonstrate that the president remained focused and was dealing actively and visibly with highly sensitive issues.[91] It was unclear who needed the summit most – the Clinton administration, Israel or the Palestinians. The debilitated and beleaguered US president was reluctant to confront the Israeli prime minister, in spite of Albright's urging.[92]

The weakness of the Americans gave Netanyahu the advantage. In his bargaining with them, he was relentless in his security demands and in stressing the internal political obstacles to implementation of the proposed 13 per cent Further Redeployments.[93] However, the façade comprising domestic political issues and security demands hid a more ambitious foreign policy aim: reducing as much as possible the transfer of land and authority from Israel to the PA.

Accordingly, during negotiations with the Americans, the Israelis insisted on collapsing the second and third Further Redeployments in the West Bank into one action. They reached an understanding with the US administration that, in exchange for transferring 13 per cent of the West Bank to Palestinian control in a second Further Redeployment – and an additional 14 per cent from area B to area A – the third Further Redeployment would not exceed 1 per cent.[94] Consequently, prior to negotiations over the permanent agreement, the Palestinians would control a maximum of 41 per cent of the West Bank, that is, 50 per cent less

---

[91] Ross, *The Missing Peace*, p. 401.

[92] Ross, *The Missing Peace*, p. 377; Nave, *Executive Secrets*, p. 98; Miller, *The Much Too Promised Land*, pp. 273–4.

[93] Albright, *Madam Secretary*, p. 372; 'Remarks by Prime Minister Netanyahu on the Peace Process, 9 June 1998', *IMFA*, http://mfa.gov.il/MFA/ForeignPolicy/MFADocuments/Yearbook12/Pages/48%20Remarks%20by%20Prime%20Minister%20Netanyahu%20on%20the%20peac.aspx; 'Briefing by Prime Minister Netanyahu to Members of the Diplomatic Corps' 3 July 1998, *IMFA*, http://mfa.gov.il/MFA/ForeignPolicy/MFADocuments/Yearbook12/Pages/56%20Briefing%20by%20Prime%20Minister%20Netanyahu%20to%20members.aspx, accessed 22 February 2019; Ross, *The Missing Peace*, pp. 378–414; Nave, *Executive Secrets*, pp. 88–103.

[94] Nave, *Executive Secrets*, pp. 101–4; Ross, *The Missing Peace*, pp. 386, 390, 412.

than the 91 per cent Arafat had expected. It is clear that this interpretation, promoted by the Israeli negotiating team, was not based solely on internal political constraints, although these were significant. It was a well-considered foreign policy, aimed at reducing the area of land the Palestinians would receive prior to negotiations over the permanent agreement. Indeed, in his later memoirs, Dani Nave describes this as 'possibly the greatest achievement of the Netanyahu government'.[95]

The Alternative not Taken

When the Netanyahu government had achieved two years in office, it had a clear balance sheet towards the Palestinians. It had been the first Likud government to sign an agreement with the PLO and to cede territory in a peace process with the Palestinians. At the same time, this government determinedly and consistently unpicked the Oslo accords. The opening of the Hasmonean Tunnel, followed by the provocative decision to build in Har Homa went against the understanding of retaining the status quo in Jerusalem in a way that could prejudge the final settlement. In stalling over Further Redeployments in the West Bank, the government reduced the process of Israeli withdrawal from the West Bank and scaling down of the occupation. These retractions occurred alongside a significant decline in terrorist attacks. The head of the GSS and the Americans were reporting the cooperation with the Palestinian security forces as unprecedented.

Israel's foreign policy to unpick the Oslo accords was, perhaps, not unexpected. Binyamin Netanyahu was elected after his denouncement of the Oslo process, which he sincerely believed posed a security threat to Israel and was a betrayal of Zionist ideology. He and most of the members of his immediate circle were convinced that the Oslo process was a mistake of historic proportions. His political power base, the ultra-orthodox, national religious and the secular Israeli right were all equally vehement in their opposition to the Oslo process. Moderate members of his inner cabinet, such as David Levy and Yitzhak Mordechai, were sidelined. Thus, faced with a US administration that was heavily invested in the Oslo peace process, Netanyahu preferred continuously to unpick rather than to formally breach the Oslo accords.

Given Netanyahu's ideological deposition, the composition of his immediate circle and his political power base did he have an alternative? The answer must be a resounding 'yes'. Throughout the period of stalemate, Eitan Bentsur, MFA director general, had implored the prime minister to take a different path. If the Oslo framework were the problem,

---

[95] Nave, *Executive Secrets*, p. 103.

168　　Unpicking the Oslo Accords

Bentsur, a committed civil servant, argued, then why not revert to the framework of the Madrid peace conference, in which Netanyahu participated and which was a product, in part, of Likud diplomacy?

However, there were some serious obstacles to this foreign policy alternative, revealed by the scepticism of the prime minister and his supporters towards the very notion of Arab-Israeli peace. 'Although Netanyahu participated in Madrid', recalled Bentsur, 'the great feat of bringing Arabs and Israelis together for the first time never really captivated him. It did not challenge his inherent concern and doubts. He shared the scepticism of Shamir, plus, plus, plus.' 'When I made some attempts to approach the Prime Minister on this issue', Bentsur recollected, 'his immediate circle of aides and confidents also proved a real obstacle. There was nobody around the Prime Minister with the foreign policy expertise or willingness necessary to reorient Israeli foreign policy back towards the Madrid framework. I had no one to work with. I was all alone.'[96]

The US peace team did not explore Bentsur's intuition, but remained bent on keeping the Oslo process intact. In clinging to the Oslo framework, which the Israeli government was all too eager to frustrate, the peace process was reduced to a quest for the next summit. However, rather than a summit that might represent a breakthrough in the process, the proposed high-level encounter between Israel and the Palestinians, under US mediation, was to focus on securing the second Further Redeployment in the West Bank. The time and political capital required by the USA to maintain negotiations over the summit are testament to the profound setback to Israeli-Palestinian relations under Binyamin Netanyahu's premiership.

---

[96] Interview 1 Mr Eytan Bentsur, former director general of the Israeli MFA, 28 February 2017, Tel Aviv.

8 Backtracking

To Engage or not to Engage?

The Rabin-Peres Labour government bequeathed Binyamin Netanyahu's incoming Likud-led coalition Israel's warm peace agreement with Jordan, fledgling ties with Arab countries in the Gulf and the Maghreb and a framework for negotiations with Syria. Would Israel's newly elected prime minister follow in the steps of former Likud leader, Prime Minister Menachem Begin, who had concluded the peace agreement with Egypt after pledging not to withdraw even an inch from the Sinai? Or would Binyamin Netanyahu's stark world view, his government's domestic political commitment to the Israeli right and the political composition of his coalition steer Israeli foreign policy away from engagement? These profound uncertainties hung over the Netanyahu government as it began engaging with an Arab world split between supporters and detractors of the peace process with Israel.

Israeli Foreign Policy towards Jordan under Binyamin Netanyahu

As negotiations over the 1994 peace agreement between Israel and Jordan progressed, King Hussein sought to extend his ties with Israeli politicians beyond the upper echelons of the Labour party. He began cultivating relationships with the then head of the opposition, Binyamin Netanyahu, in spite of his claims that the Palestinian state was in Jordan. Gradually, as Israeli-Jordanian peace negotiations advanced, Hussein's overtures proved useful. Netanyahu's pronouncements about Jordan mellowed, leading Likud, in the Knesset, to support ratification of the Israel-Jordan accord, which was passed by a majority of 105 to three.[1] Subsequently, in a rare show of Arab support for an Israeli candidate, King Hussein invited Netanyahu to visit Amman during the 1996 election

---

[1] Shamir, *The Rise and Decline of the Warm Peace with Jordan*, p. 322.

170   Backtracking

campaign. Hussein reasoned that dealing with Netanyahu, a novice statesman, would be easier than negotiating with the then Labor candidate for the prime ministership, Shimon Peres, in whom Hussein had lost trust.[2] Hussein suspected that peace agreements forged by Peres with Syria and the Palestinians might threaten Jordanian interests. This was less likely under Netanyahu given his and his party's hostility towards the PLO and opposition to withdrawal from the Golan.[3]

King Hussein's was virtually the only Arab voice expressing support for Binyamin Netanyahu following his election victory. Hussein stated publicly that: 'There is no reason to necessarily see the election of Netanyahu as an act against peace.'[4] However, these hopes were dashed by Israel's unilateral decisions to open the Hasmonean Tunnel and authorize construction in Har Homa. In both cases, which impinged on the peace with Jordan, Israel's decision-making process was shaped significantly by Netanyahu and his immediate circle. Their poor foreign policy judgement resulted in dispatching Dr Dore Gold, Netanyahu's trusted aide, to Amman, less than thirty hours before the opening of the Hasmonean Tunnel, for a routine briefing with King Hussein. Gold had not been privy to discussions about the opening and, therefore, did not raise the issue in his meeting with the King, which was leaked and received media coverage. A similar pattern was followed shortly before the dispute over Har Homa erupted. Just three days before authorizing the Har Homa construction, Netanyahu paid a well-publicized visit to Jordan.[5]

Why were these two meetings between top Israeli officials and their Jordanian counterparts so problematic? The unilateral step to open the second exit to the Hasmonean Tunnel breached Israel's fundamental commitment to Jordan, in article 9 of the peace agreement, to 'respect' and give 'high priority' to the special historic role of the Hashemite Monarchy in the Muslim Holy Shrines in Jerusalem.[6] This clear contravention of the agreement threatened bilateral relations and challenged a key tenet of the Hashemite Monarchy's legitimacy – its self-proclaimed custodianship of the Muslim Holy Shrines in Jerusalem.[7] A meeting

[2] I am grateful to Professor Avi Shlaim for drawing my attention to this last point; Halevy, *Man in the Shadows,* p. 120.
[3] Shamir, *The Rise and Decline of the Warm Peace with Jordan,* pp. 324, 328–9.
[4] Oded Granot, 'King Hussein: There Is No Reason to Worry', *Ma'ariv,* 2 June 1996.
[5] Shamir, *The Rise and Decline of the Warm Peace with Jordan,* pp. 210, 212; Shlaim, *Lion of Jordan,* p. 562.
[6] 'Treaty of Peace Between the State of Israel and the Hashemite Kingdom of Jordan', 26 October 1994, *IMFA,* www.mfa.gov.il/mfa/foreignpolicy/peace/guide/pages/israel-jordan%20peace%20treaty.aspx, accessed 10 November 2015.
[7] On the connection between the Hashemite's legitimacy and Jerusalem, see Kimberly Katz, *Jordanian Jerusalem: Holy Places and National Places* (Gainesville: University of Florida Press, 2005).

Foreign Policy towards Jordan under Netanyahu   171

between a top Israeli official and King Hussein just thirty hours before the breach of such a fundamental commitment in the peace agreement created an impression of Jordan's collusion or Israel's disregard of the commitment.

It was clear that Hussein's initial unconditional support for the Netanyahu government had backfired, while Netanyahu and his immediate decision circle had displayed poor foreign policy management in relation to Jordan. Consistent with the prime minister's blinkered historical outlook, which too easily denied the Arabs' historic ties to Jerusalem, the Netanyahu government disregarded the peace agreement clauses about preserving Hashemite interests in the Holy City. Reflecting the mood in Jordan's royal palace, Queen Noor noted that, for Jordan, the tunnel crisis emboldened critiques of the peace accord with Israel.[8]

This was the background to King Hussein's sharp comments during the October 1996 Washington Summit, which was convened by the Americans to resolve the tunnel crisis. In this closed forum, the King expressed his deep frustration: 'We are at the edge of the abyss', he told Netanyahu, 'and regardless of our best efforts, we might be just about to fall into it – all of us.'[9]

The symbolism in the decision on 26 February 1997, only a few months following the tunnel crisis, to authorize construction in Har Homa compounded the effects of the tunnel crisis. Israel's ambassador to Jordan, Shimon Shamir, noted a surge in negative Jordanian public opinion towards the agreement with Israel. In March 1997, the King's utter frustration with Israeli foreign policy was expressed publicly.[10] In two letters from Hussein to Netanyahu, which were leaked to the Israeli press, the king listed his complaints – unilateral steps in Jerusalem, stalling economic cooperation, unpicking the Oslo accords and deliberate humiliation of the Palestinians.[11]

These letters demonstrated Hussein's loss of trust and disappointment. Almost a year into Netanyahu's premiership, it was evident that Israeli foreign policy towards Jordan was driven not by the requirements of the peace process but, rather, it was determined by the commitment of the prime minister and his coalition government to their national-religious power base and their Greater Israel ideology. These domestic determinants of Israeli foreign policy, coupled with the prime minister's and his immediate circle's entrenched scepticism towards the Arab world, seriously undermined the Israeli-Jordanian peace. Gradually, as scholar

---

[8] Noor, *Leap of Faith*, p. 400.   [9] Noor, *Leap of Faith*, p. 401.
[10] Shamir, *The Rise and Decline of the Warm Peace with Jordan*, p. 230.
[11] Guy Bechor, 'The King's Nightmare', *Ha'aretz*, 12 March 1997; 'Editorial' *Ha'aretz*, 12 March 1997; Shlaim, *Lion of Jordan*, pp. 567–8.

172   Backtracking

Markus Bouillon describes, the lofty dreams of a warm peace based on economic and social cooperation faded.[12]

In this context, Israeli-Jordanian ties were tested to the limit when, on 14 March 1997, a Jordanian soldier, Ahmed Dakamesh, killed seven Israeli schoolgirls at a northern border crossing known as the 'Island of Peace'. King Hussein, quickly grasping the gravity of the incident, cut short a visit to Spain. On returning to Jordan, he travelled to Israel to pay visits of condolence to each of the grieving Israeli families. Kneeling before the mourners, he shared their and the Israeli nation's profound sorrow over the girls' murders. He insisted that this powerful human gesture be broadcast on Jordanian television, fully aware that, in some Arab and Muslim quarters, it could be construed as submitting to the Israelis. In an unpublicized gesture (which was accepted), he offered $1 million to be distributed to the victims' families.[13]

This visit to Israel made it clear that the type of peace Hussein sought was the antithesis of the peace of deterrence propagated by Binyamin Netanyahu. The king's reaction – in word and deed – left a strong impression on the Israeli leadership, creating the potential for renewed cooperation between the two states and a foundation for an improved strategic dialogue and security cooperation.[14] The Jordanians monitored Hamas headquarters in Amman and, periodically, arrested Hamas activists plotting attacks in Israel.[15] Israel reciprocated; for example, in an agreement signed on 8 May 1997, it agreed to transfer $50 million of its US aid to Jordan. It also increased water transfers by 25 million cubic metres, although this was only half the amount promised by Israel in the peace accord.[16] However, the potential for reviving the Israeli-Jordanian peace was not realized. Consistent with the monolithic world view adopted by the prime minister and his immediate decision-making circle, which was inherently suspicious of the Arabs, Israel did not consider Jordan a strategic partner. Consequently, Jordanian interests remained minor in Israeli foreign policy calculus. Before long, this led to an acute foreign policy crisis between the two states.

---

[12] Markus E. Bouillon, *The Peace Business: Money and Power in the Israeli Palestinian Conflict* (London: I.B. Tauris, 2004), pp. 75–105; Shamir, *The Rise and Decline of the Warm Peace with Jordan*, pp. 334–5.

[13] Shlaim, *Lion of Jordan*, p. 569; Noor, *Leap of Faith*, p. 405.

[14] Ashton, *King Hussein of Jordan*, p. 331.

[15] 'Jordan Arrests five Hamas Activists Planning Terrorist Attacks in Israel', *Ha'aretz*, 18 August 1997.

[16] Shamir, *The Rise and Decline of the Warm Peace with Jordan*, pp. 365–7, 369–70; Ashton, *King Hussein of Jordan*, p. 334.

A Self-Inflicted Foreign Policy Crisis – the Botched Assassination of Khaled Mashal

On 22 September 1997, King Hussein held a meeting with Mossad's David Silberg, who was responsible for its overt ties with Jordan. According to General Ali Shukri, Hussein's chief of staff, the King relayed to the Israelis a Hamas offer of a thirty-year truce. King Hussein clearly considered it a serious proposal and pledged his personal mediation were Israel to agree to negotiate with Hamas. Hussein insisted that Silberg transmit this message urgently to the prime minister and, on 22 September, Silberg confirmed it had reached Netanyahu's desk.[17]

King Hussein awaited Israel's response to this proposition, about which Head of Mossad Danny Yatom had been briefed by Silberg. Silberg was unsure about the genuineness of Hamas's proposition, but Yatom was unequivocal: 'Offers for Hudnas' [an Arabic term for a truce], he stated, 'were constantly passed to Israel via Arab members of Knesset, European envoys, informants, and the Israeli civil administration … However, they were always treated as amounting to nothing. Hamas requested cease fires while it was weak to regroup, rearm, and regain strength.'[18] Had the GSS and the IDF intelligence been privy to the offer relayed by Silberg, Yatom argued, as with previous offers, it would have been disregarded.[19]

Yatom's account is inaccurate on a number of points. For example, the GSS would not necessarily have dismissed the notion of a truce with Hamas. 'By 1997 we recognized that the notion of a Hudna with Israel was percolating Hamas', recalls then Head of GSS, Ami Ayalon, 'and by 1998 the leader of Hamas, Sheik Ahmad Yassin, theologically sanctioned it.'[20] In this light, it is unclear that Hamas's offer of a truce would have been disregarded as readily as Yatom claimed.

There is also an issue about when Prime Minister Netanyahu was made aware of the offer. While Shukri reported that the message had reached the prime minister's desk, Yatom claims that Netanyahu had not been able to review it immediately. Yatom maintains that a technical mistake meant that the prime minister, who had just returned from abroad and was reported to be exhausted, did not receive the message about the truce. The meeting, in which Yatom planned to brief Netanyahu face to face about the offer relayed by King Hussein, was delayed.[21]

---

[17] Shlaim, *Lion of Jordan*, p. 571; Shamir, *The Rise and Decline of the Warm Peace with Jordan*, p. 237.
[18] Yatom, *The Confidant*, p. 40.   [19] Ibid.   [20] Interview 2 Ayalon.
[21] Yatom, *The Confidant*, p. 41.

174   Backtracking

Whether Shukri's or Yatom's account is more accurate is difficult to determine. However, it seems clear that there was no serious foreign policy evaluation of the Hamas proposal. It certainly reached the head of Mossad and, possibly, was seen by the Israeli prime minister. However, the GSS and the MFA, as a well-placed official confirmed, were not aware of the offer.[22] Furthermore, Efraim Halevy recalls that, 'at no point was there a systematic analysis about whether engaging with Hamas solely by military means was the most effective way to deal with the organization.'[23]

A Crisis Erupts

It is against this backdrop that we need to assess the Israeli decision, on 25 September 1997, to authorize a Mossad hit squad of eight to assassinate Kahled Mashal, head of the Hamas Bureau in Amman, whom Israeli intelligence had linked to several terrorist operations.[24] In Yatom's view, the offer relayed from Hamas just three days earlier did not justify a rethinking of the assassination operation.[25] The attempt on Khaled Mashal's life was carried out by two Mossad operatives, in Amman city, in broad daylight, by means of a slow-acting poison sprayed into Mashal's ear. It was a complete blunder. The two assassins were captured and detained by Jordanian security forces, four of the team sought refuge in the Israeli embassy, the other two Mossad operatives remained at large.[26]

A few hours later and clearly alarmed, Head of Mossad Yatom was dispatched by the prime minister to brief the king on the incident before the story was broken by the media. The meeting was also attended by General Ali Shukri and General Samih Batikhi, head of Jordan's General Intelligence Department. Danny Yatom had served previously as military secretary to Yitzhak Rabin and was integral to negotiations with Jordan, which had contributed to the development of a personal relationship with King Hussein. For instance, less than two months before the botched assassination attempt, King Hussein had invited Yatom and his family to holiday in Aqaba.[27] Thus, King Hussein anticipated that Yatom's visit, on 25 September 1997, was to discuss Hamas's truce offer. As the

---

[22] Interview 2 Ayalon; Interview with high-level MFA official on condition of anonymity.
[23] Halevy, *Man in the Shadows*, p. 133.
[24] Yatom, *The Confidant*, pp. 15–16; Interview 1 Ayalon.
[25] Yatom, *The Confidant*, p. 41.
[26] Shlaim, *The Lion of Jordan*, p. 571; Shamir, *The Rise and Decline of the Warm Peace with Jordan*, pp. 235–6; Paul MacGeough, *Kill Khalid: The Failed Mossad Assassination of Khalid Mashal and the Rise of Hamas* (New York: New Press, 2009), p. 184.
[27] Yatom, *The Confidant*, p. 13; Shlaim, *Lion of Jordan*, p. 572; Halevy, *Man in the Shadows*, p. 133.

purpose of the impromptu trip to Amman became apparent, Hussein felt personally betrayed.[28]

The effect of the assassination attempt was severe. King Hussein had received no prior notice of Israel's plans neither was he made aware by the Israelis that Khaled Mashal was directly responsible for terrorist attacks.[29] Thus, in just over twelve months, Israel had violated its agreement with Jordan. Article 2, which states that Israel and Jordan will 'recognize and will respect each other's sovereignty' and 'develop good neighbourly relations', had been breached. Similarly, article 4, which acknowledged that 'mutual understanding and co-operation in security-related matters will form a significant part of their relations' was also infringed.[30]

Besides violating the Israeli-Jordanian peace accord, the failed Israeli operation put the king in an extremely awkward position vis-à-vis a number of constituencies. These included the Jordanian public, which was weary of the agreement with Israel and the Islamist groups, in particular. Likewise, Arab regimes were critical of the accommodation Jordan had shown towards Israel after Netanyahu's election. Meanwhile, the PLO resisted any move that might embolden Hamas. In this context, the botched assassination attempt so close to King Hussein's offer to mediate, not only rendered Hamas's proposal of a truce stillborn. It also suggested strongly that Jordan was either too weak to control the Israelis on its own soil or, worse, that it was collaborating with the Israelis.

'Hussein's conclusion was simple: Netanyahu was out to destroy peace.'[31] Incensed, he briefed President Clinton by phone. Hussein threatened that if Mashal died he would expose the story, suspend the peace treaty with Israel and put the attackers on public trial in Jordan. Concurrently, the Jordanians demanded the antidote to the poison that had been injected into Mashal's ear, suspended security cooperation with Israel and readied their army units to storm the Israeli Embassy to arrest the four Mossad operatives it was sheltering.[32] Thus, the assassination attempt on Khaled Mashal constituted, for Israel, a self-inflicted foreign policy crisis. It threatened a strategic asset: peace with Jordan and limited the length of time before the situation became irreversible. The potential for military escalation was real.[33]

---

[28] Shlaim, *Lion of Jordan*, p. 573.

[29] Shamir, *The Rise and Decline of the Warm Peace with Jordan*, p. 237.

[30] Quotes are from the 'Israel Jordan Peace Treaty', *IMFA*.

[31] Shlaim, *Lion of Jordan*, p. 576.

[32] Shlaim, *Lion of Jordan*, pp. 572–3; Ashton, *King Hussein of Jordan*, p. 332; Yatom, *The Confidant*, pp. 18–22, 27; Nave, *Executive Secrets*, p. 172; Halevy, *Man in the Shadows*, pp. 134–5.

[33] For a discussion on the foreign policy crisis, see Michael Brecher and Jonathan Wilkenfeld, *A Study of Crisis* (Ann Arbour: University of Michigan Press, 1997).

176   Backtracking

What led Israel to take such a perilous foreign policy course? The prime minister's decision to authorize the assassination was prompted by Hamas's 30 July and 4 September terror attacks. Yet, in the planning stages for the assassination, Mossad stressed that it would have only a 'temporary' effect on Hamas because Mashal's place would quickly be filled.[34] The GSS supported this assessment.[35] Why, then, especially given the sensitivities involved in an assassination attempt in Jordan, did the prime minister authorize the operation? The answer lies in the weakening effect that the terrorist attacks were having on Binyamin Netanyahu's domestic political standing. We have seen that the prime minister was unable to match the security credentials of his predecessors, Yitzhak Rabin and Yitzhak Shamir. His tactic was to cultivate a hardline antiterrorist stance and his promise of 'peace and security' hinged on this image. The assassination of a key member of Hamas, although it would have a fairly insignificant impact on Hamas, would sustain the image of Binyamin Netanyahu as both hardline and antiterrorist.

It is ironic, therefore, that the resolution to the self-inflicted foreign policy crisis was contingent on creating the reverse effect. In the early stages of the crisis, Hussein refused flatly to meet any Israeli.[36] This is evidence that the foreign policy pursued by the Netanyahu government since its rise to power had burned the final bridge with Israel's only ally in the Arab world. The sole potential remaining link to the Jordanian monarch was Mossad veteran, Efraim Halevy, one of the architects of the accord between the two states, who, at the time, was Israeli ambassador to the EU. Following an urgent summons to Israel, the incapability of the Israeli side to view the crisis from Hussein's perspective, was clear to Halevy: 'When I joined the initial deliberations on how to respond', he recalls, 'which were held by the Chief of Staff, Head of Mossad Yatom and others, a number of proposals were floating around'. They revolved around 'offering a supply of infrared night sights for Jordan's military tanks, or perhaps upgrading some of the Jordanian air force's aging fleet'.[37] In contemplating the possibility of resolving the crisis via these minor gestures, it was clear that the top brass in Israel's security network were unaware of the gravity of the crisis and the predicament faced by King Hussein. They were preoccupied only with the narrow perspective of Israel. As Mossad's head, Yatom, confirms: '[W]hat was at the top of my agenda during those moments was not the relationship with Jordan

---

[34] Yatom, *The Confidant*, p. 14.   [35] Interview 2 Ayalon.
[36] Shlaim, *Lion of Jordan*, p. 573; Halevy, *Man in the Shadows*, p. 133.
[37] Interview Halevy.

The Botched Assassination of Khaled Mashal 177

and with the King but how do I rescue my people and return them safely to Israel.'[38]

What Yatom did not appreciate was that the two elements were intertwined, which was the reason for Halevy's absolute rejection of his approach. Halevey later observed: 'We had to propose a deal that King Hussein could defend to his own people and that would clarify beyond any doubt that he was not a Mossad agent, which he was not.' Halevy suggested a ground-breaking idea. In exchange for freeing the Mossad agents, Israel would release Hamas's leader and founder, the blind paraplegic, Sheik Ahmad Yassin, who had been held prisoner in Israel since 1991. The idea was put to the prime minister on the evening of Friday 26 September, by Halevy, but was rejected flatly: 'Think of a different solution!' demanded Netanyahu.[39]

Two incidents that occurred on the following day, the Sabbath, 27 September, are revealing of the prime minister's foreign policy decision-making. Having returned to a Mossad facility that morning Halevy received a phone call from Binyamin Netanyahu. 'Do you recall speaking to me about someone yesterday', asked the prime minister. 'Who do you mean? I want you to say explicitly who are you talking about', retorted Halevy. 'Yassin', replied the prime minister curtly, after a pause. 'Go and finish it.'[40]

Halevy agreed, but during the same conversation, requested that his role in the affair remain secret. The Mossad veteran was aware that his relationship with the king was not merely personal, but was also an Israeli national asset. Therefore, any association with the sordid Mashal affair would erode his intimacy with King Hussein and undermine his value as a national asset. Technically, given the tight censorship imposed on the affair in Israel at the time, there should have been no problem honouring Halevy's sensible request. However, forty-eight hours after the meeting, Halevy's role in it had been leaked to the Israeli media.

Why was the prime minister reluctant to utter Yassin's name and why did the part played by Halevy reach the Israeli media? Why did Netanyahu so quickly backtrack from his initial rejection of the idea to release Yassin? International factors certainly played a part in the release decision. There was a real prospect of the Israeli-Jordanian accord collapsing. Canada was aggrieved by the Mossad agents having used Canadian passports.[41] The USA was harshly critical of Netanyahu.[42]

---

[38] Yatom, *The Confidant*, p. 21.   [39] Interview Halevy.   [40] Interview Halevy.

[41] Rory McArthy, 'The Mossad's Foreign Operations Have often Embarrassed Israel, *Guardian*, www.theguardian.com/world/2010/feb/16/mossad-operations-passports-israel-embarrassment, accessed 30 May 2019.

[42] Ross, *The Missing Peace*, pp. 356–8; MacGeough, *Kill Khalid*, p. 182.

178   Backtracking

However, Halevy was of the opinion that another factor, which was a common thread running through the prime minister's decision-making, had tilted the balance during the crisis: Netanyahu's domestic standing and political survival. It was for precisely this reason that the prime minister had tried to disassociate himself from the proposal to release Yassin during his phone conversation with Halevy and why the media got wind that the proposal made by Halevy had prepared the way to the sealing of a deal with Jordan. 'In doing so', Halevy observed presciently, 'the Prime Minister shifted the spotlight from the decision-maker to the civil servant making the proposal', creating, in the eyes of his constituency, an artificial boundary between the prime minister and the actual decision.[43]

In so doing, the prime minister had prioritized preservation of his own 'antiterrorist' domestic political image over protecting a crucial national asset. Furthermore, said Halevy, reflecting rather sombrely on his period of working with the prime minister as head of Mossad, 'you will not find a brave decision taken by Binyamin Netanyahu on a substantive matter that contradicted his own personal political interest to remain in power.'[44] GSS officials and former ministers who worked closely with the prime minister had arrived at the same conclusion as the former head of Mossad.[45]

In retrospect, there is no evidence that the attempt to assassinate Khaled Mashal was part of a coherent foreign policy attempt to destroy the peace with Jordan, which was how King Hussein perceived it initially. Only Yatom, head of Mossad, and, possibly, the prime minister, were aware of the offer made by Hussein. It would seem, rather, that the foreign policy crisis provoked by the assassination attempt was unintended, and that the assassination plan was motivated by domestic considerations – not least the prime minister's political standing. Nonetheless, the event and its subsequent management by the prime minister and the then head of Mossad posed a direct threat to the peace agreement between the two countries.

Ultimately, the Mashal affair was resolved by a negotiated deal. Israel agreed to release Ahmad Yassin and seventy Jordanian and Palestinian prisoners. In return, Jordan allowed the two remaining Mossad operatives being held in custody to return to Israel, the other six members of the assassination team having already been allowed to leave Jordan. However, the affair reflected a rapid cooling of the Israeli-Jordanian peace. From

[43] Interview Halevy.   [44] Interview Halevy.
[45] Interview 2 Ayalon; Interview with former minister in Netanyahu's government on condition of anonymity.

a peak under the Rabin government, a series of poorly managed and reckless decisions under Netanyahu brought the relationship to its nadir. As Cabinet Secretary Nave recalled: '[W]hile the Mashal affair was resolved the deep wound in Israeli-Jordanian relations continued haemorrhaging.'[46]

Whither the Israeli-Jordanian Peace?

The diminution of relations between Israel and Jordan following the Mashal affair notwithstanding, certain underlying elements of the peace remained intact. The prospect for Israeli-Jordanian security coordination resurfaced with the renewed threat of a confrontation between Iraq and the USA. Since October 1997, Iraq had been blocking a series of inspections by the United Nations Special Commission (UNSCOM). UNSCOM was put in place following the 1990–1 Gulf War to supervise the elimination of Iraq's 'weapons of mass destruction and ballistic missiles with a range greater than 150 kilometres'.[47] Over the course of two months, Iraq ordered American personnel in UNSCOM's monitoring centre in Baghdad to leave the country and declared the presidential compounds off limits for inspections. In response, the USA strengthened its forces in the Gulf and threatened use of military power.[48] The potential for renewed escalation in the Gulf, reminiscent of the 1990–1 Gulf War, prompted Prime Minister Netanyahu to declare that Israel would respond militarily if attacked.[49]

This set the background to a renewal of Israeli-Jordanian cooperation in January–February 1998. During this period, Defence Minister Mordechai and Efraim Halevy, who replaced Yatom as the head of Mossad, met with the Jordanian security top brass to coordinate Israel's and Jordan's reactions to further escalation in the Gulf. Israel's assumed that if Saddam Hussein felt his regime to be under direct threat, he would attack Israel, to transform his conflict with the USA and Britain, into an Arab-Israeli feud.[50] In this context, Jordan adopted the position it had taken during the 1990–1 Gulf War. It made clear to Israel that it would not allow its airspace to be used by Israel to attack Iraq and that any such attempts would jeopardize the peace agreement.[51]

---

[46] Nave, *Executive Secrets*, p. 176.

[47] 'United Nations Special Commission', United Nations official website, www.un.org/D epts/unscom/General/basicfacts.html, accessed 1 February 2017; Indyk, *Innocent Abroad*, pp. 186, 188.

[48] Indyk, *Innocent Abroad*, pp. 186, 188–91.   [49] Nave, *Executive Secrets*, pp. 162–3.

[50] Nave, *Executive Secrets*, p. 162.

[51] Shamir, *The Rise and Decline of the Warm Peace with Jordan*, pp. 373–4; Shlaim, *Lion of Jordan*, p. 580.

180   Backtracking

The coordination over security in the wake of the escalation in the Gulf is indicative of the type of peace that developed between Israel and Jordan under the Netanyahu government. It was a far cry from the warm peace envisaged by Hussein when Israel and Jordan signed the 1994 peace accord. Israeli foreign policy towards Jordan amounted to a strategic peace, a peace devoid of societal and economic relations between Israelis and the Jordanians and limited trust between the leaders.

This strategic peace foreign policy stance adopted by Israel hinged on three other elements: resolute US support for the accord; converging interests between Israel and the House of Hashem, especially in relation to curbing terrorism and radical Arab states; and a consensus among the Israeli and Jordanian top political echelons that peace – with all its limitations – was preferable to the alternative. Leading this process on the Jordanian side was Crown Prince Hassan Bin-Talal, who, with the publication of his book, *Search for Peace*, had laid the intellectual foundations for why peace with Israel was in Jordan's interests.[52] On the Israeli side, the process was slower, but was virtually complete by the mid-1990s. The conventional wisdom within senior Israeli foreign policymaking circles was that a stable Jordan would provide Israel with the strategic depth that, historically, it had lacked.[53] Indeed, these material and ideational foundations of the Israeli-Jordanian peace accord prevented its collapse under the perilous foreign policy adopted by Israel towards Jordan under Netanyahu.

From Negotiation to the Brink of War

Relations with Jordan and the Palestinians were not the only aspects of Israel's foreign policy towards the Arab world to be threatened by the election to power of Binyamin Netanyahu. It posed a direct challenge to the fragile Syrian-Israeli negotiations, which had been taking place in the previous four years under the Rabin-Peres government. The foreign policy tactic adopted by Netanyahu towards negotiations with Syria was similar to his foreign policy approach to the Oslo accords. Under the guise of a different negotiating tactic, Israel proposed new conditions to Syria, which would allow the prime minister to redefine the negotiating framework without formally disavowing it.

Most significant in this context was the decision to inform the Americans and Syria that Israel was not committed to the understandings

---

[52] Hassan Bin Talal, *Search for Peace: The Politics of the Middle Ground in the Arab East* (London: Macmillan, 1984).
[53] Interview with senior Israeli security official on condition of anonymity, 29 October 2012, Tel Aviv.

reached under the Rabin-Peres government. Two issues were rejected by Netanyahu as early as July–August 1996. He clarified that he did not endorse the promise, made by Rabin and Peres, that Israel would withdraw fully from the Golan to the 4 June 1967 line, conditional on adequate security arrangements and full normalization. In addition, Netanyahu emphasized that he would not be bound by the security understandings outlined on 22 May 1995, in the 'Aims and Principles of Security Arrangements' non-paper. Instead, he reverted to the Shamir government's entrenchment foreign policy stance. This depended on participation in negotiations without preconditions, and rejection of the land-for-peace formula in favour of the principle of peace for peace.[54]

Concomitantly, Israel proposed a 'Lebanon first' initiative, premised on the demand that the Lebanese government disarm Hezbollah, secure the Israeli-Lebanese border and assign an official role to Israel's proxy, Antoine Lahd, and his SLA. Only if these conditions were met would Israel withdraw its forces. Israel's proposal amounted to an extremely caveated interpretation of UNSCR 425, which called on Israel, immediately and unconditionally, to withdraw its military forces from Lebanon. Therefore, Syria and Lebanon dismissed Israel's 'Lebanon first' initiative, which was perceived as an attempt by Israel to separate their respective peace tracks and negotiate a withdrawal from Lebanon while remaining in the Golan.[55]

The Israeli decision to renege on the understandings reached by the Rabin-Peres government was driven by domestic determinants. First, a majority of Israelis and the political establishment remained opposed to withdrawal from the Golan. Second, the political composition of the coalition government included parties firmly opposed to a withdrawal. 'Israeli sovereignty over the Golan', the government baselines stated clearly, 'would form the basis for any peace agreement with Syria'.[56] Third, was the strategic significance attributed by the prime minister to the Golan Heights. Capturing the Golan in 1967, he maintained, enabled Israelis to gaze 'down at the Syrians for the first time', a strategic advantage he was unwilling to surrender.[57] These domestic factors clearly determined Israel's foreign policy stance towards Syria at the onset of the Netanyahu government.

---

[54] Nave, *Executive Secrets*, pp. 152–3; Al-Sharaa, *The Missing Account*, pp. 358–9.

[55] Patrick Seale, 'The Syria Israel Negotiations: Who Is Telling the Truth', *Journal of Palestinian Studies*, 29, 2, 2000: 77.

[56] 'The Basic Lines of the 27 Government', Knesset official website, http://main.knesset.gov.il/mk/government/documents/kaveiyesod1996.pdf, accessed 9 February 2017.

[57] Netanyahu, *A Place Among the* Nations, p. 137.

182   Backtracking

At this point, it might have been expected that the USA would put pressure on Israel to reverse its decision to reject the understandings arduously negotiated under the previous government. However, the USA demonstrated poor judgement as a mediator and failed to challenge this clear attempt by Israel to reshape the negotiating framework; in fact, the USA all but condoned it. In a confidential letter dated 18 September 1996, Secretary of State Christopher confirmed to Netanyahu that the 1995 'Aims and Principles of Security Arrangements' non-paper had no standing in international law and, therefore, was not binding on Israel.[58] Christopher was correct that a 'non-paper', by definition, is not legally binding. However, the non-paper was significant in providing an important basis for continued negotiations, which, in one diplomatic masterstroke, Christopher managed to nullify. Furthermore, as Syria's foreign minister, al-Sharaa recalls, the confidence of the Syrian leadership in the secretary of state's 'integrity' and ability to be an honest broker, was seriously undermined.[59] In this respect, Christopher's letter was 'a serious blow to the peace process'.[60]

Israel's redefinition of the negotiating framework took place against the earlier suspension of Israeli-Syrian talks, in February 1996. Following that, Israel had signed a defence treaty with Turkey and, as we have seen, in April 1996, launched a devastating attack on Lebanon in Operation Grapes of Wrath. This sequence of events, according to Patrick Seale, one of the leading chroniclers of Syria and a confidant of its regime, reconfirmed Hafez al-Assad's long-held view of Israel as an inherently aggressive and an expansionist state. The confluence of these events was perceived by the ever-suspicious top Syrian foreign policymakers as ominous. The prevailing view was that Israel was attempting to exert military pressure on Syria via a show of force in Lebanon and to marginalize it regionally and isolate Iran through its alliance with Turkey, which would destabilize the Assad regime.[61]

Based on the available evidence, it is unclear whether this was Israel's intention. However, it is apparent that Israel's decision to try to redefine the negotiating framework, rather than resume talks, created a very dangerous situation. In June 1996, after a meeting between Syrian Ambassador Walid al-Moualem and senior advisor to the Israeli prime Minister Dr Dore Gold, direct contact ceased completely, making very

---

[58] Al-Sharaa, *The Missing Account*, p. 360.   [59] Al-Sharaa, *The Missing Account*, p. 361.
[60] Ibid.
[61] Patrick Seale with Linda Butler, 'Assad's Regional Strategy and the Challenge from Netanyahu', *Journal of Palestine Studies*, 26, 1, 1996: 27–8; al-Sharaa, *The Missing Account*, p. 364.

real the prospect of foreign policy miscalculation leading to conflict between the two longstanding rivals.[62]

Syria's concern emanated from the assumption that Israel sought to coerce it into accepting its renegotiating terms by exerting military pressure. Israel's suspicion, by way of contrast, was based on a fabricated report that had been prepared by a Mossad operator, Yehuda Gil. Gil officially was retired, but remained active in Mossad under the pretext of having a Syrian source who would meet only with him. This alerted Head of Mossad, Danny Yatom, who ordered an internal investigation, which revealed that, for twenty-three years, Gil had submitted fictitious reports about supposed meetings with this alleged exclusive source.[63]

In one of these reports, submitted in September 1996, Gil claimed that he had concrete proof that the Assad regime had given up on the Netanyahu government and was planning to attack Israel militarily. This would demonstrate the cost involved in stalling negotiations with Syria and return Israel to the negotiating table. The redeployment of around one-third of Syria's forces in Lebanon, to within striking distance of Mount Hermon, lent credibility to Gil's claims. Syria's aim, according to Gil's report, involved capturing the sophisticated Israeli communication complex on Mount Hermon in a land grab rather than full-scale war. Syria, the fabricated report argued, had a shrewd foreign policy plan. It hoped the UN would impose a ceasefire and compel the two sides to negotiate, leaving Syria in control of the land it had retrieved during the surprise attack, which would provide it with an advantage in the resumed negotiations.[64]

Endorsement of the fabricated Gil report was similar in some ways to the government's endorsement of the IDF's intelligence assessment that Arafat was giving the green light to terror, as we examined in Chapter 7. In both cases, the information provided coincided with the views of the prime minister and his immediate circle that Arab violence towards Israel was unremitting. This position, which was central to the prime minister's psychological environment, too easily overlooked a number of counterarguments. For instance, the contention that Assad was a prudent leader and was deeply concerned with preserving relations with the USA and with President Clinton, who Assad 'considered to be a friend'.[65] Netanyahu and his close circle also disregarded the assessment of former

---

[62] Nave, *Executive Secrets*, p. 152; al-Sharaa, *The Missing Account*, p. 360; Yatom, *The Confidant*, p. 194.

[63] Yatom, *The Confidant*, pp. 50–1.

[64] My account is based on information inferred in Nave, *Executive Secrets*, p. 150; Yatom, *The Confidant*, pp. 47–8.

[65] Shaaban, *Damascus Diary*, p. 158.

184   Backtracking

IDF intelligence chief, General Uri Sagie, following the 1991 Madrid conference, that Syria had made a strategic choice to make peace with Israel.[66]

Why were these counterarguments not afforded more consideration? They were inconsistent with the black-and-white view of the prime minister and his close circle, of perpetual Arab hostility towards Israel. Sagie's approach, also, was incompatible with the deep political opposition from the government's supporters, to any territorial concessions towards Syria, which was a precondition for resuming the negotiations and, thus, was virtually dismissed.

Ultimately, the brewing crisis was defused by discreet Russian and US interventions, which prevented full-scale military confrontation.[67] However, the Israeli-Syrian negotiations remained frozen for several months. They were blocked by the deeply entrenched Israeli foreign policymaking view that, strategically, the Golan was indispensable; by the political consensus within the Netanyahu government against a withdrawal; and by Israeli public opinion, which, overall, was against withdrawing from the Golan.

As negotiations stalled, to Syria's chagrin, Israel expanded its military cooperation with Turkey. This included high-level meetings between Chief of Staff Lipkin-Shahak and Defence Minister Mordechai and their Turkish counterparts and joint military manoeuvres. In January 1998, following attempts to mend fences after the Mashal affair, Jordan sent an observer to the joint naval manoeuvres, which were both relatively small and civic in nature. Nonetheless, Jordan's interest indicated King Hussein's continued willingness to take a stance against Arab detractors of his ties with Israel.[68]

The joint naval manoeuvres, which were conducted facing the Syrian and Lebanese shorelines, coincided with deepening tensions between Syria and Turkey on a number of issues. These included shared use of water from the Euphrates and Syria's support for certain anti-Turkish Kurdish groups such as the PKK – the Kurdistan Workers' Party. The combination of US assaults in Iraq, on the one hand, and joint Israeli-Turkish-US manoeuvres, on the other, were perceived by the mistrustful Syrian leadership as a threat. The Syrian leadership's impression of increasing isolation in the region and stalled peace negations, made the Syrian leadership fearful of an imminent Turkish-led military offensive

---

[66] Communication from Sagie to Shamir conveyed to me by Mr Dan Meridor.

[67] Nave, *Executive Secrets*, pp. 151–2; Yevgeny Primakov, *Russia and the Arabs* (New York: Basic Books, 2009), p. 298.

[68] Neil Lochery, 'Israel and Turkey: Deepening Ties and Strategic Implications 1995–98', *Israel Affairs*, 5, 1, 1998: 54.

against it, which increased the prospect of a miscalculation leading to conflict.[69]

Missed Opportunities in the Gulf

The formative years of the Oslo process, which accelerated the slow normalization between Israel and the Arabs, prompted by the Madrid peace conference, created new foreign policy opportunities for Israel in the Gulf.[70] Israel's recognition by the PLO and the ensuing negotiations, reduced the political obstacles to the forging of official ties. Concurrently, Shimon Peres's framework for the realization of a new Middle East vision, was taking shape. The 1994 MENA Economic Summit, which took place in Casablanca, brought together Israeli and Arab business people, governments and international stake holders. It was a powerful illustration of how the new Middle East vision could be translated from theory into practice. Whereas the New Middle East vision had limited traction when it came to deepening the peace between Israel, Jordan and the Palestinians, it had more traction when it came to forging ties between Israel and the rich Arab Gulf states.

In the context of these political and economic regional breakthroughs, Israel forged its first meaningful ties with the Arab Gulf States following the end of the Cold War. Qatar was the first Arab Gulf State to exploit this opportunity. Its bold foreign policy towards Israel was led by its Emir, Hamad al-Kahlifa Al-Thani, who rose to power following the 27 June 1995 palace coup he had launched against his father, Sheik Khalifa bin Hamad al-Thani.[71] Carving out for Qatar an independent foreign policy course from its powerful neighbours, Saudi Arabia and Iran, Qatar signed a memorandum for the sale of gas to Israel, during the 1995 MENA Summit in Amman.[72] This was a significant step in that Qatar had publicly disassociated itself from the Arab states imposed boycott on companies trading with Israel. Moreover, it reinforced the underpinnings of the new Middle East vision propagated by Shimon Peres, in which economic cooperation would be the basis for Arab-Israeli peace. As a result, six months later, on 2 April 1996, Prime Minister Peres paid an official visit to Qatar. He was received in full

---

[69] Al-Sharaa, *The Missing Account*, pp. 369–70.
[70] Uzi Rabi, 'Qatar's Relations with Israel: Challenging Arab and Gulf Norms', *Middle East Journal*, 63, 3, 2009: 448.
[71] Uzi Rabi, 'Qatar's Relations with Israel', 443–59.
[72] Sammy Revel, *Israel at the Forefront of the Persian Gulf: The Story of an Israeli Mission in Qatar* (Tel Aviv: Miskal, 2009) pp. 51–2 (in Hebrew); Rabi, 'Qatar's Relations with Israel', 447–8.

186   Backtracking

state ceremony and signed an agreement to establish the first Israeli Trade Representation Office in Doha. By then, Israel had forged diplomatic relations with another Gulf Emirate, Oman, and three Maghreb countries – Morocco (1994), Tunisia (1996) and Mauritania (1996).[73]

Against this backdrop, when Binyamin Netanyahu came to power in 1996, his government was presented with a historic opportunity: consolidating ties with Arab Gulf states. The Qatari leadership certainly recognized this and adopted towards the newly elected Israeli prime minister a similar stance to that espoused by Jordan in the aftermath of the Israeli elections. Sammy Revel, an Israeli diplomat who headed the first Israeli diplomatic mission in Qatar, was well placed to observe Qatari foreign policy in the wake of Likud's return to power. Qatar's objective, recalled Revel, was to continue the peace process and safeguard the gains already achieved between the two states.[74]

However, the foreign policy adopted by the Likud towards the Israeli-Palestinian peace process proved a significant obstacle. As we have seen, during the first few months in power, Prime Minister Netanyahu refused to meet Yasser Arafat and reversed the settlements freeze imposed by the Rabin-Peres government. This produced a serious transformation in Israeli-Qatari relations. Revel explained that, a few months before the election of Netanyahu 'everyone was speaking in terms of regional cooperation and gradual normalization between Israel and the Arabs.'[75] In contrast, a few months after the rise to power of the Netanyahu government, 'advancing the bilateral relations with Israel became contingent upon Israel freezing settlements'.[76] 'We were shocked', Revel recalls, 'by the radical shift that occurred within such a short period of time.'[77]

With the benefit of hindsight, the linkage established by the Qatari leadership was perhaps not surprising. It reflected the inextricable link between resolving the Israeli-Palestinian conflict and accepting Israel into the Middle East. Accordingly, while the Oslo process was progressing, Arab states in the Maghreb and the Gulf, such as Oman and Qatar, were proactively advancing their relationship with Israel. However, the unpicking of the Oslo accords by the Netanyahu government, stopped the entente between Israel and Arab Gulf states in its tracks. Qatar put on hold its decision to establish a representation in Tel Aviv, which was to

---

[73] 'Israel Among the Nations: The Middle East and North Africa', *IMFA*', www.mfa.gov.il /mfa/aboutisrael/nations/pages/israel%20among%20the%20nations-%20middle%20ea st%20-%20north%20afri.aspx, accessed 23 March 2017.
[74] Revel, *Israel at the Forefront of the Persian Gulf*, pp. 82–3.
[75] Revel, *Israel at the Forefront of the Persian Gulf*, p. 87.   [76] Ibid.   [77] Ibid.

open in reciprocation for the establishment of the Israeli Trade Representation Office in Doha.[78]

The deterioration in relations between Israel and Qatar was compounded by Israel's decision, in August 1996, to open the Hasmonean Tunnel. The Qatari leadership perceived the decision as a deliberate Israeli attempt to undermine the peace process. Meanwhile, observed Revel, the majority of Qatari society, which subscribed to the Wahabi strand of Sunni Islam, interpreted the Israeli government's decision in starker terms. Mediated through the lens of Wahabism, which is a particular purist strand of Sunni Islam, the decision to open the tunnel was seen as an intentional religious assault, aimed at harming the third holiest site to Islam.[79]

Qatar's interpretation of Israel's decision to open the Hasmonean Tunnel exposes an interesting aspect of the interplay between domestic determinants, Israeli foreign policy behaviour and outcomes. The decision to open the Hasmonean Tunnel was shaped by several domestic factors. These included the foreign policy inexperience of the prime minister and his immediate circle, their disregard for the interests and sensitivities of Israel's Arab peace partners and the unwavering commitment of the government to its ethno-religious-nationalist power base. We have seen how the confluence of these domestic determinants produced a foreign policy behaviour that challenged the negotiations with the Palestinians and the peace with Jordan. The abrupt ending of the Israeli-Qatari entente reveals how the same domestic foreign policy determinants undermined another aspect of Israel's regional foreign policy: the embryonic framework of Arab-Israeli economic cooperation, which was intended to create a more favourable regional environment for resolving the Israeli-Palestinian conflict.

The blow dealt to Israeli-Qatari relations by the tunnel crisis was amplified by the February 1997 Israeli decision to backtrack on the memorandum to purchase Qatari gas. The final decision to withdraw from the deal was taken by the then Israeli minister of infrastructure, hardliner Ariel Sharon. It is unclear whether this decision was connected to the deteriorating relations with Qatar or resulted from an economic cost-benefit analysis. Either way, it reflected the disdain of the prime minister towards forging a new Middle East. In a wide-ranging interview with *Ha'aretz* a few months earlier, Netanyahu branded the concept of a New Middle East 'a very amusing idea' that has 'no grounding in reality'.[80]

---

[78] Revel, *Israel at the Forefront of the Persian Gulf*, p. 86.
[79] Revel, *Israel at the Forefront of the Persian Gulf*, p. 107.
[80] Ari Shavit, 'A New Middle East? What an Amusing Idea', *Ha'aretz*, 22 November 1996.

188   Backtracking

Cancelling the Israeli-Qatari gas deal just a few months after the tunnel crisis halted official relations between the Israeli and Qatari governments.[81] Likewise, the limited economic cooperation between the Israeli and Qatari business communities, in relation to joint agricultural ventures and exports of Israeli hi-tech products, also stalled. Furthermore, Revel recalled that the Qatari government conditioned any expansion of relations with Israel on progress in the Israeli-Palestinian peace process. Thus, in 1998, the stalled Israeli-Palestinian peace process prompted Qatar to rethink its foreign policy towards Israel. Qatar's Foreign Minister Hammad bin Jassim al-Thani issued the stern warning that if the Israeli-Palestinian peace process did not get back on track, Israeli representation in Qatar would be terminated.[82]

Revel recalled, sombrely, how the statement by the Qatari foreign minister cast a shadow over Israeli foreign policy towards the Emirate by giving the impression that the Israeli Trade Representation Office in Doha would soon close. Consequently, Revel and his staff devoted most of their time to damage containment rather than to exploiting the opportunities created during the heyday of the Oslo process. The main reason for continued Israeli-Qatari relations was the pleas from the USA – the guarantor of Qatari security – to maintain formal relations with Israel.[83]

The Downfall of the First Netanyahu Government

The Failed Lauder Mission

Towards the summer of 1998, Prime Minister Binyamin Netanyahu faced two foreign policy options in relation to the Arab-Israeli peace process. He could participate in an Israeli-Palestinian-US summit, which the Americans had been pressing for during the previous fourteen months or try to revive the stalled Israeli-Syrian track. On 7 August 1998, a US business tycoon, Ronald Lauder, arrived in Damascus. Lauder, the son of Estée Lauder, the cosmetics manufacture, was personally and politically close to Binyamin Netanyahu. A staunch Republican and a vocal Likudnik on all matters relating to Israel, he had backed Netanyahu since the 1980s and was a leading figure in the US Zionist Jewish Community.[84] Having no in-depth knowledge of the Arab-Israeli conflict and, not least, Syria, his main asset in his bid to rekindle the

---

[81] Revel, *Israel at the Forefront of the Persian Gulf*, p. 113.
[82] Raviv Druker, *Ma'ariv*, 23 July 1998; Al-Hayat, 2 October 1998; *Ha'aretz*, 2 December 1998; Revel, *Israel at the Forefront of the Persian Gulf*, pp. 213, 216.
[83] Revel, *Israel at the Forefront of the Persian Gulf*, p. 220.
[84] Shlaim, *The Iron Wall*, p, 620.

Israeli-Syrian negotiations was his personal charisma and contacts. Lauder's brief from Binyamin Netanyahu, as described to his first Syrian contact, Ambassador al-Mouallem, was to engage in 'very intensive and very unofficial talks'.[85] Over five weeks during summer and autumn 1998, Lauder shuttled between Jerusalem and Damascus. During this period, he held nine meetings, which produced what came to be known as the Lauder ten-point document.[86]

These negotiations, conducted by a private citizen, took place outside any governmental framework. However, a relatively large number of individuals on the Israeli and Syrian sides were made privy to their content. These individuals included Prime Minister Netanyahu, Defence Minister Mordechai, Dr Uzi Arad, the prime minister's diplomatic advisor, and Cabinet Secretary Nave. Others involved included aide to Defence Minister Mordechai, Yaakov Amidror, and Shimon Shapria, the prime minister's military secretary. On the Syrian side, President Assad, whose health was beginning to deteriorate, depended on Foreign Minister al-Sharaa and Ambassador al-Mouallem.[87]

During the talks, the Syrians made two key concessions. They agreed to maintenance of an early warning system (EWS) on Mount Hermon for ten years after total withdrawal and, according to Lauder, the EWS would be an 'American-French facility under their total auspices and responsibilities'.[88] Bouthaina Shaaban, the official interpreter and advisor to President Assad, who participated in the negotiations, maintained that the agreement included integrating Syrian personnel in the EWS.[89] Whatever the truth, the Israelis would be dependent on the good will of foreign governments for information.

The Syrians agreed, also, to extend the period of Israeli withdrawal from fourteen to eighteen months, to be effected in three stages. Shaaban claimed that normalization would deepen after each withdrawal. Accordingly, at the beginning of the withdrawal, the two countries would exchange ambassadors and achieve full normalization at the end of the third stage.[90] Lauder, in contrast, does not refer to the sequencing of the withdrawal and normalization, which had been a stumbling block

---

[85] Shaaban, *Damascus Diary*, p. 161.

[86] Information on what the document contained was gleaned from a letter of clarification sent by Lauder to President Clinton. The letter is reproduced in its entirety in Yatom, *The Confidant*, pp. 448–50. I also consulted Butheina Shaaban's record; Shaaban was present at all the talks.

[87] Daniel Pipes, 'The Road to Damascus: What Netanyahu almost Gave Away [to Assad in 1998], www.danielpipes.org/311/the-road-to-damascus-what-netanyahu-almost-gave-away, accessed 21 February 2017.

[88] Lauder letter to Clinton quoted in Yatom, *The Confidant*, p. 450.

[89] Shaaban, *Damascus Diary*, p. 166.   [90] Ibid.

190   Backtracking

since negotiations had begun under Rabin. On less disputed matters, Israel and Syria agreed to base security arrangements on the 1995 'Aims and Principles of Security Arrangements' non-paper. Water rights would be addressed in line with international norms.

The outcome of the Lauder mission – albeit limited – was significant. Documents prove that Binyamin Netanyahu was more willing than either Rabin or Peres had been to concede to Syrian demands. He relayed to the Syrians, via Lauder, that Israel was willing to withdraw to a border based on the 4 June 1967 line, while Rabin and Peres had made a hypothetical commitment only and that contingent on Syria agreeing first to Israel's demands with regard to normalization and security. In contrast, Netanyahu offered to withdraw from the Golan without conditioning the offer on Syria first providing assurances to Israel about normalization and security arrangements.[91]

Why was the prime minister so forthcoming in verbal negotiations with the Syrians conducted by his American interlocutor? The Lauder mission coincided with increasing US pressure on Israel to agree to a deal on the pending Further Redeployments in the West Bank. It is conceivable that Netanyahu maintained the Syrian track, via Lauder, solely to avoid progress on the Israeli-Palestinian track. This interpretation is reinforced by the fact that the Lauder initiative failed once it showed signs of becoming substantive. Pinning Netanyahu down to track II diplomacy that Netanyahu had himself initiated, President Assad made a simple request for a map marking what Israel perceived to be the 4 June 1967 line. 'The talks', as Lauder stated explicitly in a letter to president Clinton, 'could not be finalized until a map of the June 4 1967 line was provided by Israel', which Netanyahu refused to make available.[92]

Why did the prime minister retract at this critical juncture? Debilitated politically, Netanyahu could not afford to provide the Syrians with a map; it was clear that his immediate circle remained utterly against an Israeli withdrawal. For this reason, the prime minister's confidant and Cabinet Secretary, Danny Naveh, pressed Netanyahu not to provide the map and continued to advocate for Israel not withdrawing from the Golan.[93] Opposition from ministerial colleagues was also significant. Former head of Mossad, Danny Yatom, who had the opportunity to debrief the American peace team on the Lauder initiative, revealed that Defence Minister Mordechai objected strongly to the idea of furnishing a map. He was unhappy with the security arrangements it outlined.[94] There was

[91] Ross, *The Missing Peace*, p. 528; Yatom, *The Confidant*, p. 198; Kfir and Dor, *Barak. Wars of my Life*, p. 215.
[92] Lauder letter to President Clinton reproduced in Yatom, *The Confidant*, p. 448.
[93] Nave, *Executive Secrets*, p. 160.   [94] Yatom, *The Confidant*, p. 198.

Downfall of the First Netanyahu Government

also a clear public opinion constraint, which influenced how the Israeli prime minister operated in the negotiations. From the outset, he made it clear to the Syrians that he could not 'go public with the initiative as it contradicted the pledge he made during the election of not withdrawing from the Golan'.[95] Since Netanyahu was aware all along of these political constraints, it is doubtful that the politically beleaguered Israeli prime minister had entered the negotiations in good faith. It explains why he preferred to negotiate with the Syrians via a private citizen, Lauder, enabling him, the prime minister, and his immediate circle, to retain full deniability and stall on the Palestinian track for as long as possible.[96]

The Wye Plantation Summit

Netanyahu and his immediate circle were extremely attentive to Israeli domestic public opinion.[97] Netanyahu's chief media advisor, Aviv Bushinski, recalls that they worked under the assumption that public opinion imposed clear boundaries on their foreign policy, which was that 'the Oslo process must continue. The show must go on. We could argue about how, at what pace, and impose conditions, but we strongly believed that public expected from us to continue the Oslo process.'[98] Therefore, the retractions on every front of the Arab-Israeli peace process, exposed the Netanyahu-led government to mounting domestic pressure.

Against this backdrop and being prodded by the Clinton administration, Netanyahu agreed to a summit with the Palestinians to try to break the diplomatic deadlock. The Israeli delegation to the summit, which was convened at Wye Plantation, Maryland, between 15 and 23 October 1998, consisted of the prime minister, Defence Minister Mordechai, Absorption Minister Sheranski and Ariel Sharon, who was recently appointed foreign minister. In the months before the summit, Sharon positioned himself as staunchly opposed to a withdrawal from more than 9 per cent of the West Bank, which he rendered in the past an existential threat to Israel. However, never one to ignore an opportunity, Sharon relaxed his position slightly in return for his appointment as Israeli foreign minister. He agreed, in principle, to a 13 per cent withdrawal, which was what the US peace team had been demanding. 'I was responsible for facilitating this political deal', revealed

---

[95] Yatom, *The Confidant*, p. 195.

[96] For instance, Danny Nave's response to the piece by Daniel Pipes. 'The Road to Damascus', www.danielpipes.org/311/the-road-to-damascus-what-netanyahu-almost-gave-away, accessed 7 May 2017.

[97] Interview Bushinski.   [98] Interview Bushinski.

192   Backtracking

Aviv Bushinki.[99] It seems that, as for Sharon, personal domestic politics could trump Israeli national security considerations.

The Wye summit culminated in a twenty-seven-hour negotiation marathon during which US President Bill Clinton and an effective intervention from King Hussein secured a deal. For Hussein, it was one of his last diplomatic achievements before his death from lymphoma. The Wye agreement hinged on Israeli-occupied territory on the West Bank being exchanged for Palestinian antiterrorist measures that would be monitored by the CIA. The Palestinians committed, also, to summoning a broad assembly of Palestinian delegates to review the 1968 Palestinian National Charter and expunging the clauses that contravened the PLO's commitment to denouncing terrorism and recognizing and living peacefully alongside Israel.[100] The Israeli government and the Knesset ratified the agreement on 11 and 17 November 1998 respectively. While the government approved the deal reluctantly, the Knesset endorsed it by seventy-nine votes to nineteen, with nine abstentions.[101] The clear majority confirms the view that the Israeli public, expressed via its elected representatives, wished to see the Oslo process continue.

However, after authorizing the first of three withdrawals agreed on at Wye, on 2 December 1998, the Israeli government took a significant decision. Following an attack on an Israeli soldier in Ramallah, the cabinet charged the PA with 'encouraging acts of violence in an attempt to pressure Israel' and put a halt to the process of Further Redeployments.[102] Nevertheless, the Palestinians continued to honour their part of the bargain. On 14 December, the Palestinian National Council convened a meeting in Gaza, in the presence of President Clinton, to delete the clauses calling for the destruction of Israel.[103] A day later, Israel proposed a litany of further conditions on the

[99] Interview Bushinski.
[100] The Wye River Memorandum, *IMFA*, www.mfa.gov.il/mfa/foreignpolicy/peace/guide/pages/the%20wye%20river%20memorandum.aspx, accessed 29 March 2017; Albright, *Madam Secretary*, pp. 389–405; Miller, *The Much Too Promised Land*, pp. 275–8; Nave, *Executive Secrets*, pp. 113–38; Ross, *The Missing Peace*, pp. 415–60; Shlaim, *The Iron Wall*, p. 634.
[101] Cabinet Communiqué, 19 November 1998, *IMFA*, http://mfa.gov.il/MFA/ForeignPolicy/MFADocuments/Yearbook12/Pages/93%20Cabinet%20communique-%2019%20November%201998.aspx, accessed 29 March 2017.
[102] Cabinet Communiqué on Wye Memorandum, 2 December 1998, *IMFA*, http://mfa.gov.il/MFA/ForeignPolicy/MFADocuments/Yearbook12/Pages/99%20Cabinet%20communique%20on%20Wye%20Memorandum-%202%20Decembe.aspx, accessed 27 March 2017.
[103] 'Reactions of Prime Minister Netanyahu and Defence Minister Mordechai to the PNC Vote on the PLO Charter', 14 December 1998, *IMFA*, http://mfa.gov.il/MFA/ForeignPolicy/MFADocuments/Yearbook12/Pages/120%20Reaction%20by%20Prime%20Minister%20Netanyahu%20and%20Defen.aspx, accessed 29 March 2017.

Palestinians before Israel would implement its part of the Wye River memorandum.[104]

This was a clear attempt to upset the process, rather than a reaction to Palestinian violations. 'The penny dropped', recalled the prime minister's chief media advisor, 'right after the signing of the Wye memorandum. Netanyahu understood that it amounted to severing his ties with the ideological right', his main political base.[105] Given the fraught relations with his cabinet members, Netanyahu was completely exposed politically, so he decided to perform 'a 180 degrees turn' and effectively hollow out the Wye agreement.[106] However, this tactic, which had been effective for the prime minister following the signing of the Hebron Protocol, failed. By now, the prime minister was out of touch with his public, 74 per cent of whom supported the Wye agreement.[107] He had lost touch, also, with the Israeli parliament, which voted for a dissolution by a majority of eighty to thirty MKs. After fewer than three years in power, the countdown to the 1999 elections started.

The Consequences of Backtracking

The first Netanyahu government was the only Likud-led coalition that transferred land in exchange for peace negotiations with the Palestinians. However, this clear compromise on the ideological commitment to the Greater Land of Israel principle, was dwarfed by the overall influence exerted by the foreign policy of backtracking on the Arab-Israeli peace process. The first Netanyahu government demonstrated a clear preference for satisfying its core political constituency, overtaking the measures necessary to advance the peace process. As a result, the opening of the Hasmonean Tunnel, the decision to build in Har Homa and the prolonged stalemate in negotiations with the Palestinians undermined the Arab-Israeli peace. The Oslo process was intentionally slowed; the warm peace with Jordan became a cooler strategic peace. Relations with the Gulf countries were frozen and the Maghreb states all but severed their ties with Israel.

The retraction from the foreign policy of engagement was entirely in line with the unmitigated, hostility of the prime minister and his immediate circle towards the Arab world and the Palestinians, in particular. Despite the progress achieved by the Rabin-Peres government's foreign

---

[104] 'Statement on Israel-U.S.-PA Meeting at Erez', 15 December 1998, *IMFA*, http://mfa .gov.il/MFA/ForeignPolicy/MFADocuments/Yearbook12/Pages/122%20Statement%20o n%20Israel-US-PA%20meeting%20at%20Erez-%2015.aspx, accessed 27 March 2017.
[105] Interview Bushinski.   [106] Interview Bushinski.
[107] Survey data quoted in Shlaim, *The Iron Wall*, p. 634.

policy of engagement, Binyamin Netanyahu continued to subscribe to the world view that the Arab world was unremittingly antagonistic towards Israel. He was unable to conceive of the Arab world as a potential partner. Thus, he violated the peace agreement with Jordan, was indifferent to the moves of the Gulf States to forge closer relations with Israel and entered into negotiations with Syria in bad faith. Ultimately, Binyamin Netanyahu failed to seize the historic opportunity he was presented with. He could have emulated Menachem Begin by revisiting his erstwhile views and pursing a foreign policy aimed at improving Arab-Israeli relations via a land-for-peace deal. Lacking the leadership qualities of Begin and of his own predecessors, Shamir and Rabin, the youngest prime minister in Israel's history opted for a different foreign policy path. Driven by his reified view of history, his political power base and a right-leaning coalition, the first Netanyahu government backtracked. This approach, which was out of sync with the Israeli public and the American administration, not only posed a real threat to Arab-Israeli relations; it also brought about the downfall of Netanyahu's first government.

9   Just Beyond Reach

The 1999 Election Campaign

With few accomplishments during his three years as prime minister, it was a battered and bruised Binyamin Netanyahu who entered the 1999 general election campaign following a motion of no-confidence in his government, which received eighty-one against thirty votes. The ensuing election campaign was for prime minister and for the list of party members of the Knesset.[1] Ehud Barak, leader of the opposition and recently elected Leader of the Labour party, was locked in a fierce political battle with the incumbent prime minister, Binyamin Netanyahu. The two men, who had served and fought together in Sayeret Matkal, knew one another well.[2]

Binyamin Netanyahu presented himself as responsible for the decline in terrorist attacks since his 1996 election victory, arguing that Barak and his future administration would compromise Israeli security in their peace negotiations.[3] However, this campaigning tactic backfired. Barak, the most decorated soldier in the history of the IDF and former IDF chief of staff, had solid security credentials. They proved an important campaigning asset, swaying the votes of immigrants from the former Soviet Union in his favour.[4]

Equally important was the creation of a new alliance, One Israel. Based on the Labour party, One Israel included Meimad, a liberal religious party, and the Gesher party. David Levy, leader of Gesher, had served as a minister in all the Likud-led governments since 1977, resigning after serving as foreign minister under Binyamin Netanyahu. Barak promised Levy the Foreign Ministry and Gesher three seats in the first group of

---

[1] Daniel J. Elazar and M. Ben Mollov (eds.), *Israel at the Polls 1999* (London: Frank Cass, 2001), pp. 1–3.
[2] Kfir and Dor, *Barak. Wars of my Life*, pp. 54, 64–8, 78–80.
[3] Elazar and Mollov, 'Introduction' in *Israel at the Polls 1999*, p. 7.
[4] Vladimir Khanin, 'Israeli, Russian Parties and the New Immigrant Vote' in Elazar and Mollov, *Israel at the Polls 1999*, pp. 126 and 133 footnote 97.

thirty Labour representatives. Identified closely as a leading Sephardi politician and allied to the Israeli centre right, Levy was perceived to be an asset who would strengthen Ehud Barak's domestic legitimacy. Similarly, by including Meimad, which was promised one ministerial position, One Israel hoped to shed the highly secularist image of the Labour party that had dogged the Rabin-Peres government.[5]

One Israel's campaign tactic favoured Ehud Barak, who defeated Binyamin Netanyahu on election day, 17 May 1999, by a margin of 56 per cent to 44 per cent, in the direct election for the premiership. Barak, who had positioned himself as heir to Yitzhak Rabin, presented an image of security and strength, which he committed to combining with cautious pursuit of an agreement with the Palestinians and Syria. Crucially, Barak pledged to withdraw the IDF from Lebanon by June 2000.[6]

While Ehud Barak's personal victory over Binyamin Netanyahu was absolute, his party, One Israel, won only twenty-six seats. Likud performed even worse, securing only nineteen seats. The less than impressive results of the two largest parties reflected an important shift in Israeli politics. Labour and Likud were weakened significantly after winning forty-four and thirty-two seats respectively in the 1992 elections. Commensurately, the number of parties promoting the interests of specific groups within Israeli society – Palestinian-Israelis, Sephardi ultra-orthodox, new immigrants – grew. This result was a clear indication that the dual system of separate votes for prime minister and Knesset had fragmented the Israeli parliament, which, after the 1999 elections, was comprised of small and medium sized parties.[7]

Political Fragmentation and the Foreign Policy Decision-Making Structure

Although Barak was elected prime minister by a wide margin, his main constituency, the Zionist centre-left One Israel and Meretz parties, together secured only thirty-six out of 120 seats.[8] These parties, which would form the core of his coalition government, had several common

---

[5] Kfir and Dor, *Barak*, p. 199; Gideon Doron, 'Barak, One – One Israel, Zero, Or, How Labour Won the Prime Ministerial Race and Lost the Knesset Elections' in Arian and Shamir, *The Elections in Israel 1999*, pp. 182, 185.

[6] Gerald Steinberg, 'Foreign Policy in the 1999 Elections' in Elazar and Mollov, *Israel at the Polls 1999*, pp. 174, 195.

[7] Asher Arian and Michal Shamir (eds.), *The Elections in Israel 1999* (New York: SUNY Press, 2002), p. 12.

[8] Party composition in the 15th Knesset, http://main.knesset.gov.il/About/History/Pages/FactionHistory15.aspx, accessed 3 May 2017.

Political Fragmentation and Foreign Policy Decision-Making 197

features. They were Zionist, secular and social democratic in their economic orientation and supported Israel's foreign policy of engagement.[9] However, to secure the parliament majority needed to pass legislation and govern, Barak needed to include in his coalition at least one party from the Israeli centre right.

The offer to become the main coalition partner was made to Shas, the Association of Sephardic Torah Keepers, whose number of parliamentary seats increased from ten to seventeen. Barak was convinced that the ambiguous position adopted by Shas on the question of land for peace, provided the government with the domestic legitimacy, lacked by the Rabin-Peres government, to rekindle the peace processes.[10] Achieving legitimacy was clearly significant for Ehud Barak, who sought a wide coalition representing the various strands of Israeli Jewish society. He included in his coalition government a number of religious parties, which were located squarely within the Israeli right. These included the National Religious Party (five seats), which represented the settlers, and the ultra-orthodox Yahadut HaTorah (five seats); Israel Ba'aliya (six seats), which was formed largely of former immigrants from the USSR; and the centrist party (six seats), which included former Likud and Labour politicians. Thus, the coalition government Barak presented to the Knesset commanded a significant majority of seventy-five seats.[11]

However, this broad coalition had several innate political tensions. One was the rift between religious parties and Meretz on social issues. Another conflict was between the National Religious Party's complete rejection of Israel's engagement foreign policy, which was fully endorsed by Meretz, the majority of One Israel and parts of the Centrist Party. The politically fractured structure of the government was reproduced in the cabinet, which was too divided and too politicized to be a constructive and meaningful forum for foreign policy decision-making and deliberation. Even Barak's own party, One Israel, was unfit for that purpose. Barak sought to distinguish himself from the dovish elements in his party and to contain them politically. His party's leading figures, such as Shimon Peres, Dr Yossi Beilin, Professor Shlomo Ben-Ami and Haim Ramon – who were all well qualified to play significant foreign policy roles – were sidelined. They were appointed to ministries that had little or no bearing on Israel's foreign relations. Bitter and disappointed for the most part, these capable politicians were prevented from making any constructive

---

[9] Data on parties available on the Knesset official website, http://main.knesset.gov.il/About/History/Pages/FactionHistory15.aspx, accessed 26 April 2017.
[10] Kfir and Dor, *Barak*, pp. 206–7; Barak, *My Country My Life*, p. 327.
[11] Knesset official website, political parties since the establishment of the state, www.knesset.gov.il/faction/heb/FactionListAll.asp?view=1, accessed 12 June 2017.

198   Just Beyond Reach

contribution to the government's foreign policy process.[12] Barak, like Rabin and Peres before him, further centralized the foreign policy decision-making process by taking on the defence portfolio in addition to his position as prime minister.[13]

The composition of the new prime minister's close decision-making circle was revealing of his decision-making style. It bore clear traces of his long service in Sayeret Matkal, which, according to his authorized biography, was 'formative' of his leadership style.[14] Ehud Barak was accustomed to a hierarchical, highly secretive and centralized chain of command. Trained for many years in the art of deception, he lacked almost all trust in his subordinates. His head of Mossad, Efraim Halevy, recalls: 'Ehud Barak was extremely distrustful towards those surrounding him. He kept a distance from his civil servants, did not share with them crucial information, which created a deep sense of suspicion between him and them.'[15] The arts of persuasion, charm, negotiation and personal relationships, not always necessary in a military context, but absolutely essential in politics, eluded Barak.[16] 'He was accustomed', noted his close confidant Gilad Sher, 'to seek solitude, concentrate, and think on his own'.[17] Equally lacking was a clear ideological or principled world view. Instead, like his mentor, Yitzhak Rabin, Ehud Barak was a quintessential 'doer' and his foreign policy outlook derived from his own cost-benefit analysis. However, unlike Yitzhak Rabin, Ehud Barak lacked the political experience, diplomatic exposure and policy record that his role model had brought to his second term as prime minister.

The Contradictory Foreign Policy Agenda of Ehud Barak

Ehud Barak presented his foreign policy agenda during his first face-to-face meeting with the Clinton administration on 15–16 July 1999.[18] In line with his centralized decision-making style, before that meeting he refused to hold any preparatory discussions below presidential level. Danny Yatom, Barak's chief confidant, recalls that Barak tended to rely

[12] Gilad Sher, *Just Beyond Reach: The Israeli-Palestinian Peace Negotiations 1999–2001* (Tel Aviv: Yedioth Ahronoth, 2001), p. 19 (in Hebrew); Gil, *The Peres Formula*, pp. 223–8.
[13] Raviv Druker, *Harakiri: Ehud Barak the Failure* (TelAviv: Miskal-Yedioth Ahronoth, 2002), pp. 48–52 (in Hebrew); Kfir and Dor, *Barak*, p. 208.
[14] Kfir and Dor, *Barak*, p. 67.   [15] Halevy, *Man in the Shadows*, p. 123.
[16] Druker, *Harakiri*, pp. 22, 28–9, 56–60.   [17] Sher, *Just Beyond Reach*, p. 19.
[18] My account of the content Barak presented at the meeting is derived from: Ross, *The Missing Peace*, pp. 498–501; Indyk, *Innocent Abroad*, p. 246; Yatom, *The Confidant*, pp. 203–6; Albright, *Madam Secretary*, pp. 602–3.

Contradictory Foreign Policy Agenda of Ehud Barak

on liaising with other leaders directly and 'face to face' rather than using personal envoys.[19] During the meeting, Barak told an enthusiastic Bill Clinton that he wanted to reach an agreement with Syria and the Palestinians by spring 2000. His timeframe was determined by his concern that breaching this deadline would risk Iraq or Iran acquiring nuclear weapons. In these circumstances, Barak believed that the Israelis would recoil from any concessions to Syria and the Palestinians. In addition, Barak was convinced that Arafat and Assad, the only political leaders in their respective societies with whom he could strike a deal, might not have long to live.

Barak continued his presentation with proposals for some foreign policy changes. With respect to Syria, Barak refused to reaffirm the 'Rabin deposit', given by Rabin when he was prime minister to Secretary of State Warren Christopher, in August 1993. Subsequently, it had been reconfirmed by Peres and Netanyahu. Strategically, Barak was concerned that the terms of the Rabin deposit jeopardized Israel's control of its main freshwater source, Lake Kinneret. He was worried, also, that, were he to reaffirm the deposit, he 'would give up the only negotiating card he had vis-à-vis Syria before Assad indicated that he was serious about making peace'.[20] Politically, he was apprehensive that accepting the Rabin deposit would undermine his ability to achieve an agreement through referendum. In relation to the Palestinians, Barak proposed extending the timeframe for Further Redeployments in the West Bank from the twelve months that Israel had agreed to under the Wye River memorandum, to twenty-four months.

The demand to renegotiate previous agreements and understandings, rather than to continue negotiations from the point where they had broken off, was inconsistent with Barak's own foreign policy goals. It posed a threat to the tight timeframe for achieving peace that Barak had presented to the US president, who duly raised this concern during his meeting with the Israeli premier.[21] A further challenge to the self-imposed twelve-month deadline stemmed from how Ehud Barak envisaged the interplay between domestic Israeli politics and foreign policy. The Rabin-Peres government progressed in the peace process with the slightest of majorities in the Knesset. Conversely, to avoid the legitimacy deficit that had blighted the Rabin-Peres government, Barak wanted the 'mainstream of Israel with him on peace.'[22] However, the Israeli mainstream remained opposed to a withdrawal from the Golan and was ambivalent towards the

---

[19] Yatom, *The Confidant*, p. 200.   [20] Barak, *My Country, My Life*, pp. 333–4.
[21] Yossi Beilin, *The Path to Geneva: The Quest for a Permanent Agreement, 1996–2004* (New York: RDV Books, 2004), p. 107.
[22] Ross, *The Missing Peace*, p. 498.

200   Just Beyond Reach

Oslo peace process. Therefore, harnessing the support of the mainstream for peace with Syria and the Palestinians would have required protracted and arduous political campaigning.

When presenting his foreign policy agenda to his American hosts, Ehud Barak made clear that his first priority was peace with Syria. In addition to ending the conflict between the two states, an accord with Syria was critical for achieving the pledge made by Barak during the elections, to withdraw the IDF from Lebanon within a year.[23] In the absence of an agreement with Syria, the powerbroker in Lebanon since it had invaded the country in 1976, there was an undeniable risk that withdrawal of the IDF would not be peaceful and that attacks on Israel from south Lebanon would continue. An agreement with Syria could break this pattern once and for all and, critically, turn Syria from an ally of Iran to an ally of the USA. These significant strategic considerations were coupled with the Israeli prime minister's perception of the key decision-makers. Barak was deeply suspicious of Arafat. By contrast, he believed Hafez al-Assad to be a tough enemy, who kept his word and, unlike the Palestinian leader, commanded a real state with a formidable army. Under certain circumstances, it could wage a war against Israel.[24]

Resuming the Syrian Track

Barak assembled around him a small and discrete foreign policy team, which was cast in his own image, to negotiate with the Syrians. Former military intelligence director, Uri Sagie, who, since 1991, had maintained that Syria had taken a strategic decision to make peace with Israel, in exchange for receiving all the territories it lost to Israel in 1967, was appointed chief negotiator.[25] Fewer than half a dozen men, all from the security establishment, including Chief of Staff Shaul Mofaz and Head of Mossad Efraim Halevy, were made aware of the renewed contact with the Syrians.[26] However, apart from Barak, no member of the government was involved in the secret resumption of the Syrian-Israeli track. In fact, as a prominent member of his government recalls, most of his ministers objected to Barak's 'Syria first' strategy, which they thought made the Palestinian leader look 'humiliated, restless, alienated, and hostile'.[27] Why did the prime minister proceed nonetheless? 'He knew he would not face opposition from within the cabinet', explained the then internal

[23] Beilin, *The Path to Geneva*, pp. 103–4.
[24] Ross, *The Missing Peace*, p. 509; Kfir and Dor, *Barak. Wars of My Life*, p. 217.
[25] Uri Sagie, *The Frozen Hand* (Tel Aviv: Miskal-Yedioth Ahronoth Books, 2011), pp. 21–4 (in Hebrew).
[26] Sagie, *The Frozen Hand*, p. 39.   [27] Ben-Ami, *Scars of War Wounds of Peace*, p. 241.

Resuming the Syrian Track   201

security minister, Professor Shlomo Ben-Ami. Because the idea of negotiating with Syria might facilitate an Israeli withdrawal from Lebanon, it was supported in the government.[28] The question remained how to sequence the Syrian and the Palestinian tracks.

The sense of urgency exhibited by Ehud Barak yielded quick results. Israeli and Syrian negotiators met in secret on 26 August 1999, in Bern, Switzerland, and on 15–16 September in Washington, DC. Sagie led the negotiations on behalf of the Israeli side. The USA was represented by Dennis Ross. The Syrians sent Riad Daoudi – a businessman and former legal advisor to the Syrian MFA, who had been at the 1996 Israeli-Syrian talks at Wye. The briefing given by Barak to Sagie strongly reflected the prime minister's awareness of the domestic opposition towards negotiations with Syria.[29] Sagie was tasked with finding a formula to reopen the Israeli-Syrian track, while minimizing Barak's exposure to his domestic opponents. Thus, Sagie was instructed not to put anything in writing. 'I don't want any documents!', Sagie recalls Barak exclaiming during their preparatory meeting. Barak also banned his chief negotiator from raising the issue of the Rabin deposit or giving assurances that Israel was prepared to withdraw from the Golan to the 4 June 1967 line. The talks would be based on the principle that nothing would be agreed until everything was agreed.[30]

The Israeli team came to these secret talks extremely well prepared. During the long and often heated debates, Sagie and his team demonstrated that the so-called 4 June 1967 border line was unclear. In fact, it had not been formally delineated on a map. Sagie, reverting to maps showing Israeli and Syrian military deployments pre-5 June 1967, showed how contested the 4 June 1967 line was. Indeed, Sagie's presentation bore out an important point, namely, that according to certain interpretations, the 4 June 1967 line awarded Syria less territory than recognized by the 1923 international border.[31] Building on this claim, Sagie proposed a creative and flexible negotiating approach. 'We need', he told his Syrian counterparts, 'to find a way to draw the 4 June 1967 line to satisfy your principle and meet our needs.'[32] By Israel's 'needs', Sagie meant Israeli sovereignty extending over the shores of Lake Kinneret and the northern sections of the River Jordan.[33]

---

[28] Interview Professor Sholomo Ben-Ami, 10 July 2017, Kfar Saba; Interview 3 Beilin.
[29] Barak outlined his views on this issue in Barak, *My Country My Life*, pp. 338–9.
[30] Sagie, *The Frozen Hand*, pp. 38–9, 46; Yatom, *The Confidant*, p. 210; Ross, *The Missing Peace*, p. 518; al-Sharaa, *The Missing Account*, p. 387.
[31] Sagie, *The Frozen Hand*, pp. 57–62; Ross, *The Missing Peace*, pp. 525–6; Yatom, *The Confidant*, p. 217.
[32] Quoted in Indyk, *Innocent Abroad*, p. 248; al-Sharaa, *The Missing Account*, p. 396.
[33] Sagie, *The Frozen Hand*, p. 62; Ross, *The Missing Peace*, p. 526.

202   Just Beyond Reach

Deeply suspicious of Israel's intentions, the Syrians rejected Sagie's approach outright. An irritated Daoudi told Dennis Ross that if the USA accepted Sagie's presentation then 'it would be preferable that the [Rabin] deposit remained in President Clinton's pocket.'[34] 'Foreign Minister al-Sharaa was even blunter, accusing Sagie of trying to deliberately 'confuse' matters and to 'blow up' the Rabin deposit'.[35] Lest there be any misunderstanding, during a meeting with President Clinton and Madeline Albright on 28–29 September 1999, al-Sharaa repeated the Syrian position towards the 4 June 1967 line. He stated that Syria's territory had to extend to the body of water in the north east of Lake Kinneret and the northern section of the River Jordan.[36]

The Bern and Washington meetings did not yield substantive progress on the core issues – withdrawal, security arrangements, the timing of their implementation and normalization. However, Sagie and Daoudi developed a rapport and were able to signal to their respective leaders that the other side had come to the negotiations in good faith and with intent. This set the conditions for the first Israeli-Syrian direct, bilateral, high-level foreign policy summit since negotiations had begun.

The Israeli-Syrian Encounter at Blair House

Chief negotiator Uri Sagie lived in Kfar Biyalik, a small community in northern Israel. He was an infantry battalion commander during the fighting that led to Israel's occupation of the Golan Heights. After his appointment as chief negotiator, members of his community and some of his former soldiers confronted him. Some were anxious, others were livid; they asked how he, a seventh-generation northern Israel farmer, could lead the charge to return the Golan to Syria. As his critics grew more hostile, the GSS received information that West Bank settlers planned to harm Sagie, who was put under tight security. Concurrently, the Golan Lobby revived its fierce campaign against withdrawal.[37]

The criticism levelled at Sagie was not merely significant in terms of the stress it imposed on the chief Israeli negotiator. It also reflected the deeply emotional and political opposition that the government would need to overcome to win a referendum vote for a withdrawal from the Golan. By December, domestic opposition to an agreement with Syria had become an acute issue. President Assad, following the Bern and Washington talks, authorized direct negotiations. Syria would be represented for the first

[34] Al-Sharaa, *The Missing Account*, p. 400.
[35] Al-Sharaa, *The Missing Account*, pp. 394, 396.
[36] Ross, *The Missing Peace*, pp. 528–9; al-Sharaa, *The Missing Account*, p. 404.
[37] Sagie, *The Frozen Hand*, pp. 93–108.

The Israeli-Syrian Encounter at Blair House

time by a high-level politician, Foreign Minister Farouk al-Sharaa, which symbolized Syria's implicit recognition of Israel. Uncharacteristically, no preconditions were attached to the unprecedented level of negotiations.[38] The only Syrian request was that Ehud Barak should be the counterpart: 'Foreign Minister Levy', they told Dennis Ross, 'was not a decision-maker and did not have much influence.'[39]

Why was Assad willing to take the step he had avoided for so many years? 'Barak is serious', Assad told Dennis Ross and Madeline Albright when he met them in Damascus on 7 December 1999. 'He wants to reach agreement quickly and so do I.' In addition, Dennis Ross suspected that Assad was aware of his own deteriorating health and wanted to relieve his heir apparent, the inexperienced Bashar al-Assad, from having to take 'the difficult step to make peace with Israel'.[40]

Ehud Barak's personality was stamped significantly on the foreign policy approach Israel adopted towards the first negotiations with Syria at the political level. His secretive and suspicious nature got the better of him; concerned about leaks, Barak did not trust Foreign Minister al-Sharaa to keep the content of private conversations confidential. Therefore, Barak refused to hold any private meetings with the Syrian foreign minister on this high-profile occasion, which undermined the symbolism of the proposed encounter and the potential for a rapport between the Syrian foreign minister and the Israeli premier. Moreover, Barak insisted that the historic meeting focus on process rather than substance.[41]

Why was Barak so circumspect regarding the first political encounter with the Syrian leadership, set for 15 December 1999, at Blair House, Washington, DC? His stance was determined by his domestic opposition, which had more bearing on him personally and politically than previously. In the past, Barak had sent representatives whom he could disavow as having exceeded his instructions. However, now that Barak was negotiating himself, *he* would be held accountable for how the negotiations developed. It was clear to Barak that, in any substantive discussion, the Syrians would demand reaffirmation of the Rabin deposit.[42] US negotiator, Marin Indyk, recalled that Barak was concerned that conceding to the Syrian demand would signal to the Israeli public that he had given up on the Golan before finding out what he would be offered in return.[43] Worried that this would significantly reduce the chances of winning any

---

[38] Indyk, *Innocent Abroad*, p. 251.   [39] Ross, *The Missing Peace*, p. 537.
[40] Ross, *The Missing Peace*, p. 537; Albright, *Madam Secretary*, p. 604.
[41] Ross, *The Missing Peace*, p. 539.   [42] Ross, *The Missing Peace*, p. 540.
[43] Indyk, *Innocent Abroad*, p. 252.

204   Just Beyond Reach

referendum, the Israeli prime minister refused to discuss any substantive issues during his first encounter with al-Sharaa.

The Syrian approach to the launch of official, direct, political negotiations with Israel was similarly unhelpful. Instead of working towards creating the inspirational imagery generated by past Arab-Israeli summits, Syria's conduct during the summit exacerbated the Israeli prime minister's domestic woes. Foreign Minister al-Sharaa delivered a militant opening speech, which focused on denouncing Israel's occupation and Israeli aggression:[44] 'You killed him with your speech', President Clinton remarked to al-Sharaa in private.[45] Adding insult to injury, the Syrian delegation refused to shake hands with their Israeli counterparts 'until an agreement was signed'.[46]

Refraining from engaging in public diplomacy in this highly symbolic event spoke volumes about the rigid approach the Syrians adopted towards the negotiations, which reinforced Barak's mistrust of al-Sharaa: 'If it took al-Sharaa two minutes to break a promise he made to the US president', which was that only Clinton would deliver opening remarks at Blair House, 'what will be the fate of Syrian promises on more significant issues', protested Barak to the Americans.[47]

Moreover, US and Israeli negotiators felt that the speech delivered by al-Sharaa made Prime Minister Barak look weak and naïve before his own public and at a particularly sensitive time.[48] Although the Knesset had endorsed commencement of the negotiations, by a majority of forty-seven to thirty-one, the vote exposed the deepening opposition *within* the coalition government to agreement with Syria. During the vote, which was held on the eve of Barak's departure for Washington, there were twenty-four abstentions – mostly members of Shas. The ambiguity of Shas towards the prospect of exchanging land for peace seemed to have been replaced by a growing unease towards the prime minister's peace foreign policy. Two coalition members – the National Religious Party and Yisrael Ba'aliyah – voted against the decision to open negotiations with the Syrians.[49]

---

[44] 'Statements by Prime Minister Barak, President Clinton, and Syrian Foreign Minister al-Sharaa at the opening of Israel-Syria talks – the White House – 15 December 1999', *IMFA*, http://mfa.gov.il/MFA/ForeignPolicy/MFADocument s/Yearbook13/Pages/74%20Statements%20by%20Prime%20Minister%20Barak-%20President%20C.aspx, accessed 25 May 2017.

[45] Al-Sharaa, *The Missing Account*, p. 419.

[46] Al-Sharaa, *The Missing Account*, p. 418; Yatom, *The Confidant*, pp. 218–9.

[47] Yatom, *The Confidant*, p. 221.

[48] Sagie, *The Frozen Hand*, pp. 113–14; Ross, *The Missing Peace*, pp. 540–1; Yatom, *The Confidant*, pp. 219–21.

[49] For the voting breakdown, see 'Address to the Knesset by Prime Minister Barak, 13 December', *IMFA*, document number 73, retrieved 4 November 2015.

The awkward public display by Foreign Minister al-Sharaa was followed by a private discussion between the Israelis, the Americans and the Syrians. Al-Sharaa made it clear that he would not return for another meeting unless it would address the 'demarcation of the future Israeli-Syrian border'.[50] Barak responded evasively: 'While my government has made no commitment on territory we don't erase history.'[51]

As vague as this reference was to the Rabin deposit – and to its subsequent reaffirmation by Peres and Netanyahu – it clearly left a significant mark on the Syrian delegation. Following the meeting at Blair House, the Syrian foreign minister attended an *iftar* – the meal that breaks the daily fast in the holy month of Ramadan – at the Saudi ambassador's residence in Washington. At al-Sharaa's request, all the Arab ambassadors to Washington were invited. In this festive atmosphere, al-Sharaa asked the ambassadors to inform their governments that Syria was about to make peace with Israel. Al-Sharaa praised Barak as a statesman, emphasizing that during the Blair House meeting the two sides had agreed to establish a border demarcation committee. Under the impression that Barak had all but confirmed the Rabin deposit, a confident Syrian foreign minister claimed that Syria would be able to retrieve the territory it lost during the 1967 Arab-Israeli war.[52]

However, this was far from the Israeli prime minister's reading of the Blair House summit, which shows how flawed the communication between the two sides was. Barak emerged from the summit with growing anxiety about his domestic opposition. He 'was constantly thinking about arguments that would help him gain the support he needed in the Knesset and in a referendum to pass the agreement', noted Danny Yatom in his memoirs.[53] This was the background to demands made by Ehud Barak of the Americans during the succeeding few weeks. They included initiating peace negotiations between Israel and Lebanon in tandem with the Israeli-Syrian negotiations; bringing Tunisia to re-establish diplomatic relations with Israel, which had been cut off during the Netanyahu government; and securing an improved US military assistance package for Israel. These demands were drawn up on the basis of domestic polls, which indicated to Barak that a linkage between these issues and the negotiations with Syria would shore up domestic support for a final agreement.[54] The deadline for when Barak aimed to achieve all these complex tasks, 13 January 2000, reflected how his long years in the military had imprinted his foreign policy conduct. Under stress, he failed

---

[50] Al-Sharaa, *The Missing Account*, p. 421.   [51] Ross, *The Missing Peace*, p. 542.
[52] Indyk, *Innocent Abroad*, pp. 256–7.   [53] Yatom, *The Confidant*, p. 221.
[54] Ross, *The Missing Peace*, pp. 546–7; Indyk, *Innocent Abroad*, p. 258.

206   Just Beyond Reach

to internalize that international politics are often less compliant than the military. Predictably, the Americans declared they were unable to offer anything concrete in response to the demands made by Barak within his requested timeframe.[55]

In Shepherdstown without a Shepherd

When the Israeli and Syrian delegations resumed negotiations on 3 January 2000, in Shepherdstown, West Virginia, there was a significant gap in their expectations. The foreign policy approach of Prime Minister Barak was designed to address his domestic opposition rather than to engage with the Syrians on substantive matters. Accordingly, on his arrival in the USA, Barak made it clear that he would not reaffirm the Rabin deposit. 'I can't do it', said Barak to the astounded US negotiator, Marin Indyk, as he welcomed Barak with the plane still on the tarmac; 'Political circumstances have changed.'[56]

Barak concluded that the domestic political landscape had changed on the basis of the results of some polls following the Blair House summit. The polls were held in the wake of false news published in the Israeli press, claiming that Israel had agreed already to withdraw completely from the Golan to the 4 June 1967 line. This prompted opposition party leader, Ariel Sharon, to accuse the Barak government of surrendering to US internal politics and Syrian dictates.[57] Amid lack of Syrian engagement in public diplomacy during the Blair House summit, the Golan Lobby continued its effective campaign of portraying the Syrians as untrustworthy partners for peace. In this charged atmosphere, the polls indicated that the majority of Israeli Jews did not support any peace agreement with Syria that entailed a withdrawal to the 4 June 1967 line.[58]

This posed a significant challenge to the approach outlined earlier by the prime minister of securing the support of the Israeli mainstream for his foreign policy. Furthermore, Barak departed for the Shepherdstown summit while the Knesset was discussing the Golan referendum law. Its instigators sought a stipulation that any territorial concessions related to the Golan would require an absolute majority of registered Israeli voters, rather than a simple majority of referendum votes. As Barak departed for Shepherdstown, his pollsters warned him that this public support was simply absent.[59]

---

[55] Ross, *The Missing Peace*, p. 547.   [56] Indyk, *Innocent Abroad*, p. 251.
[57] Druker, *Harakiri*, p. 70.
[58] Indyk, *Innocent Abroad*, p. 251; Druker, *Harakiri*, pp. 71–2.
[59] Indyk, *Innocent Abroad*, p. 251.

In Shepherdstown without a Shepherd 207

The constraint imposed by public opinion on the prime minister's foreign policy stance was compounded by the increasing fragility of his coalition government. Between the meeting at Blair House and the Shepherdstown summit a number of his own coalition members, including Shas MKs, voted with the opposition on a number of key domestic legislations.[60] As the negotiations with Syria entered their most critical phase, the main coalition partner, Shas, was indicating, clearly, that its support would be tentative at best.

In light of the mounting domestic constraints faced by the Israeli prime minister, his pollsters recommended that he should adopt a tough negotiating stance towards the Syrians from the outset.[61] This explains why, contrary to chief negotiator Sagie's counsel, Barak refused to reaffirm the Rabin deposit at the start of the Shepherdstown summit.[62] Further hardening his position, Barak insisted that he would not reaffirm the Rabin deposit unless Syria supported simultaneous commencement of Israeli-Lebanese negotiations.[63] The link between the Syrian and Lebanese tracks, recalled Danny Yatom, was crucial for Barak 'because he sensed that the Israeli public was fatigued from the prolonged Israeli military presence in Lebanon'. In tying together the two peace tracks, Yatom noted that Barak was seeking to 'persuade the Israeli public that the concessions to Syria were worthwhile'.[64]

However, chief negotiator Sagie was extremely critical of the tougher position adopted by his prime minister. It created an insurmountable tension – between satisfying Israeli domestic opposition and Syrian demands – within Israel's foreign policy approach towards the most critical negotiation round with Syria to date. Sagie's judgement of how his prime minister chose to deal with his domestic constrains was harsh and unequivocal: 'The effort to sway Israeli public opinion by insisting on resuming the Israeli-Lebanese negotiations', ended up 'blowing up the negotiations' with Syria.[65]

Sagie's frustration is understandable. By the third day of the summit, the gap in Israeli and Syrian expectations had hardened. The Syrians arrived assuming that, as soon as the direct talks at Shepherdstown began, Barak would commit explicitly to the Rabin deposit. The USA, as Madeline Albright revealed candidly, 'had expected it too'.[66] There was frustration that the summit was being consumed and undermined by a fight about what to negotiate. Barak demanded that negotiations

---

[60] Sher, *Just Beyond Reach*, p. 66.   [61] Druker, *Harakiri*, p. 73.
[62] Ross, *The Missing Peace*, p. 551.
[63] Sagie, *The Frozen Hand*, p. 121; Shaaban, *Damascus Diary*, p. 177.
[64] Yatom, *The Confidant*, p. 230.   [65] Sagie, *The Frozen Hand*, pp. 122–3.
[66] Albright, *Madam Secretary*, p. 605; Sagie, *The Frozen Hand*, p. 15.

208   Just Beyond Reach

between the working groups on security and normalization should begin before discussions took place over water and borders. As negotiator Martin Indyk observed at the time, Barak 'wanted to use this sequence to help create the impression at home that he was negotiating Israel's concerns on security and peace before discussing Syria's demand for full withdrawal.'[67] As a result, progress was made only 'around the edges' with 'little substantive work taking place.'[68]

This prompted the Americans to make the bold move of tabling a document outlining their understanding of the Israeli and Syrian positions. The Americans were exploring the limits to their flexibility with the Israelis and the Syrians.[69] According to US mediator Dennis Ross, Foreign Minister al-Sharaa made a significant concession on the border question. Al-Sharaa agreed that '*the Israelis would have sovereignty over the lake; the Syrians would have sovereignty over the land, at least all the land to the east of the 10 meters of the shoreline.*'[70] The obstinate Israeli prime minister was not to be moved. He remained convinced that, to overcome his domestic opposition, he needed to have Israeli-Lebanese talks – otherwise, 'there was no way to do anything' at Shepherdstown.[71]

The two sides' respective positions led Ross to conclude that 'Barak intended to leave after a week with the objective of being able to show his public that he had made no concessions at Shepherdstown.' He believed he 'would cement the political basis on which he could move to a - conclusion'.[72] This foreign policy approach may have made sense in the context of Israeli domestic politics. However, as a negotiating tactic towards making peace with Syria, it was fatally flawed. Indyk and Ross recall that, at Shepherdstown, the Syrians showed 'uncharacteristic flexibility on every issue' – water, normalization, security and definition of the 4 June 1967 border.[73] These were bold measures, particularly since Foreign Minister al-Sharaa 'was feeling the political heat from those around Assad who doubted the wisdom of concluding a deal with Israel'.[74] Thus, although the Syrian positions fell short of Israeli demands, they should have elicited an encouraging Israeli response to these Syrian openings. However, the unyielding Israeli prime minister remained paralysed by his domestic constraints and shied away from taking the fateful decision required to advance the peace process.

[67] Indyk, *Innocent Abroad*, p. 256.
[68] Albright, *Madam Secretary*, p. 607; Ross, *The Missing Peace*, p. 552.
[69] Ross, *The Missing Peace*, p. 552.
[70] Ross, *The Missing Peace*, p. 554, emphasis in original.
[71] Ross, *The Missing Peace*, p. 555.   [72] Ross, *The Missing Peace*, p. 555.
[73] Ross, *The Missing Peace*, p. 551; Indyk, *Innocent Abroad*, p. 259.
[74] Indyk, *Innocent Abroad*, p. 258; Ross, *The Missing Peace*, p. 566.

In Shepherdstown without a Shepherd   209

In his memoirs, President Clinton reflected on his disappointment with the Israeli prime minister and, more significantly, his decision to base his foreign policy stance on poll data. As Clinton explains:

> Barak had not been in politics long, and I thought he had gotten some very bad advice. In foreign affairs, polls are often useless; people hire leaders to win for them, and it's the results that matter . . . if Barak had made real peace with Syria, it would lift his standing in Israel and across the world, and increase the chances of success with the Palestinians. If he failed, a few days of good poll numbers would vanish in the wind. As hard as I tried, I couldn't change Barak's mind.[75]

The uncompromising conduct at Shepherdstown seriously undermined the already thin Syrian confidence in Israeli intentions. Al-Sharaa noted bitterly in his memoirs 'that Barak was playing a cunning game to disavow himself from the Rabin deposit. He did not arrive to Shepherdstown to conclude a peace agreement but to play other games.'[76] The Syrian foreign minister conveyed this message powerfully during the 'Last Supper' at Shepherdstown. In the presence of US President Clinton, Prime Minister Barak and the key negotiators, al-Sharaa announced that he would be obliged to tell his president that he had been deceived at Shepherdstown and, therefore, that the talks had failed. He would refuse to resume negotiations in the future unless specifically ordered to do so by Assad.[77] Disillusioned and resentful, al-Sharaa returned to Syria empty handed from the negotiations he had believed would be decisive.

Syrian frustration was compounded by the leaking of the American draft, summarizing US understanding of the Syrian and the Israeli positions, to the Israeli broadsheet, *Ha'aretz*, on 13 January 2000, three days after the Shepherdstown talks concluded. The leaked document misrepresented the state of the talks. Whereas the purpose of the draft was to identify US understanding of the gaps in the talks, the newspaper report made the document look as if the two sides had agreed its content. It gave the impression that 'the Syrians had conceded the principles of peace to Israel without any qualifiers and had not gotten Israeli acceptance of the border in return.'[78] During a phone conversation with President Assad on 18 January 2000, President Clinton expressed his sympathy with Syria's frustrations, by laying the failure in Shepherdstown squarely at the door of the Israeli prime minister. The next opportunity to negotiate, which

---

[75] Clinton, *My Life*, p. 886.   [76] Al-Sharaa, *The Missing Account*, p. 428.
[77] Sagie, *The Frozen Hand*, pp. 13–14; Indyk, *Innocent Abroad*, p. 263.
[78] Ross, *The Missing Peace*, p. 566; Sagie, *The Frozen Hand*, p. 124; Indyk, *Innocent Abroad*, p. 260.

210   Just Beyond Reach

would be in Geneva, Switzerland, would produce a better result for Syria, promised Clinton.[79]

The Geneva Summit

The summit meeting between Presidents Clinton and Assad, which was scheduled for 26 March 2000, was eagerly anticipated. Following the debacle in Shepherdstown, the Geneva summit was the make or break moment in the Israeli-Syrian negotiations. Since the collapse of the Shepherdstown talks in January, the Israeli and US negotiating teams had worked intensively. The core group consisted of Prime Minister Barak, his close confidant, Danny Yatom, and Martin Indyk, who had been reappointed US Ambassador to Israel in January.

The Israel-US team developed a detailed proposal for peace, which hinged on three elements. One was a small land swap, which would leave Lake Kinneret, the River Jordan and a territorial corridor to the Banias springs under Israeli sovereignty. In return, the Syrians would receive land in the southern part of the lake, in the al-Hama region, which under any interpretation of the 4 June 1967 border would otherwise have been inside Israeli territory. The proposed land swaps, which consisted of between 400 metres and 500 metres on each side of Lake Kinneret, would be presented to the Syrians on a map depicting the borderlines that Israel would accept.[80] The map proposed to keep all of Lake Kinneret under Israeli sovereignty while the area occupied by five Syrian villages prior to the 1967 Arab-Israeli war, on the shores of the Lake Kinneret itself, would be under Syrian sovereignty.[81] This delineation was designed to meet al-Assad's demand that a peace agreement would involve a return to the pre-1967 borders and Israel's requirement to retain sovereignty over Lake Kinneret in its entirety.

The second element was that Israeli-Lebanese negotiations would be conducted in tandem with Israeli negotiations with Syria, which would prevent Hezbollah and Palestinian terror organizations under its control from resorting to violence. The proposal also laid down that the EWS on Mount Hermon would be managed by the Americans with seven Israelis for five years. The third element was that Assad should adopt confidence-building measures to help Barak contend with his domestic opposition.

---

[79] Transcript of Clinton-Assad phone conversation, on 18 January 2000, quoted verbatim in Shaaban, *Damascus Diary*, pp. 219–22; and al-Sharaa, *The Missing Account*, pp. 437–40.
[80] Indyk, *Innocent Abroad*, pp. 272–3; Yatom, *The Confidant*, pp. 259–62.
[81] See map presented to Assad in Yatom, *The Confidant*, p. 289.

As a concession, Barak agreed to shorten the withdrawal timeframe from three to two-and-a-half years.[82]

If Ehud Barak were to blame for the collapse of the Shepherdstown talks, President Assad was directly responsible for the failure of the Geneva summit. The Israeli proposal may not have met the final requirements of the Syrian president. However, it offered concessions on every major aspect of the Israeli-Syrian negotiations. Therefore, at the very least, it should have elicited a Syrian response. However, President Assad objected vehemently to the idea that the 4 June 1967 border would be 'commonly agreed' on. Although this terminology was taken from the sections in the Lauder document that Assad had accepted in the past, the Syrian president now deemed this formulation 'a problem'. Efforts by Dennis Ross to show Assad that, in effect, the offer by Barak left Syria with '100 percent of the Golan Heights', particularly since the waterline of Lake Kinneret had receded over the years, were in vain. 'They do not want peace', responded President Assad, who was visibly angry and lost all interest in looking at the map further.[83]

Moreover, contradicting the Syrian position at Shepherdstown, which granted the Israelis sovereignty over Lake Kinneret, Assad insisted that he would never cede any of the land. 'He wanted', he said to President Clinton, 'to sit on the shore of the lake and put his feet in the water.'[84] By the end of the meeting it was clear that Assad flatly rejected every aspect of an offer that was utterly reasonable; it would enable Syria effectively to recover the land it lost during the 1967 war while permitting Israel to meet its security and water needs.

Why did the Syrians outright reject a deal similar to that which other Arab states, such as Egypt and Jordan, had accepted in the past? One explanation is that the only decision-maker who was able to make peace with Israel, Hafez al-Assad, was simply too ill to do so. Although his advisor, Butheina Shaaban, claims that the president was healthy at the time of the Geneva summit, her assertion is unsustainable. The Israelis were receiving reports, via Mossad, that during the last months of his life Assad was on medication pills for his terminal illness that caused sharp mood swings and fits of rage.[85] Indeed, President Assad's poor physical state was confirmed by his own Foreign Minister, Farouk al-Sharaa, who,

---

[82] Indyk, *Innocent Abroad*, pp. 274–5; Ross, *The Missing Peace*, pp. 571–6, 583; Yatom, *The Confidant*, pp. 262–8. Yatom claims Barak required a 3-and-a-half year timeline for completion of the withdrawal.

[83] Ross, *The Missing Peace*, pp. 584–6; Shaaban, *Damascus Diary*, pp. 192–4; Albright, *Madam Secretary*, p. 611; al-Sharaa, *The Missing Account*, pp. 447–8.

[84] Clinton, *My Life*, p. 903.

[85] Shaaban, *Damascus* Diary, p. 189; Kfir and Dor, *Barak. Wars of my Life*, p. 226.

212   Just Beyond Reach

on the eve of the summit was concerned 'more than ever' about Hafez al-Assad's health. The president, he recalls, barely slept during the two nights preceding the Geneva summit.[86] Confirming the fears of al-Sharaa, ten weeks after the Geneva summit, on 10 June 2000, al-Assad died of a heart attack.

Yet President Assad's poor health, which sheds some light on his reaction to the proposal conveyed by President Clinton, accounts only partially for his obstinate response in Geneva. By March 2000, agreeing to make peace with Israel posed a serious threat to his last major ambition: securing a smooth succession of his rule to his son, Bashar al-Assad. The shared assessment of the Americans, the Israelis and the then President of Egypt, Husni Mubarak, was that Assad was deeply worried in this regard. He was concerned that, accepting the guidelines of the Israeli offer would provide his opponents, who for decades had been forcibly silenced by Assad, with political ammunition. These opponents included Syrian Islamist groups, certain segments of Syria's Sunni business elites and members of the Ba'ath party seeking positions of power. Granting the Israelis full sovereignty over Lake Kinneret, the northern section of the River Jordan and the territorial corridor to the Banias might be seen as a compromise, providing detractors of the regime with the opportunity to launch a serious political challenge to the leadership of the Assad family at the twilight of Hafez al-Assad's life.[87]

According to this interpretation, the anti-Israeli stance nurtured by the Ba'ath regime in Syria for decades, which became one of the fundamentals of its identity and its legitimacy, came back to haunt al-Assad at the most critical moment in Syria's post-Cold War foreign policy towards Israel. The ethos promoted for years by the Ba'ath regime, left almost no room for negotiation with Israel. For this reason, Assad, the personification of this ethos, flatly rejected the Clinton offer rather than negotiate over it.

At the same time, peace with Israel presented several opportunities for Syria and it is, therefore, worth exploring why the positive prospects of peace for Syria did not exert more influence during the Assad-Clinton summit. To a great extent, American mediation was to blame. As the Israelis and the Americans were preparing their offer, they failed to liaise sufficiently with the Syrians. Chief negotiator Sagie, who admittedly was less involved in the negotiations during this phase, was still in a position to

---

[86] Al-Sharaa, *The Missing Account*, pp. 445–6.
[87] For evidence of the link to Assad's opposition, see Indyk, *Innocent Abroad*, pp. 278–81, 283; Yatom, *The Confidant*, pp. 27–1; Kfir and Dor, *Barak. Wars of my Life*, p. 223; Sagie, *The Frozen Hand*, p. 164.

observe that, at no point before the Geneva summit, did the Americans discuss the evolving Israeli-US offer directly with Hafez al-Assad.[88]

Sagie's observation was echoed by the Syrian foreign minister. During this last critical phase of the negotiations, al-Sharaa recalls that the USA relied too heavily on the reports they received from Prince Bandar of Saudi Arabia, who was shuttling between Washington and Damascus. 'The Syrians will not stop the negotiations over a meter or two', Bandar told the Americans repeatedly.[89] However, al-Sharaa emphasizes that the Syrian position in relation to the final agreement with Israel was far less moderate than that which Bandar reported to the Americans.[90] Therefore, when the offer was finally conveyed by the Americans to Assad in Geneva, it was perceived by the Syrian president as a repeat of the discussion about what constituted the 4 June 1967 border. Assad felt cornered, which was another reason for his defensive and hostile reaction.[91]

The chief American negotiator in the meeting, Bill Clinton, was not in an ideal position to handle the situation. Prior to the meeting, revealed Indyk in his memoirs, the president became 'quite ill and had little time for his prebrief. According to some involved in [the Geneva] session, by the time he met Assad the president was eager to get the meeting over and done with.'[92] Poor American mediation, Assad's failing health and the domestic challenges to the succession were the key reasons for the collapse of the Israeli-Syrian peace process in Geneva.

A Hostage to Domestic Constraints

Israeli foreign policy towards Syria under Ehud Barak was strongly determined by the domestic constraints he faced. They included hostile public opinion to the idea of withdrawing from the Golan, a fractured coalition and attempts to impose tough conditions via legislation on passing a peace agreement with Syria via referendum. During most of the negotiations, the prime minister remained a hostage to these domestic constraints. As a result, until the Geneva summit, he adopted a highly circumspect foreign policy approach, that was designed to address his domestic constrains rather than respond to the demands of the Syrian side. Instead of advancing on substance, he focused on the foreign policy process.

---

[88] Sagie, *The Frozen Hand*, pp. 160–1.   [89] Al-Sharaa, *The Missing Account*, pp. 441–2.
[90] Al-Sharaa, *The Missing Account*, pp. 441–2.   [91] Sagie, *The Frozen Hand*, p, 173.
[92] Indyk, *Innocent Abroad*, p. 276; Sagie, *The Frozen Hand*, p. 168.

214   Just Beyond Reach

This foreign policy approach was seriously flawed. It delayed negotiations, frustrated the American mediators, did nothing to buttress the fragile coalition government and undermined Syrian trust in the peace process. Ultimately, it did not shift Israeli public opinion, which became increasingly hostile and disillusioned since the Syrians never missed an opportunity to not engage in public diplomacy. By the time Ehud Barak made a very reasonable offer to his Syrian interlocutors, President Assad was in failing health and was too domestically constrained to negotiate a compromise with the Israelis

Ehud Barak stands out in any comparison with his predecessors. Amid Iraqi missile attacks, Yitzhak Shamir was unfazed by domestic demands to retaliate. Yitzhak Rabin, for his part, sought to address his domestic constraints by pushing ahead with his foreign policy of peace towards the PLO rather than subordinating it to the domestic opposition he faced. Conversely, the politically inexperienced Ehud Barak allowed his domestic constraints to derail his foreign policy approach towards Syria, which remained incompatible with Syrian demands throughout the negotiations. This unbridgeable gap was at the heart of his failure to conclude a peace deal with Syria, which he had identified as his first foreign policy priority.

With the benefit of hindsight, the collapse of the Israeli-Syrian negotiations was, perhaps, a blessing in disguise for Israel. In 2011, a brutal civil war broke out in Syria. Had Israel withdrawn to the 4 June 1967 line proposed by Ehud Barak, the Syrian civil war would have been waged on the shores of Lake Kinneret. Contrariwise, had Israel and Syria struck a deal, opening Syria to the West and its influences, perhaps the civil war would have been averted. It impossible to say, as C.S. Lewis reminds us, as 'we can never know what might have been'.

10 Between Engagement and Unilateralism

In the Aftermath of Geneva

The failure of the Geneva summit, which ended the Israeli-Syrian peace process under the Barak government, had implications for Israeli foreign policy towards Iran. The Islamic Republic, in some respects, faced serious challenges, especially due to the US foreign policy of dual containment. This policy, imposed in 1992, involved deterring Iran by military force and applying severe economic and diplomatic sanctions. At the same time, several external threats that Iran had faced since 1979 reduced significantly. Its eight-year war with Iraq ended in 1988 and the ensuing defeat of Iraq by the US-led coalition in the 1991 Gulf War further weakened Iran's arch regional rival. Also, the threat posed by the USSR, which had invaded Afghanistan in 1979, disappeared with the breakup of the Soviet Union in 1991.

As a result, the ending of the Cold War left Iran better placed to expand its regional influence than at any time since the 1979 revolution. Iran boosted its military capabilities by developing long-range missiles capable of reaching Israel. Simultaneously, it deepened its military, economic and logistical support, via Syria, to its Lebanese proxy, Hezbollah. According to Naim Qassem, Deputy Secretary General of Hezbollah, Iran's aim to expand its regional influence converged with Syria's and Hezbollah's goal of evicting the IDF from south Lebanon via guerrilla warfare and attrition.[1]

Apart from improving its military capabilities and supporting Hezbollah in Lebanon, Iran sought to destabilize the Arab-Israeli peace process to prevent the formation of an Arab-Israeli coalition against it. To achieve this goal, Israeli and US negotiators observed that Iran supported the PIJ and Hamas. However, the relationship between Hamas and Iran was far from straightforward.[2] 'As a Sunni organization affiliated to the

---

[1] Qassem, Hizballah, pp. 235–8; see also, from the US perspective, Indyk, *Innocent Abroad*, pp. 172–4.

[2] Interview 1 Ayalon; Indyk, *Innocent Abroad*, pp. 171, 173.

216   Between Engagement and Unilateralism

Muslim Brotherhood', former head of the GSS observed, 'Hamas was uneasy about the support it obtained from Iran. Hamas operatives were being trained for months in Iran', he further noted, 'but, participating in these training camps was very difficult for them from the point of view of religious doctrine. Hamas sent Imams with its trainees in Iran to prevent them from being subjected to Shiia influences. Ideologically, Hamas did not see itself part of Iran or of its project.'[3]

Nonetheless, the convergence of Iran's and Hamas's interests trumped religious-doctrinal differences. Hamas needed an external backer that would support its conflict with Israel and its resistance to the PA's efforts to suppress it. For its part, Iran was keen to bolster its regional credentials by showing solidarity with the Palestinian groups in conflict with Israel, which resonated in the Arab Middle East.[4]

Yitzhak Rabin and Shimon Peres were well aware of the three-pronged challenge posed by Iran – its growing military capabilities, support for Islamist groups that clashed with Israel and its efforts to destabilize the Israeli-Palestinian peace process. Indeed, their foreign policy of engagement was geared towards creating an Israeli-Arab coalition against Iran. In this context, one of Israel's main motivations for pursuing peace negotiations with Syria since 1992 was to drive a wedge in Syria's alliance with Iran and Hezbollah. However, amid the collapse of the Israeli-Syrian negotiations, this foreign policy option became unviable for the foreseeable future.

Thus, Israeli policymakers faced a number of serious foreign policy dilemmas. Having failed to delink Damascus from Tehran, how should Israel respond to the direct challenges posed by Iran in its bid for regional influence? This question was related directly to another serious issue: Prime Minister Barak's election pledge to withdraw the IDF from Lebanon by July 2000. The failure of the Assad-Clinton Geneva summit made it clear that conflict with Hezbollah and Syria would persist. Therefore, for Barak's election pledge to be honoured would require the creation of a foreign policy mechanism that would enable the IDF to withdraw from Lebanon unilaterally and to defend northern Israel from the international border. The continued ties between Iran and Hamas in the wake of the collapse of the Israeli-Syrian peace process had a bearing also on the Israeli-Palestinian peace process. What would be Israeli foreign policy towards the PLO under these circumstances? Amid this uncertain regional political environment, the fractured Barak coalition government faced profound foreign policy dilemmas.

---

[3] Interview 1 Ayalon.   [4] Milton-Edwards and Farrell, *Hamas*, pp. 133, 224.

The Maturing of Israeli Foreign Policy towards Iran

Efraim Sneh, who was appointed Barak's Deputy Minister of Defence, was excellently placed to assess Israel's foreign policy response to the multiple challenges presented by Iran. Throughout the 1990s, Sneh observed that Israeli prime ministers were not involved deeply in decision-making in relation to Iran; Rabin's, Netanyahu's and Barak's priorities were relations with Syria and the Palestinians. None of them saw Iran as posing an imminent threat, a view that was echoed by the MFA.[5]

Consequently, there was no central umbrella organization coordinating Israel's foreign policy towards Iran during this period. This foreign policy vacuum was filled by the GSS, the IDF and Mossad, which were cooperating on an ad hoc basis. These three security agencies, which formed the core of the Israeli security network, achieved significant autonomy to determine de facto Israeli foreign policy towards Iran throughout the 1990s. Decision-making was bottom up, as the security agencies were determining Israeli foreign policy towards Iran. The role of the prime minister was to authorize, rather than formulate, this security-driven foreign policy course.[6]

Deputy Defence Minister Sneh introduced a subtle change in the structure of decision-making towards Iran. He established a central committee within the Ministry of Defence that brought the separate agencies dealing with Iran within one framework. Perhaps humorously, this was code-named *Amba*, which is a spicy sauce used in Middle Eastern cuisine.[7] According to Sneh, this may have been one of the first decision-making structures since the end of the Cold War devoted solely to Iran and it brought the various agencies that, hitherto had dealt with Iran under one umbrella. Up to that point, Mossad, the GSS and the IDF had coordinated their activities towards Iran – ad hoc – in the influential Heads of Security Services Committee, which met regularly to liaise over various national security issues.[8] Yet it is unclear how significantly *Amba*, which focused solely on Iran, improved the capacity to develop a coherent foreign policy response towards the Islamic Republic. In fact, as former head of GSS reveals, it was not until the premiership of Ariel Sahron that one security agency, Mossad, was designated responsible for gathering intelligence and for intercepting the Iranian nuclear project. Moreover, as head of GSS, he had no knowledge about *Amba*.[9]

---

[5] Interview Dr Sneh; Interview Bentsur.
[6] Interview with a senior GSS official; Interview with the then head of military intelligence, Moshe Ya'alon, 11 July 2017, Tel Aviv.
[7] Interview Dr Sneh; Interview with a senior GSS official.　　[8] Interview Ya'alon.
[9] Personal email correspondence with Mr Ami Ayalon, 15 April 2019.

218   Between Engagement and Unilateralism

Nevertheless, what is clear is that Israeli policy towards Iran cohered during Ehud Barak's premiership. Iran, like the rest of the international community, assumed that Israel was in possession of a nuclear weapons arsenal. Exploiting this assumption, Efraim Sneh pointed out that, 'during my time in office, we diversified the options to operate what we had.'[10] This was a direct reference from an Israeli foreign policymaker to the nuclear secondary launch capabilities potential Israel was assumed to have acquired via deployment of the Dolphin submarines that had entered service in the Israeli Navy in 1999. In addition to diversifying its deterrence options, Israel was enhancing its defensive capabilities by consolidating the Arrow missile system – in cooperation with and based on funding from the USA – which became the bedrock of Israel's defence system against long-range ballistic threats.[11]

The deterrent and defensive components of Israeli foreign policy towards Iran ran parallel to efforts to convince the USA and the EU that Iran's nuclear programme included a military component. By 1997, the Americans were convinced and by 2000, the EU was persuaded. This resulted in Israel's two-pronged foreign policy. The thrust of its foreign policy towards Iran consisted of relying on the USA to lead international efforts to curb the Iranian nuclear programme.[12] At the same time, Israeli security agencies were preparing for the possibility that these US-led efforts might fail by enhancing Israel's capabilities to intercept and delay Iran's nuclear programme.[13] A senior GSS official recalled that: 'From the mid-1990s, we developed our signal intelligence and human intelligence capabilities, which were critical for delaying the progress of the Iranian nuclear program. In this respect, our success was significant.' Concurrently, he recalled that the 'security services scuppered the efforts of Iran to develop an intelligence network in Israel by apprehending agents it tried to recruit.'[14] Thus, by 2000, Israeli foreign policy towards Iran had matured around four principles – deterrence, defence, interception and support for multilateral efforts to curb Iran's nuclear programme. This reflected a subtle, but important shift away from the Rabin-Peres vision, which hinged on harnessing Israel's foreign policy of engagement to create an Arab-Israeli coalition against Iran.

[10] Interview Dr Sneh.
[11] 'Address by Prime Minister Barak to the National Defence College', *IMFA*, http://mfa.gov.il /MFA/ForeignPolicy/MFADocuments/Yearbook13/Pages/24%20Address%20by%20Pri me%20Minister%20Barak%20to%20the%20National.aspx, accessed 8 August 2017.
[12] Interview Ya'alon.
[13] Confidential interview with minister in the Netanyahu governments, who had access to the Iran portfolio.
[14] Interview 1 Ayalon.

Corrosion of the Security Zone in South Lebanon

Ehud Barak had pledged to withdraw the IDF from the security zone in south Lebanon within twelve months from his election and had hoped to coordinate this with a peace agreement with Syria. His plan was utterly frustrated by the collapse of the Clinton-Assad Geneva summit in March 2000, at which point his government faced tough choices. Should it, given the collapse of the Israeli-Syrian peace negotiations, unilaterally withdraw the IDF from the security zone in south Lebanon? Or should Israel maintain the status quo by keeping its troops deployed in a foreign country?

The military stakes involved in unilaterally withdrawal of the IDF from south Lebanon were high. At any given time, between 1,000 and 1,500 IDF soldiers were engaged in maintaining the security zone, which extended three to twelve miles beyond the Israeli border, into Lebanon. Alongside the IDF, 2,500 soldiers from the SLA, Israel's proxy, were deployed.[15]

In certain military respects, the security zone was highly successful. Since it had been established in 1985, it had prevented infiltration across the Israeli-Lebanese border, of Hezbollah, Amal and the Palestinian rejectionist groups. Only nine guerrilla squads had succeeded in reaching the Israeli-Lebanese border; two had crossed the border, but they were killed before they could reach civilian targets.[16] In this respect, the security zone was an effective buffer between Israeli towns and villages on the northern border and Lebanese guerrilla groups. Losing this element of strategic territorial depth was one of the key reasons why the IDF objected to unilateral withdrawal from Lebanon.

However, the shortcomings of the security zone outweighed its advantages. For instance, it failed utterly to prevent mortar and Katyusha attacks on Israel. Between 1985 and 2000, more than 4,000 Katyusha rockets landed in Galilee. These attacks claimed seven lives, a relatively small number of fatalities, but the disruption to the everyday lives of the 200,000 Israelis within range of the Katyusha missiles was significant.[17] Another issue was the increasingly untenable military architecture of the security zone. Since the zone had been established, the SLA had sustained high casualty rates. It had lost more than 450 men from a total population of around

---

[15] Luft, 'Israel's Security Zone in Lebanon – A Tragedy? p. 14; a higher number of over 2,500 is reported in Amos Gilboa, *The True Story of How Israel Left Lebanon – Code Name Dawn* (Jerusalem: Efi Meltzer, 2015), p. 15 (in Hebrew).
[16] Luft, 'Israel's Security Zone in Lebanon', p. 14.
[17] Luft, 'Israel's Security Zone in Lebanon', pp. 14–15.

220   Between Engagement and Unilateralism

100,000 Lebanese linked to the SLA.[18] Gabi Ashkenazi, the then IDF Head of the Northern Command, who was in daily contact with the SLA soldiers, saw that Barak's election pledge to withdraw the IDF had provoked deep anxiety within the SLA.[19] If Israel were to withdraw unilaterally from Lebanon without an agreement with Syria, this would leave the SLA's situation very unclear. Would its soldiers be subject to legal penalties imposed by the Lebanese government on citizens collaborating with Israel? Would its soldiers be exposed to reprisals by Hezbollah? Under such a circumstance, would Israel abandon the SLA?

The prospect of a unilateral Israeli withdrawal cast a long and dark shadow over the SLA. From May 1999, the GSS recorded a hike in defections from the SLA to Hezbollah. The morale and composure of the remaining soldiers was declining rapidly.[20] The failure of the Geneva summit exacerbated the tensions within the SLA and posed a real threat to its survival as a pillar of the Israeli security zone in Lebanon. At the same time, Hezbollah's military and intelligence capabilities were improving. This was exemplified by the assassination in February 1999 of the head of the IDF's liaison unit in Lebanon, Brigadier General Erez Gerstein.[21] A double agent, Amil Nasser, an SLA commander, provided Hezbollah with information about the travel plans of Brigadier Gerstein and his three companions, who were killed instantly when their car hit a roadside bomb planted by Hezbollah.[22]

In total, since Israel had established the security zone in 1985, 256 Israeli soldiers had been killed in combat and 840 wounded.[23] Hezbollah, which was well aware of the growing domestic sensitivity within Israel to IDF casualties, embarked on an effective psychological war by transmitting live broadcasts of its successful attacks against IDF soldiers, including the assassination of Gerstein.[24]

---

[18] Luft, 'Israel's Security Zone in Lebanon', p. 14; a higher number of over 500 is reported by Amos Gilboa, *The True Story of How Israel Left Lebanon – Code Name Dawn* (Jerusalem: Efi Meltzer, 2015), p. 15 (in Hebrew).

[19] Margalit and Bregman, *The Pit* (Kinneret: Zmora-Bitan, 2011), p. 61.

[20] Interview 2 Ayalon; Margalit and Bregman, *The Pit*, p. 61.

[21] Yossi Beilin, *A Guide to an Israeli Withdrawal from Lebanon* (Tel Aviv: HaKibutz Hameuchad, 1998), p. 14 (in Hebrew).

[22] Kfir and Dor, *Barak*, pp. 230–1.

[23] Luft, 'Israel's Security Zone in Lebanon', p. 16; Gilboa records the lower figure of 235 in *The True Story of How Israel Left Lebanon* p. 15; a higher estimate of the number of wounded in 'the thousands' is reported in Belin, *A Guide to an Israeli Withdrawal from Lebanon*, p. 20.

[24] Margalit and Bergman, *The Pit*, p. 59; Beilin, *A Guide to an Israeli Withdrawal from Lebanon*, p. 30.

The continuing IDF fatalities and clear shortcomings of the security zone were not just a military problem. They constituted a strategic liability for Israeli foreign policymakers. The protracted Israeli occupation of the 328-square-mile security zone in south Lebanon was having an increasingly corrosive effect on the IDF. Israel, which never had territorial claims on Lebanon, was engaged in an inconclusive and unwinnable war against an indigenous guerrilla force, Hezbollah, which was supported by Iran and Syria.[25] Barak's confidant, Danny Yatom, recalls that Hezbollah, Iran and Syria used the security zone as a bargaining chip to impose pressure on Israel via attacks on the IDF.[26]

The military pressure exerted by Hezbollah on the IDF also had a political dimension related to the mounting domestic opposition to the Israeli quagmire in Lebanon. Dr Yossi Beilin, Justice Minister during the Barak government, was a longstanding advocate of IDF withdrawal from Lebanon. In 1997, he established the 'Citizens Movement for Leaving Lebanon in Peace', which was backed by Labour, Meretz and some Likud MKs, academics, policymakers and former army generals. Domestically, the movement was significant in that it highlighted the follies of the protracted Israeli presence in Lebanon.[27] Leading research institutes, such as the Leonard Davis Institute in the Hebrew University, were also reviewing the premises for maintaining the IDF in Lebanon.[28]

The crux of the critique was that there was no military imperative to maintain the IDF in the security zone. Instead, advocates of a withdrawal argued, Israel could defend its northern towns and villages equally well from the international border by developing deterrence, interception and defensive capabilities vis-à-vis Hezbollah.[29] Hence, the pro-withdrawal campaign was able to present an alternative security paradigm to defending the northern border, to that offered by the IDF. The effective public campaign that was unfolding drew its agenda from this alternative intellectual framework.

The opposition to the IDF's presence in Lebanon from the dovish Labour party members, such as Beilin, was predictable, but the campaign waged by more mainstream groups was perhaps less anticipated. The 'Four Mothers Movement', which was founded in 1997, is a case in point. The movement was formed by mothers of soldiers on active service and

---

[25] Shlaim, *The Iron Wall* (2nd ed.), p. 617.   [26] Yatom, *The Confidant*, p. 359.
[27] Yossi Beilin, *A Guide to Leaving Lebanon* (Tel Aviv: Kibutz Meuchad, 1998), pp. 10, 18 (in Hebrew).
[28] See, for example, Yaacov Bar Siman-Tov et al., *The Security Zone in Lebanon: A Reassessment* (Jerusalem: Leonard Davis Institute for International Relations, 1997) (in Hebrew).
[29] Beilin, *A Guide to an Israeli Withdrawal from Lebanon*, pp. 47–9, 62–75.

222 Between Engagement and Unilateralism

bereaved mothers, following a mid-air collision on 4 February 1997, between two helicopters carrying soldiers to Lebanon, which killed all seventy-three of its IDF soldier passengers. Sociologist Yagil Levy convincingly identifies the significance of the movement. He argued that it effectively mainstreamed the arguments being made by the political campaign for withdrawal from Lebanon, by linking two fundamental social roles in Israeli society: motherhood and soldiering. Israeli women were expected to express their motherhood by supporting their sons' service in the IDF. However, Four Mothers was conspicuous in its criticisms of the IDF, especially after incidents that claimed the lives of Israeli soldiers in south Lebanon. Its denunciations did not focus on the IDF as such, but rather on the protracted deployment of IDF troops in south Lebanon.[30]

The effect of the Four Mothers movement, via its social activism, was palpable and provoked a harsh reaction from within the IDF General Staff. Former Chief of Staff, Dan Haloutz, noted in his memoirs:

There can be no doubt that the Four Mothers Movement reflected a deep shift within Israeli society, as far as its willingness to make sacrifices for the national interest is concerned. The test of how many soldiers we lose became the definitive parameter. We have seen with our own eyes how the most important decision-makers get cold feet when mothers stand by their side. The feeling was that nobody wants to bear the responsibility for the last [IDF] victim in Lebanon ... I have always thought, and still think, that they, Four Mothers, and similar movements, are an unwelcome phenomenon, which cast a question mark over the survival of Israel in the long run. They represent an Israeli society of 'the here and now', a society that cannot accept the price of living in a violent neighbourhood.[31]

The former chief of staff's remarks are evidence of the degree to which the IDF was entrenched. Rather than engaging directly with the critique from the pro-withdrawal movement, he reduced it to an emotionally driven campaign reflecting flaws in Israeli society.

The Rise of Israeli Unilateralism under Ehud Barak

On balance, then, it is clear that the deficiencies of the security zone outweighed its limited military advantages, which is why Israeli foreign policymakers, for some years, had been floating the idea of withdrawing the IDF from Lebanon. As foreign minister in the Peres government, Ehud Barak had explored this idea with Dennis

[30] Yagil Levy, *The Other Army of Israel: Materialist Militarism in Israel* (Tel Aviv: Yedioth Ahronoth, 2003), pp. 204–5 (in Hebrew).
[31] Danny Halutz, *Straightforward* (Tel Aviv: Miskal-Yedioth Ahronoth, 2010), p. 218 (in Hebrew).

Ross in 1996.[32] Similarly, the Netanyahu government had examined alternatives for defending the Israeli northern border, which included withdrawing the IDF from Lebanon.[33]

Why then did Israeli foreign policy towards Lebanon continue unchanged? A key reason for remaining was that the IDF top brass opposed any change to the status quo. 'The army began to believe its own propaganda that it was essential to risk the lives of IDF soldiers in Lebanon to protect the towns and villages in northern Israel', recalled Yossi Beilin, solemnly.[34] Two informed observers reported that previous governments had preferred not to confront the IDF directly on this matter.[35] In addition, as we have seen, until the collapse of the Assad-Clinton Geneva Summit, Israel's foreign policymakers sought to withdraw the IDF from Lebanon as part of a peace agreement with Syria. Prime Minister Barak, unlike his predecessors, was willing and able to confront the IDF general staff. Bound by his election pledge to withdraw the IDF, the conviction that the security zone was a strategic liability and, backed by growing domestic support for IDF withdrawal, Ehud Barak became the first post-Cold War Israeli prime minister to develop a unilateralist foreign policy posture.[36] In his position as Minister of Defence as well as Prime Minister, Barak purposely sidelined the IDF from his development of a unilateralist stance. For example, the IDF military intelligence was not invited to present its assessment to the government before its unanimous vote on 5 March 2000 to unilaterally withdraw the IDF from Lebanon.[37]

Barak's decision to marginalize the IDF from the decision-making process was the result of friction over the issue of unilateral withdrawal between the government and the military top brass, which showed clear signs of groupthink during the period of forming Israeli unilateralism. Groupthink occurs when decision-makers seek rapid internal agreement, even at the expense of the issue at hand. Those involved cling to the consensus in the face of contradictory evidence. Criticisms of the orthodoxy – especially when associated to the group's leader – become especially difficult. Consequently,

---

[32] Ross, *The Missing Peace*, pp. 251–2.   [33] Margalit and Bregman, *The Pit*, p. 59.
[34] Interview 3 Dr Yossi Beilin, 10 July 2017, Tel Aviv.
[35] Margalit and Bregman, *The Pit*, p. 59.
[36] According to Yossi Beilin, the public polls conducted by the pro-withdrawal campaign saw a sharp rise in support from 18 per cent in 1997 to 72 per cent in 1999. Interview 3 Beilin.
[37] Gilboa, *The True Story How Israel Left Lebanon*, p. 172; *Yedioth Ahronoth*, 6 March 1997; Government resolution regarding the redeployment from Lebanon, 5 March 2000, *IMFA*, http://mfa.gov.il/MFA/ForeignPolicy/MFADocuments/Yearbook13/Pages/94%20Government%20Resolution%20regarding%20the%20redeploymen.aspx, accessed 19 July 2017.

224   Between Engagement and Unilateralism

groupthink develops dangerous gaps between the decision-makers' psychological environment and the actual foreign policy environment they face.[38]

In line with this group thinking, the IDF general staff subscribed to the view expressed by Chief of Staff Shaul Mofaz. Mofaz breached the delicate boundary between his role as chief of staff and politics, by publicly expressing his opposition to unilateral withdrawal.[39] Echoing its commander in chief, the general staff presented a unified position to the prime minister, against unilateral withdrawal, one day after the government had voted in favour of it.[40] Similarly, in April 2000, more than a month after the decision to withdraw had been taken, senior ministers expressed the view that the generals were being unduly alarmist; they were presenting worst case scenarios and were ignoring possible opportunities related to IDF withdrawal.[41]

However, by April 2000, the IDF's top brass's opposition to unilaterally withdrawing from Lebanon became unsustainable as the cracks within the SLA widened. According to a report prepared by the IDF liaison unit in Lebanon, there were acute tensions between SLA soldiers and their commanders, while the number of defectors continued to rise.[42] The evident fractures within the SLA were exacerbated by a sharp decline in the motivation of IDF soldiers serving in Lebanon, who were becoming more risk averse. The Israeli media was reporting that the troops, frequently and macabrely, were asking one another who wanted to be the last soldier to be killed in Lebanon.[43]

In these circumstances, the IDF was in no position to resist the government's decision to withdraw, which became the basis for Israel's unilateralist foreign policy approach. On 14 and 17 April 2000 respectively, the Israeli government formally informed the USA and the UN of its intention to withdraw from Lebanon in line with UNSCR 425.[44] Implementing UNSCR 425 required Israel to withdraw to the international border, which would be recognized by the UN; to cease all military activity against Lebanon, which included dismantling the SLA; and to establish a UN 'interim force for Southern Lebanon for the purpose of confirming the withdrawal of Israeli forces, restoring international peace and security

---

[38] On groupthink, see Hill, *Foreign Policy in the 21st Century*, p. 76.
[39] Kfir and Dor, *Barak. Wars of My life*, p. 228; Yatom, *The Confidant*, p. 364.
[40] Gilboa, *The True Story of How Israel Left Lebanon*, p. 65.
[41] Margalit and Bregman, *The Pit*, p. 65; Gilboa, *The True Story How Israel Left Lebanon*, pp. 99–101.
[42] Interview 2 Ayalon.
[43] *Yedioth Ahronoth*, 10 February 1997; Margalit and Bregman, *The Pit* p. 62.
[44] Yatom, *The Confidant*, p. 360.

and assisting the Government of Lebanon in ensuring the return of its effective authority in the area'.[45]

Carrying out UNSCR 425 was a highly significant step. It enabled Israel to anchor the withdrawal from Lebanon in an agreement with the international community, embodied by the UN, instead of in an agreement with Syria, the preferred Israeli option since 1992. This shift introduced a new paradigm into Israeli foreign policymaking. Rather than withdrawing from territory in exchange for peace, which was what Israel's foreign policy of engagement had hinged on, Israel sought international legitimacy to withdraw unilaterally from areas it occupied.

The logic behind grounding Israel's unilateral withdrawal from Lebanon in international legitimacy was revealed by Barak in an official testimony to the Winograd Commission a few years after he had left office. The testimony was not supposed to be made public. Therefore, the unilateralist approach presented by Barak before the commission should be seen as reflecting his genuine thinking rather than as an attempt to make political gain. He explained that, in his view, unilateral withdrawal of the IDF from Lebanon to the international border would deny Hezbollah legitimacy to continue attacks on Israel. By the same token, with the IDF deployed on the international border, there would be international and domestic legitimacy for Israel to retaliate fiercely against Hezbollah attacks to create deterrence.[46] Thus, Israeli unilateralism under Ehud Barak was designed to rest on two pillars: international legitimacy and deterrence.

In terms of Israeli-Hezbollah relations, the prime minister's analysis was broadly correct. After Israel had complied in full with UNSCR 425, Hezbollah confined its attacks on Israel to the small Sheba Farms area, which, Hezbollah argued, was Lebanese territory and, hence, under Israeli occupation. However, this claim was rejected by the UN certifying that Israel had complied with UNSCR 425, which indicated that Hezbollah was looking for a pretext to continue the military conflict with Israel. Nevertheless, the intensity of the conflict decreased substantially. Between 1985 and 2000, Israel sustained approximately twenty casualties per annum compared to the same number between 2000 and 2006. Subsequently, bar the eruption of the 2006 Israel-Hezbollah war, the level of incidents across the Israeli-Lebanese border post-withdrawal remained extremely low compared to the 1985–2000 period.

---

[45] UNSCR 425, UN official website, http://unscr.com/en/resolutions/425, accessed 19 July 2017.
[46] Ehud Barak, Testimony before the Winograd Commission, 28 November 2006, pp. 8–9, 18 (in Hebrew).

226   Between Engagement and Unilateralism

At the same time, certain aspects of Israel's unilateralist approach were problematic. The SLA, Israel's ally and proxy for the best part of the eighteen years it had maintained the security zone, imploded more rapidly than anticipated by Barak and his close circle. As the IDF reduced its forces in Lebanon in preparation for the withdrawal, the SLA was in limbo about its future. Meanwhile, Hezbollah was increasing its attacks on IDF and SLA posts and offering immunity to any SLA soldiers who defected to Hezbollah after killing an IDF soldier.[47] Moreover, Hezbollah was organizing huge human processions towards SLA posts and the remaining IDF outposts. By 21 May 2000, the situation had become unsustainable. Hezbollah attacks were intensifying and it was encouraging the ever-increasing numbers marching on the IDF and SLA outposts while Israel was offering no assurances to the SLA. Finally, the SLA imploded.

Without their Lebanese proxy to help maintain the security zone, the Israelis brought forward the planned July withdrawal, to 23 May. By 07.00hrs on 24 May 2000, Israel's fifteen-year occupation of the security zone in south Lebanon had ended after a hasty, but successful retreat by the IDF the previous night. This hurried withdrawal sent a strong signal that proxies, such as the SLA, could not rely on Israel. Some took refuge in Israel, but many had to surrender to the Lebanese authorities. Moreover, Israel's withdrawal from Lebanon under cover of darkness was perceived in Israel and portrayed by Hezbollah, as an escape and a defeat. This message was articulated most powerfully by Hezbollah General Secretary Hassan Nasserallah, in a victory speech delivered in the Lebanese town of Bint-Jbeil on 26 May 2000, celebrating Israel's withdrawal from Lebanon. Cunningly, in his first speech following Israeli withdrawal, Nasserallah linked Hezbollah's success to the Palestinian struggle to end the Israeli occupation:

O, People of Palestine, the road to Palestine and your road to freedom follows the path of resistance and *intifada* . . . I tell you: the Israel that owns nuclear weapons and has the strongest air force in the region is weaker than a spider's web. O, People of Palestine: if you put yourselves in God's hands, He will give you victory and make you strong. People of Palestine: if God is on your side, no one will ever defeat you.[48]

The speech perfectly articulated the direct linkage that had been established between Israeli unilateral withdrawal from Lebanon and the stuttering Israeli-Palestinian peace process. The successful guerrilla war

---

[47] Gilboa, *The True Story How Israel Left Lebanon*, pp. 134–5.
[48] Nicholas Hoe, *Voices of Hezbollah: The Statements of Sayyed Hassan Naserallah* (London: Verso, 2007), p. 242.

waged by Hezbollah was one of the key reasons why, after eighteen years of occupation, Israel withdrew from Lebanon. In contrast, the Palestinians were still occupied by the Israelis after nine years of negotiations. The ideology and practice of Hezbollah, which combined guerrilla warfare, complete negation of Israel and Islamist ideas inspired by the Iranian revolution, were bolstered. By contrast, the notion of ending Israeli occupation of the Palestinians via negotiations was increasingly discredited. Against this charged political backdrop, the Israeli government was redirecting its foreign policy from a focus on Syria and Lebanon to concentration on the peace process with the Palestinians, which had been on the backburner since Ehud Barak's election to office.

The Neglected Peace Track

From the outset, Ehud Barak had been highly critical of the Oslo peace process. As chief of staff, he described it as a 'Swiss cheese full of holes'. Subsequently, much to the chagrin of Prime Minister Rabin, Barak abstained from the cabinet vote that approved the Oslo II agreement.[49] On his election to prime minister, Barak continued to have reservations about the Oslo peace process, although, unlike those of Binyamin Netanyahu, they were not based on ideological grounds. Rather, as Gilad Sher, one of the chief Israeli negotiators with the Palestinians, explains, Barak's opposition was based on a cost-benefit analysis. He believed that the step-by-step approach underpinning the Oslo peace process had forced Israel to make major concessions over interim agreements, which would leave it with few bargaining chips once negotiations over the permanent agreement commenced. The prime minister was convinced that this was a very poor negotiating tactic.[50]

Also, the prime minister opposed the step-by-step approach on domestic political grounds. In his view, implementing the interim agreements Israel had committed to in the past, the most recent being the Wye accord, threatened his coalition government. The National Religious Party, representing the settlers in the West Bank and Gaza, was averse to concessions being made to the PLO. Shas, the senior coalition partner, tied its support for concessions to the Palestinians, to promotion of its own party's narrow interests. In return for supporting the peace process, it demanded government fund El-Hamaayan, an ultra-religious education system established by Shas some years earlier.

[49] Kfir and Dor, *Barak. Wars of My Life*, pp. 182–3.
[50] Sher, *Just Beyond Reach*, pp. 20, 27.

228   Between Engagement and Unilateralism

Shas's demands were anathema to the decidedly secular and liberal party, Meretz, the junior partner in the coalition, which held the education portfolio. Its leader, Yossi Sarid, vehemently rejected these demands on the grounds that El-Hamaayan did not equip its students with the tools needed to cope in the modern world.[51] This left the prime minister in a serious domestic political bind. Implementing the interim agreements stipulated by the Oslo process risked plunging the coalition government into a political crisis.

Barak's view that negotiating with the Palestinians on the basis of interim agreements was a flawed negotiating tactic and the domestic political challenge it presented to him, strongly influenced his foreign policy towards the PLO. Accordingly, one of the first foreign policy decisions taken by Ehud Barak was to reopen negotiations over the Wye River memorandum, which had taken two years of intense US diplomacy to secure. Instead of implementing another interim accord, Barak sought to subsume the Wye agreement in a permanent settlement. A two-month negotiating round during July and August 1999 culminated with the Sharm el-Sheik memorandum on 4 September 1999. This date was significant because it coincided with the original self-imposed five-year deadline laid down by the Oslo accords for Israel and the Palestinians to agree on a framework agreement to end the conflict.

However, the Sharm el-Sheik memorandum showed how far Israel and the PLO were from achieving this goal. It established 13 September 2000 as the new date for agreement on the permanent status of Israel and the Palestinians, which delayed by a year, the deadline Israel and the PLO agreed to in the 1993 DoP. The memorandum provided a milestone in the journey to an agreement on the permanent status, namely, achieving a conceptual Framework Agreement on Permanent Status (FAPS) within five months. The FAPS would address all 'outstanding issues', which were disputed issues that Israel and the PLO had agreed, in the 1993 DoP, to defer until the permanent status negotiations. These included Jerusalem and the Holy Sites, Palestinian refugees, permanent borders, settlements, security issues and relations with neighbouring states.[52] The Sharm memorandum stipulated, also, that Israel release 350 prisoners, in two phases, and laid down that the Wye Further Redeployments would be implemented between September 1999 and January 2000. For its part, the PLO reiterated its security commitments, which included collecting

---

[51] Ross, *The Missing Peace*, pp. 600–1.
[52] Declaration of Principles, *IMFA*, www.mfa.gov.il/mfa/foreignpolicy/peace/guide/pages/declaration%20of%20principles.aspx, accessed 25 July 2017.

The Neglected Peace Track

illegal weapons, arresting suspects and submitting lists of Palestinian policemen for prospective vetting by Israel.[53]

At the time, the signing of the Sharm memorandum was well received by Israeli, Palestinian, Arab and US negotiators. However, in retrospect, it should be considered as typifying a major flaw that deepened as the Oslo peace process unfolded. Instead of adhering to the obligations stipulated by the signed agreements, each new Israeli government renegotiated them. This applied to the Wye River memorandum, which renegotiated aspects of the Oslo II agreement. Subsequently, it applied to the Sharm memorandum, which reopened the Wye River accord. No deadline or interim agreement was deemed sufficiently important to stand.

Furthermore, since the Barak government was focused on negotiations with Syria and unilateral withdrawal from Lebanon, implementation of the Sharm memorandum was partial and the Israeli-Palestinian peace track was marginalized. Domestic political considerations were at the heart of the foreign policy sequencing adopted by the Israeli prime minister. As Dennis Ross recalls, Barak 'was reluctant to commit to anything with the Palestinians that might undo his political base for doing a deal with Syria'.[54] Hence, the chief negotiator with the Palestinians post remained vacant for nearly two months until the appointment of Dr Oded Eran in November. In the meantime, Barak rejected the Americans' repeated proposals for a back channel with the Palestinians. Consequently, Israel and the PLO were negotiating only via the official and open channel, between Oded Eran and his Palestinian counterpart, Yasser Abed-Rabbo.

The open channel was under constant media and political scrutiny, which deprived the negotiators of the time and space required to develop and test new ideas. Moreover, as Dennis Ross observed, while Barak might have 'proclaimed his intent to achieve the FAPS with the Palestinians, he would not grant anyone on his side the mandate to offer serious ideas for shaping such a deal.'[55] Meanwhile, the Palestinians were adopting maximalist positions and Arafat was reverting to his past practices. Bent on preventing any one negotiator from gaining too much political power, the Palestinian leader created multiple negotiating channels. Vying for power and proximity to Arafat, the negotiators constantly undermined one another's channels.[56] Consequently, as more than one close observer noticed, the Eran-Abed-Rabbo discussions were a mere formality that yielded no significant results.[57]

---

[53] Sharm el-Sheik Memorandum, *IMFA*, www.mfa.gov.il/MFA/MFA-Archive/1999/Pa ges/Sharm%20el-Sheikh%20Memorandum%20on%20Implementation%20Timel.as px, accessed 24 July 2017; Ross, *The Missing Peace*, p. 508.
[54] Ross, The Missing Peace, p. 591.   [55] Ibid.   [56] Ross, *The Missing Peace*, p. 591.
[57] Sher, *Just Beyond Reach*, pp. 63, 67, 70; Beilin, *The Path to Geneva*, pp. 118–19; Ross, *The Missing Peace*, pp. 603–9.

230 Between Engagement and Unilateralism

Between September 1999 and March 2000, Ehud Barak was hedging all his bets on negotiations with Syria. Thus, he stalled on completing the Wye River memorandum's Further Redeployments – perhaps Israel's most significant commitment in the Sharm memorandum. According to Dennis Ross, Barak conveyed to Arafat that he could not implement the last Wye Further Redeployments in January, which coincided with the culmination of his negotiations with the Syria. Insensitive to Palestinian politics, the prime minister, via the Israeli media, also publicly rejected a request made privately by Arafat that when the Further Redeployments were implemented, it would include three villages bordering Jerusalem: Abu Dis, al-Eizariya and al-Ram.[58] At this point, it became clear that the approaching deadline for completing the FAPS, February 2000, also would be breached.

The handling of the last Wye Further Redeployments is indicative. It reflects how significantly the domestic politics of the coalition government shaped the prime minister's negotiating approach to the Palestinians. Barak was convinced that his government and the Israeli public could not cope with concessions to both the Syrians and the Palestinians simultaneously.[59] He felt obliged to choose which peace track to prioritize. Up to March 2000, his choice was clear; the steps Ehud Barak took on the Palestinian track 'were derivative of those he took on Syria', which remained his priority.[60]

However, his foreign policy of marginalizing the Palestinian track as a means to contain domestic political challenges was flawed. The prime minister and his close circle failed to recognize that the government's domestic political problems were worsening irrespective of whether Israel met its commitments to the Palestinians. The National Religious Party's opposition to any concessions towards the Palestinians was increasing and Shas was unrelenting in its linking support for the peace process to funding El-Hamaayan. By 1 March 2000, the government suffered what Minister of Justice Beilin branded its worst parliamentary defeat. Twenty-six members of the coalition government voted in favour of a law proposed by Silvan Shalom, a prominent Likud opposition member, which required a supermajority in any referendum on relinquishing territory. The intent behind drafting the law in these terms was clear: to prevent Palestinian citizens of Israel from casting the deciding votes. This was the bill's first reading, but, as Beilin recalls, 'the results reverberated through Israel and around the world.'[61]

[58] Ross, *The Missing Peace*, p. 592.   [59] Interview Ben-Ami.
[60] Ross, *The Missing Peace*, p. 603.   [61] Beilin, *The Path to Geneva*, p. 132.

While stalling on the Sharm accord had little effect in terms of improving the domestic standing of the coalition government, it had serious repercussions for the Palestinians. In numerous meetings, the Palestinian leadership spelt out to its Israeli counterparts that, by dragging their feet on implementing the Wye River memorandum, the Israeli government had humiliated the Palestinian leadership and betrayed its trust. Moreover, the Palestinians emphasized that Barak's foreign policy, in certain respects, was worse than the foreign policy behaviour of Binyamin Netanyahu. The Palestinians had expected Netanyahu to stall and unpick the Oslo accords, but had envisaged that Ehud Barak would promote and enhance it. Furthermore, under Barak, several representatives of the peace camp, such as Yossi Beilin, Yossi Sarid and Shlomo Ben-Ami, had held ministerial positions.

However, although these leading peaceniks had held prominent positions, nothing seemed to have changed. In fact, in the Palestinians' view, the situation was deteriorating. The Palestinian leadership could no longer say to its constituents that, once the Israeli peace camp returned to power, things would get better. During candid conversations with their Israeli counterparts, the Palestinians voiced their profound and acute concern over the failure of the Oslo process to end Israeli occupation and the growth of settlements. During the first half of 2000, there was a 96 per cent increase in new constructions in the settlements and the settlement population grew by 12 per cent.[62] The Palestinians made clear that, at a certain point, it would become impossible to contain Palestinian frustrations. Interestingly, the individuals with most responsibility for Israeli security independently raised precisely the same concerns with the Americans.[63]

A Critical Juncture

In both Israeli and Palestinian history, 15 May is a charged date, for on that date, Israelis celebrate their Day of Independence and the Palestinians commemorate al-Nakba, 'the catastrophe', which Palestinians maintain occurred as a result of the creation of the State of Israel. Commemoration days are useful for political mobilization and 15 May 2000 was no exception. The Israeli Prime Minister, Ehud

---

[62] Data from the Israeli construction ministry quoted in Zertal and Eldar, *Lords of the Land*, pp. 238–9.

[63] Beilin meetings with leading Palestinians February–April 1999 in Beilin, *The Path to Geneva*, pp. 132–4; Ben-Ami meetings with Muhammad Dahlan, *A Front without a Rearguard*, p. 63; Ross meetings with Chief of Staff Shaul Mofaz and Head of GSS Ami Ayalon, in Ross, *The Missing Peace*, p. 593.

232   Between Engagement and Unilateralism

Barak, was engaged in a political battle to obtain the Knesset's approval to transfer the three villages bordering Jerusalem from partial to full Palestinian authority. The domestic political challenge he faced in implementing this decision was patently clear to his ministerial colleagues.[64]

As Barak was fighting in the Knesset to win this approval, Palestinian demonstrations turned extremely violent. According to Yossi Beilin, a sworn peacenik, the orders to deploy violence were given a few days earlier by the leaders of Tanzim, an organization founded by Fatah Youth in 1983, which was rehabilitated following the September 1996 tunnel crisis. Subsequently, Tanzim members took up arms and became influential players in the politics of Fatah and the PLO. In a meeting before al-Nakba Day, Beilin implored Marwan Barghouti, who had close connections to the Tanzim and recently been appointed Fatah's general secretary, to try to quell any planned violence. 'The instructions for tomorrow have already been given', replied Barghouti, callously, throwing up his hands like someone unable to deliver.[65]

The consequences were dire. During the demonstrations, Palestinian policemen opened fire on Israeli soldiers for the first time since the September 1996 tunnel crisis. In the ensuing clashes, twelve Israeli soldiers were wounded, one seriously; five Palestinians were killed and 188 were injured.[66] The violent events surrounding al-Nakba Day, which continued for a week after the Palestinians announced two 'Days of Rage' on 21 and 22 May, reflected the vulnerability of the Israeli-Palestinian peace process in May 2000.

Concurrently, the prime minister was losing his grip on the coalition because of the Shas-Meretz dispute.[67] This intractable feud, which prompted Shas to threaten to leave the government, was compounded by the deep reservations held by Yisrael Ba'Aliya, a party backed primarily by Jewish immigrants from the former Soviet Union. Its leader, Natan Sharansky, conveyed to Dennis Ross that, based on reports in the Israeli media, rather than information from the prime minister directly, Barak was planning to make concessions to the Palestinians that he, Sharansky, could not support.[68] The tendency for Barak not to confide in his coalition partners and his predilection for centralizing foreign policy were exacerbating the domestic political crisis of his coalition government. However, given the proclivity of the cabinet members to leak information, it is difficult to see how the prime minister could have squared this circle.

---

[64] Ben-Ami, *A Front without a Rearguard*, p. 65.   [65] Beilin, *The Path to Geneva*, p. 142.
[66] Beilin, *The Path to Geneva*, p. 143; Indyk, *Innocent Abroad*, p. 296.
[67] Kfir and Dor, *Barak*, pp. 247–8; Sher, *Just Beyond Reach*, p. 239.
[68] Ross, *The Missing Peace*, p. 625.

A Critical Juncture   233

Under these conditions, the influence of domestic politics on the peace process became pervasive. Shlomo Ben-Ami, Internal Security Minister, recently appointed by the prime minister to join the leading team negotiating with the Palestinians, explained the situation to his Palestinian counterpart in plain terms: 'Currently', Ben-Ami told his Palestinian counterpart, Abu Ala, 'the internal Israeli political constellation prevents from the government to implement the commitments it made to the Palestinians in the Sharm memorandum.'[69]

The coalition government's problems had a curious effect. Rather than halting the process, they forced the prime minister into a fast-track peace process with the Palestinians. As Barak explained to Dennis Ross, he felt that if he brought Israel to the brink of a historical breakthrough with the Palestinians, it would make it difficult for his coalition partners to play petty politics.[70] Therefore, he insisted that the time had come to move to an endgame summit with the Palestinians.[71]

Kissinger's dictum that Israel has no foreign policy, only domestic politics, was certainly vindicated in this particular instance. Trying to resolve the internal political difficulties of the coalition government by pushing for an endgame summit – where Israel and the Palestinians would be forced to resolve all outstanding issues – revealed Ehud Barak's political inexperience. There was no guarantee that the centre-right coalition partners would support the compromises Israel would have to make on core issues, such as Jerusalem, settlements and refugees, to achieve a permanent agreement. Neither were there indications that the internal political divides within the fragmented coalition government, which embodied core questions concerning the relationship between religion and state in Israel, would be put aside to support a peace deal.

The domestic political determinant of Barak's demand for an endgame summit was not the only factor shaping his foreign policy thinking. During a meeting with President Clinton on 1 June 2000, Barak revealed another consideration. 'In a summit', he told the president, Arafat would 'have to face up to the moment of truth, and then we would know if he was a partner for settling the conflict.'[72]

This foreign policy approach, which according to Ben-Ami conformed to the image Barak maintained of leaders meeting to take fateful, historic decisions, was problematic. In the run-up to the negotiations, the Americans were unable to get either Barak or Arafat to commit to

---

[69] Ben-Ami, *A Front without a Rearguard*, p. 95.
[70] Ross, *The Missing Peace*. 623; Kfir and Dor, *Barak*, p. 244.
[71] Ross, *The Missing Peace*, p. 622.   [72] Ross, *The Missing Peace*, p. 628.

234   Between Engagement and Unilateralism

positions that would signal that a breakthrough was possible.[73] Publicly, as Secretary of State Albright observed during her visit to the region to assess the chances of the summit, 'the two sides were committed to widely disparate positions'.[74] Moreover, the PLO issued a warning that conditions were not ripe for a summit, a message echoed strongly by the Israeli MFA. Foreign Minister Levy told Madeline Albright that failure of the summit would unleash unprecedented violence and, for this reason, Levy chose not to participate in it.[75]

These warnings were timely. Barak and Arafat had not developed any level of the trust that would be needed to bridge the various gaps and achieve a permanent agreement.[76] So, why was the prime minister demanding an endgame summit? A private conversation with Ami Ayalon, by then retired from the GSS, is revealing. Barak saw everything through the prism of his interests. Ayalon recalled that, over the Camp David talks, 'Barak told me that he will make Arafat an offer that he cannot refuse', to which Ayalon responded, rather taken aback, 'Ehud, this is not the wild west. This is a partnership. If Arafat thinks that you are not a partner he will not go with you ... he wants to shake your hand and know that in five years' time you will be with him on the same path you agreed upon [in the negotiations].' Barak chided Ayalon for his naïveté and told him that Arafat 'will not have a choice'. 'He will not have a choice', retorted Ayalon, perplexed. 'Arafat would rather return to Tunis and start all over again than enter the annals of Palestinian history as a leader who betrayed the cause of national liberation.'[77]

Ultimately, it was for the Americans to make the decision about calling a summit. Based on the available information, the success of the summit was by no means assured.[78] Nevertheless, with 'inherent optimism deeply encoded in his political DNA', President Clinton decided that 'the cost of going to a summit is far less than the cost of not trying and seeing a collapse of the process'.[79] His confidence that 'maybe he could pull this off', tilted the balance towards issuing invitations for the decisive Camp David summit.[80]

---

[73] Ross, *The Missing Peace*, pp. 630–47.   [74] Albright, *Madam Secretary*, p. 615.
[75] Interview with high-level MFA official on condition of anonymity; Akram Hanieh, 'The Camp David Papers', *Journal of Palestine Studies*, 30, 2 (2001): 76.
[76] Interview Ben-Ami; Ross, *The Missing Peace*, p. 647.
[77] Interview Ben-Ami; the same message was conveyed by President Mubarak to the Americans, see Indyk, *Innocent Abroad*, p. 301.
[78] Ben-Ami, *A Front Without a Rearguard*, p. 131.
[79] Ross, *The Missing Peace*, p. 645; Miller, *The Much too Promised Land*, p. 295.
[80] Miller, *The Much too Promised Land*, p. 295.

Playing Chess with Oneself

The Camp David summit commenced on 11 July 2000 and ended in the early hours of the morning of 25 July. It was a climactic foreign policy event, which was aimed at concluding a final status agreement between the PLO and Israel. After fourteen days of tough negotiations, it was clear that the summit had failed. The multiple accounts of the summit help to explain why.[81]

As the Camp David summit unfolded, the assumptions that had driven Barak to push for a summit collapsed. A key reason for Barak wanting the summit was to confront Arafat with 'a moment of truth'. At the same time, Barak subjected his coalition government to a moment of reckoning. However, his centre-right coalition partners did not wait to see how the summit would develop. Shas, the National Religious Party, and Yisrael Ba'aliya, resigned on the eve of the Camp David summit. The prime minister's calculation that the prospect of a fateful decision would solidify his coalition, in fact precipitated its collapse.[82] Hence, even had Israel struck a deal with the PLO at Camp David, the majority needed to pass it in the Knesset did not exist. The agreement would have had to be passed via referendum or elections, called by a minority government. This reinforced the Palestinians' doubts about Barak's leadership. Since he had not delivered on the Sharm memorandum and had arrived at Camp David as head of a minority government, was he able to implement a permanent agreement?

The domestic political latitude of the Palestinian leadership was also not wide, which was an issue the prime minister did not sufficiently appreciate given his focus on Arafat's role. The violence provoked by the Tanzim in May, indicated that, besides Hamas, elements within the PLO were seriously opposing the Oslo peace process and the PA's role in it.[83] Simultaneously, by July 2000, Israel had completely withdrawn its forces from Lebanon and the offer made by Barak to Hafez al-Assad – which, included withdrawing to the 4 June 1967 borders – was made known.

---

[81] Albright, *Madam Secretary*, pp. 616–33; Ben-Ami, *A Front Without a Rearguard*, pp. 129–235; Clinton, *My Life*, pp. 911–16; David Miller, *The Much too Promised Land*, pp. 295–315; Haniyeh, 'The Camp David Papers', pp. 75–97; Indyk, *Innocent Abroad*, pp. 306–41; ; Robert Malley and Hussein Agha, 'Camp David: The Tragedy of Errors', *New York Review of Books*, 9 August 2001; Ross, *The Missing Peace*, pp. 650–712; Sher, *Just Beyond Reach*, pp. 153–231.

[82] 'Briefing to the cabinet by Prime Minister Barak Regarding the Camp David Summit', *IMFA*, http://mfa.gov.il/MFA/ForeignPolicy/MFADocuments/Yearbook13/Pages/139%20%20Briefing%20to%20the%20cabinet%20by%20Prime%20Minister%20Bar.aspx, accessed 2 August 2017; 'Address to the Knesset by Prime Minister Barak Regarding the Camp David Summit 10 July 2000', *IMFA*, vol. 118, 1999–2001, document 140.

[83] Interview 1 Ayalon.

Martin Indyk, US Ambassador to Israel and negotiator at Camp David, observed that the confluence of these domestic and international factors reduced the degree to which the PLO could compromise.[84] If Israel withdrew from Lebanon completely and offered to return to Syria all the territory it occupied in the 1967 War in exchange for peace, why would the Palestinians settle for less?[85]

In this context, as chief negotiator Shlomo Ben-Ami observed at the time, the positions of the Israelis and Palestinians at the Camp David negotiations were very different. The Palestinian leadership entered the Oslo peace process under the assumption that it had made a major concession in 1993 DoP by recognizing Israel and, therefore, giving up 78 per cent of what they perceived as historical Palestine. By contrast, the Israelis considered the DoP the starting point for negotiations, which it saw as culminating with the Camp David summit.[86]

This is perhaps the source of the debate over the nature of the offer made by Prime Minister Barak to the Palestinians at Camp David. In a nutshell, it included a Palestinian state comprised of 100 per cent of the Gaza Strip and 91 per cent of the West Bank; negotiating a satisfactory solution to Palestinian refugees; and an end-of-conflict agreement. In addition, the Israelis proposed Palestinian sovereignty over Palestinian neighbourhoods on the outer ring of Jerusalem; divided authority in the city's Palestinian inner neighbourhoods; and Palestinian sovereignty over the Muslim and Christian quarters of the Old City. The Palestinians would be awarded custodianship of the Haram al-Sharif/Temple Mount while Israel would remain sovereign.

From the Israeli perspective, this was a generous offer, especially since, on his departure for Camp David, the prime minister had promised 'a united Jerusalem under Israeli sovereignty'.[87] Indeed, a united Jerusalem had become an integral part of the identity and geography of Israel since its annexation in 1967. Nonetheless, as Arafat's close advisor and participant in the talks relayed, in his version of the summit, from a Palestinian point of view, this offer was a difficult one to accept. The Palestinians would not be given 100 per cent of the land occupied by Israel in 1967; the Haram would remain under Israeli sovereignty; and the solution to the refugee

---

[84] Indyk, *Innocent Abroad*, pp. 295, 297.
[85] Arafat posed the question directly to Ben-Ami. See Ben-Ami, *A Front Without a Rearguard*, p. 149.
[86] Ben-Ami, *A Front Without a Rearguard*, p. 149.
[87] 'Address to the Knesset by Prime Minister Barak Regarding the Camp David Summit', 10 July 2000, *IMFA*, http://mfa.gov.il/MFA/PressRoom/2000/Pages/Address%20to%20the%20Knesset%20by%20PM%20Barak%20on%20the%20Camp%20Dav.aspx, accessed 4 August 2017.

Playing Chess with Oneself 237

problem would remain unclear.[88] The surrender of 78 per cent of historical Palestine by Arafat's signing of the DoP in 1993 raised the spectre of his being accused by the Muslim and Arab worlds of having 'sold Jerusalem to achieve [his] state'.[89] Thus, Arafat rejected all proposals made by the Americans that did not include Palestinian sovereignty over the Haram.

A personal relationship based on trust between the two leaders, Ehud Barak and Yasser Arafat, might have served to bridge these highly significant gaps. However, the essential ingredients of joint political leadership and trust did not exist. At Camp David, aside from during two joint meetings with President Clinton – on the first and last days of the summit – the two leaders never spoke directly.[90] The warning conveyed by former GSS head Ayalon to Ehud Barak came back to haunt him as Arafat refused his offer at the eleventh hour of the summit. The Palestinian leader did not oblige by making the move that the Israeli prime minister had intended. Ehud Barak was confronted with the stark reality that his idea of an endgame summit had been reduced to his playing chess against himself. Barak became a recluse for two days and disengaged from the summit negotiations.[91]

In the past, US mediation had compensated for the lack of trust and rapport between the Arab and Israeli leaders. For example, at the Madrid conference, James Baker broke the taboo against Arab and Israelis negotiating directly with one another. However, at Camp David, the gap between the position of the USA as the world's sole superpower and its influence over Israel and the Palestinians was palpable. Consequently, US mediation failed in the face of what was admittedly a more complex task than assembling the Madrid conference. More specifically, the American mediation strategy was to present Israel and the Palestinians with the parameters of an agreement and then to work on bridging the differences. Astonishingly, this negotiating approach was discarded on the first day following the first sign of opposition from Prime Minister Barak; this threw the US negotiating plan into disarray. 'We were not taking control of the summit at the outset', recalled Ross, and backed off too easily in the face of Israeli and Palestinian demands.[92] This approach was in stark contrast to the mediation style of James Baker, who, by employing carrot-and-stick tactics, had effectively brought Israel and the Arabs closer to his positions. Bill Clinton relied too much on

---

[88] Haniyeh, 'The Camp David Papers', p. 92.
[89] Indyk, *Innocent Abroad*, p. 333; see also Haniyeh, 'The Camp David Papers', pp. 86, 90.
[90] Haniyeh, 'The Camp David Papers', p. 93.
[91] Ben-Ami, *A Front Without a Rearguard*, p. 206.
[92] Ross, *The Missing Peace*, pp. 656, 662; Albright, *Madam Secretary*, p. 617; Indyk, *Innocent Abroad*, pp. 308, 329.

238   Between Engagement and Unilateralism

persuasion and soft interventions. More than one negotiator believed that Clinton lacked toughness – the courage to walk away and impose on Israel and the Palestinians the costs for saying no.[93] However, there was also a political dimension to the president's limited influence. Bound by the approach of the end of his second term in office, Clinton was negotiating with the last 'fumes of his political fuel'.[94]

The Unfulfilled Promise of Engagement

The collapse of the Camp David summit, which followed the breakdown of the Clinton-Assad meeting in Geneva, was a milestone. Taken together, these events demonstrated the limits to Israel's foreign policy of engagement. In both cases, the proposals put forward by the Israeli government were not backed by a parliamentary majority. Also, public support was questionable and Ehud Barak was not the type of prime minister to be able to influence that. He was highly inexperienced as a politician and was unable to galvanize domestic support. Neither was he successful in persuading his Arab counterparts, Hafez al-Assad and Yasser Arafat, to accept his offer. Assad remained imprisoned by Ba'thist ideology and, by March 2000, was fixated on the transfer of power to his son. Yasser Arafat was unwilling to make further concessions on the key issues of the refugees, Jerusalem and territory, beyond the compromises the Palestinian National Movement had agreed to in 1993. Similarly, although the Israeli delegation to Camp David had a strong secular tilt, it could not cross the Rubicon of relinquishing sovereignty over the Haram Al-Sharif /Temple Mount. Thus, in spite of nine years of negotiations, rigid historical, national and religious narratives were still preventing a land-for-peace exchange to end Israel's conflict with Syria and the Palestinians.

Israeli relations with Lebanon were free of these shackles, which is why Ehud Barak could order the IDF to withdraw unilaterally from Lebanon in the short timespan of three months. His foreign policy style, which was based on untying Gordian knots swiftly and decisively, was a clear advantage in this case, as the domestic political conditions were ripe and international legitimacy was forthcoming. Under certain conditions, as Barak's tenure demonstrated, Israel could benefit from taking bold unilateral steps. Against his failure to realize the promise of engagement, the imminent collapse of the peace process and unilateralism would prove to be long lasting legacies of Ehud Barak.

---

[93] Ross, *The Missing Peace*, p. 684; Miller, *The Much too Promised Land*, p. 509; Interview Ben-Ami.

[94] Ben-Ami, *A Front without a Rearguard*, p. 223; Indyk, *Innocent Abroad*, p. 304.

11 In Search of a Foreign Policy Paradigm

The Eruption of the Al-Aqsa Intifada

The failure of the Camp David summit produced a serious domestic backlash in Israel. David Levy and his Gesher faction resigned, citing differences with the prime minister over Jerusalem, joining Shas, the National Religious Party and Yisrael Ba'Aliya, who left the coalition on the eve of the Camp David summit.[1] Even members of Barak's own party – around half according to Barak's estimate – opposed him following Camp David.[2] From a political and domestic legitimacy point of view, the disintegration of the Barak government was significant. It demonstrated that the PLO was not alone in rejecting Barak's offer. The majority of the Israeli public, as reflected by the MKs, were also opposed to the peace proposal made by its government at Camp David.

This domestic political context was fertile ground for the fierce criticism mounted by the opposition against the government. The rhetoric used by opposition leader, Ariel Sharon, was suffused with religious and national jingoism, centring on Jerusalem and the Temple Mount.[3] In a highly symbolic step, Sharon asked to visit the Temple Mount/Haram al-Sharif on 28 September 2000, which coincided with the anniversary of the Oslo II accords.

Wearing dark glasses and protected by a 1,000 strong police cordon, Ariel Sharon ascended the Temple Mount/Haram Al-Sharif to 'examine archaeological sites'.[4] On the eve of the visit, Head of the PA's Preventative Security Services in the West Bank Jibril Rajoub, told Shlomo Ben-Ami, Israel's Internal Security Minister, that if Sharon

---

[1] 'Remarks to the Cabinet by Prime Minister Barak Regarding the Peace Process', 20 August 2000, *IMFA*, http://mfa.gov.il/MFA/ForeignPolicy/MFADocuments/Yearbo ok13/Pages/153%20%20Remarks%20to%20the%20cabinet%20by%20Prime%20Mini ster%20Bara.aspx, accessed 11 August 2017.

[2] Ben-Ami, *A Front Without a Rearguard*, p. 241; Kfir and Dor, Barak, p. 265.

[3] Landau, *Arik*, pp. 338–9.

[4] Ahron Bregman, *Elusive Peace: How the Holy Land Defeated America* (London: Penguin, 2005), p. 126.

239

240   In Search of a Foreign Policy Paradigm

avoided entering the mosques, the PA could control any violence.[5] Sharon, flanked by half a dozen Likud members, respected this advice and did not enter the mosques. However, standing on the holy site Sharon boasted that 'the Temple Mount is in our hands and will remain in our hands.'[6]

This statement and the ascent of Sharon to the Temple Mount/Haram al-Sharif was not prompted by any deep religious beliefs on Sharon's part – he was thoroughly secular. Rather, it had clear domestic political aims. Over the summer, in the course of thirty-eight meetings, US, Israeli and Palestinian negotiators continued batting about ideas related to how to proceed with the peace process. Sharon sought to position himself and Likud firmly against these negotiations.[7]

The day after this visit saw numerous Palestinian demonstrations, both spontaneous and planned. On the Haram itself, Israeli police responded using live ammunition against the rioters. The images of Palestinian fatalities in the Haram were contagious and the following day there were demonstrations in the West Bank and the Gaza Strip, some of which were violent. The IDF's retaliation was severe. In the first few days of the violence, more than fifty Palestinians were killed and hundreds were wounded, compared to only five Israeli civilian deaths. There was a particularly harrowing incident on 30 September when a twelve-year-old boy, Muhammad al-Dura, died in the arms of his father, Jamal, after being caught in crossfire between IDF and Palestinian militants near the Netzarim junction. Palestinian negotiator, Abu Ala, recalled that the agonising images of a helpless father and his son attempting to find cover, created the first martyr, a Shahid, of what Palestinians now refer to as the al-Aqsa Intifada.[8] Less than two weeks later, on 12 October, as the violence spiralled, two non-combatant Israeli reserve soldiers, Yossi Avrahami and Vadim Nurzhitz, were lynched after entering central Ramallah by mistake.[9] The brutality of the murderers, who displayed their bloodied hands gleefully to a cheering mob, shocked the Israeli public. Positions on both sides began to harden and a tit-for-tat dynamic of deadly violence gathered momentum.[10]

The violence spread quickly to Israel proper. Between 1 and 2 October Palestinian-Israelis organized mass demonstrations that turned violent as

[5] Ben-Ami, *A Front Without a Rearguard*, p. 287.   [6] Bregman, *Elusive Peace*, p. 126.
[7] Ross, *The Missing Peace*, pp. 712–27; Ben-Ami, *A Front Without a Rearguard*, pp. 235–50, 268–85; Sher, *Just Beyond Reach*, pp. 236–81.
[8] Ahmed Qurie, *Peace Negotiations in Palestine: From the Second Intifada to the Road Map* (London: I.B. Tauris, 2014, p. 14.
[9] Bregman, *Elusive Peace*, p. 127; Druker and Shelah, *Boomerang*, p. 28; Ross, *The Missing Peace*, p. 731.
[10] Shlaim, *The Iron Wall*, p. 690.

The IDF's Undeclared War 241

protestors blocked one of the country's main transport arteries, Highway 65. The police response to the demonstrations, which for Israeli Jews created the impression that the boundaries between the West Bank, the Gaza Strip, and Israel proper were blurring, was disproportionate: thirteen Israeli-Palestinian citizens were shot dead in counter-riots between Israeli Jews and Palestinian-Israelis. On 7 October 2000, Hezbollah tried to open another front by kidnapping three Israeli soldiers in the Mount Dov area, just four months after the unilateral withdrawal from Lebanon.[11] Despite previous pledges from Prime Minister Barak following the unilateral withdrawal – that his government would respond forcefully to Hezbollah attacks – this clear provocation by Hezbollah prompted no response.

The IDF's Undeclared War

The events following Ariel Sharon's visit to the Temple Mount/Haram al-Sharif marked the beginning of the most significant and protracted eruptions of violence since the signing of the Oslo process. Until that point, the Israeli security network had been divided between two approaches to Palestinian violence. One was personified by the outgoing head of the GSS, Ami Ayalon. He saw this violence as reflecting the humiliation, hopelessness and hatred that had been brewing in Palestinian society for some years. He explained that: 'This is what caused people to go on the streets being fully aware that some of them will be wounded or killed ... that's what people feel when they have nothing to lose.'[12]

Moshe (Bogie) Ya'alon, embodied a position at the other end of the spectrum. Since becoming the IDF's military intelligence head, he had been convinced that Yasser Arafat was not preparing the Palestinians for peace. Ya'alon first voiced his view to Prime Minister Rabin in August 1995. Later, the 1996 tunnel crisis reinforced Ya'alon's opinion about Arafat. It also increased his concern over Israeli society's internal cohesion. Instead of dealing with the fact that Arafat was not committed to peace, he recalled, 'we were arguing between ourselves and weakening our own immune system.'[13]

Subsequently, in 1999–2000 and especially during the unilateral withdrawal from Lebanon, Ya'alon perceived Palestinian violence as part of a broader campaign against Israel. 'When Hassan Nasserallah delivered the speech that compared Israel to a spider web', explained Ya'alon, 'he described Israel as a Zionist entity in retreat', a nation that 'was no longer willing to make sacrifices'. Following Nasserallah's speech, which left

[11] Druker and Shelah, *Boomerang*, p. 29.   [12] Interview 2 Ayalon.
[13] Interview Ya'alon.

242   In Search of a Foreign Policy Paradigm

a profound mark on Ya'alon while he was head of the Israeli Central Command, he summoned all battalion heads in active service and the reserve to attend a conference in May 2000. Ya'alon stated in the conference that 'in September there will be a war' and ordered the training regime of the units under his command to be intensified to prepare for what he anticipated would be a prolonged and violent clash with the Palestinians.[14]

Ya'alon was not the only senior IDF officer to subscribe to this view, which was set out formally in July 1999 in a document entitled 'Towards September'. Similar views were being endorsed by the IDF general staff and, most importantly, by its Chief of Staff, Shaul Mofaz.[15] Mofaz saw the events that unfolded following the unilateral withdrawal from Lebanon, to the violence surrounding the 15 May Nakba Day, to the outbreak of the al-Aqsa Intifada, through the same prism as Ya'alon. Accordingly, prior to the outbreak of the al-Aqsa Intifada, Mofaz had declared that 2000 would be a year of 'preparedness'.[16] Important evidence of the type of preparations made by the IDF was provided in a documentary shown on Israeli TV entitled 'A Million Bullets in October'. Brigadier General Zvika Fogel, a high ranking officer in the IDF's Southern Command, described how the IDF had increased the size of its forces in the occupied territories and improved its fortifications in preparation for conflict. Concurrently, the IDF trained additional snipers and purchased weapons considered appropriate for the type of conflict expected with the Palestinians.[17] Furthermore, as early as 1998, the IDF had prepared a contingency plan, 'Field of Thorns', to reoccupy areas A, which were under full Palestinian control.[18]

It was against this background that the IDF's violent response in the aftermath of Sharon's visit to the Temple Mount/Haram al-Sharif needs to be understood. As Ya'alon explains, it was an attempt to reverse the Oslo peace process, which, by 2000, was perceived by him and other leading IDF officers as constituting a major retreat. As Ya'alon explains:

The 'land-for-peace paradigm', which came out of a feeling of strength and power following the six day war, and out of a sincere desire by Israel to end the Arab-Israeli

---

[14] Interview Ya'alon; Ya'alon, *The Longer Shorter Way* (Tel Aviv: Yedioth Ahronoth Books, 2008), pp. 89–90.
[15] Ya'alon, *The Longer Shorter Way*, pp. 90, 98.
[16] Druker and Shelah, *Boomerang*, pp. 48–9; Ya'alon, *The Longer Shorter Way*, p. 98.
[17] 'A Million Bullets in October', scripted and directed by Moish Goldberg, transmitted on Israeli TV Channel 8, on 1 December 2007; Druker and Shelah, *Boomerang*, p. 49.
[18] Ya'alon, *The Longer Shorter Way*, p. 97.

The IDF's Undeclared War   243

conflict, has developed during the last two decades into a strategy of retreats out of an Israeli perception (wrong in my view) of weakness.[19]

It is within this context that the Israeli reaction to the al-Aqsa Intifada should be assessed. The response, as Ya'alon reveals, was not merely a counterterrorist measure:

It was a strategic response in the construction of the Iron Wall. As long as the Palestinians saw that terrorism leads to Israeli withdrawals why would they want to negotiate with us? They can bring Israel to make concessions via the use of force. Therefore, it was important to rebuild the Iron Wall and to stop withdrawing. To stand tall, pay a price, not surrender . . . change course from retreating to attacking.[20]

The strategic thinking outlined by Ya'alon explains the IDF's disproportionate use of force in the wake of the Palestinian violence that erupted in 2000. This was strongly reflected in the number of fatalities during the first six weeks of the conflict. According to the IDF's own data, a month after the outbreak of the Intifada, the Palestinian death toll soared to 129 while there were only twelve Israeli fatalities.[21] During the same period, the head of the IDF's military intelligence, Amos Malka, confirmed that the army had asked for 1 million bullets to replenish the ammunition that had been used during the first month of the confrontation with the Palestinians.[22] The IDF all but declared war on the PLO, the PA and its affiliated organizations, such as Tanzim, as well as on Hamas and PIJ. According to Palestinian negotiator, Abu Ala, the discrepancy between the number of Israeli and Palestinian casualties 'undermined the position of the Palestinian leadership.'[23]

Shlomo Ben-Ami, Israeli Internal Security Minister and chief negotiator with the Palestinians, who was well placed to observe the course of action taken by the IDF, was harsh in his judgement of its conduct. 'Whereas the government sought to contain events', he notes in his memoirs, 'the IDF's command had a different agenda', which 'expanded the vicious circle of violence rather than reduced it'.[24] 'It was conducting a war', he continues, 'as it saw fit', which 'increased the Palestinian level of rage to unprecedented levels'.[25] Thus, 'the army dictated the pace of events' while the government failed to impose its decisions on it.[26] Former chief of staff and minister in the Barak government, Amnon

---

[19] Ya'alon, *The Longer Shorter Way*, p. 31, emphasis in original.
[20] Interview Ya'alon; Ya'alon, *The Longer Shorter Way*, p. 107.
[21] 'Monthly Breakdown of Fatalities', *Ha'aretz*, www.haaretz.co.il/hasite/images/daily/D2 90905/700info.jpg, accessed 9 August 2017.
[22] Druker and Shelah, *Boomerang*, p. 28; Ya'alon, *The Longer Shorter Way*, p. 121.
[23] Qurie, *Peace Negotiations in Palestine*, p. 17.
[24] Ben-Ami, *A Front without a Rearguard*, p. 319.   [25] Ibid, 320.
[26] Ben-Ami, *A Front without a Rearguard*, p. 320.

244   In Search of a Foreign Policy Paradigm

Lipkin-Shahak, echoing Ben-Ami's view, described how decisions made by the government 'evaporated' on their way to the IDF.[27] 'These were', concluded Ben-Ami sombrely, 'dark days for our democratic rules and procedures, as far as the distance between the government and the military were concerned, with each fighting its own war with its own logic.'[28]

However, the IDF was not alone in fuelling the violence. Since May 2000, the role played by the Palestinian security services, Tanzim, Hamas and PIJ, in propelling the violence and fuelling the Intifada was also significant. Some Israeli and American policymakers argued that Arafat had orchestrated the violence with two strategic aims in mind. First, to escape being cornered into a peace agreement based on the Camp David proposal, which he did not want. Second, to exert pressure on Israel to make further concessions via the use of violence.[29]

It is true that the Palestinian leader did not make significant efforts to curb the violence. Nevertheless, arguing that the eruption of the al-Aqsa Intifada was stage managed, with Arafat a puppeteer of Palestinian violence, is a view that is not supported by the evidence. In fact, certain elements within the IDF's MID, its Planning and Policy Directorate and the GSS, refused to lay all the blame at Arafat's door. They observed that Arafat was not in complete control of his own system.[30] Moreover, Khalil Shikaki, an authoritative academic with no axe to grind, provides a further explanation for the violent eruption of the al-Aqsa Intifada. Shikaki conducted seventy-five public surveys between 1993 and 2001. Based on these reliable responses, he demonstrates forcefully that, following the Camp David summit, support for Arafat fell by 47 per cent while support for Fatah declined by 33 per cent. Shikaki argues that the violence pursued by the Palestinian security services, Hamas and PIJ, was part of a challenge to Arafat's rule – not just to Israel.[31]

An emerging young Palestinian guard, which had little influence in the PLO's political institutions, but wielded considerable power within Fatah's semi-militias, such as Tanzim and the al-Aqsa Brigades, mounted a challenge to the Oslo peace process paradigm. This young guard and the Palestinian Islamist organizations, which were inspired by the Hezbollah model, sought to end the Israeli occupation by armed popular resistance and to present an alternative to the PA's rule. As Shikaki demonstrates, the failed peace process, deteriorating economic conditions, official

---

[27] Quoted in Sher, *Just Beyond Reach*, p. 368.
[28] Ben-Ami, *A Front without a Rearguard*, P. 320.
[29] Ben-Ami, *A Front Without a Rearguard*, pp. 299–300, 302, 316; Indyk, *Innocent Abroad*, p. 352; Ross, *The Missing Peace*, p. 730.
[30] Peri, *Generals in the Cabinet Room*, p. 112.
[31] Khalil Shikaki, 'Palestinians Divided', *Foreign Affairs*, 81, 1, 2002: 92.

corruption and the failing Palestinian democracy, were bleeding Arafat and Fatah of their supporters. Thus, the poor policy record of Arafat and his close circle meant that the Palestinian leader no longer had the degree of authority and legitimacy ascribed to him by the Israeli and American policymakers, to halt the violence. Indeed, to show credibility with the younger leadership, Arafat had to tolerate their alliance with the Islamists in their violent confrontation with the IDF. This significantly constrained his and his close circle's abilities to deal with the crisis, which also explains why Arafat consistently refused to condemn Palestinian violence explicitly.[32] As Abu Ala recalls: '[W]e felt that any attempt to stem this movement would leave the leadership looking isolated from the street.'[33]

It is somewhat ironic that Ehud Barak and Yasser Arafat found themselves in similar situations. Their control over their respective security networks, which had developed their own ideas of how to confront 'the enemy', was partial. Neither leader was able to admit this publicly so each pinned the blame for the collapse of the peace process on the other.

A Janus-Faced Foreign Policy towards the PLO

In the wake of the collapse of the Camp David summit and the eruption of violence, Israeli foreign policy under the Barak government was inconsistent. On the one hand, the minority government continued on the foreign policy path begun at Camp David, which, despite the failed summit, broke important taboos. In the past, Israeli foreign policymakers had subscribed to the dictum that Jerusalem was indivisible. On the other, Camp David prompted a more informed discussion about Jerusalem's future as grounded in this binational and multi-religious city's demographic, geographic and religious realities. Likewise, the Palestinians' treatment of the Right of Return was problematized. Israeli and US negotiators underscored its incompatibility with Israel's self-determination as a Jewish state, which was supported by the overwhelming majority of its Jewish population. Following Camp David, the Israeli and Palestinian delegations continued negotiations with two aims in mind: developing the ideas promulgated at Camp David and stopping the violence. In the period July and December 2000, over fifty meetings between the Israeli and Palestinian negotiating teams were held,

---

[32] Shikaki, 'Palestinians Divided', 92–5, 97–8; A similar view was voiced by former Head of GSS Ami Ayalon, and former Chief of Staff, Amnon Lipkin-Shahak, who was still serving as a minister in the Barak government. See Indyk, *Innocent Abroad*, p. 354.

[33] Qurie, *Peace Negotiations in Palestine*, p. 26.

246   In Search of a Foreign Policy Paradigm

including summits in Paris and Sharm El-Sheik on 4 and 16 October respectively.[34]

At the same time, the government was implementing measures that undercut its own aims. Most crucially, on returning from Camp David, Prime Minister Barak stated that: 'We did not succeed because we did not find a partner prepared to make discussions on all issues.'[35] Furthermore, in a number of high-level meetings, Israeli foreign policymakers echoed the thesis promoted by Ya'alon and the generals that Arafat was orchestrating the violence.[36] Meanwhile, in negotiations with Arafat, Barak accused him of being a 'liar' and the 'leader of a gang of thugs'.[37] The harsh judgement passed on Arafat and the rendition that there was 'no partner' on the other side had an immediate effect on the Palestinians. As Abu Ala recalls, the declared Israeli positions 'sowed doubt about the very feasibility of ever reaching a negotiated solution'.[38]

Veering between negotiating with the PLO and denouncing it, amid the undeclared war between the IDF and the Palestinians, Israeli foreign policy towards the PLO resembled the behaviour of a bat flying in daylight. The PLO was equally erratic in its approach; Arafat swung between accepting agreements to stop the violence and withdrawing from them shortly thereafter.

The Clinton Parameters – Exposing the Limits of the Two-State Solution

Israeli and Palestinian negotiations entered a critical round of negotiations on 20 December at Bolling Air Force Base, near Washington, DC. It was clear to the Americans and members of the Barak government that, in the wake of the Intifada, the political ground in Israel was shifting to the right.[39] The Clinton presidency was effectively over, following confirmation that George W. Bush had won the 2000 presidential elections against Al Gore. Bush would ascend to the White House in the following January. Despite the clear sense of urgency, the negotiations remained

---

[34] Ross, *The Missing Peace*, pp. 734–42; Sher, *Just Beyond Peace*, pp. 292–9, 304–7; Ben-Ami, *A Front Without a Rearguard*, pp. 309–12, 322–4.

[35] 'Statement by Prime Minister Barak on his return to Israel from Camp David', 26 July, *IMFA*, http://mfa.gov.il/MFA/ForeignPolicy/MFADocuments/Yearbook13/Pages/14 9%20%20Statement%20by%20Prime%20Minister%20Barak%20on%20his%20retu .aspx, accessed 11 August 2017.

[36] Ben-Ami, *A Front without a Rearguard*, pp. 299–300, 302, 310, 316, 313.

[37] Sher, *Just Beyond Reach*, pp. 292, 307, 329.

[38] Qurie, *Peace Negotiations in Palestine*, p. 28.

[39] Clinton, *My Life*, p. 936; Ben-Ami, A *Front Without a Rearguard*, p. 310; Indyk, *Innocent Abroad*, p. 356.

The Clinton Parameters 247

trapped by the gaps that had separated Israel and the PLO since September. Both sides requested that the Americans break the deadlock by presenting the US position on core issues, to which Israel and the Palestinians would respond.[40]

The Americans agreed on condition that their 'proposals' be presented verbally as 'ideas'. The reason for not wanting these ideas to be presented in a formal document was due to American concern that the Palestinians would seek to negotiate over the ideas presented by the US president. This was something the Americans were not willing to do; the president's ideas would constitute the endpoint of the negotiations.[41]

Under these conditions, the Israeli and Palestinian negotiators were invited to the White House Cabinet Room on 23 December 2000 to hear the president present what came to be known as the Clinton parameters.[42] To underline the informality of the occasion, the president wore jeans and a casual shirt. When everyone had taken their seats, Clinton began reading aloud from a script. He read slowly to ensure that the negotiators could record every word. It was made clear that further negotiations within the parameters could take place, but that those parameters were themselves non-negotiable. Each side would have four days to formulate yes or no responses.[43]

The essence of the Clinton parameters was as follows.[44] On territory, Clinton recommended a Palestinian state on 100 per cent of the Gaza Strip and between 94 per cent and 96 per cent of the West Bank, with a land swap from Israel of 1 per cent to 3 per cent and an understanding that the land retained by Israel would include 80 per cent of the settlers in blocs. Territorial contiguity in the West Bank would be assured, while the number of Palestinians absorbed into the areas the Israelis annexed would be minimized.

On security, Clinton suggested that Israeli forces should withdraw over a three-year period while an international force was gradually introduced, on the understanding that a small Israeli presence in the Jordan Valley could continue for a further three years, answerable to the international forces. The Israelis also could maintain three EWS in the West Bank with a Palestinian liaison presence. In the event of an 'imminent and demonstrable threat to Israel's security', there would be provision for emergency deployments in the West Bank. The new state of Palestine would be 'non-

---

[40] Ross, *The Missing Peace*, p. 749; Ben-Ami, *A Front Without a Rearguard*, pp. 365–7; Sher, *Just Beyond Reach*, pp. 354–8.
[41] Ross, *The Missing Peace*, pp. 749–50.
[42] Sher, *Just Beyond Reach*, pp. 292–9, 304–7, 354–64; Ross, *The Missing Peace*, pp. 734–42.
[43] Ross, *The Missing Peace*, pp. 750–1; Sher, *Just Beyond Reach*, p. 360.
[44] Ross, *The Missing Peace*, pp. 752–3; Clinton, *My Life*, pp. 936–7.

248   In Search of a Foreign Policy Paradigm

militarized', but would have a strong security force, sovereignty over its air space with special arrangements to meet Israeli training and operational needs and an international force for border security.

On Jerusalem, Clinton recommended that the Arab neighbourhoods be in Palestine and the Jewish neighbourhoods in Israel and that the Palestinians should have sovereignty over the Temple Mount/Haram and the Israelis should have sovereignty over the Western Wall and the 'holy space' of which it was a part. There should be no excavations around the wall or under the Mount, at least without mutual agreement. On refugees, the new state of Palestine was designated the homeland for refugees displaced in the 1948 War and after, but without ruling out the possibility that Israel would accept some of the refugees according to its own laws and sovereign decisions, giving priority to the refugee populations in Lebanon. The president recommended an international effort to compensate refugees and assist them to find houses in the new state of Palestine, in the land-swap areas to be transferred to Palestine, in their current host countries, in other willing nations or in Israel. Both parties would agree that this solution satisfied UN resolution 194 and that the overall agreement satisfied UNSCR 242 and 338. Finally, the agreement would clearly mark the end to the conflict, the finality of all claims and an end to all violence.

The Clinton parameters were very significant. They were the first proposal by the administration of a judiciously considered package portraying what the end of the Israeli-Palestinian conflict might resemble. The Israeli and Palestinian responses to the parameters provoked extremely charged debate. The verdict of President Clinton, Secretary of State Albright and chief US negotiator, Dennis Ross, was unambiguous. They claimed that the Israeli government's response to the parameters was a historic 'yes' and that the Palestinians' response was equivocal.[45] According to Albright, in a written response, Arafat argued against Israeli sovereignty over the Western Wall, against an Israeli presence in the Jordan valley, against a compromise on the right of return and in favour of a complete Israeli withdrawal within months not years.[46] Dennis Ross described Arafat's reservations as 'deal-killers'.[47] Ben-Ami, who cites excerpts from the Palestinian letter, reached similar conclusions.[48] Prince Bandar of Saudi Arabia, who followed the last phase of the negotiations closely, branded Arafat's reply as negative and as 'a tragic mistake – a crime, really'.[49]

---

[45] Clinton, *My Life*, p. 944; Ross, *The Missing* Peace, pp. 3–5; excerpts of the Israeli response are in Sher, *Just Beyond Reach*, pp. 372–4.
[46] Albright, *Madam Secretary*, p. 631.   [47] Ross, *The Missing Peace*, p. 756.
[48] Ben-Ami, *A Front without a Rearguard*, pp. 394–5.
[49] Interview Elsa Walsh, 'The Prince', *New Yorker*, 24 March 2003.

The Clinton Parameters 249

In contrast, Clayton Swisher, who wrote an investigative report on the Camp David summit and its aftermath, disagreed. Having gained access to Arafat's response letter to the Americans, Swisher asserted that his conditions were within the Clinton parameters. Therefore, presenting them in writing was a minimal fulfilment of his historical role as a Palestinian leader.[50] Moreover, Palestinian negotiator, Abu Ala, claimed that, in a meeting on 2 January 2001, Arafat told Clinton that 'the Palestinian leadership would agree to all his proposals, which Arafat described as constituting the basis of an agreement that the Palestinians would accept.'[51] Dennis Ross, who was present at that meeting, contends that Arafat's views still fell short of meeting the parameters.[52]

Analysing the personal role played by Arafat in the fate of the Clinton parameters is important. However, any such examination should be placed in the broader context in which it took place, which is something that detractors of Arafat frequently ignore. For example, by the time the Barak government had accepted the Clinton parameters, the distrust between Ehud Barak and Yasser Arafat was profound. Indeed, it is likely that Arafat continued – and for good reason – to have reservations about whether Barak would fully implement the agreement. The Barak government's record over implementing the 1999 Sharm agreement was very poor. Moreover, the prime minister was being buffeted by the crosswinds of violence and diplomacy, which was why, by January, he was contemplating a complete discontinuance of the negotiations. However, following the collapse of his broad government, his cabinet was heavily dominated by Labour's doves and the architects of the Oslo process. This group exerted heavy pressure on Barak to continue the negotiations and was the main reason, according to Ya'alon, that the IDF recommendation to 'declare Arafat as an enemy' was rejected.[53] Moreover, Yossi Beilin threatened to accuse Barak publicly for abandoning the peace process were he to decide to suspend negotiations.[54] This would lay responsibility for the failure of the peace process squarely at the prime minister's door.

The doubts harboured by Arafat about Barak's ability to deliver on an agreement could only have been increased by the domestic response the Clinton parameters provoked in Israel. During the cabinet meeting to discuss the parameters, Chief of Staff Mofaz referred to them as an 'existential danger to the state of Israel', which was consistent with his

[50] Clayton Swisher, *The Untold about Camp David: The Untold Story about the Collapse of the Middle East Peace Process* (New York: Nation Books, 2004), pp. 399–403.
[51] Qurie, *Peace Negotiations in Palestine*, p. 7.   [52] Ross, *The Missing Peace*, pp. 11–12.
[53] Ya'alon, *The Longer Shorter Way*, p. 105.
[54] Ben-Ami, *A Front without a Rearguard*, p. 398; Ross, *The Missing Peace*, p. 737.

250   In Search of a Foreign Policy Paradigm

strategy since the outbreak of the al-Aqsa Intifada. He then made his views public in clear breach of the delicate boundary between his role as chief of staff and the political sphere.[55]

The fierce opposition mounted by Mofaz and the lack of trust between Arafat and Barak were not the only impediments to the Clinton parameters. Another serious hindrance was the Barak government's lack of domestic legitimacy to accept the parameters in the first place. At the time, the government had been left with no parliamentary base. Furthermore, Ehud Barak had already resigned as prime minister, which started the countdown to an election scheduled for February 2001. The resignation of Barak, who had been elected prime minister under the direct vote system, meant that the MKs would not stand for election. Only candidates for the premiership would seek election by the Israeli public. This created the curious situation of Barak serving as caretaker prime minister until the February elections, which would determine whether he or his rival, Likud leader, Ariel Sharon, would become the next prime minister of Israel.

This domestic political limbo understandably led Israeli Attorney General Elyakim Rubenstein to pass harsh judgement on the government's decision to accept the Clinton parameters. 'Legal but immoral' was his verdict, recalled Ben-Ami, somewhat sadly from his position as acting foreign affairs minister. Putting his finger on the heart of the problem, Israel's leading diplomat recalls that: 'We were criticized for being a minority government that was trading with strategic and historic assets.'[56] Meanwhile, the election polls were favouring the Likud candidate, Ariel Sharon, which cast doubt on the ability of the Israeli government to implement the parameters. As chief negotiator Sher noted, Barak had made it clear that before the elections he would not sign any agreement that would be subject to referendum.[57] The domestic Israeli context casts the response of the Palestinians to the Clinton parameters in a somewhat different light than presented by the detractors of the Palestinian leader. Arafat may well have equivocated in his responses to the Clinton parameters. However, the bulk of the Israeli political and military top brass also rejected them.

Could the PLO have disregarded the domestic Israeli response and placed its trust in the USA to force Israel to implement the Clinton ideas, even had Ariel Sharon ascended to power? In December 2000, this would have constituted a huge gamble by the Palestinians. By then, the

[55] Ben-Ami in 'A Million Bullets in October'; Sher, *Just Beyond Reach*, pp. 367–8.
[56] Ben-Ami, *A Front Without a Rearguard*, p. 321; Druker and Shelah, *Boomerang*, pp. 29–30.
[57] Sher, *Just Beyond Reach*, p. 374.

Palestinian leadership had no trust in the US mediation team, especially Dennis Ross. 'His name', wrote Affif Safieh, a leading Palestinian diplomat in his memoirs, 'will always be associated with bias, partiality and the absence of American even-handedness in the quest for peace in the Middle East.'[58]

Besides the issue of trust there was the question of timing, which the US mediation team seemed to have got completely wrong. Had the Clinton parameters been presented at the end of the Camp David summit, they may have stood a better chance of being accepted. The president still had five months in office and the violence had yet to become full blown. However, with the president 'no longer effective', as the Israeli acting foreign, minister put it, Barak trailing Sharon in the election campaign, relentless violence continuing and Arafat facing his own significant domestic challenges, the tabling of the Clinton parameters was too late. Thus, it is clear that several problems loomed like a dark cloud over the Clinton parameters, which is why explaining the Palestinian response, as Dennis Ross does, solely in terms of Arafat being 'unwilling to confront history and mythology' is simplistic.[59]

Given what we know now, Arafat may have well missed a historic opportunity by not accepting the Clinton parameters unequivocally. However, their presentation was badly timed and they were submitted against an extremely volatile political and military context, which made them a less solid and clear-cut offer than suggested by detractors of Arafat. In fact, the failure of the Clinton parameters to produce a final peace agreement clearly exposed the limits to Israel and the Palestinians agreeing on a peace that was based on the two-state solution. A last gasp attempt by both sides, in Taba – this time without American mediation – reproduced the pattern set at Camp David. While some of the gaps between Israel and the Palestinians narrowed, they remained unbridgeable.[60]

The Resistible Rise of Ariel Sharon

Ehud Barak was elected with a personal mandate to make peace with Syria and the Palestinians. The Geneva and Camp David summits

---

[58] Afif Sfieh, *The Peace Process: From Breakthrough to Breakdown* (London: Saqi Books, 2010), pp. 240–1.

[59] Ross, *The Missing Peace*, p. 758.

[60] On the Taba negotiations, see Ben-Ami- *A Front Without a Rearguard*, pp. 432–55; Sher, *Just Beyond Reach*, pp. 397–412; Beilin, *The Path to Geneva*, pp. 227–52; 'Joint Israeli-Palestinian statement regarding the Taba Talks', 27 January 2001, *IMFA,* http://mfa .gov.il/MFA/ForeignPolicy/MFADocuments/Yearbook13/Pages/231%20%20Joint%20 Israel-Palestinian%20statement%20regarding.aspx, accessed 13 August 2017.

252   In Search of a Foreign Policy Paradigm

exposed the limits of the land-for-peace formula, which had been at the heart of Israel's engagement stance during Barak's term as prime minister. It was against this background that Ariel (Arik) Sharon, a staunch opponent of Israel's engagement stance, won the February 2001 elections by a majority of 62.39 per cent.[61]

Sharon was born Ariel Scheinerman, on 26 February 1928, in Kfar Malal, a semi-collective farm or *moshav*. Sharon had not published a book of ideas neither was he renowned for his political speeches. Information on his complex character and main sources of influence comes from biographies written by students of Israeli history, personal accounts and interviews with his close confidants and his son, Gilad Sharon.[62] Like many of his generation, Sharon's most formative experience was his long and chequered military service in the IDF. Twice, in 1967 and 1973, he had been associated with outstanding military campaigns. In 1967, he led the Israeli forces' conquest of Abu Agheila, which opened the main axis to the IDF's advancement into the Sinai.[63] In 1973 Sharon was associated, perhaps more than any other Israeli general, with the IDF's counteroffensive to Egypt's surprise attack launched on 6 October 1973. By the end of the war, Sharon had led his forces across the Suez Canal into the Egyptian mainland, which was a turning point in the war.[64] The role he played in both these wars made him a national hero, renowned as Arik King of Israel.

At the same time, Sharon's brute force was infamous and had marked his career since his early days as commander of the IDF's 101 commando unit. This unit was instrumental in Israel's 'reprisal policy' of crossborder raids during the 1950s. In one such reprisal attack, in the West Bank village of Qibya, Ariel Sharon's unit blew up 45 houses. Sixty-nine civilians, two-thirds of them women and children, were killed in the attack. A UN report on the incident concluded that the killings were intentional.[65] Subsequently, in 1971–1972, as commander of Israel's southern front, Major General Sharon fought a merciless campaign in the Gaza Strip. Sharon used collective punishment, forced displacement

---

[61] 'Elections February 2001 – Special Update', *IMFA*, www.mfa.gov.il/mfa/aboutisrael/hi story/pages/elections%20february%202001%20-%20special%20update.aspx, accessed 14 August 2017.

[62] See, for instance, Ariel Sharon with David Cahanoff, *Warrior: An Autobiography* (London, 1989); Uri Dan, *Ariel Sharon – An Intimate Portrait* (Tel Aviv: Miskal, 2007); Nir Hefetz and Gadi Bloom, *Ariel Sharon: A Life* (New York: Random House, 2006); Landau, *Arik;* Gilad Sharon, *Sharon – The Life of a Leader* (Tel Aviv: Meter, 2011); Dov Weissglas, *Ariel Sharon – A Prime Minister* (Tel Aviv: Yedioth Ahronoth, 2012).

[63] Landau, *Arik*, pp. 62–3.

[64] Jacob Even and Simcha B. Maoz, *At the Decisive Point in the Sinai: Generalship in the Yom Kippur War* (Lexington: Kentucky University Press, 2017).

[65] Shlaim, *The Iron Wall*, p. 96.

The Resistible Rise of Ariel Sharon

and a shoot-to-kill policy to crush Palestinian resistance and confront terrorist attacks.[66]

If there were any enduring influences from his military career on the foreign policy outlook of Ariel Sharon, they were boldness, daring and the use of brute force to attain his goals. Above all, as a key member of Sharon's inner circle observed: 'Sharon always strove to maintain the initiative.'[67] These features also became the trademarks of his political career. From his early days in Israeli politics, Sharon was wedded to the settler movement in the form of Gush Emunim, the Block of the Faithful. Since his first ministerial position in Menachem Begin's 1977 government, Sharon led the charge to expand the number and size of Jewish settlements in the occupied territories. The locations were carefully chosen to restrict the expansion of Palestinian towns and, geographically, to dominate the West Bank and Israel's Coastal Plain. Above all, the drive to create 'facts on the ground', as the settlement expansion was often described in revisionist Zionist parlance, was designed to render impossible any future territorial compromise. As Jewish settlements expanded in number and size, Sharon came to be known as the bulldozer, based on his desire to build settlements and the brutal means he used to accomplish it. Perhaps more than other Likud politician of his time, Sharon was identified with Israel's settlement project and transformation into occupier.[68] 'He does not stop at a red light', was how one critical biographer summed up his conduct.[69]

The ties that bound Sharon to the settlers were not religious. He was a deeply secular man, with a strong attachment to Jewish heritage, history and culture, but not religion. As Zeev Hever, a leading figure in the settler movement, who developed an intimate relationship with Sharon, recalls, 'the ideological thinking of Ariel Sharon was designed to show the Arabs that the Jews are strongly rooted in the land. We had to show that we are not a temporary phenomenon, that this is our land, and that we are not going anywhere.'[70] In addition, Sharon's perception of Israel's possession of the West Bank and Gaza Strip was linked inextricably to demography. As his political strategist Eyal Arad put it, rather bluntly: 'Sharon ultimately believed that areas where Jews settled and lived will be ours whereas places where the number of Jews was insufficient would not remain under Israeli control.'[71] The link between demography and control over the

---

[66] Landau, *Arik*, pp. 81–4.   [67] Interview Eyal Arad, 21 January 2018, Ramat Gan.
[68] Eldar and Zertal, *Lords of the Land*, pp. 84–8; Landau, *Arik*, pp. 157–8.
[69] Uzi Benziman, *He Does Not Stop at a Red Light* (Tel Aviv: Am Oved, 1985).
[70] Zeev Hever, 'Zeev Hever (Zambish)' in Ari Shavit, *Partition: Disengagement and Beyond* (Jerusalem: Keter 2005) (in Hebrew).
[71] Interview Arad.

254   In Search of a Foreign Policy Paradigm

land was part of the deeply ethnocentric outlook of Ariel Sharon. He preferred to use the term Jews rather than Israelis and was convinced that the Jewish people were, indeed, the chosen people. 'There is nothing nobler than to be Prime Minister of Jews', he would tell his confidant, Dov Weissglass.[72]

Besides being a leading advocate of the settlers, Sharon became a driving force in domestic Israeli politics. In 1973, he became MK for the capitalist Liberal party, befitting one of Israel's largest cattle ranchers. Not one to be contained by a political shell, Sharon became instrumental in creating the Likud bloc by joining his Liberals and other smaller factions to Menachem Begin's Herut, as the senior partner. Subsequently, he contested the 1977 elections after breaking away from the Liberals to head his own Shlomtzion (Peace of Zion) party. Despite pledging not to return to Likud, he did so after Shlomtzion's poor performance in the elections, when it won only two seats. This period of political manoeuvring was critical for Sharon's consolidation as a politician. His detractors accused him of deceit, mendacity and political promiscuity. For instance, the then leader of the Liberals, Simcha Ehrlich, remarked bitterly that 'Sharon is a man without principles, without human feelings, and without any moral norms whatsoever.'[73]

The political mendacity of Ariel Sharon and his proclivity for brutal and indiscriminate use of military force to achieve his goals were displayed to the full during his tenure as defence minister in 1981–3. While holding the most important portfolio in the second Begin government, Sharon developed a plan to transform Lebanon, which was in the midst of civil war, into a vassal Israeli state. His strategy was to use the IDF's military might to destroy the PLO's infrastructure in Lebanon and to establish a new political order under the leadership of Israel's proxy, the Christian Phalanges. Their leader, Bashir Gemayel, backed by Israeli military force, would form a government that would sign a peace agreement with Israel. The then Chief of Staff Raphael Eitan, supported the plan, which was codenamed Big Pines.

However, Big Pines was rejected by the IDF intelligence chief and the head of Mossad. Most of the cabinet also objected to the plan, which led Sharon to pursue it discretely and incrementally. Rather than authorizing Big Pines, Sharon persuaded the government to sanction the more modest version, Little Pines, which was presented to the government as a military campaign to destroy PLO targets in Lebanon. However, what Sharon did not disclose to his cabinet colleagues was that the enemy's response to this limited IDF campaign would be used as a pretext to

[72] Dov Weissglas, *Ariel Sharon*, pp. 7, 95.   [73] Quoted in Landau, *Arik*, p. 151

The Resistible Rise of Ariel Sharon

expand its military operations to the scope originally envisaged by the Big Pines plan.[74]

This was the background to the 1982 Israeli invasion of Lebanon, which backfired badly, exacting a heavy personal and political price from Sharon. The main objective of the Big Pines plan – crowning Bashir Gemayal as the leader of Lebanon – collapsed with Gemayal's assassination on 14 September 1982. The Christian Phalanges seeking revenge, committed massacre on the refugee camps of Sabra and Shatila, killing at least 800 Palestinian men, women and children.[75] There was a sense of real shock and outcry in Israel, which prompted the government to set up a Commission of Inquiry, headed by Supreme Court Justice Yitzhak Kahan. The investigating committee concluded that Sharon bore personal responsibility for not anticipating that the entry of the enraged Phalanges to the refugee camps would invite carnage. Its recommendation that Sharon be dismissed from the defence ministry and denied that ministerial position in the future was implemented by the cabinet. It removed Sharon by a majority of sixteen to one votes, with Sharon's being the only dissenting vote.[76]

The 1982 Lebanon war, in contrast to the 1967 and 1973 wars, damaged Ariel Sharon's political career and public standing. 'For us the young liberals of Israel', wrote leading journalist Ari Shavit, Sharon became 'Arik the Leper, who, in 1982, led the country into a catastrophic war in Lebanon and bore a great measure of responsibility for the massacres at the Sabra and Shatila refugee camps.'[77] Confidants of Sharon saw how the personal and political price of pursuing divisive policies, deceiving his government colleagues and overreliance on the military had become ingrained in Ariel Sharon's political outlook.[78] Ehud Olmert, who would serve as Sharon's deputy and would succeed him, commented that Sharon was tempered by 'the hump he carried with him from the 1982 Lebanon war.'[79] Sharon's close aides, Eyal Arad and Dov Weissglas, also noticed a change in Sharon over the years. 'He was an idealist', remarked Weissglas, 'but over the years he also developed a deep sense of pragmatism.'[80]

The election of Ariel Sharon to prime minister at the age of seventy-three represented an astonishing political comeback after his barring,

---

[74] Shlaim, *The Iron Wall*, pp. 407–9. [75] Shlaim, *The Iron Wall*, p. 418.
[76] Shlaim, *The Iron Wall*, p. 429.
[77] Ari Shavit, 'The General: An Israeli Journalist's Six Years of Conversation with Ariel Sharon, *New Yorker* 23 January 2006, www.newyorker.com/magazine/2006/01/23/the-general-5, accessed 14 August 2017.
[78] Weissglas, *Arik Sharon*, p. 125.
[79] Interview former prime minister, Ehud Olmert, 23 January 2018, TelAviv.
[80] Interview Arad; Interview Dov Weissglas, Tel Aviv, 23 January 2018.

256   In Search of a Foreign Policy Paradigm

twenty years earlier, from ever again holding the defence portfolio. Sharon brought to the decision-making table the different strands that marked his career in the IDF and politics. An iron-fisted, renowned general and a territory-expanding Zionist, he was patron of the settlers and the nemesis of the Palestinians. His political conduct in the later part of his career was driven more by his personal contacts and his analysis of how people and political leaders operate than by ideology. Above all, Sharon was a quintessential 'doer', a man of action through and through, who sought, in his disruptive thinking, to shape rather than to be defined by reality. In light of his age, Sharon knew that he would not be prime minister for more than eight years, which instilled in him a pragmatism and 'a sense of urgency' to get things done.[81]

Having experienced, first hand, the price attached to causing public splits and attracting international condemnation, Sharon sought to govern amid national unity. This explains one of his first acts as prime minister, which was to form a broad government rather than a narrow rightist-religious coalition. He appointed Shimon Peres, architect of the Oslo process, as his foreign affairs minister, and another Labourite, Binyamin Ben-Eliezer, as his defence minister. In addition to Labour, the senior partner in the coalition, the first Sharon government included the ultra-religious Shas and Yahadut HaTora parties. Yisrael BaAliya, which was supported primarily by immigrants from the Soviet Union, the ultra-nationalist HaIchud HaLeumy-Yisrael Beiteinu and two centrist factions – Derech Hadasha and Am Echad – ensured the national unity government of Ariel Sharon an overwhelming majority in parliament.[82]

Sharon's inner decision-making circle was comprised of a small, intimate group of aides and confidants, including his sons, Omri and Gilad, who formed the locus of foreign policymaking. Uri Shani, who had been appointed Likud's general director by Sharon, became director general of the prime minister's office. After April 2002, he was replaced by Dov Weissglas, Ariel Sharon's personal attorney since the 1980s. Reuven Adler and Eyal Arad, the main campaign strategists, were also central in Sharon's immediate personal circle.[83] Arie Genger, an Israeli-turned-American businessman, acted as unofficial messenger between the Israeli prime minister and the White House until he was replaced by Weissglas.[84] It was clear that the members of intimate group were

---

[81] Weissglas, *Arik Sharon*, p. 97; Interviews Arad and Weissglas.
[82] 15th Knesset: the 29th Government, Knesset official website, www.knesset.gov.il/govt/heb/GovtByNumber.asp?govt=29, accessed 19 October 2017.
[83] Sharon, *Sharon – The Life of a Leader*, p. 331; Druker and Shelah, *Boomerang*, pp. 102–3; Interview Arad; Interview Weissglas.
[84] Landau, *Arik*, p. 361.

pragmatic rather than ideological, markedly civilian and utterly loyal to Sharon. This reflected the shift made by Sharon during the latter part of his political career. Although Sharon had, for years, been a patron of the settlers, he did not include a settler representative in his close circle.

Muddling Through

The first five months of Ariel Sharon's premiership were marked by a certain irony. The prime minister, who had a reputation of uncompromising resolve, determination and tenacity, struggled to develop a coherent foreign policy course. By his inauguration on 7 March 2001, he had had two phone conversations with his arch enemy, Yasser Arafat. Subsequently, he sent his most trusted confidant, his son Omri, and Yossi Ginossar, to prepare the ground for an accord with the PA that would end the violence. The choice of Ginossar, who had served Prime Ministers Rabin and Barak as a discreet messenger to the PA before going into business with Palestinian partners, was significant. It suggests that the intent to reach an accord along the following lines was serious.

The agreement Israel proposed was based on a commitment to withdraw the IDF to its positions prior to 28 September – the day Sharon visited the Temple Mount; reopen negotiations in April; implement the third Further Redeployment in the West Bank; and refrain from unilateral action in Jerusalem and the construction of new settlements. In return, Arafat would denounce terrorism, and the Palestinians would commit to fighting terrorism. According to two well-informed accounts and as Sharon would later state, it was Arafat who decided to back away from the plan.[85]

At the same time, Sharon was unrelenting in his demands to the military to crush the Intifada, which, by September 2001, had claimed 188 Israeli lives.[86] Since one of his election pledges was 'no negotiations under fire', the cessation of violence was important, not only from a security point of view, but also from a domestic political perspective. Thus, Sharon and Defence Minister Ben-Eliezer made it clear to the IDF that, as far as the government was concerned, it had a great deal of leeway to respond to the Palestinians, which the IDF then exploited.[87]

---

[85] Amos Harel and Avi Isacharoff, *The Seventh War* (Tel Aviv: Yehioth Ahronoth, 2004), pp. 110–11 (in Hebrew); Bregman, *Elusive Peace*, p. 153; 'PM Sharon's Address to the Knesset', *IMFA*, http://mfa.gov.il/MFA/PressRoom/2002/Pages/PM%20Sharon-s%20Address%20t o%20the%20Knesset%20-%208-Apr-2002.aspx, accessed 5 October 2017.

[86] Harel and Isacharoff, *The Seventh* War, Appendix.

[87] Harel and Isacharoff, *The Seventh War*, p. 115.

258   In Search of a Foreign Policy Paradigm

However, it was clear to the prime minister, who had waged his own war on terror in Gaza thirty years earlier, that as long as the violence continued, the IDF was failing to quash the Palestinian Intifada using military means. In fact, the rising death toll and tougher security measures imposed by the IDF in the West Bank and Gaza Strip, exemplified that the al-Aqsa Intifada was intensifying rather than abating. This had severe regional repercussions as Egypt and Jordan, with whom Israel had formal peace agreements, recalled their ambassadors.[88] For its part, Saudi Arabia beseeched the Americans to take immediate steps to curb the IDF. The Saudis threatened to stop considering US interests unless the administration took their views on the Palestinian issue more seriously. According to Elliot Abrams and Aaron David Miller, who were deeply involved in the negotiations, the clear Saudi threat prompted President Bush to commit himself, in a letter sent in August 2001 to Crown Prince Abdallah of Saudi Arabia, to a 'viable Palestinian state'.[89] The notion of a Palestinian state was, of course, integral to the peace proposals laid down by the Clinton administration. However, the letter from Bush to King Abdallah 'established for the first time that the US policy henceforth would be to support a two-state solution'.[90] Previous American administrations had not crossed this Rubicon.

What, if any, were the foreign policy determinants accounting for the seemingly inconsistent Israeli foreign policy, which sought to address the Intifada via simultaneous negotiations and brute military force? Sharon assumed the premiership heading a party of nineteen MKs and following a controversial political career. The decision to forge a national unity government with Labour was aimed at addressing these two issues. It established him as prime minister of a broad government, which secured him a wide majority in parliament. It also allowed him to pursue his foreign policy without creating the domestic divides that had exacted such a heavy personal and political price during Israel's 1982 Lebanon War. Yet Labour, which was identified directly with the Oslo process, could not disavow the PLO overnight. Therefore, to maintain his broad government and domestic consensus for his policy, Sharon was obliged to make overtures to the PLO although his preference was that the IDF crush the Intifada. However, Sharon never considered trying to strike a peace agreement with Arafat, whom he distrusted completely and loathed personally. Instead, as his close political strategist, Eyal Arad observed:

---

[88] Meital, Yoram, *Peace in Tatters* (Jerusalem: Carmel, 2004), pp. 154–5.
[89] Miller, *The Much too Promised Land*, p. 333.   [90] Ross, *The Missing Peace*, p. 786.

Muddling Through

Sharon's engagement with Arafat at this stage was purely tactical. It was aimed at concluding certain pragmatic arrangements that would reduce the violence between Israel and the Palestinians. But the fundamental assumption was, and continued to be, that Arafat was an enemy of Israel and would do anything he could to harm it.[91]

The domestic political considerations driving Ariel Sharon's foreign policy towards the PLO went hand-in-hand with another key consideration that informed the Sharon government during its early days: the prime minister's need to rehabilitate his international reputation, especially in the USA. From the outset, Sharon was at pains to establish a good working relationship with the George W. Bush administration. As the then US Ambassador to Israel, Martyn Indyk, observed:

For a decade he [Sharon] had been persona non grata in Washington after his exploits in Lebanon in the early 1980s, and his encouragement of settlement building in the early 1990s, had damaged his relationships with the Reagan and earlier Bush administrations. Now, returning as prime minister, Sharon was determined to avoid any show of daylight between himself and the new president. He had taken note of how both Yitzhak Shamir and Bibi Netanyahu, the two previous Likud leaders, had mismanaged relations with American presidents, which had contributed significantly to their electoral defeats ... He wanted to find a common language with Bush.[92]

What would be the basis of US-Israeli common language in the wake of the collapse of the peace process? US Secretary of State Colin Powell was the only member of the administration who still aspired to renewing the peace process. To this end, he tried to build US foreign policy around a fact finding report prepared by George Mitchell, which investigated the events that led to the eruption of the second Intifada. The report recommended cessation of Palestinian terrorism, Israeli withdrawal to the position held by the IDF prior to 28 September, renewed security cooperation and a settlement freeze.[93]

Whatever Powell's vision of his activities, for too many in the administration they seemed to be an unwanted continuation of Clinton's approach.[94] Elliot Abrams, deputy national security advisor and White House national security staff member in charge of Israeli-Palestinian affairs, was well placed to offer an insider assessment of US foreign policy during this period. He concluded that, although the

---

[91] Interview Arad.   [92] Indyk, *Innocent Abroad*, p. 378; Weissglas, *Arik Sharon*, p. 155.
[93] Sharm El-Sheikh Fact-Finding Committee Report 'Mitchell Report', EU official website, http://eeas.europa.eu/archives/docs/mepp/docs/mitchell_report_2001_en.pdf, accessed 8 September 2017.
[94] Abrams, *Tested by Zion*, p. 7; see also Miller, *The Much too Promised Land*, p. 330.

260   In Search of a Foreign Policy Paradigm

Bush administration endorsed the Mitchell report, there was no appetite to implement it. 'Where the administration could go with this [Mitchell] report', he noted, 'remained unclear'.[95] 'Our goal', Abrams recollects, 'was simply to calm down the region' and engage in 'conflict management'.[96]

Thus, the foreign policy of Israel was determined by different factors pushing in different directions. The strategic relationship with the USA, in which Sharon had a personal and political vested interest, had a tempering effect on the foreign policy of Israel towards the PLO. During his first few months as Israel's premier, Sharon was unable to pursue a foreign policy that would undermine the US goal of conflict management. Likewise, the position of Labour, the initiator of the Oslo peace process, as the senior coalition partner, meant that Israel would not completely reject diplomacy as a foreign policy tool towards the PLO. At the same time, the security challenge posed by the al-Aqsa Intifada prompted the government and the security network to use military means to try to quell the uprising. Under these conditions, Israeli foreign policy lacked direction and cohesion; it was simply muddling through.

In Search of a New Foreign Policy Paradigm

The period between 1967 and 2000 was characterized by two distinct foreign policy paradigms: the two-state solution and Greater Israel. The two-state solution formed the basis of Israel's foreign policy of engagement while Israel's foreign policy of entrenchment hinged on maintaining a Greater Israel. The Barak government failed to achieve its self-proclaimed goals of achieving peace with Syria and the Palestinians. Subsequently, the notion, instilled into public debate by Barak and the Clinton administration, that there was no Palestinian partner was followed by the eruption of the al-Aqsa Intifada. As a result, the idea of ending the Arab-Israeli conflict, based on a territorial compromise, descaling the occupation and diplomacy, was now seriously discredited by the majority of Israel's foreign policy and security elites. At the same time, Israel remained signed up to the Oslo peace agreement, which the USA had backed for the best part of a decade. Although the Clinton parameters were never formally consigned to the diplomatic record, they could not

---

[95] Elliot Abrams, *Tested by Zion: The Bush Administration and the Israeli-Palestinian Conflict* (Cambridge: Cambridge University Press, 2013), p.7.
[96] Abrams, *Tested by Zion*, p. 5.

simply be erased from the collective memory. Therefore, while Israel's engagement stance was discredited, the idea of restoring its foreign policy of entrenchment and its corollary of clinging to a Greater Israel also seemed unfeasible. Israeli foreign policymakers were involved in a search for a foreign policy paradigm.

12   A Perfect Storm

The 9/11 Attacks and their Immediate Aftermath

On 11 September 2001, the USA experienced the worst terrorist attack in world history. A Jihadi-Islamist terrorist global network, al-Qaeda, hijacked four civilian passenger planes and used them as flying bombs, crashing two into the World Trade Center buildings in New York City, and crashing one on the Pentagon in Washington, DC. A fourth plane that had been destined for the White House, crashed near Shanskville, Pennsylvania, killing all of its passengers and crew. A total of almost 3,000 people – including nineteen hijackers – perished in the attacks.[1]

For a short period following what came to be known as the 9/11 attacks, Israeli foreign policymakers experienced a feeling of déjà vu. During the 1990–1 Gulf War, the USA had assembled an international coalition to evict the Iraqi army from Kuwait. There had been a risk that Iraq would try to draw Israel into the conflict, to transform it from a US-led campaign against Iraq, to an Arab-Israeli war. This would have resulted in the Arab countries withdrawing their support from this US-led international effort. US concerns were similar post-9/11; it feared that the Israeli-Palestinian violence, ongoing since 2000, might hinder Arab and broader Muslim support for its imminent invasion of Afghanistan to oust the Taliban government, which was sheltering al-Qaeda. This apprehension had a clear effect on US foreign policy, as Aaron Miller, the only civil servant during the Clinton era who continued to work in the Bush administration, noted in his memoirs: 'The White House', he wrote, 'realized that mobilizing coalitions to fight the war against terror might be easier if the United States signalled interest in Arab-Israeli peace-making.'[2]

This was the background to President Bush's speech to Congress, on 2 October 2001, in which he declared that 'the idea of a Palestinian state has always been part of a vision, so long as the right to Israel to exist is

---

[1] Shlaim, *The Iron Wall*, p. 727; 'The 9/11 Terrorist Attacks', *BBC*, www.bbc.co.uk/history/events/the_september_11th_terrorist_attacks, accessed 20 February 2018.

[2] Miller, *The Much too Promised Land*, p. 336.

The 9/11 Attacks and their Immediate Aftermath 263

respected.'[3] That had been true, perhaps, since the beginning of the Oslo peace process, but had never been articulated so formally or explicitly by a US president. Further, the Americans demanded that the Sharon government take measures to reduce the violence with the Palestinians and authorized a summit between Arafat and the then Israeli Foreign Minister, Shimon Peres, who was keen to renew regular negotiations with the Palestinians. It gave him the opportunity to lead an initiative that might break the cycle of violence, possibly restore Israel's engagement stance and strengthen his position in the Sharon government.[4]

The pressure mounted on Sharon by the USA and the motivations of his foreign minister resulted in a secret negotiating track between Peres and veteran Palestinian negotiator, Abu Ala. The meetings, which took place between September and December 2001 in Jerusalem, Gaza and Rome, yielded a position paper proposing a sequenced approach to resumption of negotiations. The first phase involved ending the Palestinian military fragmentation by creating a unified Palestinian security force, which, together with the IDF, would enforce a ceasefire. After a few months with no violence, negotiations over a permanent agreement could resume. Abu Ala sought, first, the recognition of a Palestinian state according to the 4 June 1967 borders and then an immediate declaration of state in areas A and B and parts of C in the West Bank, and the whole Gaza Strip. Peres, referring to UNSCR 242, insisted that the size of the Palestinian state should continue to be negotiated.[5]

The veteran PLO leadership had a clear interest in the negotiations succeeding. Arafat had been on the wrong side of the Americans during the 1990–1 Gulf War and understood perfectly the severity of the Palestinian situation post-9/11. As Abu Ala explains:

Bush asked every country to clarify its position as either 'with America or with the terrorists'. Abu Ammar [Araft] was told that if he did not lend his support to this war, and if Sharon succeeded in his bid to portray him as the devil, that he would be condemned to political oblivion. President Arafat took this advice seriously.[6]

Arafat was put to the test amid the outpourings of joy at, and support for, the 9/11 attacks, both in the West Bank and Jerusalem. According to Abu Ala, the demonstrations were quelled by the PA's security forces on

---

[3] 'Bush Endorses Palestinian State', BBC, 2 October 2011, http://news.bbc.co.uk/1/hi/wo rld/middle_east/1575090.stm, accessed 14 September 2017.
[4] Bregman, *Elusive Peace*, pp. 161–2.
[5] Harel and Isacharoff, *The Seventh War*, pp. 174–6; Qurie, *Peace Negotiations in Palestine*, p. 60. The full document is reproduced in Qurie, *Peace Negotiations in Palestine*, pp. 269–70.
[6] Qurie, *Peace Negotiations in Palestine*, p. 58; Ya'alon reached precisely the same conclusion; see Ya'alon, *The Longer Shorter Way*, p. 123.

264   A Perfect Storm

Arafat's orders. The Palestinian president also demanded that Hamas and other Palestinian factions 'halt armed operations' and 'cease doing anything that could make the Palestinians . . . guilty of wrongdoing'.[7] This demand was significant – especially since, during September–November 2001, there was a sharp rise in Palestinian causalities from clashes with the Israelis, compared to the preceding three months.[8]

The response from the Palestinian factions reflected Arafat's limited control and how ingrained the Intifada had become. Although the suicide bombings declined in number – resulting in a corresponding reduction in Israeli fatalities – other forms of Palestinian attack, especially shootings, continued.[9] The most significant assault occurred on 17 October 2001, when a cell of the Popular Front for the Liberation of Palestine (PFLP) assassinated Rehavam Ze'evi, which was revenge for the slaying of PFLP leader, Abu Ali Mustafa, on 27 August 2001. Ze'evi was a close friend of Sharon, a cabinet minister and head of the Moledet party, which supported physical transfer of Palestinian-Israelis from Israel. His killing, like that of Abu Ali Mustafa, was a political assassination.[10]

In his memoirs, Abu Ala reports that Arafat knew the names of the assassins, whom the Israelis and the Americans demanded Arafat should arrest. However, in practice, Arafat 'was unable to detain the men, who were protected by their factions and were beyond the reach of the Palestinian Authority's security forces'.[11] Undermining Arafat's internal position further, all the commitments made by Hamas and other factions to cooperate with the PA and modify their tactics towards Israel quickly evaporated. It was, as Abu Ala recalled with some frustration, the result of 'internal squabbles between the factions' and 'the determination of some within the Palestinian opposition forces to damage the Palestinian Authority at all costs'.[12] Such was Arafat's limited control and authority over the Palestinians in October 2001.

The secret Peres-Abu Ala track also faced a formidable obstacle in Israel in the form of Prime Minister Sharon. Sharon was concerned about the overlap between President Bush's speech endorsing a Palestinian state, and US demand that he authorize the Peres-Abu Ala negotiations. The correspondence between the two events, according to close observers of the prime minister, convinced Sharon that the USA was 'going to sacrifice Israel in order to create a new coalition in the Gulf'.[13]

---

[7] Qurie, *Peace Process in Palestine*, p. 58.
[8] Harel and Isacharoff, *The Seventh War*, Appendix.
[9] On the reduction in Israeli casualties during this period, see Harel and Isacharoff, *The Seventh War*, Appendix.
[10] Bregman, *Elusive Peace*, p. 165; Harel and Isacharof, *The Seventh War*, p. 193.
[11] Qurie, *Peace Process in Palestine*, p. 59.   [12] Qurie, *Peace Process in Palestine*, p. 58.
[13] Quoted in Abrams, *Tested by Zion*, p. 21; Dan, *Ariel Sharon*, p. 285.

A Transformed Foreign Policy Environment 265

Even though US support for Israel was a staple of his foreign policy outlook, Sharon expressed his view publicly and in no uncertain terms. In a defiant public statement, delivered on 5 October 2001, he said:

> We are currently in the midst of a complex and difficult diplomatic campaign. I call on the Western democracies, and primarily the leader of the Free World – the United States. Do not repeat the dreadful mistake of 1938, when enlightened European democracies decided to sacrifice Czechoslovakia for a 'convenient temporary solution'. Do not try to appease the Arabs at our expense – this is unacceptable to us. Israel will not be Czechoslovakia. Israel will fight terrorism.[14]

The foreign policy message of the speech equated the actions of the US to Europe's appeasement of Nazi Germany in 1938 and thereby likened George W. Bush to Neville Chamberlain. While Sharon would permit his foreign minister to negotiate, he himself was adamantly opposed to any concessions – especially towards the Palestinians – that might help the USA to rally an international coalition. Thus, like his predecessors, Yitzhak Shamir and Binyamin Netanyahu, when faced by American pressure to act on foreign policy matters, Sharon was willing to concede on foreign policy process matters such as authorizing the Peres-Abu Ala negotiations. However, he was not willing to yield anything on substance. Accordingly, on 23 December, Sharon disavowed the Peres-Abu Ala understandings. Arafat echoed this rejection, despite both leaders having authorized the channel.[15] The opposition of Sharon and the majority of the Palestinian factions, to the Peres-Abu Ala negotiations, foiled the attempt to rekindle Israel's engagement foreign policy immediately following the 9/11 attacks.

A Transformed Foreign Policy Environment

The collapse of the Peres-Abu Ala secret channel reflected a decisive shift in the balance of power from the supporters to the opponents of engagement in Israel and among the Palestinians. The timing of this shift was significant in coinciding with the US launch of its Global War on Terror (GWoT), which was a sharp departure from US foreign policy towards the Middle East since the end of the Cold War. In the aftermath of the conflict between the two great powers, US foreign policy rested on three pillars: containing Iraq and Iran, maintaining the free flow of oil from the

---

[14] Statement by Israeli Prime Minister Ariel Sharon, 4 October 2001, *IMFA*, http://mfa .gov.il/MFA/PressRoom/2001/Pages/Statement%20by%20Israeli%20PM%20Ariel%2 0Sharon%20-%204-Oct-2001.aspx, accessed 20 September 2017.
[15] Harel and Isacharoff, *The Seventh War*, p. 176; Qurie, *Peace Negotiations in Palestine*, p. 69.

266   A Perfect Storm

Gulf and acting as mediator in the Arab-Israeli conflict. In contrast, post-9/11, US foreign policy hinged on pre-emptive and preventative use of military force, regime change, counterterrorism and intelligence gathering.

The GWoT frequently was justified by the US administration as necessary for promoting democracy, which became one of the main benchmarks used by the USA to distinguish friend from foe. The US administration subscribed to the notion that undemocratic regimes, such as those in Afghanistan, Iran, Iraq and Syria, were breeding grounds for terrorists and, therefore, preferably, should be replaced. Curiously, however, Saudi Arabia and Egypt, the origin countries of *all* the 9/11 hijackers, were conspicuously absent from this list. Instead, they remained designated strategic allies, which shows how, in the aftermath of the 9/11 attacks, the use of democracy and terrorism to distinguish America's supporters and opposition was selective and politicized.

The reformulation of US foreign policy in the wake of the 9/11 attacks had significant implications for Israel. Even before the attacks, key figures in the Bush administration had clearly been predisposed towards Israel. For instance, President Bush, when still governor of Texas, was introduced to the Arab-Israeli conflict in 1998 during a visit to Israel. His guide on a helicopter tour of the country was none other than the then Foreign Minister, Ariel Sharon. Bush's main takeaway from this visit was 'Israel's vulnerability in a hostile neighbourhood' and this shaped his administration's policy significantly, after he came to power.[16] His national security advisor recalled that from the first day of the George W. Bush administration, it 'was determined that [the US] would support Israel's right to defend itself.'[17] The 9/11 attacks, by the President's own admission, refined his position:

I refused to accept the moral equivalence between Palestinian suicide attacks on innocent civilians and Israeli military actions intended to protect their people. My views came into sharper focus after 9/11. If the United States had the right to defend itself and prevent future attacks, other democracies had those rights, too.[18]

Apart from strengthening the pro-Israeli orientation of the administration, the 9/11 attacks engendered a broader shift towards the Israeli-Palestinian conflict. Post-9/11, the US administration had discarded the view that hitherto had informed its foreign policy towards the conflict, namely, that it was a political dispute over specific issues: occupation, Jerusalem, settlements, refugees, security and borders. Instead, as Aaron

[16] George W. Bush, *Decision Points* (London: Virgin Books, 2010), p. 400.
[17] Condoleezza Rice, *No Higher Honor* (New York: Simon & Schuster, 2011), p. 54.
[18] Bush, *Decision Points*, p. 400.

A Transformed Foreign Policy Environment 267

Miller recalls, post-9/11, the Israeli-Palestinian conflict was viewed as subsidiary to a far more important struggle – an epic fight between democracy and authoritarianism, moderates and extremists, terrorists and antiterrorists. Through this foreign policy prism, the Bush administration saw an end to the Israeli-Palestinian conflict with only a change in the nature of the Palestinian leadership towards greater democracy.[19] As for Palestinian violence, it was viewed by the Bush-Cheney leadership as 'a war imposed on us by enemies' and was rejected utterly and branded as terrorism.[20]

Significantly, the USA had also abandoned its pretence of acting as an honest broker between Israel and the Palestinians. Bush, Rice and Cheney were all convinced that Arafat was 'a failed leader', 'a terrorist and a crook'.[21] 'As a Nobel Peace Prize recipient', Bush condemned Arafat, in his memoirs, 'he sure didn't seem very interested in peace.'[22] Secretary of Defence Donald Rumsfeld, who had never been anything other than utterly unsympathetic towards the Palestinian cause, referred to the West Bank and Gaza as 'so-called occupied territory'.[23] These uncompromisingly bleak views of Arafat greatly benefitted Israel. As Miller observed, during this period, 'when it came to fighting terror, seeking peace, and promoting democracy' Israel was perceived by the administration as 'being on the right side of the line. Arafat and the others had chosen the wrong side.'[24]

The only dissenting voice was that of Secretary of State Colin Powell, but the balance of political power within the Bush administration had turned decidedly against him. Outnumbered, Powell could only witness the diminishing scope of US diplomacy. The first peace envoy appointed by the Bush administration, General Anthony Zinni, a former commander-in-chief of the US Central Command, experienced this shift first hand. Zinni's brief was to revive the security cooperation between Israel and the Palestinians on the basis of a plan that had been drawn up in the previous June by George Tenet, then head of the CIA. Conspicuously, Zinni's remit did not include engaging with political issues and he was urged to avoid any peace plans.[25]

Aron Miller, who accompanied Zinni on his mission, knew, from his experience during the Clinton administration, that this approach was a non-starter; it would be impossible to resume security cooperation without, at the same time, addressing the political issues. During their

---

[19] Miller, *The Much too Promised Land*, pp. 325–6.   [20] Abrams, *Tested By Zion*, p. 20.
[21] Rice, *No Higher Honor*, p. 54; Cheney, *In My Time*, p. 380; Bush, *Decision Points*, p. 404.
[22] Bush, *Decision Points*, p. 399.   [23] Miller, *The Much too Promised Land*, p. 330.
[24] Miller, *The Much too* Promised Land, p. 336.
[25] Miller, *The Much too Promised Land*, pp. 337–9; Bregman, *Elusive Peace*, p. 170.

268   A Perfect Storm

meetings with Zinni, the Palestinians conveyed the same message.[26] However, Zinni had no room for manoeuvre and, as Miller recalls, had 'no mandate to do anything'.[27] Unlike his predecessor, Dennis Ross, Zinni was not backed by a president who was personally and politically invested in the peace process. President Bush made this position clear to Secretary of State Powell in the conclusion to his first briefing with general Zinni. 'Colin', he said, referring to the Zinni mission, 'this is your baby.'[28] With no mandate to engage with political matters and with little support from the White House, General Zinni was an envoy without a mission, which was why his activities between November 2001 and April 2002 yielded nothing.

In the post-9/11 transformed foreign policy environment, Miller recalls, the 'administration accorded like-minded democracies such as Israel, engaged in similar struggles against terror and extremism, high value and wide latitude of action in the common battle'.[29] Israeli policy-makers were well aware of this shift and the IDF deputy Chief of Staff Moshe Ya'alon, expressed the view that the 9/11 attacks were 'an oppor-tunity that will not return'.[30]

This backdrop produced a watershed moment on 3 January 2002 when Israeli naval commandos seized the vessel, *Karin A*, in inter-national waters in the Red Sea. The Israelis presented evidence to the Americans tying Arafat inextricably to the arms seized by the IDF's naval commandos. The *Karin A* was carrying fifty tons of weaponry, including antitank missiles, mines and explosives, which was in com-plete breach of the Oslo accord's ban on the PA's possessing such weapons. Fuad al-Shawbaki, the PA's finance officer, was shown to have handled payment for the weapons, which were supplied by Iran via Hezbollah operatives. Arafat denied involvement and proposed the establishment of a committee of enquiry, which only exacerbated his situation vis-à-vis the Americans.[31] As President Bush explains in his memoirs:

We and the Israelis had evidence that disproved the Palestinian leader's claim. Arafat had lied to me. I never trusted him again. In fact, I never spoke to him again. By the spring of 20002, I had concluded that peace would not be possible with Arafat in power.[32]

---

[26] Qurie, *Peace Negotiations in Palestine*, p. 57.
[27] Miller, *The Much too Promised Land*, p. 338.   [28] Ibid.
[29] Miller, *The Much too Promised Land*, p. 335.
[30] Ya'alon, *The Longer Shorter Way*, p. 123.
[31] Qurie, *Peace Negotiations in Palestine*, pp. 71–2.   [32] Bush, *Decision Points*, p. 401.

The *Karin A* incident was a transformative moment. It cemented the US shift during the Clinton era, from treating Arafat as a partner in US diplomacy, to considering him a 'terrorist, working with Iran and Hezbollah, at the moment when America was in a global war against terror'.[33] Fifteen months after the eruption of the al-Aqsa Intifada, the Palestinian president became persona non grata in the eyes of the Bush administration, in line with the official foreign policy stance adopted by Israel two weeks earlier. On 12 December, following a severe spate of terrorist attacks, the security cabinet communiqué stated that: 'Arafat is no longer relevant from Israel's point of view, and there will be no more communication with him.'[34] In full alignment, the USA and Israel began discussing 'alternatives to Arafat' and 'his marginalization'.[35]

To Assassinate or not to Assassinate?

Moshe Ya'alon held Ariel Sharon in high esteem during his first term as prime minister. He branded his decision-making 'very impressive' and described him as a leader with a 'very sober perception of reality', one who 'understood the environment we operated in'.[36] During Sharon's second term as prime minister, he and Ya'alon fell out, very publicly, over the direction that Israel's foreign policy should pursue. The rift deepened, which is why it is unlikely that Deputy Chief of Staff Ya'alon would have had any interest in unduly complimenting his prime minister. It would seem rather that Ya'alon's commendation reflected the agreement among key Israeli foreign policy decision-makers during Ariel Sharon's first term as Israel's prime minister.

It was against this backdrop that a gradual strategic foreign policy change vis-à-vis the Palestinians occurred, aimed at ending Israel's foreign policy of engagement. The harbingers of this foreign policy change had emerged during the first few months following the 9/11 attacks, when Israel stepped up its targeted assassinations. It also embarked on more frequent and more prolonged incursions into areas A – where the PA had

---

[33] Quoted in Abrams, *Tested by Zion*, p. 25; see also Miller, *The Much too Promised Land*, pp. 340–1, *Rice, No Higher Honor*, p. 136.

[34] Security Cabinet Decision, 12 December 2001, IMFA, http://mfa.gov.il/MFA/Pre ssRoom/2001/Pages/Security%20Cabinet%20Decision%20-%2012-Dec-2001.asp x, accessed 20 September 2017; Israel submitted an official complaint to the UN secretary general, which provides full details of what the attacks entailed; see 'Letter Dated 13 December 2001 from the Permanent Representative of Israel to the United Nations addressed to the Secretary-General', UN official website, http://mfa.gov.il/MFA/PressRoom/2001/Pages/Security%20Cabinet%20Decision% 20-%2012-Dec-2001.aspx, accessed 20 September 2017.

[35] Rice, *No Higher Honor*, p. 136; Gilad Sharon, *Sharon*, p. 402; Interview Weissglas.

[36] Ya'alon, *The Longer Shorter Way*, p. 170.

270   A Perfect Storm

full control – which was in violation of the Oslo accords.[37] The decision to assassinate Raid Karmi, a commander in the al-Aqsa Martyr Brigades in the Tulkarem area, was another sign of the gradual, but consistent shift towards terminating Israel's engagement policy. Karmi, who was twenty-eight, was charismatic, brave and admired hugely by young Palestinians. The Israelis, by contrast, considered him a terrorist with blood on his hands, who had used explosives and machine-gun fire against the IDF and civilians.[38]

On 14 January 2002, Karmi was in the sights of the Israeli GSS. The forum that was to determine whether or not to authorize his assassination was assembled and was faced with a serious dilemma. Defence Minister Ben-Eliezer had recently reported to the cabinet 'there has been a decrease in the level of violence and the scope of attacks' during the previous two weeks.[39] The relative reduced violence continued into January as the PA tried to contain the fallout from the *Karin A* incident. Ben-Eliezer's concern was that assassinating Karmi would destroy any chance of achieving a full ceasefire that might restore Israel's engagement stance towards the Palestinians. On these grounds, Ben-Eliezer objected to the GSS plan to assassinate Karmi.

However, the defence minister was opposed by Prime Minister Sharon, Chief of Staff Mofaz, Deputy Chief of Staff Ya'alon, and GSS head Avi Dichter, who supported the assassination on pure security grounds. They argued with Ben-Eliezer that Karmi was, by virtue of his past, 'a ticking bomb'. For this group of men, once a terrorist always a terrorist. So, if the opportunity were presented to exterminate Karmi, and Israel had the capability and the political will to do it then he should be assassinated. The longer term political ramifications, such as whether the assassination would reduce the prospects of a ceasefire and restore engagement, were regarded as secondary.[40]

This aspect of the decision-making process was extremely disturbing. In fact, it prompted four former GSS heads – Yaakov Shalom, Carmi Gilon, Ami Ayalon and Yaakov Peri – to question whether the GSS had lost capacity for independent thinking vis-à-vis the government. In a highly unusual step, these former GSS heads requested a meeting

---

[37] Ya'alon, *The Longer Shorter Way*, pp. 125, 180; Harel and Isacharoff, *The Seventh War*, pp. 172–4, 224–5.

[38] Bregman, *Elusive Peace*, p. 173.

[39] Cabinet Communiqué – 22 December 2001, *IMFA*, http://mfa.gov.il/MFA/Press Room/2001/Pages/Cabinet%20Communique%20-%2022-Dec-2001.aspx, accessed 27 September 2017.

[40] On the decision-making process leading to the assassination, see Bregman, *Elusive Peace*, p. 174; Harel and Isacharoff, *The Seventh War*, pp. 186, 230–1; More, *Gate Keepers*, pp. 290, 297.

with the current head of the GSS, Avi Dichter, to voice their concerns. During a stern interchange with Dichter, he was told that he had too readily transformed the practice of targeted assassinations from being a counterterrorist tactic to being state policy. The result, these veteran GSS chiefs continued, was that the number of targeted assassinations was growing exponentially, the number of innocent civilians killed in 'collateral damage' was increasing and the capacity to monitor the utility of targeted assassinations was diminishing. This was the essence of the problem related to increased use of targeted assassinations as an Israeli state policy, a change that the veteran GSS chiefs considered was being driven primarily by Sharon. The four expressed themselves adamantly to Dichter that the GSS should have exercised more independence and resisted Sharon's line.[41]

It is, of course, unclear whether not assassinating Karmi would have led to an eventual ceasefire or created the conditions for restoring Israel's engagement stance. However, what is evident is that the assassination erased all chances of a ceasefire and a return to engagement. 'If there will not be security in Tulkarem there will be no security in Tel-Aviv', declared Marwan Bargouti, head of the Tanzim, following the assassination. 'The ceasefire is cancelled', he continued, 'Sharon has opened the gates of hell before the Israelis.'[42]

The unveiled threat from Barghouti was acute; the al-Aqsa Martyr Brigades, the group to which Karmi had belonged, intensified their terrorist attacks to avenge his death. Other secular Palestinian factions, such as Tanzim, joined the Palestinian Islamists in dispatching suicide bombers. In the absence of a physical barrier between the West Bank and Israel, the effect was immediate. Within a month, between mid-January and mid-February, Israeli fatalities soared from thirty to seventy-six.[43] The removal of one 'ticking bomb', Karmi, had highlighted the complexity of the situation. Although an individual terrorist could be eliminated, as long as his ideologies and the environment fuelling further attacks remained intact, there would always be a supply of willing people ready to engage in attacks. The death toll in March 2002 showed that dealing with one ticking bomb had merely detonated multiple others.

As the number of Israeli and Palestinian fatalities rose, Jibril Rajoub and Muhammad Dahlan, two of the heads of the PA's security apparatus, embarked on talks with the Israelis. GSS head, Avi Dichter, and Major General Giora Eiland, head of the IDF's planning unit, represented the Israeli side. At the end of February, Defence Minister Ben-Eliezer joined

---

[41] More, *Gate Keepers*, pp. 286–7.   [42] Harel and Isacharoff, *The Seventh War*, p. 213.
[43] Harel and Isacharoff, *The Seventh War*, pp. 214–5, Appendix.

272 A Perfect Storm

the talks in a last-ditch attempt to set the terms for a ceasefire, which he then submitted to the cabinet. However, by then, the political balance had shifted from Labour to the parties opposing engagement. The proposal presented by Ben-Eliezer was duly rejected and the cycle of reciprocal violence escalated.[44] March 2002 proved the most fatal month since the outbreak of the al-Aqsa Intifada: in one month alone, 133 Israelis and 239 Palestinians were killed.[45]

A particularly horrific suicide attack occurred on 27 March. Guests had assembled at the seaside Park Hotel in Netanya to celebrate Seder, the ritual feast for the Jewish celebration of Passover. In the midst of the traditional dinner, a twenty-five-year-old Hamas terrorist, Muhammad Abd al-Basset Oudeh, entered the hotel. Oudeh, who once had worked at the Park Hotel, detonated his explosive belt, blowing himself up, killing another thirty people instantly and wounding close to 150 more.[46] It was the most devastating single suicide bombing since the outbreak of the al-Aqsa Intifada in 2000. Defence Minister Ben-Elizer broke the news to Prime Minister Sharon. 'Arik', he told him over the phone, 'a catastrophe has happened', to which Sharon responded furiously: 'Listen, we have to destroy, destroy!'[47] Sharon's son, Gilad, who was observing his father as he took the phone call, felt that, for the prime minister, 'that was it. He had had enough'.[48] Two ensuing suicide bombings just four days later meant the die was cast.[49]

A Frontal Attack on Engagement

Sharon's Chief of Staff, Dov Weissglas, once explained that, 'after his bitter personal and political experience during the 1982 invasion of Lebanon the Prime Minister was well aware that any prolonged military campaign was doomed to fail unless it is widely supported domestically.'[50] In this respect, the attack on the Park Hotel was a watershed moment. 'It was only then', Weissglas recalled, 'that Sharon was convinced that he enjoyed a "wall-to-wall" support from the Israeli-Jewish public to embark upon a prolonged military campaign.'[51] Against this background, the government authorized

---

[44] Harel and Isacharoff, *The Seventh War*, pp. 230–1.
[45] Harel and Isacharoff, *The Seventh War*, Appendix.
[46] More, *Gate Keepers*, p. 275; Bregman, *Elusive Peace*, p. 182; 'Passover Suicide Bombing at Park Hotel in Netanya', 27 March 2002, *IMFA*, https://mfa.gov.il/MFA/MFA-Archive/2002/Pages/Passover%20suicide%20bombing%20at%20Park%20Hotel%20in %20Netanya.aspx, accessed 11 March 2019.
[47] Bregman, *Elusive Peace*, pp. 182–3.   [48] Sharon, *Sharon – Life of a Leader*, p. 408.
[49] 'Israel's History of Bomb Blasts', BBC, http://news.bbc.co.uk/1/hi/world/middle_east/1 197051.stm, accessed 8 October 2017.
[50] Weissglas, *Arik Sharon*, p. 126.
[51] Weissglas, *Arik Sharon*, p. 127; Ya'alon, *The Longer Shorter Way*, p. 128.

A Frontal Attack on Engagement 273

the launch of Operation Defensive Shield, which Sharon described as part of a 'war forced upon us'.[52] 'Its goal', stated the prime minister in his address to the nation, was one of 'uprooting the terrorist infrastructure which Arafat built to continue attacking us'. Israelis, he declared, were fighting for their 'home'.[53]

Depicting Operation Defensive Shield, which was launched on 29 March 2002, solely in terms of a war of no choice, waged to quash Palestinian terrorism, does not reveal the full foreign policy agenda behind the military offensive authorized by the government. Indeed, Operation Defensive Shield epitomized Sharon's disruptive thinking, his tendency to shape reality by wielding brute force rather than allowing the external environment to determine his foreign policy course. Alongside being a counterterrorist campaign, Operation Defensive Shield was designed to dismantle the last vestiges of Israel's foreign policy of engagement, which first emerged as the country's foreign policy towards the Middle East in 1993. Accordingly, during Operation Defensive Shield, Israel reoccupied the West Bank by taking control of large parts of area A. This contravened a founding principle of engagement, namely, scaling down the occupation. The notion of using diplomacy and negotiation as the main foreign policy tools in Israel's dealings with the Palestinians – another tenet of engagement – was replaced by use of brute military force. Arafat was besieged for forty days in his headquarters, the *Muqataa* compound, which was reduced mostly to rubble, and was banned from attending the 2002 Beirut Arab League Summit.

Israel conditioned the lifting of the siege on Arafat on surrendering the killers of Minister Ze'evi and Fuad al-Shawbaki, who had financed the purchase of the arms found on the *Karin A*. Security cooperation with the PA ceased with the IDF's intent, revealed by its then deputy chief of staff, to 'demolish the military rationale of the Oslo process'.[54] This goal was achieved as Israel reoccupied the West Bank and restored its control over the whole area, the government's rendition of Arafat as an 'enemy' and the decision to isolate him in his headquarters.[55] Amid this

---

[52] There are various accounts of the operation and its impact, among them Qurie, *Peace Negotiations in Palestine*, pp. 79–82; Bregman, *Elusive Peace*, pp. 187–222; Harel and Isacharoff, *The Seventh War*, pp. 235–69; 'Operation Defensive Shield', *IMFA*, https://mfa.gov.il/MFA/MFA-Archive/2002/Pages/Operation%20Defensive%20Shield.aspx, accessed 11 March 2019.

[53] 'PM Sharon's Address to the Nation', *IMFA*, www.mfa.gov.il/mfa/pressroom/2002/pages/pm%20sharon-s%20address%20to%20the%20nation%20-%2031-mar-2002.aspx, accessed 5 October 2017.

[54] Ya'alon, *The Longer Shorter Way*, pp. 129, 135.

[55] Cabinet Communiqué 29 March 2002, *IMFA*, www.mfa.gov.il/mfa/pressroom/2002/pages/cabinet%20communique%20-%2029-mar-2002.aspx, accessed 5 October, 2017.

274   A Perfect Storm

demolition of engagement, Abu Ala summed up the view of Operation Defensive Shield from Ramallah:

On the night when the Israeli army crossed its last remaining red line by invading the city of Ramallah and the *Muqataa* complex, the headquarters of the Palestinian President, Yasser Arafat, the peace process completely collapsed, and its remaining validity was lost.[56]

The frontal attack on engagement – encapsulated by Operation Defensive Shield – had broader regional aims, which were made explicit by deputy chief of staff, Ya'alon. Since the eruption of the al-Aqsa Intifada, Ya'alon had portrayed the conflict with the Palestinians as a test case for the idea conveyed by Hassan Nasserallah – that Israel appeared strong, but was, in fact, as weak as a spider's web. Ya'alon was convinced that Israel must challenge the spider's web conception if it wanted to avoid being regarded as a 'wounded animal by its enemies, who would be thinking only about how and when to attack it'.[57]

In this respect, Ya'alon perceived the al-Aqsa Intifada in existential terms, branded it as the most significant conflict Israel had engaged in since 1948, and regarded Operation Defensive Shield as a decisive moment in this confrontation. Ya'alon's view reflected a broad consensus, which emerged among the Israeli policymaking top brass. Emblematically, a cabinet communiqué issued in the midst of the operation described Defensive Shield as a 'fateful fight for our homeland'.[58] Ya'alon had no qualms about admitting that the use of military force was designed to 'sear into the consciousness of the Palestinians' that the use of violence does not pay, demonstrate Israel's material power and steadfastness and deter its regional enemies.[59] 'Defensive Shield began as a show of force', recalled Ya'alon; it proved that we were 'not made out of spider webs'.[60] Similarly, Head of the GSS Avi Dichter remarked that the 'generation of Palestinians that was born in the territories after 1967 experienced for the first time the real military prowess of Israel. The idea that Israel could be defeated by terrorism', he told two senior Israeli journalists, 'which gained traction within the Palestinians after the withdrawal from Lebanon, was powerfully disproven.'[61]

The use of military force towards the Palestinians also had an explicit domestic political engineering dimension. 'The people of Israel', Ya'alon

---

[56] Qurie, *Peace Negotiations in Palestine*, p. 82.
[57] Ya'alon, *The Longer Shorter Way*, p. 107.
[58] Cabinet Communiqué 7 April 2002, *IMFA*, http://mfa.gov.il/MFA/PressRoom/2002/P ages/Cabinet%20Communique%20-%207-Apr-2002.aspx, accessed 5 October 2017.
[59] Ya'alon, *The Longer Shorter Way*, pp. 107–8.
[60] Ya'alon, *The Longer Shorter Way*, p. 133.
[61] Harel and Isacharoff, *The Seventh War*, p. 266.

contended, 'were awash by a propaganda campaign that peace was just beyond reach and was rejected by us.' We needed to 'change this mind-set to instil into the Israeli people's awareness that they were in conflict'.[62] The idea of the IDF transforming the domestic Israeli environment from above was not new. Israel's founding father and first Prime Minister, David Ben-Gurion, saw it as central to the evolution of the Jewish state, to Zionism and to the creation of a new type of Jew in Israel, the Warrior-Sabra. Similarly, Ya'alon subscribed to the view that the IDF was entitled to engage in domestic political engineering and that this would instil in Israeli the consciousness that the country would face a long and arduous struggle for many years to come.[63]

A Diplomatic Alternative

By the end of March 2002, as the Israeli government's decision was being taken to implement Operation Defensive Shield, another foreign policy alternative emerged. The Arab summit in Beirut, on 27–28 March 2002, adopted a resolution that came to be known as the Arab Peace Initiative (API). This was a modified version of a Saudi proposal devised by Crown Prince Abdallah and outlined in an interview with the American journalist, Thomas Friedman, a month earlier.[64]

The API required Israel to withdraw fully from the territories seized in the 1967 war and agree to the establishment, in the Gaza Strip and West Bank, of a Palestinian state, with East Jerusalem as its capital. It laid down that the Palestinian refugee problem should be resolved in accordance with UN Resolution 194, which required that Palestinian refugees who wanted to return to their homes and live in peace with their neighbours should be permitted to do so at the earliest practicable date. The API also stipulated that the manner in which UN 194 would be implemented must be agreed by all parties, which clearly included Israel.[65] These conditions attached to the API not only agreed to recognition of Israel's existence and the right of Israelis to live in peace, it also expressed a willingness to establish full, normal relations with Israel.[66] The opaque phrasing of the API suggests that whatever the sides could agree on would be accepted by the Arab League with a view to achieving an end to the Arab-Israeli

---

[62] Ya'alon, *The Longer Shorter Way*, p. 105.

[63] Ya'alon, *The Longer Shorter Way*, p. 105.

[64] Elie Podeh, *Chances for Peace: Missed Opportunities in the Arab-Israeli Conflict* (Austin: University of Texas Press, 2015, p. 304.

[65] Elie Podeh, 'Israel and the Arab Peace Initiative, 2002–2014: A Plausible Missed Opportunity', *Middle East Journal*, 68, 4, 2014: 588.

[66] For a full text of the API, see 'Arab Peace Initiative', *Guardian*, www.theguardian.com /world/2002/mar/28/israel7, accessed 6 October 2017.

276   A Perfect Storm

conflict. Thus, the API constitutes the most conciliatory pan-Arab negotiation position towards Israel since the beginning of the Arab-Israeli conflict.

However, it elicited little response from Jerusalem. There were some indications that the Israelis tried to establish direct contact with the Saudis via 'Adil al-Jubayar, a top Saudi foreign ministry advisor, and through Andrey Vdovin, a special Russian envoy to the Middle East'.[67] Also, in a public address to the Knesset, Sharon offered to meet with the leaders of the Arab states.[68] These secret and public overtures were rejected outright by the Arab states, which saw the Israeli response as an attempt to achieve formal recognition before negotiations had even started.

Henceforth, Israel ignored the API, a stance shaped decisively by Prime Minister Sharon. While acknowledging that there was a 'positive component' to the API, Sharon underlined 'the extreme demands included in the resolutions of the conference of Arab leaders in Beirut'.[69] Subsequently, during a meeting with President Bush on 5 May, Sharon presented the Americans with an intelligence dossier implicating the Saudis in funding the families of suicide bombers.[70] This was a clear effort to further undermine the standing of Saudi Arabia, the sponsor of the API, in US eyes. Sharon's opposition to the API was a product of his political outlook throughout his tenure as prime minister that no agreement was possible as long as Yasser Arafat remained leader of the Palestinians. In this sense, as Sharon's chief of staff would observe later, the API was 'premature'.[71]

The obstacle posed by Sharon's disposition towards Arafat before the API was compounded by the political shackles imposed by his own party, Likud. In May 2002, members of Likud's central committee, the party's main member electing body, adopted a resolution, promoted by Binyamin Netanyahu, which restated Likud's unequivocal opposition to a Palestinian state. The resolution constituted a significant domestic obstacle to Israel's further exploration of the API.[72] Likud's resistance was predictable, but the fact that the Labour party, still the senior partner in the government, did not demand that the API should be explored further is somewhat baffling. Even Foreign Minister Shimon Peres's response was unwaveringly lukewarm. While he acknowledged that the

---

[67] Podeh, 'Israel and the Arab Peace Initiative, p. 587.
[68] PM Sharon's address to the nation, *IMFA*.
[69] PM Sharon's address to the nation, *IMFA*.
[70] Sharon, *Arik Sharon – A Life of Leader*, p. 423.
[71] Interview Weissglas, 22 January 2018, Tel Aviv.
[72] Weissglas, *Arik Sharon*, pp. 170–1.

A Diplomatic Alternative 277

API was 'important', Peres hastened to add that 'it is liable to flounder if terrorism is not stopped' and that Israel cannot 'ignore the problematic aspects which arose at the Beirut Summit and the harsh and rejectionist language used by some of the speakers'.[73]

The foreign minister's reaction, which so closely echoed Sharon's remarks, reflected a deeper trend in Israeli domestic politics. After two years of Intifada, appalling violence and a security establishment bent on demolishing the foundations of Israel's engagement foreign policy, the centre ground of Israeli domestic politics had shifted firmly to the right. This is exemplified by the API's being not only ignored by the Israeli government but also receiving no public support for its further examination. Even Israeli intellectuals were not interested at the time; the first international academic conference to discuss the API, which was organized in Israel by Professor Yoram Meital, did not take place until eight years later.[74] The first academic study of the API in Hebrew was published only in 2010.[75]

The underwhelming response to the API was symptomatic of a profound trend within the Israeli Zionist left. During this period, politicians and intellectuals were describing how they had 'sobered up' from their dreams that Israel-Palestinian peace was achievable. Benny Morris, who during the late 1980s, emerged as part of a group known as the New Historians, which refuted many myths of Zionist historiography, is an excellent case in point. In an article published in the *Guardian*, a British broadsheet, on 21 February 2002, he stated that 'my thinking about the current Middle East crisis and its protagonists has in fact radically changed during the past two years.' 'Peace?' he asks in the article rhetorically. 'No chance!'[76] The claims of Morris and others such as

---

[73] 'Response by FM Peres to the Decisions Taken at the Arab Summit in Beirut', *IMFA*, http://mfa.gov.il/MFA/PressRoom/2002/Pages/Response%20of%20FM%20Peres%20t o%20the%20decisions%20of%20the%20Arab.aspx, accessed 6 October 2017; see also 'Response by Deputy Prime Minister and Foreign Minister Shimon Peres to a Tabled Agenda on the Subject of the Saudi Initiative, *Yearbook of Official Documents 2002, IMFA*, pp. 79–91, https://issuu.com/israelmfa/docs/yearbook2002?layout=http%253A%252F %252Fskin.issuu.com%252Fv%252Fcolor%252Flayout.xml&backgroundColor=2 a5083&showFlipBtn=true, accessed 6 October 2017.

[74] Akiva Eldar, 'How Israel managed to Dry Up the Arab Peace Initiative, *Ha'aretz*, 22 June 2010.

[75] Efraim Lavie (ed.), *Israel and the Arab Peace Initiative* (Tel Aviv: Tammy Steinmetz Centre for Peace Research, 2010) (in Hebrew).

[76] Benny Morris, 'Peace? No Chance', *Guardian*, www.theguardian.com/world/2002/f eb/21/israel2, accessed 13 October 2017; Morris continued to advocate similar line publically, see, for instance his interview with Ari Shavit, 'Survival of the Fittest', *Ha'aretz*, 8 January 2004, www.haaretz.com/survival-of-the-fittest-1.61345, accessed 13 October 2017.

278   A Perfect Storm

renowned author and peacenik, Amos Oz, who in an interview also claimed to have sobered up, represented a forceful intellectual challenge to the very essence of Israel's erstwhile engagement stance.[77]

Its de-legitimation by intellectuals was amplified by prominent Israelis' depictions of Palestinian behaviour as bordering on racism. For example, former Prime Minister Ehud Barak described Arafat's 'mendacity' during their negotiations as the 'product of a culture in which to tell a lie ... creates no dissonance. They [the Palestinians] don't suffer from the problem of telling lies that exists in Judeo-Christian culture.'[78]

Such equivocal claims made by leading Israeli intellectuals and a former prime minister are revealing. They reflect the extent to which the Israeli centre left was plunged into political and intellectual crisis following the collapse of the Camp David summit and two years of the al-Aqsa Intifada. Under these circumstances, the political constituency, which, once, would have demanded 'peace now' in response to an initiative such as the API, had all but vanished in under three years.

Explicit US backing for the API might have given it the diplomatic impetus it needed given its unenthusiastic response from Israel. However, being fully aware of Sharon's disposition brought Rice to the conclusion that the API's 'timing could not have been worse.' 'Sharon', she explains, 'was elected to defeat the intifada – not to make peace. There was no trust in Arafat as a partner, an assessment we shared.'[79] President Bush clearly attached little importance to the API; it is not mentioned once in his presidential memoir, *Decision Points.*

A New Vision for Peace?

The end of Operation Defensive Shield brought to a head a number of processes. The greatest Israeli military offensive against the Palestinians in the West Bank since 1967 had weakened the PA significantly. Forced to rely on a fragmented, enfeebled and defeated security apparatus, Arafat's and the PA's already limited control over the Palestinian territories became even weaker. Local Palestinian militias gained more influence in the main cities of the West Bank and were disinclined to take orders from the PA.[80]

A more significant challenge to the PA and to Arafat, in particular, came from the USA. Since the launch of the GWoT, the Bush

---

[77] Interview Amos Oz, *Ha'aretz*, 10 January 2003 (in Hebrew).
[78] 'Camp David and After: An Exchange' (Interview 1 Barak), *New York Review of Books*, June 13 2002 issue, www.nybooks.com/articles/2002/06/13/camp-david-and-after-an-exchange-1-an-interview-wi/, accessed 13 October 2017.
[79] Rice, *No Higher Honor*, p. 136.
[80] Harel and Isacharoff, *The Seventh War*, pp. 288–9.

A New Vision for Peace? 279

administration had paid little attention to the Israeli-Palestinian conflict. In the words of Elliot Abrams, it was 'pushed back' after previous administrations had tried and failed.[81] At the same time, the administration could no longer remain disengaged since, by April 2002, US foreign policy towards the Israeli-Palestinian conflict had become increasingly entwined with the diplomatic and military preparations related to the US-led invasion of Iraq. The Saudis, whose support the USA required, were frustrated by the lack of an American response to the API. Tony Blair, Britain's Prime Minister, and the USA's main ally in the preparations for the offensive against Iraq, was, according to Abrams, peppering the president with advice about how to move things forward. Blair argued, both publicly and privately, that to take action on Iraq required an initiative on Israeli-Palestinian peace and was urging the Americans to reengage as mediators.[82] As the planning for the attack on Iraq intensified, President Bush became more receptive to his allies' requests, in order to secure their support.

At this point, as Miller observed during his time in office, George W. Bush had to choose between conflicting approaches to how to deal with Blair's request. The state department under Colin Powell's leadership expressed the view that the USA should design a proposal based on previous US diplomacy and propose a peace conference.[83] However, Vice President Cheney and Defence Secretary Rumsfeld were against the USA adopting any type of initiative. They argued that 'supporting a Palestinian state in the midst of an intifada would look like rewarding terrorism.'[84] The president was unwilling to revert to the foreign policy course pursued by the Clinton administration but, at the same time, feared that ignoring the Saudi and British pleas might alienate his allies. Striking a balance of his own, he opted for a different foreign policy approach, which he outlined in an important speech delivered on 24 June 2002.[85]

The speech, which was pitched as a vision for peace, was, in fact, something rather different. As Dov Weissglas, Sharon's chief of staff, quickly recognized, it was a blueprint for how the US intended to '*manage*' Israeli-Palestinian relations.[86] As the president's speech progressed, it became clear that it consolidated the Bush administration's departure

---

[81] Abrams, *Tested by Zion*, p. 19; Marwan Muasher, *The Arab Center: The Promise of Moderation* (New Haven: Yale University Press, 2008), p. 104.

[82] Abrams, *Tested By Zion*, p. 39.   [83] Rice, *No Higher Honor*, p. 142.

[84] Rice, *No Higher Honor*, p. 143; Miller, *The Much Too Promised Land*, p. 347; Bush, *Decision Points*, p. 404.

[85] Full text available at 'President Bush Calls for New Palestinian Leadership, *White House*, https://georgewbush-whitehouse.archives.gov/news/releases/2002/06/20020624-3.html, accessed 10 October 2017.

[86] Weissglas, *Ariel Sharon*, p. 182, emphasis in original.

from US foreign policy towards the Israeli-Palestinian conflict under Clinton and George Bush Sr. It made clear that US foreign policy towards the Israeli-Palestinian conflict would no longer hinge on mediation. Instead, it would be based on transformative diplomacy, regime change and democratization. It was in this context that, in his speech, President Bush called on the Palestinians to 'elect new leaders', making it clear that the USA no longer considered Yasser Arafat a legitimate leader. The president urged the Palestinians also to conduct reforms, 'which will require entirely new political and economic institutions'.[87] This was presented as a precondition for future US support for the Palestinians.

The speech's absence of specific reference to the political issues underpinning the Israeli-Palestinian conflict was conspicuous. There were only general calls to freeze the settlements, end the Israeli occupation and make peace on the basis of UNSCR 242 and 338.[88] However, these rather general calls did not impose a price in the event that Israel did not comply. Also, they represented a dramatic withdrawal from the positions expressed by President Clinton a mere eighteen months earlier. Based on Bush's 24 2002 June speech, the Palestinians could look forward in the immediate future only to a state with provisional borders. In its tone and its content, President Bush's speech encapsulated how politically weakened the Palestinians had become by the al-Aqsa Intifada. So much so that, in his memoirs, Dov Weissglas reports that, following the speech, Sharon was convinced that Israel would not in the foreseeable future be subject to international pressure to negotiate a final agreement with the current PA.[89]

The shift in US policy has been mostly connected to the foreign policy agenda being pursued by the president's national Security Advisor, Condoleezza Rice. The dialogue she was conducting with Sharon's Chief of Staff Dov Weissglas and Minister Natan Sheranski was instrumental in shaping the president's speech.[90]

However, there was a more deep-seated element to the 24 June 2002 speech, which stemmed from the close liaison between the Israeli and US security intelligence services. According to the then Head of Mossad, Ephraim Halevy, during Operation Defensive Shield, Mossad had begun advocating a new foreign policy approach to the Palestinians. The intention was to create an alternative power centre to President Arafat, within the Palestinian parliamentary system. To this end, the Palestinians should consolidate their fragmented security forces and create a new post of

[87] 'Bush Calls for New Palestinian Leadership', *White House*.
[88] 'President Bush Calls for New Palestinian Leadership', *White House*.
[89] Weissglas, *Ariel Sharon*, p. 178.
[90] Miller, *The Much too Promised Land*, pp. 349–50; Interview Weissglas.

prime minister, who, effectively, would become leader of the Palestinian executive branch. Mossad's plan included the appointment of a finance minister, who would restructure the Palestinian financial system and report directly to the new prime minister rather than to Arafat. The architects of this plan envisaged the balance of power within the PA shifting from President Arafat's office to the office of the prime minister, which eventually would achieve sufficient authority and power to replace Arafat in negotiations with Israel. The plan, Halevy recalled with some pride, 'was an ambitious attempt of regime change directly within our chief rival'.[91]

Before the 24 June speech, Halevy and Prime Minister Sharon's Military Secretary, Moshe Kaplinski, had sought support for Mossad's plan in Arab capitals, in Europe and in the USA. Halevy could assess the impact of his endeavour after listening to the 24 June speech. 'At 3:47 in the afternoon', Halevy noted in his memoirs, after the speech ended, 'I could not recall a case where the intelligence community was able to reach such an achievement in terms of setting in motion regional strategic trends.'[92]

News of regional strategic trends, however, was premature since Israeli foreign policymakers faced some profound questions. How would the rhetoric used by the president in his 24 June speech translate into practice? At what point would the US-led invasion of Iraq commence and how would it affect the regional landscape? Would the attempt at regime change succeed? If so, who would replace Arafat and what foreign policy direction would his replacement pursue? As these weighty questions remained hanging in the air for several months, the influence of US foreign policy reformulation outlined by Bush remained unclear.

A Perfect Storm

The 9/11 attacks and the launch of the GWoT radically changed the foreign policy environment in which Israel had operated since the beginning of the al-Aqsa Intifada. Post-9/11, the IDF was given more legitimacy to act against the Palestinians and, eventually, to destroy the last vestiges of Israel's foreign policy engagement stance. Prime Minister Sharon and his immediate circle were instrumental in exploiting the international context generated by the 9/11 attacks, to push for this change in Israeli foreign policy. Centring Israeli foreign policy on quashing the Palestinian Intifada by force and promoting regime change, was

---

[91] Halevy, *Man in the Shadows*, pp. 167–8. [92] Halevy, *Man in the Shadows*, pp. 166–7.

282 A Perfect Storm

entirely consistent with the foreign policy outlook espoused by Prime Minister Sharon throughout his military and political career.

The foreign policy direction promoted by the prime minister and his immediate circle was backed fully by the security network. Since the eruption of the al-Aqsa Intifada, the IDF general staff, under the leadership of Mofaz and Ya'alon, and the GSS, under the stewardship of Avi Dichter, had been seeking to end Israel's foreign policy of engagement. They perceived this foreign policy direction as posing a mortal threat to the country. Post-9/11, as Ya'alon stated repeatedly, Israel had to refute the notion of Israel likened to a spider's web, which had been promoted by Hassan Nasserallah.

This monochromatic foreign policy outlook explains the lack of support for exploring the API in more detail. Such a response a few years earlier would have been opposed by the Israeli left. However, by the time of Operation Defensive Wall, this constituency had mostly disappeared. The Labour party, the champion of the Oslo peace process, was the senior partner in the coalition that sought to dismantle Israel's engagement stance. Thus, there was no political alternative to the foreign policy path pursued by Sharon and the generals. Furthermore, the collapse of the Camp David summit and the eruption of the al-Aqsa Intifada stripped the Israeli centre left of its previous wide intellectual support. The notion that Israel had no choice but, via the use of force, to sear into Palestinian consciousness that violence does not pay off, rapidly gained traction. Amid these domestic trends in Israel, the USA washed its hands of its mediator role. The Bush administration was steadily applying the principles that shaped its GWoT, to its foreign policy towards the Israeli-Palestinian conflict. A perfect domestic and international political and military storm left Israel's foreign policy engagement stance in tatters.

13 The Road Map for Regime Change

The 2003 Election Campaign

On 5 November 2002, Ariel Sharon asked the Israeli President, Moshe Katzav, to dissolve the Knesset and announce an early election. The prime minister's decision was prompted by the departure of One Israel from the coalition government on the pretext of its opposition to the proposed annual budget.[1] In previous elections – 1996, 1999 – Israelis had been asked to vote for a prime minister and for MKs.[2] Following these elections, it had become clear that this seriously fragmented the domestic parliamentary system. Therefore, one of earliest measures taken by the first Sharon government was to rescind the law allowing direct election of the prime minister.[3] Consequently, the 28 January 2003 election was based on the erstwhile proportional representation single ballot system.

The 2003 election campaign pitted Likud and Labour against one another, after David Levy's Gesher party broke away from One Israel – the political compact created by Ehud Barak in the midst of the 1999 election campaign. In the run-up to the elections, which took place on 28 January 2003, the Labour party elected a new Chairman, Amram Mitzna, a former army general and mayor of Haifa. Mitzna defeated the incumbent Chair, Binyamin Ben-Eliezer, who was accused by a powerful group of dovish Labour MKs of kowtowing to Sharon. The party platform for the 2003 campaign reflected the strong influence of Labour doves such as Yossi Beilin, Haim Ramon and Avraham Burg. They were all strong supporters of Mitzna, sometimes described as 'Beilin with a beard'.[4] Essentially, Labour's platform comprised a bid to restore

---

[1] Asher Arian and Michal Shamir, *The Elections in Israel—2003* (New Brunswick: Transaction Publishers, 2005), pp. 3–4; Sandler and Mollov, 'Israel at the Polls 2003, p. 6.

[2] The 2001 elections were solely for the premiership. MKs did not stand for election.

[3] Gideon Alon, 'The Direct Voting Electoral Law is Erased from the Law Book', *Ha'aretz 7 March 2003*, https://www.Ha'aretz.co.il/misc/1.684838, accessed 19 October 2017.

[4] Beilin, *The Path to Geneva*, p. 260.

Israel's foreign policy of engagement or, failing that, to revert to unilateralism. It committed in its platform to resuming negotiations with the Palestinians from the point at which, under Barak, they had halted and to sign a peace deal based on the Clinton parameters. If the peace negotiations failed, Labour pledged to 'separate from the Palestinians' by developing 'a unilateral plan founded on security considerations.[5] Labour's platform presented Israelis with a starkly different prospect from the foreign policy record of the first Sharon government, which hinged on quashing the Intifada by military force.

Faced with two clear alternatives, the verdict of the Israeli electorate in the 2003 national election was decisive. Likud secured thirty-eight MKs compared to Labour's nineteen. Labour's devastating defeat was due, in part, to personal factors. Amram Mitzna was a novice in national politics whereas, by 2003, Ariel Sharon had become almost a father figure in Israel. Having presided over a national unity government since 2001, Sharon was no longer regarded as a divisive politician. In fact, he had garnered wide domestic support, which is perhaps why several corruption scandals surrounding Sharon and his sons left him untainted. Sharon's political support at home was reinforced by the US president's backing – an important electoral asset. At the same time, Sharon's toning down of his erstwhile hawkish views was helping to cultivate his new image as respectable statesman. Frequently during the campaign he declared himself willing to make 'painful territorial concessions' for a political settlement with the Palestinians.[6]

While these factors might explain Labour's defeat by Likud, they do not explain the distribution of votes between right and left in parliament. The block of right-wing parties in the Knesset won sixty-nine of the Knesset's 120 seats whereas parties associated with the centre left secured only thirty-six. This resounding victory by the right-wing party block broke the political tie between the Israeli left and right that had existed since the mid-1980s. In this respect, the outcome of the 2003 elections was extremely significant in reflecting a decisive shift to the right of the domestic Israeli political centre ground. Clearly, the potential of Israel's engagement foreign policy stance to inspire voters and galvanize sufficient political support to win an election was exhausted. The main foreign policy plank of the Israeli Zionist-Liberal left had reached the end of its domestic political road.

---

[5] The 2003 Labour Party Platform, The Moshe Sharet Labour Party Archive, www.Ha'ar etz.co.il/misc/1.684838, accessed 19 October 2003.

[6] Diana Bachur, 'Sharon in the Editors' Committee: Ready for Painful Concessions', Ynet 5 December 2002, www.ynet.co.il/articles/0,7340,L-2296153,00.html, accessed 19 October 2017.

The Second Sharon Government
and the Decision-Making Process

By the time Ariel Sharon formed his coalition government, the tally of Likud MKs had increased by two, going from thirty to forty following a merger with Natan Sheranski's party, Yisrael BaAliya, which in 1999 had secured seven seats. The decline in the support for Yisrael BaAliya reflected a broader sociological phenomenon. Over the preceding decade, the 1 million-strong community of immigrants from the former USSR had become increasingly integrated into Israeli politics, society, economy and culture and this affected the voting patterns. In a shift from supporting parties, such as Yisrael BaAliya, which represented needs specific to the absorption process, more and more immigrants from the former Soviet Union were backing parties with a national agenda such as Likud.[7]

Sharon was keen to maintain the broad domestic support he had obtained during his first term and, therefore, positioned Likud at the centre of his coalition government. On its right flank was the National Union – a compact of four ultra-nationalist secular parties – and the National Religious Party, which represented the settlers. Shinui, meaning change, which was positioned on Likud's left, was led by the media firebrand, Yossef (Tommy) Lapid. It was anti-clerical on social matters, economically it was neoliberal and was centrist in its foreign policy. It appealed to voters who found Meretz and Labour too left leaning on foreign policy and the economy, which explains why its number of MKs leapt from six in 1999 to fifteen in the 2003 elections.[8]

Ariel Sharon's coalition government commanded a majority sixty-eight seats. Its broad political contours provided it with wide foreign policy manoeuvring space. While recognizing the importance of settlement, 'in all its forms, as a national project', the government's basic lines acknowledged also that making peace would entail 'painful concessions'. Furthermore, these basic lines stated that government would seek to make peace with Syria and the Palestinians on the basis of UNSCR 242 and 338, principled on 'land-for-peace'. Significantly, the prospect of establishing a Palestinian state was not ruled out completely.[9]

Within these wide foreign policy contours, Prime Minister Sharon had significant autonomy. Empowered by his enhanced domestic standing

---

[7] Sandler and Mollov, 'Israel at the Polls, 2003', p. 15.

[8] Efraim Torgovnik, 'Shinui's to Capture the Centre of Israeli Politics in Shmuel Sandler, in M. Ben Mollov and Jonathan Rynhold, *Israel at the Polls 2003: A New Turning Points in the History of the Jewish State?* (London: Routledge, 2005).

[9] 'The 30th Government Basic Lines under the Premiership of Ariel Sharon', Knesset official website, www.knesset.gov.il/docs/heb/kaveiyesod2003.htm, accessed 19 October 2017.

with the Israeli public and within Likud, Sharon was in a position to exploit the full autonomy inherent in the prime minister's office by centralizing the foreign policy decision-making process. His ministerial appointments strongly reflected this. The only Likud member who could challenge Sharon's decisions politically, Binyamin Netanyahu, was removed from the foreign policy circle after grudging acceptance of the finance ministry portfolio. Silvan Shalom, a leading Likud politician, but not someone who could challenge Sharon, was appointed to the foreign affairs ministry, but with reduced responsibility. Sharon and his confidants made it clear to Shalom that Middle East affairs and relations with the USA were outside his purview.[10] Consequently, as a senior American observer concluded, Shalom would never be a 'powerful member of the government' and Sharon's Chief of Staff, Weissglas, was 'in effect his foreign minister and chief interpreter – interpreter of the world to Sharon and of Sharon to the world'.[11]

Sharon perhaps would have liked to follow his predecessors – Rabin, Peres and Barak – and assume the defence portfolio in tandem with his prime ministerial duties. However, as we have seen, there was a legal ban on his doing so. Sharon addressed this issue with characteristic cunningness by appointing former Chief of Staff Shaul Mofaz as his minister of defence. Having retired from the IDF only in July 2002, Mofaz was in a cooling-off period and was not eligible to contest a seat for the Knesset. This was advantageous for Sharon; without an independent political base of his own the defence minister could not counterbalance the prime minister. In fact, Mofaz was virtually subordinate to Sharon and depended on his good will to stay in office. This fundamental imbalance in the decision-making structure was deliberate and designed to centralize the foreign policy decision-making process in Sharon and his immediate circle of confidants. Moshe Ya'alon, then IDF Chief of Staff, recalls his deep unease at witnessing Sharon 'castrating his security cabinet'.[12]

The tightknit group of individuals around Sharon became known as the 'Ranch Forum' because they often met at Sharon's Sycamores Ranch. The Ranch Forum was the locus of Israeli foreign policy decision-making during the second Sharon government and included Sharon's Chief of Staff, Weissglas, the prime minister's sons, Omri and Gilad, and the political strategists, Eyal Arad and Reuven Adler. The main criterion for inclusion in this forum, which Sharon frequently consulted and encouraged to engage in free-flowing discussion, was personal loyalty.[13]

---

[10] Interview Weissglas.   [11] Abrams, *Tested by Zion*, pp. 63, 73.
[12] Ya'alon, *The Longer Shorter Way*, p. 168.   [13] Interviews Arad and Weissglas.

Lobbying Efforts

The second Sharon government, which was sworn in on 28 February 2003, faced an uncertain international environment. Since summer 2002, it had become clear that the USA was planning to invade Iraq to topple Saddam Hussein, which it did on 20 March 2003. The memory of Iraq's unprovoked attack on Israel twelve years earlier was still fresh. Equally vivid, was recollection of US proactive diplomacy following the 1991 Gulf War, to promote Arab-Israeli peace negotiations, which yielded the Madrid peace conference. President Bush's speech on 24 June 2002 was delivered in a similar context. As Jordan's Foreign Minister Muashar put it, the USA had to make a credible effort to further the peace process before invading Iraq if it was to convince the Arab public 'that America meant what it said about democracy and freedom'.[14]

However, Bush's 24 June speech merely sketched the US view of Israeli-Palestinian negotiations. Since the USA was preparing to invade Iraq, the specifics of its diplomacy had yet to be formulated. This was the context for Israel's and the pro-western Arab countries – Egypt, Jordan and Saudi Arabia – two-level diplomatic lobbying to influence the course of US diplomacy towards the Arab-Israeli conflict. It consisted of traditional bilateral diplomacy between these states and the USA and diplomatic liaisons with the 'Quartet' – the diplomatic foursome including the UN, the USA, the EU and the Russian Federation, established in April 2002.

The Quartet was an initiative of Colin Powell. According to Jordan's Foreign Minister, Marawan Muasher, who was immersed in these diplomatic efforts during this period, it enabled Powell to 'articulate a position that was more balanced than that of the United States but in which the United States would be represented'.[15] Elliot Abrams saw the Quartet as serving a different aim, namely, curbing the diplomacy of individual European states and Russia by incorporating them under a US umbrella.[16] Muashar's and Abram's perspectives constitute two sides of the same coin. The Quartet would indeed play a continuing role in coordinating the views and policies of the US administration, the Europeans, the UN and Russia throughout the tenure of George W. Bush.

Jordan, Saudi Arabia and Egypt led the Arab lobby efforts, which are described in Foreign Minister Muasher's memoirs. Ahmed Maher, the then Egyptian Foreign Minister, his Saudi counterpart, Crown Prince

---

[14] Marwan Muasher, *The Arab Center: The Promise of Moderation* (New Haven: Yale University Press, 2008), p. 166.
[15] Muasher, *The Arab Centre*, p. 136.   [16] Abrams, *Tested By Zion*, pp. 33, 58.

288   The Road Map for Regime Change

Saud and Muasher himself took the diplomatic lead. Notably, for the first time since the 1991 Madrid peace conference, the Palestinians did not represent themselves in diplomatic discussions that had direct bearing on them. This was an illustration of how the ongoing Intifada in the post-9/11 context had significantly weakened the Palestinians' international diplomatic standing.

The stakes were highest for Jordan. Its economy, energy supplies, demographic composition and security were threatened by the imminent US invasion of Iraq and the ongoing Israel-Palestinian conflict.[17] Jordan's goal was to reduce the threat posed to it by the Israeli-Palestinian conflict by bringing about a US-sponsored peace plan. To this end, Jordan's King Abdallah II and Muasher broached the idea of a road map for peace, in a meeting with President Bush on 1 August 2002. The Jordanian-led road map proposed a Quartet-led peace plan, with the API at its centre, designed to rekindle and link the Israeli-Lebanese, Israeli-Syrian and Israeli-Palestinian peace tracks. All parties would fulfil their commitments in parallel to prevent any from stalling of the process. A Palestinian state would be established within three years, which corresponded with the timeline proposed by President Bush in his 24 June 2002 speech.[18]

Dov Weissglas, Prime Minister Sharon's closest confidant, was responsible for coordinating the Israeli counter-lobbying effort. He was assisted by Shalom Tourgeman, the prime minister's chief political aide. 'The pair', recalls Elliot Abrams, who in autumn 2002 was US NSC director for Near East and North African affairs, 'had become Israel's two-man foreign ministry when it came to dealing with the United States'.[19]

The Israelis were presented with a first version of the road map during a planned state visit by Sharon to the USA in mid-October 2002. This was the seventh of his twelve visits to the United States as prime minister. The draft, which was prepared by William Burns, US Assistant Secretary of State for Near Eastern Affairs, so dismayed the Israelis that they refused even to discuss it; they promised a response after returning to Israel.[20] Subsequently, Weissglas established a steering committee comprised of representatives from Mossad, the MFA, the prime minister's office, the IDF and the NSC. The steering committee, which reported directly to Sharon, was responsible for negotiating with the Americans over the final draft of the road map and coordinating the lobbying effort.[21] Weissglas's

---

[17] On the ramifications of the war in Iraq for Jordan, see Muasher, *The Arab Centre*, pp. 168, 180.
[18] Muasher, *The Arab Centre*, pp. 154–63; Miller, *The Much too Promised Land*, pp. 350–1.
[19] Abrams, *Tested by Zion*, p. 50.
[20] Podeh, *Chances for Peace*, p. 328; Abrams, *Tested by Zion*, p. 50.
[21] Weissglas, Arik *Sharon*, p. 181; Sharon, *Sharon*, p. 470.

first action was to buy some time. He argued that the road map should not be published before the outcome of the Israeli elections, to avoid its becoming politicized during the campaign. The Israelis also demanded that, before the road map was published, the Palestinians should appoint an 'empowered' prime minister. Ultimately, although the text of the road map had been approved for publication by 20 December 2002, it was not published until 30 April 2003.

Weissglas's memoirs of this period reveal the profound gap between what Israel and the three Arab states sought to achieve by the road map. While the Arab states hoped it would become a peace plan, the Israelis wanted to use it to '*manage*' the negotiations with the Palestinians.[22] The team led by Weissglas used the excellent lobbying capacity of AIPAC to influence Congress and rally public opinion towards the Israeli position.[23] In addition, it capitalized on the support of neoconservative officials in the White House, especially Elliot Abrams. Abrams described himself as a 'neocon' and strong proponent of the closest possible relations between the USA and Israel, which made him a key point of contact for the Israelis.[24] His appointment as director of Near East and North African affairs in the NSC spoke volumes about the position of national security advisor, Condoleezza Rice, on the issues raised during discussions over the road map.

A Road Map for Peace?

The final version of the road map was published on 30 April 2003, one day before the end of US military operations in Iraq. It was devised by the Quartet and presented as a 'Performance-Based Roadmap to a Permanent Two-State Solution to the Israeli-Palestinian Conflict'.[25] Tony Blair, then UK Prime Minister, had been urging the Americans to time publication of the road map to coincide with the end of the Iraq invasion. Blair argued that some demonstration by the USA and the UK of progression towards a peace plan leading to a Palestinian state would add to the legitimacy in the Middle East of their invasion of Iraq.[26]

The road map, which was launched as the first US-sponsored peace initiative since Ronald Reagan's peace plan published in 1982, involved

[22] Weissglas, *Arik Sharon*, p. 182, emphasis in original.
[23] Bregman, *Elusive Peace*, p. 245; Harel and Isacharoff, *The Seventh War*, p. 302.
[24] Abrams, *Tested by Zion*, p. 59.
[25] 'A Performance-Based Road Map to a Permanent Two State Solution to the Israeli Palestinian Conflict', *IMFA*, www.mfa.gov.il/mfa/foreignpolicy/peace/guide/pages/a%20 performance-based%20roadmap%20to%20a%20permanent%20two-sta.aspx, accessed 27 October 2017.
[26] Bush, *Decision Points*, p. 405; Abrams, *Tested by Zion*, pp. 38–9.

290   The Road Map for Regime Change

three phases. Phase one was aimed at 'ending terror and violence, normalizing Palestinian life, and building Palestinian institutions'. Phase two was portrayed as a 'transition' stage that included 'the option of creating an independent Palestinian state with provisional borders and attributes of sovereignty, based on the new constitution, as a way station to a permanent status settlement'. Phase three aimed at 'a permanent status agreement and end of the Israeli-Palestinian Conflict'.[27]

A close reading of the document shows that it represented something other than a peace plan and clearly reflected Israeli priorities. For instance, the demands of Jordan, Egypt and Saudi Arabia to establish the API as the basis for US diplomacy were ignored and there was no recognition of the API. The road map referred merely to the 'initiative of Crown Prince Abdullah', describing it as a 'vital element of international efforts to promote a comprehensive peace'. Similarly, the Arab troika's request for an immediate linkage between the Syrian-Lebanese-Israeli and the Palestinian-Israeli peace tracks was kicked into the long grass. The road map set out only that it would 'support progress toward a comprehensive Middle East settlement between Israel and Lebanon and Israel and Syria, to be achieved as soon as possible'.[28]

The road map's stipulations regarding the Israeli-Palestinian conflict reveal a similar tilt towards Israeli positions. The Palestinians were required to 'immediately undertake an unconditional cessation of violence', 'have leadership acting decisively against terror' and carry out a security and 'comprehensive political reform' as part of the first stage. Security reforms included consolidating all Palestinian security forces into 'three services reporting to an empowered Interior Minister' – rather than to President Arafat. Financial reforms required all donor countries to channel their funds 'through the Palestinian Ministry of Finance's single Treasury Account', which would not be accessible to Arafat. Clearly, both sets of reforms were designed to curb President Arafat's power.

The performance-based process governing implementation of the road map also reflected Israeli preferences. It followed a sequential method – an Israeli demand – rather than the Arab's request that Israel and the Palestinians should meet their benchmarks simultaneously. As Elliot Abrams recalls, this was highly significant as it required, 'first an end to terror, then Palestinian reform and the departure from power of Arafat, and only then the negotiations that would lead to Palestinian statehood'.[29]

---

[27] Podeh, *Chances for Peace*, p. 324.   [28] 'A Performance-Based Road Map', *IMFA*.
[29] Abrams, *Tested by Zion*, p. 55.

A Road Map for Peace? 291

In other words, a prerequisite for resuming peace negotiations was an internationally sanctioned plan for a regime change in the Palestinian territories, which bore a striking resemblance to the plan for regime change developed by Mossad in April 2002. Thus, it was not surprising that the road map was attractive to Sharon, who 'suspected that the Palestinians were unwilling or unable to fulfil the first stage of the Road Map'. Therefore, as Weissglas explains, since the map's progress depended on the milestones specified in each stage being achieved, Sharon saw it 'as a guarantee that Israel would not have to negotiate under any external pressure'.[30] Indeed, Weissglas speculated that it was possible that Sharon thought that the road map would not reach the third phase of realization of the two-state solution, because meeting the benchmarks would fail.[31]

Content with the final version of the road map, on 25 May 2003 Sharon presented it to his government for discussion. At the end of intense debate it was accepted by a majority of twelve votes to seven with four abstentions, but not before fourteen reservations were raised in the government decision.[32] The Americans refused to include these conditions in the final version of the road map, but agreed to address them 'fully and seriously' as and when the need arose.[33] Nonetheless, the fourteen reservation conditions included by the Israeli government were important. Their fulfilment would hinder progress from the first to subsequent phases of the road map and rendered its fulfilment more difficult – perhaps even impossible – compared to the original text. For instance, Israel reinforced the requirement for the Palestinians to cease their violence. The Israeli government's first reservation required the PA's 'complete the dismantling' of all Palestinian factions and 'collect[ion of] illegal weapons' – something that the IDF had failed to do in the two and half years of the Intifada. How, after being dealt the severe blow by Operation Defensive Shield, the Palestinian security apparatus could meet these demands could be described as a mystery wrapped in an enigma. Even with full security capacity, dismantling the violent Palestinian factions would have required all-out war against them and would have taken months, if not years.

---

[30] Weissglas, *Arik Sharon*, p. 182.   [31] Weissglas, *Arik Sharon*, p. 183.
[32] 'Government Meeting about the Prime Minister's Statement on the Road Map', 25 May 2003, *IMFA*, www.mfa.gov.il/MFA/PressRoom/2003/Pages/Goverment%20meet ing%20about%20the%20Prime%20Minister-s%20state.aspx, 'Israel's Response to the Road Map', *IMFA*, www.mfa.gov.il/MFA/ForeignPolicy/Peace/MFADocuments/Pages/Isr ael%20Response%20to%20the%20Roadmap%2025-May-2003.aspx, both links accessed 27 October 2017.
[33] Bregman, *Elusive* Peace, p. 253; Abrams, *Tested by Zion*, p. 68.

292   The Road Map for Regime Change

The fifth Israeli reservation was equally inhibiting. It insisted that the provisional Palestinian state would embody only 'certain aspects of sovereignty' and that it would be subject to severe limitations on freedom of movement. Weissglas was clear that Sharon envisioned this situation as lasting for years if not decades.[34] Thus, besides breeching the three-year outline stipulated by the road map, the fifth Israeli reservation meant that the Palestinian state might be temporary and subject to reversal. This formula resembled some of the ideas explored by Yitzhak Rabin on the eve of his assassination in 1995. Were the Palestinians to accept the same position in 2003, it would reverse the diplomatic progress achieved during the 1990s, by almost a decade. The sixth reservation introduced a wholly new feature – making explicit reference to the right of Israel to exist as a Jewish state. The Oslo accords confined recognition of Israel to a state.[35]

No, Prime Minister

Mahmoud Abbas, popularly known as Abu Mazen, was appointed first Palestinian prime minister, by Yasser Arafat, on 19 March 2003. Since September 2002, Abu Mazen had championed a domestic challenge to Yasser Arafat, which, ultimately, resulted in the Palestinian president's cabinet resigning.[36] The main criticisms were set out in a letter to Arafat on the second anniversary of the al-Aqsa Intifada. It was signed by Abu Mazen and thirteen leading members of Fatah. Arafat was accused of allowing a corrupt and undemocratic PA and of presiding over a failed violent campaign against Israel. The signatories demanded that the armed Palestinian factions be dismantled and that the violent attacks on Israel end.[37] The budding internal opposition to Arafat emerged alongside demands from the Quartet for Arafat to relinquish some of his power. Prior to the publication of the road map, Arafat had responded to this internal and domestic pressure by appointing Abu Mazen. On 30 April, following four weeks of haggling with President Arafat, Abu Mazen presented his cabinet.[38]

---

[34] Ari Shavit, 'In the Name of his Client, *Ha'aretz*, 7 October 2004, www.Ha'aretz.co.il/misc/1.1004558, accessed 7 November 2017; Abrams, *Tested by Zion*, p. 68.
[35] 'Israel's Response to the Road Map', *IMFA*.
[36] Molly Moore, 'Cabinet Resigns as Legislators Challenge Arafat, *Washington Post*, 12 September 2002, www.washingtonpost.com/archive/politics/2002/09/12/cabinet-resigns-as-legislators-challenge-arafat/5614d353-e9b2-4d88-8fb3-6dad08ebac10/?utm_term=.d0640d1ceefb, accessed 6 November 2017.
[37] Arnon Regular, 'For the First Time Arafat Comes Out Against Reformers: They Are Plotting', *Ha'aretz*, 29 September 2002, www.Ha'aretz.co.il/misc/1.827819, accessed 6 November 2017.
[38] Qurie, *Peace Negotiations in Palestine*, pp. 112–13; Bregman, *Elusive Peace*, pp. 248–50.

One of the Abu Mazen government's first decisions was to accept the road map 'as it stood' and without reservations.[39] However, meeting first-phase milestones set for the Palestinians was impeded by a number of factors. Abu Ala, speaker of the Palestinian Legislative Council (PLC), who was well placed to follow events, offered an erudite explanation of the domestic constraints faced by Abu Mazen. Abu Mazen, he recalled, was in charge of a 'mixed system in which the president and the prime minister shared authority'.[40] Arafat refused to delegate authority to his prime minister and was unwilling, in particular, to share control over the PA's security apparatus, which 'remained under the President's general oversight'.[41] Abu Mazen was never able fully to exercise his authority, particularly since President Arafat had the legal power to remove the prime minister from office at any given moment.[42] This friction, which was never resolved, led eventually to a complete breakdown of trust between Arafat and Abu Mazen.[43]

The obstacles presented by the limited authority of Abu Mazen in the bifurcated Palestinian political system were compounded by Israeli impediments. These were revealed during the first meeting between Abu Mazen and Sharon, held on 18 May 2003. Abu Mazen was accompanied by the speaker of the PLC, Abu Ala, and by Palestinian Minister of State, Muhammad Dahlan, who had vied unsuccessfully for control of the PA's security apparatus. Prime Minister Sharon, Dov Weissglas, Shalom Tourgeman and Yoav Galant, the prime minister's military secretary, represented the Israeli side.[44]

Abu Ala chronicled the meeting in detail and recalls that Abu Mazen began by pledging to end the violence. He then set out a number of requests to the Israelis, aimed at consolidating his domestic position in the Palestinian territories and alleviating civilian suffering. These included freezing the settlements, lifting the closures, reducing the number of checkpoints, transferring to the Palestinians $850 million of tax monies collected by Israel on behalf of the PA, lifting the siege of Arafat and releasing prisoners. He asked for priority to be given to political prisoners, such as members of the PLC Marwan Barghouti and Hussam Khader, who Israel regarded as terrorists because of their involvement in attacks against civilians.[45]

---

[39] Qurie, *Peace Negotiations in Palestine*, p. 119.
[40] Qurie, *Peace Negotiations in Palestine*, p. 111.
[41] Qurie, *Peace Negotiations in Palestine*, p. 112.
[42] Qurie, *Peace Negotiations in Palestine*, pp. 110–11; Muasher, *The Arab Centre*, p. 184.
[43] Qurie, *Peace Negotiations in Palestine*, pp. 113–15.
[44] Qurie, *Peace Negotiations in Palestine*, pp. 121–22.
[45] Qurie, *Peace Negotiations in Palestine*, pp. 123–4; $850 million is the figure quoted in Druker and Shelah, *Boomerang*, p. 329.

294   The Road Map for Regime Change

Significantly, Abbas rejected Israel's offer of a speedy withdrawal of the IDF from the centre of Palestinian cities. 'We are too weak at the moment', he told Sharon, which showed how enfeebled the Palestinian security forces had remained following Operation Defensive Shield. Abu Mazen warned that if the IDF withdrew prematurely this would create a 'security vacuum' that would be 'filled by negative elements' and this persuaded Sharon to hold back on any withdrawal.[46] This was the only Palestinian request to which Israel acceded. Sharon was, in Weissglas's words, very 'stingy' with regard to discussing what would happen after the road map's first phase was completed.[47] He refused to disclose, either publicly or privately, his plans for a future Palestinian state, which meant that Abu Mazen had no political prospects to offer the Palestinians in return for fulfilling the demands set out in the first phase of the road map. Israel also refused to reduce the sentences of Palestinian political prisoners, something that would have bolstered Palestinian popular support for Abu Mazen. Instead, it released some 400 prisoners – mostly petty criminals – an act that constituted a public humiliation for the beleaguered Palestinian premier. At the same time, Sharon reneged on his promise to dismantle the settlement outposts. The situation was described, eloquently, by Condoleezza Rice: '[T]he illegal outposts were *going* to be moved but [were] never quite moved', while expansion to existing settlements continued unabated.[48]

Furthermore, by May 2003, Israel was involved in constructing a physical barrier, between the West Bank and Israel proper, that had been authorized by government the previous summer amid a sharp rise in terror attacks. The barrier was constituted by a network of concrete walls, electric fences, ditches and guard towers, which stretched for hundreds of miles around the West Bank to stop suicide bombers from crossing into Israel. Although still under construction in 2003, the barrier was already proving effective and the number of suicide bombers getting through had decreased. However, it was causing immense upheaval to the lives of thousands of Palestinians living in its vicinity. Crucially, it deviated from the Green Line, the internationally accepted border between Israel and the West Bank. Combined with the expansion of Jewish settlements and bypass roads, the effect of the barrier was to dissect the West Bank into cantons and to cut off Arab East Jerusalem from part of the West Bank. It eventually was to complicate the process of drawing up borders. The Palestinians were well aware of the barrier's implications, which was

---

[46] Weissglas, *Arik Sharon*, p. 193.   [47] Weissglas, *Arik Sharon*, pp. 196–7.
[48] Harel and Isacharoff, *The Seventh War*, pp. 311–15; Qurie, *Peace Negotiations in Palestine*, p. 135; Rice, *No Higher Honor*, p. 219, emphasis in original.

No, Prime Minister 295

why Abu Mazen asked Sharon and the Americans to stop its construction, to which the Israelis responded with a flat refusal.[49]

At the same time, targeted assassinations against the Hamas and PIJ leadership persisted while President Arafat remained imprisoned in the *Muqataa*. Wining and dining with US official and the Israelis while Arafat remained besieged, the Palestinian prime minister was viewed increasingly as an Israeli collaborator, perhaps even a traitor. Faced with these constraints, how Abu Mazen could implement the first stage of the road map was unclear. Even the then IDF Chief of Staff, Moshe Ya'alon – no friend of the Palestinians – felt that Israeli foreign policy towards the Abu Mazen government was a missed opportunity. Ya'alon conceded that Israel had failed to support Abu Mazen's government and demonstrate to the Palestinians that, under a moderate leadership, their situation might improve dramatically.[50] Instead, Israel's policies were undermining the legitimacy and capabilities of the Abu Mazen government.

Was Israeli foreign policy towards the Abu Mazen government warranted? The answer is a resounding no. The Palestinian prime minister was utterly committed to ending the Israeli-Palestinian conflict in line with the road map. The speech he delivered at the 4 June Aqaba summit, which officially launched the road map, reflected his sincerity towards its orientation. After publicly acknowledging the suffering of the Jewish people throughout history, Abu Mazen went on to say that 'the armed intifada must end', emphasizing that 'there is no military solution to our conflict'. He continued by denouncing 'terrorism against Israelis wherever they might be' and pledging to create a Palestinian state based on 'the rule of law, a single political authority, and weapons only in the hands of those charged with upholding law and order'. He promised 'a complete end to violence and terrorism' and that the Palestinians would be a 'full partner in the international war against terrorism'. Conspicuously, his speech made no mention of Yasser Arafat, who remained besieged; neither did it dwell on Palestinian grievances.[51]

Muashar, Jordan's foreign minister, and Weissglas, Sharon's closest confidant, commended the 'courageous' speech delivered by Abu Mazen, especially amid the negative reaction it prompted within the Palestinian territories. Abu Ala recalled that the five major Palestinian factions, Fatah, Hamas, Islamic Jihad, the PFLP and the DFLP, pledged to

[49] Bregman, *Elusive Peace*, pp. 268–71; on the implications of the barrier from a Palestinian perspective, see Qurie, *Peace Negotiations in Palestine*, p. 164.
[50] Ya'alon, *The Longer Shorter Way*, pp. 158–9.
[51] Abbas Statement: Full Text, BBC website, news.bbc.co.uk/1/hi/world/middle_east/2963516.stm, accessed 6 November 2017.

296 The Road Map for Regime Change

continue the armed Intifada. Demonstrations organized by Hamas in the Gaza Strip condemned the Aqaba summit, underscoring that it ignored the Palestinians' key problems.[52]

This notwithstanding, the Palestinian prime minister matched his actions to his words by taking a significant political and personal risk. In early June, Abu Mazen persuaded Hamas to accept an Egyptian-brokered ceasefire with Israel, for an initial period of six months.[53] The results were felt immediately and the first weeks following the Aqaba summit were the quietest since the Intifada had begun.[54] Dr Salam Fayyad, who took up the PA's finance portfolio after a successful tenure at the World Bank and the IMF, presided over the fiscal reforms. Nathan Brown, an expert on Palestinian politics, notes that Fayaad wrested control of some of Arafat's funds and began building state institutions to serve the interests of the general Palestinian public rather than Arafat's cronies.[55] According to Weissglas, who was following events closely, Muhammad Dahlan survived at least one assassination attempt during the period when his proposed security policies were taking effect.[56]

Why, given the rhetoric and practice of the Abu Mazen government, did Israel impose obstacles that were self-defeating for its foreign policy aim of regime change in the Palestinian territories? For years, Weissglas recalled, Sharon had seen the creation of a Palestinian state as a threat to Israel. Therefore, he was never wedded to the second and third phases of the road map – the stages leading to a Palestinian state – and did not want to talk about them.[57] Thus, constraining the Palestinians ability to advance implementation of the road map's first phase was in line with his continued objection to a Palestinian state.

It was consistent, also, with maintenance of his crucial domestic political support. During his meetings with Abu Mazen, he stated that certain 'points in the road map create problems for us because of internal opposition inside Israel.'[58] Here, Sharon was alluding to the references to a Palestinian state, which was anathema to several of his party members and his ultra-nationalist coalition partner, the National Union. Furthermore, the recent election result was a reminder to Sharon that the Israelis were against a return to engagement, the central plank of

---

[52] Qurie, *Peace Negotiations in Palestine*, p. 133.
[53] Harel and Isacharoff, *The Seventh War*, pp. 311–12; Miller, *The Much too Promised Land*, p. 352; Qurie, *Peace Negotiations in Palestine*, p. 134.
[54] Weissglas, *Arik Sharon*, p. 203.
[55] Nathan J. Brown, 'Evaluating Palestinian Reform', *Carnegie Endowment Papers*, No. 59, 2005, pp. 10–11, http://carnegieendowment.org/files/CP59.brown.FINAL.pdf, accessed 8 November 2017.
[56] Weissglas, *Arik Sharon*, p. 203.   [57] Weissglas, *Arik Sharon*, p. 197.
[58] Qurie, *Peace Negotiations in Palestine*, p. 126.

No, Prime Minister 297

Labour's platform, and the two-state solution it entailed. Accordingly, concessions to Abu Mazen posed a potential threat to the Sharon government because of the political backlash from the ultra-right elements of his government they would have unleashed. Clearly, Sharon had no faith in Abu Mazen to risk his government in such a way. In a typically demeaning way, Sharon referred to his Palestinian counterpart as 'a chick that's not grown feathers'.[59]

When reminded about the Palestinian prime minister's qualities, Sharon hastened to tell his audience that 'Abu Mazen, too, is after all an Arab.'[60] The huge reservoir of distaste and distrust towards Israel's neighbouring nation and its leaders is critical for understanding Sharon's policy towards the Abu Mazen government. It was at the heart of his distrust of the most moderate Palestinian leader with whom Israel had negotiated and Sharon's suspicions about the second and third phases of the road map.

During the Clinton administration, American mediation sometimes helped the Palestinians to deal with impasses in the negotiations. For example, during the first Netanyahu government, the Hebron and Wye River memoranda were secured thanks to US mediation. Abu Mazen certainly understood this. During his first meeting with George W. Bush, he commented that 'he seems to have gained worldwide support, but his backing among the Palestinian population is not so strong.' He pleaded with the US president, saying: 'You are the only person who can help me by working with Sharon to change the situation.'[61]

Frustratingly for the Palestinian prime minister, American diplomacy towards the Israeli-Palestinian conflict during 2003 was high in symbolism, but low on substance. Two highly choreographed summits – in Sharm El Sheik and Aqaba – took place in June 2003 to support the road map. During the summits, President George W. Bush made even more demands on the Israelis.[62] Yet, US diplomats, such as Aaron Miller, remained unsatisfied, since no serious American diplomacy followed the president's speech in Aqaba, and 'for the remainder of the president's first term'.[63] Indeed, the Americans failed to repeat their diplomatic feat following the 1991 Gulf War, which had enabled the Madrid peace conference. Unlike James Baker, who was empowered in 1991, by George Herbert Bush, to pursue a serious diplomatic manoeuvre with Israel and the Arabs, Colin Powell's position in Bush junior's administration remained trimmed. As

[59] 'Sharon: Abu Mazen is a Chick that's Not Grown Feathers', *Walla*, https://news .walla.co.il/item/399612, accessed 8 November 2017.
[60] Quoted in Druker and Shelah, *Boomerang*, p. 324.
[61] Qurie, *Peace Negotiations in Palestine*, p. 139.   [62] Bregman, *Elusive Peace*, p. 258.
[63] Miller, *The Much too Promised Land*, p. 352.

298   The Road Map for Regime Change

Elliot Abrams reports, the state department 'was informed and asked to perform various helpful supporting roles', but did not formulate policy.[64] Instead, the president was represented by Condoleezza Rice, whose meetings with the Israeli and the Palestinian leadership seem symbolic rather than substantive.[65] Neither did the administration appoint a high-level envoy, of the calibre of Dennis Ross, to represent the president. Instead, the administration chose John Wolf, a veteran foreign service officer with little Middle East experience, who claimed, revealingly, that he was appointed precisely because of his inexperience in Middle East affairs.[66]

At a Dead End

Constrained by Arafat and the Israelis and lacking significant American involvement, Abu Mazen's premiership resembled the 1980s' British political satirical sitcom *Yes, Prime Minister*. Unable to deliver, recalled Abu Ala, his 'domestic situation went from bad to worse'.[67] The fragile ceasefire he brokered with Hamas broke down after Israel and Hamas resumed their tit-for-tat attacks. On 14 August, Israel assassinated Muhammad Seder, Head of the PIJ's military wing in Hebron. Hamas and PIJ felt that if they did not respond they would appear weak.[68] Three deadly terrorist attacks followed: the first on 19 August followed by two more on 10 September. In the interim, Israel assassinated Ismail Abu Shaenb, a member of Hamas's political leadership and launched a failed assassination attempt on Sheik Ahmad Yasin, the founder and spiritual leader of Hamas.[69]

It was clear to Abu Mazen that the al-Aqsa Intifada had restarted. According to Dov Weissglas, the Palestinian prime minister requested that President Arafat authorize emergency measures to curtail Hamas and Islamic Jihad, which Arafat refused to do.[70] This was the last straw for Abu Mazen, who stepped down and disengaged temporarily with the Palestinian political scene. In summing up the reasons for his resignation, the embittered former Palestinian prime minister identified 'Israel's unwillingness to implement its road map commitments' as the 'fundamental problem'. He blamed the Americans for not 'exerting sufficient influence' while accusing Arafat and his allies of 'harsh and dangerous

---

[64] Abrams, *Tested by Zion*, p. 69.   [65] Rice, *No Higher Honor*, p. 219.
[66] Miller, *The Much too promised Land*, p. 353.
[67] Qurie, *Peace Negotiations in Palestine*, p. 140.
[68] Shlaim, *The Iron Wall*, 2nd ed., pp. 769–70.
[69] Bregman, *Elusive Peace*, pp. 272–6; Jean-Pierre Filiu, *Gaza: A History* (London: Hurst, 2012), pp. 269–70.
[70] Interview Weissglas.

incitement against the government and the obstruction of its functions'.[71] His successor, speaker of the PLC, Abu Ala, was more concerned with maintaining Palestinian unity and his position vis-à-vis President Arafat than advancing the road map. Thus, although never officially abrogated, the road map to peace had reached a dead end.

---

[71] Quoted in Chris McGreal 'Ridiculed and Betrayed: Why Abbas Blames Arafat', *Guardian*, 8 September 2003, www.theguardian.com/world/2003/sep/08/israel, accessed 8 November 2017.

14   The Resurgence of Unilateralism

The Unexpected Disengager

On a number of occasions since he rose to power in 2001, Ariel Sharon's statements contrasted with his erstwhile hawkish position on policies supporting Greater Israel and the Jewish settler movement.[1] His conciliatory remarks, prior to December 2003, may have been mere lip service to maintain good relations with the Bush administration and his position at the centre of Israeli domestic politics. Against this backdrop, the speech he delivered on 18 December 2003 at the Herzliya Conference represented a watershed.

Sharon did not simply recycle his previous mollified rhetoric. Instead, he used this high-profile forum to announce a strategic foreign policy change towards unilateralism vis-à-vis the Palestinians. Sharon told his audience that 'he did not intend' to wait 'indefinitely' for the Palestinians. If progress on the road map was not forthcoming, which seemed the case, then, Sharon declared, 'Israel will initiate the unilateral security step of disengagement from the Palestinians.' To achieve this, Israel would redeploy the IDF along new security lines and change the positions of the settlements, 'to reduce as much as possible the number of Israelis located in the heart of the Palestinian population'. Sharon proposed to 'relocate' the settlements, as he put it, which he was convinced 'would not be in the territory of the State of Israel in the framework of any possible future permanent agreement'. By the same token, Sharon sought to

---

[1] For instance, 'Statement by PM after the Aqaba Summit Meeting'. 4 June 2003, *IMFA*, www .mfa.gov.il/MFA/PressRoom/2003/Pages/Statement%20by%20PM%20Ariel%20Sharon%2 0after%20the%20Aqaba%20Summi.aspx, accessed 10 November 2017; 'Statement of Sharon in Likud's Central Committee on 4 June 2003', see Ilan Marsiano, 'In Response to Attacks in His Own Party Sharon Responds: The Occupation Must End', Y*net*, 26 May 2003, www.ynet.co.il/articles/0,7340,L-2635195,00.html, accessed 10 November 2003; 'Sharon's Speech at the Herzliya Forum Conference', 4 December 2002, *IMFA*, http://mfa.gov.il/MFA/ PressRoom/2002/Pages/Speech%20by%20PM%20Sharon%20at%20the%20Herzliya%20 Conference%20-%204.aspx, accessed 10 November 2017.

The Unexpected Disengager 301

strengthen Israeli control over areas he considered would 'constitute an inseparable part of the State of Israel in any future agreement'.

Sharon pledged to carry out what came to be known as the unilateral disengagement plan, in line with the two foreign policy determinants that had guided him since he had first assumed office: full coordination with the USA and a 'broad domestic consensus'.[2] Six weeks after the Herzliya speech, the prime minister made his plans more concrete: 'I have ordered to evacuate, sorry, redeploy 17 settlements and their 7500 inhabitants from the Gaza Strip to Israel', plus 'three problematic settlements' in Samaria, he told *Ha'aretz* columnist, Yoel Marcus.[3]

The unilateral disengagement plan was to have significant ramifications for Israel. It redrew Israel's southwestern border and created a precedent for the evacuation of Jewish settlements from the occupied Palestinians territories without any reciprocal gesture from the Palestinians. This decision to adopt a unilateralist posture towards the Palestinians was taken without any consultation with the top brass of the Israeli security establishment and foreign policymakers, including the government. It was deliberated solely within the Ranch Forum. The subsequent interview with Yoel Markus rendered the shift to unilateralism a fait accompli. Dov Weissglas, Sharon's closest confidant, explains why Sharon chose not to discuss with his cabinet his decision to disengage:

The Prime Minister will never come to the cabinet with an idea that has not first been tested within his intimate circle ... Members of the cabinet are not people that you brainstorm with. For better or for worse, in our political system they are [the Prime Minister's] enemies. Those who sit with him around the table want to substitute him. Nine out of ten want to replace him, nine out of ten are legitimately waiting for the prime minister's downfall. Therefore, they are not an appropriate forum for consultation.[4]

What drove Sharon to perform this dramatic foreign policy volte face? Since he had assumed power, he had pursued two foreign policy stances towards the Palestinians. In the first two years, he had tried to bring the Palestinians to surrender by using military force to quash the Intifada. By September 2003, it was clear that this foreign policy course was not being

---

[2] 'Address by PM Sharon to the 4th Herzliya Conference', 18 December 2003, *IMFA*.
[3] Yoel Marcus, 'The Planned Evacuation: Twenty Settlements in the Gaza Strip and the [West] Bank Within One or Two Years', *Ha'aretz*, 2 February 2004, www .haaretz.co.il/misc/1.943057, accessed 13 November 2017. Number of settlers was in fact 9,000, see 'Israel's Disengagement from Gaza and Northern Samaria (2005)', *IMFA*, https://mfa.gov.il/MFA/AboutIsrael/Maps/Pages/Israels%20Disengagement% 20Plan-%202005.aspx, accessed 16 December 2019.
[4] Interview Weissglas.

302   The Resurgence of Unilateralism

entirely effective. Hamas resumed its suicide bombing campaign, something that Israel had hoped to curb with its assassination of the Islamic Resistance Movement leadership. The limits to the Israeli response were quickly exposed. By October 2003, Hamas terrorist attacks had claimed seventy Israeli lives.[5] It had become clear, also, that with the resignation of Abu Mazen, Sharon's second foreign policy direction vis-à-vis the Palestinians – engendering regime change in the occupied Palestinians territories through the road map – had failed.

Privately, Sharon conceded that the status quo with the Palestinians was 'very, very bad'.[6] The Americans agreed. In September 2003, during a sobering meeting with Weissglas, Condoleezza Rice acknowledged that the road map had stalled and that Arafat was immovable. She warned that, before long, even if the violence continued, the international community would begin to pressurize Israel to negotiate with the Palestinians over a state. Cautioning Weissglas, she warned Sharon's seasoned confidant that the Bush administration might no longer be in office and have the power to deflect this pressure. To avoid this situation, Rice told Weissglas: '[W]e need something to break in the region; we need to shake up the dynamics.' She implored him to talk to Sharon and do something 'dramatic'.[7]

Weissglas provided Sharon, who, since assuming power had regarded US support as almost sacrosanct, with a verbatim account of this meeting. The seeming wavering US resolve it reflected coincided with domestic changes. By September–October 2003, a deepening rift was developing within the top brass of Israel's security decision-making circle, manifested in the increasingly acrimonious relationship between Chief of Staff Ya'alon and Defence Minister Mofaz. Mofaz informed Sharon that he could no longer work with Ya'alon. He demanded that Sharon curtail the chief of staff's term in office, stating that, otherwise, he (Mofaz) could not continue to serve as defence minister.[8]

This growing rift among the security top brass was exacerbated by signs of unease in parts of the elite IDF reserve units. For instance, on 23 September 2003, a group of twenty-seven Israeli reserve pilots signed a letter addressed to the then head of the IAF, General Dan Haloutz, and copied it to the editor of the popular broadsheet, *Yedioth Ahronoth*. In this letter, which clearly left a deep impression on Haloutz, the pilots stated that they *'refused to participate in aerial attacks over civilian centres'*. They

---

[5] Harel and Isacharoff, *The Seventh War*, Appendix.
[6] Conversation between Sharon and his military advisor, General Moshe Kaplinski, quoted in Abrams, *Tested by Zion*, p. 89.
[7] Weissglas, *Arik Sharon*, pp. 208–9; Abrams, *Tested by Zion*, p. 87.
[8] Interview Weissglas.

The Unexpected Disengager 303

also warned that '*the on-going occupation fatally harms Israel's security and moral standing*'.[9] This letter was part of a wider phenomenon. Two months later, a group of reserve officers in the semi-secret Israeli commando unit, Sayeret Matkal, signed a letter that stated their refusal to 'take part in the oppressive regime in the occupied territories'.[10]

The prime minister and his close circle were quick to comprehend the salience of these Refuseniks' letters. They were written not by 'a bunch of ponytailed esoteric youngsters shrouded in clouds of weed', explains Dov Weissglas, but 'by the best of the best'.[11] 'During the same period, a joint interview, conducted by Yedioth Ahronoth, with four former GSS heads – Avraham Shalom, Yaakov Peri, Carmi Gillon and Ami Ayalon – served to reinforce the view of the prime minister's closest confidant.[12] These prominent members of Israel's security network warned that the current situation means 'Israel is in danger.'[13] The Refusnik letters and the criticism levelled by the former GSS heads struck a deep personal cord with Sharon, whose fall from grace as defence minister in 1982 was precipitated by scathing critique from the IDF's reserve core. They also exposed cracks in the domestic consensus Sharon had sought assiduously to cultivate since his rise to power.

These were alarming signs for the prime minister. However, up to December 2003, the unease exhibited by a small, but significant group within the policymaking circle and the military, remained fragmented and not able to develop into a foreign policy alternative. In this context, publication of the Geneva Agreement was a tipping point. It was developed jointly by Labour MK, former minister Yossi Beilin and Yasser Abed-Rabbo, a former PLO politician. In a nutshell, it proposed an end to the Israeli-Palestinian conflict through the establishment of a demilitarized Palestinian state in the Gaza Strip and near the whole of the West Bank. The Palestinians would gain sovereignty over Haram al-Sharif in exchange

---

[9] Letter quoted in Haloutz, *Straightforward*, p. 251, emphasis in the original.

[10] Ynet, 'Refusniks'; also in Sayeret Matkal, *Ynet*, www.ynet.co.il/articles/0,7340,L-2845 620,00.html#n; in January 2002, a group of fifty officers in IDF field units signed a letter expressing their refusal to serve in the occupied Palestinian territories on the same moral grounds, Haim Tal, 'we will not continue to control, destroy, deport, eliminate, and disgrace', *Ynet*, www.ynet.co.il/articles/1,7340,L-1581749,00.html, both links accessed 24 November 2017.

[11] Ari Shavit, 'In the Name of His Client', *Ha'aretz*, www.haaretz.co.il/misc/1.1004558, accessed 6 March 2019.

[12] Interview Doron More, Director of the Gate Keepers, by Nirit Anderman, 'Former Head of the Shabak Compares the IDF to the German Army During WW2', *Ha'aretz*, www .haaretz.co.il/gallery/cinema/1.1901878, accessed 15 December 2017.

[13] Sima Kadmon and Alex Fishman, 'Four Shin Bet Chiefs Warn: Israel is in Danger', *Yedioth Ahronoth*, 14 November 2003.

304   The Resurgence of Unilateralism

for complete Israeli discretion over the number of Palestinian refugees it would accept. Half of the Israeli settlements would remain intact and under Israeli control.[14] The proposed agreement was supported by former high-profile members of the Israeli security establishment, some left-wing politicians and international figures including former US President, Jimmy Carter. Arafat was made aware of the agreement that was being promoted by left-leaning members of the PLO.

Yossi Beilin had a proven track record in breaking foreign policy moulds. He was the driving force behind Israel's decision in 1993 to recognize the PLO and the subsequent campaign to withdraw the IDF unilaterally from Lebanon. Belin's intention with the Geneva Agreement was to achieve a resumption of public debate: 'With the peace camp wounded and withered', he recalls, seeming 'wall-to-wall support for Sharon, and a national consensus that there was "no one to talk to" on the other side, I believed it was imperative to present an alternative.'[15]

His timing was prescient in that the Geneva Agreement coincided with two other attempts to challenge Israel's foreign policy stalemate with the Palestinians. Former GSS head, Ami Ayalon, and Palestinian intellectual, Sari Nusseiba, obtained more than 300,000 signatories to their blueprint agreement. This hinged on complete Israeli withdrawal from the occupied territories in return for the Palestinians abandoning the right of return.[16] After its publication in the media and some favourable reactions recorded in Israeli public polls, the agreement was signed in Geneva, with former US President Jimmy Carter, acting as master of ceremonies.[17] Significantly, Colin Powell agreed to meet the authors of the Geneva accord, which signalled that the US State Department had not ruled it out as an alternative to the current stalemate.[18] In combination, the Geneva Agreement and the Ayalon-Nusseiba national referendum punctured the myth propagated by Ehud Barak, namely, that Israel had 'no partner' on the Palestinian side.

The Geneva Agreement was not a formal accord. It was an agreement signed by Israeli and Palestinian politicians who had become marginal in their respective domestic peace camps. Therefore, according to Eyal Arad, one of Sharon's chief political strategists, the Ranch Forum did not see the Geneva accord as an initiative that could galvanize support for a domestic political alternative to Sharon. Nevertheless, Sharon perceived the Geneva Agreement as a threat. He was concerned that, if the road map continued to stall, the template offered by the Geneva accord

---

[14] Beilin, *The Path to Geneva*, pp. 326–62.   [15] Beilin, *The Path to Geneva*, p. 261.
[16] Drooker and Shelah, *Boomerang*, p. 357; Shlaim, *The Iron Wall*, 2nd ed., p. 774.
[17] Beilin, *The Path to Geneva*, pp. 254–63; Harel and Isacharoff, *The Seventh War*, p. 316.
[18] Abrams, *Tested By Zion*, p. 87.

The Unexpected Disengager 305

might be adopted as an alternative, especially by the EU.[19] Adamant about keeping the initiative under his control, the prime minister proposed an alternative to the stalled road map.

Sharon's Ranch Forum was like a council of sages that deciphered the world with the prime minister. Their social and personal profiles were related to Israel's globalized business community rather than to the ideology and practice of the Jewish settler movement. Driven by a strong sense of pragmatism and loyalty to Sharon, the Ranch Forum members' deliberations resounded as in an echo chamber. The unilateral disengagement was presented as a panacea for the domestic woes facing the prime minister and potential erosion of Israel's international standing. For example, Weissglas told Sharon, repeatedly, that the 'only thing' that could reverse current foreign policy, domestic and military trends was 'to get out of Gaza'. This would, he continued, 'directly address the grumblings of the IDF, reduce the territorial dispute between ourselves and the Palestinians, and restore international support for Israel'.[20]

Sharon's sons, Omri and Gilad, concurred, emphasizing that 'the Israeli public was fed up with the death toll exacted by the Gaza Strip.'[21] By the same token, Sharon's confidants predicted that unilaterally withdrawing from the Gaza Strip would boost Israeli public morale, which they considered to be very low. They warned Sharon that a renewed terrorist campaign by Hamas and an ongoing economic recession in Israel had taken their toll on the Israeli public and Sharon's standing. Some polls suggested that his approval rate had plummeted from 80 per cent to 30 per cent. Failure to act was presented by Sharon's intimate circle as very risky. It had the potential to submerge Ariel Sharon's premiership under waves of violence, demoralization and failed foreign policy initiatives.[22]

At the same time, Sharon was made abundantly aware of the domestic political constraints he faced were he to adopt a unilateral foreign policy stance towards the Palestinians. Eyal Arad, somewhat glibly, estimated that 'within three months you won't have a government, within six months the Knesset will be dissolved, within nine months you don't have a party, and within 12 months you are at home and out of office.' 'What's wrong with being at home', retorted the prime minister wryly.[23] Yet, on considering the changing environment around him more seriously, Ariel Sharon was departing from his previous views in support of a Greater Israel. As his closest confidant, Dov Weissglas, explains:

---

[19] Interview Arad.   [20] Weissglas, *Arik Sharon*, p. 209.   [21] Sharon, *Sharon*, p. 488.
[22] Weissglas, *Arik Sharon*, p. 210; Harel and Isacharoff, *The Seventh War*, p. 321.
[23] Weissglas, *Ariel Sharon*, p. 211.

306   The Resurgence of Unilateralism

What pushed Sharon towards taking the decision to disengage from the Gaza Strip was the reality. As Prime Minister, it became clear to Sharon that not one country in the world, including and especially the United States, supported Israel's desire to remain in the Gaza Strip, Judea and Samaria. He concluded that the nations of this world would simply not allow it ... Once he reached the conclusion that remaining in all the territories Israel occupied in 1967 was unfeasible the decision to withdraw from the Gaza Strip became self-evident.[24]

Implementing Unilateralism

International actors

Fully aware of the domestic political constraints he faced, Ariel Sharon first secured international support for the unilateral disengagement plan. Egypt's cooperation was crucial because it was the only other country that shared a land border with the Gaza Strip. Weissglas was dispatched, in secret, to meet Hosni Mubarak, then president of Egypt, to brief him about Sharon's decision to disengage unilaterally. It was significant that this was revealed to the Egyptians while the IDF and the Israeli government remained unaware of Sharon's plan.[25] This discrete liaison attests to a level of strategic cooperation, confidence and trust between Israel and Egypt, unimaginable under Sharon's predecessors, Binyamin Netanyahu and Ehud Barak. What was it that led to this change?

During his premiership, Sharon had developed a level of personal intimacy, confidence and, eventually, mutual trust with Mubarak. Weissglas reveals in his memoirs that Mubarak showed much affection for Sharon; their meetings involved mutual compliments and also jokes, especially 'at the expense of other leaders'. 'There was [between them] a kind of "old-boy camaraderie"', reflected Weissglas, 'of officers who in the past had fought each other and now engaged in discussion'.[26] By December 2004, Mubarak was describing Sharon as 'the best chance for peace'.[27]

The unilateral disengagement plan added a strategic dimension to the personal rapport between Sharon and Mubarak. As a result, the cold peace Egypt and Israel had maintained since they had signed an accord in 1979 was shifting gradually to a peace marked by common strategic

---

[24] Interview Weissglas.
[25] Weissglas, *Arik Sharon*, p. 269; Ya'alon, *The Longer Shorter Way*, pp. 171–2.
[26] Weissglas, *Arik Sharon*, pp. 117, 268; see also reports of phone conversations with Mubarak in Sharon, *Sharon*, pp. 520, 523–4.
[27] AP, 'Mubarak to the Palestinians: Sharon is the Only Chance for Peace', *Ynet*, www .ynet.co.il/articles/0,7340,L-3012687,00.html, accessed 14 December 2017.

Implementing Unilateralism

interests. As American sources reveal, Egypt and Israel had a common interest in containing Hamas – an offshoot of the Muslim Brotherhood movement which opposed the military-led presidential rule of Hosni Mubarak.[28] Abdel Monem Said, the then Head of the al-Ahram Centre for Political and Strategic Studies, a think tank that worked extremely closely with the Egyptian president, expanded on the reasons for Israeli-Egyptian cooperation. 'The whole Gaza issue', explained Said, 'needed a lot of cooperation between Egypt and Israel ... because Gaza was a problem for us and the Israelis ... Egypt sought to keep the pressure on Hamas whilst preventing a humanitarian disaster occurring'.[29]

In its liaison capacity, Egypt engaged in negotiations with the Palestinian factions, including Hamas and PIJ, over how Gaza would be run. Its aim was to establish a long period of calm or *tahadi'a*, without formal commitment to a ceasefire.[30] In addition, the then Egyptian Intelligence Minister, Omar Suleiman, played an important part in coordinating between Israel and the Palestinians throughout the period leading to unilateral disengagement.[31] Eventually, Egypt was entrusted with oversight of the security arrangements between the Sinai Peninsula and the Gaza Strip.

As much as Egyptian cooperation was desirable for the success of the disengagement plan, US support was a sine qua non. It is against this backdrop that a meeting was arranged with Elliot Abrams at the Cavalieri Hilton in Rome, on 17 November 2003, a month before the Herzliya speech. Abrams was eagerly anticipating this meeting and looking forward to dining with Sharon. On entering the prime minister's suite, he reports seeing Sharon feasting on a platter of meat, which, Abrams recalled, 'sure looked like ham to me'. Abrams, an observing Jew, did not eat pork and assumed that Sharon also did not. Unable to contain his curiosity, he asked the prime minister of the Jewish State 'what meat, exactly, is that? 'Elliot', Sharon replied, 'sometimes it is best not to ask.'[32]

Sharon was less equivocal when it came to discussing foreign policy substance. He began by rejecting a proposal from Abrams to renew negotiations with Syria. 'A nation', he told Abrams, 'has only a certain ability to face problems ... don't drag Israel now into an internal struggle.'[33] Like Rabin and Barak before him, Sharon maintained that

---

[28] Congressional Research Service, Report RL33003, pp. 23–4, http://wikileaks.org/wiki/CRS-RL33003, accessed 18 April 2013; see also US-Egyptian dialogue in Abrams, *Tested by Zion*, p. 103.

[29] Interview Mr Abdel Moneim Said, 5 November 2012, Cairo.

[30] Qurie, *Peace Negotiations in Palestine*, pp. 177, 208–10, 215–17.

[31] Weissglas, *Arik Sharon*, p. 270.   [32] Abrams, *Tested by Zion*, p. 88.

[33] Abrams, *Tested by Zion*, p. 88.

308   The Resurgence of Unilateralism

Israel, politically, could not absorb simultaneous engagement on two peace tracks. Sharon was also concerned that negotiating with Syria would afford the Assad regime international legitimacy at a period when its relations with the USA were fraught. Sharon was keen to avoid this.[34]

Having concluded discussion on Syria, Sharon turned to the Palestinian issue. Surprising his guest, Sharon made the case for his plan for unilateral disengagement from the Gaza Strip and demanded US assistance. Over the next two months, the Americans deliberated over Sharon's plan, which they committed to backing with one condition: something also had to happen in the West Bank. Otherwise, explained the Americans, the USA might be seen to be colluding with an Israeli ploy to withdraw from Gaza, only to tighten its grip on the West Bank.[35]

A Defiant Chief of Staff

Having secured US and Egyptian support, the most significant challenge to realizing the disengagement plan was a domestic one. In this specific respect, the IDF's Chief of Staff, Moshe Ya'alon, was potentially a bitter rival. Ya'alon saw the unilateral disengagement plan as 'a disaster'. 'We created a precedent of withdrawing to the last millimeter in Gaza' he explained in an interview. 'The world might have applauded us but one day they would demand that we do exactly the same thing in Judea and Samaria.' Furthermore, Ya'alon reflected sombrely, until the idea to disengage was made public: 'We were on the offensive and the Americans were on the offensive (in Iraq). Suddenly, we revert back to unilateralism?! We thus destroyed a big chunk of the iron wall that we built with blood and toil. In addition, we put the brakes on the attack launched by the civilized Western world in Iraq on extremist Islam, providing a tail wind to Islamic Jihadists.' The chief of staff could not reconcile Sharon's strategic foreign policy course up to that point with his disengagement. Therefore, he was convinced that Sharon had announced the disengagement plan to deflect police investigations into allegations of bribery against himself and his sons.[36]

These serious allegations, ultimately, were settled by Israel's Attorney General Menachem Mazuz. In a forensic report published in 2004, Mazuz argued that the facts and findings against Sharon 'didn't even come close to a reasonable chance of conviction'. An appeal to the Israeli

[34] Sharon, *Sharon*, p. 510.
[35] Weissglas, *Arik Sharon*, pp. 211–12, 226–8; Abrams, *Tested by Zion*, p. 100; Rice, *No Higher Honor*, p. 281.
[36] Direct quotations from interview with Ya'alon; see also, Ya'alon, *The Longer Shorter Way*, pp. 160, 174.

A Defiant Chief of Staff 309

Supreme Court, after Mazuz's report was published, was quashed by a six to one majority.[37] Ze'ev Zambish Hever, one of the few among the settler leadership that had developed a genuine intimacy with Sharon, also rejected Ya'alon's theory outright. As he stated unequivocally: 'I do not believe that Sharon did what he did [that is, the disengagement] because of his legal problems. I do not believe that personal motivations drove Sharon to sacrifice national interests.'[38]

Ya'alon was convinced that his principled opposition to the disengagement plan was perceived by Sharon and his confidants as a 'strategic threat' to Sharon and to the disengagement itself.[39] The prime minister and his close circle responded in kind. Traditionally, Israel's chief of staff is appointed for a three-year term, with its being customary to extend to a fourth year unless there are serious reasons not to. Sharon quashed the domestic threat posed by Ya'alon simply by breaking with custom. In February 2005, he authorized Defence Minister Mofaz – whose personal relationship with Ya'alon had broken down irretrievably – to relieve the chief of staff of his office after three years.[40] Almost offhandedly, Mofaz informed Ya'alon that when his three years were up, he would be replaced by Dan Haloutz, then Deputy Chief of Staff and former commander of the IAF.

Ya'alon argues bitterly in his memoirs that his successor, Dan Haloutz, was appointed IDF chief of staff because: 'He wined and dined with the Sharon family, befriended them, and served their personal interests.'[41] It is, of course, impossible to fully corroborate this accusation, which Haloutz denied vehemently.[42] However, Haloutz's memoirs reinforce the impression that discontinuing Ya'alon's term was part of a broader strategy to eliminate domestic opposition to the unilateral disengagement plan. Typically blunt, Sharon told Haloutz in his first briefing after taking office, that 'he expected him to command an army that implements the decisions of the government rather than thwarts them.'[43]

While the IDF general staff may have been split over its view of disengagement, it was united around a fundamental issue related to the plan. Israel could not be seen as scurrying away from Gaza in disarray, defeated, which was the impression that was left after its unilateral retreat from Lebanon in 2000. This led to a qualitative shift in Israel's targeted assassination policy. In the run up to disengagement, Israel focused on

[37] Quoted in Landau, *Arik*, pp. 476, 479.
[38] Hever 'Ze'ev Hever', in *Partition: Disengagement and Beyond*, p. 125.
[39] Ya'alon, *The Longer Shorter Way*, p. 188.
[40] Ya'alon, *The Longer Shorter Way*, p. 188; Weissglas, *Arik Sharon*, pp. 224–5.
[41] Ya'alon, *The Longer Shorter Way*, pp. 188–90.   [42] Haloutz, *Straightforward*, p. 296.
[43] Haloutz, *Straightforward*, p. 297.

310   The Resurgence of Unilateralism

the top echelons of the Hamas leadership while, previously, its assassination plans had been aimed primarily at the movement's military wing. By April 2004, almost the whole of Hamas's political leadership, including Sheik Ahmad Yassin – following a double suicide attack at the port of Ashdod – had been assassinated by the Israelis.

Yassin, founder and spiritual leader of Hamas, was accused by the Israelis of promoting, motivating and overseeing terrorism. However, in the Gaza Strip he was iconic. The austere manner of a quadriplegic, who was nearly blind and was confined to a wheelchair, contrasted sharply with the corrupt life styles adopted by large segments of Fatah and the PA bureaucrats. His assassination by three Hellfire missiles, fired from an Israeli helicopter as his wheelchair was pushed, frantically, down the street following his emergence from his morning prayers, rendered him in the eyes of the Palestinians, a *Shahid*, a martyr.[44]

The assassination of Yasin enhanced the popularity of Hamas.[45] At the same time, the targeted assassination of Hamas's political leadership significantly weakened the movement. Its consultative council, Majlis al-Shura, recognized that it needed time to regroup, reorganize and cultivate a new leadership. Thus, as Hamas expert, Shlomi Eldar, revealed, it offered to stop the suicide bombings if Israel would halt the targeted assassinations of Hamas's political leadership. As we have seen, in the past, Israel had flatly rejected such offers. However, in the context of the run-up to the disengagement, Hamas's proposal served both parties' converging interests. Hamas was allowed time to recover, rebuild and plan its next step of becoming integrated into the PA. Israel, particularly after the assassination of Yasin, was able to continue its cultivation of an image of not disengaging under military pressure from Hamas.[46]

Although the vicious circle of political assassinations and suicide bombings was put on hold, the IDF and Hamas continued to clash militarily. Hamas fired Kassam rockets into Israel and engaged, militarily, with the IDF and the settlers in the Gaza Strip. For its part, Israel launched large-scale military offensives into the Palestinian territories in the Gaza Strip. They included Operations Rainbow, Active Shield and Days of Penitence, this last being the final large-scale incursion into the Palestinian territories in the Gaza Strip before the disengagement.[47]

The use of large-scale military force included the demolition of houses and factories, workshops and physical infrastructure and the uprooting of

---

[44] Eldar, *Getting to Know Hamas* (Jerusalem: Keter, 2012), pp. 53–6.
[45] Filiu, *Gaza*, p. 273.   [46] Eldar, *Getting to Know Hamas*, pp. 62–63, 126–7.
[47] 'Weapon Smuggling Tunnels in Rafah – Operation Rainbow', *IMFA*, www.mfa.gov.il/mfa/foreignpolicy/terrorism/palestinian/pages/weapon%20smuggling%20tunnels%20in%20rafah%20may%202004.aspx, accessed 10 December 2017.

The Political Challenges to Disengagement 311

many trees. Above all, the huge discrepancy in the loss of lives between Israelis and Palestinians reflected the scale of the military offensive. For example, between May and July 2004, 234 Palestinians were killed compared to twenty-seven Israeli lives lost. Since Israel was about to withdraw from rather than retain control of Gaza, the main thrust of this large-scale military attack had two aims.[48] First, to weaken Hamas and PIJ and pave the way for PA forces led by local strong man, Muhammad Dahlan, to take control of the Strip once the IDF pulled out. It was designed, also, to reinforce the image that Israel was not withdrawing under fire as had happened when it pulled out of Lebanon in May 2000.

The Political Challenges to Disengagement

While Sharon was able to deal directly with the opposition within the IDF, his control over domestic politics was more tenuous. Following his Herzliya speech, the National Union, the National Religious Party and a large segment of Likud's MKs declared their opposition to the prime minister's plan. For Weissglas, the situation was crystal clear: the prime minister was facing a 'political mutiny'.[49] Sharon employed a number of tactics to fend off this acute domestic political challenge. One was to enlist 'political backing from the US', which, as Abrams recalls, prompted President Bush's letter to Ariel Sharon on 14 April 2004.[50]

This was an extraordinary document; the domestic problems being experienced by Israel's prime minister triggered what Condoleezza Rice described as a 'major departure of US policy toward the Middle East'.[51] As Abrams recalls, 'when we met with Sharon [in March 2004] he again pleaded for US help and support. There was a nasty campaign and energetic campaign against him and his plans. If what the President says isn't clear', emphasized Sharon, 'I won't be able to win the battle in Likud; and that would be the end of disengagement, he added.'[52]

The president responded to the prime minister's plea by writing an official letter, delivered at a meeting between the two men on 14 April 2004. In this letter, the president committed the USA formally to supporting Israel on two key matters, determined by the Oslo accords as final-status issues. On the subject of Palestinian refugees, the letter restricted the 'right of return' only to the future Palestinian state. This statement contrasted starkly to the Palestinians' demand to apply the right of return principle to Mandatory Palestinian in its entirety. On the

---

[48] Harel and Issacharoff, *The Seventh War*, Appendix.
[49] Weissglas, *Arik Sharon*, p. 214.   [50] Abrams, *Tested by Zion*, p. 102.
[51] Rice, *No Higher Honor*, p. 283.   [52] Abrams, *Tested By Zion*, p. 103.

312   The Resurgence of Unilateralism

subject of territory, the letter stated that: '[I]n light of new realities on the ground, including already existing major Israeli population centers, it is unrealistic to expect that the outcome of final status negotiations will be a full and complete return to the armistice lines of 1949.'[53] Thus, the US president all but officially legitimized the de facto annexation by Israel of large settlement blocks – Gush Etzion, Ma'ale Adumim, Ariel – in the West Bank. This was in contrast to previous presidents' references to Israeli settlements as obstacles to peace.

It is true that the letter merely validated certain aspects of the Clinton ideas. However, they had been presented as an informal offer. In contrast, Bush's letter constituted an official US foreign policy shift towards Israel on two principles that the Palestinians had held dear since the onset of the negotiations – Israeli withdrawal to the 1967 borders and the right of Palestinians refugees to return to their former homes. The letter was a severe blow for the Palestinians as their then Prime Minister, Abu Ala, explained to Condoleezza Rice: '[W]ith the issues of borders and refugees off the table', he told her, 'our negotiating position is intolerably weak. If these issues were to be settled according to Sharon's plans', he continued, 'we would lose half of our negotiating objectives before any talks could even begin.'[54]

The 14 April Bush letter became legally binding in June after it was approved by Congress and Senate with majorities of respectively 407 to nine and 95 to three. A week earlier, the G8 summit had expressed its support for the plan after its earlier endorsement on 5 May by the Quartet.[55] Having garnered international support and legitimacy, the unilateral disengagement plan replicated the foreign policy tactic used by Ehud Barak when he presided over Israeli unilateral withdrawal from Lebanon. Amid failure to reach an agreement with an Arab partner – Syria, in Barak's case – Israel grounded its steps towards unilateral withdrawal from Arab occupied territory, in the legitimacy and support afforded to it by international fora.

After receipt of the letter setting out the US commitments, Sharon and his close confidants returned to Israel. Weissglas and Gilad Sharon recall that the euphoria among the prime minister's team was boosted further by

---

[53] 'Exchange of Letters Between PM Sharon and President Bush', *IMFA*, www.mfa.gov.il /mfa/foreignpolicy/peace/mfadocuments/pages/exchange%20of%20letters%20sha ron-bush%2014-apr-2004.aspx, accessed 6 December 2017.

[54] Qurie, *Peace Negotiations in Palestine*, p. 175.

[55] Mazal Mualem, Shlomo Shamir, Aluf Ben, 'The US and Europe: It Is Necessary to Implement the Disengagement from Gaza', *Ha'aretz*, 5 May 2004, www.haaretz.co.il/ misc/1.963870; Yitzhak Ben Horin, 'The Senate also Approves the Commitments of President Bush', *Ynet*, 25 June 2004, www.ynet.co.il/articles/0,7340,L-2937376,00 .html#n, both links accessed 14 December 2017.

The Political Challenges to Disengagement 313

the favourable public opinion polls supporting disengagement. Complacently, the prime minister and his close circle calculated that Likud members would not dare to torpedo the disengagement plan and risk forfeiting the achievements represented by the Bush letter. However, they were severely off mark. Sharon and his intimate circle underestimated the principled nature of the opposition within Likud to the disengagement plan, which betrayed Likud's and the settlers' Greater Israel ideology. Indeed, the Bush letter was to have little effect on the Israeli nationalist and religious right, which set out to thwart the disengagement plan. The leaders of this effort, former Refusenik Natan Sheranski and hardliner Uzi Landau, soon flexed their political muscles. On 2 May 2004, Sharon suffered a political defeat as the Likud convention voted against the unilateral disengagement plan by a 60 per cent to 40 per cent majority.[56]

Reeling from this result and facing a revolt in Likud and a defiant cabinet, the prime minister convened the Ranch Forum to discuss his next steps. The link between party politics and foreign policy was at the heart of the discussion. Weissglas, who managed relations with the USA, objected fiercely to the proposal made by Sharon's political advisors. Eyal Arad, Rueven Adler and Uri Shani pressed Sharon to retract or otherwise risk losing his position as leader of Likud. They warned that, politically, going against the results of the party referendum was unthinkable. However, private polls commissioned by Sharon and his team showed a growing divergence between the views expressed by the referendum in Likud and the broader Israeli public, which overwhelmingly supported the disengagement plan.[57]

The gap between public support for the disengagement plan and the opposition within Likud explains Sharon's action during the ensuing few months. The challenge he faced was how to translate public support into political strength. Against this backdrop, the cabinet met on 30 May 2004 to vote on the disengagement plan. The decision-makers were presented with an 'amended' version, which Sharon had devised as a response to the vote in Likud against his original scheme. The so-called revised plan, which was brokered by Minister Tzipi Livni, did not differ in its content. Rather, the difference was in the 'phased' sequencing approach towards evacuating the settlements, which were split into four groups.[58] The cabinet was asked to approve the entire plan at the meeting, with the

---

[56] Weissglas, *Arik Sharon*, pp. 240–2; Sharon, *Sharon*, pp. 501–2.
[57] Quoted in Weissglas, Arik *Sharon*, pp. 240–3.
[58] See revised disengagement plan in 'The Cabinet Resolution Regarding the Disengagement Plan', *IMFA*, www.mfa.gov.il/MFA/ForeignPolicy/Peace/MFADocuments/Pages/Revised%20Disengagement%20Plan%206-June-2004.aspx, accessed 18 December 2017.

314   The Resurgence of Unilateralism

proviso that a further vote would be held before each of the four settle-ments clusters was evacuated.

This change notwithstanding, Sharon was poised to lose the cabinet vote because eight Likud ministers threatened to side with the right-wing parties in his coalition government. Faced by an imminent defeat, Sharon adjourned the meeting, but not before issuing a clear threat to his unruly cabinet ministers. 'Likud', he declared, 'is very dear to us but Israel is dearer. Therefore', he continued, 'I am determined to implement the disengagement plan even if I have to change the composition of the government or take other far-reaching measures.'[59]

The steps Sharon took over the next week befitted his political nick-name, the bulldozer. His track record of creating Likud in the early 1970s, its reinvigoration from nineteen to thirty-eight seats in the 2003 elections, and his unparalleled security credentials and long history of supporting the settlers, gave Sharon sufficient political standing to ruthlessly quell the domestic opposition he faced. He sent two letters of dismissal to the National Union ministers, Transport Minister Avigdor Lieberman and Tourism Minister Benny Elon. This highly unorthodox measure, which the judiciary criticized as autocratic, but declared legal, ensured the revised disengagement plan would receive majority support in the cab-inet. On 6 June 2004, it was approved by fourteen to seven votes.[60] Yet, to an experienced politician such as Sharon, it was clear that the cracks within Likud were deepening. His inner circle estimated that at any given moment he faced between thirteen and seventeen Likud rebels. This acute domestic political threat cast doubt on the coalition govern-ment's survival and Sharon's ability to implement the unilateral disen-gagement plan.[61]

The tension between domestic politics and the reorientation of Israeli foreign policy vis-à-vis the Palestinians, to unilateralism, culminated, on 25 October 2004, in Sharon seeking Knesset approval for his disengage-ment plan. In his speech to the house, Sharon described the decision it was about to make as 'fateful' and the most difficult of his life. He recapped the thinking that had caused him to embark on the disengage-ment, citing demography as the main factor. He told the Knesset: 'We

---

[59] Mazal Mualem and Gideon Alon 'Sharon to the Government: The Likud is Very Dear to Us but Israel is Dearer', *Ha'aretz*, 31 May 2004, www.haaretz.co.il/misc/1.970047, accessed 14 December 2017.

[60] Weissglas, *Arik Sharon*, p. 248; Landau, *Arik*, pp. 491–2; 'The Cabinet Resolution Regarding the Disengagement Plan', *IMFA*, http://mfa.gov.il/MFA/ForeignPolicy/Peac e/MFADocuments/Pages/Revised%20Disengagement%20Plan%206-June-2004.aspx# C, accessed 17 December 2017.

[61] Shavit, 'In the Name of his Client'; Weissglas, *Arik Sharon*, pp. 248–50; Sharon, *Sharon*, p. 503.

The Political Challenges to Disengagement 315

have no desire to permanently rule over millions of Palestinians who double their numbers every generation. Israel', he continued, 'which wishes to be an exemplary democracy, will not be able to bear such a reality over time.' His speech also included a personal and explicit message to the Jewish settler movement, which he charged with developing 'a messianic complex'.[62]

This stinging accusation from Sharon was part of a tactic he had employed throughout the campaign over the disengagement, which hinged on delegitimizing the settler opposition to his plan. The settlers employed the same tactic they had used against Rabin and Barak. The more extreme groups sought to derail the process violently, recalled the then GSS head, Yuval Diskin. There were plans to trigger a regional conflagration that would halt the disengagement by launching a Jewish terror attack on Haram al-Sharif (Temple Mount) in Jerusalem. There was much talk, he continued, about harming Sharon.[63] The settlers hoped, also, to interrupt the disengagement operation by flooding the Gaza Strip with supporters from other parts of the country. Opting for yet a different method, several rabbis issued religious decrees permitting soldiers to refuse an order to evacuate the settlers on D-Day.[64]

Amid the broader public support for the disengagement plan, the settlers were engaged in a rear-guard battle, which made Sharon's poignant charge that they were being 'messianic', effective. When the time came for the Knesset to vote on the disengagement, the majority of Israelis had concluded that the Gaza Strip was a liability. Economically, as Sara Roy shows quite clearly, the Gaza Strip was de-developed and was becoming one of the world's poorest regions.[65] On the military front, the IDF was complaining about defending isolated settlements in the Gaza Strip and the long defence lines necessary to secure the transportation routes to and from the settlements.[66] Demographically, the 9,000-strong Jewish settler community was completely outnumbered by the 1.5 million Palestinian residents of the Gaza Strip. Most importantly, perhaps, for the vast majority of Israelis, the Gaza Strip invoked no religious or

---

[62] 'Prime Minister Ariel Sharon's Address to the Knesset – The Vote on the Disengagement Plan', *IMFA*, www.mfa.gov.il/MFA/PressRoom/2004/Pages/PM%20 Sharon%20Knesset%20speech%20-%20Vote%20on%20Disengagement%20Plan% 2025-Oct-2004.aspx, accessed 18 December 2017.

[63] More, *The Gatekeepers*, pp. 329–30.

[64] Efrat Weis, 'Against Disengagement: Rabbis will Distribute Leaders Calling to Disobey Orders, *Ynet*, www.ynet.co.il/articles/0,7340,L-2886634,00.html; Amos Harel and Nir Hason, 'Yesh Council: We Will Bring Thousands of People into Gush Katif', *Walla*, ne ws.walla.co.il/item/750414, both links accessed 21 February 2018.

[65] Sara Roy, *Failing Peace: Gaza and the Palestinian-Israeli Conflict* (London: Pluto Press, 2007).

[66] See Weissglas meeting with Rice in Rice, *No Higher Honor*, p. 280.

316 The Resurgence of Unilateralism

nationalist sentiments. On these grounds, Sharon's speech comfortably separated him from the settler movement. As Weissglas revealed in an interview, Sharon no longer viewed Gaza as 'an area that Israel has any national interests in'.[67]

The content of Sharon's speech not only reflects the rupture with the Jewish settler movement, it also exhibited Sharon's distance from the right-wing faction of Likud, which was plotting a political coup against him. Binyamin Netanyahu was at the forefront of this effort. In the midst of the charged two-day debate in the Knesset on the disengagement plan, Netanyahu threatened that, unless the prime minister allowed national referendum on the disengagement plan, he, Netanyahu, would vote against it. The National Religious Party, which had four members in the coalition government and represented the Jewish settler movement, issued an identical ultimatum.

Adamant, Sharon would neither budge nor negotiate. Sphinx like, he remained seated at the government table in the parliament as Likud's conspirators plotted to derail his plan via a parliamentary vote. This political melodrama was aired live on Israeli television, leaving the nation transfixed and glued to their screens. Sharon calculated that a centrist-left coalition government of MKs – spanning the Jewish Zionist parties and Palestinian-Israelis – would allow the vote to be passed. This broad coalition, which reflected public support for the disengagement plan, was a hurdle the Likud plotters could not clear. After a debate lasting two days, the unilateral disengagement plan, including compensation for would-be evacuees, was approved on 26 October by a majority of sixty-seven to forty-five, with seven MKs abstaining and one absent due to illness.[68]

Nevertheless, domestic politics and the unilateral disengagement plan remained entangled. The next hurdle Sharon faced was the vote on the annual budget, which became entwined with the politics of disengagement. Shinui, the staunchly anti-clerical centrist coalition partner, refused to the support the 2005 annual budget. It objected to transferring 290 million New Israeli shekels – a modest allurement in relative terms – that had been earmarked for ultra-orthodox *yeshiva*s and schools. Weissglas pleaded with Shinui's leader, Tommy Lapid, to reverse his party's position. Otherwise, he warned, the disengagement plan, which Lapid wholly supported, would collapse under the pressure of the feud over the national budget.[69] The déjà vu of Prime Minister Barak's pleas to

---

[67] Sahvit, 'In the Name of his Client'.

[68] Weissglas, *Arik Sharon*, p. 270; Sharon, *Sharon*, p. 516; Gideon Alon, 'Knesset Approves PM Sharon's Disengagement Plan', *Ha'aretz*, www.haaretz.com/1.4726464, accessed 12 March 2019.

[69] Weissglas, *Arik Sharon*, pp. 253–4; Sharon, *Sharon*, pp. 516–17.

The Political Challenges to Disengagement 317

his junior coalition partner, the left-leaning Meretz, to reconcile its differences with Shas, in the midst of the negotiations with the Palestinians, was inescapable. Shinui, like Meretz before it, would not countenance what it perceived to be a nefarious political bribe. It voted against the first reading of the budget bill, at which point Sharon sacked its five ministers from the government.

This was the background to the invitation from Sharon to the Labour party and Yahadut HaTora, a Lithuanian ultra-orthodox party, to join his coalition government. These two parties would replace Shinui, the National Union and the NRP, which had seceded from the government following the disengagement vote. Sharon's thirty years of experience in Israeli politics and the personal rapport he had developed with his erstwhile political rival, the then head of the Labour party, Shimon Peres, were critical for clinching the deal with Labour. On 10 January 2005, the third Sharon government was sworn in, after an earlier vote of support in the Likud convention.[70] It commanded a majority of sixty-four MKs.

The new structure of the coalition government enabled Sharon to govern amid the rebellion from Likud. The inclusion of Yahadut HaTorah in the coalition government was important in another sense. The ultra-orthodox spiritual leader of Yahadut HaTorah, Rabbi Yosef Shalom Elyashiv, legitimized the disengagement plan by allowing his party to join the coalition government. The respect that the 94-year-old rabbi commanded beyond his own immediate followers, persuaded other clerics, such as Rabbi Ovadia Yosef, the spiritual leader of Shas, not to publicly oppose the unilateral disengagement plan. As a result, only one strand of Orthodox Judaism, the national religious settler movement, publicly and collectively opposed the unilateral disengagement plan. Consequently, the third Sharon government's legitimacy was based on segments of the Jewish ultra-orthodox clerical establishment that had eluded the Rabin and Barak governments.

Sharon and the top echelon of the IDF exploited the legitimacy afforded to the foreign policy shift towards unilateralism, to deploy the police and the IDF against the mass demonstrations being mounted by the settlers. In one particular incident, a group of 30,000 settlers were besieged in the small Israeli village of Kfar Maimon, en route to offering support to the prospective evacuees in the Gaza Strip. The combination of legitimacy and state power crushed the settler's resistance. In the space of eight days, between 15 and 22 August 2005, 9,000 settlers, spread across twenty-one settlements in the Gaza Strip and the IDF's military forces and four small settlements (Ganim, Kadim, Chomesh and Sa-Nur)

---

[70] Weissglas, *Arik Sharon*, pp. 255–7.

318   The Resurgence of Unilateralism

in the north of the West Bank were evacuated. After the wreckers, at the request of the PA, had demolished all the buildings, all that was left standing were the synagogues, emptied of their Torah Arks, pulpits and pews.[71]

A 'Blown Opportunity'?

On 29 October 2004, in the midst of the period leading to the Israel's unilateral disengagement, Yasser Arafat was released from his imprisonment in the *Muqataa*. He was in a visibly critical condition and was flown by a Jordanian helicopter to Amman and, thence, was taken by a French military aircraft to the Percy Military Training Hospital in Clamart, outside Paris. He was diagnosed with a serious blood disorder – disseminated intravascular coagulation (DIC) and nine days later, on 11 November 2004, after suffering a stroke three days earlier, the Palestinian leader died. Rumours circulated that Arafat had been poisoned by the Israelis, who had gained access to him through a member of his entourage. However, no evidence was ever produced while Israel categorically denied the accusations. Moreover, according to Weissglas, he personally had to convince Sharon to grant the release of Arafat based on information he received from his Palestinian contacts; the IDF was arguing that Arafat was suffering from a minor illness. Despite extensive tests, the French doctors never discovered the specific cause of the infection that led to the DIC.[72]

Mahmoud Abbas, who had resigned from the post of prime minister in the previous August, became Arafat's immediate successor. By virtue of his position as number two in the PLO, and founder of the Fatah party, Abbas was nominated president of the PLO Executive Committee and a candidate for PA president. For sixty days, before the elections took place, Rawhi Fattouh, speaker of the PLC, took on the presidency. Shortly, thereafter, during December 2004–January 2005, Abbas contested his first Palestinian elections against six minority candidates. Hamas boycotted the elections on the grounds that they derived from the Oslo agreements, which the Islamic Resistance Movement refused to recognize or legitimate. Following Abbas's victory by 62 per cent of the

---

[71] The PA's request that Israel demolish the buildings and infrastructure in the settlements that were evacuated was to avoid the difficult political decision of how to redistribute the properties among Palestinians. Qurie, *Negotiations in Palestine*, p. 222; Eldar, *Getting to Know Hamas*, p. 132.

[72] 'Q&A: Investigation into Yasser Arafat's Death', *BBC*, www.bbc.co.uk/news/world-middle-east-20512259, accessed 20 December 2017; Qurie, *Negotiations in Palestine*, pp. 186–93; Interview Weissglas.

A 'Blown Opportunity'? 319

votes, the head of the elections monitoring team, former President Jimmy Carter, described the vote as a clear expression of the democratic will of the Palestinian people.[73]

The eminent historian, Avi Shlaim, observed that Abu Mazen 'represented the obliging, nonviolent alternative to Arafat' that Israel had been calling for.[74] Why then did Israel proceed with its unilateralist stance after this well-known, self-professed Palestinian leader was elected Palestinian president? Did Israel, as some American officials thought at the time, 'blow an opportunity' to rekindle the peace process?[75] Theoretically, the death of Arafat could have prompted the Israelis to abandon the road to disengagement and leap immediately towards final status negotiations. In practice, however, this was not a viable foreign policy option. Most crucially, perhaps, because Abu Mazen had not yet consolidated his position, the Palestinians themselves decided 'not to consult with the Israelis over the withdrawal', except on security issues and certain logistical arrangements.[76] They chose to remain 'completely detached' from the disengagement process, which they feared was an Israeli ploy to withdraw from Gaza only to tighten the grip on the West Bank.[77] In the context of consolidating his domestic position following the death of Arafat, the risk of being perceived to be colluding with the Israelis was one Abu Mazen could not afford to take. Abu Mazen had to contend with the Arafat loyalists still in power, lawlessness throughout the Palestinian territories resulting from the breakdown of the security forces, and the political challenge posed by Hamas.[78] The Israelis were aware that Abu Mazen did not want to be associated politically with the disengagement. As Eyal Arad recalls, he was given strict orders to 'disassociate Abu Mazen from the political process accompanying the disengagement plan'.[79]

This was not the only obstacle to using the unilateral withdrawal from Gaza as a springboard to restoring Israel's engagement stance. Veering from the disengagement track would have weakened the political support for his plan that Sharon was assiduously building. In this respect, Aron Miller's assessment, 'that if we pressed Sharon to negotiate Gaza the Israelis would still be there today', seems sound.[80] As we have seen, the wide support of Israeli public opinion was oiling the wheels of the political

---

[73] Grant Rumeley and Amir Tibon, *The Last Palestinian: The Rise and Reign of Mahmoud Abbas* (Amherst: Prometheus Books, 2011), pp. 106–11; Qurie, *Peace Negotiations in Palestine*, pp. 195–6, 203.
[74] Shlaim, *The Iron Wall*, p. 770, 2nd ed.
[75] Miller, *The Much too Promised Land*, p. 355. [76] Interview Weissglas.
[77] Abrams, *Tested by Zion*, p. 120; Qurie, *Peace Negotiations in Palestine*, pp. 163, 211, 218.
[78] Rumley and Tibon, *The Last Palestinian*, pp. 114–15; Qurie, *Peace Negotiations in Palestine*, pp. 227–9.
[79] Interview Arad. [80] Miller, *The Much too Promised Land*, p. 355.

320 The Resurgence of Unilateralism

vehicle advancing the disengagement plan when Sharon was facing his most serious domestic political challenges. This wide public support emanated from the peripheral sentimental, strategic and economic value of Gaza to the majority of Israelis. A return to negotiations over a permanent status agreement, in the midst of the disengagement process, would have evoked the opposition experienced by Rabin and Barak.

Could Sharon have succeeded where his predecessors failed? Perhaps, but he was not willing to take the risk because Arafat's death had not changed his fundamental mistrust of the Palestinians and the Arab world generally. His feelings were shared by his main confidants. For instance, Sharon's biography by his son, Gilad, is replete with pejorative references to 'the Arabs'.[81] Dov Weissglas, while emphasizing that Sharon as a leader had some respect for the Palestinians, recalls two 'slight flaws' the prime minister often cited when referring to them: '[T]hey are murderous and treacherous.'[82] Ze'ev Hever, based on many years of intimacy with the prime minister, maintained that 'a basic assumption of Sharon was that the Arabs are unreliable.'[83] This unremitting mistrust is key to understanding why Sharon did not divert from his unilateral foreign policy course even after the demise of his nemesis, Arafat. While Sharon had met with Abbas and developed a rapport with him and agreed to transfer security back to the PA in the main cities of the West Bank, his distrust of the Palestinians steered him towards maintaining a wholly unilateral position towards the PA.

The Consequences of Unilateralism

The shift to unilateralism towards the Palestinians was born out of the failure of alternative foreign policy paradigms. The collapse of the Camp David summit and the attempts to forge an agreement based on the Clinton parameters, brought an end to the two-state solution paradigm. Similarly, the failed attempt to quash the Palestinian intifada by military might and to enforce regime change via the road map demonstrated the limits to what was achievable using force. After three years of bloodletting, Ariel Sharon reached the conclusion that had been reached by three of his predecessors, Yithak Rabin, Shimon Peres and Ehud Barak: that the status quo with the Palestinians was not supported internationally, was unsustainable demographically and posed a threat to the Jewish and democratic identity of the state. Unilateralism was an attempt to address those same issues that Labour governments had grappled with and with which Sharon himself had been contending since he had assumed power.

---

[81] Sharon, *Sharon*.   [82] Weissglas, *Arik Sharon*, p. 117.
[83] Ze'ev Hever (Zambish) in Shavit, *Disengagement and Beyond*, p. 121.

The Consequences of Unilateralism

With the benefit of hindsight, we can see that implementation of the unilateral disengagement plan had three key consequences. It created a geographical divide between the Palestinian territories in the West Bank and the Gaza Strip, which exacerbated the political and bureaucratic rift that had been developing throughout the al-Aqsa Intifada, between the PA and the Palestinian Islamists. In this respect, the successful implementation of the disengagement from Gaza had significantly weakened the Palestinian National Movement, which, since that point, had been deeply divided split between the PA and Hamas. In this context, Hamas clearly gained politically from the disengagement by arguing that the 'resistance' against the Israelis had driven them out of Gaza, while the negotiations pursued by the PA had yielded no results. However, the Palestinians' ability to pursue the struggle for an independent state as a unified national movement was weakened.

The disengagement from Gaza put an end to an Israeli presence in that part of Mandatory Palestine, but significantly strengthened its hold in the West Bank, a key aim of the disengagement plan.[84] The 14 April 2004 Letter of Assurance, written by President Bush, which was supported by the Quartet, the US Senate and Congress, legitimized the de facto annexation of the main settlement blocks. Furthermore, having withdrawn completely from the Gaza Strip, Israel would able to deploy the IDF even more forcefully in any future confrontation with the Palestinians.

Sharon may have won the battle, but it was far from clear that he had won the domestic political war. The disengagement plan may have been the boldest move since the end of the Cold War to free the country's foreign policy from its grip by the settlers; even left-leaning governments refrained from evacuating settlements. However, while the settler movement was bruised it was by no means defeated. In addition, the long political journey Sharon had embarked on with the launch of his disengagement plan split his own party, Likud. By August 2005, as unilateral disengagement was completed, it was clear that Sharon's leadership of Likud would be perpetually contested. Binyamin Netanyahu, who had resigned on the eve of the disengagement, was ideally placed to carry the anti-Sharon banner. Conscious of the limited time he had available by virtue of his seventy-seven years of age, Sharon remained adamant about the need to move forward – Kadima. Could he quell the opposition in Likud or would he, as he had done in the past, be forced to form a new political framework? The prime minister was presented with an existential political dilemma.

---

[84] Interview Weissglas; Shavit, 'In the Name of his Client'.

Figure 14.1 Soldiers and family in Hebron
A Palestinian family walking by an IDF patrol, in Hebron. Taken 30 October 2001. Courtesy Avi Ohayon, Israel Government Press Office

Figure 14.2 Separation barrier
The separation barrier near the Palestinian village of Baka al-Garbiya in the West Bank. Taken 2 March 2004. Courtesy Moshe Milner, Israel Government Press Office

Figure 14.3 Handshake between Foreign Minister Levy and his Chinese counterpart
Handshake between Chinese Foreign Minister Qian Qichen and Israeli Foreign Minister David Levy following the establishment of diplomatic relations between Israel and China in Beijing. Taken 24 January 1992. Courtesy Ya'acov Sa'ar, Israel Government Press Office

Figure 14.4 Prime Ministers Sharon and Vajpayee
Prime Minister Sharon's (R) meeting with Indian Prime Minister Shri Atal Bihari Vajpayee in New Delhi. Taken 9 September 2003. Courtesy Avi Ohayon, Israel Government Press Office

Figure 14.5 PM Ehud Barak, Chief of Staff Shaul Mofaz and Major General Gabi Ashkenazi
Prime Minister Ehud Barak speaking to soldiers following the IDF's withdrawal from south Lebanon. (R) Chief of Staff Shaul Mofaz and (L) OC of Northern Command Gabi Ashkenazi. Taken 24 May 2000. Courtesy Avi Ohayon, Israel Government Press Office

Figure 14.6 Acting PM Ehud Olmert and Cabinet Secretary Israel Maimon
A special cabinet meeting to approve the appointment of Ehud Olmert as Interim Prime Minister to replace Prime Minister Ariel Sharon, who had fallen into a coma. Taken 11 April 2006. Courtesy Amos Ben Gershom, Israel Government Press OfficeFig

Figure 14.7 Mass demonstration
A mass demonstration at Rabin Square, Tel Aviv, calling for a State Commission of Inquiry regarding the 2006 Lebanon War. Taken 9 September 2006. Courtesy Moshe Milner, Israel Government Press Office

Figure 14.8 Prime Minister Netanyahu and President Barak Obama
Prime Minister's Binyamin Netanyahu visit in Washington to start direct negotiations between Israel and the Palestinian National Authority. Taken 1 September 2010. Courtesy Israel Government Press Office

15   Events Dear Boy, Events

Following the unilateral withdrawal from the Gaza Strip, the opposition to Ariel Sharon from within Likud mounted. Yet Sharon was determined to maintain the political initiative. On 21 November 2005, he left Likud to form a new party, Kadima or Forward, causing political upheaval. Since 1977, Likud and Labour had dominated Israeli politics. Now, emboldened by the unilateral withdrawal and Sharon's national stature, Kadima was set to emerge as Israel's largest party in the 28 March 2006 national elections. However, Ariel Sharon's term ended abruptly on 4 January 2006, when he suffered a massive stroke, which left him in a vegetative state.[1] His enduring legacies remain the brutal suppression of the al-Aqsa Intifada and Israel's unilateral withdrawal from the Gaza Strip.

Deputy Prime Minister Ehud Olmert was nominated acting prime minister and leader of Kadima. Olmert was born in Nachlat Jabotinsky to a staunch Zionist-Revisionist family. He rose to the highest position in the land as a career politician. In 1974, he became the youngest MK ever to be elected to parliament. As his political career evolved, Olmert was associated to a group of prominent Likud MKs that included Benny Begin, Tzipi Livni, Dan Meridor and Binyamin Netanyahu. They were described as 'princes' based on the leading roles played by their parents' in the pre-state Revisionist-Zionist movement.[2] Olmert's father, Mordechai, had been a member of the Irgun and Menachem Begin's Herut Party.[3]

When Ehud Olmert was appointed prime minister, on 4 May 2006, he had experience of numerous ministerial positions and had held the posts of deputy prime minister and acting prime minister.[4] In addition to his

---

[1] Shlaim, *The Iron Wall*, 2nd ed., p. 792; Michal Shamir, Raphael Ventura, Asher Arian and Orit Kedar, 'Kadima', in Asher Arian and Michal Shamir, *The Elections in Israel 2006* (New York: Transaction Publishers, 2008), p. 15.

[2] Gil Samsonov, *The Princes: How Did the Sons of the Warrior Family Conquer the Leadership of the State* (Or Yehuda: Kineret, Zmora-Bitan, 2015), pp. 32–9, 44–5, 98, 109–18 (in Hebrew).

[3] Samsonov, *The Princes*, p. 97.

[4] Knesset official website, http://main.knesset.gov.il/mk/Pages/MKGovRoles.aspx?MKID=3, accessed 20 February 2018.

The Foreign Policy Decision-Making Circle 327

ministerial experience, he had political decision-making skills and in-depth knowledge of Israeli politics, governance and bureaucracy. For most of his career, Olmert identified strongly with Revisionist-Zionism's Greater Israel ideology. He was so strongly committed to it that he voted against the 1979 Camp David agreements with Egypt and evacuation of the Jewish settlements in Sinai.[5]

In 1993, Olmert was elected mayor of Jerusalem, a post he held for the next decade. This period, as he explains, triggered in him a dramatic political shift:

What led me to move away from my position within the Israeli right to the moderate political centre was a process of sobering up. When I was mayor, we were talking about integrating 250,000 Palestinians [of East Jerusalem] and about the unity of the city. We were talking about Jews and Palestinians living together in Jerusalem, which is a precondition for anyone who subscribes to the Greater Israel ethos involving annexing the territories. And yet, I saw that where it is most sensitive, most necessary, and most significant, precisely the opposite was happening and that this will never change. In Jerusalem we are destined to live with the Arabs as second class citizens and we can't do anything about it. We are unwilling to pay the political and the economic price so that East Jerusalem will be like the rest of Israel ... I would often ask myself as mayor ... what does it mean that the city is unified and in what ways? Actually, there is no connection between the people who live in the western and eastern parts of the city. It is all fake, deception, a lie.

Like his predecessor, Ariel Sharon, Olmert was a once ardent supporter of the Greater Israel ideology, who, over time, became committed to the idea that the Israeli occupation should be scaled down.

The Foreign Policy Decision-Making Circle

The 2006 election result defined the foreign policy decision-making circle surrounding Ehud Olmert. His Kadima party achieved twenty-nine votes while Labour and Likud won nineteen and twelve seats, respectively. This clear fragmentation of domestic Israeli politics compelled Olmert to form a coalition government that included sixty-seven MK. Its seven-MK majority included Kadima, Labour, Shas and the new Pensioners' Party.[6]

The composition of the coalition government, which eschewed parties from the nationalist and religious Israeli right, was intentionally designed by Olmert in line with the foreign policy agenda he had presented during his election campaign. In relation to the Palestinians, Olmert argued that

---

[5] Samsonov, *The Princes*, p. 144.
[6] Knesset official website, http://main.knesset.gov.il/About/History/Pages/FactionHistor y17.aspx, accessed 5 March 2018.

328   Events Dear Boy, Events

Israel 'must establish a border as soon as possible that will reflect the demographic reality on the ground'.[7] Olmert vowed to resume negotiations with the Palestinians to end the conflict, promising that, should these fail, he would act unilaterally and implement his Hitkansut or convergence plan. Hitkansut hinged on a unilateral Israeli withdrawal from 90 per cent of the West Bank and parts of Jerusalem, and the establishment of a permanent border based on the barrier fence that Israel had been constructing since the 2002 wave of terrorist attacks. The notion of the wall forming a barrier between Israel and the Palestinians, which was mooted in the first Sharon government by the Labour party, now became central to Ehud Olmert's policy towards the Palestinians. Like Barak and Sharon before him, Olmert intended to obtain international support for his unilateral action.[8]

By his own admission, Olmert lacked Ariel Sharon's 'halo of a hero' and this affected his authority over his senior ministers.[9] Foreign Minister Tzipi Livni never fully accepted Olmert's rise to the premiership, despite his having led Kadima to an election victory. 'She clearly dreamed to replace me', wrote Olmert in his memoirs, describing Livni as 'lacking in leadership and decision-making ability'.[10]

The conflict between the prime minister and his Defence Minister, Amir Peretz, was political rather than personal. Peretz emerged into Israeli politics as a dovish MK and a dynamic Labour union leader. His appointment as leader of the Labour party was the first time a major political party had nominated a Sephardi candidate for the post of prime minister.[11] However, Peretz never achieved a ministerial position, which is why he found Ehud Olmert's offer of the defence portfolio extremely tempting. A successful term would have supported his contestation for the position of prime minister in the next elections. Keen to bolster his political credentials, Peretz accepted, but blinded by his ambition, refused to appoint a deputy despite his profound lack of experience.

The leading foreign policy troika – Prime Minister Olmert, Defence Minister Peretz and Foreign Minister Livni – was distinctive in its limited

---

[7] 'Transcript of Acting Prime Minister Ehud Olmert's Speech at the Hertzliya Conference', 4 February, 2006, *Ha'aretz*, www.haaretz.co.il/misc/1.1080167, accessed 20 February 2018.

[8] Nachum Barnea and Shimon Shifer, 'These Are my Borders', *Yedioth Ahronoth*, 10 March, 2006 (in Hebrew); Abrams, *Tested By Zion*, pp. 170–2; see also the speech by Olmert on introducing his government, 'Knesset Protocol', 4 May 2006, pp. 16–19 (in Hebrew); Ehud Olmert, *In Person* (Miskal-Yedioth Ahronoth, 2018), p. 658 (in Hebrew).

[9] Olmert, *In Person*, p. 653.   [10] Olmert, *In Person*, p. 11.

[11] Arian and Shamir, *The Elections in Israel 2006*, p. 4; 'MK Amir Peretz', Knesset official website, http://main.knesset.gov.il/mk/pages/MkPersonalPrint.aspx?MKID=105, accessed 26 February 2019.

foreign policy and security decision-making experience. The problem was exacerbated by Olmert's sidelining of veteran foreign policymakers, whom, he suspected, might challenge his authority. Former Defence Minister and IDF Chief of Staff Shaul Mofaz and the veteran Shimon Peres were both given marginal ministerial portfolios.[12]

The personal and political friction between Olmert and his senior ministers meant that the prime minister was threatened politically by his own cabinet, which he preferred not to use for foreign policy formulation. Olmert was more inclined to deliberate over foreign policy with his inner circle. Its most senior members were Chief of Staff Dr Yoram Turbowics, a doctoral graduate from Harvard, a former trade restrictions authority commissioner and a successful businessman.[13] Shalom Tourgeman, one of Ariel Sharon's chief foreign policy advisors, maintained this role in Ehud Olmert's inner circle.[14]

From Containment to War

Summer 2006 significantly tested Israel's leading foreign policy decision-makers. On 25 June, members of three Palestinian cells – Hamas, the Popular Resistance Committees and the Army of Islam – tunnelled from Gaza into Israel, killed two soldiers and kidnapped Corporal Gilad Shalit.[15] Less than three weeks later, on 12 July, under cover of heavy shelling, a Hezbollah fighter unit ambushed an IDF patrol on the northern border, killing three Israeli soldiers, wounding two and kidnapping Ehud Goldwasser and Eldad Regev. Two hours after the attack an Israeli Merkava tank went in pursuit of the kidnapped soldiers, but hit a landmine which killed its crew of four.[16]

---

[12] Knesset official website, http://main.knesset.gov.il/mk/Pages/MKGovRoles.aspx?MKID=720; Knesset official website, http://main.knesset.gov.il/mk/Pages/MKGovRoles.aspx?MKID=104, both accessed 20 February 2018.
[13] Amira Lam, 'Olmert's Right Hand Man', *Ynet*, www.ynetnews.com/articles/1,7340,L-3285552,00.html, accessed 19 February 2018.
[14] Interview Olmert; Lam, 'Olmert's Right Hand Man'.
[15] Amos Harel and Nir Hason, 'The Abduction of Gilad Shalit Stage by Stage', *Ha'aretz*, www.haaretz.co.il/news/politics/1.1267807, accessed 20 April 2018.
[16] The dramatic events of 12 July led Israel into what came to be known as the 2006 Lebanon War. Two reports prepared by a government-appointed commission of enquiry following the war, the Winograd Commission, and the testimonies given to the commission, were made publicly available. The reports and most of the testimonies are available on the Winograd Commission website, www.vaadatwino.gov.il (in Hebrew). The documents were retrieved from the website on 19 July 2017. The events of 12 July are described in the Winograd interim report, p. 11. The Winograd Commission was authorized to investigate the performance of the political and military echelons in relation to all aspects of the war. These included the decision to go to war, its management by the top political and security brass, the readiness of the IDF, the military achievements, the

330   Events Dear Boy, Events

The 12 July Hezbollah attack was part of a policy towards Israel, post the 2000 unilateral withdrawal, to maintain a low-intensity conflict. Hezbollah variously justified its attacks on military and civilian targets as deterring Israel; putting pressure on Israel to release Lebanese prisoners; and contributing to the effort to 'liberate' the Shebaa Farms, a small strip of disputed land at the intersection of the Syria-Lebanon-Israel border. Hezbollah maintained that Israel must withdraw its forces from the Shebaa Farms, which, Hezbollah argued, were on Lebanese territory. By contrast and challenging Hezbollah's claims, UN maps show that the farms were on the Syrian side of the border, which meant that Israel had complied with the conditions laid down by UNSCR 425 of fully withdrawing its forces from Lebanon.[17]

Israel adopted a policy of containment towards Hezbollah, which, its proponents argued, placed Hezbollah in a bind. Up to the IDF's unilateral withdrawal in 2000, the Lebanese government had deemed Hezbollah's armed struggle against the IDF national resistance.[18] However, following the IDF's withdrawal, various groups in Lebanon demanded Hezbollah halt its attacks on Israel and disarm.[19]

These internal challenges were compounded by external pressures. In September 2004, the USA and France initiated UNSCR 1559, calling for a 'disbanding and disarmament of all Lebanese and non-Lebanese militias' in accordance with the 1990 Ta'if agreement, which ended the Lebanese civil war.[20] In addition to Hezbollah, the Resolution referred

attention to the civilian rear and the ending of the war. See Winograd interim report, p. 13.

[17] Augustus R. Norton, *Hezbollah: A Short History* (Princeton: Princeton University Press, 2007), pp. 92–3; D. Sobleman, 'Four Years after the Withdrawal from Lebanon: Refining the Rules of the Game', *Strategic Assessment*, 7, 2 (2004): 31, www.inss.org.il/wp-content/u ploads/systemfiles/Four%20Years%20after%20the%20Withdrawal%20from%20Lebanon %20Refining%20the%20Rules%20of%20the%20Game.pdf, accessed 19 March 2019; details of the attacks are available at 'Main Events on the Israeli-Lebanese Border since the IDF Withdrawal', *IMFA*, www.mfa.gov.il/MFA/MFAArchive/2000_2009/2003/8/Mai n%20Events%20on%20the%20Israel-Lebanese%20Border%20since%20th; 'Resolution 425 Israel-Lebanon', United Nations official website, http://unscr.com/en/resolutions/425, both links accessed 13 July 2018.

[18] Eyal Zisser, 'Hezbollah: Between Armed Struggle and Domestic Politics', in Barry Rubin (ed.), *Revolutionaries and Reformers: Contemporary Islamic Movements in the Middle East* (New York: State University of New York Press, 2003)', pp. 91–6; Krista E. Wiegand, 'Reformation of a Terrorist Group: Hezbollah as a Lebanese Political Party', *Studies in Conflict and Terrorism*, 32, 2019: 675.

[19] For example, Gibran Tueni quoted in Norton, *Hezbollah*, p. 118; Walid Junblat, leader of the Lebanese Druze and *al-Mustakbal*, the newspaper of Lebanon's then prime minister, Rafiq al-Hariri, also criticized Hezbollah; see Eyal Zisser, 'Hezbollah and Israel: Strategic Threat on the Northern Border', *Israel Affairs*, 12, 1, 2006: 98.

[20] 'Security Council Resolution 1559', UN official website, http://daccess-dds-ny.un.org/doc/ UNDOC/GEN/N04/498/92/PDF/N0449892.pdf?OpenElement, accessed 17 November 2009.

From Containment to War 331

to the 30,000 strong Syrian military force that had been present in Lebanon since 1976. US and French pressure mounted, especially following the assassination of Lebanese Prime Minister, Rafiq al-Hariri, on 14 February 2005, in which Syria and Hezbollah were implicated. Finally, on 29 April 2005, following a presence of twenty-nine years, Bashar al-Assad withdrew the entire Syrian military contingent from Lebanon.[21]

Israel's containment foreign policy stance was designed to exacerbate these internal and external tensions, which the Israelis believed tempered Hezbollah's behaviour and, ultimately, would force it to disarm.[22] Containment also enabled Israel to avoid opening a 'second front' against Hezbollah during the al-Aqsa Intifada.[23] Nevertheless, containment attracted criticism, which was championed by then IDF Chief of Staff, Dan Haloutz. Critics of containment argued that it eroded Israeli deterrence, allowed Hezbollah to strengthen its military capabilities uninterrupted, deploy its forces right across the Israeli border, train and fund Palestinian organizations.[24] Haloutz, who was keen to terminate containment, had voiced his reservations to Prime Minister Olmert, in March 2006.[25]

Against the background of this charged debate, the Israeli government convened on 12 July 2006 at 20:00, to discuss how to respond to Hezbollah's most recent attack. Following a two-and-half-hour session, the government authorized a large-scale IAF reprisal operation, code-named Specific Gravity, which was carried out that night.[26] In the space of thirty-five minutes, Israeli jets had destroyed most of Hezbollah's long-range rocket launchers. On 14 July, the IAF bombarded the Dahia compound in southern Beirut, which, according to IDF reports, housed Hezbollah's command centre. Concurrently, Israel imposed a sea blockade on Lebanon and bombed parts of Beirut's International Airport and the Beirut-Damascus highway.

---

[21] 'Syrian Troops Leave Lebanon after 29 Years Occupation', www.nytimes.com/2005/04/26/international/middleeast/syrian-troops-leave-lebanon-after-29year-occupation.html, accessed 17 April 2018; Bush, *Decision Points*, p. 411.

[22] Ya'alon, *Longer Shorter Way*, p. 214

[23] Winograd interim report, p. 44; Shaul Mofaz testimony to the Winograd Commission, p. 7.

[24] Weissglas, pp. 19–20; Binyamin Ben-Eliezer, 'Testimony to the Winograd Commission', Winograd interim report, pp. 39, 40, 45–6.

[25] Winograd interim report, p. 45.

[26] My account of the 2006 Lebanon War is derived from a number of sources. They include Avi Kober, 'The Israel Defense Forces in the 2006 Lebanon War: Why the Poor Performance? *Journal of Strategic Studies*, 31, 1, 2008: 1–8; Ofer Shelah and Yoav Limor, *Captives in Lebanon* (Tel Aviv: Miskal-Yedioth Ahronoth, 2007) (in Hebrew); Amos Harel Avi Issacharoff, *Spider Webs (34 Days)* (Tel Aviv: Miskal-Yedioth Ahronoth, 2008) (in Hebrew); for a useful table of the main events during the war, see Winograd interim report, pp. 156–64.

332   Events Dear Boy, Events

After two days of conflict, Israel was at a critical juncture. On 15 July, Fuad Siniora, then Prime Minister of Lebanon, proposed a ceasefire. Israel rejected the proposal on the grounds that it would merely restore the status quo ante that, initially, had led to the confrontation. This paved the way to a serious diversion from the original government decision. Foreign Minister Livni explained that: '[A]s far as I was concerned on 12 July we embarked upon an operation, which was due to end on the same night or at the latest by noon the following day.'[27]

These factors notwithstanding, on 17 July 2006, Prime Minister Olmert delivered a defining speech in the Knesset, scaling up the large-scale reprisal government had approved on 12 July to full-blown war; the government neither voted on nor approved this. 'When missiles are launched at our residents', stated Olmert, 'our answer will be war with all the strength, determination, valour, sacrifice and dedication that characterizes this nation.'[28] The ensuing communiqué from the political-security cabinet outlined Israel's conditions for ending the conflict. They included unconditional release of abducted soldiers; a halt to the rocket attacks on Israeli targets; and full and complete implementation of UNSCR 1559 including disarming of all armed militias, extension of the sovereignty of the Lebanese government over all its territory and deployment of the Lebanese army along the border with Israel.[29]

The shift from a large-scale military reprisal to full-blown conflict launched the second phase of the 2006 Israel-Hezbollah confrontation. During the next two weeks, Israel used the IAF and limited ground forces, mostly Special Forces, to damage Hezbollah's military capabilities and remove its presence from across the Israeli border. Hezbollah, which anticipated Israel's military tactics, withstood the offensive and continued to launch hundreds of rockets daily into Israel. Its fighters used simple, but effective anti-tank and anti-ship missile, and guerrilla hit-and-run and evasion tactics, which benefited from Hezbollah's familiarity with the terrain and the population. Hezbollah's concealed bunker system – the so-called nature reserves – remained intact and the organization's decentralized command and control system continued operating. 'I cannot see how the army creates for me the victory I need', Olmert solemnly remarked to his top security brass, in a closed meeting nine days into

[27] Livni testimony before the Winograd Commission, p. 4.
[28] 'Prime Minister's Olmert Address to the Knesset During the Conflict in the North', PMO official website, www.knesset.gov.il/docs/eng/olmertspeech2006_eng.htm, accessed 9 March 2018.
[29] 'Political-Security Cabinet Communiqué', *IMFA*, http://mfa.gov.il/MFA/PressRoo m/2006/Pages/Political-Security%20Cabinet%20communique%2019-Jul-2006.aspx, accessed 3 May 2018.

From Containment to War 333

the conflict.[30] A week later, Chief of Staff Haloutz was hospitalized for a few hours with severe stomach pains, which may have reflected the immense stress he was under given the IDF's unconvincing performance.[31]

The third and last stage of the conflict began on 5 August, with the Israeli decision to prepare for a large-scale ground offensive involving three divisions.[32] The military aim of the plan was to reduce Hezbollah's rocket-launching capability by seizing, within ninety-six hours, the area between the Israeli border and the Litani River. Subsequently, the IDF would need four to six weeks to clear the area of Hezbollah presence.[33] On 9 August, the plan was put before the Israeli cabinet, which faced a tough choice: rejecting the only plan presented by the IDF or approving it. It reluctantly chose the latter. Several ministers, including the prime minister, were uneasy about authorizing a ground offensive since deliberations in the UN over the terms of the ceasefire seemed to have entered their final stages.[34]

Prime Minister Olmert hoped a UNSCR, favourable to Israeli demands, could be achieved without a large-scale ground offensive, which is why he delayed authorization of the ground operation. However, Defence Minister Peretz and IDF Chief of Staff Haloutz were keen for the attack to begin, believing it would put pressure on the UNSC deliberations. A UNSCR draft received by Israel on 11 August cast the die. Chief Israeli negotiator, Shalom Tourgeman, deemed it a 'disaster' and 'a victory for Hezbollah and a loss for Israel'.[35] Agonized, Olmert authorized the major ground offensive, on Friday 11 August at 16:00, with the intention of swaying the diplomatic discussions in Israel's favour. As Haloutz explained, 'a wider maneuver by us will serve our diplomatic efforts because it clarifies ... that there are some lines that we are not prepared to compromise upon and we are moving forward.'[36]

Israel's final ground manoeuvre at the end of the war was a military failure. The IDF failed to gain control over the area between the Israeli border and the Litani River. Meanwhile, Hezbollah held strong and continued daily to launch salvos of rockets into Israel until the war ended.[37] However, it seemed to have influenced diplomacy. According

---

[30] Winograd final report, p. 98. [31] Winograd final report, p. 128.

[32] For a detailed analysis of the ground offensive, see Winograd final report, pp. 377–92.

[33] Winograd final report, pp. 176, 178, 377, 520.

[34] Winograd final report, pp. 141, 172, 180, 531–3; Olmert, *In Person*, p. 724.

[35] Winograd final report, pp. 197, 202; Foreign Minister Livni testimony, p. 57; Haloutz, *Straightforward*, p. 462.

[36] Winograd final report, pp. 202–3; Defence Minister Peretz pursued the same line of argument in his meeting with Olmert on the same day; Winograd final report, p. 201.

[37] Winograd final report, p. 535.

334 Events Dear Boy, Events

to the Winograd Commission, the changes made to the draft resolution, received by Israel on 11 August and UNSCR 1701, which ended the war, helped to ensure that some of Israel's key demands were met.[38] Most importantly, UNSCR 1701 established that the area between the Israeli border and the Litani River was a buffer zone 'free of any armed personnel assets and weapons other than those of the Government of Lebanon and of UNIFIL'.[39] The buffer zone would be controlled by a 15,000-strong Lebanese army force and a UNIFIL contingent, operating under Chapter VI of the UN Charter, which authorized use of peaceful means to uphold the terms of the ceasefire.[40] Thus, Hezbollah was prevented from returning to the positions it held prior to the war across the border. In addition, the large ground offensive may well have pushed the Lebanese government to accept UNSCR 1701 and Hezbollah's decision to respect the ceasefire when it came into force at 08:00 on 14 August.[41]

Hindsight allows a clearer picture of the 2006 Lebanon War. It was a war of choice initiated by Israel, which fought under unprecedentedly favourable conditions. The IAF had superiority in the air. Israel did not face a conventional army since Syria was deliberately kept out of the war.[42] The Israeli government received domestic support and, during the initial phases of the war, from Western countries and pro-Western Arab states. Admittedly, international support reduced significantly following an IDF air strike on the village of Qana on 30 July 2006, which killed twenty-eight civilians, half of them children.[43]

Israel achieved some gains from the war. From its ending to the time of writing (May 2020), Hezbollah has not launched any cross-border attacks on Israel. A comment from Hezbollah's General Secretary, Hassan Nasserallah, immediately after the war, to the effect that he would not have ordered the kidnapping of the Israeli soldiers had he known Israel's reaction would be so fierce was significant. It suggests that Israeli deterrence played a part in Hezbollah's restraint towards Israel since 2006.[44] However, other factors besides Israeli deterrence were also at play. Since the beginning of the Syrian civil war in 2011, Hezbollah had diverted

---

[38] Winograd final report, p. 537.
[39] 'Security Council Calls for End to Hostilities between Hezbollah, Israel, Unanimously Adopting Resolution 1701', www.un.org/press/en/2006/sc8808.doc.htm, accessed 9 March 2018.
[40] Ibid.   [41] Winograd final report, p. 567.   [42] Haloutz, *Straightforward*, p. 460.
[43] See 'Statement by Group of 8 Leaders-G-8 Summit 2006, *IMFA*, http://mfa.gov.il/MF A/MFA-Archive/2006/Pages/Statement%20by%20Group%20of%20Eight%20Leaders %20-%20G-8%20Summit%202006%2016-Jul-2006.aspx, accessed 17 April 2018; Haloutz, *Straightforward*, p. 393; Winograd Final Report, pp. 88, 119; Abrams, *Tried by Zion*, pp. 186–188; Olmert, *In Person*, pp. 693, 716; Rice, *No Higher Honor*, p. 477.
[44] Nasserallah: 'Soldiers Abductions a Mistake, *CNN*, http://edition.cnn.com/2006/WOR LD/meast/08/27/mideast.nasrallah/, accessed 27 April 2018.

From Containment to War   335

significant resources and attention from its conflict with Israel to the civil war by supporting the brutal repression of the Syrian uprising by the Bashar al-Assad regime.

Alongside these achievements, the war exposed numerous and profound failures. Forty-four Israeli civilians and 119 IDF soldiers were killed, 300,000 residents were displaced and more than 1 million people were forced to live in shelters. Almost one-third of Israel's population – over 2 million people – were exposed directly to the threat posed by the 4,000 missiles that Hezbollah fired into Israeli territory.[45] Indeed, as summarized by the Winograd commission: '*[F]or the first time in the history of the wars of Israel, a war Israel was involved in ended without a clear military victory . . . A semi military organization of a few thousand fighters withstood for weeks the attack by the strongest army in the Middle East.*'[46]

Across the border, at least 1,109 Lebanese were killed by Israeli attacks, 4,399 were injured, and an estimated 1 million were displaced.[47] Israeli bombings, which included illegal use of cluster and phosphorous bombs, affected civilian life for a considerable period after the war, while Lebanon's infrastructure was seriously damaged.[48] With regard to Hezbollah, it is clear that it recovered from the war. Elliot Abrams and others report that, although UNSCR 1701 called for full control of the Lebanese territory by the government of Lebanon and the Lebanese army, Hezbollah remained the dominant force in south Lebanon. It replenished its rocket arsenal through shipments from Iran and Syria, despite UNSCR 1701 declaring there should be no supplying of arms without authorization from the Lebanon government. UNIFIL, as might have been expected, was ineffective in resisting Hezbollah's contraventions of UNSCR 1701 and previous UNSCR resolutions, which called for the disbanding and disarming of all Lebanese and non-Lebanese militias.[49]

---

[45] 'Israel-Hezbollah Conflict: Victims of Rocket Attacks and IDF Casualties', *IMFA*, www.mfa.gov.il/mfa/foreignpolicy/terrorism/hizbullah/pages/israel-hizbullah%20conflict-%20victims%20of%20rocket%20attacks%20and%20idf%20casualties%20july-aug%202006.aspx; 'The 2006 Lebanon War', *IMFA*, http://mfa.gov.il/MFA/ForeignPolicy/Terrorism/Hizbullah/Pages/Hizbullah%20attack%20in%20northern%20Israel%20and%20Israels%20response%2012-Jul-2006.aspx both links accessed 27 March 2018.
[46] Winograd interim report, p. 11, emphasis in original.
[47] 'Why They Died: Civilian Casualties in Lebanon During the 2006 War', *Human Rights Watch*, www.hrw.org/report/2007/09/05/why-they-died/civilian-casualties-lebanon-during-2006-war, accessed 9 March 2018.
[48] 'Factbox: Costs of War and Recovery in Lebanon and Israel', *Reuters*, www.reuters.com/article/us-lebanon-war-cost/factbox-costs-of-war-and-recovery-in-lebanon-and-israel-idUSL0822571220070709, accessed 27 March 2018.
[49] Abrams, *Tried by Zion*, p. 189; Ya'alon, *Longer Shorter Way*, p. 215; Olmert, *In Person*, p. 710; see UNSCR 1559 and UNSCR 1680, which was adopted on 17 May, 2006, 'Resolution 1680', http://unscr.com/en/resolutions/1680, accessed 7 May 2018; Foreign

336   Events Dear Boy, Events

Explaining a Botched War of Choice

Thus, in the final analysis, Israel botched the 2006 Lebanon War. To a certain extent, long-term processes determined the poor result. During the previous two decades, the IDF had become, primarily, a policing force in the occupied territories and suffered from budget cuts.[50] As a result, its fighting capabilities were weakened significantly and its stockpiles were neglected. This was evident most acutely in the reserve units, which arrived on the Lebanese battlefield undertrained and lacking equipment and basic supplies.[51]

The weakening of the IDF's combat capabilities was compounded by a profound change in its military doctrine. Traditionally, the IDF based its military doctrine on ground manoeuvres aimed at swiftly transferring the war into the enemy's territory to minimize exposure of the Israeli rear.[52] However, following the US-led campaigns in Iraq (1991, 2003) and the Balkan Wars of the mid-1990s, the IDF adopted a new doctrine: revolutions in military affairs (RAM). The RAM doctrine, of which Chief of Staff Haloutz was one of the chief proponents, maintained that precision firepower would allow for swift campaigns with relatively low numbers of combat casualties.[53] Notably, in Iraq and the Balkans, the US-led military forces faced standing armies, which did not pose a threat to the civilian populations of the attacking forces. By contrast, in Lebanon Israel faced a 'populist-based guerrilla group, entrenched in densely populated civilian areas', which used well-hidden and mobile rocket launchers to bombard civilians.[54] The 2006 Lebanon War demonstrated the flaws in extrapolating the RAM doctrine to other combat arenas.

Application of RAM to the conflict with Hezbollah cannot be understood without considering the legacy of Israel's first Lebanon war in 1982. The anxiety about entering another Lebanese quagmire was a key consideration in Haloutz's, Peretz's and Olmert's preference for firepower and resistance rather than a large ground manoeuvre.[55] The potential for high casualty rates, involvement in a prolonged guerrilla war and

---

Minister Livni testimony before the Winograd Commission, p. 5; Rice, *No Higher Honor*, p. 494.

[50] Winograd final report, p. 247.

[51] Kover, 'The IDF in the 2006 Lebanon War', p. 30; Asaf Siniver and Jeffrey Collins, 'Airpower and Quagmire: Historical Analogies and the 2006 Lebanon War', *Foreign Policy Analysis*, 11, 2, 2015: 222; Olmert, *In Person*, p. 735; Winograd final report, p. 253

[52] Winograd final report, p. 253.

[53] Winograd final report, pp. 273–4; Siniver, 'Airpower and Quagmire', p. 221.

[54] On the influence of RAM, see Kover, 'The IDF in the 2006 Lebanon War', 17–22.

[55] Haloutz, *Straightforward*, pp. 376, 378; Winograd interim report, p. 61; Winograd final report, pp. 82, 90, 106, 125; Amir Peretz testimony before the Winograd Commission, p. 56; Olmert, *In Person*, p. 679.

Explaining a Botched War of Choice

reoccupation of Southern Lebanon as well as fears that Israeli society was unwilling to pay these prices were compelling reasons against a large ground offensive.[56] Thus, the thrust of the IDF's war effort consisted of massive firepower and short-term individual 'raids', which caused some damage to Hezbollah's forces and infrastructure, but did not have a decisive influence on the battlefield.[57]

These long-term processes influencing the IDF certainly affected the outcome of the 2006 Lebanon War. However, the fateful decisions taken by Israel's primary decision-makers were also crucial. The scathing language in the Winograd Commission report portrays Ehud Olmert, Amir Peretz and Chief of Staff Haloutz as possessing significant decision-making autonomy. The formal foreign policy and security forums operating during the war – government, the cabinet, the inner war cabinet and the IDF general staff – were rarely convened and, thus, were marginalized. Fear of the deliberations being leaked by participants and by the IDF was the main reason for not exploiting these fora.[58] Cabinet met only three times during the war, with the first meeting held two weeks into the war.[59] The IDF general staff convened only once, on 12 July.[60] The inner war cabinet met twice during the war compared to daily and sometimes twice-daily meetings during previous wars.[61] Consequently, the most experienced Israeli decision-makers, such as former Chief of Staff Mofaz and veteran Shimon Peres, had little influence on the course of the confrontation.

The government, which was convened only to authorize military reaction to the 12 July attacks and resolution 1701, was not privy to the deliberations over key decisions.[62] Yitzhak Hertzog, who had served as cabinet secretary previous to his various ministerial positions in the Olmert government, elaborated on this in his testimony to the Winograd Commission:

The decisive part of the decision-making process, which we are not part of, is undoubtedly before the government meeting. I have no idea how it took place, nor at what level did the deliberations take place. In the [government] meeting we talk, we take a decision, hear the briefings, but everything is by then very well cooked. There is no real dialogue ... things are done in a rush because, ultimately, whoever wants to pass the decision in the government knows what he wants. He dictates the decision in his spirit, because he is the leader of the people.[63]

---

[56] Winograd final report, p. 526.   [57] Winograd final report, pp. 313, 520, 551.

[58] Livni testimony before the Winograd Commission, p. 29, 34; Olmert testimony before the Winograd Commission, pp. 36, 39; Haloutz, *Straightforward*, pp. 472–3.

[59] Winograd final report, pp. 160, 516–17.   [60] Winograd final report, pp. 296, 408.

[61] Winograd final report, p. 573.   [62] Winograd final report, p. 517.

[63] Winograd interim report, p. 78.

338   Events Dear Boy, Events

Shimon Peres, who participated in the critical decision-making fora during the war, concurred. He observed that 'there has always been a preliminary discussion between the Prime Minister, the Defence Minister, and the military, so what was brought before the cabinet [or the government] was to some extent cooked.'[64] The defence minister and the prime minister, Peres continued, 'are the key decision-makers and the dominant politicians in the coalition-government, so if they come with a focused proposal, it is very difficult to move one of them, they are tied.'[65]

Crucially, the deliberations within the leading Israeli troika to which Hertzog and Peres referred were marked by an internal imbalance in favour of Haloutz. He was the only person with a proven track record in security, which is why he emerged as the driver of Israel's response to the 12 July attacks and the ensuing war. Less than three hours after the 12 July attacks, Haloutz had taken the lead. He argued that the kidnapping of the two IDF soldiers, the shelling of the Israeli northern border and the abduction of Gilad Shalit were linked and insisted that Hezbollah had escalated the conflict.[66] During his initial meetings with his defence minister, Haloutz was already urging Peretz to 'bang on the table in the hardest possible way and where it hurts the most' and 'take a number of aggressive measures to establish new rules of the game' with Lebanon.[67] To Prime Minister Olmert, Haloutz made a particularly extreme proposal, namely, 'to bomb Lebanon back to the stone age'.[68] This astonishing recommendation was based on the unproven assumption that collective punishment was the most effective to deal with the threat posed by Hezbollah's rockets.[69] Pressure from the Americans would seem to be the main reason why Olmert and Peretz rejected Haloutz's extreme proposal. As Condoleezza Rice explained: '[W]e agreed to press the Israelis on all fronts to refrain from attacks that punished our allies in Beirut.'[70] Rice was referring to the Lebanese government of Fuad Siniora, which the USA perceived as critical to pursuit of its freedom agenda – a policy that called for democratization of the Arab world as a means to prevent terrorism.[71]

Olmert and Peretz did not challenge the chief of staff's underlying premise that Israel should respond forcefully to the 12 July attacks and

---

[64] Winograd interim report, p. 81.
[65] Winograd interim report, p. 81; Peres testimony before the Winograd Commission, p. 12.
[66] Defence Minister Peretz testimony before the Winograd Commission, pp. 15–16.
[67] Winograd interim report, p. 69.   [68] Olmert, *In Person*, p. 695.
[69] Haloutz, *Straightforward*, p. 443.
[70] Rice, *No Higher Honor*, pp. 481, 491; Haloutz, *Straightforward*, p. 453.
[71] Rice, *No Higher Honor*, p. 491.

Explaining a Botched War of Choice 339

abandon containment.[72] The prime minister and his defence minister, having very limited foreign policy or security experience, were overly reliant on the IDF chief of staff. Bewilderingly, neither of them asked to review the contingency plans prepared by the IDF in case the conflict with Hezbollah snowballed into full-blown war. This was a serious oversight. The Winograd Commission established that the last contingency plan approved by the IDF had been dated 2002. However, following the 2005 withdrawal of Syrian forces from Lebanon, large parts of this plan became irrelevant and required modification. A new plan, code named Sky Waters, which had been under development, was approved by the Northern Command in June 2006. Chief of Staff Haloutz was scheduled to authorize a revised version of Sky Waters, but only after it had been tested in a second large-scale manoeuvre in October 2006. Inopportunely for the Israelis, the 12 July attacks interrupted the process.[73] So when the decision to break with containment was presented to the Israeli government on 12 July, the IDF had no approved contingency plan for war with Hezbollah. This critical issue, which clearly undermined the IDF's entire performance, was not brought to the attention of the Israeli government.[74]

The preeminent position of the chief of staff in the decision-making process created other problems. Olmert and Peretz tended to reflect the positions assigned by the IDF rather than shaping them. Olmert frequently told his government colleagues that 'he had always authorized the plans submitted to him by the IDF', but was hard pressed to find an occasion when either he or his defence minister had determined the IDF's actions.[75]

Consequently, Chief of Staff Haloutz was able to reject foreign policy alternatives. For instance, in the 12 July government meeting, former Prime Minister and Defence Minister Shimon Peres argued that applying military pressure would yield little because the Lebanese government was too weak to enforce its authority over Hezbollah. Peres also did not think that it would weaken Hezbollah sufficiently since he believed Hezbollah was already deployed in defence positions and prepared for IAF assaults. Therefore, Peres proposed to apply the financial leverage of France and the USA to the Lebanese government, to exacerbate the internal and external pressure on Hezbollah to temper its behaviour and to disarm. Clearly concerned, Peres urged Haloutz 'to think one or two steps ahead. Let's say we do [what is proposed], they respond, what then?' Haloutz,

---

[72] Olmert, *In Person*, p. 696. [73] Winograd interim report, pp. 55–7.
[74] Winograd final report, p. 300.
[75] Peretz testimony before the Winograd Commission, p. 53.

340   Events Dear Boy, Events

taking advantage of his dominant position within the decision-making troika, replied dismissively: 'I think two steps ahead, I also think four steps ahead, but all these steps seem like the same step multiplied by four.' 'Can anyone here give me a scenario that sees three or four steps ahead', Haloutz asked rhetorically. 'I can't', he continued 'but if anyone can may he please put it on the table and I am happy to debate this scenario.'[76]

Having secured departure from containment, Chief of Staff Haloutz had a virtually free hand to determine the military tactics Israel deployed during the 2006 Lebanon War. They reflected the confidence of Haloutz – a former IAF commander – that airstrikes and firepower would be the most effective military strategy against Hezbollah. Notably, Mossad objected to this line of thinking. Its chief, Meir Dagan, argued that Israel could not achieve its goals by relying predominantly on airstrikes and firepower. Presciently, Dagan foresaw that Israel would have to engage in a prolonged confrontation with Hezbollah, which, eventually, would require ground troops, on a large scale, to neutralize Hezbollah's rocket-launching capabilities. However, these critical objections were never integrated into a foreign policy alternative. Reflecting the preeminent position of Haloutz, the IDF was the only agency to present its foreign policy position to the Israeli government.[77] Accepting the foreign policy course proposed by Haloutz on 12 July, but with no exit plan, was a critical error. Moreover, at no point during the war did the Israeli troika initiate debate over whether the course of action championed by Haloutz should be retained, terminated or abandoned even when it proved ineffective.[78] Instead, Olmert, Peretz and Haloutz dithered, clinging to the flawed concept of engaging with Hezbollah.[79]

In his memoirs, Prime Minister Olmert defended his decision to respond forcefully to Hezbollah's 12 July attacks and to depart from containment, which, he contended, had exacted a heavy price on Israeli deterrence. Olmert also defended his decision to respond swiftly to the attack in order take advantage of 'the international outrage and the identification of world leaders with our right to defend ourselves'.[80] However, the balance sheet related to Israel's war of choice would seem not to favour this. Israel entered a war it initiated with its military, unprepared and without clearly defined objectives. Israel's political and military top brass did not fully internalize engagement in a war as opposed to a large-scale military campaign. Tellingly, only in March 2007, almost

---

[76] Winograd interim report, p. 78.
[77] Winograd interim report, pp. 61–2, 71, 123; Winograd final report, pp. 88, 105.
[78] Winograd final report, p. 521.   [79] Winograd final report, pp. 250, 524–5, 545–6.
[80] Olmert, *In Person*, p. 693; Olmert testimony before the Winograd Commission, p. 61.

a year after the confrontation with Hezbollah ended was the conflict recognized officially as a war.[81]

Derailed by War

It is said that former British Prime Minister Harold Macmillan was asked by a journalist what might steer governments off course. He is said to have replied, with Edwardian languor: 'Events dear boy, events.' In the first six months of its term, Ehud Olmert's government felt the full force of Macmillan's insight. The association with the failures of the 2006 Lebanon War politically weakened the leading Israeli troika, Ehud Olmert, Amir Peretz and Chief of Staff Haloutz. In addition, the conflict with Hezbollah, just six years after the unilateral withdrawal from the Gaza Strip, cast doubt on a unilateral withdrawal from the West Bank. If Israel withdrew, who could guarantee that the West Bank would not be used by Hezbollah and Hamas to launch attacks? Six months after his election, Ehud Olmert found himself weakened politically by a war that derailed his flagship foreign policy plan.

[81] Winograd interim report, p. 11.

16   The End of the Road

The Political Fallout of the Second Lebanon War

The 2006 Second Lebanon War debilitated the leading Israeli troika. Prime Minister Olmert remained in power but, on his own admission, was 'an unpopular Prime Minister'.[1] Chief of Staff Haloutz stepped down in January 2007 and was replaced by General-in-Reserve Gabi Ashkenazi. Ehud Barak forced Amir Peretz to resign from the defence ministry after defeating him in the June Labour party leadership contest.[2] Olmert recalls that Barak's appointment as defence minister exacerbated the discord within Israel's foreign policy leadership:

> It was clear to me that he would do anything to become Prime Minister again. Barak did not hide this. In one of our conversations he said that 'there is only one really interesting post. Which, I replied. Prime Minister, he answered'. I told him that he may be right, but his record in that job was abysmal.[3]

In his weakened state, Prime Minister Olmert faced constant political threats from his two key ministers, Barak and Livni, who were untainted by the Winograd Report. The fraught relationship among these three leading ministers was to dog foreign policy decision-making throughout Olmert's time in office.

Between War and Peace with Syria

In the early days of March 2007, Mossad agents broke into the Vienna flat of Ibrahim Othman, head of the Syrian Atomic Energy Commission. They downloaded top-secret documents from his computer that proved that Syria was secretly constructing a plutonium nuclear reactor in the

---

[1] Mazal Mualem, 'Olmert: I Am Unpopular but Here to Get on With the Job', *Ha'aretz*, 15 March 2007 (in Hebrew).
[2] Hanan Greenberg, 'An Earthquake: Chief of Staff Haloutz Resigns', *Ynet*, www.ynet.co.il /articles/0,7340,L-3353265,00.html; Atila Shumplavi, 'Peretz Resigns, *Ynet*, www .ynet.co.il/articles/0,7340,L-3413386,00.html, both links accessed 24 October 2018.
[3] Olmert, *In Person*, p. 12.

342

northeastern district of Deir ez-Zur. The installation was almost identical to that of the Yongbyon reactor in North Korea, which was assisting the Syrians. Prime Minister Olmert convened an Israeli expert panel to review the material; the panel concluded that the sole purpose of the reactor was to produce an atomic bomb and recommended it be destroyed.[4]

Israel's preference was that the USA should carry out the attack. Olmert made the case for this in a meeting with President Bush on 16 June. He argued that Syria would not respond to a US strike, which also would signal to Iran the risks involved in running a nuclear programme.[5] The Bush administration was divided. Vice President Cheney argued that a US strike would demonstrate that the USA was serious about non-proliferation and would enhance its credibility in the Middle East.[6] Secretaries Gates and Rice thought differently. Elliot Abrams, note taker during the deliberations, reported that Gates was absolutely against attacking a third Muslim country while still engaged in the Afghanistan and Iraq wars. Rice, in her turn, was heavily influenced by a CIA position paper, published during the deliberations.[7] Still discredited by its failure to find any weapons of mass destruction in Iraq, the CIA was unwilling to certify with 'anything other than low confidence that the reactor was part of a nuclear program'.[8] Thus, Gates and Rice supported a diplomatic route that would require Syria to shutter and close the reactor under International Atomic Energy Association (IAEA) supervision.[9] Faced with a split among his leading policymakers, President Bush decided he could not authorize a military strike on a sovereign country on the basis of an inconclusive CIA report.[10]

On 13 July, Bush informed Olmert that, in the case of Syria, the USA would pursue a diplomatic route backed by the use of force.[11] This decision posed a number of problems for Israel. Syria's supporters in

---

[4] Olmert, *In Person*, pp. 199, 204; Amos Harel and Aluf Ben, 'The End of Ambiguity: How Israel Attacked the Syrian Nuclear Reactor', *Ha'aretz*, www.haaretz.co.il/news/politics/MAGAZINE-1.4675626, accessed 21 March 2018. Elliot Abrams, 'Bombing the Syrian Reactor: The Untold Story', *Commentary*, www.commentarymagazine.com/articles/bombing-the-syrian-reactor-the-untold-story/, accessed 17 May 2018, pp. 6–7.

[5] Olmert, *In Person*, p. 200.   [6] Cheney, *In My Time*, p. 471.

[7] David Makowski, 'The Silent Strike', *New Yorker*, www.newyorker.com/magazine/2012/09/17/the-silent-strike, p. 18, accessed 18 May 2008; Abrams, *Tested By Zion*, p. 177; Abrams, 'Bombing the Syrian Reactor', 10.

[8] Rice, *No Higher Honor*, p. 708.

[9] Elliot Abrams, 'Bombing the Syrian Reactor: The Untold Story, *Commentary*, February 2013, www.commentarymagazine.com/articles/bombing-the-syrian-reactor-the-untold-story/, p. 7, accessed 28 February 2019

[10] David Makovsky, 'The Silent Strike', *New Yorker*, 17 September 2012, p. 20.

[11] Bush, *Decision Points*, p. 421.

344   The End of the Road

the UN, especially Russia, were likely to protect it during the prolonged diplomatic process; the IAEA's record in relation to halting nuclear programmes was poor; and were the reactor to be activated during diplomatic negotiations, the threat of a military strike would become all but void. Once the reactor went 'hot', radiation resulting from its destruction could harm millions of people and contaminate the Euphrates River, which was the reactor's cooling water source. Thus, Olmert was defiant in his response to the American decision: 'George', he told the US president, 'this leaves me surprised and disappointed. I cannot accept it.'[12] 'If you won't do it we will!'[13] Bush raised no objections and assured Olmert that the Americans would remain 'buttoned up' and, after ending the phone call, remarked to Elliot Abrams that Olmert 'has guts'.[14]

Ehud Barak, Olmert's defence minister, was less impressed. He was concerned that the IDF had yet to develop a failsafe plan of attack on the reactor that would not spark full-scale war with Syria and, probably, Hezbollah.[15] Shockingly, according to Olmert, Barak would not rule out striking the reactor after it became 'hot', the inevitable catastrophic environmental damage notwithstanding.[16] Olmert, by way of contrast, was convinced that the IDF attack plan was sound and that delaying it could jeopardize the whole operation, especially if the reactor were to be activated.

The rift between Israel's primary decision-makers came to head during a security cabinet meeting on 1 August. During this meeting, General Ido Nehoshtan presented the IDF's unequivocal recommendation to destroy the reactor and began to outline the IAF's operation plan. Barak, still determined to halt the attack cut the presentation short, shouting 'Sit down! I forbid you to continue.'[17] The awkward silence was broken by Olmert. Conscious that Nehoshtan was legally subordinate to Barak, the prime minister completed the presentation in lieu of the astounded general.[18]

The incident exposed how the personal rivalry between Olmert and Barak impinged on the very heart of Israel's foreign policymaking. Following the 1 August meeting, Barak continued to lobby security cabinet members to delay the attack. Olmert, who also held lengthy consultations with all relevant foreign policy agencies and cabinet members, was advocating an immediate strike.[19] Olmert invoked the Begin

---

[12] Quoted in Abrams, 'Bombing the Syrian Reactor', 16; Bush, *Decision Points*, pp. 421–2.
[13] Olmert, *In Person*, p. 206.
[14] Makovsky, 'The Silent Strike', 25; Abrams, 'Bombing the Syrian Reactor', 17.
[15] Ehud Barak, *My Country My Life*, p. 411.   [16] Olmert, *In Person*, pp. 202, 218.
[17] Olmert, *In Person*, p. 214.   [18] Ibid.
[19] Makovsky, 'The Silent Strike', 32; Olmert, *In Person*, pp. 214–15, 217–21, 225–8; Harel and Ben, 'The End of Ambiguity', 4–5.

Doctrine, which was established after Israel destroyed Iraq's nuclear reactor in 1981. The essence of this was that no Israeli adversary in the Middle East should be allowed to acquire a nuclear weapon. Olmert's methodical decision-making process, which contrasted sharply with the haste preceding the 2006 Isarael-Hezbollah War, secured the support needed by the politically vulnerable prime minister. On 5 September, cabinet approved the attack, granting Olmert, Barak and Livni authority to decide on its method and timing. Sometime between 12:40 and 12:53 am on 6 September 2007, IAF pilots uttered the computer-generated codeword of the day, 'Arizona', indicating that seventeen tons of explosives had been dropped on their target, which had been destroyed. The Israeli strike was deliberately low signature in being aimed solely at destroying the reactor. Israel did not take credit for the attack until eleven years later, which allowed the Syrian president to deny that it had taken place.[20] The military balance of power favouring Israel and its assured support from the USA seem to have been the main factors determining Syrian forbearance.

Assad's decision to hold back was highly significant. Israel's attack on his nuclear facility took place in the midst of covert negotiations under Turkish mediation, which had begun in February 2007.[21] Again, as with the decision to destroy the Syrian reactor, Olmert was the driving force behind the resumption of negotiations with Syria after a seven-year hiatus.[22] Olmert perceived Turkey as a Syrian ally.[23] Its prime minister, Recep Tayyip Erdoğan, was a devout Muslim, leader of the Welfare and Development Islamist party and political leader of a Muslim country. This convinced Olmert that Turkey would be acceptable to Assad as a mediator.[24] Olmert's choice of Turkey to mediate between the two sides was unusual in that, traditionally, Israel preferred US mediation. However, the USA objected to the Israeli-Syrian negotiations. It believed that Syria was deliberately undermining the US campaign in Iraq and it had no faith in Assad.[25]

Olmert's confidants, Tourgeman and Turbowicz, took charge of the talks. Ehud Barak and Tzipi Livni were notified about the process, but excluded from it.[26] At the outset, Olmert presented his conditions for peace with Syria. They included open borders, diplomatic and trade relations and Syrian commitment to sever relations with Iran and

---

[20] Harel and Ben, 'The End of Ambiguity', 9–12; Makovsky, 'The Silent Strike', 26–8; Olmert, *In Person*, pp. 226–8.
[21] Interview Shalom Tourgeman 23 January 2018, Tel Aviv.   [22] Interview Olmert.
[23] Interview Olmert.   [24] Olmert, *In Person*, p. 756.
[25] Interview Olmert; Olmert, *In Person*, p. 759.   [26] Olmert, *In Person*, pp. 758, 760.

346   The End of the Road

Hezbollah and close its border to terrorists wanting to fight US forces in Iraq.[27] Significantly, Olmert refused to commit to the Rabin Deposit.[28]

Syria, which was isolated internationally and motivated to conclude an association agreement with the EU, was keen to negotiate, but not necessarily to conclude a deal based on Olmert's conditions. Syria's representative at the talks was Dr Riad Daudi, who had negotiated with the Israelis previously and was a close confidant of Assad. Heading the Turkish mediation team were Ahmet Davutoğlu, Prime Minister's Erdogan's key foreign policy advisor at the time, and Deputy Foreign Minister and former ambassador to Israel, Feridun Sinirlioğlu.[29]

Assad's decision not to respond to the Israeli strike enabled these indirect negotiations to continue beyond September 2007. However, Olmert's refusal to endorse the Rabin Deposit remained a serious impediment to progress. Thus, whereas in 2000, top Israeli and Syrian political leaders had met face to face, the peace talks under Olmert remained indirect. The Israeli and Syrian delegations were housed in different hotels in Ankara and the Turkish mediators shuttled between them.

It would seem that domestic constraints were the main reason for Olmert's opening gambit's not being bolder. Israeli public opinion remained consistently against withdrawing from the Golan Heights.[30] The 2006 Second Lebanon War and the ongoing conflict with Hamas around the Gaza Strip stiffened opposition to voluntary withdrawal from territory, including the Golan. Olmert, who, by his own admission, was profoundly unpopular at the time, could not reverse this deep-seated public sentiment. In addition, he lacked parliamentary support for a more forthcoming position towards Syria. Even Olmert's own party, Kadima, Ha'aretz correspondent, Aluf Ben, reported at the time, 'was split on the question of the Golan'.[31] Heavily constrained by domestic factors and lacking US support, the indirect Israeli-Syrian negotiations were driven by process rather than substance. Frustrated, in April 2008, Olmert described the talks as a car 'driving full gas in neutral'.[32]

---

[27] Olmert, *In Person*, pp. 756–7.   [28] Interview Olmert.
[29] Olmert, *In Person*, p. 757; Interview Olmert.
[30] A number of polls reported consistently that 73–75 per cent of Israelis opposed full withdrawal from the Golan. See August 2007 and April 2008 peace index polls; *Yedioth Ahronoth*, 23 May 2008.
[31] Aluf Ben, 'A Convergence of Interests: A Necessary but Insufficient Precondition', *Strategic Update*, 11, 1, 2008; 9 (in Hebrew).
[32] Olmert, *In Person*, p. 760.

Abandoning the Convergence Plan

The negotiations with Syria were not the only diplomatic impasse facing Israel. The 2006 Second Lebanon War forced Olmert to abandon his flagship foreign policy project, the convergence plan. As Olmert's close confidant, Yoram Turbowicz, explained to Condoleezza Rice, the convergence plan had very little support because Israel was being attacked from south Lebanon and Gaza after unilaterally withdrawing from both. Dejected, Turbowciz conceded that Olmert was too weak to overcome that resistance.[33]

Retreat from the convergence plan created a foreign policy vacuum at a very delicate moment. Nine months earlier, on 26 January 2006, Hamas had won a landslide victory in the Palestinian elections, securing seventy-four out of the 132 PLC seats. Its main rival, Fatah, won only forty-five seats, due to internal splits, corruption and the poor Oslo Process record. Hamas's decisive victory was overseen by an eighty-four-member delegation of international monitors, which reported a 77 per cent turnout of the 1.2 million registered Palestinian voters and deemed the elections free and fair.[34]

Following its election victory, Hamas was caught between a rock and a hard place. The Quartet – comprised of the USA, the EU, Russia and the UN – attached clear conditions to continuing foreign aid to the Palestinians. It demanded from any future Palestinian government a commitment to 'nonviolence, recognition of Israel, and acceptance of previous agreements and obligations'.[35] To govern, Hamas was in desperate need of foreign aid. However, accepting the Quartet's conditions would compromise Hamas's political and ideological stance since the signing of the Oslo accords. Politics and ideology trumped the government's practical considerations as Hamas rejected the Quartet's conditions, which was a serious mistake. As Condoleezza Rice reveals, had Hamas complied with the Quartet's conditions, the USA would have had to reconsider its position towards Hamas, sowing division between Israel and the Americans.[36]

Rejecting the Quartet's conditions gave to the Hawkish elements in the Bush administration, the EU and Israel, a pretext to launch a fierce, coordinated, international offensive.[37] The USA and the EU severed

---

[33] Abrams, *Tested by Zion*, p. 200.
[34] Filiu, *Gaza*, p. 290; Eldar, *Getting to Know Hamas*, p. 168; Baconi, *Hamas Contained*, pp. 94–5; Rumley and Tibon, *The Last Palestinian*, p. 125.
[35] Quartet Statement, London, 20 January 2006, www.un.org/news/dh/infocus/mid dle_east/quartet-30jan2006.htm, accessed 25 May 2018.
[36] Rice, *No Higher Honor*, p. 419.
[37] Eldar, *Getting to Know Hamas*, pp. 148–51, 163–6.

348   The End of the Road

economic ties with the Hamas-led government, formed in March 2006 under the leadership of Ismail Haniyeh. Egypt and Saudi privately made it clear that they would tailor their aid to ensure it could not reach Hamas. Foreign aid to the Palestinians reduced following severe restrictions on the banks dealing with the PA.[38] Meanwhile, Israel froze its monthly transfers of taxes, tariffs and other fees it collected on the PA's behalf.[39] In addition, Hamas's PLC members based in Gaza were banned from travelling to the West Bank. Gazan workers were not allowed to enter Israel and the customs envelope allowing goods from Gaza and the West Bank to enter Israel was withdrawn.[40]

Concurrently, Israel intensified its military assaults on the Gaza Strip. In June, it launched Operation Summer Rains, following the abduction of Corporal Gilad Shalit by Palestinian factions, and this was followed by Operation Autumn Clouds in November. By the end of November, these large-scale military offensives and associated attacks had killed 524 Palestinians.[41] According to an Amnesty International report, some eighty of those killed and more than 300 of the injured were children. The collective punishing of the population caused 'deliberate and wanton destruction of civilian infrastructure and property in the Gaza Strip'.[42]

Israel claimed that its attacks were aimed at freeing Corporal Gilad Shalit and countering Palestinian terrorist and rocket attacks.[43] These last referred to the 861 rocket hits sustained by Israel during 2006, which had severely disrupted the everyday life of residents in the Western Negev. However, the casualty rate – four deaths – was relatively low. In fact, the majority (fifteen out of thirty-two) of Israeli casualties during 2006 were

---

[38] Michele K. Esposito, 'Quarterly Update on Conflict and Diplomacy', *Journal of Palestine Studies*, 35, 4, 2006: 101–4; Filiu, *Gaza*, p. 291; Milton-Edwards and Farrell, *Hamas*, pp. 270–1; Rice, *No Higher Honor*, p. 420.

[39] Cabinet Communiqué 19 February 2006; Filiu, *Gaza*, p. 291.

[40] 'The Gaza Strip: March Access Report, Closure at Karni Crossing', *United Nations: Office for the Coordination of Humanitarian Affairs*, https://unispal.un.org/DPA/DPR/unispal.nsf/0/9321873EB12052608525714F004D346B, accessed 27 February 2018.

[41] 'Palestinian Killed in the Gaza Strip by the Israeli Security Forces from the Second Intifada to Operation Cast Lead (not including)', *B'Tselem*, www.btselem.org/hebrew/statistics/fatalities/before-cast-lead/by-date-of-event/gaza/palestinians-killed-by-israeli-security-forces, accessed 4 June 2018.

[42] 'Israel and the Palestinians: The Road to Nowhere', Amnesty International, December 2006, pp. 8–10.

[43] 'Operation Summer Rains: IDF Enters Southern Gaza Strip to Secure Release of Abducted Soldier', *IMFA*, http://mfa.gov.il/MFA/PressRoom/2006/Pages/IDF%20enters%20southern%20Gaza%20Strip%20to%20secure%20release%20of%20abducted%20soldier%2028-Jun-2006.aspx; 'Beit Hanoun: A Hub for Terrorist Activity: IDF Concludes Operation Autumn Clouds in Bet Hanoun', *IMFA*, www.mfa.gov.il/mfa/foreignpolicy/terrorism/palestinian/pages/beit%20hanoun-%20a%20hub%20of%20terrorist%20activity%205-nov-2006.aspx, both links accessed 25 May 2018.

Abandoning the Convergence Plan   349

caused by four suicide bombing attacks carried out by Fatah and the PIJ.[44]

The scope of the military force used by Israel towards the Palestinians seems not to have been aimed solely at tackling these security threats. Rather, as Olmert wrote in his memoirs, 'we were conducting a punitive campaign against Hamas.'[45] Following Shalit's kidnap, Olmert wrote that Israel 'intended to convey a message to the population of the Gaza Strip that their lives would become intolerable'.[46] This helps to explain why Prime Minister Olmert ruled out two political initiatives relating to the kidnap of Shalit. Gershon Baskin, a prominent Israeli peace activist, recounts in his memoirs, how he established contact with Razi Hamed, then close advisor to Prime Minister Haniyeh. Transcripts of the correspondence Baskin conducted separately with Hamed and Olmert – via his daughter Dana – reveal that the Israeli prime minister rejected an offer from Baskin to mediate between Israel and Hamas to negotiate a prisoner exchange.[47]

Khaled Mashal, Head of the Hamas bureau in Damascus, also approached Olmert with an offer to negotiate, via a mediator, over Shalit. According to a leading researcher on Hamas, Mashal's proposals were set out in a non-paper that was delivered to Olmert in September 2006. GSS head, Yuval Diskin, and Israeli go-between, Dr Nimrod Novik, were privy to this information. Mashal's non-paper proposed a prisoner exchange – including Shalit – and a plan for a twenty-five-year ceasefire between Israel and Hamas.[48] It is unclear whether either initiative would have yielded results. However, what is evident is that Prime Minister Olmert rejected these political alternatives to his policy of isolating and undermining the Hamas-led government by employing large-scale military force, harsh economic sanctions and imposing a blockade on the Gaza Strip.

Fatah, President Abbas's political party, fully supported Olmert's harsh stance. Since its election defeat, it had disagreed with Hamas on basic issues including how to control the Palestinian security forces, how to respond to the Quartet's conditions and the division of labour between the Hamas-led government and the Palestinian president's office under Abbas.[49] Consequently, as a former aide to President Abbas recalled, after Hamas's

---

[44] 'The Nature and Extent of Palestinian Terrorism', *IMFA*, www.mfa.gov.il/mfa/foreign policy/terrorism/palestinian/pages/palestinian%20terrorism%202006.aspx, accessed 30 May 2018.
[45] Olmert, *In Person*, p. 688.   [46] Olmert, *In Person*, p. 685.
[47] Gershon Baskin, *Freeing Gilad: The Secret Back Channel* (Or-Yehuda: Kineret Zmora Bitan, 2013), pp. 26–37, 42–7 (in Hebrew).
[48] Eldar, *Getting to Know Hamas*, pp. 236–8.
[49] Baconi, *Hamas Contained*, pp. 100–12.

350 The End of the Road

election victory he was concerned primarily with 'how to preserve his control' amid the deepening political crisis with Hamas.[50]

As the internal Palestinian political crisis intensified, Hamas and Fatah engaged in deadly clashes, especially in the Gaza Strip. In 2006 alone, forty-seven Palestinians were killed in internecine fighting.[51] Egypt, Saudi Arabia and Qatar sought to mediate between Fatah and Hamas. As the crisis in governance deepened, Hamas sought to form a national unity government with Fatah to deal with the Quartet's position. Saudi Arabia, which was able to capitalize on this shift, in 8 February 2007, brokered the Mecca Agreement between Hamas and Fatah. The two leading Palestinian political movements agreed to form a cabinet that would 'respect' – rather than recognize – past agreements and the right of return based on UN resolution 194 and that the PLO should negotiate with Israel.[52] However, the agreement did not resolve the recurrent differences over how to control the security forces and reform the PLO to include Hamas, which impeded implementation of the accord. On 14 June 2007, amid an irreparable domestic political Palestinian crisis, the agreement collapsed completely. In a dramatic turn of events, Hamas forces gained control of the Gaza Strip in a brutal takeover that lasted four days and involved killing, torture and execution several Fatah members in the process.[53] In its defence, Hamas argued that the takeover was a pre-emptive strike, which was correct. Only a few weeks earlier, a military plan to crush Hamas in the Gaza Strip had been presented to Ehud Olmert by Muhammad Dhalan, Head of the PA's Security Forces in the Gaza Strip.[54]

Yet, while Hamas may have protected itself, the violent takeover of the Gaza Strip ushered in a profound crisis. Split between the West Bank and the Gaza Strip, the Palestinian National Movement was ruptured politically, economically, militarily and bureaucratically. Moreover, the Gaza Strip was subjected to a tighter closure. All five crossings from Gaza to Israel were closed as was the Rafah crossing between Gaza and Egypt. Food shortages and a healthcare crisis emerged instantly as the Gazan economy contracted rapidly. To meet the basic needs of the population in

---

[50] Quoted in Rumley and Tibon, *The Last Palestinian*, p. 129; see also Baconi, *Hamas Contained*, pp. 101–2.

[51] 'Palestinians Killed by Palestinians from the Outbreak of the Outbreak of the Second Intifada to Operation Cast Lead (not inclusive)', *B'Tselem*, www .btselem.org/hebrew/statistics/fatalities/before-cast-lead/by-date-of-event/gaza/pales tinians-killed-by-palestinians, accessed 1 June 2018.

[52] Baconi, *Hamas Contained*, pp. 121–2, 125–9; Eldar, *Getting to Know Hamas*, pp. 185, 188–9, 245, 257–60.

[53] Baconi, *Hamas Contained*, pp. 131–3; Eldar, *Getting to Know Hamas*, pp. 257–60.

[54] Olmert, *In Person*, p. 805.

Gaza, Hamas relied increasingly on aid organizations, such as the UN Relief and Rehabilitation Agency and a growing 'tunnel economy' of goods smuggled from the Sinai underground.[55] Meanwhile, President Abbas dissolved the short-lived national unity government formed by Hamas and Fatah following the Mecca Agreement, replacing it with an emergency cabinet under Prime Minister Salam Fayyad.

The takeover of the Gaza Strip by Hamas also produced a significant change to the international politics of the Israeli-Palestinian conflict. Pro-Western Arab states and Israel supported the Fatah-led PA against Hamas and its supporters – Iran, Syria and Hezbollah. A summit convened in Sharm el-Sheik, a week after Hamas completed the takeover, reflected this shift. Egypt hosted the summit, which included King Abdullah of Jordan, Olmert and Abbas. Olmert used it to launch the foreign policy of propping up the new Fatah-led PA government while isolating and punishing Hamas. He announced that Israel would pass on the frozen Palestinian tax monies it had collected on behalf of the PA, release 250 Fatah prisoners and renew security and economic cooperation with the PA. In addition, Abbas and Olmert agreed to meet every other week to advance 'all issues on their shared agenda'.[56]

The Annapolis Conference and its Aftermath

The military takeover of the Gaza Strip by Hamas prompted US Secretary of State Rice to reevaluate US foreign policy towards the Israeli-Palestinian conflict. Rice had come to see the terms laid down in the 2003 road map, which conditioned Israeli-Palestinian negotiations on cessation of violence, as an impediment. Fatah's defeat by Hamas in the legislative elections and the takeover of the Gaza Strip reinforced her concern that, in the absence of negotiations, the balance of power in Palestinian domestic politics was shifting towards Hamas. Indeed, Rice concluded that the only way President Abbas and Fatah could recover politically was by negotiating an agreement with Israel.[57] To this end, Rice advocated a new approach, namely, resuming negotiations irrespective of whether or not violence continued. Were negotiations to be successful, only the implementation phase would be conditioned on cessation of violence.[58]

---

[55] Baconi, *Hamas Contained*, pp. 135, 138, 14–3.
[56] 'Statement by PM Olmert at the Sharm el-Sheik Summit, *IMFA*, www.mfa.gov.il/mfa/pressroom/2007/pages/statement%20by%20pm%20ehud%20olmert%20at%20the%20sharm%20el-sheikh%20summit%2025-jun-2007.aspx, accessed 7 June 2018.
[57] Rice, *No Higher Honor*, p. 381.
[58] Abrams, *Tested by Zion*, pp. 192, 196, 201, 215–16.

352   The End of the Road

Olmert, who was against revising the sequence of the road map, was hardly in a position to resist. The takeover of the Gaza Strip by Hamas further weakened Olmert's political standing. It cast the unilateralist approach he had championed in his election campaign as another serious error of judgement. Weakened domestically, Olmert could not afford a public spat with Rice. Olmert's Foreign Minister, Tzipi Livni, supported Rice's efforts to unpick the road map, which rendered Olmert even more vulnerable. His position reflected the deep personal and political rift within the Israeli cabinet. An apprehensive Olmert, as Abrams recounts, was concerned that 'Rice was building a relationship with Foreign Minister Livni that went beyond their diplomatic business and looked more like Rice trying to pick his successor.'[59]

In summer 2007, a buoyant Rice concluded that 'the pieces were falling into place for a big push towards a resolution of the Israeli-Palestinian conflict.'[60] Rice's optimism was fuelled, in part, by the subtle, but significant realignment of international politics in the Arab-Israeli conflict as pro-Western Arab states – Saudi Arabia, the United Arab Emirates, Egypt and Jordan – were liaising covertly with Israel, against Iran.[61] This tacit cooperation and the divide between Fatah and Hamas created the conditions for obtaining the backing of pro-Western Arab states for the peace process.[62]

This was the impetus for the Annapolis Peace Conference, which Rice anticipated would give a 'real push' to the two-state solution.[63] The conference, which epitomized Rice's internationalizing of the Israeli-Palestinian peace process, was held on 27 November 2007, at the US Naval Academy in Annapolis, Maryland. It attracted representatives from thirteen Arab countries, including Egypt, Saudi Arabia, Jordan and Syria, the G8 group of industrialized countries, permanent members of the UN Security Council, the Quartet, the Organization of the Islamic State, the IMF and the World Bank.[64]

The impressive size and scope of the gathering masked the profound gap between symbolism and substance. The minutes of the meetings held between the Israeli and Palestinian negotiators in preparation for Annapolis reveal that the two sides could not bridge the gaps related to core issues.[65] For this reason, the Joint Understanding, issued at the end

[59] Abrams, *Tested by Zion*, p. 205.   [60] Rice, *No Higher Honor*, p. 582.
[61] Olmert, *In Person*, p. 816.   [62] Abrams, *Tested by Zion*, p. 255.
[63] Rice, *No Higher Honor*, pp. 600–1.
[64] Carol Migdalovitz, 'Israeli-Palestinian Peace Process': The Annapolis Conference', *CRS Report for Congress*, p. 2, https://fas.org/sgp/crs/mideast/RS22768.pdf, accessed 28 February 2019.
[65] See minutes of the negotiations in Clayton E. Swisher, *The Palestine Papers: The End of the Road?* (Chatham: Hesperus, 2011), pp. 76–101.

Annapolis Conference and its Aftermath 353

of the conference, focused solely on the structure of the negotiations and ignored substantive matters entirely.[66]

Domestic constraints contribute to explaining why Israel and the Palestinians were immovable. Hamas, which controlled the Gaza Strip and won the Palestinian legislative elections, was excluded conspicuously from the conference. Consequently, as Palestinian chief negotiator, Abu Ala, observed, Hamas's parameters for success in Gaza were 'steadfastness in the face of the occupier with no peace process working'.[67] Thus, Abbas's legitimacy to address substantive topics was challenged from the outset.

In turn, Olmert's negotiating position was curtailed by his coalition partners. Shas, the Sephardi ultra-religious party, threatened to leave the coalition government if the subject of Jerusalem were raised in the negotiations – this being a prerequisite for any agreement with the Palestinians.[68] Avigdor Liberman, head of the ultra-nationalist party, Israel is Our Home, which joined the government shortly after the 2006 Second Lebanon War, rejected President Abbas as a viable negotiating partner. Lieberman described Abbas as 'surviving thanks to Israeli bayonets' and as 'not being able to deliver the goods'.[69] Thus, any significant progress in the negotiations between Olmert and Abbas would certainly have triggered a coalition government crisis.

Following the Annapolis Conference, Israeli-Palestinian negotiations resumed amid these formidable domestic constraints. Foreign Minister Livni and veteran Palestinian negotiator, Abu Ala, led their negotiating teams.[70] The negotiation framework, comprising twelve subcommittees, was extremely cumbersome. Livni and Abu Ala presided over the committee dealing with the core issues of Jerusalem, refugees, borders, settlements, water and security.[71]

The negotiations reached a critical phase between June and August 2008. Minutes of the meetings, which were published on the WikiLeaks website and collated in *The Palestine Papers*, reveal important

---

[66] 'Joint Understanding Read by President Bush at the Annapolis Conference, *US Department of State*, https://2001-2009.state.gov/p/nea/rls/95696.htm, accessed 8 June 2018.

[67] 'Minutes from the Security Session Post Annapolis, Thursday 28 February 2008', in Swisher, *The Palestine Papers*, p. 122.

[68] 'Rabbi Ovadia Yossef: If Jerusalem Is Divided Shas Is Out', *Ynet*, www.ynet.co.il/articles/0,7340,L-3476007,00.html, accessed 8 June 2018.

[69] Roni Sopher, 'Liberman, Abu Mazen Lives in Judea and Samaria on Our Bayonets', *Ynet*, www.ynet.co.il/articles/0,7340,L-3470012,00.html, accessed 8 June 2018.

[70] Omer Zanani, *Annapolis Process (2007–2008): Oasis or Mirage?* (Tel Aviv: Steineitz Centre for Peace, 2015), p. 38 (in Hebrew).

[71] Interview Foreign Minister Tzipi Livni, 24 January 2018, Jerusalem; 'Minutes From 7th Negotiation Meeting, 12 November 2007', in *The Palestine Papers*, p. 81.

354   The End of the Road

details of the discussions.[72] The Palestinians made a number of proposals to break the impasse. For instance, they declared themselves willing to accept key Israeli security requirements, including maintaining EWS in the West Bank provided they were manned by a third party. They suggested that a joint operations room be created between Israel, the Palestinians, third-party forces, Egypt and Jordan.[73] However, the Israeli side remained entrenched in a conflict mentality and, seemingly, was unable to make the cognitive leap towards a post-conflict peace scenario. As chief Israeli negotiator, Udi Dekel, explained to his Palestinian counterpart, Saeb Erikat: 'I know that you think when there is peace there will be security. We can't and don't think that way. For us, in order to have peace, we need security first.'[74]

Similarly, the Palestinians tried to initiate constructive discussion over Jerusalem, which hit the brick wall of the domestic pressures the Olmert government faced. Shas, a key coalition partner, checked with Livni weekly on the negotiations; to prevent Shas from leaving the government, Livni was obliged to give assurances that 'nothing has been agreed upon' in relation to Jerusalem.[75] This tough political constraint posed an obstacle to discussion of Palestinian offers regarding Jerusalem, including formulations that went beyond what the Palestinians had proposed at the 2000 Camp David summit.[76] For instance, during a critical meeting, held on 30 June 2008, to evaluate the state of the negotiations, Abu Ala hoped to tackle the issue of Jerusalem head on. 'I want to put to you our position on Jerusalem', he appealed to Livni. 'Since I cannot refer to it', Livni responded, 'I am going to just listen.'[77] Abu Ala's presentation was duly received with a deafening silence.

Unlike the previous Israeli Foreign Ministers, Shimon Peres and Shlomo Ben-Ami, Livni was immovable and, thus, it was impossible to push the boundaries to the negotiations to achieve a breakthrough. Livni's lack of experience in negotiating with the Palestinians combined with the unwieldy twelve subcommittee structure was a further impediment to progress. Consequently, the negotiations yielded meagre results at a time when major advances were needed. It was clear to all parties that the end of President Bush's second term marked the end of the Annapolis peace process.

[72] Swisher, *The Palestine Papers*.
[73] 'Minutes of Security Meeting, 2 July 2008', in *The Palestinian Papers*, pp. 189–91.
[74] Minutes of Security Meeting, 2 July, 2008', in *The Palestinian Papers*, p. 190.
[75] 'Meeting Minutes, 22 January 2008', *The Palestinians Papers*, p. 102.
[76] 'Minutes of the Trilateral Meeting, 15 June 2008', in *The Palestine Papers*, p. 163.
[77] 'Minutes of the General Plenary Meeting, 30 June, 2008', in *The Palestinian Papers*, p. 185.

Take it or Leave it

Ehud Olmert was not surprised by the stalemate in the Livni-Abu Ala negotiations. When he had appointed Livni, he had anticipated that she and Abu Ala 'would have good chemistry, they would talk, there would be several meetings, but peace would not come out of it'.[78] This trajectory suited Olmert, who, throughout, had intended to resolve the core issues in his meetings with President Abbas.[79] During his premiership, Ehud Olmert met President Abbas thirty-six times, with the first meetings starting in December 2006.[80] The most critical phase, during which President Bush expressed unwavering support for Olmert, followed the Annapolis Conference. Poignantly, in intimate meetings with the Israeli cabinet, Bush underlined that an Israeli-Palestinian peace agreement was possible only while he and Olmert were in office.[81] Bush's strong support was a political asset for the otherwise vulnerable Israeli prime minister.

Another advantage for Olmert was the personal relationship he had forged with Abbas. Feeling that his predecessors were 'patronizing' in their negotiations with the Palestinians, Olmert adopted a different stance.[82] Conscious of the importance of symbols, during the bilateral meetings between Abbas and Olmert, the Palestinian flag was hoisted, for the first time, at the Israeli prime minister's residence. Attentive to detail, Olmert agreed to release more Palestinian prisoners than the Palestinians had requested, to transfer more funds than they had demanded and to authorize bids for military equipment from the PA.[83] An auspicious atmosphere allowed the two leaders a readier recognition of one another's limitations than in previous Israeli-Palestinian negotiations. For instance, Olmert recalls the Palestinian president telling him that he did not 'want to change the nature of the state of Israel'.[84] This extremely significant comment suggested that the Palestinian president would be content with a symbolic gesture rather than full implementation of the Palestinian right of return. For his part, Olmert accepted the principle that a peace agreement required Israeli withdrawal to the 1967 lines or an equivalent area, which would involve a one-for-one land swap.[85] This was a significant retreat from the April 2004 letter, presented by President Bush to Israel, which defined the starting point of the negotiations as the 1967 border minus the three large Israeli settlement blocks.

---

[78] Interview Olmert in 'Hamakor', broadcast 16 December 2015 on Israel's TV Channel 10 (in Hebrew).
[79] Olmert, *In Person*, p. 794.   [80] Interview Shalom Tourgeman.
[81] Abrams, *Tested by Zion*, p. 264.
[82] Olmert, *In Person*, pp. 789, 802; Interview Olmert (in 'Hamakor').
[83] Olmert, *In Person*, pp. 792–3.   [84] Olmert, *In Person*, p. 795.
[85] Olmert, *In Person*, p. 808.

356   The End of the Road

Olmert hoped to exploit President Bush's strong support and his personal rapport with Abbas to secure a permanent agreement. The first policymaker to whom he presented his ideas in confidence was Condoleezza Rice. 'Given the several meetings Rice had conducted with Israel and the Palestinians', Olmert noted in his memoirs, 'she would be a reliable indicator to whether I could harness Abu Mazen to my plan.'[86] This might have been true, but his decision to confide in Rice rather than his own cabinet speaks volumes about the prime minister's political isolation. Over a dinner, held on 3 May 2008, a clearly emotional Olmert made his pitch to Rice. Rice was riveted by the presentation, but kept reminding herself to *'concentrate, concentrate'* and overcome her disbelief at Olmert's words.[87] Her first comment after he concluded was 'Prime Minister, this is remarkable' and 'I will try to help.'[88]

Rice's reception of Olmert's ideas, which were very close to the offer he made to President Abbas four months later, on 16 September 2008, was understandable. On territory, Olmert proposed to Abbas that Israel annex 6.3 per cent of the West Bank, which included the Jewish neighbourhoods around Jerusalem and the large settlement blocks. As compensation, Israel would transfer to the Palestinians 5.8 per cent of the land within Israel proper. The remaining 0.5 per cent would be compensated for by a forty-kilometre-long passage connecting the Gaza Strip and the West Bank, which the Palestinians would control.

On Jerusalem, Olmert proposed that the Jewish neighbourhoods should remain part of Israel and that the Palestinian neighbourhoods should constitute the Palestinian state capital. Management of the Holy Basin, home to the Holy Shrines for Judaism, Islam and Christianity, would be entrusted to a five-state international committee. These included Saudi Arabia, whose king was Custodian of Islam's Two Holy Shrines in Mecca and Medina, Jordan, whose peace agreement with Israel granted it special status in Jerusalem's holy sites, Israel and the Palestinian state, by virtue of their historical and religious ties to the Holy Basin, and the USA, which Olmert thought should represent the Christian world.

On refugees, Olmert refused to accept the principle of the right of return or the notion of family unification, claiming that the numbers of some Palestinian extended families could be in the hundreds of thousands. Instead, he proposed a symbolic gesture. At the time of his offer to President Abbas, around a thousand illegal immigrants and asylum seekers were entering Israel annually from the Sinai Peninsula. Olmert

---

[86] Olmert, *In Person*, p. 829.   [87] Rice, *No Higher Honor*, p. 652, emphasis in original.
[88] Rice, *No Higher Honor*, p. 653.

proposed that, for a period of five years, a similar number of Palestinians should be allowed into Israel and that Israel would have full discretion over who was allowed to enter. In return, the Palestinians would submit a written declaration of the end to the conflict and its demands of Israel.

On security, Olmert emphasized that there would not be free passage between the Palestinian state and Jordan. However, unlike his predecessors, he did not require Israel to retain a presence in the Jordan Valley. Instead, he proposed deployment, on the east bank of the Jordan River, of an international force whose composition would be agreed by Israel, Jordan and the Palestinians.[89]

President Abbas, who took notes during Olmert's presentation, could not have failed to recognize its novel aspects. Jerusalem was to be divided and internationalized. Israel would acknowledge the suffering of Palestinian refugees, but not accept responsibility for it. The land swap would produce a Palestinian state of an equivalent size to the areas Israel occupied in 1967. President Abbas would recognize that Israel would not retain its presence in the Jordan valley. As one might have expected, President Abbas requested he be allowed a few days to study the map proposed by Olmert, to which Olmert consented, on condition that the Palestinian president agreed with its general principles by initialling a copy of the map. Clearly, Olmert was concerned that the Palestinians would 'pocket' his proposal and demand that negotiations continue.[90]

More than a decade later, there has still been no official Palestinian response to Olmert's offer, which critiques of the Palestinians could argue proves they are not partners for peace. However, this argument does not bear scrutiny. Olmert's proposal was unprecedented, but the prospects for its implementation were weak. A few months earlier, in May, it had become known that the Israeli police were investigating Olmert's relationship with an American businessman, Moshe Talansky, from whom, it was suggested, Olmert had accepted a bribe. The enquiry was just one of eight police investigations that plagued Olmert during his time in office. The police investigations of the prime minister not only undermined his political standing with the Israeli public but also dealt a mortal blow to his – already shaky – position in his cabinet and the parliament. Unlike Prime Ministers Rabin and Sharon, who imposed dramatic decisions on their cabinets at the height of their political powers, Olmert had lost command and authority over his colleagues.

Foreign Minister Livni told Rice that Olmert 'has no standing in Israel' and urged the US secretary of state 'not to enshrine the Olmert

[89] Olmert, *In Person*, pp. 838–40.   [90] Olmert, *In Person*, p. 840.

358   The End of the Road

proposal'.[91] Defence Minister Barak was even more outspoken. After Moshe Talanksy's witness evidence in Jerusalem's District Court some three months prior to Olmert's proposal to Abbas, Barak had stated publicly that 'Olmert could not continue leading the country while resolving his "personal matters".'[92] Bowing to this mounting political pressure, before he made his offer to Abbas, Olmert announced that he would step aside. In effect, Olmert's offer to Abbas was made after it was abundantly clear to all sides that he could not be Kadima's prime ministerial candidate.

However, under Israeli law, he would remain prime minister until his successor, Foreign Minister Livni, could form a government or call an early election. Years later, Olmert explained that he intended to use this approximately five-month period to realize the offer he made to Abbas:

My starting point was that if I reached an understanding with the Palestinians, which was signed and initialized, I would know how to sell it to the Israeli public in my own way, regardless of whether they [Barak and Livni] agreed. It would not even be dependent on the composition of the government or the Knesset. I was thinking about a process that involved bringing our agreement to the UN, which would approve it unanimously. We would then have a joint session of the US Houses of Representatives, followed by the EU. Abu Mazen and I would then invite the leaders of the world to a meeting point in Jerusalem at, say, the Holy Basin. We would raise our hand and say peace, peace. We would then stand for elections. I would receive the required support and he, Abu Mazen, would obtain it. There is a difference between a theoretical proposal and an offer that had been accepted by the UN and now needed to be approved. 70 percent of the Israeli public would have supported me. I had no doubt about that.[93]

It is clear that after securing international support for his proposal, Olmert would try to escape from his evident political predicament by appealing directly to the Israeli public. It is impossible to know whether such a plan would have succeeded, although its prospects could not have been high. Olmert did not have domestic political backing within either parliament or his own party. In addition, although Rice supported Olmert, some of the US president's advisors were extremely sceptical about his proposed plan of action. Elliot Abrams, for instance, believed that 'Olmert was in no position to bind Israel to anything'.[94] 'Any deal he offered Abbas', Abrams assessed, 'would be seen by many Israelis as designed to rescue his prime ministership, or at least his reputation'.[95]

[91] Rice, *No Higher Honor*, p. 713.
[92] Barak, *My Country, My Life*, p. 413; Amnon Meranda and Roni Sopher, 'Barak: Olmert Cannot Run the Government', *Ynet*, www.ynet.co.il/articles/0,7340,L-3548876,00 .html, accessed 5 July 2018.
[93] Interview Olmert.   [94] Abrams, *Tested By Zion*, p. 279.
[95] Abrams, *Tested by Zion*, p. 275.

Indeed, Abrams thought that Olmert promoted his offer to 'prove that he was a consequential historical figure, not an accidental prime minister who had failed in Lebanon and was mired in corruption charges'.[96] 'The weaker he became politically', commented Abrams, 'the more Olmert seemed willing to risk.'[97]

The profound doubts raised by Olmert's own cabinet ministers and American officials, such as Abrams, are significant in the context of the debate over whether the Palestinians were a partner for peace. The Palestinians had not rejected a viable peace offer; rather, they preferred not to respond to an offer from a prime minister whose public legitimacy was in tatters following police investigations, a failed war and a flawed unilateralist plan. Had they signed the agreement, they would have risked forsaking two key demands – the right of return and sovereignty over Jerusalem – only to see Olmert overtaken by his untenable political position. Flanked by Hamas amid an irreparable chasm within the Palestinian National Movement, this would have been an extremely high risk, one that President Abbas was unwilling to take.

Between Ankara and Gaza

Unlike previous Israeli prime ministers, Ehud Olmert made no distinction between the Syrian and the Palestinian peace tracks. As he explained, 'this myth that it is impossible to negotiate in parallel is baseless. If the process is positive, and you believe that it will be backed by the public, then why not do it all at once?'[98] Guided by this belief, as Olmert entered the critical phase of his negotiations with the Palestinians, the government made public the negotiations with Syria.[99]

The Americans remained opposed to the Israeli-Syrian negotiations. Convinced that Syria was assisting the insurgency in Iraq, the Bush administration was bent on isolating Bashar al-Assad's regime. Israel's public announcement that it was negotiating with Syria made it virtually impossible for the Americans to maintain this stance. As Abrams reveals, 'no one in the Bush administration, or at least the White House, could figure out what Olmert was doing. The President told him so when they spoke on the phone on June 4. "You are giving freebies to Assad".'[100]

---

[96] Abrams, *Tested by Zion*, p. 206.   [97] Abrams, *Tested by Zion*, p. 233.
[98] Interview Olmert.
[99] Interview Olmert; Pinhas Wolf, 'Negotiations with Syria and the Palestinians – in Parallel', *Ynet*, https://news.walla.co.il/item/1285834, accessed 5 July 2018; Olmert, *In Person*, p. 760.
[100] Abrams, *Tested by Zion*, p. 276.

360   The End of the Road

Having neither domestic backing nor US support, Olmert's foreign policy of peace towards Syria relied wholly on his Turkish mediators and the goodwill of President Assad. By August 2008, the Israeli and Syrian delegations had conducted four rounds of talks. Each was devoted to one of the core issues necessary to seal an agreement: security, normalization, the border and water resources.[101] At this point, having already stated that he would not seek re-election, Olmert told the Turkish interlocutors that he would agree to a summit with President Assad in Ankara. However, this did not happen. During a marathon telephone conversation between Erdoğan and Assad with Olmert sitting in a room adjacent to the Turkish prime minister's office, the Syrians backtracked. According to Olmert, the Syrians had demanded that the summit should be about 'the return of the Golan Heights to Syria', which was a far cry from what Olmert had in mind.[102] As he made clear from the outset, he would only participate in a summit that would include discussion of a full peace agreement, open borders and full diplomatic relations.[103] The two sides were unable to reconcile these gaps.

There are two possible explanations for the Syrian retraction. One was Olmert's untenable domestic position. As he himself noted, the police investigations made 'a big impression' in Israel and around the world at a time when his negotiations with Syria were entering their most critical phase.[104] Also, the Syrians were aware that Olmert, a weak prime minister, could not deliver on an agreement that involved full withdrawal from the Golan. A second explanation was that Syria had not entered negotiations in good faith. Rather, as the USA had always suspected, Syria's aim was to undermine the US policy of Syrian isolation rather than to conclude a peace agreement with Israel. When Olmert returned from Ankara, it was clear that his strategy towards Syria and the Palestinians had failed.

While these delicate negotiations were underway, in June 2008 Egypt brokered a ceasefire between Israel and Hamas, which was based on two elements. Hamas, which controlled the Gaza Strip, would call a halt to attacks by Palestinian armed groups against Israel and Israel would cease its military operations in the Gaza Strip. The agreement also required Israel gradually to lift the blockage it had imposed on the Gaza Strip since 2007.[105] Olmert, rather ominously, predicted that the 'truce would be fragile and could be short-lived' while Hamas's leader in Gaza, Ismail Haniya, said the truce would 'bring stability to Israel if they commit themselves to it'.[106]

---

[101] Interview Tourgeman; Olmert, *In Person*, p. 762.   [102] Olmert, *In Person*, p. 763.
[103] Olmert, *In Person*, p. 762.   [104] Olmert, *In Person*, p. 761.
[105] 'Israel and Hamas Cease Fire Begins', *BBC*, http://news.bbc.co.uk/1/hi/world/mid dle_east/7462554.stm, accessed 10 January 2019.
[106] Ibid.

The political context surrounding the June 2008 ceasefire was combustible. Attempts to achieve Palestinian domestic reconciliation failed and Hamas maintained its official rejection of the conditions proposed by the Quartet. This context notwithstanding, three months into the truce it was clear that the ceasefire had produced a rather dramatic effect. A report compiled by a leading Israeli research centre shows that the number of rockets and mortars fired at Israel fell dramatically compared to previous months. In the first six months of 2008, 179 rockets were fired from Gaza into Israel every month on average. Following the truce, between July and October, the monthly average plummeted to three.[107] This sharp decrease indicated that Hamas was observing the ceasefire but was unable to prevent other armed groups from firing the occasional rocket.

On 4 November 2008, the delicate ceasefire was dealt a serious blow when Israel launched a military raid into the Gaza Strip. The IDF said that the target was a tunnel, which, it claimed, Hamas was planning to use to capture Israeli soldiers positioned on the border fence 250 metres distant. Hamas denied the claim.[108] While it is difficult to verify either side's claims, building a tunnel on the Gazan side of the border was not a breach of the ceasefire whereas the military incursion most certainly was. Israel and Hamas were on thin ice as it became apparent that Israel had stalled on the second condition of the ceasefire, lifting of the blockade which had been only slightly alleviated.[109]

This was the background to the two-pronged tactic employed by Hamas as the six-month ceasefire period ended. On 18 December, Hamas stated publicly that it would not agree to a renewal of the ceasefire on the grounds that it had been violated by Israel's raid on Gaza and the continuing blockade.[110] Over the next week, Hamas renewed its attacks

---

[107] 'Summary of Rocket Fire and Mortar Shelling in 2008', *Intelligence and Terrorism Information Centre* at the Israeli Intelligence Heritage & Commemoration Centre, pp. 6–7, https://web.archive.org/web/20110524125511/http://www.terrorism-info.org.il/m alam_multimedia/English/eng_n/pdf/ipc_e007.pdf, accessed 10 January 2018.

[108] Rory McCarthy, 'Gaza Truce Broken as Israeli Raid Kills 6 Hamas Gunmen', *Guardian*, 5 November 2008, www.theguardian.com/world/2008/nov/05/israelandthepalesti nians; Amir Buchbut, 'Gaza: IDF Force Operated to Dismantle a "Ticking Tunnel"', *Ma'ariv*, 4 November 2008, www.makorrishon.co.il/nrg/online/1/ART1/807/233.html? hp=0&loc=1&tmp=9926; Baconi, *Hamas Contained*, p. 154.

[109] Measures taken by the Israelis to alleviate the blockage are available in 'Humanitarian Assistance to Gaza During the Period of Calm (19 June –18 December 2008), *IMFA*, https://mfa.gov.il/MFA/PressRoom/2008/Pages/Humanitarian_assistance%20_to_Gaz a_since_June_19_calm_understanding_18_Nov_2008.aspx, accessed 11 January 2019.

[110] Associated Press, 'Hamas: The Period of Calm with Israel is over', *Ma'Ariv*, 18 December 2008, www.makorrishon.co.il/nrg/online/1/ART1/827/576.html? hp=0&loc=1&tmp=6383.

362   The End of the Road

on Israel, launching more than one hundred rockets and mortars on Ashkelon, Nevtivot and the broader western Negev area, and attempting to plant an explosive device near the border fence.[111]

In parallel with Hamas's stepping up of its military attacks, it dispatched a proposal to the Israelis about a renewal of the ceasefire, via Professor Bob Pastor. Pastor, who was working with former US President, Jimmy Carter, had perhaps spent more time than any US official with Hamas's senior leadership. In his capacity as Senior Advisor on Conflict Resolution in the Middle East to the Carter Centre, he and former President Carter met with Khaled Mashaal, Chairman of the Politbureaux of Hamas, in Damascus in mid-December 2008. Mashal gave Pastor a written proposal for how to restore the ceasefire, which was essentially the same agreement that Israel and Hamas had reached in June 2008. Pastor travelled to Tel Aviv and delivered Hamas's proposal a few days later to Major General (ret.) Amos Gilad, then director of the defence ministry's political affairs bureau. He told Gilad that if Israel accepted and agreed to implement the proposal, to which it had previously consented, but had not implemented, Hamas would stop firing rockets. According to Pastor, Gilad promised to communicate the proposal directly to Minister of Defence Barak and expected an answer either that evening or the following day. The next day, Pastor phoned Gilad's office three times, but received no response.[112] Shortly afterwards, on 27 December 2008, Israel launched Operation Cast Lead.

Operation Cast Lead began with a ferocious air assault, followed by an air-ground phase. Hamas and other Palestinian factions responded with rocket fire into towns in southern Israel, maintaining a battery of around thirty-five rockets and mortar shells a day on average.[113] The fighting lasted three weeks, ending with a unilateral ceasefire, issued by Israel, on 16 January 2009. The toll of the conflict reflected Israel's utter military superiority over Hamas and the ferociousness of the assault. According to the Israeli human rights organization, B'Tselem, 1,391 Palestinian were killed in the Gaza Strip, 759 of whom were non-combatants and 344 of whom were minors. On the Israeli side, six security personnel and three

---

[111] 'Behind the Headlines: Rockets Rain Down on Southern Israel', *IMFA*, https://mfa.gov.il/MFA/ForeignPolicy/Issues/Pages/Behind_the_Headlines_Rockets_on_souther n_Israel_Dec_2008.aspx, accessed 10 January 2019.

[112] 'The Hamas File', private papers of Professor Robert Pastor. I am grateful to Professor Avi Shlaim for giving me access to the documents chronicling Pastor's diplomacy attempt.

[113] 'Operation Cast Lead: Israel Strikes at Hamas Terror in Gaza', *IMFA*, http://mfa.gov.il/MFA/ForeignPolicy/Terrorism/Pages/Israel_strikes_back_against_Hamas_terror_infr astructure_Gaza_27-Dec-2008.aspx, accessed 17 July 2018; Baconi, *Hamas Contained*, pp. 156–7.

Israeli civilians were killed.[114] Similarly, physical damage on the Israeli side was limited, whereas the destruction Israel wrought on the Gaza Strip was extensive. Despite charged debate over the legality of the Israeli attacks, it is undisputed that it caused major destruction in the Gaza Strip via attacks on private property and numerous civilian infrastructures, the destruction of mosques, government and UN Relief and Works Agency buildings, food production areas, water and sewage infrastructure facilities.[115]

Why, given the message relayed to the Israelis via Pastor, a very credible messenger, did the diplomatic option of renewing and implementing the 2008 ceasefire not elicit a response from the Israelis? It is, perhaps, because Operation Cast Lead had already been planned.[116] Olmert explains in his memoirs, that Israel waited 'for the right time – in terms of our ability to respond forcefully towards Hamas and reduce its motivation to attack us, and harnessing the international community to support our forceful response'.[117] Therefore, it is clear that the operation was part of Israel's broader strategy towards Hamas, which could not be reconciled with further exploration of the diplomatic option proposed by Pastor. Comments made prior to the launch of Operation Cast Lead (March 2008) by General Gadi Eisenkott, the then chief of the northern command, and by other non-serving, but well-placed military thinkers, provide insights into what this strategy might have entailed.[118] These statements reflect the belief that Hamas should be deterred by punitive military force, destruction of civilian infrastructure and assets and pressure on the civilian population. This approach to confronting Hamas was articulated in the Dahiya Doctrine, a plan developed and approved following the destruction wrought by the IDF on Hezbollah's headquarters in Dahiya, south Beirut, during the 2006 Israel-Hamas War.[119]

---

[114] 'Deaths During Operation Cast Lead', *B'Tselem*, www.btselem.org/hebrew/statistics/fatalities/during-cast-lead/by-date-of-event, accessed 16 July 2018.

[115] For the debate, see United Nations Human Rights Council, *Report of the United Nations Fact Finding Mission on the Gaza Conflict* (henceforth, the Goldstone Report), 2009, pp. 17, 19, 105–15; ' Gaza Operations Investigations: Second Update', www.mfa.gov.il/NR/rdonlyres/1483B296-7439-4217-933C-653CD19CE859/0/GazaUpdateJuly2010.pdf, accessed 16 January 2012.

[116] See the Goldstone Report, pp. 324–9; statement by DM Barak, Israeli Ministry of Foreign Affairs, www.mfa.gov.il/MFA/Government/Communiques/2009/Statement_DM_Ehud_Barak_3-Jan-2009.htm, accessed 13 December 2011.

[117] Olmert, *In Person*, p. 765.

[118] Reuters, 'Israel Warns Hezbollah War will Invite Destruction', *Ynet*, 10 March 2008, www.ynetnews.com/articles/0,7340,L-3604893,00.html, accessed 23 October 2018; Giora Eiland, 'The Third Lebanon War: Target Lebanon', *Strategic Assessment*, 11, 2, 2008: 9–17; Dr Mati Steinberg, a former senior advisor to the Israeli General Security Service, quoted in the Goldstone Report, p. 95.

[119] Reuters, 'Israel Warns Hezbollah War will Invite Destruction'.

364   The End of the Road

The tactics used by the IDF during Operation Cast Lead encapsulated the Dahiya Doctrine. IAF data state that '99 percent of the firing that was carried out hit targets accurately', meaning that the damage inflicted during the first week of the aerial attacks was intentional, not collateral.[120] Intensive use of unarmed aerial vehicles during the ground phase of the operation suggests that high levels of accuracy in managing firepower were maintained.[121] Thus, Israel's attack on Gaza during Operation Cast Lead should be seen as part of the broader policy it had employed towards Hamas since its 2006 election victory. It was designed to deter Hamas, keep it isolated via the blockade and collectively penalize Gaza's civilian population with the political aim of putting pressure on it to repudiate Hamas. However, there was also a personal element to the ferocious attack launched by Israel on Gaza. Defence Minister Ehud Barak wanted to stop the operation after a few days because he felt its objectives had been achieved. Yet Olmert was intent on prolonging the attacks. Reflecting retrospectively on this episode, Barak suggested that Olmert perhaps wanted to 'balance the failures in Lebanon with "success" in Gaza' by 'expand[ing] our attacks'.[122]

Imprisoned

Ehud Olmert's government launched the botched 2006 Lebanon War and the most ferocious military attack on the Gaza Strip since the 1948 Arab-Israeli War. The prime minister had presided over the destruction of a Syrian nuclear reactor while, simultaneously, negotiating with President Assad. During Olmert's time in office, the most forthcoming peace proposal from an Israeli prime minister was made to the Palestinians. Olmert's ability to launch severe military strikes was not surprising and they were supported by the Israeli public, the parliament and Olmert's cabinet. In contrast, his peace overtures to the Palestinians and Syria were politically unviable. Indeed, Olmert's proposals to Syria and the Palestinians are a reflection more of Olmert's personal journey from the Revisionist Israeli right to the centre ground of Israeli politics. Plainly, his interlocutors, Presidents Abbas and Assad, were aware of this, which might explain why they did not respond when the crucial offers were put on the table.

Throughout his term, Olmert was a beleaguered prime minister. Delegitimized early on by the botched Israel-Hezbollah War, he lost command over his cabinet – as well as parliament and the public – and

---

[120] Quoted in the Goldstone Report, p. 327.   [121] Goldstone Report, p. 328.
[122] Barak, *My Country, My Life*, p. 415.

was unable to carry through his ambitious plans. The numerous police investigations as his time in office progressed weakened him further and, eventually, brought about his downfall. These domestic constraints limited his foreign policy of peace and determined his personal future. After stepping down from office, Olmert became embroiled in numerous trials. At the age of seventy, he became the first former Israeli head of government to be charged with bribery and given a prison sentence, when one of the numerous cases against him was upheld by Israel's Supreme Court.[123] His failure to conclude a peace deal with either the Palestinians or Syria marked the end of the road for Israel's foreign policy of exchanging land for peace.

[123] 'Ehud Olmert, Corruption Cases', *BBC*, www.bbc.com/news/world-middle-east-1642 6018, accessed 17 July 2018.

17   Vulnerable Ties

Immediately after the end of the Cold War, the USA was established as the sole world superpower. However, the 2003 invasion of Iraq and the later 2008 financial crash weakened US dominance and gave rise to a de-centred international system. China has continued its 'peaceful rise'; the EU's ranks have expanded; and new powers, such as India, were becoming increasingly influential internationally. These changes to the global landscape had raised serious questions for Israeli foreign policy. Should Israel diversify its alliances or try to further deepen its ties with the USA? Could the rising powers in Asia, such as China and India, constitute an economic alternative to the EU as Israel's chief trading partner? Could Israel separate its protracted conflicts in the Middle East, especially with the Palestinians, from its foreign policy beyond that region?

The Enduring US-Israeli Strategic Alliance

Israel's most consistent strategic foreign policy aim during the post-Cold War period was to deepen and consolidate its strategic alliance with the USA. As a Congressional report reveals, Israeli foreign policy has been very successful in this respect. As of 2019, Israel has been the largest cumulative recipient of US foreign assistance since WWII, averaging $3 billion annually since the 1980s, mainly in the form of Foreign Military Financing (FMF).[1] Civic aid, via Economic Support Fund grants, was scaled down and then was discontinued in 2008 with recognition of Israel as a fully industrialized state.[2]

Using FMF, Israel purchased various US-manufactured military ordinances, including M-16 rifles, supersonic jet fighters, global position-

---

[1] Jeremy M. Sharp, 'US Foreign Aid to Israel', 7 August 019, *Congressional Research Service*, https://fas.org/sgp/crs/mideast/RL33222.pdf, accessed 19 December 2019.

[2] Jeremy M. Sharp, 'US Foreign Aid to Israel', Congressional Research Service, 2010, p. 1.

The Enduring US-Israeli Strategic Alliance 367

ing systems and Patriot missiles.[3] Israel was allowed to use approximately 25 per cent of its FMF for in-country weapons procurement, a benefit not granted to any other recipient of US military assistance.[4] This allowed Israel's defence industries to achieve economies of scale and produce highly sophisticated equipment for certain niche markets. Thus, FMF has been integral to Israel's ascendance to a leading arms-exporting country.[5] FMF is also essential for Israel's defence proper. It has been used to fund joint US-Israeli missile defence cooperation, which focuses on systems intercepting rockets, conventional missiles and missiles with nuclear-tipped warheads, which include the Iron Dome, David's Sling and the Arrow antimissile systems.[6]

US direct aid, via FMF, has been complemented by US-backed loan guarantees, which have helped to lower the rates related to Israel's borrowing from commercial sources. The benefits of this indirect form of aid are significant. As we have seen, the Rabin government secured $10 billion in loan guarantees to assist its absorption of immigrants from the former Soviet Union. Subsequently, the Sharon government received $12 billion in loan guarantees, which it used to alleviate Israel's 2003 economic recession and to fund preparations for possible attacks during the US war with Iraq. Congress extended authority to provide loan guarantees to financial year 2023, with the proviso that they should be used only within Israel's pre-5 June 1967 borders. However, since the Israeli budget is fungible, US loan guarantees free up resources that Israel then can use in areas beyond these borders.[7] The US-Israel Strategic Partnership Act, passed in 2014, puts decisions by any future Administration to sell arms to other states in the Middle East under further scrutiny and requires the USA to provide further capabilities and training should Israel deem it necessary as a result of such sales.[8]

The deepening US-Israeli alliance is evident not only in various forms of US aid but also in stronger politico-military ties. Significant among these, the longstanding US pledge to maintain Israel's 'Qualitative Military Edge' (QME) over neighbouring militaries. This pledge obtained legal grounds with the Naval Vessel Transfer Act, passed by Congress in 15 October 2008. The Act defines QME as:

---

[3] Stuart A. Cohen, 'Light and Shadows in US-Israeli Military Ties', in Robert Freedman (ed.), *Israel and the United States: Six Decades of US-Israeli Relations* (Boulder: Westview Press, 2012), p. 145.
[4] Sharp, 'US Foreign Aid to Israel', p. 5.   [5] Sharp, 'US Foreign Aid to Israel', pp. 5, 7.
[6] Sharp, 'US Foreign Aid to Israel', p. 10.
[7] Sharp, 'US Foreign Aid to Israel', 7 August 2019, p. 1.
[8] Sharp, 'US Foreign Aid to Israel', 7 August 2019, pp. 3–4.

368   Vulnerable Ties

The ability to counter and defeat any credible conventional military threat from any individual state or possible coalition of states or from non-state actors, while sustaining minimal damage and casualties, through the use of superior military means, possessed in sufficient quantity ... that in their technical characteristics are superior in capability to those of such other individual or possible coalition of states or non-state actors.[9]

In addition, the Act requires the US president to carry out an 'empirical and qualitative assessment on an ongoing basis of the extent to which Israel possesses a qualitative military edge over military threats to Israel'.[10] It requires 'certification' for proposed arms sales to 'any country in the Middle East other than Israel' to include 'a determination that the sale or export of the defense articles or defense services will not adversely affect Israel's qualitative military edge over military threats to Israel'.[11]

What accounts for the expansion and deepening US-Israeli relations? Eminent political scientists John Mearsheimer and Stephen Walt ascribe it to 'the political power of the Israel lobby', defined as 'a loose coalition of individuals and groups that seeks to influence American foreign policy in ways that will benefit Israel'.[12] According to Mearsheimer and Walt, the lobby 'played key roles in shaping US foreign policy towards the Israeli-Palestinian conflict, the ill-fated invasion of Iraq, and the on-going confrontations with Syria and Iran'.[13]

Although this analysis offers food for thought, it is inadequate. We have seen, in contrast to the claim made by Walt and Mearsheimer that US and Israeli foreign policy towards Syria diverged during Prime Minister Olmert's term. Israel engaged in peace talks with Syria, via Turkish mediation, while the USA sought to isolate and penalize the Assad regime. Similarly, Mearsheimer and Walt ignore foreign policy differences over Iran that were evident during the George W. Bush administration. In a private meeting with Ehud Olmert and Ehud Barak, Bush outlined the US government's formal position: 'We are', he explained, 'totally against any action by you to mount an attack on the [Iranian] nuclear plants ... We expect you not to do it. And we're not going to do it, either, as long as I am president. I wanted it to be clear.'[14]

The depiction of Israel's role in the US-led invasion of Iraq is similarly inaccurate. According to Dan Meridor, who was intimately involved in the US-Israeli strategic liaison over Iraq, Israel supported the invasion

---

[9] Public Law 110–429, 15 October 2008, US Congress Official Website, p. 3, www .congress.gov/110/plaws/publ429/PLAW-110publ429.pdf, accessed 26 July 2018.
[10] Ibid, p. 3.   [11] Ibid, p. 3.
[12] The chief exponents of the Israel lobby thesis are John Mearsheimer and Stephen Walt; see Mearsheimer and Walt, *The Israel Lobby*, p. viii.
[13] Ibid.   [14] Barak, *My Country My Life*, p. 418.

The Enduring US-Israeli Strategic Alliance   369

'because Saddam Hussein was a strong Arab leader who spoke about the destruction of Israel. We would not stand in the way of anyone who wanted to attack him.'[15] This position is consistent with the ample public statements, made by Israeli politicians and pro-Israel groups in the USA, supporting the invasion of Iraq.[16] However, Meridor hastened to add that the invasion of Iraq 'was not an Israeli initiative; it came purely from the US. In fact, we always prioritized the threats posed by Syria and Iran', a point made repeatedly by Israeli officials.[17]

Apart from overstating Israel-US foreign policy convergences, the 'Israel lobby thesis' also exaggerates the degree of cohesion in the pro-Israel lobby. In fact, on certain issues it is divided internally and, at times, is at odds with the Israeli government. For instance, AIPAC, the most powerful pro-Israel group, for years lobbied against the PLO, which is why it did not support the Rabin-Peres government peace process.[18] Afterwards, during the GWoT, the pro-Israel lobby was split over Israel's foreign policy towards the Palestinians. AIPAC focused on harnessing US support for Israel – via Congress – to deal with its security threats. Its backing of attempts to revive the peace process was very slight. J-Street, a lobby group established in April 2008, which described itself as a 'pro peace, pro-Israel movement', adopted a different stance. It reflected the growing criticism of Israel's policies towards the Palestinians from within segments of the US Jewish community and backed the peace process strongly. Although no match for AIPAC, in 2010, it boasted 110,000 online supporters and a budget of $3 million.

At the other end of the political spectrum were the right-wing lobby groups such as the Zionists of America and the Christian Zionist organizations. These groups have benefited from close ties with Israeli prime ministers, especially from Likud, and burgeoning institutional ties. For example, in 2004, MK Dr Yuri Stern and MK representatives of the broad Israeli electorate established the Knesset Christian Allies Caucus, whose aim was 'to strengthen the cooperation between Christian leaders and the State of Israel'.[19] Right-wing Israel lobby groups supported

---

[15] Interview 2 Dan Meridor.   [16] Mearsheimer and Walt, *The Israel Lobby*, pp. 229–43.

[17] Interview 2 Dan Meridor; Barak, *My Country, My Life*, p. 418; Alan Sipress, 'Israel Emphasizes Iranian Threat', *Washington Post*, 7 February 2002, www.washingtonpost.com/archive/politics/2002/02/07/israel-emphasizes-iranian-threat/b033e c97-9ad4-4ed2-8b2c-c13e3dc823f0/?utm_term=.e717a8d6c697, accessed 1 August 2018.

[18] Dov Waxman, 'The Pro-Israel Lobby in the United States: Past, Present and Future in Freedman', *Israel and the United States*, pp. 90–1; Neil Rubin, 'The Relationship Between American Evangelical Christians and the State of Israel' in Freedman, *Israel and the United States*, p. 241.

[19] Knesset Christian Allies Caucus formal website, http://cac.org.il/site/about/, accessed 31 July 2018.

370   Vulnerable Ties

Israel's use of strong military force while opposing Israel's territorial concessions, especially in Jerusalem. J-Street rejected these views while AIPAC offered selective support.[20] In addition, the broader US Jewish community majority was suspicious of Christian Zionist organizations' end-time theology which sees a strong Jewish State as figurative and literal cannon fodder for Armageddon. It is wary, also, of the Christian evangelical emphasis on proselytizing, and its domestic politics towards abortion, gun control and the separation between Church and state.[21]

Given its flaws, the Israel lobby thesis does not help to explain the enduring US-Israeli alliance. An alternative, which centres on decision-makers, is more appropriate. Despite some instances of discord, overall, all Israeli prime ministers since the end of the Cold War have aligned Israeli foreign policy to the USA. Yitzhak Shamir acceded to the US request not to respond to Iraq's attacks during the 1991 Gulf War. Then, throughout the Clinton administration, according to Dennis Ross, the USA and Israel were 'strategic partners for peace'.[22] Ross's depiction captures US-Israeli alignment during the peace negotiations under Rabin, Peres and Barak, although not Netanyahu.

Similarly, albeit in a distinctly different context, Israel and the USA were aligned strategically during George W. Bush's presidency. In a highly symbolic speech in the Knesset, marking the sixtieth anniversary of the State of Israel, Bush forcefully expressed his views on Israeli and US foreign policy alignment. As he put it:

Israel's population may be just over 7 million. But when you confront terror and evil, you are 307 million strong, because the United States of America stands with you. America stands with you in breaking up terrorist networks and denying the extremists sanctuary. America stands with you in firmly opposing Iran's nuclear weapons ambitions. Permitting the world's leading sponsor of terror to possess the world's deadliest weapons would be an unforgivable betrayal for future generations.[23]

These comments were not mere rhetorical flourish. Under Bush Jr, the US-Israeli strategic alliance had expanded and had become more institutionalized via legislation, loan guarantees and FMF.

---

[20] Waxman, 'The Pro-Israel Lobby, pp. 91–4; Rubin, 'The Relationship Between American Evangelical Christians', p. 239.

[21] Rubin, 'The Relationship Between Evangelical Christians and Israel', p. 247

[22] Dennis Ross, *Doomed to Succeed: The U.S.-Israel Relationship from Truman to Obama* (New York: Farrar, Straus, & Giroux, 2015), p. 215; Rabin's chief negotiator with Syria, Itamar Rabinovich, conveyed the same message; see Rabinovich, *Yitzhak Rabin*, p. 180.

[23] 'Address of President George Bush to the Knesset', 15 May 2008, *IMFA*, https://knesset .gov.il/description/eng/doc/speech_bush_2008_eng.htm, accessed 1 August 2018.

The Enduring US-Israeli Strategic Alliance

In the same speech, Bush recognized a new element – the rise of Israel as a start-up nation – which went beyond state-to-state relations and served to deepen the US-Israeli strategic alliance. 'When Americans look at Israel', the president told the Knesset, 'we see a pioneer spirit that worked an agricultural miracle and now leads a high-tech revolution. We see world-class universities and a global leader in business and innovation.'[24] Indeed, economic ties have become an important facet of the US-Israeli alliance. When the US-Israeli FTA was signed in 1985, exports to the USA totalled $2.1 billion, representing approximately three-quarters of the aid Israel received.[25] By 2009, exports had increased more than tenfold, to $28 billion, placing Israel among America's top twenty trading partners.[26] Hi-tech cooperation is also important. Several joint foundations generate collaborations in industrial R&D, technological innovation and agricultural and scientific research.[27] Remarkably, by 2008, Israel accounted for more NASDAQ listed hi-tech companies than any other country outside North America.[28]

However, beneath this public veneer, Bush and some of his close ministerial circle were aware of a developing gap between Israeli and US 'shared values'. Secretary of State Rice reveals in her memoirs that she and the president were deeply disturbed by the visible and enduring signs of Israeli occupation. Rice recalls that:

The President decided, against the wishes of the Israelis, to travel *by car* to Bethlehem in the West Bank. When one goes by helicopter, it is easy to miss the ugliness of the occupation, including the checkpoints and the security wall. I insisted that the President needed to see it for himself and it would have been an insult to the Palestinians if he didn't. Riding in the car with him, I could see the look on his face. We sped through wide-open barriers, but the graffiti-laden wall couldn't be ignored, even at high speed. "This is awful", he said quietly.[29]

These privately shared sentiments had little influence on US-Israeli relations, which remained underpinned by foreign policy alignment, institutionalized US aid and increasing economic and technological ties. Mutual public support reinforced these strong foundations. Eytan Gilboa,

---

[24] 'Address of President George Bush to the Knesset', 15 May 2008.
[25] '1985: U.S. Trade in Goods with Israel, US Census Bureau', www.census.gov/foreign-trade/balance/c5081.html#1985, accessed 29 July 2018.
[26] '2009: U.S. Trade in Goods with Israel, US Census Bureau', www.census.gov/foreign-trade/balance/c5081.html#2009, accessed 29 July 2018; 'Israel and the United States: The Special Bond between Two Nations and Two Peoples', p. 8.
[27] 'The United States and Israel', p. 128; 'Factsheet U.S-Israel Economic Relations', US Embassy in Israel website, https://il.usembassy.gov/our-relationship/policy-history/fact-sheet-u-s-israel-economic-relationship/, accessed 30 July 2018.
[28] 'The United States and Israel', p. 132.
[29] Rice, *No Higher Honor*, pp. 622–3, emphasis in original.

372   Vulnerable Ties

a leading expert on US public opinion trends, maintains that some two-thirds of Americans demonstrated a consistently favourable opinion of Israel during the post-Cold War era. They identified Israel as a loyal ally and the most reliable in the Middle East. Meanwhile, public support in Israel for the alliance was overwhelming, which adds a domestic political incentive for its foreign policy alignment to the USA.[30] Clearly, within this broader context, the Israel lobby is highly significant. However, its influence is confined to – rather than defines – the foreign policy parameters set by US presidents and broader public sentiment. This important point is glossed over by the Israel lobby thesis.

Israel and China: A Partnership of Convenience

Israeli-Chinese relations, forged during the 1990s against the backdrop of the Arab-Israeli process, solidified during the post-Cold War era. Various Israeli government agencies were instrumental in expanding economic and scientific bilateral ties. These included the foreign affairs, science and technology, economy and trade ministries. Israel's branding as a start-up nation, its vibrant hi-tech community and private organizations, such as the Israel Chamber of Commerce in China and Silicon Dragon Israel, brought together Israeli and Chinese companies.[31] Israel's hi-tech and chemical, communications, medical optics and agriculture sectors were attractive for China's post-Cold War modernizing and its rapidly growing economy.[32]

Within a decade, these activities resulted in a sharp rise in trade, from $750 million in 2000 to $5.5 billion in 2008, positioning China as Israel's second largest trading partner in 2010.[33] In addition, since the signing of joint scientific research and development agreements in 1993, 1995 and 2000, more than fifty joint projects have been completed in diverse fields including: neuroscience, nanotechnology and computerized learning.[34] By 2010, these scientific ties were upgraded with the signing of

---

[30] Eytan Gilboa, 'The Public Dimension in U.S.-Israeli Relations', in Eytan Gilboaand Efraim Inbar, *US-Israeli Relations in a New Era: Issues and Challenges after 9/11* (London: Routledge, 2009), pp. 56–9.

[31] Israel Chamber of Commerce official website, www.ischam.org and Silicon Dragon Israel official website, www.silicondragonventures.com/, both links accessed 16 August 2018.

[32] Aron Shai, 'The Evolution of Israeli-Chinese Friendship', *Research Paper No. 7* (Tel Aviv: Daniel Abraham Centre for International and Regional Studies, 2014), p. 24.

[33] 'Israel's Foreign Trade 2000–2010', *Central Bureau of Statistics*, p. 6, www.cbs.gov.il/www/statistical/trade_115_e.pdf, accessed 6 August 2018; Yoram Evron, 'Economics, Science and Technology in Israel-China Relations', in Goldstein and Shichor, *China and Israel*, p. 202.

[34] 'International Relations China', Israeli Ministry of Science and Technology website, www.gov.il/en/Departments/General/most_intl_countries_cn, accessed 8 August 2018.

the China-Israel Cooperation Program for Industrial R&D, which complemented similar agreements between Israel and Chinese provinces.[35]

The expanding economic and scientific ties are linked inextricably to the changing international political context of Israel-China relations. Hussein Agha and Ahmad Khalidi, who negotiated on behalf of the Palestinians at different points during the post-Cold War era, witnessed this trend first hand. They explain that, during the Cold War, the Palestinian national struggle found a natural home within the liberationist and anti-colonial movements in Algeria and Vietnam, and was embraced by emerging Asian powers as part of their new sense of independence. However, the ending of the Cold War had the effect of ending this 'Third World Moment'. Emerging powers, such as China, chose 'economic self-interest in place of ideological commitment to their erstwhile partners in the Third World'.[36]

At the same time, there were certain constraints on Israel's foreign policy towards China. Paramount were US concerns over Israeli-Chinese military ties. A formal report, issued by the US House of Representatives in 1999 (the Cox Report), found that 'significant transfers of U.S. military technology' took place 'in the mid-1990s through the re-export by Israel of advanced technology transferred to it by the United States'.[37] These findings formed the background to the US veto of two major deals Israel struck with China. In the mid-1990s, Israel agreed to the sale to China of Phalcon, an Israeli improved version of the US AWACS. Then, in 2004, Israel pledged to service and supply spare parts for the Harpy-armed drone aircraft, several units of which it had sold to China in 1994.

The American response to and outcomes of these deals are instructive. The Pentagon was stiffly opposed to both. It referred to the risks involved in transferring derivative US technologies to China, which might use the weapons against Taiwan, a US ally. Under US pressure, which included threats to cut FMF, Israel cancelled both transactions and compensated China. In addition, Israel signed a memorandum of understanding with the Pentagon, which required that Israel obtain authorization from US

---

[35] 'China and Israel', Israel Innovation Authority official website, www.matimop.org.il/ch ina.html, accessed 16 August 2018.

[36] Hussein Agha and Ahmad Samih Khalidi, 'The End of this Road: The Decline of the Palestinian National Movement', *New Yorker*, 8 August 2017, p. 8, www.newyorker.co m/news/news-desk/the-end-of-this-road-the-decline-of-the-palestinian-national-move ment, accessed 6 August 2018.

[37] Christopher Cox et al., *The Cox Report*, Volume I (Washington: US House of Representatives, 1999), pp. 26–7, https://china.usc.edu/sites/default/files/legacy/AppIm ages/ch1.pdf, accessed 7 August 2018.

374   Vulnerable Ties

officials to allow the sale to China of products containing civilian/military US-Israeli dual technology.[38]

Another constraint was China's heavy dependence on Middle East oil. Saudi Arabia, China's largest supplier of crude oil from 2000 to 2010, provided 20 per cent of the PRC's crude oil needs. In 2009, trade between the two states had reached $41.8 billion.[39] During the same period, Iran was China's third largest supplier of crude oil. Moreover, as Western and European companies reduced their investments in Iran in response to stricter US sanctions, Chinese companies moved in. In fact, the largest of China's national oil companies' upstream projects in the Middle East are in Iraq and Iran. Chinese firms have signed service contracts to develop several large oilfields in both countries. China National Petroleum Corporation's (CNPC) development of the Rumaila oilfield in conjunction with BP is CNPCs top-producing overseas project, accounting for almost half of CNPC's net overseas oil and natural gas production.[40]

The US factor and China's heavy reliance on Middle East oil may explain the meagre political dividends Israeli foreign policy gained from its relations with China since normalization. Chinese weapons sales are an example. Former head of Mossad, Efraim Halevy, and Israeli diplomats claim that 'China supports our most extreme enemies, refusing successive Israeli requests not to supply them the knowhow and equipment to develop WMDs.'[41] There is evidence to support Halevy's claims. During the 2006 Lebanon War, Hezbollah struck an Israeli Saar-5 destroyer with a C-802 radar-guided, anti-shipping missile, manufactured in Iran using Chinese technology.[42] Similarly, contrary to Israel's requests, Beijing maintained its 'balanced approach' towards Iran's nuclear

---

[38] 'Fear for Early Warning Planes Hangs Over Jinang's arrival in Israel', *New York Times*, www.nytimes.com/2000/04/13/world/deal-for-early-warning-plane-hangs-over-jiang-s-arrival-in-israel.html, accessed 8 August 2018; Scott Wilson, 'Israel Set to End China Arms Deal Under US Pressure', *Washington Post*, 27 June 2005, www.washingtonpost.com/wp-dyn/content/article/2005/06/26/AR2005062600544.html, accessed 8 August 2018; Aron Shai, 'Beijing and Jerusalem: Diplomatic Relations and the International Arena', in Goldstein and Shichor, p. 180.

[39] 'Chinese President Meets Saudi Arabian King on Ties', *People's Daily Online*, http://en.people.cn/90001/90776/90883/6589772.html, accessed 16 August 2018.

[40] Yoram Evron, 'China's Diplomatic Initiatives in the Middle East: The Quest for a Great Power Role in the Region', *International Relations*, 31, 2, 2017: 126; Erica S. Downs Testimony before the U.S.-China Economic and Security Review Commission, 'China-Middle East Energy Relations', *Brookings Institute*, 6 June 2013, pp. 2–3, www.brookings.edu/testimonies/china-middle-east-energy-relations/m, accessed 8 August 2018.

[41] Suffot, *A China Diary*, p. 144; Navit Zumer, 'Foreign Control of a Strategic Asset Like Tnuva – A Danger', *Ynet*, www.ynet.co.il/articles/0,7340,L-4489097,00.html, accessed 9 August 2018.

[42] News Agencies and Amos Harel, 'Soldier Killed, 3 Missing After Navy Vessel Hit off Beirut Coast', Ha'aretz website, www.haaretz.com/1.4857613, accessed 9 August 2006.

programme, which hinged on diplomacy.[43] Another Chinese-Israeli foreign policy divergence is towards the Arab-Israeli conflict. Historically, as Binyamin Netanyahu and Israeli diplomats recognized, Israel's and China's pattern of voting in the UN was not 'in consonance'.[44] In this vein, China opposed the financial sanctions and boycott imposed on Hamas by Israel and the West.[45]

Israel's and China's foreign policy divergences towards the Middle East and Israel's tilt towards the USA explain Israel's reticence about China's involvement in the Arab-Israeli peace process. In 2002, acceding to a request from the Arab states, China appointed Wang Shijie its first special envoy to the region. Since then, Shijie and other Chinese officials have made several attempts to establish the PRC as a mediator between Israel and the Arabs.[46] However, so far, China continues to be excluded from being a potential mediator in the Arab-Israeli peace process and remains outside the Quartet.

The stark contrast between expanding Chinese-Israeli economic relations and the limited political cooperation is significant. Israel's strategic alliance with the USA, China's interests in the Gulf Cooperation Council (GCC) and Iran and the different approaches to Arab-Israeli relations have restricted Israel-China relations. As long as these factors prevail, Israel-China ties will continue to represent a partnership of convenience.

Israel and India: A New Strategic Partnership?

Has Israel's foreign policy towards India developed into more than a partnership of convenience? The rise to power of the Hindunationalist Bharatiya Janata Party (BJP), following its 1996 election victory, promoted Israeli-Indo ties following normalization in 1992.

---

[43] Aluf Ben, 'Olmert Request from the Chinese: Do not Support Iran', *Ha'aretz*, 8 January 2007, reported by *Walla*, https://news.walla.co.il/item/1037010, accessed 9 August 2018.

[44] Suffot, *A China Diary*, p. 144; Raphael Ahren and Yifeng Zhou, 'Netanyahu to Times of Israel: I hope China's "Superb" Economic Relations with Israel will Affect its UN Votes', *Times of Israel*, www.timesofisrael.com/netanyahu-to-tois-chinese-site-i-hope-beijings-superb-relations-with-israel-will-affect-its-un-votes/, accessed 16 August 2018.

[45] 'Israel Protests Chinas Invitation to Hamas Foreign Minister', *Ha'aretz*, www.haaretz.com/1.4906601, accessed 7 August 2018; Haim Levinson and Amos Harel, 'GSS Documents Reveal: This is how Hamas Transfers Money to Banks in China', *Ha'aretz*, www.haaretz.co.il/news/politics/.premium-1.2127897 (in Hebrew), both links accessed 18 October 2018.

[46] 'Steps to Advance the Middle East Peace Process and to Promote the Establishment of a Nuclear-Weapon-Free Zone in the Middle East', Report Submitted by the People's Republic of China, Ministry of Foreign Affairs of the People's Republic of China official website, www.fmprc.gov.cn/mfa_eng/wjb_663304/zzjg_663340/jks_665232/kjfywj_665252/t196479.shtml, accessed 16 August 2018.

376   Vulnerable Ties

Traditionally, the BJP, unlike the Congress party, had supported rapprochement with Israel. Its Hindu-nationalist agenda chimed well with the definition of Israel as a Jewish and democratic state. Moreover, BJP hardliners perceived Israel as 'anti-Muslim' and, therefore, expected Israel to support India in its prolonged conflict with Pakistan and radical Islamists.[47]

The rise to power of the BJP coincided with a change in the foreign policy perceptions of Indian civil servants and parts of the political elite outside the BJP. Throughout the Cold War, India had supported the Palestinians. In return, it had expected Arab states' backing during its conflict with Pakistan, but this was not forthcoming; instead, Pakistan was supported on grounds of Islamic solidarity. The growing disappointment within India's foreign policy circles over the Arab states' pro-Pakistan stance coincided with the launch, during the 1990s, of the Arab-Israeli peace processes. This concurrence diminished India's erstwhile concern about antagonizing the Arab world by forging closer relations with Israel.[48]

The shift in India's stance towards the Arab world, combined with the ascent to power of the BJP, created auspicious political conditions for the expansion of Israel-Indo ties based on military cooperation. India sought military support following the collapse of the USSR and its Eastern European satellite regimes, which, together, supplied 70 per cent of India's military equipment. India's financial constraints did not allow it to fill this gap by purchasing modern military hardware. Instead, it was forced to rely on upgrading its existing armaments, acquiring force multipliers and forging joint R&D projects in critical sectors. Israel's defence industries were well placed to supply India's post-Cold War requirements.[49] As N.A.K. Browne, India's first military attaché in Tel Aviv-turned IAF chief explains:

Israel enjoyed certain unique advantages over other arms suppliers. These included its experience with weapons and systems of both the former Cold War blocs, the no-questions-asked policy that governs its arms trade, its reputation as a reliable supplier coupled with its expertise in technological innovation and upgradation skills.[50]

These considerations lay behind India's decision to extend its military ties with Israel and to establish a defence wing in its embassy in Tel Aviv in

[47] Achin Vanaik, 'Making India Strong: The BJP Government's Foreign Policy Perspectives', *South Asia: Journal of South Asian Studies*, 25, 3, 2002: 333.
[48] Kumaraswamy, *India's Israel Policy*, pp. 267–8.
[49] Farah Naaz, 'Indo-Israel Military Cooperation, *Strategic Analysis*, 24, 5, 2008: 970–1.
[50] N.A.K. Browne, 'A Perspective on India-Israel Defence and Security Ties', *Strategic Analysis*, 41, 4, 2017: 332.

1997.[51] Initially, military ties were confined to upgrading ancient MiG aircraft and supplying patrol boats. Subsequently, they expanded to include avionics, border management, small arms, missiles and anti-missile systems and cooperation in space.[52] According to various high-ranking Indian serving officers, Israel increased its credibility by providing several strategic weapons systems to India during its 1999 Kargil conflict with Pakistan. Critically, at that point, India was subjected to international sanctions following its 1998 nuclear tests in Pokhran.[53]

The GWoT added a political facet to the security ties. Historically, India had been exposed to violence and terrorist attacks from non-state Islamist groups. For instance, the late 1980s saw the emergence of Pakistan-based groups, such as the Lashkar-e-Taiba and Jaish-e-Muhammad, which opposed India's sovereignty over Kashmir. Subsequently, in the 1990s, home-grown groups, such as the Indian Mujahedeen, emerged against the backdrop of Hindu-Muslim inter-communal tensions.[54]

Following the outbreak of the al-Aqsa Intifada, Israel's and India's exposure to violence and terrorism converged. As Barry Buzan argues convincingly, both countries linked violence and terrorist attacks directed against them in the context of local and regional conflicts, to the GWoT.[55] This common approach strengthened counterterrorism cooperation and intelligence sharing between Mossad and its Indian counterpart, the Research and Analysis Wing. Two years into the GWoT, an Indo-Israel Joint Working Group on Counterterrorism had been established. Meanwhile, India's national security advisor, Shri Brajseh Mishra, publicly discussed Israeli-Indian cooperation against the 'same ugly face of modern day terrorism'.[56]

[51] Browne, 'A Perspective on India-Israel Defence and Security Ties', 326; Naaz, 'Indo-Israel Military Cooperation', 970–1.

[52] P.R. Kumaraswamy, 'Redefining 'Strategic Cooperation', *Strategic Analysis*, 41, 4, 2017: 361.

[53] Alok Deb, 'India-Israel Defence Engagement: Land Forces Cooperation', *Strategic Analysis*, 41, 4, 2017: 337; Browne, 'A Perspective on India Israel Defence and Security Ties', 329–30.

[54] Harsh V. Pant and Ivan Lidarev, 'Indian Counterterrorism Policy and the Influence of the Global War on Terror', *India Review*, 17, 2, 2018: 181–5.

[55] Barry Buzan, 'Will the Global War on Terrorism be the New Cold War?', *International Affairs*, 82, 6, 2006: 1104.

[56] 'India-Israel Joint Working Group on Counterterrorism Communiqué', 28 May 2002, *India Ministry of Foreign Affairs*, www.mea.gov.in/press-releases.htm?dtl/13665/India+Israel+Joint+Working+Group+on+Counterterrorism; Address by Shri Brajesh Mishra, National Security Advisor, at the American Jewish Committee Annual Dinner, Indian Ministry of Foreign Affairs, www.mea.gov.in/Speeches-Statements.htm?dtl/4526/Address+by+Shri+Brajesh+Mishra+National+Security+Advisor+at+the+American+Jewish+Committee+Annual+Dinner, both links accessed 23 August 2018.

378   Vulnerable Ties

The expansion of these closer and more visible political ties was showcased during the official state visit of Ariel Sharon in September 2003. This first-ever visit by an Israeli prime minister and Palestinians' nemesis, at the height of the al-Aqsa Intifada, put the spotlight on Indo-Israeli rapprochement. The Delhi Statement of Friendship and Cooperation, which concluded the visit, reflected Israel's and India's interest-driven relationship. It underscored their joint fight against terrorism and their expanding bilateral economic relations and formalized new bilateral cooperation agreements in several areas including protection of the environment, medicine, culture, education and the fight against trafficking illicit substances. The Middle East peace process was conspicuously marginalized, mentioned only fourteenth among the eighteen clauses in the document.[57]

Expanding military and political ties fuelled economic relations. Bilateral trade rose from $200 million in 1992, when relations were normalized, to $4,747.1 million in 2010. Machinery and equipment, chemicals and fertilizers constituted 75 per cent of Israel's exports to India. These trade figures exclude the significant arms trade: Blarel's careful study shows that India's cumulated arms procurements from Israel grew from $US914 million to $US8,553 between 2000 and 2010.[58] By 2010, India was ranked sixth among Israel's trade partner countries and third in Asia after China and Hong Kong.[59]

Importantly, the arms trade increased under both the Congress-led and BJP-led governments, which shows that the gaps between the two parties on India's Israel policy had narrowed. The Bush Jr administration played a significant role in the process by encouraging rapprochement between Israel and India, two self-proclaimed partners in the US-led GWoT.[60] In this context, the USA consented to Israeli sales to India of hi-tech military ordinances, such as the Phalcon radar system, which had been denied to China.[61]

The significant progress in relations between Israel and India notwithstanding, upgrading these ties to a strategic alliance remained impeded by

---

[57] Delhi Statement on Friendship and Cooperation between India and Israel, *IMFA*, www.mfa.gov.il/mfa/foreignpolicy/bilateral/pages/delhi%20statement%20on%20friendship%20and%20cooperation%20betw.aspx, accessed 24 August 2018.

[58] Blarel, *The Evolution of India's Israel Policy*, p. 323.

[59] Ranking and trade data in 'Overview of India-Israel Bilateral Trade and Economic Relations', *Israeli Ministry of Economy and Industry*, https://itrade.gov.il/india/israel-india/, accessed 24 August 2018.

[60] Nicolas Blarel, 'Assessing US Influence over India-Israel Relations: A Difficult Equation to Balance', *Strategic Analysis*, 41, 4, 2017: 394–5.

[61] Ron Ben-Yishai, 'The Weapons Deal: A First Israeli Phalcon Lands in India, *YNET*, www.ynet.co.il/articles/0,7340,L-3721379,00.html, accessed 24 August 2018.

Israel and India: A New Strategic Partnership? 379

the foreign policy divergences between the two countries towards the Middle East. The foreign policy stance towards the GCC countries is an example. Israel's incipient ties with the GCC countries, such as Qatar and Oman, and the prospects for Israel-Saudi diplomatic relations remained unrealized amid the collapse of the Israeli-Palestinian peace process. By contrast, India's interests in the GCC countries deepened during the post-Cold War period. The 2006 Delhi Declaration between India and Saudi-Arabia – the mainstay among the GCC countries, strongly reflects this trend and called for a wide-ranging partnership in, inter alia, trade, energy and counterterrorism.[62]

By 2010, these goals had largely been achieved. Indian-GCC bilateral trade grew from \$5.6 billion in 2001 to almost \$102 billion post-2010 with the emergence of the GCC as India's second largest trading partner.[63] Crucially, it supplied 45 per cent of India's petroleum.[64] In addition, a common interest in securing the Straits of Hurmuz and Bab el-Mandeb led to a series of joint naval exercises involving the Indian navy and the GCC states.[65] These strategic interests were complemented by migration, cultural and religious ties. In 2010, there were 5.4 million Indians living in the GCC countries – the largest expatriate community in the region, which, according to the World Bank, transferred \$25.5 billion in remittances to the Indian economy.[66]

Israel's and India's foreign policy differences vis-à-vis Iran were more pronounced than those towards the GCC states. Since the 1979 Islamic Revolution, Israel and Iran have been in direct confrontation while, since 2003, India and Iran have been committed to mutual 'strategic' engagement.[67] By 2010, according to India's Foreign Affairs Ministry, bilateral relations with Iran had acquired 'a strategic dimension,

---

[62] 'Delhi Declaration', Indian Ministry of Foreign Affairs official website, www .indianembassy.org.sa/india-saudi-arabia/delhi-declaration, accessed 26 August 2018.

[63] 'India-GCC Relations', Embassy of India in Saudi Arabia's official website, www .indianembassy.org.sa/india-saudi-arabia/india-gcc-relations, accessed 26 Aug 2018.

[64] Harsh V. Pant, 'India's Relations with Iran: Much Ado about Nothing', *Strategic Analysis*, 34, 1, 2011: 68.

[65] Ibid.

[66] 'Migration and Remittances Data 2010, World Bank official website, www.world bank.org/en/topic/migrationremittancesdiasporaissues/brief/migration-remittances-da ta, accessed 26 August 2018; figures on size of Indian community in GCC drawn from Samir Pradhan, 'India and the Gulf Cooperation Council: An Economic and Political Perspective', *Strategic Analysis*, 34, 1, 2010: 94–5.

[67] 'Tehran Declaration', 10 April 2001, Indian Ministry of Foreign Affairs, http://mea .gov.in/in-focus-article.htm?20048/Tehran+Declaration; 'The Republic of India and the Islamic Republic of Iran The New Delhi Declaration', 25 January 2003, Indian Ministry of Foreign Affairs, http://mea.gov.in/bilateral-documents.htm?dtl/7544/The+ Republic+of+India+and+the+Islamic+Republic+of+Iran+quotThe+New+Delhi+Dec larationquot, both links accessed 27 August 2018.

380   Vulnerable Ties

flourishing in the fields of energy, trade, commerce, information, technology, transit' and curbing terrorism emanating from Pakistan.[68] Critically, India opposed a military solution to Iran's nuclear programme and maintained its right to peaceful use of nuclear energy in line with the Treaty on the Non-Proliferation of Nuclear Weapons (NPT).[69] The Israeli-Palestinian conflict was another source of disagreement. India consistently supports Palestinian rights and statehood, calls for 'an end of Israeli settlements in the occupied Palestinian territory' and refuses to recognize Jerusalem as the capital of Israel.[70]

Israel's rapprochement with India is not an emerging strategic alliance. Instead, it should be seen as part of India's drive to diversify its Middle East foreign policy and to position itself as a great power, however exaggerated this self-image. In this context, Israel has carved out a foreign policy niche for itself, defined by its role of key security supplier and its close ties to the USA. However, retaining this position will be contingent on India delinking its foreign policy stance towards Israel, Iran and the GCC countries and keeping domestic opposition groups at bay. The political left and certain segments of India's Muslim community continue staunchly to oppose closer ties with Israel on the grounds of its policy towards the Palestinians.

Israel and the EU: Decoupling Political and Economic Relations

The EU remained salient to Israeli foreign policy throughout the post-Cold War era. As the number of its member states expanded from fifteen to twenty-eight, the EU continued to be Israel's chief trading partner and the largest international donor to the Palestinians.[71] However, EU-Israeli relations have been shaped heavily by mutual differences over the Israeli-Palestinian process. Since the EU's 1980 Venice Declaration, the EU has maintained its support for Palestinian self-determination while branding Israel's settlement building and policies in East Jerusalem contrary to international law. In 2005, EU officials accused Israel of intending 'to

---

[68] 'Annual Report 2006–2007', Indian Ministry of External Affairs, pp. vi, 45–6, www.mea .gov.in/Uploads/PublicationDocs/168_Annual-Report-2006-2007.pdf; 'Annual Report 2009–2010', Indian Ministry of External Affairs, pp. vi, 42, www.mea.gov.in/Uploads/ PublicationDocs/171_Annual-Report-2009-2010.pdf, both links accessed 27 August 2018.

[69] India-Iran New Delhi Declaration.   [70] 'Annual Report 2009-2010', p. 111.

[71] 'New Assistance Package for Palestine', *Office of the European Union Representative*, http s://eeas.europa.eu/delegations/palestine-occupied-palestinian-territory-west-bank-and-gaza-strip/39197/new-assistance-package-palestine-eu-strongly-committed-support-soc io-economic-revival-east_en, accessed 17 September 2018.

Israel and the EU: Decoupling Political and Economic Relations 381

turn the annexation of Jerusalem into a concrete fact', in violation of both Israel's 'Road Map obligations and International Law'.[72]

These criticisms, which created friction in EU-Israel relations, have been coupled to disputes at critical junctures in the Israeli-Palestinian peace process.[73] For instance, the EU claimed that 'fears of the Palestinians that their position in Jerusalem was being eroded' triggered the 1996 Hasmonean Tunnel Crisis whereas Israel maintained that the PA had provoked it deliberately.[74] Likewise, the EU deplored Israel's reneging on its obligations in the 1998 Wye River memorandum, while Israel alleged that Palestinian violations had caused it to falter.[75] Subsequently, amid the collapse of the peace process, the EU continued supporting Yasser Arafat's leadership while, after 2002, Israel refused any dealings with him.[76] The separation fence/wall/barrier has been another source of contention. Israel declared it to be an indispensable security measure, but the EU subscribed to the International Court of Justice advisory opinion that the barrier was illegal and supported a UN General Assembly Resolution condemning Israel for its construction.[77] The rare moments of Israel-EU foreign policy convergence, such as around the 1997 Israel-PLO Hebron Accord and the 2005 unilateral withdrawal

---

[72] Report obtained from the official website of MEP Jil Evans, www.jillevans.net/english/jill_evans_mep_eu_jerusalem_report_2005.pdf, accessed 10 September 2018.

[73] Evidence reflecting EU-Israeli friction over core issues include 'Reaction by Foreign Minister Sharon on the EU Stand on Jerusalem', 11 March 1999, *IMFA*, http://mfa.gov.il/MFA/Fo reignPolicy/MFADocuments/Yearbook12/Pages/149%20Reaction%20by%20Foreign%20 Minister%20Sharon%20on%20the%20EU.aspx; 'EU Troika Representatives Meet with Foreign Ministry Acting D-G 25 February 1997', *IMFA*, http://mfa.gov.il/MFA/PressRoo m/1997/Pages/EU%20TROIKA%20MEET%20WITH%20FOREIGN%20MINISTRY %20ACTING%20D-G%20-.aspx; 'Foreign Ministry Director-General: Israel Will Reconsider Europe's Involvement in the Peace Process', 7 March 1997, *IMFA*, http://mfa .gov.il/MFA/PressRoom/1997/Pages/FM%20Dir-Gen-%20Reconsider%20Europe-s%20I nvolvement%20in%20the.aspx, all links accessed 14 September 2018.

[74] 'Council Declaration on Middle East Peace Process', 1 October 1996, *European Commission Press Release Data Base*, http://europa.eu/rapid/press-release_PRES-96-253 _en.htm, accessed 28 October 2018.

[75] 'Foreign Ministry Regrets EU Statement', *IMFA*, http://mfa.gov.il/MFA/PressRoom/1 998/Pages/Foreign%20Ministry%20Regrets%20EU%20Statement.aspx; 'Declaration by the Presidency on Behalf of the European Union on the Decision by the Israeli Government to Halt Implementation of the Wye Memorandum', http://europa.eu/rapi d/press-release_PESC-98-156_en.htm; 'Summary of a Meeting between Foreign Minister Sharon and EU Envoy Moratinos', http://mfa.gov.il/MFA/ForeignPolicy/MF ADocuments/Yearbook12/Pages/138%20Summary%20of%20a%20meeting%20betwe en%20Foreign%20Minister.aspx, all links accessed 14 September 2018.

[76] Miller, *Inglorious Disarray*, pp. 162–3.

[77] 'Israel: UN Vote Encourages Palestinian Terrorism', *IMFA*, www.mfa.gov.il/mfa/press room/2004/pages/israel%20disappointed%20by%20eu%20stand%20at%20unga%202 1-july-2004.aspx, accessed 21 September 2018.

382   Vulnerable Ties

from Gaza, failed to alter the overriding pattern of political tension and discord.[78]

There has been a sharp decline in support and sympathy for Israel in European public opinion. Consecutive surveys conducted during the 2000s, which identified Israel as a major threat to world peace, reflect the growing abhorrence in Europe of Israel's policies towards the Palestinians. Several civil society groups, academics and cultural institutions have campaigned for the imposition of sanctions and for divestment and boycotting of Israel.[79] Clearly concerned by these actions, a confidential report prepared by the Israeli MFA in 2004 warned that Israel was on course to becoming 'a pariah state' in Europe.[80]

European criticism touched a sensitive Israeli domestic nerve. It reinforced what scholars Harpaz and Shamis refer to as the 'antagonistic approach' in Israel towards the EU. Proponents of this approach are prevalent in the conservative and Jewish religious segments of the Israeli public and foreign policy elite. They argue that, whereas the EU claims to pursue its foreign policy on the basis of values such as human rights, peace, liberty and respect for public international law, Europe, in fact, is interest driven and, worse, anti-Semitic. Consequently, advocates of the antagonistic approach contend that the EU and most of its member states are unbalanced and anti-Israeli.[81] The antagonistic approach, which draws traction from the memory of Jewish persecution in Europe and anti-Semitism, is significant. It provides domestic legitimacy to Israel's foreign policy of rejecting the EU's positions on the peace process and its bids to act as a mediator.

[78] 'Javier Solana, EU High Representative for the CFSP, Comments on Israeli Disengagement from Gaza and the Northern West Bank', 17 August 2005, *United Nations*, https://www.un.org/unispal/document/eu-high-representative-comments-on-is raeli-disengagement-from-gaza-and-northern-west-bank-eu-press-release-non-un-docu ment/, accessed 20 September 2018.

[79] Rory Miller, 'Troubled Neighbours: The EU and Israel', *Israel Affairs*, 12, 4, 2006: 646, 654–55; calls to boycott Israeli academics and BDS activity in Europe movement are cases in point; see 'British Lecturers Renew Calls to Boycott Israeli Academics', *Ha'aretz*, 6 April 2005, www.haaretz.com/1.4788678 'Palestinian Civil Society Groups Call for BDS', BDS official website, https://bdsmovement.net/call, both links accessed 11 October 2018.

[80] Agencies, 'Israel Could Become a Pariah State, WReport arns', *Guardian*, 14 October 2004, www.theguardian.com/world/2004/oct/14/israel1, accessed 11 October 2018.

[81] Guy Harpaz and Asaf Shamis, 'Normative Power Europe and the State of Israel: An Illegitimate EUtopia, *Journal of Common Market Studies*, 48, 3, 2010; 587–8; for an indicative poll, see Konrad Adenauer Stiftung and Sharon Pardo, 'Measuring the Attitudes of Israelis towards the European Union and its Member States' (Jerusalem: Konrad Adenauer Stiftung, 2007); for a view from a public officeholder's perspective, see Avraham Burg, *Victory Over Hitler* (Tel Aviv: Yedioth Ahronoth and Chemed Books, 2007) (in Hebrew).

Israel and the EU: Decoupling Political and Economic Relations 383

In contrast to the fraught EU-Israeli political relations, economic ties have thrived. Bilateral economic relations were defined by the 1995 EU-Israel AA, which entered into force on 1 June 2000.[82] The AA reinforced the free trade area between Israel and the EU in industrial goods, liberalized trade in agricultural goods and enhanced cooperation in several areas: energy, transportation, agriculture, tourism, competition and provision of services.[83] Concurrently, Israel was integrated into the EU's key foreign policy framework towards the MENA region: the European Mediterranean Partnership (EMP). The EMP, or Barcelona Process, which was launched in 1995, mirrored EU efforts to export its successful peace model based on democracy, democratization, financial cooperation and dialogue. Ambitiously, the then EU15 and the twelve Mediterranean partnership countries, including Israel, contracted to promote a common area of peace and stability around three baskets of cooperation: economic, political and cultural.[84]

In 2003, the EU replaced the EMP with the European Neighbourhood Policy (ENP). The ENP hinged on a differentiated, bilaterally driven, tailor-made approach to integrate the economies of neighbouring countries, including Israel, with the enlarged EU, according to their specific economic needs.[85] Its benefits for Israel included reinforcing political dialogue, economic cooperation, trade, and integration of Israel's internal market in the EU.[86] A further series of bilateral agreements, initiated or concluded in 2008, liberalized trade in services, the aviation sector and further trade in processed food and agricultural and fishery products.[87]

---

[82] 'The Israel-EU Association Agreement', June 2000, *IMFA*, https://mfa.gov.il/MFA/M FA-Archive/2000/Pages/The%20Israel-EU%20Association%20Agreement%20-%20Ju ne2000.aspx, accessed 13 March 2019.

[83] Harpaz and Shamis, 'Normative Power Europe and the State of Israel', 586.

[84] 'Barcelona Declaration Adopted at the Euro-Mediterranean Conference 27 and 28 November 1995', *European Commission*, http://europa.eu/rapid/press-release_DOC-95-7_en.htm, accessed 18 September 2018; Amichai Magen, 'Israel and the Many Pathways of Diffusion', *West European Politics*, 35, 1, 2012: 101.

[85] 'The European Neighbourhood Policy and Israel', *2004, Volume 4, European Union*, htt p://eeas.europa.eu/archives/delegations/israel/documents/home/010_070810_eu_focu s_enp_final_he.pdf, accessed 20 September 2018 (in Hebrew); Joel Peters, 'Europe and the Israel-Palestinian Peace Process: The Urgency of Now', *European Security*, 19, 3, 2010: 519.

[86] Peters, 'Europe and the Israel-Palestine Peace Process', 522.

[87] On fishery and food process agreements, see 'Countries and Regions: Israel', *European Commission*, http://ec.europa.eu/trade/policy/countries-and-regions/countries/israel/inde x_en.htm; 'Council Decision of 20 October 2009', *Official Journal of the European Union*, https://eur-lex.europa.eu/LexUriServ/LexUriServ.do?uri=OJ:L:2009:313:0081:0082:E N:PDF; 'EU/Israel Relations', *European* Commission, http://europa.eu/rapid/press-release_MEMO-95-127_en.htm, all links accessed 24 September 2018; on aviation and services agreements, see Raffaella Del-Sarto, 'Plus Ça Change ... ? Israel, the EU and the Union for the Mediterranean', *Mediterranean Politics*, 16, 1, 2011: 121.

384   Vulnerable Ties

The deepening economic relations have yielded significant dividends for Israel. Between 1990 and 2010, exports to Israel grew from €5.4 to €14.5 billion while EU imports from Israel trebled from €3.6 to €11 billion.[88] Concurrently, the AA and the ENP have enhanced EU-Israeli scientific and technological cooperation. In 1996, Israel became the first non-European country to participate in the EU's Framework Programmes for Research and Technological Development, which, in 2010, became Israel's second-largest source of research funding.[89] Israel has participated in EUREKA, the EU's leading research network since 2000 and in the Galileo EU satellite navigation programme, since 2005.[90]

How did Israel succeed in decoupling the economic and political elements of its foreign policy towards the EU? Internal EU divisions over its policy towards Israel have been a significant factor. Some governments, such as Germany and the Tony Blair/Gordon Brown UK governments, sought close relationships with Israel. Others, such as France's Jacques Chirac government and the government of Ireland have been staunch critiques. Consequently, the EU was unable to achieve a consensus over which foreign policy measures to apply – sticks or carrots – to tilt Israel's foreign policy closer to the EU's positions. Instead, the EU converged around the only possible common denominator, namely, a critical foreign policy rhetoric towards Israel.[91]

Amid internal divisions, the EU refrained from conditioning its economic agreements on Israel's foreign policy shifting closer to the EU's position. The exception was when Israel was forced to accept the EU's distinction among exports from Israel proper and those from the territories it occupied in 1967. In 2004, following seven years of tedious negotiations, Israel succumbed to the EU's decision not to exempt exports from the occupied territories from custom duties. The then Israeli Trade Minister, Ehud Olmert, justified this climb-down on the grounds that the continued export of all Israeli products to the twenty-five EU countries was at stake.[92]

---

[88] 'European Union Trade with Israel', *European Commission*, http://trade.ec.europa.eu/d oclib/docs/2006/september/tradoc_113402.pdf, accessed 24 September 2018.

[89] Pardo and Peters, *Uneasy Neighbours*, p. 50.

[90] 'EU-Israel Research and Innovation Cooperation – 20 Years of Success, Partnership, and Friendship', *European Commission*, https://ec.europa.eu/research/iscp/index.cfm?pg=is rael, accessed 23 September 2018.

[91] Musu, *European Union Policy towards the Arab-Israeli Peace Process*, pp. 12–21.

[92] For an elaboration of the Rules of Origin Dispute, as it became to be known, see Pardo and Peters, *Uneasy Neighbours*, pp. 52–7.

Olmert's comments reflect a deep-seated pragmatism towards the EU, prevalent among the centre-left Israeli foreign policy political elite, the business community, left-leaning organized civil society and intellectuals. This powerful domestic constituency, which counterbalanced Israeli critiques of the EU, underscores the importance of bilateral economic ties and stresses EU-Israeli 'common values'.[93] EU counterparts have been receptive to this message. In contrast to the political divisions in the EU over its Israel policy, there is a Brussels consensus that deepening economic-technological ties are beneficial. Israel's growing purchasing power is increasingly evident in its ranking within the EU's top twenty-five trading partners. In addition, Israel's high-value-added production sectors and advanced technologies make it attractive to the EU economies.[94] Thus, while political differences persist, economic ties have developed apace.

Taking Stock

During the post-Cold War era Israel has expanded its bilateral ties with the EU, the USA and rising powers in Asia, notably China and India. This trend has been manifested clearly in its growing bilateral economic ties, the persistent conflict between Israel and the majority of the Arab world notwithstanding. In this respect, Israeli foreign policy has been highly successful. At the same time, the EU, India and China remain firmly opposed to Israel's policies towards the Palestinians. Even in the USA, which offered stalwart support to Israel throughout the post-Cold War era, there are signs of concern over the enduring Israeli occupation.

---

[93] This theme is consistent. See 'Address by Deputy Prime Minister and Foreign Minister Silvan Shalom before the European Union Council of Ministers 21 July 2003', *IMFA*, www.mfa.gov.il/mfa/pressroom/2003/pages/address%20by%20fm%20silvan%20sha lom%20before%20the%20european%20un.aspx; remarks by Foreign Minister Livni in 'The European Union Upgrades its Relations with Israel', *IMFA*, http://mfa.gov.il/MFA/ PressRoom/2008/Pages/The%20EU%20and%20Israel%20upgrade%20relations%20 %2016-June-2008.aspx; for a business perspective see 'Address by Acting PM Ehud Olmert to the 6th Annual Israel-Europe Conference', 6 February 2006, *IMFA*, pp. 1–2, www.mfa.gov.il/mfa/pressroom/2006/pages/address%20by%20acting%20pm%20ehud %20olmert%20to%20the%206th%20annual%20israel-europe%20conference%206-fe b-2006.aspx; the Israel-European Union Chamber of Commerce and Industry official website, http://www.ileucc.co.il/; and Magen, 'Israel and the Many Pathways of Diffusion', pp. 99, 108–111; a vibrant intellectual Israel-EU forum has been the 'Israeli Association for the Study of European Integration, www.iasei.org.il/en/, all links accessed 1 October 2018.

[94] Comparative data ranking Israel as an EU partner obtained from European Commission, *External and Intra-European Trade – Statistical Yearbook data 1958–2010* (Luxemburg: Office for Official Publications of the European Communities, 2010), pp. 32–5. On technological advantages, see Del-Sarto, 'Plus Ça Change ... ? p. 126; Miller, 'Troubled Neighbours', 657–9.

Furthermore, maintaining the current foreign policy trajectory towards the EU, USA, India and China is dependent on their delinking their interests in the Arab world – and to a lesser degree Iran – and their policy towards Israel. Thus, as long as Israel's conflict with the majority of the Arab world persists, its ties with its key international partners remain vulnerable.

Epilogue: Israel's Wondrous Decade?

The elections for the eighteenth Knesset took place on 10 February 2009. Binyamin Netanyahu's right-wing party, Likud, which secured twenty-seven seats, finished a close second behind the centrist Kadima party, which won twenty-eight seats. This slimmest of margins masked the more significant outcome of the elections. Labour and Meretz, the two parties that had championed Israel's foreign policy of engagement over the previous two decades, secured thirteen and three seats, respectively, while the centre-right block of parties achieved sixty-five seats. This marked the collapse of the Zionist-political left block in the Knesset and the die was cast according to simple political arithmetic. Following the declaration by Tzipi Livni, Kadima's leader, that she had no desire to join a broad coalition, President Shimon Peres asked Binyamin Netanyahu to form the country's next government and assume the office of prime minister.[1]

Ten years later, Netanyahu has completed his third consecutive term as prime minister and has surpassed David Ben-Gurion in being Israel's longest serving prime minister. Since 2009, his premiership has been the main element of continuity in an otherwise changing decision-making forum. Over time, policymakers who challenged Netanyahu either left government or were removed from their posts. Remarkably, at the end of his third successive term in office, Prime Minister Netanyahu also held the health, defence and foreign affairs portfolios.

Netanyahu's decade in power has been marked indelibly by what quickly became known as the Arab uprisings, which erupted when Mohamed Bouazizi, a Tunisian street vendor, on 17 December 2010 set fire to himself after a municipal officer confiscated his wares. The despair signalled by this young man's self-immolation sparked a wave of anti-government demonstrations in Tunisia, Algeria, Bahrain, Egypt, Libya, Yemen, Syria and Jordan and caused ripple effects throughout

---

[1] 'The 34th Government – Current Composition', Knesset Official Website, www .knesset.gov.il/govt/heb/GovtByNumber.asp, accessed 6 February 2019.

388   Israel's Wondrous Decade?

the Middle East. Nine years later, Libya, Yemen and Syria have all but imploded through their being plunged into civil war. Egypt's longstanding President, Hosni Mubarak, who had ruled the country since 1981, was ousted on 11 February 2011. Just over a year later Mubarak was replaced by Muhammad Mursi, a candidate fielded by the Muslim Brotherhood, in the first democratically held elections in modern Egypt. Muhammad Abdel Fatah el-Sisi, an army general, launched a military coup that toppled Mursi, who, subsequently, was imprisoned and died in jail. Meanwhile, Jordan's and Saudi Arabia's monarchies, the Gulf sheikdoms and Lebanon have managed to weather the regional political storms.

Netanyahu's prolonged time in office and the concentration of power in his hands have enabled him to significantly shape Israel's response to the Arab uprisings. Nine months into the unrest, Netanyahu portrayed the uprisings as a 'political earthquake of historic proportions' which unleashed an 'epic struggle between "good" and "evil"'.[2] Iran and the Islamist groups, argued Netanyahu, were leading the Middle East region into 'medieval barbarism' and turning it into 'a dark, savage, and desperate Middle East'.[3] He argued that Israel, in contrast, 'stood out as a towering beacon of enlightenment and tolerance'.[4]

The epic struggle within the Arab world, which sent the region into flux, was seen, from the outset, by Netanyahu as inherently threatening. 'We are in a turbulent region', Netanyahu told the Knesset, as demonstrations against former Egyptian President, Hosni Mubarak, began:

In such situations, we must look around with our eyes wide open. We must identify things as they are, not as we'd like them to be. We must not try to force reality into a preconceived pattern. We must accept that a huge change is taking place, and while it is happening keep a watchful eye.[5]

---

[2] 'Statement by PM Netanyahu Following Events in Cairo', *IMFA*, https://mfa.gov.il/MFA/PressRoom/2011/Pages/Statement_PM_Netanyahu_events_Cairo_10-Sep-2011.aspx, accessed 17 January 2019.
[3] 'PM Netanyahu's Speech at the AIPAC Policy Conference', 2 March 2015, *IMFA*, http s://mfa.gov.il/MFA/PressRoom/2015/Pages/PM-Netanyahu's-speech-at-the-AIPAC-Pol icy-Conference-2-March-2015.aspx, accessed 17 January 2019.
[4] 'PM Netanyahu Addresses the UN General Assembly', *IMFA*, https://mfa.gov.il/MFA/PressRoom/2015/Pages/PM-Netanyahu-addresses-the-UN-General-Assembly-1-Oct-2 015.aspx, accessed 17 January 2019.
[5] 'PM Netanyahu Addresses the Knesset: The Situation in Egypt', *IMFA*, https://mfa.gov.il/MFA/PressRoom/2011/Pages/PM_Netanyahu_addresses_Knesset_situation_Egypt_2-Feb-2011.aspx, accessed 19 January 2019.

Israel's Wondrous Decade? 389

A few months later, he told parliament that: 'Despite all our hopes, the chances are the Islamist wave will wash over the Arab countries, an anti-West, anti-Liberal, and ultimately an anti-democratic wave.'[6]

This monochrome view of the Arab uprisings had significant implications for Israel's negotiations with the Palestinians. Prior to the Arab uprisings, Binyamin Netanyahu had grudgingly conceded the need for a Palestinian state in a speech delivered at Bar Ilan University – where Yigal Amir, Prime Minister Rabin's assassin, attended as a student. In this speech on 14 June 2009, Netanyahu laid down his principles for a peace settlement between Israel and the Palestinians. 'In my vision of peace', he stated, 'the Palestinians must clearly and unambiguously recognize Israel as the state of the Jewish People' and the 'territory under Palestinian control must be demilitarized with ironclad security provisions for Israel.'[7] This demand that the Palestinians recognize Israel as a Jewish state was extraordinary; it effectively asked the Palestinians to validate Israel's identity, something that, arguably, was for Israelis to decide on. Netanyahu's stipulation was also unprecedented in that, when signing peace accords with Egypt and Jordan, Israel had not required explicit recognition as a Jewish state. For this reason, some members of Netanyahu's cabinet, such as Ehud Barak, queried the prime minister's demand and were convinced that 'his move was political and tactical, aimed at staking out a position of power in the diplomatic process'.[8]

The Obama administration, which sought to capitalize on the Bar-Ilan speech, continued to put pressure on Israel to advance the peace process. Four months later, on 25 November 2009, Israel approved a ten-month partial moratorium on settlement expansion. This included a freeze on new residential housing construction in the West Bank settlements, but excluded neighbourhoods inside the expanded city limits of Jerusalem and works that were already underway.[9]

The partial settlement freeze was not a sufficient guarantee for the Palestinians, who have witnessed a dramatic expansion of Israeli settlements since the end of the Cold War. By 2009, the number of settlers,

---

[6] Excerpts from Netanyahu's statement at the Knesset, 23 November 2011, *IMFA*, https://mfa.gov.il/MFA/PressRoom/2011/Pages/PM_Netanyahu_statement_Knesset_23-Nov-2011.aspx, accessed 19 January 2019.

[7] https://mfa.gov.il/MFA/PressRoom/2009/Pages/Address_PM_Netanyahu_Bar-Ilan_University_14-Jun-2009.aspx, accessed 17 January 2019.

[8] Barak, *My Country my life*, pp. 420–1.

[9] 'Behind the Headlines: The Ten-Month Israeli Moratorium on Settlement Building, *IMFA*, https://mfa.gov.il/MFA/ForeignPolicy/Issues/Pages/Behind-the-Headlines-The-Ten-Month-Israeli-Moratorium-on-Settlement-Building-26-Nov-2009.aspx, accessed 21 January 2019.

390 Israel's Wondrous Decade?

excluding in east Jerusalem, had reached 276,100 whereas in 1990 it was but 81,900.[10] The Palestinians demanded a complete cessation of settlement building, including in Jerusalem, which the Israelis refused.[11] The USA was unable to resolve this impasse and the Israeli-Palestinian peace process stalled.

The eruption of the uprisings provided a pretext for Netanyahu to kick negotiations further into the long grass. In an important statement, a few months into the uprisings, he rendered any exchange of land for peace – a prerequisite for realizing his Bar-Ilan framework – as perilous and leading to uncertainty. 'No one can foresee who would control the territory that would be transferred', the prime minister told one audience:

> We left Lebanon, every inch of it, and Iran walked in. We left every inch of Gaza and Iran walked in. The state of Israel cannot afford to step out without making security arrangements, without suitable barrier from Judea and Samaria because we cannot have this happen a third time.[12]

Netanyahu's statement was significant because it removed the land-for-peace option from the negotiating table shortly after his government had refused to extend the partial settlement freeze. Moreover, the then US Secretary of State, John Kerry, revealed that Israel had refused to take even modest collaborative measures towards the Palestinians. These included requests from the USA and the Quartet to cooperate over agriculture, natural resources and granting more building permits. According to Kerry, these measures could have been taken 'without negatively impacting Israel's legitimate security concerns'.[13]

Closer to home, the policy of stalling rather than intensifying the negotiations was criticized by prominent figures in Netanyahu's own cabinet and Israel's security network. For example, Defence Minister Barak, head of Mossad, Meir Dagan and GSS chief, Yuval Diskin, argued that *not* resolving the Israeli-Palestinian conflict was a 'disaster' on two critical counts: it directly threatened the Jewish and democratic nature of the Israeli state and it undermined Western allies' support for

---

[10] 'Number of Settlers by Years', *Israeli Bureau of Statistics*, http://peacenow.org.il/settle ments-watch/matzav, accessed 31 January 2019.

[11] Vita Bekker, Daniel Dombey and Harvey Morris, 'Netanyahu Offers Freeze on Settlements', *Financial Times*, 26 November 2009, www.ft.com/content/8c8320c4-d9d3-11de-ad94-00144feabdc0, accessed 28 January 2019.

[12] Excerpts from PM Netanyahu's remarks in the Knesset, 23 February 2011, *IMFA*, https:// mfa.gov.il/MFA/PressRoom/2011/Pages/PM_Netanyahu_remarks_Knesset_23-Feb-201 1.aspx, accessed 17 January 2019.

[13] 'Full Transcript: Kerry Blasts Israeli Government Presents Six Points of Future Peace Deal', *Ha'aretz*, www.haaretz.com/israel-news/criticizing-netanyahu-warning-against-one-state-kerry-s-full-speech-1.5479380, accessed 18 January 2019.

Israel.[14] In this vein, in private conversations, Barak told Netanyahu repeatedly that 'it was nonsensical to argue that we were so threatened by everything around us that we could not "risk" taking the initiative required to disentangle ourselves from the Palestinians on the West Bank.'[15] As he led Likud's 2015 national election campaign, Netanyahu, who rejected this analysis outright, stated categorically that there would be no Palestinian state on his watch.[16]

Kerry, who throughout his term was indefatigable in his attempts to break the logjam, worked on developing a regional peace initiative that would include an Israeli-Palestinian accord. A first draft of his proposal was seen by Prime Minister Netanyahu during a meeting with Kerry in Davos, Switzerland, on 21 January 2016. A month later, on 21 February 2016, he was presented with another version in Aqaba, Jordan. Crucially, this version was commensurate with the Bar-Ilan conditions in three key respects: agreement would be based on recognizing Israel as a Jewish state; the Palestinian state would be demilitarized; and Israel would be given security assurances from the USA. Further, Jordan's King Abdullah and President of Egypt Abdel Fattah el-Sisi both supported this proposal. Likewise, the then head of the Israeli opposition, Yitzhak Hertzog, confirmed in private to Netanyahu that he would join his coalition if the prime minister embraced the Kerry initiative.[17]

In this context, on 17 May 2016, Hertzog spoke publicly about 'a unique opportunity that may never return' giving Netanyahu, should he wish it, the option to form a unity government with Labour and promote

---

[14] Ronen Bregman, 'Shimon Peres on Obama, Iran and the Path to Peace', *New York Times*, 9 January 2013, www.nytimes.com/2013/01/13/magazine/shimon-peres-on-obama-iran-and-the-path-to-peace.html?pagewanted=4&_r=0; Barak Ravid, 'Netanyahu's Aides: Ex-Shin Bet Chief is "Frustrated and Sanctimonious"', *Ha'aretz*, 4 December 2013, w ww.haaretz.com/israel-news/.premium-1.561866; Spencer Ho, 'Ex-Shin Bet Chief. Iranian Threat Dwarfed by Danger of Failed Peace Talks', *Times of Israel*, 4 December 2013, www.timesofisrael.com/ex-shin-bet-chief-iranian-threat-dwarfed-by-danger-of-failed-peace-talks/; Stuart Winer, . 'Former Mossad Chief: We Don't Need Jordan Valley', *Times of Israel*, 5 January 2014, www.timesofisrael.com/former-mossad-chief-we-dont-need-jordan-valley/; Gidi Weitz, 'Former PM Barak: Netanyahu Leading Israel to Disaster', *Haaretz*, 8 January 2015, www.haaretz.com/israel-news/.premium-1 .635978, all links accessed 21 January 2019.

[15] Barak, *My Country, My Life*, p. 437.

[16] Maayan Lubell, 'Netanyahu Says No Palestinian State as Long as he Is Prime Minister', *Reuters*, www.reuters.com/article/us-israel-election/netanyahu-says-no-palestinian-state-as-long-as-hes-prime-minister-idUSKBN0MC1I820150316, accessed 23 January 2019.

[17] Barak Ravid, 'Kerry Presented Netanyahu a Regional Peace Initiative During Secret Meeting with El-Sisi and Abdullah a Year Ago; the PM was Reluctant', *Ha'aretz*, 19 February 2017, www.haaretz.co.il/news/politics/.premium-1.3870153 (in Hebrew), accessed 7 January 2018.

the Kerry initiative.[18] Two weeks after Hertzog's announcement, Binyamin Netanyahu took a rather different path, sounding the death knell to the secret Kerry initiative. Instead of creating a national unity government with Labour, Netanyahu widened his coalition by including the ultra-nationalist Israel is Our Home party and appointing its leader, Avigdor Lieberman, a settler and ardent opponent of the land-for-peace formula, minister of defence.

Rejecting the Kerry peace initiative is highly revealing of Netanyahu's foreign policy path towards the Palestinians since the eruption of the Arab uprisings. Rather than embrace a stance of engagement, which the Kerry initiative would have facilitated, Netanyahu opted to revert to a foreign policy of entrenchment. Thus, he rejected the Kerry initiative, which would have involved exchanging land for peace, scaling down Israeli occupation and a premium on negotiations and diplomacy. Instead, in line with Netanyahu's entrenchment foreign policy stance, Israel would explore peace with the Arab world in exchange only for peace, not territory, would rely on its iron wall of military force rather than prioritizing diplomacy and negotiations and would keep the Palestinians under occupation by strengthening its grip on the West Bank.

The Toll of Wars

Israel's entrenchment policy had severe implications for the Palestinians in the Gaza Strip, which has been controlled by Hamas since 2007. Since the return of Netanyahu to power, Israel and Hamas have been involved in countless military skirmishes and two major clashes. In November 2012, Israel launched Operation Pillar of Defence and in summer 2014 the two sides clashed in a fifty-six-day war that Israel called Operation Protective Edge. The Israelis argued that they were forced into the ongoing conflict as an act of self-defence against Hamas attacks, which included, but were not limited to, 6,572 rockets launched from the Gaza Strip into Israel between 2009 and 2016.[19]

Hamas's attacks on Israel, which resulted in casualties and severe disruption to everyday life, especially in the western Negev, could not be ignored. Nevertheless, the IDF's use of force seems to have far

---

[18] Arik Bendar, 'Hertzog in a Last Attempt to Promote a National Unity Government: "There is an Opportunity that May Never Return"', *Ma'ariv*, 17 May 2016 (in Hebrew), www.maariv.co.il/news/politics/Article-541971, accessed 7 January 2018.

[19] 'Rocket Fire from Gaza and Cease Fire Violations since Operation Cast Lead', *IMFA*, www.youtube.com/watch?v=_03uXQiz6eY&list=RD_03uXQiz6eY&start_radio=1& t=3, accessed 21 January 2019. This figure does not include mortar shells fired or misfired rockets that fell inside the Gaza Strip.

The Toll of Wars 393

exceeded the requirements of self-defence. This claim is particularly relevant to the use of force during the Pillar of Defence and Protective Edge operations, which has been examined judiciously in a recent study by Yagil Levy and the Israeli human rights NGO, B'Tselem.[20] Levy's analyses the figures provided by different agencies such as the IDF, B'Tselem and Palestinian organizations. He demonstrates clearly that B'Tselem's data are the most reliable because each Palestinian fatality in the 2014 war was investigated individually by the organization's researchers. Levy also shows that B'Tselem was subject to less institutional bias than the IDF and the Palestinian agencies, which were affiliated respectively to the Israeli government and Hamas.

During Operation Protective Edge, Israel used massive air power and artillery to reduce the risks for Israeli soldiers engaged in ground warfare, which, in turn, increased the number of civilian Palestinian deaths and their proportions relative to Palestinian combatant fatalities.[21] Based on B'Tselem data, 1,390 Palestinian non-combatants and 765 Palestinian combatants were killed during the 2014 Israel-Hamas war.[22] Moreover, the ratio of Gaza civilians killed by IDF fire to combatants killed is the highest among previous Israeli military offensives in Gaza.[23] Levy argues persuasively that Israel practiced 'excessive lethality with relatively limited distinction between combatants and non-combatants'.[24]

B'Tselem's account of the ratio of combatant to civilian fatalities during Operation Pillar of Defence provides a similar picture. This operation took place between 14 and 21 November 2012. It was shorter in duration than the 2014 Israel-Hamas war and, further, did not include an IDF ground offensive. Nevertheless, the ratio of civilian fatalities caused solely by Israeli aerial and artillery attacks during the operation involved a high proportion of civilian Palestinian casualties. At least eighty-seven out of a total of 167 deaths were civilians.[25]

Could Israel have pursued a different foreign policy route vis-à-vis Hamas which refuses to recognize Israel, previous agreements between

---

[20] Yagil Levy, 'The Gaza Fighting: Did Israel Shift the Risk from its Soldiers to Civilians?' *Middle East Policy*, 24, 3, 2017: 117–32; ' Human Rights Violations during Operation Pillar of Defense', *B'Tselem*, www.btselem.org/download/201305_pillar_of_defense_o peration_eng.pdf; '50 Days: More than 500 Children: Facts and Figures on Fatalities in Gaza', *B'Tselem*, www.btselem.org/2014_gaza_conflict/en/, both links accessed 9 January 2018.

[21] Levy, 'The Gaza Fighting', 127.

[22] The UN reports 1,523 civilians and 669 combatant deaths (Amnesty International, 2014) while Israeli MFA (2015) data report 936 combatant deaths and 761 civilian fatalities out of a total of 2,125 casualties that includes 428 fatalities that the MFA claims cannot be definitively categorized.

[23] Levy, The Gaza Fighting', 129.   [24] Levy, 'The Gaza Fighting', 118.

[25] 'Human Rights Violations during Operation Pillar of Defence', 9.

394   Israel's Wondrous Decade?

Israel and the Palestinians and to renounce violence? The answer, according to former US Secretary of State Kerry, would seem unequivocally to be yes. Kerry revealed Israeli refusal of consistent calls during his term, which began in 2013, to ease 'the movement and access restrictions to and from Gaza,' made 'with due consideration for Israel's need to protect its citizens from terrorist attacks'.[26]

Instead, Israel maintained the foreign policy stance that emerged with Operation Cast Lead, in 2009, namely, deterrence of Hamas by massive use of military force, keeping it isolated via a joint Egyptian-Israeli blockade on the Gaza Strip and penalizing Gaza's civilian population collectively, with the political aim of pressurizing it to repudiate Hamas. Ten years later, this foreign policy seems to have failed. Hamas remains entrenched in the Gaza Strip; its ongoing conflicts with Israel suggest that it is undeterred; the toll on Gazan lives is immense; and the security of Israelis residing in the western Negev remains tenuous.

A New Arab-Israeli Axis?

Israel's foreign policy of entrenchment under Binyamin Netanyahu was linked inextricably to his view that the Arab uprisings opened new opportunities for Arab-Israeli cooperation in the face of two common dangers: a nuclear-armed Iran and militant/terrorist Islamist movements gaining ground in the Sunni world. As he explained in a speech at the UN assembly in 2013:

> The dangers of a nuclear-armed Iran and the emergence of other threats in our region have led many of our Arab neighbours to finally recognize that Israel is not their enemy. This affords us the opportunity to overcome historic animosities and build new relationships, new friendships, and new hopes. Israel welcomes engagement with the wider Arab world. We hope that our common interests and common challenges will help us forge a more peaceful future.[27]

To some extent the prime minister's approach has been vindicated. In January 2019, Egyptian President Abdel Fattah al-Sisi confirmed that Egypt's military cooperation with Israel has reached unprecedented levels, referring, primarily, to security cooperation against militant and

---

[26] 'Full Transcript: Kerry Blasts Israeli Government Presents Six Points of Future Peace Deal', *Ha'aretz*.

[27] PM Netanyahu's Speech at the United Nation's General Assembly, *Prime Minister's Office*, www.pmo.gov.il/English/MediaCenter/Speeches/Pages/speechUN011013.aspx, accessed 23 January 2019.

A New Arab-Israeli Axis? 395

terrorist groups in the northern Sinai.[28] This statement came after an Egyptian court, in 2015, listed Hamas a terrorist organization, which, effectively, banned Hamas within Egypt.[29] Also, Netanyahu has become the first Israeli prime minister since 1996 to make an official visit to Oman, a country with no diplomatic relations with Israel, where he met the country's leader, Sultan Qaboos Bin Said, on 27 October 2018.[30]

Less visible, but perhaps more significant, contacts have been developing secretly between Israel and Saudi Arabia, whose ruling royal family has been threatened by Iran since the 1979 Islamic Revolution. Addressing this issue directly, the Crown Prince of Saudi Arabia and power behind the throne, Mohammed Bin Salman, referred to Iran's Supreme Leader, Ali Khamenei, as 'the new Hitler of the Middle East'. 'But', he continued, 'we learned from Europe that appeasement doesn't work. We don't want the new Hitler in Iran to repeat what happened in Europe in the Middle East.'[31]

Revealingly, on 16 November 2017, that is, one week before Bin Salman's comments, the then IDF Chief of Staff, Gadi Eisenkot, declared that 'Saudi Arabia and Israel share common interests and that Israel is willing to provide intelligence to Saudi Arabia if necessary.'[32] Dr Yuval Steinitz, a member of the government's inner cabinet, went further by stating that Israel's relations with 'the moderate Arab world, including Saudi Arabia, is helping us to halt Iran'.[33] The chances these comments from such high-profile policymakers in Saudi and Israel were coincidental are highly unlikely.

[28] 'Egypt's Sisi Confirms Unprecedented Military Cooperation with Israel', *Ha'aretz*, 4 January 2019, www.youtube.com/watch?v=hVN9ckrREWY, accessed 23 January 2019.

[29] 'Egypt Court Puts Hamas on Terrorist List', *BBC*, www.bbc.co.uk/news/world-middle-east-31674458, accessed 23 January 2019.

[30] Noa Landau and Jack Khoury, 'Netanyahu Visit Oman, which has no Diplomatic Ties with Israel, *Ha'aretz*, 27 October 2018, www.haaretz.com/middle-east-news/netanyahu-secretly-visits-oman-which-has-no-diplomatic-ties-with-israel-1.6594761, accessed 5 February 2019.

[31] Thomas Friedman, 'Saudi Arabia's Arab Spring, At Last', *New York Times*, 23 November 2017, www.nytimes.com/2017/11/23/opinion/saudi-prince-mbs-arab-spring.html, accessed 23 January 2019.

[32] Yoav Zeitun and Roi Kais, 'Chief of Staff in a Rare Interview to a Saudi Website: 'Full Agreement in Relation to Iran'', *Ynet*, 16 November 2017, www.ynet.co.il/articles/0,7 340,L-5043847,00.html, accessed 23 January 2019.

[33] Yuval Steinitz interview on Israel's military radio daily programme, Wilensky and Yaacov Bardugo, https://glz.co.il/%D7%92%D7%9C%D7%A6/%D7%AA%D7%95%D7%9 B%D7%A0%D7%99%D7%95%D7%AA/%D7%95%D7%99%D7%9C%D7%A0% D7%A1%D7%A7%D7%99-%D7%90%D7%AA-%D7%91%D7%A8%D7%93%D7 %95%D7%92%D7%95/%D7%95%D7%99%D7%9C%D7%A0%D7%A1%D7%A7 %D7%99-%D7%90%D7%AA-%D7%91%D7%A8%D7%93%D7%95%D7%92%D 7%9519-11-2017-1701, accessed 23 January 2019.

396   Israel's Wondrous Decade?

Saudi-Israeli secret ties, although perhaps significant, face serious impediments; above all, the unresolved conflict between Israel and the Palestinians. The former Head of Saudi Intelligence, Turki al-Faisal, discussed this issue during the highly visible 2016 Munich security forum. While not denying the encounters between Israel and the Gulf countries, al-Faisal emphasized that 'Sunni Arab countries are furious with Israel over the occupation and its treatment of the Palestinians.' 'Why', he asked rhetorically, 'should the Arabs feel friendship to you when you do that [to the Palestinians]?'[34] A year later, Saudi's Foreign Minister, Adel al-Jubeir, echoed al-Faisal's position, stating that normalization between Israel and Saudi Arabia and other moderate Arab states will take place only after an Israeli-Palestinian peace accord is achieved.[35] In this vein, Israel's foreign policy of entrenchment remains an obstacle to rather than a catalyst for forging a new Arab-Israeli axis.

The Offensive against Iran

Prior to Binyamin Netanyahu's return to power, Israel had relied on the USA to lead the international effort to curb Iran's nuclear programme. Since resuming premiership, Netanyahu has shifted his country's foreign policy, positioning Israel at the forefront of the international campaign against Iran.[36] This change in Israel's posture produced a serious clash with the Obama administration, which, throughout its eight-year term, had sought to engage Iran diplomatically. The dispute reached a climax in March 2015 when, in a speech in the US Congress, Netanyahu delivered a scathing critique of the then US-led proposed deal with Iran regarding its nuclear programme.[37] Netanyahu's analysis of the deal, known as the Joint Comprehensive Plan of Action (JCPoA), or the Iran nuclear deal, prompted fierce reactions from within the Democratic party. President Obama rejected it outright, arguing that Netanyahu had not presented 'any viable alternatives' for how to prevent Iran from obtaining a nuclear weapon.[38]

---

[34] Barak Ravid, 'Ya'alon: Israelis Secretly Meeting with Officials from the Gulf States', *Haaretz*, 14 February 2016, www.haaretz.com/middle-east-news/.premium-ya-alon-israelis-secretly-meeting-with-officials-from-gulf-states-1.5404184, accessed 28 January 2019.

[35] Roi Kais, 'Saudi FM: This Is the Condition for a Peace with Israel', *Ynet*, 21 November 2017, www.ynet.co.il/articles/0,7340,L-5045690,00.html, accessed 28 January 2019.

[36] Interview Ya'alon.

[37] The complete transcript of Netanyahu's address to Congress, *Washington Post*, www.washingtonpost.com/news/post-politics/wp/2015/03/03/full-text-netanyahus-address-to-congress/?noredirect=on&utm_term=.62a1679c0104, accessed 24 January 2019.

[38] 'Obama Says Netanyahu's Iran Speech Contains "Nothing New"', *BBC*, www.bbc.co.uk/news/world-middle-east-31722493, accessed 27 January 2019.

The Offensive against Iran   397

Three months later, on 14 July 2015, the Iran nuclear deal was signed between the Islamic Republic, five members of the UN Security Council plus Germany and the EU. In a nutshell, it required Iran to limit its nuclear programme in exchange for the lifting of certain Western sanctions.

These glitches notwithstanding, Netanyahu continued his diplomatic offensive against the deal and this has borne fruit following the election of Donald J. Trump as President of the USA in November 2016. Some eighteen months later, on 8 May 2018, President Trump withdrew the USA from the JCPoA, which has had severe implications for Iran's economy and international standing. The Trump administration reimposed economic sanctions, targeting core sectors of Iran's economy including oil exports, shipping, port operations and central bank transactions. Iran's purchase or acquisition of US dollars and its ability to trade in gold, coal, steel, cars, currency and debt have been significantly curbed. Companies with existing contracts in Iran were demanded to wind down their operations within ninety to 180 days, while companies seeking to trade with Iran would be subject to the US sanctions.[39]

In tandem with mounting a diplomatic campaign against Iran, Israel invested significant resources in developing the capability to launch a military strike on Iran's nuclear installations. According to Ehud Barak, the plan was to attack Iran before it entered what Israel defined as the 'zone of immunity'. This, as Barak explained, referred to 'the point at which the amount of damage we could do, and the delay we could cause, to their nuclear program, would be too negligible to worth the operational political and diplomatic risks from such an attack'.[40] According to Barak's account, by mid-2010, Israel had acquired the operational capacity to launch an attack, which was being seriously considered by Netanyahu's inner cabinet, the Forum of the Eight.[41]

Israel's offensive approach was shaped strongly by Netanyahu's perception that Iran's regime was 'evil' and negotiation was impossible. The then Defence Minister Barak and Foreign Minister Avigdor Lieberman backed the prime minister's position whereas President Shimon Peres challenged it. He portrayed the conflict with Iran as a 'policy problem' rather than a struggle between good and inherent

---

[39] Katrina Manson, 'What the US Withdrawal from the Iran Nuclear Deal Means', *Financial Times*, www.ft.com/content/e7e53c72-538c-11e8-b3ee-41e0209208ec ; Jonathan Marcus, 'Trump Re-imposes Iran Sanctions: Now What? *BBC*, 3 November 2018, www.bbc.co.uk/news/world-middle-east-46075179, both links accessed 28 January 2019.
[40] Barak, *My Country, My Life*, pp. 424–5.   [41] Barak, *My Country, My Life*, p. 425.

398   Israel's Wondrous Decade?

evil, and stated his willingness to 'meet Rouhani', the recently elected president of Iran.[42]

IDF Chief of Staff (2011–15) Benny Ganz also distanced himself from the prime minister, referring to Iran as a 'rational player' rather than 'evil' and portraying its leadership as 'full of rational individuals.'[43] Echoes of this view came from members of Netanyahu's inner cabinet, including the Strategic Affairs Minister Moshe Ya'alon, Finance Minister Yuval Steinitz and Deputy Prime Minister Dan Meridor, who, significantly, also held the intelligence and atomic agency portfolios. Meridor proposed the persuasive argument that an Israeli strike would only temporarily set back the Iranian nuclear programme. However, subsequently, Iran would have the political legitimacy, on the grounds of self-defence, to accelerate its nuclear programme including its military components.[44]

The opposition to a military strike on Iran from within Israel doubtlessly constrained the prime minister, but the most significant impediment to an Israeli attack was US objection. Throughout the discussions between Defence Minister Barak and his US counterparts, held between 2010 and 2012, the Americans consistently opposed an Israeli strike, making it clear that diplomacy was their preferred option for dealing with Iran's nuclear programme.[45] What was likely to have been a very costly war was narrowly averted.

Although the option of an Israeli military strike on Iran's nuclear installations was 'effectively off the agenda' by 2012, the prospect of a clash between the two countries persisted.[46] Since the 1979 Revolution Iranian foreign policymakers have made frequent statements explicitly denying Israel's very right to exist and called for its destruction.[47] Since Iran began supporting Syria's President Bashar al-

---

[42] Lazar Berman, 'Peres: I Would Meet Rouhani; Iran Is not an Enemy', *Times of Israel*, 8 December 2013, www.timesofisrael.com/peres-i-would-meet-rouhani-iran-is-not-an-enemy/, accessed 1 July 2016.

[43] Amos Ha'erl, 'IDF Chief to Ha'aretz: I Do Not Believe Iran will Decide to Develop Nuclear Weapons', Ha'aretz, 25 April 2012, www.haaretz.com/idf-chief-to-haaretz-i-do-not-believe-iran-will-decide-to-develop-nuclear-weapons-1.5216849, accessed 1 July 2016.

[44] Interview 2 Meridor; Barak, *My Country, My Life*, pp. 426–8.

[45] Barak, *My Country, My Life*, pp. 428–36.   [46] Barak, *My Country, My Life*, p. 436.

[47] These include, inter alia, former Foreign Minister Ali Akbar Velayati, *Iran and the Question of Palestine* (Tehran, 1997), p. 13; Ali Akbar Hashemi Rafsanjani, *Israel and the Beloved Jerusalem* (Qom, 1984), p. 45; Ayatollah Khomeini, *The Imam vs. Zionism* (Tehran, Ministry of Guidance, 1984), p. 21; 'Ayatollah Khamenei, Illegitimate Regime of Israel Will not Last', *Press TV*, 15 June 2018, www.presstv.com/DetailFr/2018/06/15/565033/Iran-Leader-United-States-Middle-East-Trump-Muslim-nations-economy; 'Leader's Speech in Meeting with Students', 23 July 2014, official website of Ali Khamenei, http://english.khamenei.ir/news/1934/Leader-s-Speech-in-Meeting-with-Students, accessed 6 February 2019.

The Offensive against Iran 399

Assad's brutal suppression of the opposition to his regime, it has established a significant military and political presence in Syria. Israel, which, in response, has adopted a strategy of 'zero tolerance' to Iranian military presence in Syria, carried out more than 200 airstrikes in Syria between 2016 and 2018 alone. The attacks, which targeted the forces of Iran's Revolutionary Guard, the Syrian army, and weapons shipments from Iran to Hezbollah, were one element of Israel's military effort against Iran's growing presence in Syria. Another element involved Israel's secret arming, funding and humanitarian support to at least twelve Syrian rebel groups in southern Syria. In exchange, these groups were given the task of preventing Iranian-affiliated forces from establishing their positions near the Israeli border.[48]

As Iran's efforts to consolidate in Syria continue, the prospects of a direct and major confrontation with Israel remain acutely real. The risks to Israel were a major confrontation to erupt are significant. In addition to defending against Iran and its proxy, Hezbollah, and the remaining Syrian army, Israel may face a threat from Russia, the key international patron of Bashar al-Assad's dictatorial regime. Unlike during the Cold War, when the USA could be expected to counter any Soviet expansion in the Middle East, Israel currently seems more exposed. President Trump, who described Syria in two words, 'sand' and 'death' has reduced US involvement in Syria, giving Russia the opportunity to increase its grip over the country. Amid these developments, Amir Eshel, until 2017 chief of the IAF and the man responsible for orchestrating Israel's air strikes on Syria, made these sobering remarks: 'There is no military capability', he argued, 'that can get [Iran] out of Syria. The only one who can get Iran out of Syria is Russia.' However, he warned, 'there is a real possibility that the Russians will turn on us.' Eshel's comments, which chime with Russia's emphatic 'ruling out' of Israel's continuous attacks on Syria, underscore Israel's predicament.[49]

---

[48] Dan Williams, 'Israel Says it Struck Iranian Targets in Syria 200 Times in Last Two Years', *Reuters*, www.reuters.com/article/us-mideast-crisis-israel-syria-iran/isr ael-says-struck-iranian-targets-in-syria-200-times-in-last-two-years-idUSKCN1L K2D7; Elizabeth Tsurkov, 'Inside Israel's Program to Back Syrian Rebels', *Foreign Policy*, https://foreignpolicy.com/2018/09/06/in-secret-program-israel-armed-and-funded-rebel-groups-in-southern-syria/, both links accessed 24 January 2019.

[49] Eshel's comments and Russia's position were cited in Yaniv Kubovich, 'Israel's Ex-air Force Chief: Military Capability Won't Get Iran Out of Syria, Only Russia Can Do It', *Ha'aretz*, 29 January 2019, www.haaretz.co.il/news/politics/1.6883415, accessed 30 January 2019.

400   Israel's Wondrous Decade?

A Wondrous Decade?

'This was a wondrous decade', announced Binyamin Netanyahu in his speech to the Knesset at the opening of the 2018 winter session.[50] Netanyahu cited Israel's stronger relations with the EU, which remains its largest trading partner, and also highlighted the significant economic development achieved in the last decade by Israel since becoming a member of the OECD in 2010. Indeed, according to an OECD report, in 2018, Israelis were 'more satisfied with their lives than the residents of most other OECD countries', while the Israeli economy has continued to record 'remarkable' macroeconomic and fiscal performance.[51] The prime minister also celebrated the burgeoning diplomatic and economic relations with China and India and, especially, 'the further consolidation of our strong alliance with the US. Despite the disagreements I had with the previous [Obama] administration', he continued, 'President Obama and I agreed upon a $38 billion military support package' over the next ten years. 'Under the Trump administration', continued the prime minister, boasting of his foreign policy achievements, 'our relations have soared to new heights'.[52] Here, Netanyahu was referring to President Trump's resolution to withdraw from the nuclear agreement with Iran and his unprecedented decision to recognize Jerusalem as Israel's capital.

In a characteristically polished and buoyant speech, the prime minister conveniently glossed over some of the less attractive aspects of the previous ten years. While Israel maintains a democracy within its original borders, within the West Bank it is an ethnocracy – a political system in which one ethnic group has rule over another. The Jewish nationhood law, which the fourth Netanyahu government celebrated as one of its main achievements, cemented Israel's deepening ethnocracy in what is a de facto binational state.[53] The Jewish nationhood law was passed on 19 July 2018, as a basic law, which means that it becomes part of the country's constitutional foundation. Its text, which includes not one mention of the word 'equality' – a crucial ingredient of 'democracy' – a word also not mentioned is unequivocal. Plainly and simply, it asserts that the Jewish people have an exclusive right to self-determination in the state of Israel. This exclusionary terminology stands in stark contrast to

---

[50] 'Prime Minister's Remarks at the Opening of the 5th Session of the 20th Knesset', 15 October 2018, *Prime Minister's Office*, www.gov.il/he/Departments/news/speech_kneset151018, accessed 16 January 2016.
[51] 'Economic Survey of Israel 2018', *OECD*, www.oecd.org/israel/economic-survey-israel.htm, accessed 31 January 2019.
[52] 'Prime Minister's Remarks at the Opening of the 5th session of the 20th Knesset.'
[53] 'Basic Law: Israel-The Nation State of the Jewish People', *Knesset*, https://knesset.gov.il/laws/special/eng/BasicLawNationState.pdf, accessed 4 February 2020.

A Wondrous Decade? 401

Israel's declaration of independence, which recognizes the equality of all the state's citizens 'without distinction of religion, race, or sex'.[54]

Israel's foreign policy of entrenchment throughout Binyamin Netanyahu's decade in power has deepened Israel's occupation of the Palestinians in east Jerusalem and the West Bank. The only peace plan that Israel accepted during this period is the so-called 'Deal of the Century', announced by the Trump administration on 28 January 2020.[55] This peace plan, which was concocted without consulting the Palestinians, envisages the creation of a highly constrained future Palestinian state. The plan stipulates that Israel will maintain control of the airspace west of the River Jordan, will retain at least one early warning station in the Palestinian territory and will have 'overriding security responsibility for the State of Palestine', which will be 'fully demilitarized'.[56] In addition, several existing Jewish settlements will remain 'Israeli Community Enclaves' under Israeli sovereignty within the 'contiguous Palestinian territory', thus, fragmenting the future Palestinian state. In terms of territory, the plan envisions land swaps providing the State of Palestine with 'land reasonably comparable in size to the territory of pre-1967 West Bank and Gaza', although it is less land than offered to the Palestinians in previous peace plans and the Jordan Valley would remain under Israeli sovereignty.[57]

On the most symbolic and emotionally charged issues, the Trump peace plan satisfies key Israel's demands and outright rejects Palestinian claims. Jerusalem will remain the 'undivided' sovereign capital of the State of Israel, which will retain control over the city's Holy Sites.[58] On the issue of Palestinian refugees, the plan rejects the right of return by or absorption of any Palestinian refugee into the State of Israel. Instead, Palestinian refugees will be absorbed by the future Palestinian state, with Israel having the right to disallow individual entries on security grounds. Alternatively, refugees could be integrated in their host countries if those countries agreed. Another route would entail 5,000 refugees a year, for up to ten years, being resettled in individual Organization of Islamic Cooperation member countries.[59] The plan envisages a 'potential' $50 billion new investment over ten years in a future Palestinian state, requires Israel to impose a four-year moratorium on settlement expansion

---

[54] The Israeli Declaration of Independence is available on the Knesset's official website, https://main.knesset.gov.il/About/Occasion/Pages/IndDeclaration.aspx, accessed 20 February 2019.

[55] 'Peace to Prosperity: A Vision to Improve the Lives of the Palestinian and Israeli People', White House official website, www.whitehouse.gov/wp-content/uploads/2020/01/Peace-to-Prosperity-0120.pdf, accessed 30 January 2020.

[56] *Peace to Prosperity*, pp. 3, 21–2. [57] *Peace to Prosperity*, p. 12

[58] *Peace to Prosperity*, pp. 17–18. [59] *Peace to Prosperity*, p. 32.

402   Israel's Wondrous Decade?

and demands that the Palestinians 'dismiss all pending actions, against the State of Israel' and the USA 'and any of their citizens before the International Criminal Court of Justice, and all other tribunals'.[60] Finally, an Israeli Palestinian Peace Agreement based on the plan, 'will end the conflict between Israelis and Palestinians, and end all claims between the parties'.[61]

The plan would establish a truncated and fragmented Palestinian entity, more akin to a subservient than an independent state. It is an instrument of Palestinian surrender, a Palestinian Versailles. Its realization, amid Palestinian division between Fatah and Hamas and an increasingly fragmented Arab world, would represent the apex of the Israeli right's politics and a vindication of Prime Ministers Netanyahu's and Shamir's entrenchment foreign policy stance. However, it is for precisely this reason that any Palestinian national leader would need to be extremely hard pressed to accept this plan. Indeed, as long as the Palestinians continue to reject the Trump peace plan, which they have, its implications for Israel will be severe. The plan is more likely to deepen the Israeli occupation than to deliver a longlasting Israeli-Palestinian peace and erode Israel's democratic and Jewish foundations while straining Israel's relations with Arab states. In the longer run, the continued occupation of the Palestinians and denial of their rights puts into serious doubt the notion of common values based on democracy and human freedoms, with the USA and the EU, Israel's traditional allies. Meanwhile, Iran continues to expand in the Middle East, under the auspices of Russia, expansion that Israel cannot halt using military means alone.

In this scenario, which is somewhat bleaker than that sketched by Binyamin Netanyahu, Israel's most recent decade does not seem so 'wondrous'. Rather, Israel under Binyamin Netanyahu could be compared to the Grande Armée under Napoleon Bonaparte. Netanyahu, like Napoleon in 1812, appears to be leading his country from one victory to another, during a period when, arguably, Israel has reached the apex of its power. However, similar to Napoleon's advances on Russia, it might as well be that these triumphs will lead Israel to its own 'harsh winter'. From this gloomy perspective, as Israel ceases to be a Jewish and democratic state, it will be unable to maintain its ties with Western liberal democracies on the basis of the shared values of human freedom and democracy and all this at a time when the Middle East is becoming increasingly violent and unpredictable and, possibly, owning nuclear capabilities. In this eventuality, the hand of history will be heavy and unforgiving.

---

[60] *Peace to Prosperity*, pp. 19, 38–9.   [61] *Peace to Prosperity*, p. 38.

Appendix   List of Persons Interviewed

Interviewee	Principal posts	Date
Eyal Arad	Political and media advisor to Prime Minister Ariel Sharon	21 January 2018
Moshe Arens	Foreign Minister Minister of Defence	5 July 2014
Ami Ayalon	Head of GSS	27 February 2017 12 July 2017
Dr Yossi Beilin	Deputy Foreign Minister Minister of Justice	2 November 2014 1 November 2015 10 July 2017
Professor Shlomo Ben-Ami	Foreign Minister Internal Security Minister	10 July 2017
Eytan Bentsur	Director of Minister of Foreign Affairs	28 February 2017 10 July 2017
Aviv Bushinki	Media Advisor to Prime Minister Binyamin Netanyahu	12 July 201
Kalman Gayer	Pollster for Prime Minister Yitzhak Rabin	22 December 2014
Carmi Gillon	Head of GSS	1 March 2017
Eitan Haber	Prime Minister Rabin's Chief of Staff	3 November 2014 2 November 2015
Elyakim HaEtzni	Member of Yesha Council Steering Committee MK for Tehiya	6 November 2014
Efraim Halevy	Head of Mossad	5 November 2015
Israel Harel	Head of Yesha Council	4 November 2014
Tzipi Livni	Foreign Minister	24 January 2018
Reuven Merhav	Director of Minister of Foreign Affairs	22 August 2016
Dan Meridor	Minister of Justice Deputy Prime Minister Minister of Intelligence	7 July 2014 26 February 2015
Sallai Meridor	Ambassador to Washington	9 July 2014
Yitzhak Mordechai	Defence Minister	8 July 2017
Ehud Olmert	Prime Minister	23 January 2018
Professor Itamar Rabinovich	Chief Negotiator with Syria Ambassador to Washington	2 November 2015

403

404   Appendix

(cont.)

Interviewee	Principal posts	Date
Dr Abdel Moneim Said	Head of the al-Ahram Centre for Strategic Studies	5 November 2012
Dr Efraim Sneh	Deputy Minister of Defense Minister of Health	21 August 2016
Dr Mina Tzemach	Leading Israeli Pollster	4 November 2014
Shalom Tourgeman	Diplomatic and Political Advisor to Prime Minister's Sharon and Olmert	23 January 2018
Dov Weissglas	Prime Minister's Sharon Chief of Staff	22 January 2018
Moshe Ya'alon	IDF Chief of Staff Defence Minister	11 July 2017

References

Abbas, Mahmoud, *Through Secret Channels* (Reading: Garnett, 1995).

Abrams, Elliot, 'Bombing the Syrian Reactor: The Untold Story', *Commentary*, February 2013.

Abrams, Elliot, *Tested By Zion: The Bush Administration and the Israeli-Palestinian Conflict* (Cambridge: Cambridge University Press, 2013).

Albright, Madeline, *Madam Secretary* (New York: Hyperion, 2003).

Alden, Chris and Aran Amnon, *Foreign Policy Analysis: New Approaches* (London: Routledge, 2016).

Al-Moualem, Walid, 'Fresh Light on the Syrian-Israeli Peace Negotiations', *Journal of Palestine Studies*, 26, 2, 1997: 81–94.

Al-Sharaa, Farouk, *The Missing Account* (Doha: Arab Center for Research and Policy Studies, 2015) (in Arabic).

Amnesty International, International Secretariat, 'Israel and the Palestinians: Road to Nowhere', *Amnesty International* (London: Abacus Printing, 2006).

Amidror, Yaakov, 'The Hizballah-Syria-Iran Triangle', *Middle East Review of International Affairs*, 11, 1, 2007: 1–5.

Aran, Amnon and Rami Ginat, 'Revisiting Egyptian Foreign Policy towards Israel under Mubarak: From Cold Peace to Strategic Peace', *Journal of Strategic Studies*, 37, 4, 2014: 556–83.

Arens, Moshe, *Broken Covenant: American Foreign Policy and the Crisis between the US and Israel* (New York: Simon & Schuster, 1995).

Arian, Asher and Michal Shamir, 'Two Reversals in Israeli Politics: Why 1992 Was not 1977', *Electoral Studies*, 12, 4, 1993: 315–41.

Arian, Asher and Michal Shamir (eds.), *The Elections in Israel 1999* (New York: State University of New York Press, 2002).

Arian, Asher and Michal Shamir, *The Elections in Israel – 2003* (New Brunswick: Transaction Publishers, 2005).

Arnon, Arie, 'Israeli Policy towards the Occupied Palestinian Territories: The Economic Dimension, 1967-2007', *Middle East Journal*, 61, 4, 2007: 573–95.

Art, Robert J., 'Bureaucratic Politics and American Foreign Policy: A Critique', *Policy Sciences*, 4, 1973: 467–90.

Ashrawi, Hannan, *This Side of Peace* (New York: Touchstone, 1996).

Ashton, Nigel, *King Hussein of Jordan: A Political Life* (New Haven: Yale University Press, 2008).

Avineri, Shlomo, *The Making of Modern Zionism* (London: Basic Books, 1983).

406 References

Axelrod, Robert (ed.), *Structure of Decision: The Cognitive Maps of Political Elites* (Princeton: Princeton University Press, 1976).

Azevedo, Mario J., Richard J. Payne and Eddie Ganaway, 'The Influence of Black Americans on US Policy towards Southern Africa', *African Affairs*, 79, 317, 1980: 567–85.

Azoulay, Orly, *The Man Who Didn't Know How To Win* (Tel Aviv: Yedioth Ahronoth, 1996) (in Hebrew).

Bachar, Giora, *India – A Diplomatic Diary: The Story of Forging Diplomatic Relations between India and Israel 1989–1992 from a Personal Perspective* (Azur: Reuveni Books, 2013) (in Hebrew).

Baconi Tareq, *Hamas Contained: The Rise and Pacification of Palestinian Resistance* (Stanford: Stanford University Press, 2018).

Baker, James A., *The Politics of Diplomacy: Revolution, War, and Peace* (New York: G.P. Putnam's Sons, 1995).

Bar Siman-Tov, Yaacov et al., *The Security Zone in Lebanon: A Reassessment* (Jerusalem: Leonard Davis Institute for International Relations, 1997) (in Hebrew).

Barak, Ehud, *My Country My Life: Fighting for Israel, Searching for Peace* (New York: Macmillan, 2018).

Barak, Oren and Gabriel Sheffer, *Israel's Security Network: A Theoretical and Comparative Perspective* (Cambridge: Cambridge University Press, 2013).

Barak, Oren and Eyal Tsur, 'The Military Careers and Second Careers of Israel's Military Elite', *Middle East Journal*, 66, 3, 2012: 476–83.

Bard, Mitchell G., 'AIPAC and US Middle East Policy', in *US–Israeli Relations in a New Era* (London: Routledge, 2009).

Bar-Yoseph, Uri, *The Watchman Fell Asleep: The Surprise of the Yom Kippur War and Its Consequences* (New York: State of New York University Press, 2005).

Bar-Zohar, Michael, *Shimon Peres: The Biography* (New York: Random House, 2007).

Baskin, Gershon, *Freeing Gilad: The Secret Back Channel* (Or-Yehuda: Kineret, Zmora Bitan, 2013) (in Hebrew).

Begin, Binymain Ze'ev, 'The Likud Vision for Israel at Peace', *Foreign Affairs*, 70, 4, 1991: 21–35.

Beilin, Yossi, *A Guide to an Israeli Withdrawal from Lebanon* (Tel Aviv: HaKibutz Hameuchad, 1998) (in Hebrew).

Beilin, Yossi, *A Guide to Leaving Lebanon* (Tel Aviv: Kibutz Meuchad, 1998).

Beilin, Yossi, *Touching Peace: From the Oslo Accord to a Final Agreement* (London: Weidenfeld & Nicolson, 1999).

Beilin, Yossi, *The Path to Geneva: The Quest for a Permanent Agreement, 1996–2004* (New York: RDV Books, 2004).

Ben, Aluf, 'A Convergence of Interests: A Necessary but Insufficient Precondition', *Strategic Update*, 11, 1, 2008 (in Hebrew).

Ben Meir, Yehuda, *Civil-Military Relations in Israel* (New York: Columbia University Press, 1995).

Ben Porat, Guy, *Between State and Synagogue* (Cambridge: Cambridge University Press, 2013).

References

Ben Porat, Shayke, *Talks with Yossi Beilin* (Tel Aviv: HaKibbutz Hameuchad, 1996 (in Hebrew).

Ben-Ami, Shlomo, *Scars of War Wounds of Peace: The Israeli-Arab Tragedy* (London: Weidenfeld & Nicolson, 2005).

Ben-Ami, Shlomo, *A Front Without a Rearguard* (Tel Aviv: Chemed Books, Yedioth Ahronoth, 2004) (in Hebrew).

Bengio, Ofra, *The Turkish-Israeli Relationship* (Basingstoke: Palgrave, 2004).

Ben-Horin, Michael et al., *Blessed Be the Man* (Jerusalem: Shalom Al-Yisrael, 1995) (in Hebrew).

Bentsur, Eytan, *Making Peace: A First-Hand Account of the Arab-Israeli Peace Process* (Westport: Praeger Publishers, 2001).

Benziman, Uzi, *He Does Not Stop at a Red Light* (Tel Aviv: Am Oved, 1985).

Berda, Yael, *The Bureaucracy of the Occupation* (Jerusalem: Van-Leer Jerusalem Institute, 2012) (in Hebrew).

Berda, Yael, *Living Emergency: Israel's Permit Regime in the Occupied West Bank* (Stanford: Stanford University Press, 2017).

Bin Talal, Hassan, *Search for Peace: The Politics of the Middle Ground in the Arab East* (London: Macmillan, 1984).

Blarel, Nicolas, *The Evolution of India's Israel Policy: Continuity, Change, and Compromise since 1922* (Oxford: Oxford University Press, 2015).

Blarel, Nicolas, 'Assessing US Influence over India-Israel Relations: A Difficult Equation to Balance', *Strategic Analysis*, 41, 4, 2017: 384–400, 394–95.

Bouillon, Markus E., *The Peace Business: Money and Power in the Israeli Palestinian Conflict* (London: I.B. Tauris, 2004).

Brecher, Michael and Jonathan Wilkenfeld, *A Study of Crisis* (Ann Arbour: University of Michigan Press, 1997).

Bregman, Ahron, *Elusive Peace: How the Holy Land Defeated America* (London: Penguin, 2005).

Brown, Nathan J., 'Evaluating Palestinian Reform', *Carnegie Endowment Papers*, No. 59, 2005.

Browne, Norman A.K., 'A Perspective on India-Israel Defence and Security Ties', *Strategic Analysis*, 41, 4, 2017: 325–35.

Burg, Avraham, *Victory Over Hitler* (Tel Aviv: Yedioth Ahronoth and Chemed Books, 2007) (in Hebrew).

Bush, George W., *Decision Points* (London: Virgin Books, 2010).

Buzan, Barry, 'Will the Global War on Terrorism be the New Cold War?' *International Affairs*, 82, 6, 2006: 1101–18.

Cheney, Dick, *In My Time: A Personal and Political Memoir* (New York: Threshold Editions, 2011).

Christopher, Warren, *Chances of a Lifetime: A Memoir* (New York: Scribner, 2001).

Clinton, Bill, *My Life* (New York: Knopf Publishing Group, 2004).

Cohen, Stuart A., 'Changing Civil-Military Relations in Israel: Towards an Over Subordinate IDF?', *Israel Affairs*, 12, 4, 2006: 769–88.

Cohen, Stuart A., 'Light and Shadows in US-Israeli Military Ties, 1948-2010', in Robert O. Freedman (ed.), *Israel and the United States: Six Decades of US-Israeli Relations* (Boulder: Westview Press, 2012).

Cohen, Yinon, Yitchak Haberfeld and Irene Kogan, 'Who Went Where? Jewish Immigration from the Former Soviet Union to Israel, the USA, and Germany, 1990-2000', *Israel Studies*, 17, 1, 2011: 7–20.

Dan, Uri, *Ariel Sharon – An Intimate Portrait* (Tel Aviv: Miskal, 2007) (in Hebrew).

Dawisha, Adeed, *Arab Nationalism in the 20th Century: From Triumph to Despair* (Princeton: Princeton University Press, 2003).

Deb, Alok, 'India-Israel Defence Engagement: Land Forces' Cooperation', *Strategic Analysis*, 41, 4, 2017: 336–40.

Del-Sarto, Rafaella, 'Plus Ça Change ...? Israel, the EU and the Union for the Mediterranean', *Mediterranean Politics*, 16, 1, 2011: 117–34.

Dixit, Jyotindra N., *My South Block Years: Memoirs of a Foreign Secretary* (New Delhi: UBS Publishers, 1996).

Doron, Gideon, 'Barak, One – One Israel, Zero, Or, How Labour Won the Prime Ministerial Race and Lost the Knesset Elections', in Asher Arian and Michael Shamir, *The Elections in Israel* 1999 (New York: State University of New York Press, 1992).

Dror, Yehezkel *Israeli Statecraft* (London: Routledge, 2011).

Druker, Raviv Harakiri, *Ehud Barak: the Failure* (Tel Aviv: Miskal-Yedioth Ahronoth, 2002) (in Hebrew).

Druker, Raviv and Offer Shelah, *Boomerang* (Jerusalem: Keter, 2005) (in Hebrew).

Elazar, Daniel J. and Shmuel Sandler, *Israel at the Polls 1996* (London: Frank Cass, 1998).

Eldar, Akiva and Idit Zartal, *Lords of the Land: The Settlers and the State of Israel* (Or-Yehuda: Kinneret-Zmora Bitan, 2004) (in Hebrew).

Eldar, Shlomi, *Eyeless in Gaza: Recollection of an Israeli Reporter* (Tel Aviv: Miskal, 2005) (in Hebrew).

Eldar, Shlomi, *Getting to Know Hamas* (Jerusalem: Keter, 2012) (in Hebrew).

Elitzur, Uri and Hagai Uberman, *The Oslo Agreement: A Report on Its Achievements, September 93-September 94* (Beit-El: Ha Likud, Mafdal, Tzomet, and Yesha Council, 1994) (in Hebrew).

Esposito, Michele K., 'Quarterly Update on Conflict and Diplomacy', *Journal of Palestine Studies*, 35, 4, 2006: 101–30.

European Commission, *External and Intra-European Trade – Statistical Yearbook data 1958–2010* (Luxembourg: Office for Official Publications of the European Communities, 2010).

Even, Jacob and Simcha B. Maoz, *At the Decisive Point in the Sinai: Generalship in the Yom Kippur War* (Kentucky: Kentucky University Press, 2017).

Evron, Yoram, 'Economics, Science and Technology in Israel-China Relations', in Jonathan Goldstein and Yitzhak Shichor, *China and Israel: From Discord to Concord* (Jerusalem: Magnes, 2016).

Evron, Yoram, 'China's Diplomatic Initiatives in the Middle East: The Quest for a Great Power Role in the Region', *International Relations*, 31, 2, 2017: 125–44.

Ezrahi, Yaron, *Rubber Bullets* (New York: Farrar, Straus, & Giroux, 1997).

Feiglein, Moshe, *In the Place Where There Are No People Strive to Be a Person* (Jerusalem: Metzuda, 1997) (in Hebrew).

References

Fein, Aharon, 'Voting Trends of Recent Immigrants from the Former Soviet Union', in Asher Arian and Michael Shamir (eds.), *The Elections in Israel 1992* (New York: State University of New York Press, 1992).

Filiu, Jean-Pierre, *Gaza: A History* (London: Hurst, 2012).

Fischer, Stanley, Patricia Alonso-Gamo and Ulrich Erickson von Allmen, 'Economic Developments in the West Bank and Gaza since Oslo', *Economic Journal*, 111, 2001: 254–75.

Freilich, Charles, 'National Security Decision-Making in Israel: Processes, Pathologies, and Strengths', *Middle East Journal*, 60, 4, 2006: 635–63.

Freilich, Charles D., *Zion's Dilemmas: How Israel Makes National Security Policy* (Cornell: Cornell University Press, 2013).

Galili, Lili and Roman Bronfman, *The Million that Changed the Middle East: The Soviet Aliya to Israel* (Tel Aviv: Matar, 2013) (inHebrew).

Gil, Avi, *The Peres Formula: Diary of a Confidant* (Hevel Modi'in: Kineret, Zmora Bitan, 2018) (in Hebrew).

Gilboa, Amos, *The True Story of How Israel Left Lebanon – Code Name Dawn* (Jerusalem: Efi Meltzer, 2015) (in Hebrew).

Gilboa, Eytan, 'The Public Dimension in US-Israeli Relations', in Eytan Gilboa and Efraim Inbar (eds.), *US-Israeli Relations in a New Era: Issues and Challenges after 9/11* (London: Routledge, 2009).

Gillon, Carmi, *Shin-Beth Between the Schisms* (Tel Aviv: Yedioth Ahronoth, 2000) (in Hebrew).

Giora Eiland, 'The Third Lebanon War: Target Lebanon', *Strategic Assessment*, 11, 2, 2008: 9–17.

Gold, Dore, 'Following the American Elections: Preparing for Trends in Israel-US Relations', *Memorandum No. 37*, December 1992, p. 1 (Tel Aviv: Centre for Strategic Studies).

Goldberg, Giora, 'The Electoral Fall of the Israeli Left', in Daniel J. Elazar and Shmuel Sandler (eds.), *Israel at the Polls 1996* (London: Frank Cass, 1998).

Goldstein, Jonathan and Yitzhak Shichor, *China and Israel: From Discord to Concord* (Jerusalem: Magnes, 2016) (in Hebrew).

Gordon, Neve, *Israel's Occupation* (Berkeley: University of California Press, 2008).

Greenberg, Lev. L., *The Histadroot Above All* (Jerusalem: Nevo, 1993) (in Hebrew).

Hadar, Leon T. 'The 1992 Electoral Earthquake and the Fall of the "Second Israeli Republic"', *Middle East Journal*, 46, 4, 1992: 594–616.

Hagai, Segal, *Dear Brothers: The West Bank Jewish Underground* (Jerusalem: Keter, 1987) (in Hebrew).

Halevy, Efraim, *Man in the Shadows: Inside the Middle East Crisis with a Man Who Led the Mossad* (Tel Aviv: Matar, 2006) (in Hebrew).

Halevy, Efraim, 'The Man, the Statesman, and the Strategist: As I Knew Him', in Anita Shapira and Nurit Cohen-Levinovsky (eds.), *Three Shots and Twenty Years* (Tel Aviv: The Yitzhak Rabin Center, 2015) (in Hebrew).

Haloutz, Danny, *Straightforward* (Tel Aviv: Miskal-Yedioth Ahronoth, 2010) (in Hebrew).

410   References

Haniyeh, Akram Hanieh, 'The Camp David Papers', *Journal of Palestine Studies*, 30, 2 (2001): 75–97.

Harel, Amos and Avi Issacharoff, *The Seventh War* (Tel Aviv: Yehioth Ahronoth, 2004) (in Hebrew).

Harel, Amos and Avi Issacharoff, *Spider Webs (34 Days)* (Tel Aviv: Miskal-Yedioth Ahronoth, 2008) (in Hebrew).

Harpaz, Guy and Asaf Shamis, 'Normative Power Europe and the State of Israel: An Illegitimate Eutopia', *Journal of Common Market Studies*, 48, 3, 2010: 579–616.

Hazan, Reuven Y. 'Intraparty Politics and Peace-Making in Democratic Societies: Israel's Labour Party and the Middle East Process, 1992-1996', *Journal of Peace Research*, 37, 3, 2000: 363–78.

Hefetz, Nir and Gadi Bloom, *Ariel Sharon: A Life* (New York: Random House, 2006).

Hermann, Charles F., 'Changing Course: When Governments Choose to Redirect Foreign Policy', *International Studies Quarterly*, 34, 1, 1990: 3–21.

Hermann, Tamar, *The Israeli Peace Movement: A Shattered Dream* (Cambridge: Cambridge University Press, 2009).

Hermann, Tamar, Efraim Yaar and Arieh Nadler, *The 'Peace Index Project: Findings and Analyses* (Tel Aviv: Steineitz Center for Peace, 1996).

Hever, Ze'ev, 'Zeev Hever (Zambish)', in Ari Shavit, *Partition: Disengagement and Beyond* (Jerusalem: Keter, 2005) (in Hebrew).

Hill, Christopher, *Foreign Policy in the 21st Century* (London: Palgrave, 2016).

Hinnebusch, Raymond A., 'Does Syria Want Peace? Syrian Policy in the Syrian-Israeli Peace Negotiations', *Journal of Palestine Studies*, 26, 1, 1996: 42–57.

Hirschfeld, Yair P., *Oslo: A Formula for Peace from Negotiations to Implementation* (Tel Aviv: Am Oved, 2000) (in Hebrew).

Hirst, David, 'South Lebanon: The War that Never Ends?', *Journal of Palestinian Studies*, 28, 3, 1999: 5–18.

Hoe, Nicholas, *Voices of Hezbollah: The Statements of Sayyed Hassan Nasrallah* (London: Verso, 2007), p. 242.

Horwitz, Dan, 'The IDF: A Civilianized Military in a Partially Militarized Society', in R. Kolkowitz and A. Korbonski (eds.), *Soldiers, Peasants and Bureaucrats* (London: Allen & Unwin, 1982).

Hroub, Khaled, *Hamas: Political Thought and Practice* (Washington: Institute for Palestine Studies, 2000).

Hudson, Michael C., 'The United States in the Middle East', in Louise Fawcett, *International Relations of the Middle East* (Oxford: Oxford University Press, 2013).

Inbar, Efraim, 'Netanyahu Takes Over', in Daniel J. Elazar and Shmuel Sandler (eds.), *Israel at the Polls 1996* (London: Frank Cass, 1998).

Indyk, Martin, *Innocent Abroad: An Intimate Account of the American Peace Diplomacy in the Middle East* (New York: Simon & Schuster, 2009).

Israeli Labour Party, *The Israeli Labour Party Manifesto to the 13th Knesset* (Tel Aviv: Israeli Labour Party, 1992).

References 411

Karpin, Michael and Ina Friedman, *Murder in the Name of God: The Plot to Kill Yitzhak Rabin* (London: Granta Publications,1998).

Karsh, Ephraim and Lawrence Freedman, *The Gulf Conflict, 1990–1991: Diplomacy and War in the New World Order* (London: Faber & Faber, 1993).

Katz, Kimberly *Jordanian Jerusalem: Holy Places and National Places* (Gainesville: University of Florida Press, 2005).

Keren, Michael, 'Elections 1996: The Candidates and the "New Politics"', in Daniel J. Elazar and Shmuel Sandler (eds.), *Israel at the Polls 1996* (London: Frank Cass, 1998).

Kfir, Ilan and Danny Dor, *Barak: Wars of My Life* (Or-Yehuda: Zmora Bitan, 2015) (in Hebrew).

Khanin, Vladimir, 'Israeli Russian Parties and the New Immigrant Vote'. in Daniel J. Elazar and Shmuel Mollov, *Israel at the Polls 1999* ((London: Frank Cass, 1998).

Kober, Avi, 'The Israel Defense Forces in the Second Lebanon War: Why the Poor Performance?', *Journal of Strategic Studies*, 31, 1, 2008: 3–40.

Konrad Adenauer Stiftung and Sharon Pardo, *Measuring the Attitudes of Israelis towards the European Union and its Member States* (Jerusalem: Konrad Adenauer Stiftung, 2007).

Kumaraswamy, P.R., *Israel's China Odyssey* (New Delhi: Institute for Defence Studies and Analysis, 1994).

Kumaraswamy, P.R., 'Redefining "Strategic Cooperation"', *Strategic Analysis*, 41, 4, 2017: 355–68.

Kumaraswamy, P.R., *India's Israel Policy* (New York: Columbia University Press, 2010).

Landau, David, *Arik: The Life of Ariel Sharon* (New York: Alfred A. Knopf, 2013).

Lavie, Efraim (ed.), *Israel and the Arab Peace Initiative* (Tel Aviv: Tammy Steinmetz Centre for Peace Research, 2010) (in Hebrew).

Lehman-Wilzig, Sam, 'The Media Campaign: The Negative Effects of Positive Campaigning', in Daniel J. Elazar and Shmuel Sandler (eds.), *Israel at the Polls 1996* (London: Frank Cass, 1998).

Levy, Yagil, *The Other Army of Israel: Materialist Militarism in Israel* (Tel Aviv: Yedioth Ahronoth, 2003) (in Hebrew).

Lewis, Samuel W. 'The United States and Israel: Evolution of an Unwritten Alliance', *Middle East Journal*, 53, 3, 1999: 364–78.

Liberman, Avigdor, *My Truth* (Tel Aviv: Maariv, 2004) (in Hebrew).

Lochery, Neil, 'Israel and Turkey: Deepening Ties and Strategic Implications, 1995-1998', *Israel Affairs*, 5, 1, 1998: 45–62.

Luft, Gal, 'The Israeli Security Zone – A Tragedy?', *Middle East Report*, 3, 2000: 13–20.

MacGeough, Paul, *Kill Khalid: The Failed Mossad Assassination of Khalid Mashal and the Rise of Hamas* (New York: New Press, 2009).

Magen, Amichai, 'Israel and the Many Pathways of Diffusion', *West European Politics*, 35, 1, 2012: 98–116.

Mahler, Gregory S., 'The Forming of the Netanyahu Government: Coalition-Forming in a uasi-Parliamentary Setting', *Israel Affairs*, 3, 3–4, 1997: 3–27.

412   References

Makovsky, David, 'The Silent Strike', *New Yorker*, 17 September 2012, www .newyorker.com/magazine/2012/09/17/the-silent-strike, accessed 15 March 2019.

Malley, Robertand Agha Hussein, 'Camp David: The Tragedy of Errors', *New York Review of Books*, 9 August 2001: 1–18.

Margalit, Avishai, 'The Violent Life of Yitzhak Shamir, *New York Review of Books*, 14 May 1992.

Margalit, Dan and Ronen Bergman, *The Pit* (Or-Yehuda: Kineret, Zmora Bitan, 2011) (in Hebrew).

Mearsheimer, John and Stephen Walt, *The Israel Lobby and US Foreign Policy* (New York: Farrar, Straus, & Giroux, 2007).

Medzini, Meron, *Israel's Foreign Relations: Selected Documents, 1988–1992*, vol. 12 (Jerusalem: Ministry of Foreign Affairs, 1993).

Meital, *Peace in Tatters: Israel, the Palestinian and the Middle East* (Jerusalem: Carmel, 2004) (in Hebrew).

Merhav, Reuven, 'The Dream of the Red Chambers – From the Scented Port to the Forbidden City/from Hong-Kong to Beijing', in *The Ministry of Foreign Affairs: The First 50 Years* (Jerusalem: Keter, 2002) (in Hebrew).

Migdalovitz, Carol, 'Israeli-Palestinian Peace Process': The Annapolis Conference', *CRS Report for* Congress, https://fas.org/sgp/crs/mideast/R S22768.pdf, accessed 19 March 2019.

Miller, Aaron D., *The Much Too Promised Land* (New York: Bantam Books, 2009).

Miller, Rory, 'Troubled Neighbours: The EU and Israel', *Israel Affairs*, 12, 4, 2006: 642–64.

Miller, Rory, *Inglorious Disarray: Europe, Israel and the Palestinians since 1967* (London: Hurst, 2010).

Milton-Edwards, Beverly and Stephen Farrel, *Hamas* (Cambridge: Polity, 2010).

Misgav, Haim, *Conversations with Yitzhak Shamir* (Tel Aviv: Sifriyat Poalim, 1997) (in Hebrew).

Misgav, Haim, *Not the Same Sea: Conversations with Shimon Peres* (Tel Aviv: Poalim Library, 2004) (in Hebrew).

Mishal, Shaul and Avraham Sela, *The Palestinian Hamas: Vision, Violence and Co-Existence* (New York: Columbia University Press, 2006).

More, Dror, *The Gatekeepers* (Tel Aviv: Yedioth Ahronoth, 2014) (in Hebrew).

Morris, Benny, *Righteous Victims: A History of the Zionist-Arab Conflict 1881–2001* (New York: Vintage Books, 2001).

Moualem, Walid, 'Fresh Light on the Syrian-Israeli Peace Negotiations', *Journal of Palestine Studies*, 26, 2, 1997: 81–94.

Muasher, Marwan, *The Arab Center: The Promise of Moderation* (New Haven: Yale University Press, 2008).

Musu, Constanza, *European Union Policy towards the Arab-Israeli Peace Process* (Basingstoke: Palgrave-Macmillan, 2010).

Naaz, Farah, 'Indo-Israel Military Cooperation', *Strategic Analysis*, 24, 5, 2008: 969–85.

Nave, Danny, *Executive Secrets* (Tel Aviv: Yedioth Ahronoth, 1999) (in Hebrew).

Neriah, Jaques, *Between Rabin and Arafat: A Political Diary* (Jerusalem: Jerusalem Centre for Public Affairs, 2016) (in Hebrew).

References 413

Netanyahu, Binyamin and Ido Netanyahu, *The Letters of Jonathan Netanyahu* (Jerusalem: Gefen, 1980).

Netanyahu, Binyamin, *A Place among the Nations* (London: Bantam, 1993).

Noor, Queen of Jordan, *Leap of Faith: Memoirs of an Unexpected Life* (London: Phoenix, 2003).

Norton, Augustus R., *Hezbollah: A Short History* (Princeton: Princeton University Press, 2007).

Olmert, Ehud, *In Person* (Tel Aviv: Miskal-Yedioth Ahronoth, 2018) (in Hebrew).

Pant, Harsh V. 'India's Relations with Iran: Much Ado about Nothing', *Strategic Analysis*, 34, 1, 2011: 61–74.

Pant, Harsh V. and Ivan Lidarev, 'Indian Counterterrorism Policy and the Influence of the Global War on Terror', *India Review*, 17, 2, 2018: 181–5.

Pardo, Sharon and Joel Peters, *Uneasy Neighbours: Israel and the European Union* (Lanham: Lexington Books, 2010).

Pedahtzur, Ami, *The Triumph of Israel's Radical Right* (Oxford: Oxford University Press, 2012).

Peled, Yoav, 'Towards a Redefinition of Jewish Nationalism in Israel? The Enigma of Shas', *Ethnic and Racial Studies*, 21, 4, 1998: 703–27.

Peleg, Ilan and Dov Waxman, *Israel's Palestinians: The Conflict Within* (Cambridge: Cambridge University Press, 2011).

Peres, Shimon, 'Ministry of Foreign Affairs Brief' (Jerusalem: Ministry of Foreign Affairs, 1993) (in Hebrew).

Peres, Shimon, *The New Middle East: A Framework and Processes Towards an Era of Peace* (Tel Aviv: Steimatzky, 1993) (in Hebrew).

Peri, Yoram, *Generals in the Cabinet Room: How the Military Shapes Israeli Policy* (Washington: United States Institute of Peace Press, 2006).

Peters, Joel, 'Europe and the Israel-Palestinian Peace Process: The Urgency of Now', *European Security*, 19, 3, 2010: 511–29.

Podeh, Elie, 'Israel and the Arab Peace Initiative, 2002–2014: A Plausible Missed Opportunity', *Middle East Journal*, 68, 4, 2014: 584–603.

Podeh, Elie, *Chances for Peace: Missed Opportunities in the Arab-Israeli Conflict* (Austin: University of Texas Press, 2015).

Pradhan, Samir, 'India and the Gulf Cooperation Council: An Economic and Political Perspective', *Strategic Analysis*, 34, 1, 2010: 93–103.

Primakov, Yevgeny, *Russia and the Arabs* (New York: Basic Books, 2009).

Primor, Avi, 'Israel and the EU', in Yager et al., *The Ministry of Foreign Affairs: The First 50 Years* (Jerusalem: Keter, 2002) (in Hebrew).

Pundak, Ron, *Secret Channel* (Tel Aviv: Aliyat Gag, 2013) (in Hebrew).

Qassem, Naim, *Hizbullah: The Story Within* (London: Saqi Press, 2005).

Qurie, Ahmed, *From Oslo to Jerusalem: The Palestinian Story of the Secret Negotiations* (London: I.B. Tauris, 2006).

Qurei, Ahmed (Abu Ala) *Peace Negotiations in Palestine: From the Second Intifada to the Roadmap* (London: I.B. Tauris, 2015).

Rabi, Uzi, 'Qatar's Relations with Israel: Challenging Arab and Gulf Norms', *Middle East Journal*, 63, 3, 2009: 443–59.

414   References

Rabin, Yitzhak, 'A Response to the Likud No-Confidence Measure in the Wake of Increasing Terrorism, 21 December, 1992', in *Pursing Peace: The Peace Speeches of Prime Minister Yitzhak Rabin* (Tel Aviv: Zmora Bitan, 1995) (in Hebrew).

Rabin, Yitzhak, 'Opening Speech of the Knesset Winter Session, 26 October, 1992', in *Pursing Peace: The Peace Speeches of Prime Minister Yitzhak Rabin* (Tel Aviv: Zmora Bitan, 1995).

Rabin, Yitzhak, 'Peace and Security or War: In Conclusion of the Discussion Following the Presentation of the Rabin Government, 13 July 1992', in *Pursing Peace: The Peace Speeches of Prime Minister Yitzhak Rabin* (Tel Aviv: Zmora Bitan, 1995) (in Hebrew).

Rabin, Yitzhak, *The Rabin Memoirs* (Berkeley: University of California Press, 1996).

Rabinovich, Itamar, *The Brink of Peace: The Israeli-Syrian Negotiations* (Princeton: Princeton University Press, 1998).

Reich, Bernard, *Securing the Covenant: United States-Israel Relations after the Cold War* (Westport: Praeger, 1995).

Revel, Sammy, *Israel at the Forefront of the Persian Gulf: The Story of an Israeli Mission in Qatar* (Tel Aviv: Miskal, 2009) (in Hebrew).

Rice, Condoleezza, *No Higher Honor: A Memoir of My Years In Washington* (New York: Simon & Schuster, 2011).

Ross, Dennis, *The Missing Peace: The Inside Story of the Fight for Middle East Peace, 1988–2000* (New York: Farrar, Straus, & Giroux, 2004).

Ross, Dennis, *Doomed to Succeed: The U.S.-Israel Relationship from Truman to Obama* (New York: Farrar, Straus, & Giroux, 2015).

Roy, Sara, 'Separation or Integration: Closure and the Economic Future of the Gaza Strip Revisited', *Middle East Journal*, 48, 1, 1994: 11–30.

Roy, Sara, 'De-Development Revisited: Palestinian Economy and Society since Oslo', *Journal of Palestine Studies*, 28, 3, 1999: 64–82.

Roy, Sara, *Failing Peace: Gaza and the Palestinian-Israeli Conflict* (London: Pluto Press, 2007).

Rubenstein, Elyakim, *Ways of Peace* (Tel Aviv: Maarachot, 1992).

Rubenstein, Elyakim, 'The Peace Agreement with Jordan', *Hamishpat*, 6 December, 1995: 6–12.

Rubin, Barry, 'US-Israeli Relations and Israel's 1992 Elections', in Asher Arian and Michal Shamir (eds.), *The 1992 Elections in Israel* (New York: State University of New York Press, 1992).

Rubin, Neil, 'The Relationship Between American Evangelical Christians and the State of Israel' in Robert Freedman, *Israel and the United States* (Boulder: Westview Press, 2012).

Rumley, Grant and Amir Tibon, *The Last Palestinian: The Rise and Reign of Mahmoud Abbas* (New York: Prometheus Books, 2017).

Rynhold, Jonathan, 'Labour, Likud, the "Special Relationship", and the Peace Process', *Israel Affairs*, 3, 3–4, 2007: 239–62.

Sagie, Uri, *Lights within the Fog* (Tel Aviv: Yedioth Ahronoth, 1998) (in Hebrew).

Sagie, Uri, *The Israeli-Syrian Dialogue* (Houston: Rice University Press, 1999).

References 415

Sagie, Uri, *The Frozen Hand* (Tel Aviv: Miskal-Yedioth Ahronoth Books, 2011) (in Hebrew).

Samsonov, Gil, *The Princes: How did the Sons of the Warrior Family Conquer the Leadership of the State* (Or-Yehuda: Kineret, Zmora-Bitan, 2015) (in Hebrew).

Sandler, Shmuel and Daniel Mollov, 'Israel at the Polls 2003: A New Turning Point in the Political History of the Jewish State', *Israel Affairs*, 10, 4, 2004: 1–19.

Savir, Uri, *The Process* (Tel Aviv: Yedioth Ahronoth Books, 1998) (in Hebrew).

Savir, Uri, *Peace First* (Tel Aviv: Yedioth Acronoth Books, 2007) (in Hebrew).

Schiff, Ze'ev, 'Israel after the War', *Foreign Affairs*, 70, 2, 1991: 19–33.

Seale, Patrick, 'The Syria Israel Negotiations: Who is Telling the Truth', *Journal of Palestine Studies*, 29, 2, 2000: 65–77.

Seale, Patrick with Linda Butler, 'Assad's Regional Strategy and the Challenge from Netanyahu', *Journal of Palestine Studies*, 26, 1, 1996: 27–41.

Segal, Hagai, *Dear Brothers: The West Bank Jewish Underground* (Jerusalem: Keter, 1987).

Senor, Dan and Saul Singer, *Start Up Nation: The Story of Israel's Economic Miracle* (Boston: Twelve Books, 2011).

Sfieh, Afif, *The Peace Process: From Breakthrough to Breakdown* (London: Saqi Books, 2010).

Shaaban, Bouthania, *Damascus Diary: An Inside Account of Hafez Al-Assad's Peace Diplomacy, 1990–2000* (Boulder and London: Lynne Rienner Publishers, 2013).

Shaath, Nabil, 'The Oslo Agreement. An Interview with Nabil Shaath', *Journal of Palestine Studies*, 23, 1, 1993: 5–13.

Shafir, Gershon and Yoav Peled (eds.), *The New Israel: Peace Making and Liberalization* (Boulder: Westview Press, 2000).

Shafir, Gershon and Yoav Peled, *Being Israeli: The Dynamics of Multiple Citizenship* (Cambridge: Cambridge University Press, 2003).

Shai, Aron, 'The Evolution of Israeli-Chinese Friendship', *Research Paper No. 7* (Tel Aviv: Daniel Abraham Centre for International and Regional Studies, 2014).

Shai, Aron, 'Beijing and Jerusalem: Diplomatic Relations and the International Arena', in Jonathan Goldstein and Yitzhak Shichor, *China and Israel: From Discord to Concord* (Jerusalem: Magnes, 2016).

Shai, Aron, *China and Israel: Equivocal Ties: Jews, Chinese, Jerusalem, Beijing* (Tel Aviv: Miskal, 2016) (in Hebrew).

Shalhevet, Joseph, *China and Israel: Science in the Service of Diplomacy* (Kiryat Ono: Smirim, 2009) (in Hebrew).

Shamir, Michael, *The 1992 Elections in Israel* (New York: State University of New York Press, 1992).

Shamir, Michal, Raphael Ventura, Asher Arian and Orit Kedar, 'Kadima', in Asher Arian and Michal Shamir, *The Elections in Israel 2006* (New York: Transaction Publishers, 2008).

Shamir, Shimon, *The Rise and Decline of the Warm Peace with Jordan: Israeli Diplomacy in the Hussein Years* (Tel Aviv: Hakibbutz Hameuchad Publishing House, 2012) (in Hebrew).

416 References

Shamir, Yitzhak, *Summing Up* (Tel Aviv: Yedioth Ahronoth, 1994) (in Hebrew).

Sharon, Ariel with David Cahanoff, *Warrior: An Autobiography* (New York: Simon & Schuster, 1989).

Sharon, Gilad, *Sharon – The Life of a Leader* (Tel Aviv: Meter, 2011) (in Hebrew).

Sharp, Jeremy M., *US Foreign Aid to Israel* (Washington: Congressional Research Service, 2010).

Sheffer, Gabriel and Oren Barak, *Israel's Security Networks: A Theoretical and Comparative Perspective* (Cambridge: Cambridge University Press, 2013).

Shelah, Ofer and Yoav Limor, *Captives in Lebanon* (Tel Aviv: Miskal-Yedioth Ahronoth, 2007) (in Hebrew).

Sher, Gilad, *Just Beyond Reach: The Israeli-Palestinian Peace Negotiations 1999–2001* (Tel Aviv: Yedioth Ahronoth, 2001) (in Hebrew).

Shichor, Yitzhak, 'Israel Military Transfers to China and Taiwan', *Survival*, 40, 1, 1998: 68–91.

Shiftan, Dan, *Palestinians in Israel: The Arab Minority and the Jewish States* (Or-Yehuda: Kineret, Zmora Bitran, 2011).

Shikaki, Khalil, 'Palestinian Divided', *Foreign Affairs*, 81, 1, 2002: 89–105.

Shindler, Colin, 'Likud and the Search for Eretz Israel', *Israel Affairs*, 8, 1–2, 2001: 91–117.

Shindler, Colin, *The Land Beyond Promise: Israel, Likud and the Zionist Dream* (London: I.B. Tauris, 2002).

Shlaim, Avi, *Collusion Across the Jordan* (Oxford: Oxford University Press, 1988).

Shlaim, Avi, *The Iron Wall: Israel and the Arab World* (London: Penguin, 2000).

Shlaim, Avi, *Lion of Jordan: The Life of King Hussein in War and Peace* (London: Penguin, 2007).

Shlaim, Avi, *The Iron Wall: Israel and the Arab World*, 2nd ed. (London: Penguin, 2014).

Shuval, Zalman, *Diplomat* (Rishon Le Zion: Miskal, 2016) (in Hebrew).

Siniver, Asaf and Jeffrey Collins, 'Airpower and Quagmire: Historical Analogies and the 2006 Lebanon War', *Foreign Policy Analysis*, 11, 2, 2015: 215–31.

Smith, Karen E., *European Union Foreign Policy in a Changing World*, 3rd ed. (Cambridge: Polity, 2014).

Smooha, Sammy and Don Peretz, 'Israel's 1992 Knesset Elections: Are They Critical?', *Middle East Journal*, 47, 3, 1993: 444–63.

Sneh, Efraim, 'The Place of Israel in a Changing World', transcript of a lecture given at the Davis Institute for International Relations at the Hebrew University of Jerusalem, April 1993.

Sneh, Efraim, *Responsibility: Israel After Year 2000* (Jerusalem: Yedioth Ahronoth Books, 1996) (in Hebrew).

Sobleman, D., 'Four Years after the Withdrawal from Lebanon: Refining the Rules of the Game', *Strategic Assessment*, 7, 2, 2004: 30–8.

Steinberg, Gerald, 'Foreign Policy in the 1999 Elections', in Daniel Elazar and Shmuel Mollov, *Israel at the Polls 1999* (London: Frank Cass, 1998).

Sufott, E. Zev, *A China Diary: Towards the Establishment of China-Israel Diplomatic Relations* (London: Frank Cass, 1997).

References

Swisher, Clayton E., *The Untold about Camp David: The Untold Story about the Collapse of the Middle East Peace Process* (New York: Nation Books, 2004).

Swisher, Clayton E., *The Palestine Papers: The End of the Road?* (Catham: Hesperus, 2011).

Tesler, Ricky, *In the Name of God: Shas and the Religious Revolution* (Jerusalem: Keter Books, 2003), pp. 59–60 (in Hebrew).

Torgovnik, Efraim, 'Shinui's to Capture the Centre of Israeli Politics in Smuel Sandler', in M. Ben Mollov and Jonathan Rynhold (eds.), *Israel at the Polls 2003: A New Turning Point in the History of the Jewish State?* (London: Routledge,2005).

Tripp, Charles, *A History of Iraq* (Cambridge: Cambridge University Press, 2007).

Vanaik, Achin, 'Making India Strong: The BJP Government's Foreign Policy Perspectives', *South Asia: Journal of South Asian Studies*, 25, 3, 2002: 321–41.

Warner, Michael, *Publics and Counterpublics* (New York: Zone Books, 2002).

Waxman, Dov, 'The Pro-Israel Lobby in the United States: Past, Present and Future', in Robert O. Freedman (ed.), *Israel and the United States: Six Decades of US-Israeli Relations* (Boulder: Westview Press, 2012).

Weissglas, Dov *Ariel Sharon – A Prime Minister* (Tel Aviv: Yedioth Ahronoth, 2012) (in Hebrew).

Wiegand, Krista E., 'Reformation of a Terrorist Group: Hezbollah as a Lebanese Political Party', *Studies in Conflict and Terrorism*, 32, 2019: 669–80.

Ya'alon, Moshe, *The Longer Shorter Way* (Tel Aviv: Miskal-Yedioth Ahronoth Books, 2008) (in Hebrew).

Yafe, Nurit, 'The Population of Israel 1990–2009: Demographic Statistics', in *The Israeli Central Bureau of Statistics* (Jerusalem: Central Bureau of Statistics, 2010) (in Hebrew).

Yatom, Danny, *The Confidant: From Sayeret Matkal to the Mossad* (Tel Aviv: Yedioth Ahronoth, 2009) (in Hebrew).

Yegar, Moshe, *The Long Journey to Asia: A Chapter in the Diplomatic History of Israel* (Haifa: Haifa University Press, 2004) (in Hebrew).

Yuchtman-Yaar, Ephraim, Tamar Herman and Arieh Nadler, *Peace Index Project: Findings and Analysis, June 1994–May 1996* (Tel Aviv: Steinmatz Centre for Peace Research, 1996) (in Hebrew).

Zak, Moshe, *King Hussein Makes Peace* (Ramat-Gan: Bar-Ilan University Press, 1996) (in Hebrew).

Zanani, Omer, *Annapolis Process (2007–2008): Oasis or Mirage?* (Tel Aviv: Steineitz Centre for Peace, 2015) (in Hebrew).

Zertal, Idit, *Israel's Holocaust and the Politics of Nationhood* (Cambridge: Cambridge University Press, 2011).

Zisser, Eyal, 'Hizballah: Between Armed Struggle and Domestic Politics', in Barry Rubin (ed.), *Revolutionaries and Reformers: Contemporary Islamic Movements in the Middle East* (New York: State University of New York Press, 2003).

Zisser, Eyal, 'Hizballah and Israel: Strategic Threat on the Northern Border', *Israel Affairs*, 12, 1, 2006: 86–106.

418 References

Official Reports

Annual Report 2006–2007, *Indian Ministry of External Affairs*, p. vi, pp. 45–6, www.mea.gov.in/Uploads/PublicationDocs/168_Annual-Report-2006–2007.pdf.

Annual Report 2009–2010, *Indian Ministry of External Affairs*, pp. vi, 42, www.mea.gov.in/Uploads/PublicationDocs/171_Annual-Report-2009–2010.pdf.

Cox Report, Washington: US House of Representatives, 1999.

'The Gaza Strip: March Access Report, Closure at Karni Crossing', *United Nations: Office for the Coordination of Humanitarian Affairs*, https://unispal.un.org/DPA/DPR/unispal.nsf/0/9321873EB12052608525714F004D346B.

Israeli Labour Party Report summarizing two years of the labour government, July 1993–June 1994.

Sharm El-Sheikh Fact-Finding Committee Report 'Mitchell Report', EU Official Website, http://eeas.europa.eu/archives/docs/mepp/docs/mitchell_report_2001_en.pdf.

Uri Elitzur and Hagai Uberman, *The Oslo Agreement: A Report on Its Achievements, September 93–September 94* (Beit-El: Ha Likud, Mafdal, Tzomet, and Yesha Council, 1994) (in Hebrew).

United Nations Human Rights Council, *Report of the United Nations Fact Finding Mission on the Gaza Conflict* (New York: United Nations, 2009).

Winograd Commission's interim and final reports into the Second Lebanon War, www.vaadatwino.gov.il.

Newspapers

Guardian
Ha'aretz
New York Times
Ma'ariv
Washington Post
Yedioth Ahronoth

Index

Abbas, Mahmoud (Abu Mazen), 45, 48, 54–5
  Abu Mazen-Beilin agreement, 109
  Beilin negotiations with, 108–10
  Olmert and, negotiations with, 355–9
  as prime minister, 292–9
  administration failures, 298–9
  Israel Defence Force and, 294–5
  limited authority of, 293
  Road Map for Peace, 293
Abdel-Shafi, Haider, 29, 40
Abed-Rabbo, Yasser, 229, 303–4
Abrams, Elliot, 258, 259–60, 287, 290, 297–8, 307–8, 335, 358–9
Abu Ala (Ahmed Qurie), 45–6, 53, 94, 263–4, 273–4, 293
Abu Mazen (Mahmoud Abbas). *See* Abbas, Mahmoud
Abu Mazen-Beilin agreement, 109
Adler, Reuven, 256, 313
Agha, Hussein, 373
AIPAC. *See* American-Israel Public Affairs Committee
Albright, Madeleine, 165, 166, 202–3, 207–8
Aloni, Shulamit, 48
American-Israel Public Affairs Committee (AIPAC), 28, 128, 369
Amidror, Yaakov, 189
Amir, Yigal, 106–7, 118, 389
Annapolis Peace Conference, 351–4
API. *See* Arab Peace Initiative
Al-Aqsa intifada, 3–4, 239–41, 270, 272, 274, 298–9
Arab Gulf States. *See also specific countries*
  Netanyahu and, foreign policy approach towards, 185–8
Arab Peace Initiative (API), 275–8
Arab uprisings, 387–9, 390, 392, 394
Arab-Israeli negotiations, 23–7, 394–6
  European Economic Community in, Israel objections to, 25

land-for-peace exchange in, 14–15
loan guarantees feud as factor in, 27–8, 129
Madrid Peace Conference and, 28–31, 39–45
Palestinian Liberation Organization in, 26–7
under Rabin. *See* Rabin, Yitzhak
settlement expansion and, 27
under Shamir. *See* Shamir, Yitzhak
Sharon, as obstacle to, 25, 27
Soviet Union role in, 26
two-state solution in
  Clinton parameters of, 247–51
  as new foreign policy paradigm, 260–1
United Nations role in, Israel objections to, 25
US role in, 23–8
  Baker and, 24–7, 41
Arab-Israeli Wars. *See also* Netanyahu, Binyamin; Olmert, Ehud; Second Lebanon War
Gaza Strip and, Palestinians in, 1
India during, 142
Israeli occupation of territories after, 12–13
Rabin and, 34–5
Shamir and, 14–15
territorial acquisition after, 14–15
unilateral foreign policy after, 2
West Bank and, Palestinians in, 1
Arad, Eyal, 253–4, 255, 256, 258–9, 304–5, 313
Arad, Uzi, 189
Arafat, Yasser, 45, 121, 122, 123. *See also* Palestinian Liberation Organization
Barak and, 234, 235–6, 237, 238, 241–5
  lack of trust between, 249–50, 278
Declaration of Principles on Self-Government Arrangements and, role in, 53
election of, 117

419

420 Index

Arafat, Yasser (cont.)
 Israel-EU foreign policy and, 381–2
 Netanyahu and, 158
  refusal to meet with Arafat, 154–5, 186
 after 9/11 attacks, negotiations with,
  263–4
 Nobel Peace Prize for, 79
 Ross and, 158
 Sharon and, 257, 276–7, 318
 US assessment of, as legitimate leader,
  279–80
Arens, Moshe, 13, 14–15, 127, 148, 153.
  See also Gulf War
Ashkenazi, Gabi, 219–20, 324, 342
Ashrawi, Hannan, 40
al-Assad, Bashar, 83, 202–3, 398–9
al-Assad, Hafez, 41, 80–1, 83–5, 103, 118,
  182. *See also* Syria
 Barak and, 211–13, 235–6, 238
 as monarchical president, 83
assassinations, political
 of Ayash, 114–16
 against Mashal, attempts at, 173–9
 of Rabin, 104–8
  by Amir, 106–7
  din mosser as justification for, 107
  din rodef as justification for, 107
  Peres ascension after, 108–13
 Sharon government and, 269–72
Association of Sephardic Torah Keepers.
  See Shas Party
autonomy. *See* relative autonomy
Avineri, Shlomo, 35
Avrahami, Yossi, 240
Ayalon, Ami, 115–16, 155, 234, 270–1, 303
Ayash, Yahya "the Engineer," assassination
  of, 114–16
Azoulay, Orly, 120

Ba'athist ideology, in Syria, 83–4
Baker, James, 237–8, 297
 Arab-Israeli negotiations and, 24–7, 41
 shuttle diplomacy of, 24–5
Barak, Ehud, 2, 18, 22, 37–8, 84, 96,
  108, 324
 Al-Aqsa Intifada and, 3–4, 239–41
 Arafat and, 234, 235–6, 237, 238, 241–5
  lack of trust between, 249–50, 278
 Beilin and, 231, 249
 Clinton and, 199, 209–10, 213, 237–8,
  246–51
  parameters of two-state solution,
  247–51
 coalition government of
  political fragmentation of, 196–8

religious fragmentation in, 197–8
 domestic policy of
  constraints against, 213–14
  Knesset and, 204, 231–2
  legitimacy of, 195–6
 foreign policy under, 196–200
  Camp David Summit and, 235–8
  commemoration days as influence on,
  231–4
  contradictions in policy agenda,
  198–200, 245–6
  decision-making structure for, 196–8
  engagement approach in, 238
  towards Palestinian Liberation
  Organization, 245–6
  political fragmentation through, 196–8
  unilateralism approach in, 219–27
  US involvement in, 235–8
 Hamas and, 215–16
 Indyk and, 203–4, 206, 208, 210
 Iran and, foreign policy towards,
  215–18, 397
  defensive components of, 218
  deterrent components of, 218
  maturation of, 217–18
 Israel Defence Force and, 241–5
 Lebanon and, foreign policy towards,
  219–22
  Four Mothers Movement and, 221–2
  Hezbollah activities as factor in, 220–1
  unilateralism approach in, 219–22
 1999 election campaign, 195–6
 Olmert and, 344, 345–6
 One Israel Party, 195–8, 283
 Oslo Peace process and, 227–31, 236
 Peres and, 117
 Ross and, 202–3, 208, 211, 229–30, 248
 security zones under, 219–22
 Sharon and, 206
 Shas Party and, 197
 Syria and, foreign policy towards, 200–14
  al-Assad, Hafez, and, 211–13,
  235–6, 238
  at Blair House summit, 202–6
  and Geneva summit, 210–13
  resumption of, 200–2
  at Shepherdstown summit,
  206–10, 211
  US involvement in, 201, 202–10
 unilateral foreign policy under, 2
 US and, foreign policy involvement by,
  235–8
 Yatom and, 198–9, 210
Barcelona Process, 134
Barghouti, Marwan, 271, 293

Index

Batikhi, Samih, 174–5
Bechar, Giora, 143–4
Begin, Benny, 30, 161, 326
Begin, Menachem, 253
Begin Doctrine, 344–5
Beilin, Yossi, 45, 59, 146, 197–8, 283, 303–4
  Abu Mazen-Beilin agreement, 109
  Barak and, 231, 249
  negotiations with Abbas, 108–10
Ben, Aluf, 346
Ben-Aharon, Yossi, 18, 131
Ben-Ami, Shlomo, 197–8, 200–1, 231, 233, 236, 243–4
Ben-Eliezer, Binyamin, 256, 270
Ben-Gurion, David, 130
Bentsur, Eytan, 167–8
Bharatiya Janata Party (BJP), 375–7
Bin Laden, Osama. *See* 9/11
Bin Salman, Muhammad, 395
Bin Shaker, Zeid, 18
Bin-Talal, Hassan (Crown Prince), 180
BJP. *See* Bharatiya Janata Party
'Black September', 125–6
Blair, Tony, 279, 289
Brown, Bill, 18–19
Browne, N. A. K., 376
Burg, Avraham, 283
Burns, Williams, 288–9
Bush, George H. W., 28–9, 127–8, 279–80. *See also* Gulf War
Bush, George W., 246–7, 259, 265, 287, 297
  Blair and, 279
  Israel-US strategic alliance, 368, 370–1
  9/11 attacks and. *See* 9/11 attacks
Bushinski, Aviv, 191
Buzan, Barry, 377

Camp David Summit, 56, 235–8
Carter, Jimmy, 303–4, 362
Chamberlain, Neville, 265
Cheney, Richard, 15, 20
  Gulf War and, 20–1
China
  dependence on Middle East oil, 374–5
  Israel foreign policy and, 134–41, 372–5
    during Gulf War (1990–1991), 140
    Hong Kong transfer and, 136–7
    Israel Liaison Office and, 138–9
    after Israeli-Egyptian peace agreement, 135–6
    during Korean War, 134–5
    Oslo Process and, 140–1
    US opposition to, 373–4

PLO recognized by, 3, 135
  support of Arab states, 3, 135
Chirac, Jacques, 384
Christopher, Warren, 44–5, 50–1, 53, 121, 199
Clark, Bill, 144
Clinton, Bill, 44–5, 54–5, 123
  Barak and, 199, 209–10, 213, 237–8, 246–51
    Clinton parameters for two-state solution, 247–51
  Netanyahu and
    on Netanyahu as threat to peace, 154–5
    during Washington Summit (1996), 157–8
  Peres and, political support for, 114–17
  Summit of Peacemakers and, 117
  Rabin and, 128
  at Wye Plantation Summit, 192
Cold War
  Eisenhower Doctrine during, 124–5
  Middle East foreign policy after, 15–20. *See also* Iraq
  Nixon Doctrine during, 124–5
concentric circles, in Israeli foreign policy, 8–10
convergence plan, abandonment of, by Olmert, 347–51

Dagan, Meir, 390–1
Dahiya Doctrine, 363–4
Dahlan, Muhammad, 271–2, 296, 311
Dakamesh, Ahmed, 163, 172
Daoudi, Riad, 201, 345–6
Davutoğlu, Ahmet, 346
Dayan, Uzi, 59
decision-makers, in Israeli foreign policy, 5–6, 12–15. *See also* Prime Ministers; *specific persons*
  political parties and, 12–13. *See also specific parties*
Declaration of Principles on Self-Government Arrangements (DoP), 53–6
  advantages of, for Israel, 56
  Arafat role in, 53, 65–6
  domestic response to, in Israel, 62–3
    anti-peace campaign, 62–3
    Netanyahu opposition to, 62
  Hamas and, 64–7
    terrorist attacks by, 66–7
  Jordan political interests and, 68–72
  King Hussein and, 69–75
  Oslo I Agreement and, 67–8
  Oslo Peace Process and, 53–4, 60–1

422 Index

Declaration of Principles (cont.)
  Palestine statehood and, 61
  peace-making approach under, 55–6
  Peres and, 54–5
  security-driven approach to
    implementation of, 59–61
  settlement demands in, 61
  settlements under, 64–7
    expansion of, 64
    Hebron, 65–6
    Kiryat Arba settlement, 64–5
    in security-driven approach to
      implementation, 61
    terrorist responses to, 64–5
    US role in, 53–4
    Yesha Council and, 64
Dekel, Udi, 354
democracy
  in Gaza Strip, for Palestinians, 9
  Israel foreign policy and, 9
  in West Bank, for Palestinians, 9
Deng Xiaoping, 135, 143
Deri, Arye, 54, 60–1
Dichter, Avi, 270, 271–2, 282
din mosser, 107
din rodef, 107
Diskin, Yuval, 349
DoP. *See* Declaration of Principles on Self-
  Government Arrangements
al-Dura, Muhammad, 240

Eagleburger, Lawrence, 22
Economic Emergency Stability Plan
  (EESP) (1985), 1
EEC. *See* European Economic Community
EESP. *See* Economic Emergency Stability
  Plan
Egypt. *See also* Arab-Israeli War; Gaza Strip
  Israeli-Egyptian peace negotiations, 35,
    37, 51, 56
    China-Israeli relations influenced by,
      135–6
    Madrid Peace Conference and, 28–9
    Sharon and, 307
    Sinai I/II Agreements, 35
Eiland, Giora, 271–2
Eisenskott, Gadi, 363, 395
Eitan, Raphael, 19, 21
Eldar, Shlomi, 115
Elon, Benny, 314
Elyashiv, Yosef Shalom, 317
EMP. *See* European Mediterranean
  Partnership
engagement, as foreign policy, 147
  in Barak government, 238

in Netanyahu government, 169
in Peres government, 118–20
in Rabin government, 56–8, 79,
  102–3, 118
entrenchment, as foreign policy, 392–4. *See
  also* Shamir, Yitzhak
  in Golan Heights, 100–1
  in India-Israeli foreign policy, 143
  limitations of, 2
  by Netanyahu, 402
  by Shamir, 402
Eran, Oded, 229
Erbakan, Necmettin, 113
Erdoğan, Recep Tayyip, 345
Erikat, Saeb, 354
Etzion, Yehuda, 107
EU. *See* European Union
European Economic Community (EEC)
  Israel and, 2–3, 124–34
    Arab-Israeli negotiations and, 25
    free trade agreements between, 130,
      132–3
    Maastricht Treaty and, 130–1
    Palestinian Liberation Organization
      endorsed by, 130
European Mediterranean Partnership
  (EMP), 134, 383
European Union (EU)
  Israel foreign policy and, 129–34, 380–6
    Arafat and, 381–2
    in Barcelona Process, 134
    bilateral economic relationship
      between, 130
    exports and, economic importance of,
      384–5
    public opinion on, 382
    Wye River memorandum and, 381–2

al-Faisal, Turki, 396
Fighters for the Freedom of Israel (Lehi), 15
Flapan, Simha, 3
FMF. *See* Foreign Military Financing
Fogel, Zvika, 242
forbearance approach, by Israel, during
  Gulf War, 22–3
Foreign Military Financing (FMF), 366–8
foreign policy, Israel. *See also* Barak, Ehud;
    Declaration of Principles on Self-
    Government Arrangements;
    engagement; entrenchment;
    Netanyahu, Binyamin; Olmert,
    Ehud; Peres, Shimon; Rabin,
    Yitzhak; Shamir, Yitzhak; Sharon,
    Ariel; unilateralism
  China and. *See* China

Index

423

data sources for, 10–11
domestic sources of, 4–10. *See also*
 decision-makers; security network
 concentric circles in, 8–10
 national narratives for, 8–10
EU and. *See* European Union
Holocaust shadow as factor in, 8
India and. *See* India
Israel as democratic state and, 9
Israel as Jewish state as factor in, 8
Kissinger on, 4–5, 233
Labour Party and, 9–10, 34–9
Likud Party and, 9–10, 20–3
New Middle East in, 110–11,
 118–19, 185
new paradigms in
 Greater Israel as, 260–1
 two-state solution as, 260–1
overview of, 31–2
relative autonomy in, 6
US alliance as element of. *See* United
 States
Zionism as factor in, 8
Four Mothers Movement, 221–2
Framework Agreement on Permanent
 Status (FPS), 228–9
free trade agreements (FTAs), between
 European Economic Community
 and Israel, 130, 132–3
Freilich, Charles, 5
FTAs. *See* free trade agreements
Further Redeployments
 in West Bank, Palestinian control of,
 162–3, 166–7
 under Wye River memorandum, 230

Galant, Yoav, 293
Gandhi, Indira, 143
Gandhi, Mahatma, 141–2
Gandhi, Rajiv, 143
Gantz, Benny, 398
Gaulle, Charles de, 129
Gaza Strip
 Arab-Israeli War and, Palestinians in, 1
 democracy in, for Palestinians, 9
 Hamas control of, 349–51
 Palestinians in
 during Arab-Israeli War, 1
 democracy for, 9
 population demographics for, 14
Gemayel, Bashir, 254
General Security Services (GSS), 6
 assassination of Ayash by, 114–16
 Netanyahu and, 158, 163–5
 under Sharon, 270–1

Geneva Agreement, Sharon and, 304–5
Genger, Arie, 256
Gerstein, Erez, 220
Gil, Avi, 52, 53, 108, 109
Gil, Yehuda, 182–3
Gilad, Amos, 362
Gilat, Yoel, 138
Gilboa, Eytan, 371–2
Gillon, Carmi, 91, 94–6, 114, 270–1, 303
Ginossar, Yossi, 257
Golan Heights, 12–13
 in Arab-Israeli negotiations, lobbying for,
 42, 43
 entrenchment policy in, 100–1
 Israel withdrawal from, 81–2
Gold, Dore, 170, 182–3
Goldstein, Baruch, 64, 107
Gorbachev, Mikhail, 28–9
Gore, Al, 246–7
Greater Land of Israel principle
 as foreign policy paradigm, 260–1
 Jordan and, 171–2
 Olmert and, 326–7
GSS. *See* General Security Services
Gulf War (1990–1991)
 Cheney and, 20–1
 China-Israeli relations during, 140
 foundations of, 20–1
 Hussein, Saddam, and, military response
 to, 20–1, 179
 Israel response to, 20–3
 as deterrence policy, 22
 domestic factors in, 22
 forbearance approach in, 22–3
 among hardliners, 21
 Israel Defence Force and, 22
 Israel-US alliance during, 370
 Jordan during, 73–4, 179
 Shamir during, 20–3
 Soviet Union and, 20–1
 US special relationship with Israel
 during, 126–7
Gur, Mordechai, 82
Guyer, Kalman, 62–3

Haber, Eitan, 35, 36, 37–8, 59, 90, 93
Halevy, Efraim, 17, 18, 70–1, 72, 153–4,
 174, 176, 200, 280–1
Haloutz, Dan, 222, 302–3, 309, 331, 336.
 See also Second Lebanon War
El-Hamaayan (education system), 227–8
Hamas (Harakat al-Muqawamah al-
 Islamiyya), 392–3
 Ayash and, assassination plot against,
 114–16

424 Index

Hamas (cont.)
 Barak and, 215–16
 Declaration of Principles on
  Self-Government Arrangements
  and, 64–7
 terrorist attacks by, 66–7
 electoral successes of, 347–8
 Gaza Strip controlled by, 349–54,
  359–64
  Dahiya Doctrine and, 363–4
  Operation Cast Lead and, 362–4, 394
 Netanyahu and, 176
 Peres and, 120
 under Rabin, 42–5, 120, 122
  deportation of Hamas members, 44–5
Haniyeh, Ismail, 347–8, 360
Harakat al-Muqawamah al-Islamiyya. *See*
  Hamas
Haram al-Sharif (Temple Mount), 107,
  236, 238, 242–3, 315
 Israel Defence Force and, 240
 Palestinian sovereignty over, 248
 Sharon at, 239–40, 241, 257
 violence at, 240
al-Hariri, Rafiq, 330–1
Hashemite Monarchy, 170–1
Hasmonean Tunnel crisis, 155–7, 187–8
Hebron, 65–6, 322
Hebron Massacre, 64–5, 66–7, 107
Hebron Protocol
 Begin, B., and, resistance to, 161
 Netanyahu and, 159–67, 193
  construction limitations under, 161–3
  Likud-PLO agreement and, 159, 161
  reciprocity principle and, 160–1
 Sharon, resistance to, 161
Hertzog, Yitzhak, 337, 391–2
Hever, Ze'ev, 253–4, 308–9
Hezbollah, 49–51
 Barak and, 220–1
 in Lebanon, 101–2
 Olmert response to, containment strategy
  for, 330–5
Hirschfeld, Yair, 45–6
Holocaust, 8
Holst, Joergen, 53
Hussein (King of Jordan), 17–18, 123. *See*
  also Israeli-Jordan Peace Treaty;
  Jordan
 assassination attempt against Mashal,
  173–9
 'Black September', 125–6
 Netanyahu and, conditional support of,
  169–72, 173–9
Hussein, Saddam

during Gulf War, military response to,
  20–1, 179
 international reputation of, 23
 invasion of Kuwait by, 17, 19
 Palestinian Liberation Organization
  response to, 26
 threats to Israel, 16–17
al Husseini, Haj-Amin, 152–3

IAF. *See* Israel Air Force
IDF. *See* Israel Defence Force
India
 during Arab-Israeli War, 142
 Bharatiya Janata Party, 375–7
 independence from British rule, 141–2
 Israel foreign policy and, 141–7, 375–80
  bilateral trade as part of, 378–80
  entrenchment approach to, 143
  Iran and, 379–80
  normalization trajectory, 145–6
  security cooperation as element of,
   146–7
  timing of diplomatic ties between, 145
 Pakistan and, 142
 Peres and, 146
 support of Arab states, 3
 on Zionism, 142
Indyk, Martin, 73, 80
 Barak and, 203–4, 206, 208, 210
 Sharon and, 259
invasion of Iraq (2003), 279, 281, 288, 366,
  368–9
Iran, 396–9
 Barak government policy towards. *See*
  Barak, Ehud
 Hezbollah and, 101–2
 India-Israel foreign policy and, 379–80
 Joint Comprehensive Plan of Action and,
  396–7
 Peres and, 216
 during Rabin government, as emerging
  challenge to Israel, 101–2, 216
  Hezbollah and, 101–2
 Syria and, 398–9
Iraq. *See also* Invasion of Iraq
 invasion of Kuwait by, 17, 19
  US response to, 17–18, 19–20
 Jordan and, military alliance with, 17–18
 Shamir and, 15–20
  invasion of Kuwait, US response to,
   17–18, 19–20
  threats by Hussein, Saddam, 16–17
 US invasion of, 279, 281, 288, 366,
  368–9
Iron Wall, of military strength, 15

Index

425

The Iron Wall (Shlaim), 3
Israel. *See also* Arab-Israeli War;
 Declaration of Principles on
 Self-Government Arrangements;
 entrenchment; foreign policy;
 security network; unilateralism;
 specific topics
 electoral system in, 5–6
 Prime Ministers, 5–6. *See also*
 Netanyahu, Binyamin; Olmert,
 Ehud; Peres, Shimon; Rabin,
 Yitzhak; Shamir, Yitzhak; Sharon,
 Ariel
 European Economic Community and,
 2–3, 124–34
 Arab-Israeli negotiations and, 25
 free trade agreements between, 130,
 132–3
 during Shamir government, 131–2
 under Treaty of Rome, 129
 in European Mediterranean Partnership,
 134, 383
 Framework Agreement on Permanent
 Status and, 228–9
 during Gulf War, foreign policy response
 to, 20–3
 deterrence policy, 22
 domestic factors in, 22
 forbearance approach in, 22–3
 among hardliners, 21
 Israel Defence Force and, 22
 Israeli-Egyptian peace negotiations, 35,
 37, 51, 56
 Jordan and, strategic alliance between, 18
 Peres and, 70–2
 Rabin and, 72–9
 US role in, 74–5
 Knesset, 5, 6, 114
 Members of the Knesset, 12–13
 loan guarantees feud with USA,
 27–8, 129
 Ministry of Foreign Affairs, 6
 One Israel, 195–8, 283
 security network in, 6–7
 Third Way movement in, 112
 Washington Declaration and, 75, 77
Israel Air Force (IAF), 20–1
Israel Ascending (Party), 119
Israel Defence Force (IDF), 7
 Abbas and, 294–5
 Barak and, 241–5
 during Gulf War (1990–1991), 22
 under Military Basic Law, 7
 Netanyahu and, 158, 163–5
 Operation Accountability, 50, 101–2

 Rabin and, 34–5, 99, 116
 Sharon, redeployment of, 300–1, 302–6
 as military force, 258
 Syria and, 99, 110
Israeli-Egyptian peace negotiations, 35, 37,
 51, 56
Israeli-Jordan Peace Treaty, 75–9
 Netanyahu on, 76, 179–80
 Washington Declaration and, 75, 77
Israeli-Palestinian Agreements, 87. *See also*
 Oslo Accords
Israeli-US-Jordanian Trilateral Economic
 Community, 70
Israel-Jordan Common Agenda, 69
Ivri, David, 22, 146

Jabotinski, Ze'ev, 148, 153
Jaruzelski, Wojciech, 12
Jerusalem, internationalization of, 357
Jewish people
 Israel as nation for, 8
 nationhood law, 400–1
Jewish Settler Movement, 9, 316–18
Joint Comprehensive Plan of Action (Iran
 nuclear deal), 396–7
Jordan
 'Black September', 125–6
 Declaration of Principles on Self-
 Government Arrangements and,
 68–75
 Greater Land of Israel principle and,
 171–2
 during Gulf War (1990–1991), 73–4,
 179
 Hashemite Monarchy, 170–1
 Iraq and, military alliance between,
 17–18
 Israel and, strategic alliance between, 18
 Peres and, 70–2
 Rabin and, 72–9
 US role in, 74–5
 Israeli-Jordan Peace Treaty, 75–9
 Netanyahu on, 76, 179–80
 Washington Declaration and, 75, 77
al-Jubayar, 'Adil, 276, 396

Kahalani, Avigdor, 100
Kahan, Yitzhak, 255
Kaplinski, Moshe, 281
Karmi, Raid, 270
Katzav, Moshe, 283
Kerry, John, 390, 391
Khader, Hussam, 293
Khalidi, Ahmad, 373
Kiryat Arba settlement, 64–5

426 Index

Kissinger, Henry, on Israeli foreign policy, lack of, 4–5, 233
Knesset, 5, 6, 114
Barak and, 204, 231–2
Members of the Knesset, 12–13
Korean War, China-Israel relations during, 134–5
Kuwait, Iraq invasion of, 17, 19
US response to, 17–18, 19–20

Labour (Party). *See also* Rabin, Yitzhak
foreign policy platform, 9–10, 34–9
parliamentary majority for, 34–9
Peres and, 1–2, 119–20
Lahad, Antoine, 50, 181
Landau, Uzi, 312–13
land-for-peace exchange, 14–15
under Rabin, 37
Lapid, Yossef (Tommy), 285, 316–17
Larsen, Terje Rod, 45
Lauder, Estee, 188–9
Lauder, Ronald, 188–91
Lebanon
Arab-Israeli negotiations and, 49–50
Barak and, foreign policy and, 219–22
Four Mothers Movement and, 221–2
Hezbollah activities as factor in, 220–1
unilateralism approach in, 219–22
Hezbollah in, 101–2
Israel invasion of, unilateral foreign policy after, 2
Madrid Peace Conference and, 28–9
Operation Grapes of Wrath in, 117–18, 182
Second Lebanon War, 329–30, 336, 346, 347, 353
Israel Defence Force and, 336–41
political fallout from, 341, 342
RAM Doctrine and, 336–7
South Lebanese Army, 50, 101, 181, 219–20, 224–5, 226
'Lebanon first' initiative, 181–2
Lebanon War (1982), 255
Lehi. *See* Fighters for the Freedom of Israel
Levy, David, 13, 28–9, 149, 154, 165, 195–6, 283, 323
Levy, Yagil, 222
Lewinski, Monica, 165, 166
Lewis, C. S., 214
Lewis, Samuel L., 129
Libai, David, 37–8
Lieberman, Avigdor, 153, 314, 353, 397–8
Likud (Party). *See also* Shamir, Yitzhak
electoral losses, 33–4
foreign policy under, 9–10, 20–3

Hebron Protocol and, 159, 161
leadership of, 1, 12–13
Netanyahu and, 1, 120, 149–50. *See also* Netanyahu, Binyamin
opposition to unilateral disengagement, 313–15
Oslo II and, response to, 89–91
Lipkin-Shakah, Amnon, 15–16, 59, 94–5, 97
Livni, Tzipi, 313–14, 326, 328, 345–6, 352, 387

Maastricht Treaty, 130–1
Macmillan, Harold, 341
Madrid Peace Conference
Arab-Israeli negotiations and, 28–31, 39–45
Middle East participants in, 28–9
Palestinian Liberation Organization and, 26–7, 28–31
Rabin and, 39–45
Shamir and, 30, 121
Maimon, Israel, 324
The Man Who Did Not Know How to Win (Azoulay), 120
Mao Ze Dong, 135
Markus, Yoel, 301
Marzuk, Musa Abu, 115–16
Mashal, Khaled, 115, 173–9, 349, 362
Masharawi, Samir, 115
mass demonstrations, 325
Matkal, Sayeret, 148
Mazuz, Menachem, 308–9
Melamed, Eliezer, 107
Members of the Knesset (MKs), 12–13
Merhav, Reuven, 136–7
Meridor, Dan, 13, 326, 398
Meridor, Sallai, 13
MFA. *See* Ministry of Foreign Affairs
Military Basic Law, Israel (1976), 7
Miller, Aaron David, 258, 262, 267–8, 297
Miller, Rory, 134
Ministry of Foreign Affairs (MFA), 6
Mishra, Shri Brajseh, 377
Mitchell, George, 259
Mitzna, Amram, 283, 284
MKs. *See* Members of the Knesset
Mofaz, Shaul, 200, 224, 242, 286, 324, 329
Molcho, Yitzhak, 154
Mordechai, Yitzhak, 149, 154
Morris, Benny, 3–4, 277–8
Mossad, 6
assassination attempt against Mashal, 173–9
Sharon and, 217

Index

Yatom and, 37–8, 72, 94–5, 173–4
al-Moualem, Walid, 84, 113, 182–3
Muasher, Marawan, 287–8
Mubarak, Hosni, 121, 306–7, 387–8
Mursi, Muhammad, 387–8
Muslim Brotherhood Movement, 42
Mustafa, Abu Ali, 264
My Truth (Liberman), 153

Nasser, Amil, 220
Nasserallah, Hassan, 226, 241–2, 282,
    334–5
Naval Vessel Transfer Act, USA (2008),
    367–8
Nave, Danny, 149, 153, 157–8
Ne'eman, Yuval, 21
Nehoshtan, Ido, 344
Nehru, Jawaharlal, 141–2
Neriah, Jacques, 40
Netanyahu, Binyamin (Bibi), 104,
    150–1, 326
  Arab uprisings and, 387–9, 390, 392, 394
  Arafat and, 158
    refusal to meet with, 154–5, 186
  Clinton and
    on Netanyahu as threat to peace, 154–5
    during Washington Summit (1996),
      157–8
  coalition government of, 148–50, 165–6
    downfall of, 188–93
    Sharon, in, 149
  domestic policy approach
    Hasmonean Tunnel crisis, 155–7,
      187–8
    Israel Defence Force and, 158, 163–5
    to settlement expansion, 155–7
  early years of, 148
  foreign policy approach, 150–4
    in Arab-Israeli relations, 151–2
    engagement approach, 169
    entrenchment approach, 402
    to Gulf States, 185–8
    influences on, 150–1
    Oslo Peace Process and, 156–7, 165,
      167–8, 227
    Palestinian Liberation Organization
      agreement, 167
    peace of deterrence, 152
    as territorial maximalist, 151
    Washington Summit (1996) and,
      157–8
  Greater Land of Israel principle, 193
  Hamas and, 176
  Hebron Protocol and, 159–67, 193
  historic length in office, 387–9, 400–2

  inner decision-making circle for, 150–4
    Nave as part of, 153
    political inexperience of, 153–4
  Jordan and, foreign policy towards,
    169–80
    assassination attempt against Mashal,
      173–9
    Greater Israel ideology and, 171–2
    Hashemite Monarchy and, 170–1
    Israeli-Jordan Peace Treaty, 76,
      179–80
    King Hussein and, conditional support
      of, 169–72, 173–9
  Lauder mission, 188–91
    Syrian involvement in, 189–91
  'Lebanon first' initiative, 181–2
  Likud and, 1, 120, 149–50
  1999 election campaign, 195–6
  Obama and, 325
  opposition to Declaration of Principles on
    Self-Government Arrangements, 62
  overview of, 193–4
  Qatar and, 185–8
  security approach under, 163–5
    General Security Services, 158, 163–5
    Israel Defence Force and, 158, 163–5
  Shamir and, 161
  Sharon and, 149, 286
  Syria and, foreign policy towards, 180–5
    Lauder Mission and, 189–91
    redefinition of, 182–3
    as threat to peace, 154–7
    Clinton on, 154–5
  Turkey and, foreign policy towards,
    184–5
  unilateral foreign policy under, 2
  Wye Plantation Summit, 191–3
    Clinton at, 192
  on Zionism, 150–1
Nevo, Azriel, 13
New Middle East, in Israel foreign policy,
    under Peres, 110–11, 118–19, 185
9/11 attacks, 262
  aftermath of, 262–9
  Israel foreign policy after, 262–72
    Karin A seizure, 268–9
    negotiations with Palestinian
      Liberation Organization, 263–4
    US involvement in, transformation of,
      265–9
  US foreign policy after
    Global War on Terror, 265–9
    Israel-US relations, transformations of,
      265–9
    marginalization of Arafat, 267–9

428 Index

Noor (Queen), 78. *See also* Jordan
Novik, Nimrod, 349
Nurzhitz, Vadim, 240

Obama, Barack, 325
Olmert, Ehud, 2, 324
  Abbas and, negotiations with, 355–9
  Barak and, 344, 345–6
  early political career of, 326–7
  foreign policy for
    containment policy, 329–35
    convergence plan, abandonment of,
      347–51
    decision-making circle in, 327–9
    military response to Hezbollah, con-
      tainment strategy in, 330–5
    political legacy of, 364–5
  Greater Land of Israel principle and,
    326–7
  Hamas takeover of Gaza Strip, 351–4,
    359–64
    ceasefire in, 361–2
    Dahiya Doctrine and, 363–4
    Operation Cast Lead, 362–4, 394
  Rice and, 355–9
  on Right of Return, 356–7
  Second Lebanon War and, 336
    Israel Defence Force and, 336–41
    political fallout from, 341, 342
    RAM Doctrine and, 336–7
  Sharon and, 255
  Shas Party under, as coalition part-
    ner, 354
  Syria and, foreign policy towards, 342–6
    Annapolis Peace Conference and,
      351–4
    Begin Doctrine and, 344–5
    Turkey involvement in, 359–64
    US involvement in, 343–4, 351–4
  unilateral foreign policy under, 2
  in Winograd Commission of Inquiry,
    337–8
One Israel (Party), 195–8, 283
Operation Accountability, 50, 101–2
Operation Cast Lead, 362–4, 394
Operation Defensive Shield, 272–8
Operation Desert Storm, 20. *See also*
  Gulf War
Operation Grapes of Wrath, 117–18, 182
Operation Pillar of Defence, 392–4
Operation Protective Edge, 392–3
Oslo Accords (I/II), 87–9
  Declaration of Principles on Self-
    Government Arrangements
    and, 67–8

foreign policy towards Syria after, 81
Palestinian state under, 105–6
purpose and goals of, 88–9
Rabin and, 88–9
  Likud Party response to, 89–91
  parliamentary support for, 89–91
Oslo Peace Process
  Barak and, 227–31, 236
  China-Israel relations and, 140–1
  Declaration of Principles on Self-
    Government Arrangements and,
    53–4, 60–1
  Netanyahu and, 156–7, 165, 167–8, 227
Othman, Ibrahim, 342–3
Oudeh, Muhammad Abd al-Basset, 272
Oz, Amos, 277–8

Pakistan, India and, 142
Palestine. *See also* Palestinian Liberation
    Organization; Palestinians
  closures in, by Rabin government, 91–3
    as collective punishment, 92–3
  under Declaration of Principles on
    Self-Government Arrangements, 61
  Haram al-Sharif and, sovereignty
    over, 248
  Muslim Brotherhood Movement, 42
  under Oslo II Agreement, 105–6
  refugees from, 401–2
  Right of Return, 245–6, 356–7
  statehood for, 61, 290. *See also* two-state
    solution
  unemployment in, 92
Palestinian Covenant, 54
Palestinian Legislative Council (PLC), 293
Palestinian Liberation Organization (PLO),
    1. *See also* Declaration of Principles
    on Self-Government Arrangements
  Arab-Israeli negotiations and, 40–1,
    45–9, 52–3
  Barak and, 245–6
  'Black September', 125–6
  China's recognition of, 3, 135
  European Economic Community
    endorsed by, 130
  Framework Agreement on Permanent
    Status and, 228–9
  Hebron Protocol and, 159, 161
  Iraq invasion of Kuwait supported by, 26
  Madrid Peace Conference and, 26–7
  Netanyahu and, 167
  after 9/11 attacks, Israel foreign policy
    and, 263–4
  Peres and, negotiations with, 108–10
  Shamir and, 26

Index 429

Sharon and, 259
   Operation Defensive Shield and,
     272–8
as terrorist organization, 26–7
Palestinian National Council, 54
Palestinians
   Al-Aqsa intifada, 270, 272, 274
   Barak and, 3–4, 239–41
   Operation Defensive Shield and,
     272–8
   in Gaza Strip, after Arab-Israeli War, 1
   as refugees, 401–2
   Right of Return for, 245–6, 356–7
   in West Bank, after Arab-Israeli War, 1
Pappe, Ilan, 3
Pastor, Bob, 362
Pawar, Sharad, 146
Peace Now, 62, 105–6
peace of deterrence, 152
People's Republic of China. *See* China
Peres, Shimon, 121, 197–8, 256, 317,
   397–8
   ascension of, after Rabin assassination,
     108–13, 119
   Barak and, 117
   Clinton and, 114–17
   Summit of Peacemakers and, 117
   Declaration of Principles on Self-
     Government Arrangements
     and, 54–5
   domestic policy under, 108–13
   Operation Grapes of Wrath,
     117–18, 182
   election campaign of, 114–17
   foreign policy under, 108–13
     Abu Mazen-Beilin agreement, 109
     administrative appointments for,
       108
     engagement approach to, rejection of,
       118–20
     New Middle East vision, 185
     Palestinian Liberation Organization in,
       negotiations with, 108–10
     Turkey and, 113
     unilateral approach to, 2
   Hamas and, 120
   in India, 146
   Iran and, 216
   Jordan and, in foreign policy towards,
     strategic alliance with Israel, 70–2
   Labour Party and, 1–2, 119–20
   Nobel Peace Prize for, 79
   on Second Lebanon War, 338, 339–40
   Syria and, foreign policy towards, 110–18
     Israel Defence Force and, 110

     in New Middle East approach, 110–11,
       118–19
Peretz, Amir, 328, 337
Peri, Yaakov, 270–1, 303
Pinchasi, Raphael, 60–1
A Place Among Nations (Netanyahu), 150–1
PLC. *See* Palestinian Legislative Council
PLO. *See* Palestinian Liberation
   Organization
Poland, Solidarity trade union in, 12
political assassinations. *See* assassinations
Powell, Colin, 259, 267, 279, 287, 297
Prime Ministers, 5–6. *See also* Barak, Ehud;
   Netanyahu, Binyamin; Olmert,
   Ehud; Peres, Shimon; Rabin,
   Yitzhak; Shamir, Yitzhak; Sharon,
   Ariel
   relative autonomy of, 6
Primor, Avi, 132
Pundak, Ron, 45–6

Qassem, Naim, 215
Qatar, 185–8
Qian Qichen, 141, 323
Qualitative Military Edge (QME), 367–8
Qurie, Ahmed. *See* Abu Ala

Rabin, Yitzhak, 121, 122, 123
   Arab-Israeli negotiations under, 38–53.
     See also Declaration of Principles on
     Self-Government Arrangements
     definition of peace in, 80
     Golan Heights and, lobbying for,
       42, 43
     Lebanon and, 49–50
     Madrid Peace Conference and, 39–45
     Oslo Process, 45–9, 52–3
     Palestinian Liberation Organization
       involvement in, 40–1, 45–9, 52–3
     Syria and, 39–40, 41, 50–3
   Arab-Israeli War and, 34–5
   assassination of, 104–8
     by Amir, 106–7
     din mosser as justification for, 107
     din rodef as justification for, 107
     Peres ascension after, 108–13
   Clinton and, 128
   domestic policy, challenges in, 91–4, 214
     closures in Palestinian areas, 91–3
   foreign policy under, 34–9, 83–5. *See also*
     specific countries
     changes in, 91–6
     domestic factors in, 57
     engagement approach to, 56–8, 79,
       102–3, 118

430   Index

Rabin, Yitzhak (cont.)
  entrenchment approach to, 56–8, 79
  hawkishness of, 35
  historical legacy of, 85–6
  land-for-peace approach, 37
  Shamir approach compared to, 56–7
    unilateral, 2
  US involvement in, 37–8
  Hamas attacks under, 42–5, 120, 122
    deportation of Hamas members
      after, 44–5
  Hezbollah attacks, 49–51
  Iran as emerging challenge under,
    101–2, 216
    Hezbollah and, 101–2
  Israel Defence Force and, 34–5, 116
  Israel special relationship with USA
    under, 127–9
  Israeli-Jordan Peace Treaty and, 75–9
    Netanyahu on, 76
    Washington Declaration and, 75, 77
  Jordan's strategic alliance with Israel
    under, 72–9
  Labour Party and, 1–2
  Nobel Peace Prize for, 79
  Oslo II and, 88–9
    Likud Party response to, 89–91
    parliamentary support for, 89–91
  Peace Now and, 62, 105–6
  Peres as political rival, 36–7, 46
  reciprocity principle and, 160
  security networks and, authority
    over, 36–7
  security zones under, establishment of,
    49–50
  security-driven approach of, 59–61
    settlement demands in, 61
  Syria and, foreign policy towards, 79–82,
    96–101
    al-Assad, Hafez, role in, 80–1, 83–5
    domestic factors in, 79–80
    Israel Defence Force and, 99
    negative public opinion towards, 86
    after Oslo I agreement, 81
    security dialogue as element of, 84–5
    withdrawal from Golan Heights as
      requirement, 81–2
    tunnel vision of, 95
Rabinovich, Itamar, 39–40, 41, 84, 95, 99
Rabinovitch, Nachum, 107
RAM Doctrine. See Revolutions in Military
  Affairs Doctrine
Ramon, Haim, 197–8, 283
Reagan, Ronald, 289–90
reciprocity principle, Rabin and, 160

redeployments. See Further Redeployments
relative autonomy, of Prime Ministers, 6
religious edicts. See din mosser; din rodef
Revel, Sammy, 186
Revolutions in Military Affairs (RAM)
  Doctrine, 336–7
Rice, Condoleezza, 280, 289, 294, 297–8,
  302, 311–12, 338, 347
  Annapolis Peace Conference and, 351–4
  Olmert and, 355–9
Right of Return, 245–6, 356–7
Righteous Victims (Morris), 3
Ross, Dennis, 51, 53, 63, 73–4, 96–7, 99,
  108, 110
  Arafat and, 158
  Barak and, 202–3, 208, 211, 229–30, 248
  on US-Israeli alliance, 370
Rothschild, Dani, 59
Roy, Sara, 315–16
Rubinstein, Elyakim, 13, 18, 40, 250
Rumsfeld, Donald, 267

Safieh, Afif, 251
Sagie, Uri, 96, 101–2, 183–4, 200, 201–3
Said, Abdel Monem, 307
Sarid, Yossi, 227–8, 231
Savir, Uri, 47–8, 53, 59, 60, 108, 162–3
Schichor, Yitzhak, 141
Seale, Patrick, 182
Second Lebanon War (2006), 329–30, 336,
  346, 347, 353
  Israel Defence Force and, 336–41
  Peres on, 338, 339–40
  political fallout from, 341, 342
  RAM Doctrine and, 336–7
security network, 6–7. See also Israel
  Defence Force
  General Security Services, 6
    assassination of Ayash by, 114–16
    Netanyahu and, 158, 163–5
  Mossad, 6
    assassination attempt against Mashal,
      173–9
    Sharon and, 217
    Yatom and, 37–8, 72, 94–5, 173–4
    Rabin and, authority over, 36–7
security zones
  under Barak, 219–22
  under Rabin, establishment of, 49–50
Seder, Muhammad, 298
Segev, Gonen, 90
settlements. See also Gaza Strip; Golan
  Heights; West Bank
  under Declaration of Principles on Self-
    Government Arrangements, 64–7

Index

expansion of settlements, 64
Hebron, 65–6
Kiryat Arba settlement, 64–5
in security-driven approach to
implementation, 61
under Netanyahu government, expansion
strategy, 155–7
under Sharon, 316–18
Shaaban, Butheina, 211–12
Sha'ath, Nabil, 61
Shachor, Oren, 93
Shalhevet, Yoseph, 138
Shalit, Gilad, 329, 338, 348–9
Shalom, Avraham, 303
Shalom, Silvan, 230
Shalom, Yaakov, 270–1
Shamir, Yitzhak
Arens and, as defense minister, 14–15
collapse of governmental coalition
under, 33–4
domestic policy of, 214
early years of, 13–14
European Economic Community and,
131–2
foreign policy under, 13–15
Arab-Israeli War and, territorial
acquisition after, 14–15
entrenchment approach in, 402
Iron Wall of military strength, 15
land-for-peace exchange, 14–15
Rabin approach compared to, 56–7
as unilateral, 2
US alliance as foundation of, 15
Gulf War (1990–1991) and, 20–3
Iraq and, 15–20
invasion of Kuwait, US response to,
17–18, 19–20
threats by Hussein, Saddam, 16–17
Likud Party and, 1, 12–13
loan guarantees feud with US, 27–8, 129
Madrid Peace Conference and, 30, 121
Netanyahu and, 161
Palestinian Liberation Organization
and, 26
Sharon as political rival, 13
US and, alliance between, 15
on US-Israel strategic alliance, 370
on Zionism, 13–14
Shanab, Ismail Abu, 298
Shani, Uri, 256, 313
Shapria, Shimon, 189
al-Sharaa, Farouk, 29, 202–3, 205, 211–12
Sharansky, Natan, 232, 285
Sharon, Ariel, 2, 19, 116
Arab-Israeli negotiations and, 25, 27

Arafat and, 257, 276–7, 318
Barak and, 206
early military history of, 252
foreign policy under. *See also*
unilateralism, as foreign policy
Arab Peace Initiative, 275–8
development of, struggles in, 257–60
engagement approach to, 272–5
General Security Services and, 270–1
legacy of, 326
peace initiatives as element of, 278–81
political assassinations as element of,
269–72
US influence on, 281–2, 289–92. *See
also* 9/11 attacks
on Gulf War (2003), 21
at Haram al-Sharif, 239–40, 241, 257
Hebron Protocol and, resistance to, 161
in India, 378
Indyk and, 259
Israel Defence Force and
redeployment of, in unilateral
disengagement foreign policy
approach, 300–1, 302–6
use of, as military force, 258
Lebanon War (1982) and, 255
Mossad and, 217
Mubarak and, 306–7
Netanyahu and, 149, 286
Olmert and, 255
Palestinian Liberation Organization and,
259. *See also* Arafat, Yasser
Operation Defensive Shield and,
272–8
political rise of, 251–7
second coalition government, 285–99
lobbying of, 287–9
political global context for, 287–9
political parties in, 285
road map for peace by, 289–92
US involvement in, 287–9
Shamir as political rival, 13
2000 election of, 250–1
2003 election of, 283–4
unilateral disengagement as foreign policy, 300–8
consequences of, 320–1
domestic political constraints of, 305–6
Egyptian role in, 307
implementation of, 306–8
international actors in, 306–8
Israel Defence Force in, redeployment
of, 300–1, 302–6
Jewish settler movement and, 316–18
Likud opposition to, 313–15

432   Index

Sharon, Ariel (cont.)
  political challenges to, 311–18
  public support for, 313–16
  redrawing of borders in, 301
  US involvement in, 311–12
  Ya'alon role in, 308–11
  unity government of
    decision-makers in, 256–7
    Peres in, 256
  use of military force, 254
    through Israel Defence Force, 258
Sharon, Gilad, 252, 256, 272, 286, 305,
    312–13, 320
Sharon, Omri, 256, 286, 305
Shas Party (Association of Sephardic Torah
    Keepers), 12–13, 37, 60–1, 79–80,
    197, 204, 232
  El-Hamaayan and, 227–8
  under Olmert, as coalition partner, 354
Shavit, Ari, 255
Shavit, Shabtai, 15–16
Sher, Gilad, 198, 227
Sheranski, Natan, 119, 280, 312–13
Sheves, Shimon, 37–8
Shihabi, Hikmat, 84, 96
Shikaki, Khalil, 244
Shilo, Dov Lior Daniel, 107
Shitrit, Shimon, 54
Shlaim, Avi, 3
Shukri, Ali, 173, 174–5
Shuval, Zalman, 19, 126–7
Silberg, David, 173
Sinai I/II Agreements, 35
Singer, Yoel, 48, 52
Siniora, Fuad, 332
Sinirlioğlu, Feridun, 346
al-Sisi, Abdel Fattah, 387–8, 391, 394–5
SLA. See South Lebanese Army
Smith, Karen, 131
Sneh, Efraim, 37–8, 48, 101–2, 217
Solidarity (trade union), 12
Soster, Harry, 15
South Lebanese Army (SLA), 50, 101, 181,
    219–20, 224–5, 226
Soviet Union
  in Arab-Israeli negotiations, 26
  Eisenhower Doctrine and, 124–5
  expansionism of, USA's special relation-
    ship with Israel and, 125–6
  Nixon Doctrine and, 124–5
start-up nation, Israel as, 8
Steinitz, Yuval, 395, 398
Stern, Yuri, 369–70
Stern Gang, 15
Sufott, Zev, 139

Suleiman, Omar, 307
Summit of Peacemakers, 117
Swisher, Clayton, 249
Syria
  Arab-Israeli negotiations and, 39–40,
    41, 50–3
  al-Assad, Hafez, and, as monarchical
    president, 83
  Ba'athist ideology in, 83–4
  Barak and, foreign policy of. See Barak,
    Ehud
  foreign policy towards
    under Barak. See Barak, Ehud
    under Netanyahu, 180–5, 189–91
    under Olmert. See Olmert, Ehud
    under Peres, 110–19
    under Rabin. See Rabin, Yitzhak
  Iran and, 398–9
  Lauder mission and, 189–91
  Madrid Peace Conference and, 28–9

Talansky, Moshe, 357, 358
Temple Mount. See Haram al-Sharif
Tenet, George, 267
al-Thani, Hammad bin, 188
Third Way movement, in Israel, 112
Tourgeman, Shalom, 293, 333
Treaty of Rome, 129
Trump, Donald, 397
Tunnel vision, of Rabin, 95
Turbowicz, Yoram, 347
Turkey
  Israel-Syria foreign policy and,
    involvement in, 359–64
  Netanyahu and, 184–5
  Peres and, 113
two-state solution
  Arab Peace Initiative and, 275–8
  Clinton parameters of, 247–51
  as new foreign policy paradigm, 260–1

UN. See United Nations
unilateralism, as foreign policy, 2
  in Barak government, 2, 219–27
  by Sharon, A. See Sharon, Ariel
United Nations (UN), in Arab-Israeli
  negotiations, 25
United States (USA). See also Gulf War
  Arab-Israeli negotiations and, role
    in, 23–8
  on Arafat as legitimate leader, 279–80
  China-Israel relations, opposition to,
    373–4
  Cold War foreign policy and
    Eisenhower Doctrine and, 124–5

Index

Nixon Doctrine and, 124–5
Declaration of Principles on
Self-Government Arrangements
and, 53–4
invasion of Iraq by, 279, 281, 288, 366, 368–9
Iraqi invasion of Kuwait and, military response to, 17–18, 19–20
Israel and, strategic alliance with, 366–72. *See also* Clinton, Bill
during Bush, George H. W., administration, 28–9, 127–8, 279–80
during Bush, George W., administration, 368, 370–1
Foreign Military Financing as part of, 366–8
during Gulf War, 370
under Naval Vessel Transfer Act, 367–8
during Obama administration, 325
Qualitative Military Edge as result of, 367–8
Ross on, 370
Shamir on, 370
during Trump administration, 397
Israel foreign policy and
under Barak, 201, 202–10, 235–8
under Olmert, 343–4, 351–4
under Rabin, 37–8
under Shamir, 15
under Sharon, 281–2, 287–92, 311–12. *See also* 9/11 attacks
unilateral disengagement as policy approach, 311–12
Israeli-US-Jordanian Trilateral Economic Community, 70
Israel-Jordan alliance and, 74–5
Joint Comprehensive Plan of Action and, 396–7
loan guarantees feud with Israel, 27–8, 129
Operation Desert Storm, 20
special relationship with Israel, 124–9
through economic assistance, 125–6
during Gulf War (1990–1991), 126–7
under Rabin, 127–9
through security cooperation, 126
Soviet expansionism limited by, 125–6
Wye River memorandum and, mediation in, 297

Vajpayee, Shri Atal Bihari, 323
Vdovin, Andrey, 276

Walesa, Lech, 12
Washington Declaration, 75, 77
Washington Summit (1996), 157–8
Weissglas, Dov, 255, 256, 272, 279–80, 288, 293, 298–9, 301, 320
Weitzman, Ezer, 116
West Bank, 322
Arab-Israeli War and, Palestinians in, 1
democracy for Palestinians in, 9
expansion of settlements in, during Arab-Israeli negotiations, 27
Further Redeployments in, for Palestinian control of, 162–3, 166–7
geographical division of, 87–8
Winograd Commission of Inquiry, 225, 329–30, 333–4, 335, 337–8, 339
Wolfowitz, Paul, 15
Wu Xueqian, 137
Wye Plantation Summit, 191–3
Clinton at, 192
Wye River memorandum, 111, 192–3, 199, 228, 229, 230, 231
EU involvement in, 381–2
Further Redeployments under, 230
US mediation in, 297

Ya'alon, Moshe, 241–3, 268, 269, 286, 295, 398
Sharon and, 308–11
Yad Vashem Museum, 8
Yang Fuchang, 139
Yassin, Ahmad (Sheik), 173, 178–9, 298, 310
Yatom, Danny, 37–8, 72, 94–5, 173–5, 176–7, 182–3
Barak and, 198–9, 210
Yegar, Moshe, 140–1, 144
Yesha Council, 64
Yortner, Yehoshua, 137
Yosef, Ovadia (Rabbi), 37, 317

Ze'evi, Rehavam, 264
Zinni, Anthony, 267–8
Zionism, 8
India on, 142
Netanyahu and, 150–1
Shamir on, 13–14

Books in the Series

1 Parvin Paidar, *Women and the Political Process in Twentieth-Century Iran*
2 Israel Gershoni and James Jankowski, *Redefining the Egyptian Nation,*
  1930–1945
3 Annelies Moors, *Women, Property and Islam: Palestinian Experiences,*
  1920–1945
4 Paul Kingston, *Britain and the Politics of Modernization in the Middle East,*
  1945–1958
5 Daniel Brown, *Rethinking Tradition in Modern Islamic Thought*
6 Nathan J. Brown, *The Rule of Law in the Arab World: Courts in Egypt and the*
  Gulf
7 Richard Tapper, *Frontier Nomads of Iran: The Political and Social History of*
  the Shahsevan
8 Khaled Fahmy, *All the Pasha's Men: Mehmed Ali, His Army and the Making of*
  Modern Egypt
9 Sheila Carapico, *Civil Society in Yemen: The Political Economy of Activism in*
  Arabia
10 Meir Litvak, *Shi'i Scholars of Nineteenth-Century Iraq: The Ulama of Najaf*
  and Karbala
11 Jacob Metzer, *The Divided Economy of Mandatory Palestine*
12 Eugene L. Rogan, *Frontiers of the State in the Late Ottoman Empire:*
  Transjordan, 1850–1921
13 Eliz Sanasarian, *Religious Minorities in Iran*
14 Nadje Al-Ali, *Secularism, Gender and the State in the Middle East: The*
  Egyptian Women's Movement
15 Eugene L. Rogan and Avi Shlaim, eds., *The War for Palestine: Rewriting the*
  History of 1948
16 Gershon Shafir and Yoar Peled, *Being Israeli: The Dynamics of Multiple*
  Citizenship
17 A. J. Racy, *Making Music in the Arab World: The Culture and Artistry of Tarab*
18 Benny Morris, *The Birth of the Palestinian Refugee Crisis Revisited*
19 Yasir Suleiman, *A War of Words: Language and Conflict in the Middle East*
20 Peter Moore, *Doing Business in the Middle East: Politics and Economic Crisis in*
  Jordan and Kuwait
21 Idith Zertal, *Israel's Holocaust and the Politics of Nationhood*
22 David Romano, *The Kurdish Nationalist Movement: Opportunity,*
  Mobilization and Identity

23 Laurie A. Brand, *Citizens Abroad: Emigration and the State in the Middle East and North Africa*
24 James McDougall, *History and the Culture of Nationalism in Algeria*
25 Madawi al-Rasheed, *Contesting the Saudi State: Islamic Voices from a New Generation*
26 Arang Keshavarzian, *Bazaar and State in Iran: The Politics of the Tehran Marketplace*
27 Laleh Khalili, *Heroes and Martyrs of Palestine: The Politics of National Commemoration*
28 M. Hakan Yavuz, *Secularism and Muslim Democracy in Turkey*
29 Mehran Kamrava, *Iran's Intellectual Revolution*
30 Nelida Fuccaro, *Histories of City and State in the Persian Gulf: Manama since 1800*
31 Michaelle L. Browers, *Political Ideology in the Arab World: Accommodation and Transformation*
32 Miriam R. Lowi, *Oil Wealth and the Poverty of Politics: Algeria Compared*
33 Thomas Hegghammer, *Jihad in Saudi Arabia: Violence and Pan-Islamism since 1979*
34 Sune Haugbolle, *War and Memory in Lebanon*
35 Ali Rahnema, *Superstition as Ideology in Iranian Politics: From Majlesi to Ahmadinejad*
36 Wm. Roger Louis and Avi Shlaim eds., *The 1967 Arab-Israeli War: Origins and Consequences*
37 Stephen W. Day, *Regionalism and Rebellion in Yemen: A Troubled National Union*
38 Daniel Neep, *Occupying Syria under the French Mandate: Insurgency, Space and State Formation*
39 Iren Ozgur, *Islamic Schools in Modern Turkey: Faith, Politics, and Education*
40 Ali M. Ansari, *The Politics of Nationalism in Modern Iran*
41 Thomas Pierret, *Religion and State in Syria: The Sunni Ulama from Coup to Revolution*
42 Guy Ben-Porat, *Between State and Synagogue: The Secularization of Contemporary Israel*
43 Madawi Al-Rasheed, *A Most Masculine State: Gender, Politics and Religion in Saudi Arabia*
44 Sheila Carapico, *Political Aid and Arab Activism: Democracy Promotion, Justice, and Representation*
45 Pascal Menoret, *Joyriding in Riyadh: Oil, Urbanism, and Road Revolt*
46 Toby Matthiesen, *The Other Saudis: Shiism, Dissent and Sectarianism*
47 Bashir Saade, *Hizbullah and the Politics of Remembrance: Writing the Lebanese Nation*
48 Noam Leshem, *Life After Ruin: The Struggles over Israel's Depopulated Arab Spaces*
49 Zoltan Pall, *Salafism in Lebanon: Local and Transnational Movements*
50 Salwa Ismail, *The Rule of Violence: Subjectivity, Memory and Government in Syria*
51 Zahra Ali, *Women and Gender in Iraq: Between Nation-Building and Fragmentation*

52 Dina Bishara, *Contesting Authoritarianism: Labour Challenges to the State in Egypt*
53 Rory McCarthy, *Inside Tunisia's al-Nahda: Between Politics and Preaching*
54 Ceren Lord, *Religious Politics in Turkey: From the Birth of the Republic to the AKP*
55 Dörthe Engelcke, *Reforming Family Law: Social and Political Change in Jordan and Morocco*
56 Dana Conduit, *The Muslim Brotherhood in Syria*
57 Benjamin Schuetze, *Promoting Democracy, Reinforcing Authoritarianism: US and European Policy in Jordan*
58 Marc Owen Jones, *Political Repression in Bahrain*
59 Dylan Baun, *Winning Lebanon: Populism and the Production of Sectarian Violence, 1920–1958*
60 Joas Wagemakers, *The Muslim Brotherhood in Jordan*
61 Amnon Aran, *Israeli Foreign Policy since the End of the Cold War*

Lightning Source UK Ltd.
Milton Keynes UK
UKHW021447091220
374873UK00003B/34